THE UNITING STATES

THE UNITING STATES

The Story of Statehood for the Fifty United States
Volume 2: Louisiana to Ohio

☆★☆

Edited by
Benjamin F. Shearer

GREENWOOD PRESS
Westport, Connecticut • London

Library of Congress Cataloging-in-Publication Data

The uniting states: the story of statehood for the fifty United States/edited by
Benjamin F. Shearer.
    p. cm.
   Includes bibliographical references and index.
    ISBN 0-313-33105-7 (v. 1 : alk. paper) — ISBN 0-313-33106-5 (v. 2 : alk. paper) —
  ISBN 0-313-33107-3 (v. 3 : alk. paper) — ISBN 0-313-32703-3 (set : alk. paper)
    1. Statehood (American politics). 2. U.S. states. I. Shearer, Benjamin F.
JK2408.U65 2004
320.473'049–dc22   2004042474

British Library Cataloguing in Publication Data is available.

Library of Congress Catalog Card Number: 2004042474
ISBN: 0-313-32703-3 (set)
      0-313-33105-7 (Vol. I)
      0-313-33106-5 (Vol. II)
      0-313-33107-3 (Vol. III)

First published in 2004

Greenwood Press, 88 Post Road West, Westport, CT 06881
An imprint of Greenwood Publishing Group, Inc.
www.greenwood.com

Printed in the United States of America

The paper used in this book complies with the
Permanent Paper Standard issued by the National
Information Standards Organization (Z39.48-1984).

10 9 8 7 6 5 4 3 2 1

Contents

List of Maps

Maps

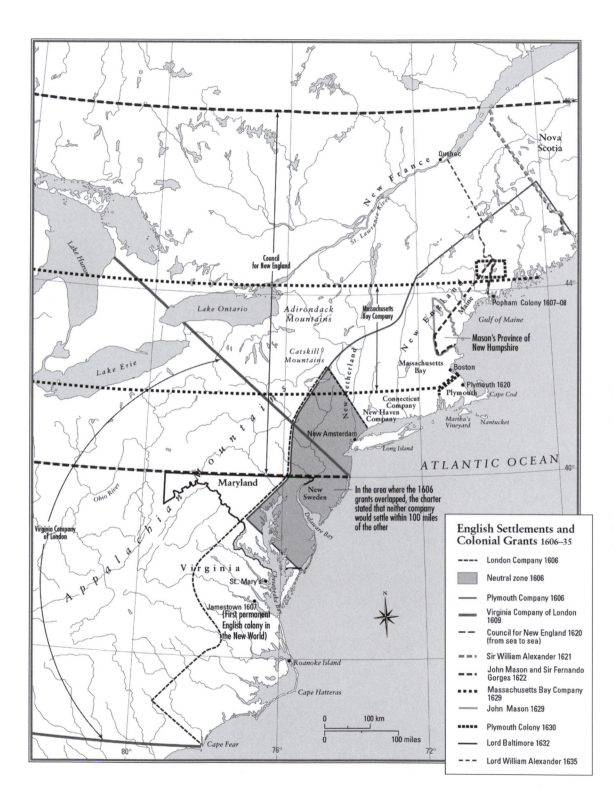

Lake Huron

Lake Ontario

Adirondack
Mountains

Catskill
Mountains

Lake Erie

New France

St. Lawrence River

Quebec

Nova
Scotia

Council
for New England

Massachusetts
Bay Company

New England

Maine

Popham Colony 1607–08

Gulf of Maine

Mason's Province of
New Hampshire

New Netherland

Massachusetts
Bay

Boston

Plymouth 1620

Plymouth

Cape Cod

Connecticut
Company
New Haven
Company

Martha's
Vineyard

Nantucket

New Amsterdam

Long Island

ATLANTIC OCEAN

Appalachian Mountains

Ohio River

Maryland

New
Sweden

Delaware Bay

Chesapeake Bay

In the area where the 1606
grants overlapped, the charter
stated that neither company
would settle within 100 miles
of the other

Virginia Company
of London

Virginia

St. Mary's

Jamestown 1607
(First permanent
English colony in
the New World)

N

Roanoke Island

Cape Hatteras

0   100 km

0   100 miles

80°   76°   72°

Cape Fear

English Settlements and Colonial Grants 1606–35

- - - - - London Company 1606

▨ Neutral zone 1606

——— Plymouth Company 1606

━━━ Virginia Company of London 1609

– – – Council for New England 1620 (from sea to sea)

–·–·– Sir William Alexander 1621

— —— John Mason and Sir Fernando Gorges 1622

▪▪▪▪ Massachusetts Bay Company 1629

——— John Mason 1629

•••• Plymouth Colony 1630

——— Lord Baltimore 1632

- - - - Lord William Alexander 1635

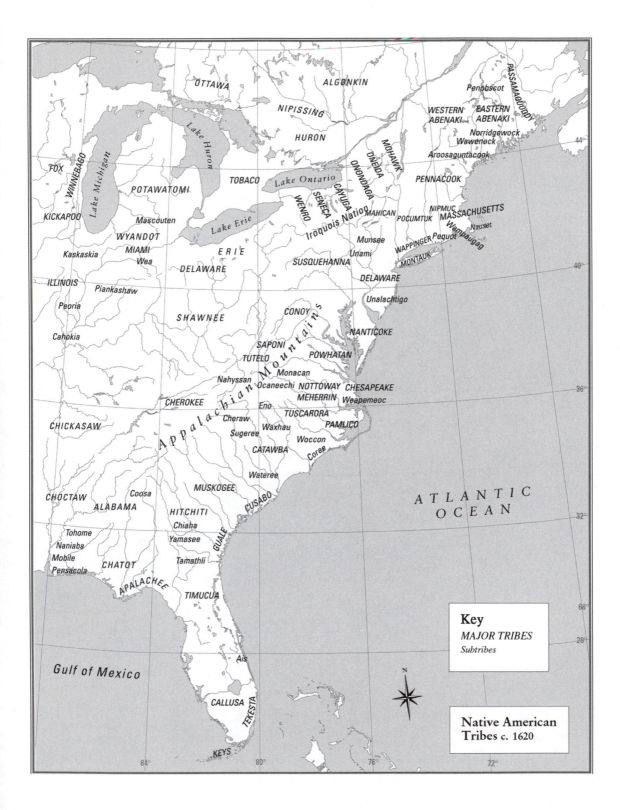

OTTAWA

ALGONKIN

Penobscot

PASSAMAQUODDY

NIPISSING

WESTERN ABENAKI

EASTERN ABENAKI

Norridgewock

Wawenock

HURON

Lake Huron

Aroosaguntacook

FOX

WINNEBAGO

Lake Michigan

MOHAWK

ONEIDA

ONONDAGA

PENNACOOK

POTAWATOMI

TOBACO

Lake Ontario

CAYUGA

NIPMUC

MASSACHUSETTS

KICKAPOO

WENRO

SENECA

MAHICAN

POCUMTUK

Nauset

Mascouten

Lake Erie

Iroquois Nation

Wampaugag

WYANDOT

Munsee

WAPPINGER

Pequot

Kaskaskia

MIAMI

ERIE

Unami

MONTAUK

Wea

DELAWARE

SUSQUEHANNA

ILLINOIS

Piankashaw

DELAWARE

Peoria

SHAWNEE

Unalachtigo

Cahokia

CONOY

NANTICOKE

Appalachian Mountains

SAPONI

POWHATAN

TUTELO

Nahyssan

Monacan

Ocaneechi

NOTTOWAY

CHESAPEAKE

CHEROKEE

Eno

MEHERRIN

Weapemeoc

Cheraw

TUSCARORA

CHICKASAW

Sugeree

Waxhau

PAMLICO

Woccon

CATAWBA

Coree

Wateree

ATLANTIC OCEAN

Coosa

MUSKOGEE

CHOCTAW

ALABAMA

CUSABO

HITCHITI

Tohome

Chiaha

GUALE

Naniaba

Yamasee

Mobile

Tamathli

Pensacola

CHATOT

APALACHEE

TIMUCUA

Gulf of Mexico

Ais

CALLUSA

TEKESTA

N

KEYS

44°

40°

36°

32°

68°

28°

84°

80°

76°

72°

Key

MAJOR TRIBES

Subtribes

Native American Tribes c. 1620

xiv

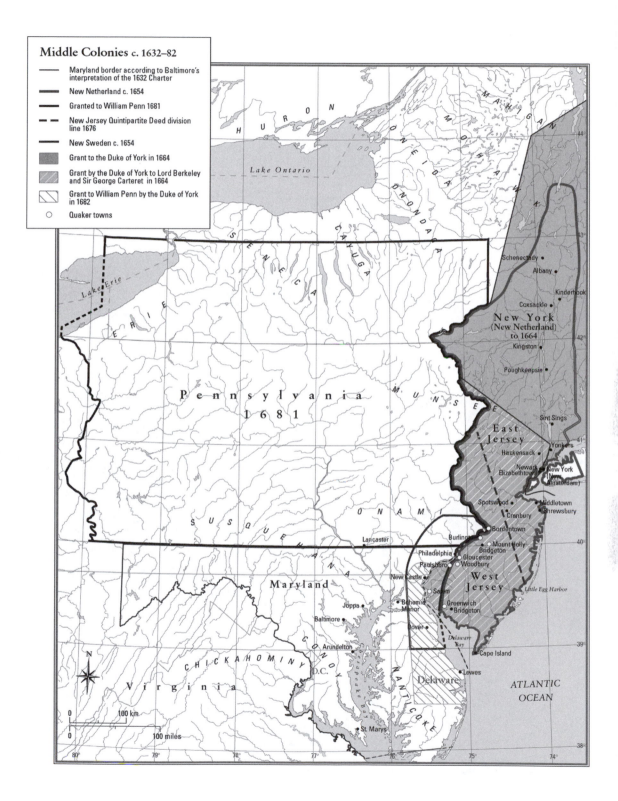

Middle Colonies c. 1632–82

- .... Maryland border according to Baltimore's interpretation of the 1632 Charter
- ——— New Netherland c. 1654
- ——— Granted to William Penn 1681
- – – – New Jersey Quintipartite Deed division line 1676
- ——— New Sweden c. 1654
- Grant to the Duke of York in 1664
- Grant by the Duke of York to Lord Berkeley and Sir George Carteret in 1664
- Grant to William Penn by the Duke of York in 1682
- ○ Quaker towns

HURON

Lake Ontario

M A H I C A N

M O H A W K

Schenectady •
Albany •
Kinderhook •
Coxsackie •

SENECA

CAYUGA

ONONDAGA

ONEIDA

Lake Erie

ERIE

New York
(New Netherland)
to 1664

Kingston •

Poughkeepsie •

P e n n s y l v a n i a
1 6 8 1

M U N S E E

Sint Sings •

East Jersey

Hackensack •
Yonkers •

Newark •
Elizabethtown •
New York
(New Amsterdam)

SUSQUEHANNA

O N A M I

Spotswood •
Cranbury •

Middletown •
Shrewsbury •

Bordentown ○
Burlington ○

Lancaster •

Mount Holly ○
Bridgeton

Philadelphia ○
Paulsboro ○
Gloucester ○
Woodbury ○

West Jersey

Little Egg Harbor

Maryland

New Castle •

Salem ○

Joppa •

Bohemia Manor •

Greenwich ○
Bridgeton •

Baltimore •

Dover •

Delaware Bay

Arundelton •

CHICKAHOMINY

CONOY

D.C.

Cape Island •

Lewes •

Delaware

V i r g i n i a

Chesapeake Bay

NANTICOKE

ATLANTIC OCEAN

N

0   100 km
0   100 miles

St. Marys •

XV

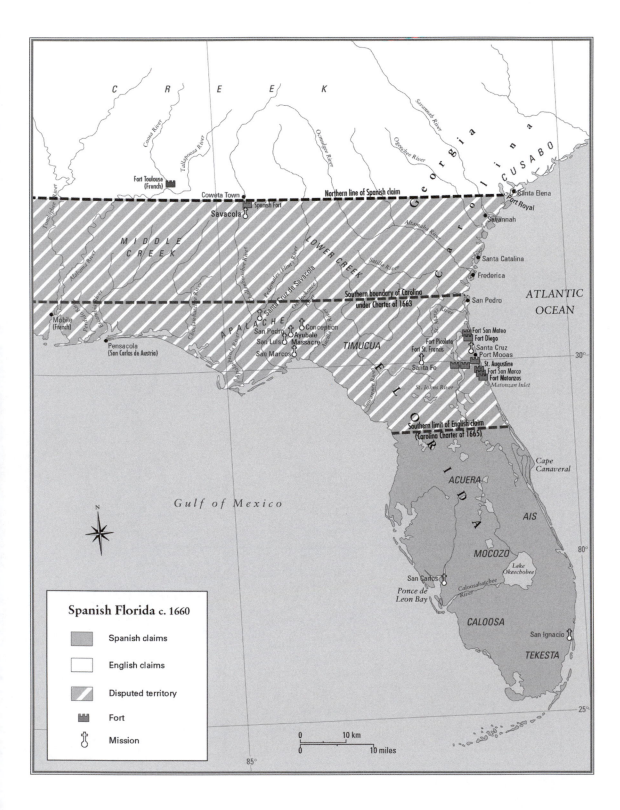

Spanish Florida c. 1660

	Spanish claims
	English claims
	Disputed territory
Fort
Mission

C R E E K

Coosa River

Tallapoosa River

Fort Toulouse
(French)

Coweta Town

Savacola

Spanish Fort

Northern line of Spanish claim

Ocmulgee River

Oconee River

Savannah River

Georgia

Carolina

CUSABO

Santa Elena
Fort Royal

Savannah

MIDDLE
CREEK

Alabama River

Chattahoochee River

Flint River

LOWER CREEK

Altamaha River

Satilla River

Southern boundary of Carolina
under Charter of 1663

Santa Catalina

Frederica

San Pedro

ATLANTIC
OCEAN

Tombigbee River

Perdido River

Escambia River

Apalachicola River

Santa Cruz de Savacola

Mobile
(French)

Pensacola
(San Carlos de Austria)

APALACHE

San Pedro
San Luis

Conception
Ayubale
Massacre

San Marcos

Suwannee River

TIMUCUA

FLORIDA

St. Marys River

Santa Fe

St. Johns River

Fort San Mateo
Fort Diego
Santa Cruz
Port Mooas

Fort Picolata
Fort St. Francis

St. Augustine
Fort San Marco
Fort Matanzas

Matanzan Inlet

30°

Southern limit of English claim
(Carolina Charter of 1665)

Gulf of Mexico

N

ACUERA

Cape
Canaveral

AIS

MOCOZO

Lake
Okeechobee

80°

San Carlos

Ponce de
Leon Bay

Caloosahatchee River

CALOOSA

San Ignacio

TEKESTA

25°

| 0 | 10 km |
| 0 | 10 miles |

85°

xvi

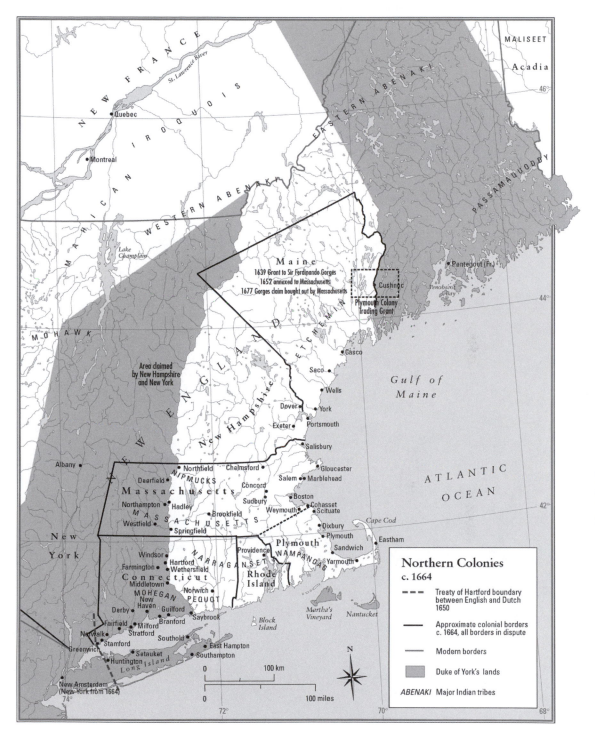

MALISEET

Acadia

N E W   F R A N C E

St. Lawrence River

M O H I C A N   I R O Q U O I S

Quebec

46°

Montreal

E A S T E R N   A B E N A K I

W E S T E R N   A B E N A K I

PASSAMAQUODDY

Lake Champlain

Maine
1639 Grant to Sir Ferdinando Gorges
1652 annexed to Massachusetts
1677 Gorges claim bought out by Massachusetts

Cushnoc

Pentegoet (Fr.)

Penobscot Bay

44°

M O H A W K

Plymouth Colony Trading Grant

Area claimed
by New Hampshire
and New York

E T C H E M I N

Casco

Saco

Wells

Gulf of
Maine

N   E   W   G   L   A   N   D

Albany

Dover

York

Exeter

Portsmouth

New Hampshire

Salisbury

Northfield

Chelmsford

Gloucester

Deerfield

NIPMUCKS

Concord

Salem Marblehead

ATLANTIC
OCEAN

42°

Massachusetts

Northampton   Hadley

Sudbury

Boston

M A S S A C H U S E T T S

Brookfield

Weymouth

Cohasset
Scituate

Westfield

Springfield

Duxbury

Cape Cod

New
York

NARRAGANSET

Plymouth

Sandwich

Eastham

Windsor

Providence

Plymouth

WAMPANOAG

Yarmouth

Farmington

Hartford
Wethersfield

Rhode
Island

Connecticut

Middletown

Norwich

MOHEGAN

PEQUOT

New
Haven

Martha's
Vineyard

Nantucket

Derby

Guilford

Fairfield   Milford   Branford   Saybrook

Block
Island

Stratford

Stamford

Southold

East Hampton

Norwalk

Greenwich

Setauket

Southampton

Huntington

Long   Island

N

New Amsterdam
(New York from 1664)

0   100 km

0   100 miles

74°

72°

70°

68°

Northern Colonies
c. 1664

- - - - Treaty of Hartford boundary
        between English and Dutch
        1650

———   Approximate colonial borders
        c. 1664, all borders in dispute

———   Modern borders

▓▓▓   Duke of York's lands

ABENAKI Major Indian tribes

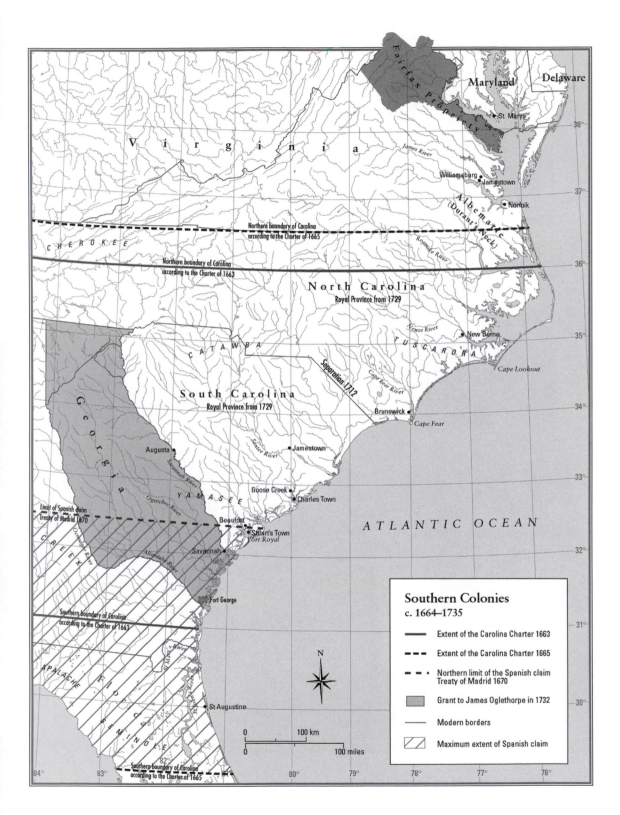

Maryland

Delaware

Fairfax property

St Marys

V i r g i n i a

James River

Williamsburg
Jamestown

Norfolk

Albemarle (Durant's Neck)

C H E R O K E E

Northern boundary of Carolina according to the Charter of 1665

Roanoke River

Northern boundary of Carolina according to the Charter of 1663

North Carolina
Royal Province from 1729

C A T A W B A

Neuse River

T U S C A R O R A

New Berne

Cape Lookout

Separation 1712

Cape Fear River

G e o r g i a

South Carolina
Royal Province from 1729

Y A M A S E E

Brunswick

Cape Fear

Augusta

Savannah River

Ogeechee River

Santee River

Jamestown

C R E E K

Limit of Spanish claim Treaty of Madrid 1670

Goose Creek

Charles Town

ATLANTIC OCEAN

Ocmulgee River

Beaufort

Stuart's Town
Port Royal

Altamaha River

Savannah

Fort George

Southern boundary of Carolina according to the Charter of 1663

A P A L A C H E

F L O R I D A

S E M I N O L E

Mary River

St Augustine

N

Southern boundary of Carolina according to the Charter of 1665

Southern Colonies
c. 1664–1735

——	Extent of the Carolina Charter 1663
– – –	Extent of the Carolina Charter 1665
- - -	Northern limit of the Spanish claim Treaty of Madrid 1670
▓	Grant to James Oglethorpe in 1732
——	Modern borders
▨	Maximum extent of Spanish claim

0   100 km

0   100 miles

38°

37°

36°

35°

34°

33°

32°

31°

30°

84°   83°   82°   80°   79°   78°   77°   76°

HUDSON'S BAY COMPANY

Lake Superior

Lake Huron

Lake Ontario

Lake Erie

FRENCH CANADA

• Québec

• Montréal

Nova Scotia

(To Massachusetts)

New Hampshire

New York

Massachusetts
• Salem
• Boston

Conn.
Hartford

Providence •
R.I. • Newport

Cape Cod

New Haven •

• New York

Pennsylvania

New Jersey

Philadelphia •

N E W   F R A N C E

B R I T I S H   A M E R I C A

Maryland
Baltimore •

Delaware

Virginia

Richmond •
Jamestown •
Williamsburg •

Chesapeake Bay

ATLANTIC OCEAN

North Carolina

Pamlico Sound

South Carolina

Charles Town •

Georgia

Savannah •

East Florida

N

48°

44°

40°

36°

32°

68°

84°

80°

76°

72°

The 1763 Proclamation Line

– – – Proclamation Line of 1763

A general map of New France, the British Colonial Frontier, and New England, as they evolved over the course of the seventeenth and eighteenth centuries.

0 ──── 200 km

0 ──── 200 miles

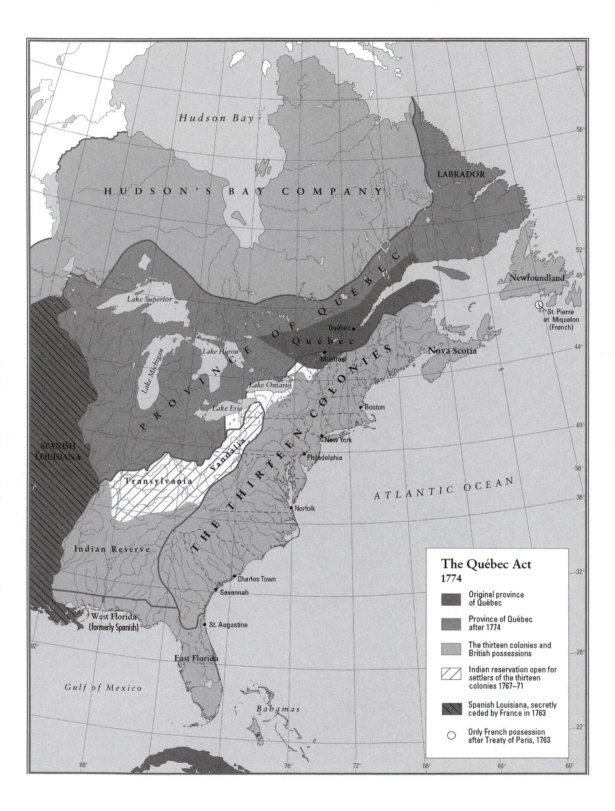

Hudson Bay

HUDSON'S BAY COMPANY

LABRADOR

Newfoundland

St. Pierre
et Miquelon
(French)

Lake Superior

Lake Huron

Lake Michigan

Québec

Québec

Montréal

Nova Scotia

Lake Ontario

Lake Erie

Boston

SPANISH
LOUISIANA

Transylvania

Vandalia

New York

Philadelphia

ATLANTIC OCEAN

Norfolk

Indian Reserve

Charles Town

Savannah

West Florida
(formerly Spanish)

St. Augustine

East Florida

Gulf of Mexico

Bahamas

P R O V I N C E   O F   Q U É B E C

T H E   T H I R T E E N   C O L O N I E S

The Québec Act
1774

Original province
of Québec

Province of Québec
after 1774

The thirteen colonies and
British possessions

Indian reservation open for
settlers of the thirteen
colonies 1767–71

Spanish Louisiana, secretly
ceded by France in 1763

Only French possession
after Treaty of Paris, 1763

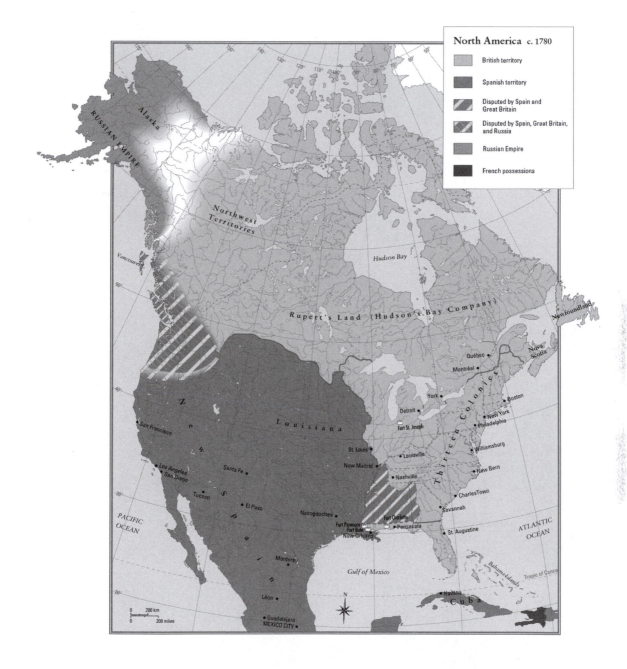

North America c. 1780

- British territory
- Spanish territory
- Disputed by Spain and Great Britain
- Disputed by Spain, Great Britain, and Russia
- Russian Empire
- French possessions

RUSSIAN EMPIRE

Alaska

Northwest Territories

Vancouver

Hudson Bay

Rupert's Land (Hudson's Bay Company)

Newfoundland

Nova Scotia

Québec

Montréal

York

Detroit

Fort St. Joseph

Louisiana

St. Louis

Louisville

Williamsburg

Boston

New York

Philadelphia

Thirteen Colonies

New Bern

CharlesTown

New Escombia

New Madrid

Nashville

Savannah

San Francisco

Los Angeles
San Diego

Santa Fe

Tucson

El Paso

Nacogdoches

Fort Panmure
Fort Bute
New Orleans

Fort Charlotte
Pensacola

St. Augustine

PACIFIC OCEAN

ATLANTIC OCEAN

Monterey

Gulf of Mexico

Bahama Islands

Tropic of Cancer

Havana

Cuba

Léon

N

Guadalajara
MEXICO CITY

0   200 km
0   200 miles

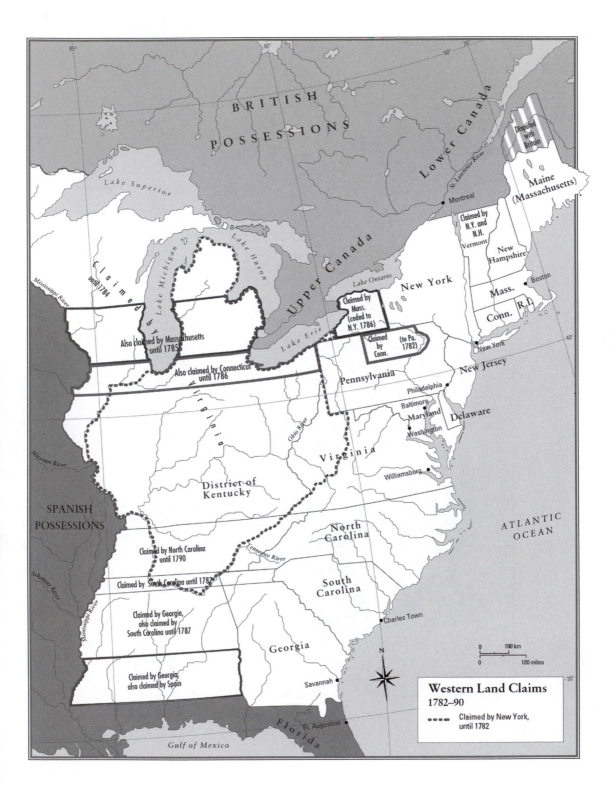

Western Land Claims
1782–90

- - - - Claimed by New York, until 1782

BRITISH POSSESSIONS

Lower Canada

Upper Canada

Lake Superior

Lake Michigan

Lake Huron

Lake Erie

Lake Ontario

Claimed by until 1784

Also claimed by Massachusetts until 1785

Also claimed by Connecticut until 1786

Claimed by Mass. (ceded to N.Y. 1786)

Claimed by Conn. (to Pa. 1782)

New York

Claimed by N.Y. and N.H. Vermont

New Hampshire

Mass.

Conn. R.I.

Boston

Montreal

St. Lawrence River

Maine (Massachusetts)

Disputed with Britain

New York

40°

New Jersey

Pennsylvania

Philadelphia

Baltimore

Maryland

Washington

Delaware

Virginia

Virginia

District of Kentucky

Ohio River

Williamsburg

Mississippi River

Missouri River

SPANISH POSSESSIONS

Arkansas River

Mississippi River

Claimed by North Carolina until 1790

Claimed by South Carolina until 1787

Tennessee River

North Carolina

South Carolina

Claimed by Georgia, also claimed by South Carolina until 1787

Georgia

Charles Town

Claimed by Georgia, also claimed by Spain

Savannah

St. Augustine

Florida

ATLANTIC OCEAN

Gulf of Mexico

0   100 km
0   100 miles

85°   80°   50°   70°

BRITISH

NORTH AMERICA

Lower Canada

Lake Superior

Disputed with Britain

Maine (to Mass.)

• Montreal

Vt.

N o r t h w e s t

Ceded by Virginia 1784

Lake Michigan

Lake Huron

Upper Canada

Lake Ontario

New York

N.H.

• Boston

Mass.

Conn. R.I.

Mississippi River

Ceded by Massachusetts 1785

Ceded by Connecticut 1786

T e r r i t o r y

Lake Erie

Ceded by Conn. 1800

Pennsylvania

New York •

New Jersey

Philadelphia •

Ohio River

Baltimore •

Md.

Delaware

Washington •

Missouri River

Ceded by Virginia 1789 (Kentucky)

Virginia

Williamsburg •

ATLANTIC OCEAN

N

L o u i s i a n a

Ceded by Spain to France 1800

Ceded by North Carolina 1790 (Tennessee)

Tennessee River

North Carolina

Arkansas River

Ceded by South Carolina to Georgia 1787

Mississippi River

Ceded by Georgia 1802

South Carolina

Charleston •

0   100 km
0   100 miles

Western Land Cessions
1782–1802

- - - Boundary of territory ceded by New York 1782

——— Boundary of territory ceded by Virginia 1784

Original thirteen states by 1782

Lands ceded by individual states to the federal government with date

Spanish possessions

British possessions

Georgia

Ceded by Spain 1795

Savannah •

Spanish Florida

St. Augustine •

Gulf of Mexico

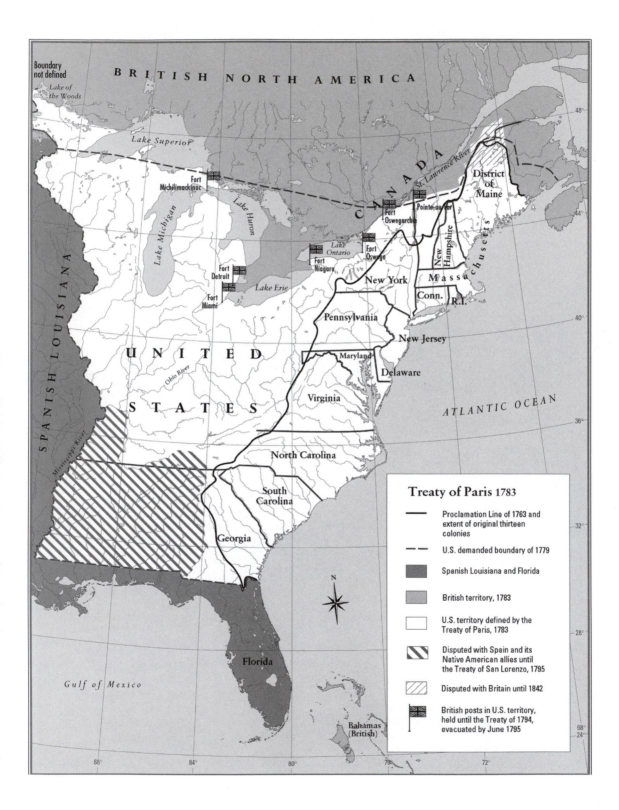

Boundary not defined

Lake of the Woods

BRITISH NORTH AMERICA

Lake Superior

Fort Michilimackinac

C A N A D A

St. Lawrence River

Fort Oswegarchie

Pointe-au-fer

District of Maine

Lake Michigan

Lake Huron

Lake Ontario

Fort Niagara

Fort Oswego

New Hampshire

Fort Detroit

Lake Erie

New York

M a s s a c h u s e t t s

Fort Miami

Conn.

R.I.

Pennsylvania

New Jersey

S P A N I S H   L O U I S I A N A

Ohio River

U N I T E D

Maryland

Delaware

Mississippi River

S T A T E S

Virginia

ATLANTIC OCEAN

North Carolina

South Carolina

N

Georgia

Florida

Gulf of Mexico

Bahamas (British)

Treaty of Paris 1783

—— Proclamation Line of 1763 and extent of original thirteen colonies

– – – U.S. demanded boundary of 1779

Spanish Louisiana and Florida

British territory, 1783

U.S. territory defined by the Treaty of Paris, 1783

Disputed with Spain and its Native American allies until the Treaty of San Lorenzo, 1795

Disputed with Britain until 1842

British posts in U.S. territory, held until the Treaty of 1794, evacuated by June 1795

48°

44°

40°

36°

32°

28°

68° 24°

88°

84°

80°

76°

72°

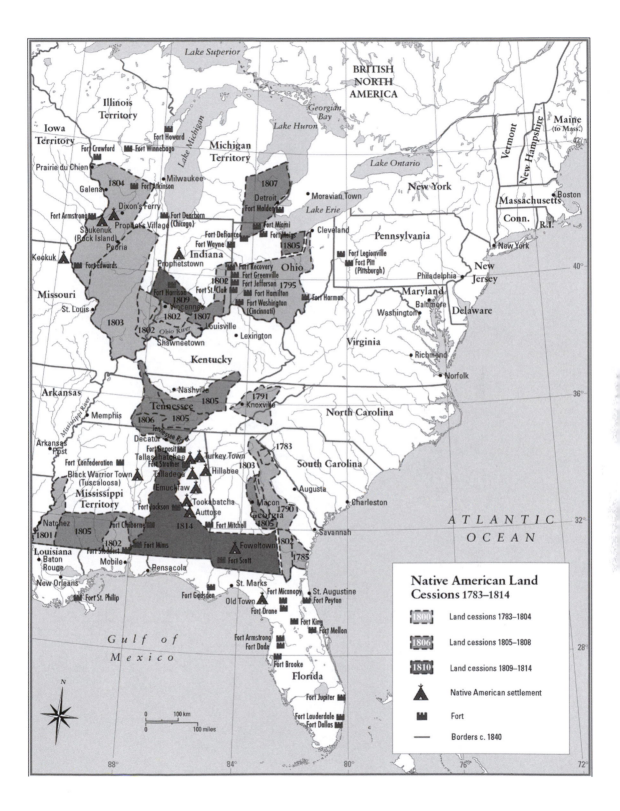

Native American Land Cessions 1783–1814

Lake Superior

BRITISH
NORTH
AMERICA

Illinois
Territory

Iowa
Territory

Fort Howard
Fort Crawford   Fort Winnebago

Prairie du Chien

Lake Michigan

Michigan
Territory

Georgian
Bay

Lake Huron

Lake Ontario

New York

Vermont

New Hampshire

Maine
(to Mass.)

47

Boston

Massachusetts

Conn.

R.I.

Galena   1804   Fort Atkinson

Dixon's Ferry

Fort Armstrong

Saukenuk
(Rock Island)

Keokuk

Missouri

St. Louis

1803

• Milwaukee

Prophets Village

Peoria

Fort Edwards

1802

Ohio River

Shawneetown

Fort Dearborn
(Chicago)

Indiana

Prophetstown

Fort Harrison

1809
Vincennes

1802   1807

Louisville

• Lexington

Kentucky

1807
Detroit
Fort Malden

Fort Miami
Fort Defiance   Fort Meigs   • Cleveland
Fort Wayne   1805

Fort Recovery
Fort Greenville
1802   Fort Jefferson   Ohio
Fort St. Clair   1795
Fort Hamilton
Fort Washington
(Cincinnati)

Moravian Town

Lake Erie

Pennsylvania

Fort Legionville
Fort Pitt
(Pittsburgh)

Fort Harman

Maryland

Washington •

• Philadelphia

Baltimore

New
Jersey

New York

Delaware

40°

Virginia

• Richmond

• Norfolk

Arkansas

Mississippi River

• Memphis

Arkansas
Post

• Nashville   1805

Tennessee

1806   1805

Tennessee River

Decatur
Fort Deposit
Tallasahatchee
Fort Strother
Fort Confederation

Black Warrior Town
(Tuscaloosa)

Mississippi
Territory

Natchez   1805

1801

Louisiana

Baton
Rouge

New Orleans

Mobile

Fort St. Philip

1802
Fort Stoddert

Turkey Town

Talladega

Emuckfaw

Fort Jackson

1814

Fort Claiborne

Fort Mims

Hillabee   1803

Tookabatcha
Auttose

Fort Mitchell

1791
• Knoxville

North Carolina

1783

South Carolina

• Augusta

Macon   1790

Georgia   1805

Fort Scott

• Pensacola

St. Marks

Fort Gadsden

Gulf of
Mexico

N

1802

• Charleston

Savannah

Foweltown

1785

36°

ATLANTIC
OCEAN

32°

Fort Micanopy   • St. Augustine
Old Town   Fort Peyton
Fort Drane

Fort King

Fort Armstrong
Fort Dade

Fort Brooke

Florida

Fort Jupiter

Fort Lauderdale
Fort Dallas

28°

0   100 km

0   100 miles

88°   84°   80°   76°   72°

**Native American Land
Cessions 1783–1814**

1800	Land cessions 1783–1804
1806	Land cessions 1805–1808
1810	Land cessions 1809–1814
▲	Native American settlement
▥	Fort
—	Borders c. 1840

XXV

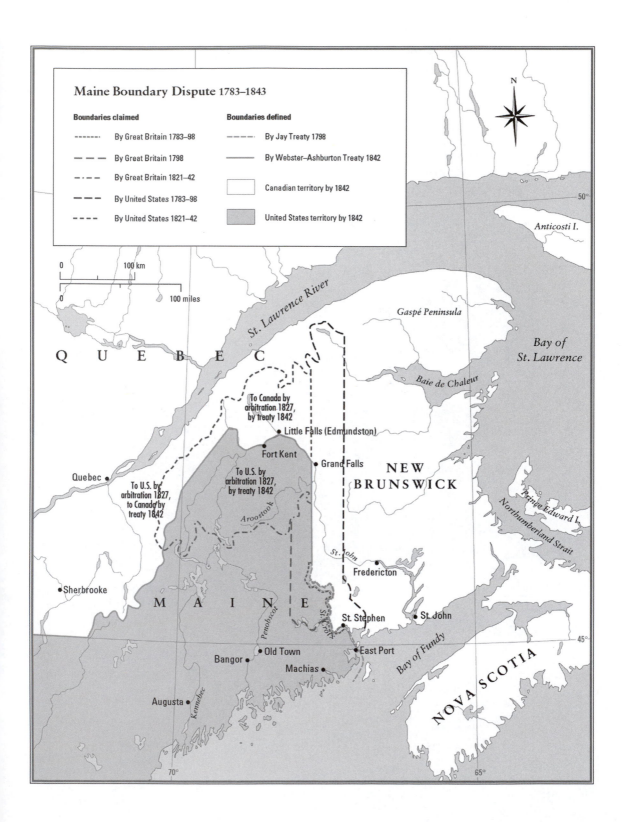

Maine Boundary Dispute 1783–1843

Boundaries claimed
- By Great Britain 1783–98
- By Great Britain 1798
- By Great Britain 1821–42
- By United States 1783–98
- By United States 1821–42

Boundaries defined
- By Jay Treaty 1798
- By Webster–Ashburton Treaty 1842
- Canadian territory by 1842
- United States territory by 1842

0   100 km

0   100 miles

N

50°

Anticosti I.

St. Lawrence River

Gaspé Peninsula

Bay of
St. Lawrence

Baie de Chaleur

QUEBEC

To Canada by
arbitration 1827,
by treaty 1842

Little Falls (Edmundston)

Fort Kent

Grand Falls

NEW
BRUNSWICK

Quebec

To U.S. by
arbitration 1827,
to Canada by
treaty 1842

To U.S. by
arbitration 1827,
by treaty 1842

Aroostook

Prince Edward I.

Northumberland Strait

Sherbrooke

MAINE

St. John

Fredericton

Penobscot

St. Croix

St. Stephen

St. John

Old Town

East Port

Bay of Fundy

45°

Bangor

Machias

NOVA SCOTIA

Augusta

Kennebec

70°

65°

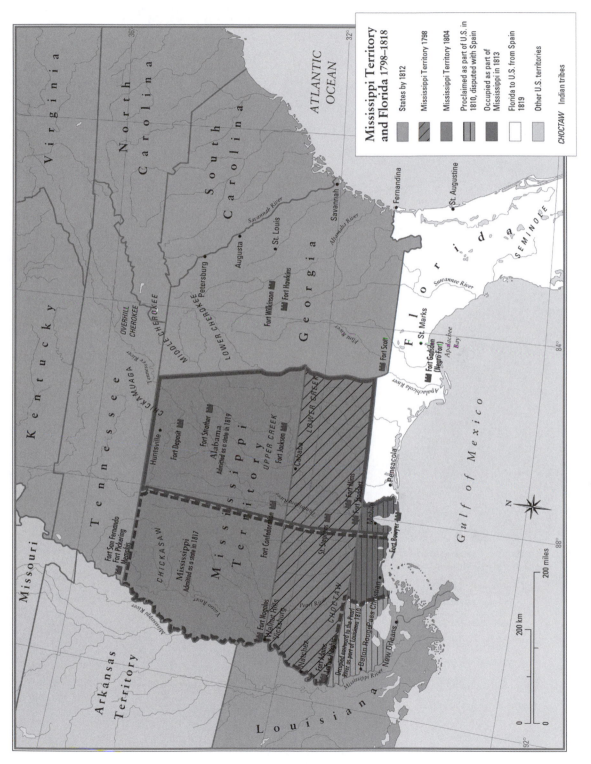

Mississippi Territory and Florida 1798–1818

States by 1812
Mississippi Territory 1798
Mississippi Territory 1804
Proclaimed as part of U.S. in 1810, disputed with Spain
Occupied as part of Mississippi in 1813
Florida to U.S. from Spain 1819
Other U.S. territories
CHOCTAW Indian tribes

Virginia

North Carolina

South Carolina

ATLANTIC OCEAN

Kentucky

Tennessee

Missouri

Arkansas Territory

OVERHILL CHEROKEE

MIDDLE CHEROKEE

LOWER CHEROKEE

CHICKAMAUGA

Tennessee River

Georgia

Savannah River

Augusta

• St. Louis

Petersburg •

Fort Wilkinson

Fort Hawkins

Flint River

Altamaha River

Savannah •

Fernandina •

• St. Augustine

F l o r i d a

S E M I N O L E

Suwannee River

St. Marks •

Fort Scott

Fort Gadsden (Negro Fort)

Apalachicola River

Apalachee Bay

CHICKASAW

Huntsville •

Fort Deposit

Fort Strother

Alabama Admitted as a state in 1819

Mississippi Territory

UPPER CREEK

LOWER CREEK

Fort Jackson

• Coosa

Fort Confederation

Tombigbee River

St. Stephens

Fort Mims

Fort Stoddert

Mobile

Fort Bowyer

Pensacola •

Gulf of Mexico

Mississippi Admitted as a state in 1817

Mississippi Territory

Fort San Fernando
Fort Pickering
Memphis

Yazoo River

Fort Nogales
Walnut Hills
Vicksburg

Pearl River

CHOCTAW

Fort Adams •

Fort Dearborn

Natchez •

Baton Rouge
Pass Christian

New Orleans •

Organized westward to the Pearl River as part of Louisiana 1810

Mississippi River

L o u i s i a n a

N

200 miles

200 km

0

0

xxvii

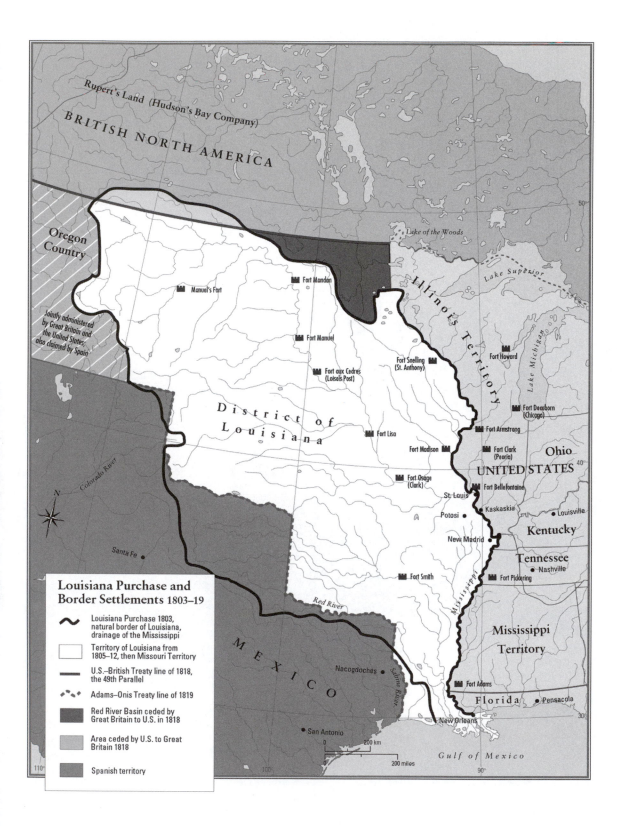

Rupert's Land (Hudson's Bay Company)

BRITISH NORTH AMERICA

Oregon
Country

Jointly administered
by Great Britain and
the United States;
also claimed by Spain

Lake of the Woods

Lake Superior

50

Illinois Territory

Lake Michigan

Manuel's Fort

Fort Mandan

Fort Manuel

Fort aux Cedres
(Loisels Post)

Fort Snelling
(St. Anthony)

Fort Howard

Fort Dearborn
(Chicago)

District of
Louisiana

Fort Lisa

Fort Madison

Fort Armstrong

Fort Clark
(Peoria)

Ohio

Fort Osage
(Clark)

Fort Bellefontaine

UNITED STATES

40

Colorado River

St. Louis

Potosi

Kaskaskia

Louisville

Kentucky

N

Santa Fe

New Madrid

Tennessee

Nashville

Fort Smith

Fort Pickering

Red River

Mississippi
Territory

Mississippi

Louisiana Purchase and
Border Settlements 1803–19

Louisiana Purchase 1803,
natural border of Louisiana,
drainage of the Mississippi

Territory of Louisiana from
1805–12, then Missouri Territory

U.S.–British Treaty line of 1818,
the 49th Parallel

Adams–Onis Treaty line of 1819

Red River Basin ceded by
Great Britain to U.S. in 1818

Area ceded by U.S. to Great
Britain 1818

Spanish territory

M E X I C O

Nacogdoches

Sabine River

Fort Adams

Florida

Pensacola

30

San Antonio

New Orleans

Gulf of Mexico

0   200 km

0   200 miles

110

100

90

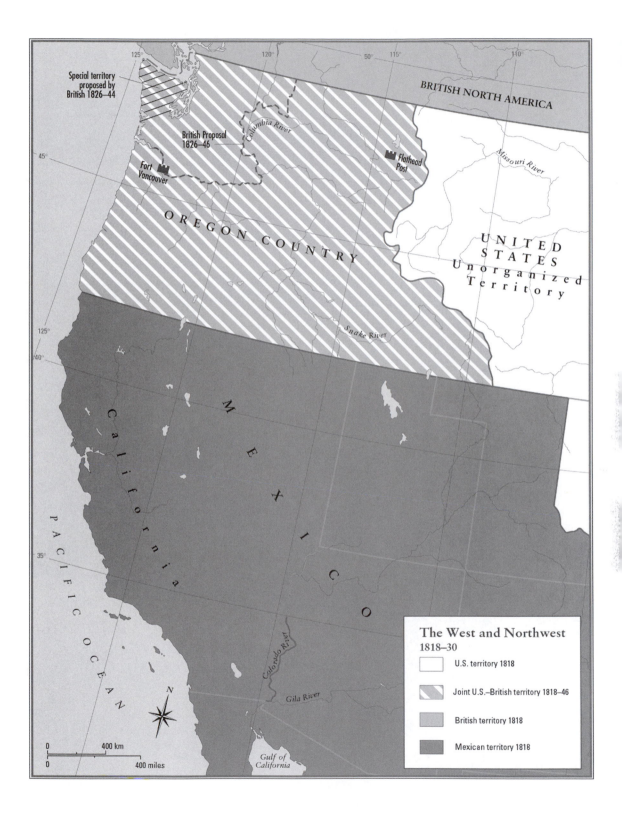

Special territory
proposed by
British 1826–44

British Proposal
1826–46

Fort
Vancouver

Flathead
Post

Columbia River

BRITISH NORTH AMERICA

Missouri River

UNITED
STATES
Unorganized
Territory

O R E G O N   C O U N T R Y

Snake River

M E X I C O

C a l i f o r n i a

P A C I F I C   O C E A N

Colorado R.

Gila River

*Gulf of
California*

N

0   400 km
0   400 miles

The West and Northwest
1818–30

☐ U.S. territory 1818

▨ Joint U.S.–British territory 1818–46

▨ British territory 1818

▨ Mexican territory 1818

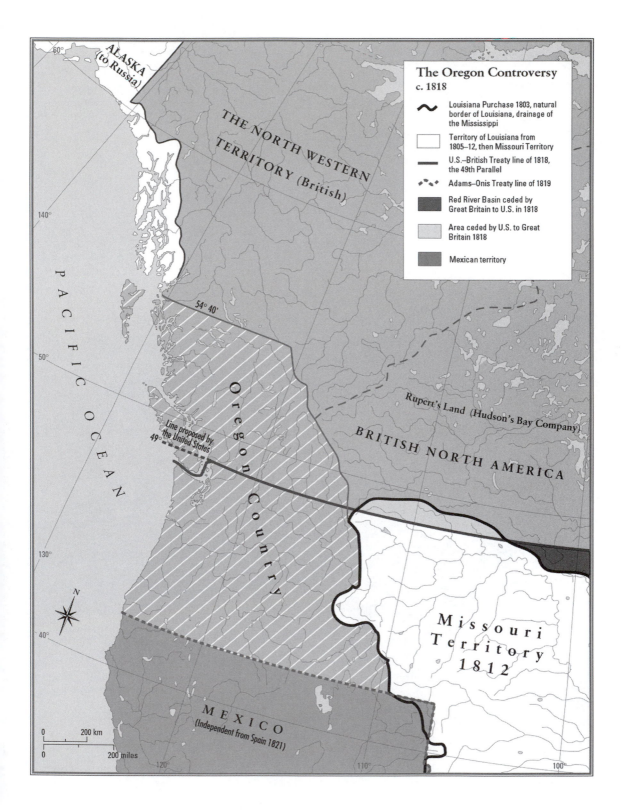

The Oregon Controversy
c. 1818

~ Louisiana Purchase 1803, natural border of Louisiana, drainage of the Mississippi

Territory of Louisiana from 1805–12, then Missouri Territory

U.S.–British Treaty line of 1818, the 49th Parallel

Adams–Onis Treaty line of 1819

Red River Basin ceded by Great Britain to U.S. in 1818

Area ceded by U.S. to Great Britain 1818

Mexican territory

ALASKA (to Russia)

THE NORTH WESTERN TERRITORY (British)

PACIFIC OCEAN

54° 40'

Oregon Country

Rupert's Land (Hudson's Bay Company)

BRITISH NORTH AMERICA

Line proposed by the United States

49°

Missouri Territory 1812

N

MEXICO
(Independent from Spain 1821)

0   200 km
0   200 miles

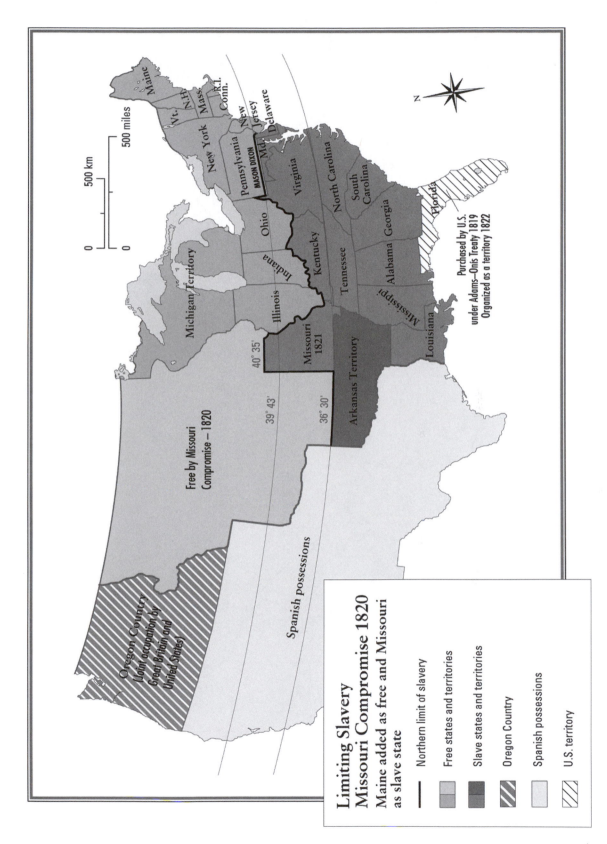

Limiting Slavery
Missouri Compromise 1820
Maine added as free and Missouri
as slave state

— Northern limit of slavery

Free states and territories

Slave states and territories

Oregon Country

Spanish possessions

U.S. territory

Maine
Vt. N.H.
Mass.
R.I.
Conn.
New York
New Jersey
Pennsylvania
Delaware
Md.
MASON DIXON
Ohio
Virginia
North Carolina
South Carolina
Kentucky
Tennessee
Georgia
Alabama
Mississippi
Louisiana
Michigan Territory
Indiana
Illinois
Missouri 1821
Arkansas Territory
40° 35'
39° 43'
36° 30'
Free by Missouri Compromise — 1820
Spanish possessions
Oregon Country (Joint occupation by Great Britain and United States)

Florida
Purchased by U.S. under Adams–Onís Treaty 1819 Organized as a territory 1822

500 miles
500 km
0
0

N

xxxi

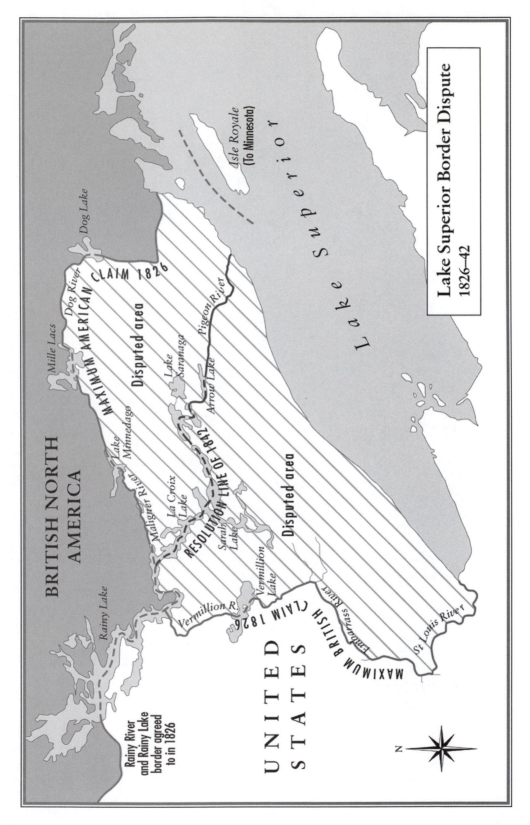

Lake Superior Border Dispute
1826–42

Lake Superior

Isle Royale
(To Minnesota)

BRITISH NORTH
AMERICA

Dog Lake

Dog River

MAXIMUM AMERICAN CLAIM 1826

Disputed area

Mille Lacs

Pigeon River

Lake
Saganaga

Arrow Lake

Lake
Minnedago

La Croix
Lake

Maligner River

RESOLUTION LINE OF 1842

Sarah
Lake

Vermillion
Lake

Disputed area

Rainy Lake

Vermillion R.

MAXIMUM BRITISH CLAIM 1826

Embarrass River

St. Louis River

UNITED
STATES

Rainy River
and Rainy Lake
border agreed
to in 1826

N

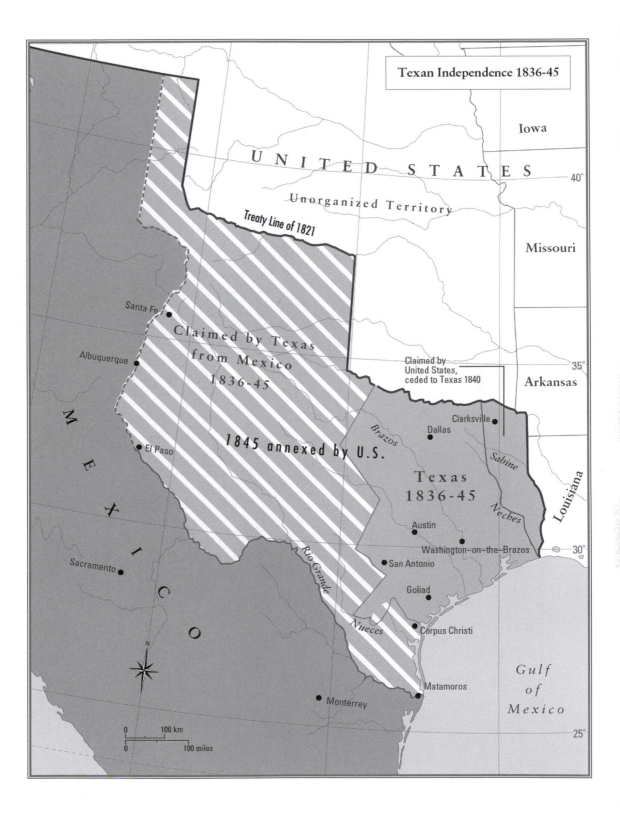

Texan Independence 1836-45

Iowa

UNITED STATES
40°

Unorganized Territory

Missouri

Treaty Line of 1821

Santa Fe
Albuquerque
35°
Claimed by
United States,
ceded to Texas 1840
Arkansas

Claimed by Texas
from Mexico
1836-45

Clarksville
Dallas

M E X I C O

El Paso

1845 annexed by U.S.

Brazos
Sabine
Louisiana

Texas
1836-45

Neches

Austin

Washington-on-the-Brazos
30°

Sacramento

Rio Grande

San Antonio

Goliad

Nueces

Corpus Christi

N

Gulf
of
Mexico

Matamoros

Monterrey

0   100 km
0   100 miles
25°

xxxiii

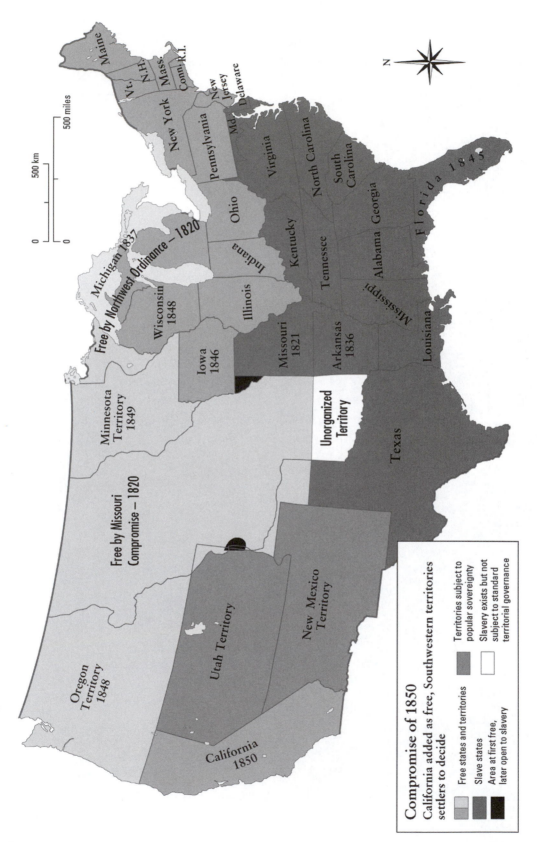

Compromise of 1850
California added as free, Southwestern territories settlers to decide

Legend:
- Free states and territories
- Slave states
- Area at first free, later open to slavery
- Territories subject to popular sovereignty
- Slavery exists but not subject to standard territorial governance

Maine

N.H.

Vt.

Mass.

Conn. R.I.

New York

New Jersey

Delaware

Pennsylvania

Md.

Virginia

North Carolina

South Carolina

Florida 1845

Ohio

Kentucky

Tennessee

Alabama Georgia

Indiana

Mississippi

Illinois

Michigan 1837

Free by Northwest Ordinance – 1820

Wisconsin 1848

Missouri 1821

Arkansas 1836

Louisiana

Iowa 1846

Unorganized Territory

Minnesota Territory 1849

Texas

Free by Missouri Compromise – 1820

New Mexico Territory

Utah Territory

Oregon Territory 1848

California 1850

500 miles

500 km

N

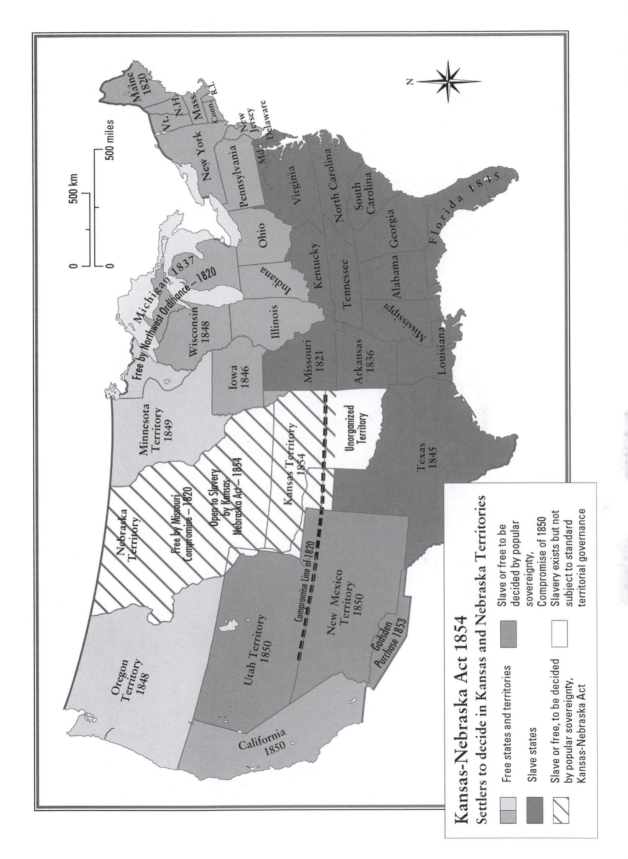

Kansas-Nebraska Act 1854

Settlers to decide in Kansas and Nebraska Territories

Free states and territories

Slave states

Slave or free, to be decided by popular sovereignty, Kansas-Nebraska Act

Slave or free to be decided by popular sovereignty, Compromise of 1850

Slavery exists but not subject to standard territorial governance

---

Maine 1820

Vt.

N.H.

Mass.

Conn. R.I.

New York

Pennsylvania

New Jersey

Md.

Delaware

Virginia

North Carolina

South Carolina

Georgia

Florida 1845

Ohio

Michigan 1837

Free by Northwest Ordinance – 1820

Wisconsin 1848

Indiana

Illinois

Kentucky

Tennessee

Alabama

Mississippi

Louisiana

Missouri 1821

Arkansas 1836

Iowa 1846

Minnesota Territory 1849

Kansas Territory 1854

Unorganized Territory

Texas 1845

Nebraska Territory

Free by Missouri Compromise – 1820

Open to Slavery by Kansas-Nebraska Act – 1854

Compromise Line of 1820

New Mexico Territory 1850

Gadsden Purchase 1853

Utah Territory 1850

Oregon Territory 1848

California 1850

N

500 miles

500 km

0

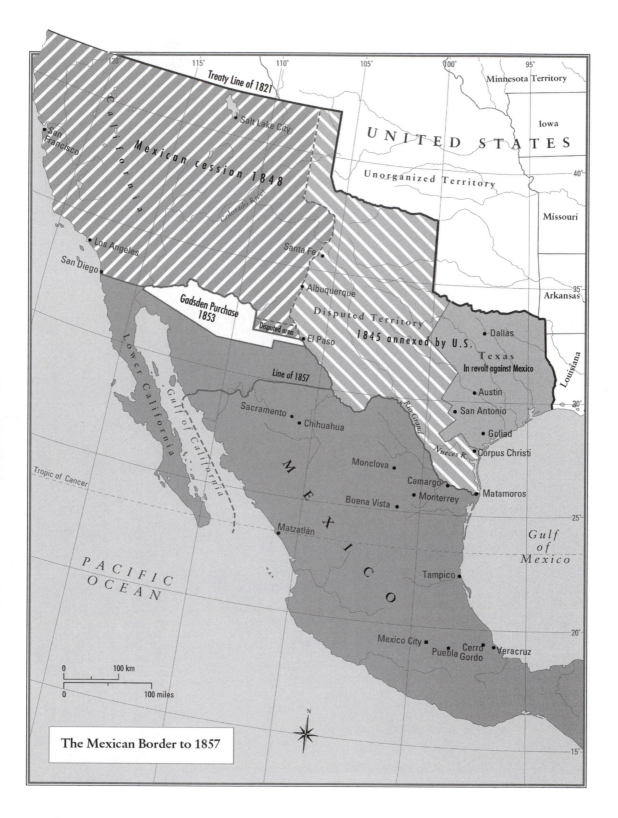

The Mexican Border to 1857

Treaty Line of 1821

Salt Lake City

San Francisco

UNITED STATES

Mexican cession 1848

Unorganized Territory

Iowa

Minnesota Territory

Missouri

Los Angeles

Colorado River

Santa Fe

Arkansas

San Diego

Albuquerque

Gadsden Purchase 1853

Disputed Territory

Disputed area

El Paso

1845 annexed by U.S.

Dallas

Texas
In revolt against Mexico

Louisiana

Line of 1857

Sacramento

Chihuahua

Austin

San Antonio

Lower California

Gulf of California

MEXICO

Monclova

Rio Grande

Goliad

Nueces R.

Corpus Christi

Tropic of Cancer

Buena Vista

Camargo

Monterrey

Matamoros

Matzatlán

Gulf
of
Mexico

PACIFIC
OCEAN

Tampico

Mexico City

Cerro
Gordo

Veracruz

Puebla

0   100 km

0   100 miles

N

The Mexican Border to 1857

xxxvi

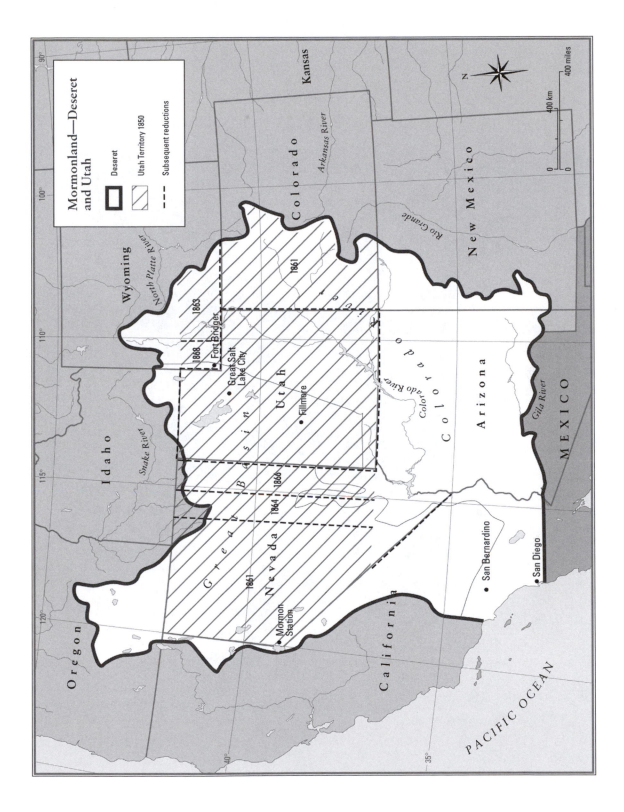

1775

MINNESOTA

WISCONSIN

MICHIGAN

IOWA

ILLINOIS INDIANA OHIO

KANSAS MISSOURI

KENTUCKY

OKLAHOMA ARKANSAS

TENNESSEE

TEXAS

MISSISSIPPI ALABAMA

LOUISIANA

VT.

N.H.

NEW YORK

MASSACHUSETTS

CONN.

R.I.

PA.

NEW JERSEY

MD.

DELAWARE

VIRGINIA

Proclamation Line of 1763

NORTH CAROLINA

SOUTH CAROLINA

GEORGIA

FLORIDA

United States Territorial Growth
1775–1960

Thirteen Colonies

British Territories

Spanish Territories

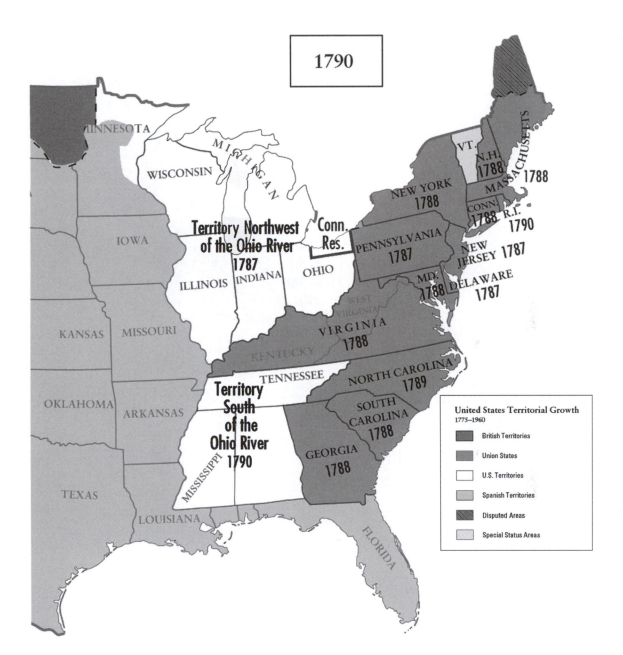

1790

MINNESOTA

MICHIGAN

WISCONSIN

VT.

N.H.
1788

MASSACHUSETTS 1788

NEW YORK
1788

CONN.
1788 R.I.
1790

IOWA

Territory Northwest
of the Ohio River
1787

Conn.
Res.

PENNSYLVANIA
1787

NEW
JERSEY 1787

ILLINOIS INDIANA OHIO

MD.
1788 DELAWARE
1787

WEST
VIRGINIA

KANSAS MISSOURI

VIRGINIA
1788

KENTUCKY

TENNESSEE

NORTH CAROLINA
1789

Territory
South
of the
Ohio River
1790

SOUTH
CAROLINA
1788

OKLAHOMA

ARKANSAS

MISSISSIPPI

GEORGIA
1788

TEXAS

LOUISIANA

FLORIDA

United States Territorial Growth
1775–1960

British Territories

Union States

U.S. Territories

Spanish Territories

Disputed Areas

Special Status Areas

xxxix

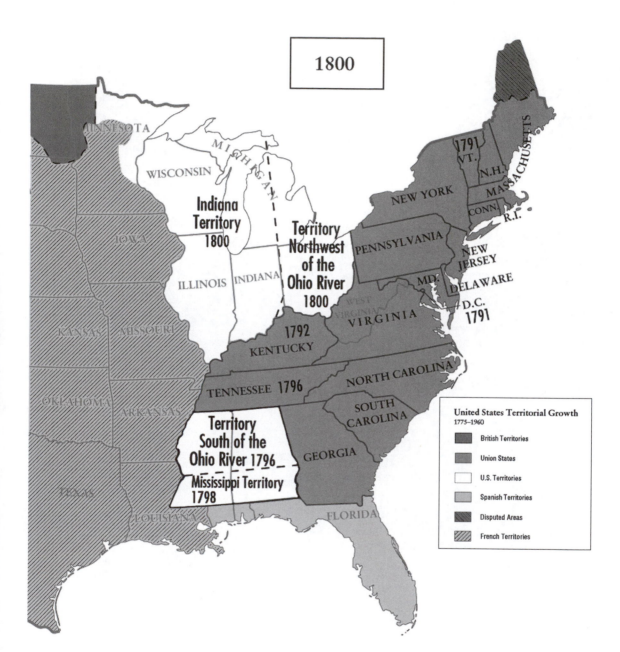

1800

MINNESOTA

MICHIGAN

WISCONSIN

Indiana
Territory
1800

IOWA

ILLINOIS   INDIANA

Territory
Northwest
of the
Ohio River
1800

NEW YORK

1791
VT.

N.H.

MASSACHUSETTS

CONN.

R.I.

PENNSYLVANIA

NEW
JERSEY

MD.

DELAWARE

WEST
VIRGINIA   VIRGINIA

D.C.
1791

KANSAS   MISSOURI

1792
KENTUCKY

OKLAHOMA   ARKANSAS

TENNESSEE 1796

NORTH CAROLINA

SOUTH
CAROLINA

Territory
South of the
Ohio River 1796

Mississippi Territory
1798

GEORGIA

TEXAS

LOUISIANA

FLORIDA

United States Territorial Growth
1775–1960

■	British Territories
■	Union States
□	U.S. Territories
■	Spanish Territories
▨	Disputed Areas
▨	French Territories

xl

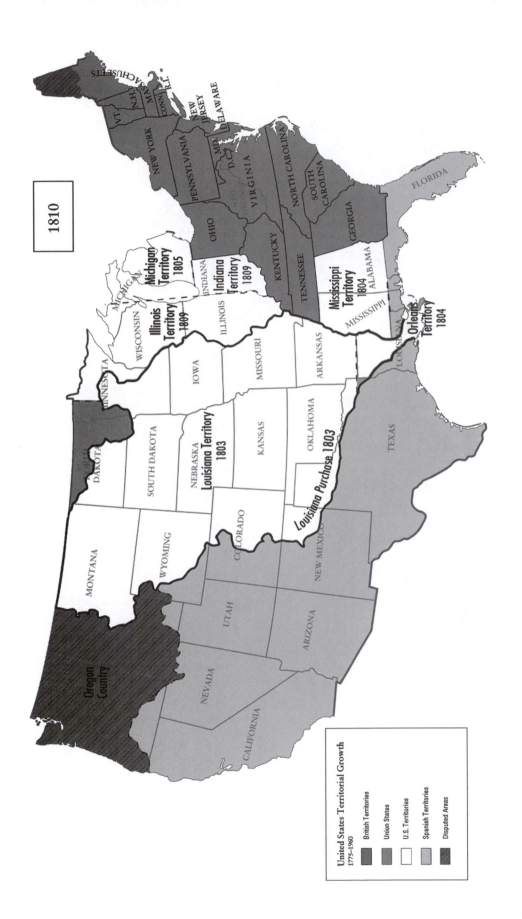

1810

Oregon Country

MONTANA

NORTH DAKOTA

SOUTH DAKOTA

WYOMING

NEVADA

UTAH

COLORADO

CALIFORNIA

ARIZONA

NEW MEXICO

Louisiana Purchase 1803

NEBRASKA
Louisiana Territory
1803

KANSAS

OKLAHOMA

TEXAS

IOWA

MISSOURI

MINNESOTA

WISCONSIN

ILLINOIS

ARKANSAS

MICHIGAN

Michigan Territory
1805

Illinois
Territory
1809

INDIANA
Indiana
Territory
1809

OHIO

KENTUCKY

TENNESSEE

Mississippi
Territory
1804

ALABAMA

MISSISSIPPI

LOUISIANA

Orleans
Territory
1804

VIRGINIA

NORTH CAROLINA

SOUTH CAROLINA

GEORGIA

FLORIDA

D.C.
MD.

DELAWARE

PENNSYLVANIA

NEW YORK

NEW JERSEY

CONN.

R.I.

MASS.

MASSACHUSETTS

N.H.

VT.

United States Territorial Growth
1775–1960

British Territories

Union States

U.S. Territories

Spanish Territories

Disputed Areas

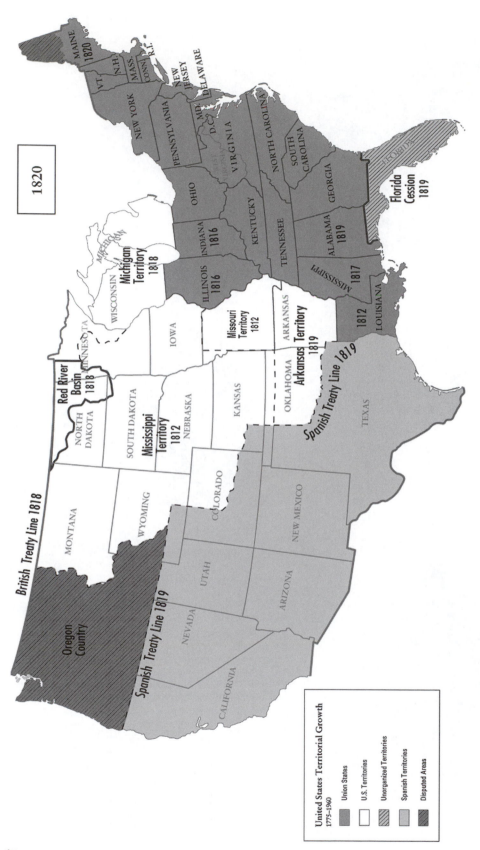

United States Territorial Growth
1775–1960

	Union States
	U.S. Territories
	Unorganized Territories
	Spanish Territories
	Disputed Areas

1820

MAINE 1820
N.H.
VT.
MASS.
CONN.
R.I.
NEW YORK
NEW JERSEY
PENNSYLVANIA
MD.
DEL.
D.C.
WEST VIRGINIA
VIRGINIA
NORTH CAROLINA
SOUTH CAROLINA
GEORGIA
OHIO
KENTUCKY
TENNESSEE
ALABAMA 1819
MISSISSIPPI 1817
1812
LOUISIANA
Florida Cession 1819
INDIANA 1816
ILLINOIS 1816
Michigan Territory 1818
MICHIGAN
WISCONSIN
IOWA
MINNESOTA
Missouri Territory 1812
ARKANSAS Arkansas Territory 1819
Red River Basin 1818
NORTH DAKOTA
SOUTH DAKOTA
Mississippi Territory 1812
NEBRASKA
KANSAS
OKLAHOMA
Spanish Treaty Line 1819
TEXAS
COLORADO
NEW MEXICO
British Treaty Line 1818
MONTANA
WYOMING
UTAH
ARIZONA
Oregon Country
Spanish Treaty Line 1819
NEVADA
CALIFORNIA

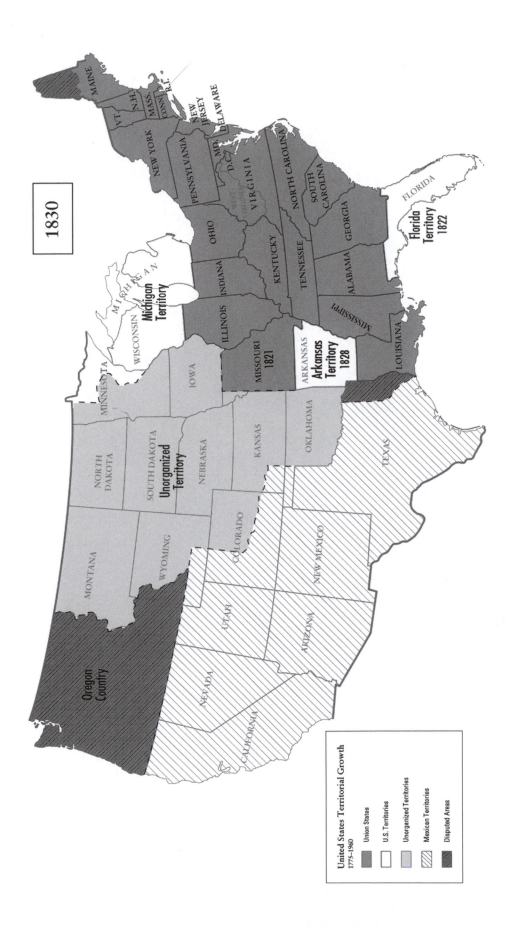

1830

MAINE

VT. N.H. MASS. CONN. R.I.

NEW YORK

NEW JERSEY

DELAWARE

PENNSYLVANIA

MD.

D.C.

WEST VIRGINIA

VIRGINIA

NORTH CAROLINA

SOUTH CAROLINA

GEORGIA

OHIO

KENTUCKY

TENNESSEE

INDIANA

ALABAMA

ILLINOIS

MISSISSIPPI

LOUISIANA

MISSOURI 1821

ARKANSAS

Arkansas Territory 1828

FLORIDA

Florida Territory 1822

MICHIGAN

Michigan Territory

WISCONSIN

MINNESOTA

IOWA

NORTH DAKOTA

SOUTH DAKOTA

Unorganized Territory

NEBRASKA

KANSAS

OKLAHOMA

TEXAS

MONTANA

WYOMING

COLORADO

NEW MEXICO

UTAH

ARIZONA

Oregon Country

NEVADA

CALIFORNIA

United States Territorial Growth
1775–1960

Union States

U.S. Territories

Unorganized Territories

Mexican Territories

Disputed Areas

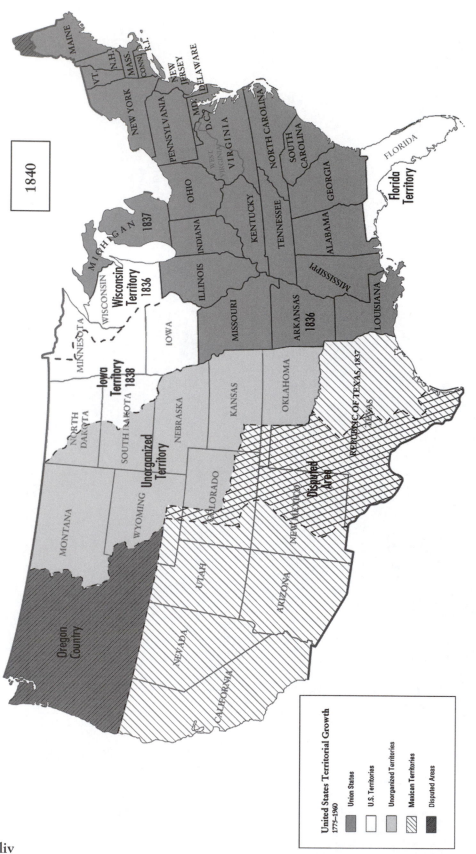

1840

United States Territorial Growth
1775–1960

- Union States
- U.S. Territories
- Unorganized Territories
- Mexican Territories
- Disputed Areas

MAINE

VT
N.H.
MASS.
CONN.
R.I.

NEW YORK

NEW JERSEY
DELAWARE

MD.
D.C.

PENNSYLVANIA

WEST VIRGINIA

VIRGINIA

NORTH CAROLINA

SOUTH CAROLINA

FLORIDA

Florida Territory

OHIO

KENTUCKY

TENNESSEE

ALABAMA

GEORGIA

MICHIGAN 1837

INDIANA

ILLINOIS

MISSISSIPPI

WISCONSIN
Wisconsin Territory 1836

MINNESOTA

IOWA

MISSOURI

ARKANSAS 1836

LOUISIANA

Iowa Territory 1838

NORTH DAKOTA

SOUTH DAKOTA

NEBRASKA

KANSAS

OKLAHOMA

REPUBLIC OF TEXAS, 1837
TEXAS, 1845

Unorganized Territory

WYOMING

COLORADO

NEW MEXICO

Disputed Area

MONTANA

UTAH

ARIZONA

Oregon Country

NEVADA

CALIFORNIA

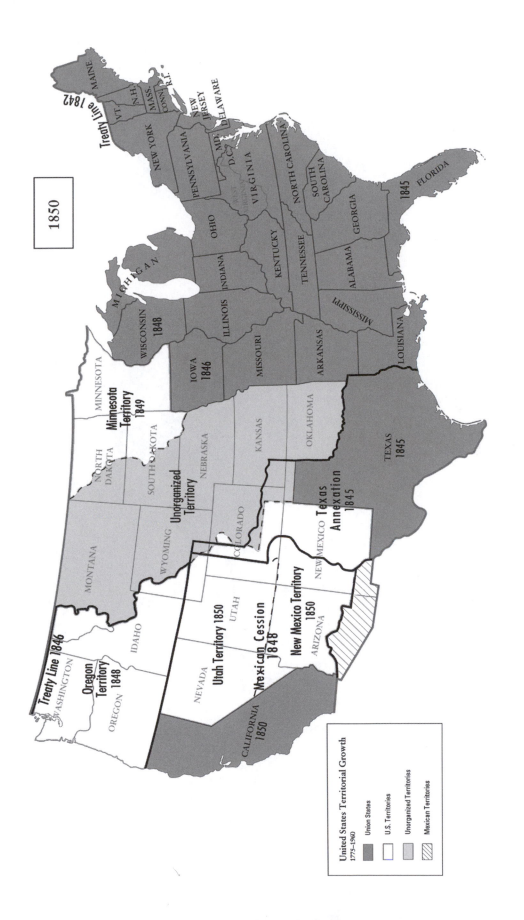

1850

United States Territorial Growth
1775–1960

■ Union States
□ U.S. Territories
▨ Unorganized Territories
▨ Mexican Territories

MAINE

Treaty Line 1842

VT. N.H. MASS. CONN. R.I.

NEW YORK

NEW JERSEY

DELAWARE

PENNSYLVANIA

MD.

D.C.

WEST VIRGINIA

OHIO

VIRGINIA

NORTH CAROLINA

SOUTH CAROLINA

KENTUCKY

GEORGIA

TENNESSEE

ALABAMA

FLORIDA 1845

MICHIGAN

INDIANA

ILLINOIS

MISSISSIPPI

WISCONSIN 1848

IOWA 1846

MISSOURI

ARKANSAS

LOUISIANA

MINNESOTA

Minnesota Territory 1849

NORTH DAKOTA

SOUTH DAKOTA

NEBRASKA

KANSAS

OKLAHOMA

TEXAS 1845

Unorganized Territory

MONTANA

WYOMING

COLORADO

Texas Annexation 1845

NEW MEXICO

IDAHO

UTAH

Utah Territory 1850

Mexican Cession 1848

New Mexico Territory 1850

ARIZONA

Treaty Line 1846

WASHINGTON

Oregon Territory 1848

OREGON

NEVADA

CALIFORNIA 1850

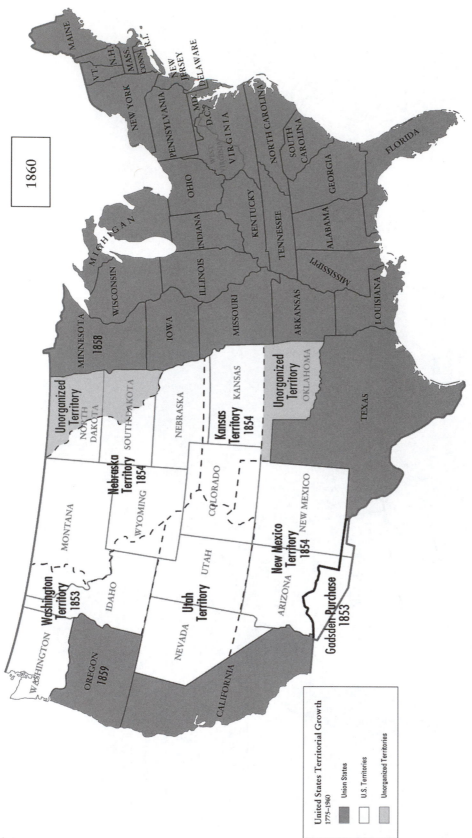

1860

United States Territorial Growth
1775–1960

Union States
U.S. Territories
Unorganized Territories

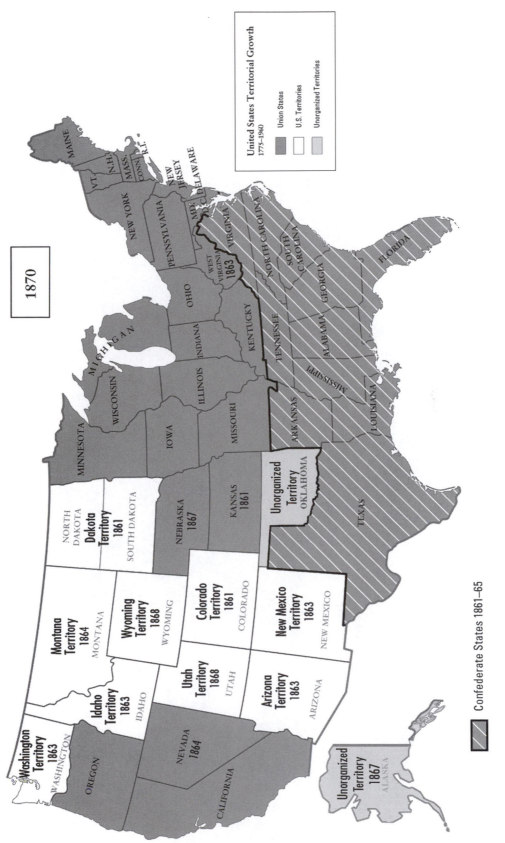

United States Territorial Growth
1775–1960

Union States
U.S. Territories
Unorganized Territories

1870

MAINE
VT
N.H.
MASS.
CONN
R.I.
NEW YORK
NEW JERSEY
PENNSYLVANIA
MD.
DELAWARE
D.C.
VIRGINIA
WEST VIRGINIA 1863
OHIO
NORTH CAROLINA
SOUTH CAROLINA
GEORGIA
FLORIDA
MICHIGAN
WISCONSIN
ILLINOIS
INDIANA
KENTUCKY
TENNESSEE
ALABAMA
MISSISSIPPI
MINNESOTA
IOWA
MISSOURI
ARKANSAS
LOUISIANA
NORTH DAKOTA
Dakota Territory 1861
SOUTH DAKOTA
NEBRASKA 1867
KANSAS 1861
Unorganized Territory OKLAHOMA
TEXAS
Montana Territory 1864
MONTANA
Wyoming Territory 1868
WYOMING
Colorado Territory 1861
COLORADO
New Mexico Territory 1863
NEW MEXICO
Washington Territory 1863
WASHINGTON
Idaho Territory 1863
IDAHO
Utah Territory 1868
UTAH
Arizona Territory 1863
ARIZONA
OREGON
NEVADA 1864
CALIFORNIA
Unorganized Territory 1867
ALASKA

Confederate States 1861–65

xlvii

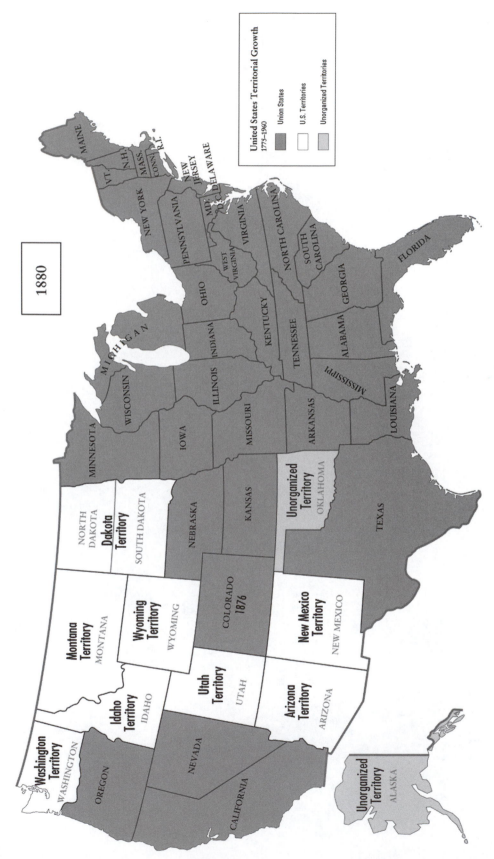

United States Territorial Growth
1775–1960

Union States
U.S. Territories
Unorganized Territories

1880

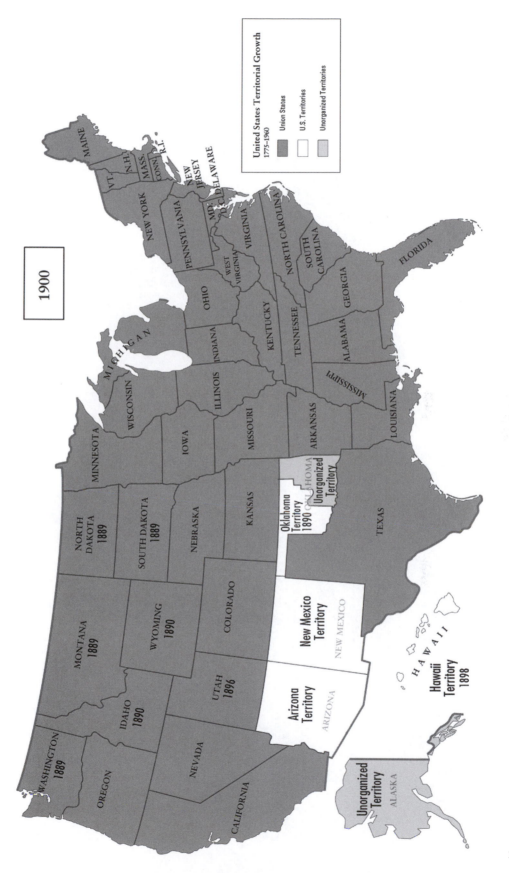

1900

United States Territorial Growth
1775–1960

Union States
U.S. Territories
Unorganized Territories

MAINE
VT.
N.H.
MASS.
CONN.
R.I.
NEW YORK
NEW JERSEY
MD.
DELAWARE
PENNSYLVANIA
WEST VIRGINIA
VIRGINIA
OHIO
KENTUCKY
NORTH CAROLINA
SOUTH CAROLINA
TENNESSEE
GEORGIA
ALABAMA
FLORIDA
MICHIGAN
INDIANA
ILLINOIS
WISCONSIN
MISSISSIPPI
MINNESOTA
IOWA
MISSOURI
ARKANSAS
LOUISIANA
NORTH DAKOTA 1889
SOUTH DAKOTA 1889
NEBRASKA
KANSAS
Oklahoma Territory 1890
OKLAHOMA
Unorganized Territory
TEXAS
MONTANA 1889
WYOMING 1890
COLORADO
New Mexico Territory
NEW MEXICO
WASHINGTON 1889
IDAHO 1890
UTAH 1896
Arizona Territory
ARIZONA
OREGON
NEVADA
CALIFORNIA
H A W A I I
Hawaii Territory 1898
Unorganized Territory
ALASKA

xlix

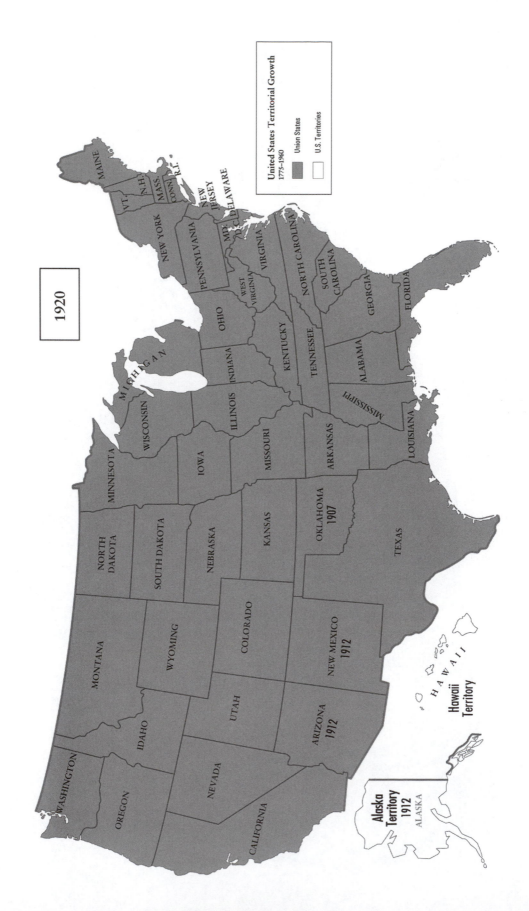

United States Territorial Growth
1775–1960

Union States
U.S. Territories

1920

MAINE
VT.
N.H.
MASS.
CONN.
R.I.
NEW YORK
NEW JERSEY
PENNSYLVANIA
MD.
DEL.
DELAWARE
WEST VIRGINIA
VIRGINIA
NORTH CAROLINA
SOUTH CAROLINA
GEORGIA
FLORIDA
OHIO
KENTUCKY
TENNESSEE
ALABAMA
MISSISSIPPI
LOUISIANA
MICHIGAN
INDIANA
ILLINOIS
WISCONSIN
MINNESOTA
IOWA
MISSOURI
ARKANSAS
NORTH DAKOTA
SOUTH DAKOTA
NEBRASKA
KANSAS
OKLAHOMA
1907
TEXAS
MONTANA
WYOMING
COLORADO
NEW MEXICO
1912
ARIZONA
1912
IDAHO
UTAH
WASHINGTON
OREGON
NEVADA
CALIFORNIA

HAWAII
Hawaii
Territory

Alaska
Territory
1912
ALASKA

1

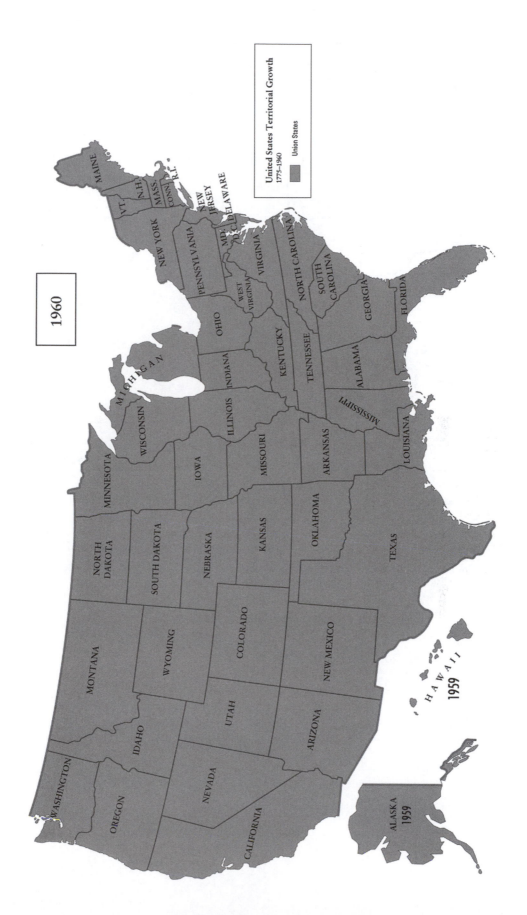

1960

United States Territorial Growth
1775–1960

Union States

MAINE
N.H.
VT.
MASS.
CONN. R.I.
NEW YORK
NEW JERSEY
PENNSYLVANIA
MD.
DELAWARE
D.C.
WEST VIRGINIA
VIRGINIA
NORTH CAROLINA
SOUTH CAROLINA
GEORGIA
FLORIDA
OHIO
KENTUCKY
TENNESSEE
ALABAMA
MISSISSIPPI
INDIANA
ILLINOIS
MISSOURI
ARKANSAS
LOUISIANA
MICHIGAN
WISCONSIN
IOWA
OKLAHOMA
TEXAS
MINNESOTA
NORTH DAKOTA
SOUTH DAKOTA
NEBRASKA
KANSAS
COLORADO
NEW MEXICO
MONTANA
WYOMING
UTAH
ARIZONA
WASHINGTON
OREGON
IDAHO
NEVADA
CALIFORNIA
HAWAII
1959
ALASKA
1959

Louisiana

Territorial Development:

- The United States obtains portions of the future state of Louisiana from France through the Louisiana Purchase, April 30, 1803
- Future state of Louisiana organized as the Territory of Orleans, March 26, 1804
- Louisiana admitted into the Union as the eighteenth state, April 30, 1812
- Spain cedes lands to the United States through the Adams-Onís Treaty, February 22, 1819, part of which is added to the state of Louisiana
- The United States annexes Texas on December 29, 1845, a small portion of which is added to the state of Louisiana

Capitals Prior to Statehood:

- Biloxi, until 1723
- New Orleans, 1723–1812

State Capitals:

- New Orleans, 1812–1830
- Donaldsonville, 1830
- New Orleans, 1830–1849
- Baton Rouge, 1849–1862
- Opelousas, 1862
- Shreveport, 1862–1865
- New Orleans, 1865–1882; legislation was passed that made Baton Rouge the capital as early as 1880, but it seems that the capital was not firmly established there until 1882
- Baton Rouge, 1882–present

Origin of State Name: Sieur de La Salle named Louisiana in honor of Louis XIV in 1682.

First Governor: W.C.C. Claiborne
Governmental Organization: Bicameral
Population at Statehood: 153,407 (figure taken from 1820 Census)
Geographical Size: 43,562 square miles

THE STATE OF LOUISIANA

Admitted to the Union as a State: April 30, 1812

John R. Kemp

INTRODUCTION

Louisiana is a state whose name conjures up images of a romantic Gallic-Hispanic past more Caribbean in flavor than other states in the Union. It was founded by French Canadians on the banks of the lower Mississippi River in 1699, secretly ceded to Spain in 1762 during the French and Indian War, regained by Napoleon in 1800, and sold to the United States in 1803. At the time of the Louisiana Purchase in 1803, the Louisiana Territory was vast but sparsely settled. Most colonists lived in the present-day state of Louisiana, primarily in and around New Orleans. The huge land acquisition, which almost doubled the size of the young American nation, would later be divided into thirteen other states or parts of states. The Americanization of Louisiana did not come about easily, however. The French-speaking population of Louisiana resented the purchase and the replacement of their laws, customs, and institutions with an American system of law and self-government as foreign to them as the newly arriving, English-speaking Americans.

New Orleans, Louisiana's capital, was still, in a way, a frontier city but one unlike any other frontier city in the nation. It was a cosmopolitan city of legendary vices, grand opera, and ballet. The city's West Indian flavor, with its Roman Catholic sensibilities, was strange to the more conservative, Protestant Americans from the Eastern Seaboard moving into the city to take advantage of new commercial opportunities. Despite these challenges, Louisiana between 1803 and statehood in 1812 moved from a colonial pawn in a European power struggle to a full partner in the new American nation. In late 1814 all Louisianans—French, Spanish, Anglo-American, white, and black—stood together to defeat an invading British army at the gates of New Orleans. This victory against a foreign invader and over internal uncertainties left little doubt that Louisianans were now Americans and a vital part of a growing young nation.

THE LOUISIANA PURCHASE

"There on the globe one single spot, the possessor of which is our natural and habitual enemy. It is New Orleans, through which the produce of three-eights of our territory must pass to market.... The day France takes possession of N. Orleans...[f]rom that moment we must marry ourselves to the British fleet and nation."[1]

So wrote President Thomas Jefferson to Robert Livingston, the American minister to France, in April 1802 when Jefferson learned that Spain had secretly ceded Louisiana back to the French two years earlier. The situation was serious, and Jefferson's reaction was extreme, for he knew well that joining with England would have allied the United States with the one country it distrusted more than France. "Every eye in the United States," he continued, "is now fixed on the affairs of Louisiana. Perhaps nothing since the revolutionary war has produced more uneasy sensations through the body of the nation."[2] Pressures from emerging territories in the American West, which needed unfettered use of the Mississippi River and the port of New Orleans to conduct trade with the East Coast and Europe, and from Napoleon's imperial wars required a resolution to the Louisiana problem. War between France and the United States was narrowly averted by the Louisiana Purchase of 1803, which doubled the territory of the United States and ensured its future position as a world power.

To avoid war with France, Jefferson instructed Livingston to negotiate with Napoleon to buy New Orleans and East and West Florida, which included Baton Rouge and today's Mississippi and Alabama Gulf Coast. That purchase would have given the United States possession of the entire eastern bank of the Mississippi River and thus free navigation of the river from the Illinois territory to the mouth of the river and the open Gulf. The price the Americans had in mind was $6 million "for New Orleans and the two Floridas," with France keeping title to all land west of the Mississippi River. Livingston made little headway at first. Napoleon's France "is no longer a republic," he wrote to James Madison, "it is the government of one man whose will is law."[3]

Napoleon had more immediate concerns than his backwater frontier in North America. For more than three years after the retrocession of Louisiana from Spain to France, Napoleon permitted Spain to govern the colony, which had been a Spanish colony since 1762, when Louis XV of France gave the colony to his cousin Carlos III of Spain to help end the Seven Years' War (known as the French and Indian War in the British colonies) between Great Britain, France, and Spain. Tensions between the Spanish in New Orleans and the westward-expanding Americans increased during the 1790s, especially in the face of expanding American shipping on the Mississippi and Ohio rivers. War seemed almost imminent. Finally, in 1795, Spain and the Americans signed the Treaty of San Lorenzo (also known as the Pinckney Treaty) in which Spain granted the Americans free navigation of the Mississippi and the right to deposit American goods in New Orleans for three years. Although the right of deposit legally expired in 1798, the privilege continued until October 1802, when Spanish officials in New Orleans ordered it stopped. By 1802 ships flying the American flag greatly outnumbered the ships of other nations, even Spain and France. American seamen, enjoying the tawdry delights of the city's river front saloons and bordellos, were quick to express their resentment toward Spanish officials with a word, gesture, and sometimes a fist fight.

In January 1803, when news reached Jefferson that the Spanish had ended the right of deposit in New Orleans, he sent his friend James Monroe to assist Livingston with his negotiations. In a letter to Monroe dated January 13, 1803, Jefferson pressed upon Monroe the importance of his mission not only to the well-being of the United States but also in Jefferson's struggle with the Federalists in Congress:

> The agitation of the public mind on occasion of the late suspension of our right of deposit at N. Orleans is extreme. In the western country it is natural and grounded on honest motives. In the seaports it proceeds from a desire for war which increases the mercantile lottery; in the federalists generally and especially those of Congress the object is to force us into war if possible, in order to derange our finances, or if this cannot be done, to attach the western country to them, as their friends, and thus get again into power.[4]

He went on to write that if the United States "cannot by a purchase of the country to insure ourselves a course of perpetual peace and friendship with all nations, then as war cannot be distant, it behooves us immediately to be preparing for that course, without, however, hastening it, and it may be necessary (on your failure on the continent) to cross the channel." Later that month Jefferson informed the British chargé d'affaires that the United States would never relinquish its claim to free navigation of the Mississippi River, so essential to the development of the West, and would resort to war if necessary to ensure access. In February a Senate resolution that would have authorized Jefferson to occupy portions of the Isle of Orleans failed, but another resolution calling for the outfitting of 80,000 militiamen passed.

Because war between France and Great Britain seemed imminent, Napoleon surprised the United States by agreeing to sell the Americans not just the land they had requested but all of Louisiana. This decision probably had less to do with the protracted negotiations than with Napoleon's failure to put down the slave rebellion in Haiti on the Island of St. Domingue and his desperate need for money to continue his war in Europe. With the retrocession of Louisiana from Spain to France, Napoleon had hoped to regain for France a glorious colonial empire in North America to rival the one lost almost a half-century earlier during the Seven Years' War.

To do so, he first had to quell the slave rebellion in Haiti led by the brilliant tactician, statesman, and former slave Toussaint L'Ouverture. Louisiana, Napoleon thought, would be the breadbasket to supply a renewed French presence in the Caribbean. A French expedition to end the revolt left Dunkerque under the command of General Victor Emmanuel Leclerc, Napoleon's brother-in-law. Although revolutionary France had abolished slavery in all its possessions, Leclerc's mission was to crush the rebel armies and reimpose slavery in St. Domingue. At first, Napoleon's expeditionary force enjoyed some success. L'Ouverture was captured and sent to France where he died in prison. In the end, the rebels won the day and their continued freedom, but at a high cost. More than 350,000 Haitians died or were killed, as were approximately 60,000 French troops who were either killed in battle or perished from yellow fever. General Leclerc himself died from the dreaded fever in November 1802. A year later, the remnants of the French army were driven from the island and into the hands of the British. Less than two months later, on January 1, 1804, Haiti proclaimed its independence.[5] Defeat in St. Domingue ended Napoleon's dreams of retaking and reestablishing the Louisiana colony. He also doubted his ability to hold the territory against British or American attacks. If France could not control the Mississippi River, Napoleon would much rather see it in the hands of the United States than of his ancient rival England.

On April 12, 1803, during a dinner party given by Livingston to celebrate Monroe's arrival in Paris, Barbé-Marbois arrived and shocked the Americans with the announcement that Napoleon was willing to sell not just New Orleans but the entire Louisiana territory. Negotiations over the price lasted more than two weeks. The United States finally agreed on April 29 to pay $11.25 million for the land and to assume French debts of $3.75 million owed to American citizens during the recent wars, bringing the total purchase price to $15 million. The treaty was dated April 30, although it was not actually signed until May 2. Livingston's remarks at the signing would prove prophetic: "We have lived long, but this is the noblest work of our lives...from this day the United States take their place among the powers of the first rank."[6]

Napoleon's comments after the sale would likewise come true: "This accession of territory affirms forever the power of the United States, and I have just given England a maritime rival that sooner or later will lay low her pride." Had the British been able to foresee the future, they might have gone forward with their own plans to invade New Orleans, which were to be carried out with the resumption of the war between France and Great Britain. Livingston learned of the invasion plan a week after the signing of the treaty, and he quickly informed London of the purchase. When the time came actually to pay France the approximately $15 million for Louisiana, however, the United States found itself embarrassed. The fledgling country simply did not have that much money in its treasury. Arrangements were made to sell bonds to the banking houses of Baring in London and Hope in Amsterdam to pay Napoleon. The total cost of the purchase, including interest and claims against the government, eventually came to $23,527,872.

Acquiring sufficient funds was not the only problem that Louisiana presented its American purchasers. The extent and exact boundaries of the vast territory had never been delineated. When Livingston asked the French foreign minister Talleyrand for information, he replied, "I can give you no direction; you have made a noble bargain for yourselves and I suppose you will make the most of it."[7] The treaty did give some hint as to the boundaries, a hint that caused even more confusion a few years later. Article 1 described the Treaty of San Ildefonso between the French Republic and the king of Spain and the retrocession of Louisiana from Spain to France: "His Catholic Majesty promises and engages on his part to cede to the French Republic...the Colony or Province of Louisiana, with the same extent that it now has in the hands of Spain, and that it had when France possessed it." The treaty went on to say that the inhabitants of the ceded "territory shall be incorporated in the Union of the United States, and admitted as soon as possible, according to the principles of the Federal Constitution, to the enjoyment of rights, advantages, and immunities, of citizens of the United States."[8]

Not all Americans, however, were happy with the Louisiana Purchase. Jefferson's Federalist opponents in Congress argued that the Constitution made no provision for acquiring land in such a way or for administering it. During the November 1803 Senate debates over ratification of the purchase treaty, a senator from Delaware argued that Louisiana was still in the hands of Spain, and therefore France had no authority to sell Louisiana. In effect, the United States was purchasing war with "the Catholic King of Spain," who opposed the purchase and the neutrality of France. After long debates over the constitutionality of the measure, possible war with Spain, and Napoleon's claim to Louisiana, the Senate ratified the treaty twenty-six to five. Senator White from Delaware, who opposed the treaty, summed up the feelings of many Senate opponents of the measure as follows:

> I wish not to be understood as predicting that the French will not cede to us the actual and quiet possession of the territory. I hope to God they may, for possession of it we must have—I mean New Orleans, and of such other positions on the Mississippi as may be necessary to secure to us forever the complete and uninterrupted navigation of that river. This I have ever been in favor of; I think it essential to the peace of the United States, and to the prosperity of our Western country. But as to Louisiana, this new, immense, unbounded world, if it should ever be incorporated into this Union, which I have no idea can be done but by altering the Constitution, I believe it will be the greatest curse that could at present befall us; it may be productive of innumerable evils.[9]

New Englanders complained that a large sum was being paid for land that would benefit only Americans residing in the West. They also were reluctant to have New Orleans as a rival for their own port cities. The reaction to the purchase in New Orleans itself was, for the most part, positive. At first, Pierre Clement Laussat, the envoy sent by Napoleon to officiate the return of the colony from Spain to France, could not believe the rumors he had heard about the purchase. He wrote to his superiors in France, describing the "[i]ncredible falsehoods." The Americans in the city were wild with joy over the news, he wrote, while the Spanish residents expressed pleasure that New Orleans would not be returned to the French. The local French Creole population, who looked forward to a reunion with France, were now in despair, he continued, and were considering selling their possessions and moving away. Laussat soon received word that the rumors were indeed true, and he was ordered to receive the colony from Spain and hold it for the United States. Finally, during special ceremonies in New Orleans, Spain transferred the colony to France on November 30, 1803. The United States took possession twenty days later.

At the time of the purchase, New Orleans was still, in a way, a frontier city, but it was unlike any other city in the new nation. The population in 1803 had risen to more than 10,000, with another 3,000 residents living along the river below the city. The population consisted primarily of descendants of European settlers, primarily from France and Spain, free people of color, Anglo-Americans, slaves and a few Native Americans. By 1810 New Orleans was the largest city in the South, boasting a population of more than 24,000 residents, and it was the fifth-largest city by population in the nation. Between 1804 and 1810, the population of the city increased dramatically as French-speaking whites, free blacks, and their slaves fled to the city to escape revolutions in the French West Indies. In 1809 alone more than 5,700 emigrants sought refuge in New Orleans. The Louisiana Territory was vast but sparsely settled, with approximately 75,000 inhabitants, excluding Native Americans. Most people resided in the present-day state of Louisiana, primarily in and around New Orleans, along the river and nearby bayous. Of that number, approximately 40 percent were slaves who had lost many of the rights that they had enjoyed under both the French and Spanish.[10]

LOUISIANA BECOMES A U.S. POSSESSION

New Orleans was a prosperous city that would add considerable wealth to the nation. Assimilating the city and the port's trade into the nation's economy would be simple, because American merchants already had considerable business interests in the city at the time of the purchase. Political assimilation was a more difficult task. Since New Orleans had been founded in 1699, Louisianans had lived under one monarchy or another. Government and laws had been dictated by either France or Spain. Transforming a hodge-podge of French and Spanish laws and administrative procedures to the American political and legal system proved to be a great challenge, especially for a proud people who demanded immediate statehood.

When the United States took possession of its new territory, Jefferson named his young friend and fellow Virginian, William Charles Cole Claiborne, governor. Jefferson had first offered the job to the popular Marquis de Lafayette and later to James Monroe. To interest Lafayette, Jefferson exchanged a large Revolutionary War land grant that had been given to Lafayette in the Ohio Valley for an area just outside New Orleans. Lafayette politely refused the offer.[11] In January 1804, Jefferson wrote to Monroe, asking him to take the post, but Monroe also refused. Jefferson asked Monroe three additional times as late as 1809, but Monroe was not interested in the post. Finally, Jefferson settled upon Claiborne. One of Claiborne's first official duties came on December 20, 1803, during ceremonies in New Orleans, when he and General James Wilkinson, reportedly a spy for the Spanish government, took possession of Louisiana for the United States—just twenty days after a disappointed French commissioner received the colony from Spain.

Thus, Claiborne became the first American to take possession of a foreign territory that was being annexed to the United States. "All previous U.S. territories had been inhabited in the main by English-speaking Protestants who shared a British tradition of self government," noted Louisiana historian Judith Kelleher Schafer. "Claiborne for a time became virtual dictator over people from radically different cultures who spoke different languages, practiced a different religion from the vast majority of U.S. citizens, and had no experience whatsoever with representative government." Jefferson gave Claiborne the difficult assignment "to prevent any insurrection against the United States, but he also expected the governor to rule these people justly, to introduce them to representative government, and to make them loyal new citizens of a republic then only twenty-seven years old." The predominantly French population of Louisiana disliked the Spaniards who ruled Louisiana from 1768 to 1803, but they liked the newly arriving Americans even less.[12]

Jefferson gave Claiborne full executive, legislative, and judiciary powers. He had complete control. Claiborne came to Louisiana after a rather colorful career as a congressional clerk, later a member of the Tennessee Supreme Court, a congressman from that state, and governor of the new Mississippi Territory. A long-time Jefferson friend and activist in Republican politics, Claiborne remained loyal to Jefferson in the bitter presidential election of 1800 between Jefferson and Aaron Burr. Claiborne refused to back Burr, and Jefferson never forgot the favor. Claiborne's career blossomed. He was an ardent Republican who did not believe in a dictatorial or oppressive government. Unfortunately, he was anything but ready for the people of Louisiana, who had no tradition of self-government and were ethnically and socially foreign to his Anglo-Saxon Virginian sensibilities.

The Virginia-born Protestant could not speak French, and the American legal system was confusing to his new charges. They resented the ban on importing slaves, a practice they had pursued throughout French and Spanish colonial days, and rumors persisted that Louisiana would soon be returned to either France or Spain. After arriving in Louisiana, Claiborne chose not to live in the ostentatious style of former Spanish and French governors, and he ordered the French-speaking Municipal Council of New Orleans to print its acts in English. He moved slowly in establishing new political institutions in the territory, and he refused to back immediate statehood for the region.[13] In a letter to Secretary of State James Madison dated January 2, 1804, Claiborne described his feeling about the subject and the people he found in the new territory:

> The tranquility in which I found this Province is uninterrupted, and every appearance promises a continuation of it. This is the Season of Festivity here, and I am pleased to find that the change of Government has given additional Spirit to the Public amusement.
>
> It gives me great satisfaction to learn from every side the favourable inclinations of the People and their confidence in the justice and generous intentions of the American Government towards the Province.... I feel sensibly the weight of the responsibility which rests on me; I however indulge an anxious hope that Congress will soon relieve me from that difficulty. The establishment of a Government for this Province will I presume be a matter of immediate consideration, and cannot be determined more speedily than I wish. In the mean time I propose no exercise of my Authority except such as the peace of the Province and the conciliation of general confidence in the Government shall peremptorily require.
>
> To attempt a General renovation of the late System of Government would be a vain labour. The original principals of the System have been long lost sight of;—Government had scarcely a nerve not wounded by corruption; the Business in every department was wrapped up in Mystery and intrigue and has been left in confusion perhaps inexplicable.
>
> The merchants as well as the planters in this Country appear to be wealthy, their habits of living are luxurious and expensive, but by far the greater part of the people are deplorably uninformed. The wretched Policy of the late government having discouraged the Education of youth. The attainments of some of the first people consist only of a few exterior accomplishments. Frivolous diversions seem to be among their primary pleasures, and the display of Wealth and the parade of power constitute their highest objects of admiration.[14]

Education, he continued, was essential to good citizenship, and a system of public schools was imperative to help Louisianans participate in a new representative form of government. "When the minds of the people become a little expanded," he stated in his letter to Madison,

> I doubt not they will be useful, if not zealous members of our Common Wealth. Among the first objects therefore to be attended to is some effectual plan of immediately introducing into this Province some system of Education.... The Sons of ignorance and affluence are too apt to be content with their

condition.... I therefore hope that the Government will take early Measures to erect Schools, and as soon as possible, some superior seminaries of Literature in this Province.[15]

The twenty-nine-year-old governor then completed his scathing commentary on the state of local social values by describing his low opinion of the political abilities of his new countrymen:

> When the charms of novelty have faded, and the people have leisure to reflect, they will I fear become very impatient in their present situation. I could wish that the Constitution to be given to this District may be as republican as the people can be safely intrusted with. But the principles of a popular Government are utterly beyond their comprehension. The Representative System is an enigma that at present bewilders them. Long inured to passive obedience they have, to an almost total want of political information, superaded [sic, superadded] an inveterate habit of heedlessness as to measures of Government, and of course are by no means prepared to make any good use of such weight as they may prematurely acquire in the national Scale.[16]

Meanwhile, Jefferson continued to receive letters from Louisianans complaining about Claiborne's actions and fearing the uncertainties that faced them under the new government of the United States. Once such letter came from the mother superior of the Ursuline nuns, a French Catholic teaching order that had been in New Orleans since the early 1720s. The nuns were concerned about the affect of the purchase on the order's religious practices. In a letter dated May 15, 1804, Jefferson assured the nuns that "the principles of the constitution and government of the United States are a sure guarantee to you that it will be preserved to you sacred and inviolate, and that your institution will be permitted to govern itself according to its own voluntary rules, without interference from the civil authority."[17]

In addition to the local Creole leadership, Claiborne soon found himself at odds with Daniel Clark, the Irish-born American Consul in New Orleans and a close friend of Jefferson whose information about Louisiana had been helpful to the president before and after the purchase. Initially, Jefferson asked Clark to assist Claiborne, but the two quickly fell out. Claiborne described Clark as a dictator who, with other prominent Americans, was conspiring to turn the local people against him. Clark in return had little regard for Claiborne.[18]

By spring 1804, Claiborne was so alarmed by rumors of conspiracies and popular uprisings among the French population that he considered reactivating the local militia. He was particularly concerned about the activities of the French and Spanish officials who remained in the territory after the transfer of the colony from Spain to France and then to the United States. Claiborne feared they were secretly plotting a revolt among the French and Spanish inhabitants. He also accepted the services of two companies of free people of color that had existed during the French and Spanish regimes. After consultation with Washington, Claiborne decided to keep the companies rather than have another group of malcontents working against his administration. The only stipulation was that white officers head the companies. Claiborne's first years in office were marked by increased friction between the Americans and local inhabitants, troubles with the Spanish over borders with Texas and Spanish West Florida, and the arrival of refugees, both free and slave, from the slave revolt in Haiti.[19]

THE TERRITORY OF ORLEANS

On March 26, 1804, Congress divided Louisiana into the Territory of Orleans (present state of Louisiana minus the Florida parishes, or counties, in southeast Louisiana and an area in the west near Texas and the Sabine River) and the Louisiana Territory, which comprised the rest of the acquisition. John Quincy Adams and other New Englanders objected, stating the Constitution made no provision for determining how the people of a purchased territory would govern themselves. That same month Congress created the Territory of Orleans's first government and legislature. The government would include a governor, a secretary, three judges and a Legislative Council of thirteen men appointed by the president with the consent of the Senate. Actually, Jefferson permitted Claiborne to appoint its members. Despite Claiborne's low opinion of the native "ancient population," he appointed several to his council. As with any other legislature, the council could make laws for the territory. The judicial system included a superior court and "such inferior courts, and justices of the peace, as the legislature of the territory may from time to time establish." The act also established a federal district court for the territory. The act also outlawed the foreign slave trade in Louisiana: although it approved the domestic slave trade, it forbade the selling of slaves brought into the United States after May 1, 1798. A year later Claiborne wrote to Jefferson again complaining of his problems with the new assembly: "I always thought that an early extension of the Representative system in this Territory was a hazardous experiment; and of this I am now convinced."[20]

Creation of the Territory of Orleans apparently did not satisfy everyone. Creoles and Anglo-Americans complained that they were being denied the rights of other Americans and that all power was concentrated in the hands of the governor. They sent memorials to Congress complaining of the situation. Free people of color, angry because they were not permitted to attend the meetings to draw up the memorials for Congress, decided to hold a meeting of their own. When the announcement appeared in a local newspaper, city officials feared an insurrection was underway and petitioned Claiborne for help. The governor met with the free men of color who promptly assured the governor that they were not plotting rebellion. They simply wanted to participate in the new government as free men. Some people, however, did have trouble in mind. A month after Congress formed the territory, handbills appeared around New Orleans describing the "United States as a wicked devour'ing Nation" and urging the inhabitants to rise in rebellion. Local prominent Creoles wanted to offer a reward for the name of its author, but Claiborne dismissed the idea.[21]

A month later, another poster appeared with similar invective. Again Claiborne ignored the call. In a letter to President Madison, Claiborne described the wording as similar to those found in France during the French Revolution. Although this was an isolated incident, Claiborne did have enemies who attacked him at every chance. They assailed his character, administration, and performance, personally and in the press. In late 1804, a strongly worded pamphlet, *Esquisse de la Situation Politique et Civil de La Louisiane depuis le 30 Novembre 1803 jusqu'a l er Octobre 1804, par un Louisianais*, whose author remained anonymous, claimed that Claiborne and his policies were the root of all problems between the American and local French populations. The treatise admonished the governor for instituting an American-controlled court, for appointing mostly Americans to important government positions, for giving preference to his volunteer militia rather than the regular French-speaking militia units, and for requiring the use of English in all government publications and actions. The document also accused the governor of being an outsider unfamiliar with the customs of the people he was sent to govern.[22]

Defending himself, Claiborne on October 16, 1804, wrote to Secretary of State James Madison, proclaiming that he had made some mistakes but refuting claims made in the pamphlet:

> The enclos'd political Pamphlet, is circulating in this Territory; it is written with Ingenuity, and is, certainly well calculated to encrease [sic] the existing Discontents.—[T]hat a part of the statements in this Pamphlet are true, I will readily admit; but on some occasions, the writer has manifested an Ignorance of facts, or a great want of Candour.[23]

He went on to refute an allegation that he appointed mostly "native" Americans to "lucrative" government posts. He presented a list of "ancient" French-speaking Louisianans who received important government positions. One by one, he denied each of the charges against him, except that he could not speak French. Even then, he said, he always made use of a qualified translator when presiding over the supreme court and conducting other governmental duties.

> To conciliate public opinion, and to promote Harmony, have been my favorite objects:—but I have been less fortunate, than I had anticipated!—Unfortunate Divisions, certainly exist in Louisiana; but the seeds of discontent, were sown, previous to my arrival in the province, and they have deriv'd nourishment from causes, which I cou'd neither controul [sic] or counteract.

The news-paper scribbling, which has excited so much sensibility, I have seen and sincerely regretted; but it does not devolve upon me, to correct the Licentiousness, of the press.—It's Liberty I will never invade![24]

As one student of the era noted, "If Governor Claiborne was uncomfortable during his temporary governorship, he would be even more so during the first year of territorial government as political controversy swirled about him."[25]

Adding to Claiborne's problems were former French and Spanish colonial administrators who remained in Louisiana after the purchase. Pierre Clement Laussat, the man Bonaparte sent to take possession of the colony, remained behind, hoping Napoleon would change his mind and take back the colony. The Marquis de Casa Calvo, the former Spanish governor, stayed in Louisiana, inciting the local population against the American government. Eventually, Claiborne ordered Casa Calvo to leave Louisiana.[26]

Establishing an American-style government in Louisiana proved difficult. The French population, still smarting over the Louisiana Purchase, was completely unfamiliar with American government and institutions. Debates for and against the imposition of the new government in Louisiana were incessant throughout late 1804 and early 1805. In July Jefferson reminded a despondent Claiborne of the importance of his task and the great value of New Orleans and Louisiana to the United States: "The Position of New Orleans certainly destines it to be the greatest city the World has ever seen. There is no spot on the Globe to which the produce of so great an extent of fertile Country must necessarily come."[27]

From December 1804 through February 1805, delegates from Louisiana worked hard to convince Congress to give Louisiana more autonomous powers and to reopen the slave trade. On March 1, the Congress passed another bill pertaining to the governance of the Territory of Orleans. Contrary to petitions from Louisiana requesting that the old Province of Louisiana be reunited, the foreign slave trade resumed, and immediate statehood granted, the new act gave the territory a government similar to that of the neighboring Mississippi Territory. Voters could now elect a General Assembly. The new legislature would consist of a popularly elected lower house of twenty-five representatives and a five-member upper house appointed by the president from a list of candidates submitted by the lower house. The president, with the consent of the Senate, would continue to appoint territorial officials. The most important provision of the law was a mechanism for eventual statehood. It stated that once the population of the territory reached 60,000 free inhabitants, they could write a constitution and petition for statehood. Although those who favored immediate statehood were disappointed, the new legislation provided the mechanism for statehood once the population reached the prescribed number. Equally important, voters in the territory for the first time had the right to elect their legislators and make their own laws.

The first legislature met in New Orleans on March 26, 1806. From the first, its members and Claiborne were at odds. The Legislative Council, elected by the full legislature, consisted mostly of white, French-speaking Creoles who enjoyed their new powers. A major cause of friction between the new legislature and Claiborne was the territory's new legal system, specifically the replacement of the old French system with American laws. To help smooth the transition between the two systems, Claiborne retained as much Spanish law as possible, especially in noncriminal matters, as long as those laws were not in opposition to the U.S. Constitution. In criminal matters, he imposed the common law practices, including trial by jury, used in other American states. Contrary to the governor's wishes and veto, the legislature in 1808 adopted a civil code based on Spanish law and the French Napoleonic Code rather than on the English common law found in other states. This code remained the law of the land until the Louisiana Civil Code of 1824, which has been described as "one of the most original of codes...[that] blended French, Spanish, and common-law forms into a skillful, efficient whole." Eventually, relations between Claiborne and native French-speaking legislators improved. The natives became more adept at self-government, and Claiborne realized that his real enemies were not the local natives but English-speaking Americans who had not been appointed to high positions or who came to the territory looking for get-rich opportunities.[28]

The first decade or so of the American era in New Orleans was a hubbub of excitement, uproar, flux, boom and bust, disasters, disappointments, and achievements. "The arrival of Americans in New Orleans," noted one historian,

> introduced a new and vital dynamic into the life of the city. This dynamic—compounded of unabashed idealism, a vision of an unexampled future for the city, uninhibited opportunism, directed materialism, and technical competence—operated in a milieu relatively free from restraint and enjoying advantages of French and Spanish beginnings. The mixture of this dynamic with residual qualities produced the New Orleans of Antebellum days.[29]

In addition, thousands of people died in the yellow-fever epidemics of 1804, 1807, 1808, 1811, and 1813. American and foreign sailors frequently slugged it out on the levees and in taverns, while Creoles lavished their contempt on Anglo-Americans. In 1809 Collector of Customs William Brown absconded with $150,000 in customs receipts, and one year later a slave insurrection just above the city in St. John the Baptist Parish (county) was brutally suppressed. The heads of the revolt's leaders were mounted on poles along the levee for other slaves to see and take heed.

THE AARON BURR CONSPIRACY

Aside from the purchase itself, the events that left the most significant impressions on the collective imagination in those years were the Aaron Burr conspiracy of 1808–1807, Jefferson's Embargo Act of 1807, statehood in 1812, and the British invasion of 1814–1815.

Former Vice President Aaron Burr, whose political career ended when he killed Alexander Hamilton in a duel in 1804, allegedly conspired with General James Wilkinson and others to wrest Louisiana and western territories away from the United States or a part of Mexico from Spain to set up his own country. In the summer of 1805 Burr visited New Orleans to meet with Edward Livingston, Daniel Clark, and members of the Mexican Association, a group of traders and adventurers that wanted to invade Mexico. To New Orleans Burr carried a letter of introduction from Wilkinson, then governor of the Louisiana Territory, not including the Territory of Orleans. Burr's true intentions may never be known. Burr had previously told British, French, and Spanish ministers in Washington of his plans to separate the western territories and states from the Union. To others he spoke of his intentions to invade Mexico.

In 1806 and 1807 New Orleans was alive with rumors of Burr's advancing army, and every new arrival from upriver, especially from Kentucky and Tennessee, was suspect. Many New Orleanians believed the Spanish in neighboring West Florida were working with Burr to regain Louisiana. Governor Claiborne interviewed all newcomers arriving in the city from upriver to satisfy himself that they were not vanguards of Burr's army. The coup d'état did not take place, and Burr later was arrested, tried, and acquitted.

THE EMBARGO ACT OF 1807

Although fears of the Burr invasion subsided in 1807, naval war continued on the Atlantic between Great Britain and France. Although the United States professed neutrality in the conflict, hundreds of American ships were seized at sea by England and France. Repeated appeals by President Jefferson were ignored, so the president and Congress reacted by passing the Embargo Act of 1807, prohibiting all exportation of American goods to either of the warring powers.

This act had devastating effects on the American economy, particularly on port cities such as New Orleans. Smuggling became commonplace, and American exports fell from $108 million in 1807 to $20 million the following year. Imports dropped from $138 million to less than $57 million. Jefferson adhered to the act and his course of action, hoping to force the British and French to respect America's rights on the seas. In New Orleans, mercantile companies foundered, and young men who came to the city with dreams of making their fortune became destitute. Such was the case of young Nathaniel Cox, who came from Kentucky to New Orleans in 1806. Writing to business associates back home on May 2, 1808, he described the effect of the Embargo Act on their business: "This infernal Embargo has so effectively stopped our

Commercial career that the prospects once so flattering have become extremely gloomy—and the profits arising from the business we are now doing will not justify the step."[30] Lamenting his inability to build a home and settle down, Cox wrote again on September 15, 1809:

> If there had been no failures in New Orleans, no frays with the Chesapeake— no Embargo—no non-intercourse—no Burr—no Wilkinson, no proclamations— and in short, if the usual commertial [sic] arrangements had continued between the United States and Europe my calculations might in some measure been realized.[31]

THE STATEHOOD MOVEMENT

By 1812 British depredations upon the American nation, coupled with American expansionist ideas, led the young nation into a war that until then had been a European affair. In 1811 and well into the next year, while the nation directed its attention to the growing menace of war with Great Britain, Louisianans pressed Congress for statehood. The 1810 census showed the population of the Territory of Orleans had risen to more than 76,500 residents, and a population of only 60,000 was required for statehood. As early as 1804, a delegation of prominent Louisianans traveled to Washington seeking immediate statehood for the territory. They tried again in 1809 by having the territorial legislature to petition Congress. Claiborne, as in the past, remained opposed to the idea, stating the people were not yet ready for statehood or self-government.[32] In a May 18, 1809, letter to Secretary of State Robert Smith, the governor wrote:

> I am not from principle an advocate for Territal. [territorial] systems of Govt., nor during my Agency in their Administration, have I experienced as much satisfaction, as to have created a personal Bias in their favour; but really it seems to me that the system as relates to this District, cannot yet be done away without hazarding the Interest of the U.S. and the welfare of this Community.... They nevertheless are not prepared for self Govt. to the extent solicited by the Legre [legislature].... [Our] population is a mixed one, & composed of very discordant materials; But the Mass of the Inhabitants still entertain strong prejudices in favor of their ancient Laws and usages....
>
> I much doubt, whether "if a question as to the early reception of the Territory into the Union as a State," was submitted to the People, there would be found a majority in its favour. Of one fact I am assured, that a great majority of the native Citizens of the U.S. residing here are against the measure, as are also many of the native Louisianians.[33]

In March 1810 Senator William Giles of Virginia introduced another statehood request from the Territory of Orleans legislature. It went to a

Senate committee that reported out a bill calling for the territory to form a state constitution and government. The full Senate approved the bill and sent it to the House of Representatives where it died.

Meanwhile, the United States annexed the West Florida Territory from the Mississippi River and Baton Rouge east to the Perdido River, the present boundary between the states of Alabama and Florida. Earlier that year, the mostly Anglo-American population of the region had rebelled against the Spanish administration that claimed the province for Spain. The successful rebels set up the independent Republic of West Florida. On October 27, 1810, President Madison annexed the territory to the United States, proclaiming the territory was rightfully part of the purchase in 1803.

> Whereas the territory south of the Mississippi Territory and eastward of the River Mississippi and extending to the River Perdido, of which possession was not delivered to the United States in pursuance of the treaty concluded at Paris, on the 30th of April, 1803, has at all times, as is well known, been considered and claimed by them, as being within the colony of Louisiana conveyed by the said treaty, in the same extent that it had in the hands of Spain, and that it had when France originally possessed it.[34]

Less than two months later, delegates from the Territory of Orleans presented another petition to the House of Representatives requesting statehood. It was referred to a special committee, and ten days later it reached the floor, where it was debated by the Committee of the Whole. Federalists tried to block it, fearing a new state in the southwest would increase Republican power in Congress. Debates also centered on the proposed state's eastern border. Many objected to the inclusion of West Florida. Still others, such as Laban Wheaton and Josiah Quincy of Massachusetts, opposed statehood for Louisiana. They did not believe Congress had the right to add new states. They also believed the addition of new states would adversely affect the strength of the original states in the Union. Despite attempts to block statehood for Louisiana, the House on January 15, 1811, approved the enabling legislation by a vote of seventy-seven to thirty-six, with the strongest opposition centered in the New England delegation.[35]

The bill went to the Senate where it was referred to committee. Ten days later the measure was sent to the full Senate with amendments, establishing the state's eastern and western boundaries. The Senate also amended the bill to limit suffrage to all white, male citizens of the U.S. Senator Samuel Dana of Connecticut tried to derail the enabling legislation by offering an amendment that would require the consent of every state or a constitutional amendment to admit new states to the Union. Dana's measure failed. On February 7, 1811, the Senate approved the legislation and returned it to the House to concur with the Senate's amendments. The House approved the boundary amendment but balked at the idea of specifying "white" in the suffrage requirement. The Senate stood by its amendment, and the House agreed, although reluctantly.

The House approved the legislation with the Senate's amendments on February 13, 1811, and President Monroe signed it on February 16. The way was now clear for the Territory of Orleans to elect delegates to a constitutional convention in New Orleans.[36]

> According to the enabling legislation, the state's boundary would include
> All that part of the territory or country ceded under the name of Louisiana, by the treaty made at Paris on the thirtieth day of April, one thousand eight hundred and three, between the United States and France, contained within the following limits, that is to say: Beginning at the mouth of the river Sabine [present boundary between the states of Louisiana and Texas]; thence by a line to be drawn along the middle of the said river, including all islands, to the thirty-second degree of latitude; thence due north to the northernmost part of the thirty-third degree of north latitude; thence along the said parallel to the river Mississippi; thence down the said river to the river Iberville [a small stream south of Baton Rouge]; and from hence, along the middle of the said river and Lakes Maurepas and Pontchartrain, the Gulf of Mexico; thence bounded by the said gulf to the place of beginning, including all islands.[37]

In other words, the state would include its present-day boundaries plus West Florida.

THE CONSTITUTIONAL CONVENTION

By early 1811 Claiborne had changed his mind and now supported statehood. With the annexation of West Florida and the addition of Anglo-Americans to the Territory of Orleans, Claiborne felt more comfortable with his new political base. News of the bill's passage did not reach New Orleans until April 9, 1811, when a local newspaper printed the measure word-for-word. Claiborne, although not receiving official word form Washington, immediately set to work. After the election of delegates to the convention, mostly drawn from the territory's leading social and political figures, the convention began meeting in New Orleans on November 4, 1811. According to one Louisiana historian, although the delegates "may not have equaled the assembly of demigods who performed the miracle at Philadelphia, they were not lacking in distinction. All were men of property and standing whose education and attainments surpassed by some distance those of the voters who chose them." Of the forty-six delegates, more than half were of French origin, reflecting the Territory's Gallic origins. The second-largest group was Americans who came to Louisiana from Kentucky, Virginia, New York, and New England. Others were from Ireland, Switzerland, Germany, and Spain.[38]

Although the convention was open to the press, editors did not feel any great need to give their readers thorough accounts of the proceedings. Once underway, the convention elected officers, established procedures, and fought off an early attempt to prevent statehood. To establish clearly why the convention was meeting, a member offered a motion that the Territory of Orleans become a "sovereign and independent state" and that the convention proceed to write a constitution. His motion was seconded immediately. During debates on the motion, a small faction argued that statehood was premature, contending that the "common people, or rather the great mass of the people, were not educated in the principles of freedom." Others argued against the enabling legislation's wording that would separate the new state of Louisiana from Upper Louisiana and West Florida east of the Perdido River. The discussion lasted more than three days, but in the end the nay-sayers lost. With that bit of work finished, the convention went about its business. It adopted the Constitution of the United States, addressed vacant land issues, and created a committee to ask Congress to annex to Louisiana portions of West Florida along the Mississippi River from just below Natchez to just south of Baton Rouge. To tackle the difficult assignment of drafting a constitution, the convention elected a committee composed of French and Anglo-Americans. The convention then recessed to give the committee time to do its work.[39]

The committee went to work, examining the federal Constitution and other state constitutions, especially the Kentucky constitutions of 1792 and 1799. Two members of the committee had been members of the first Kentucky constitutional convention and, therefore, had some knowledge of state constitutions and their structures. Once the committee reviewed and refined the document, it submitted the draft to the full convention on November 29. Like the federal Constitution, Louisiana's delineated separate and balanced powers. Draft copies were distributed to members on December 9. The convention quickly agreed that the new state would be called Louisiana, not Lower Louisiana as suggested by the committee. Not everyone was pleased with the document. One historian described the reaction as running "the gamut from approval to hostility." Delegates examined every word in the document. Two sections in the draft proved the most contentious—senatorial districts and the judiciary. The judiciary clause primarily addressed the number of state Supreme Court judges, the length of their appointments, and other procedural issues. The delegates quickly worked out a compromise, agreeable to most, concerning the Supreme Court but could not come to agreement concerning the number and powers of the local district courts. The convention eventually decided not to decide but to allow future legislatures to determine the number and powers of these courts.[40]

The second issue, one of great interest to New Orleans delegates, was representation in the Senate. The draft called for members of the House of Representatives to be determined by population. Senators would be chosen by district. The New Orleans delegation did not like the wording in the original draft, because it would give the city only one senator. Meeting privately, they drew up a plan to divide the state into thirteen districts with two districts representing the New Orleans area, one for the city of New Orleans and the other for the remaining parts of the parish. This suggestion failed, at first. In January, when the final portions of the draft came up for approval by the full convention, the New Orleans delegates again tried to rewrite the senatorial district clause. Again they failed. This time the entire New Orleans delegation walked out of the convention and boycotted all further proceedings. Finally, the remaining delegates acquiesced, and New Orleans was allotted two senators.

The final hurdle was the provision of the constitution that determined how governors would be elected. Debates centered on three possibilities—direct election by the voters, election by the legislature, or by some other method. After long debates, delegates choose the federal model. Governors were to be chosen indirectly. The names of the two gubernatorial candidates receiving the most votes in a popular election would be submitted to both houses of the legislature meeting in the House of Representatives. Ballots would be cast, and the candidate receiving the highest vote would be governor. The convention approved the new constitution on January 22, 1812. The next day it approved a petition asking Congress to annex West Florida to Louisiana.[41]

The constitution of 1812 began with a preamble, "We, the Representatives of the People." Article 1, following the federal model, created three separate seats of government—legislative, executive, and judiciary. Article 2 provided for the election of representatives and senators and specified their districts (including two for New Orleans) and powers. Representatives had to be free, white males, citizens of the United States, at least twenty-one years of age, residents of the state for the two preceding years, and own property worth $500 or more. Senators had to meet most of the same requirements, but they had to have resided in the state at least four years preceding election and own property worth at least $1,000.

Article 3 set forth the powers of the governor, the gubernatorial term, and the means for his election and qualifications for candidacy. To qualify for election, the minimum requirements called for a candidate to be at least thirty-five years old, a citizen of the United States, a resident of the state for at least six years prior to the election, and own property valued at $5,000. Article 4 created the judiciary, providing for a Supreme Court and specifying its composition, powers, and jurisdiction. The convention's indecision over the powers of the lower courts was reflected in the wording: "The legislature is authorized to establish such inferior courts as may be convenient to the administration of justice." Remaining articles dealt with matters such as impeachment of public officials, suffrage, oaths of office, treason, methods for revising the constitution, and other matters of government.[42]

FEDERAL APPROVAL OF STATEHOOD

President Madison presented the constitution of Louisiana to the House and Senate on March 3, 1812. Congress ratified the document on April 8,

1812. In the House, the vote to approve statehood fell mostly along partisan lines. The proposal passed seventy-nine to twenty-three. Of those voting against statehood, seventeen were Federalists from New England, three were southern Federalists, and three were Republicans from New England and the Middle States. The 1812 constitution of Louisiana has been described as not particularly remarkable but important in that it "set the foundations for institutions that exist to this day. It started traditions of self-government that are acknowledged still. It contributed to the blending of Anglo-American precepts of law and constitutionalism with continental European practices into customs that give the state its distinctive legal coloration."

At first, West Florida east to the Pearl River (today's boundary between the states of Mississippi and Louisiana) was not included in the state's boundaries. The House had approved inclusion, but the Senate rejected it. Two days later, however, a congressional amendment added that portion of West Florida to the new state. Louisiana became the nation's eighteenth state on April 30, 1812. During the subsequent gubernatorial election, Claiborne—appointed governor six times by Jefferson—defeated a popular local Creole by a slim margin of thirty-three to thirty-nine in the Legislature.[43]

THE WAR OF 1812 AND THE BATTLE OF NEW ORLEANS

The first true test of Louisiana's loyalty to its new nation soon followed. Slightly more than a month after Louisiana gained statehood, Congress declared war on Great Britain. Since the end of the American Revolution, the young nation had endured repeated insults to its national sovereignty at the hands of the British, including the boarding of American ships at sea and impressing American seamen. British ships blockaded American ports. In violation of the treaty ending the Revolution, Great Britain maintained forts in American territory near the Great Lakes from which they encouraged Indians to attack westward-moving settlers. British harassment was not the only reason for the War of 1812. War Hawks in Congress and Americans in the western territories believed that, in the event of war, Canada and Spanish Florida would easily fall to the United States. Some Westerners also believed that war would solve their agricultural problems and enable them to obtain higher prices for their cotton, tobacco, and wheat. Despite opposition in New England states, war came, and the United States was hardly prepared to fight.

Americans enjoyed some success early in the war, notably Oliver Hazard Perry's victory in the Battle of Lake Erie. The British successes, however, were more impressive. They defeated the Americans at Fort Dearborn and Detroit. They captured and burned Washington, D.C., and effectively blockaded American ports. America's dreams of capturing Canada vanished when several invasion forces were soundly defeated and turned back.

In Louisiana, Governor Claiborne busily prepared for a defensive war while two British blockade ships sat at the mouth of the Mississippi. Not all Louisianans were enthusiastic in their support of the American war effort. Some French Creoles asked the French consul in New Orleans for protection, claiming they were French, not American citizens. Other New Orleanians were ready to fight the British, but still others were suspected of supplying the enemy with important intelligence. In early 1814 General Andrew Jackson marched south from Tennessee to suppress the Creek Indians who, at the instigation of the British, had massacred white settlers along the Alabama River. Meanwhile, Claiborne met with Caddo Indian chiefs in northern Louisiana to make sure they did not follow the lead of the Creeks.

By spring 1814, Louisianans learned that the British were planning to attack New Orleans and the Gulf Coast. Claiborne moved quickly to prepare the city's defenses. On August 24 he wrote to Jackson, complaining about the lack of cooperation from the local populace: "I have a difficult people to manage; native Americans, native Louisianans, Frenchmen, Spanish, with some English."[44]

In September 1814, the British brig *Sophia* dropped anchor south of New Orleans near Grande Terre, the stronghold of the celebrated pirate Jean Lafitte. Captain Nicholas Lockyer presented Lafitte with a letter from British Lieutenant Colonel Edward Nicholls, who had occupied Pensacola with an expeditionary force in July. Nicholls offered Lafitte the rank of captain in the British forces and land and money in return for his help against the Americans. While Lafitte was passing this information along to state officials, Claiborne and the Committee of Defense sent a force of regular U.S. soldiers and sailors in the U.S. Navy to capture Lafitte and to break up his sanctuary. Although most of the pirates escaped, including the Lafitte brothers, others were taken prisoner.

Even the British were not sure about the loyalties of these new American citizens. Nicholls soon left no doubt in the minds of Louisianans about the British intentions when a proclamation began appearing all over the city:

> Natives of Louisiana! On you the first call is made to assist in liberating from a faithless, imbecile government, your paternal soil: Spaniards, Frenchmen, Italians, and British...you also I call to aid me in this just cause. The American usurpation of this country must be abolished, and the lawful owners of the soil put in possession.

In response, Jackson, playing on centuries-old rivalries between England and France, issued his own proclamation, which read in part:

> Louisianans! The proud British, the natural and sworn enemies of all Frenchmen, has called upon you, by proclamation, to aid him in his tyranny, and to prostrate the holy temple of our liberty. Can Louisianans, can Frenchmen, can Americans, ever stoop to be the slaves or allies of Britain?

Word also circulated that the British planned to arm slaves and give them their freedom if they would rise up against their owners.

In September Jackson drove off a British attack on nearby Mobile. The next month Jackson moved successfully against Pensacola, sending Nicholls and his troops back to their ships. Claiborne flooded Jackson with dispatches describing the problems—both real and imagined—the governor was facing in preparing Louisiana to defend itself. Not enough troops, not enough money, spies, and trouble with the state legislature were the complaints that filled the governor's letters to the general. Jackson often lost his temper with Claiborne's seeming inability to take hold of the situation.

Meanwhile, reports continued to arrive in Washington describing the massive buildup of British troops and supplies in Jamaica in preparation for the invasion of Louisiana. With this information in hand, Jackson set out from Mobile to New Orleans on November 22, only days before the British set sail on their Gulf Coast expedition. Jackson arrived in New Orleans on December 2.

Eight days later the British fleet of fifty ships dropped anchor off North Chandeleur Island, just off the southeastern Louisiana coastline. Aboard was an army of more than ten thousand troops commanded by General Sir Edward Pakenham, the Duke of Wellington's brother-in-law. The fleet was under the command of Admiral Sir Alexander Cochrane. So confident were the British of victory that aboard their ships they brought civil officials to take over the Louisiana government as well as their wives and the wives of the military officers. Also aboard was a government printing press to promulgate the new government's policies and proclamations.

Upon his arrival in New Orleans, Jackson immediately prepared the city for war. He ordered Major Arsene Lacarriere Latour, an engineer sent to Louisiana by Napoleon in 1802, to rehabilitate and strengthen the city's defenses. With the help of Mayor Nicholas Girod, every available person— white and black, free and slave—worked furiously. Batteries and earthworks were thrown up at the two major passages from the Gulf to Lake Pontchartrain on the city's northeastern edge and at two forts below the city on opposite banks of the Mississippi River.

Jackson did not have to wait long to learn the direction of the British attack. On December 14 Admiral Cochrane sent troops from the south in oared barges to destroy the small American naval force in Lake Borgne. The British concentrated their forces on a small island in Lake Borgne southeast of the city. On December 22 British forces began moving across the lake to Bayou Bienvenue and set up camp on a large plantation facing the Mississippi River. In a brilliant strategic move, Jackson attacked the British on the night of December 23. The weary British army was taken completely by surprise.

For the rest of December, the British landed troops and supplies, and Jackson dug in about three miles below the city's gates along the Rodriguez Canal on the Chalmette Plantation. Behind hastily built fortifications of dirt mounds, cotton bales, and cypress logs, Jackson waited. On December 28 the British attacked the American line to determine its strength but then retreated. The British right actually turned Jackson's left flank in the cypress swamp. They might have driven the American main force from its lines had Pakenham not lost control of his reconnaissance. He sounded recall when victory was within reach.

When the fog lifted on the morning of New Year's Day, 1815, the British artillery brought in from the ships opened a barrage on the American line. The American artillery responded, and after almost five hours of bombardment in both camps, a considerable proportion of the British cannon had been silenced. On January 7 the armies on both sides prepared behind their lines for what they knew would be the decisive battle. Shortly before daybreak on January 8, the British attacked the American lines in full force. American cannon fire savagely ripped through British lines, but still the British marched on. American riflemen joined the artillery to mow broad swaths through British ranks. American sharpshooters managed to dispatch the few attackers who reached American lines. Finally, the carnage was too much even for the disciplined British troops. They broke rank and ran to the rear, discarding weapons along the way. Pakenham himself was killed when he rode forward to rally his troops. Reports differ slightly as to the number of casualties suffered on both sides. One participant on the American side placed fatalities at 13 dead, 39 wounded, and 19 missing. The British reported 858 dead, 2,468 wounded, and many others missing.

British forces lingered in the area for several more weeks before rejoining the fleet on January 27. The fleet then moved to Mobile Bay, where it was met by fresh reinforcements from England. The battle for New Orleans had only begun. Fort Bowyer at the entrance of Mobile Bay fell to the British as they planned a new overland attack against New Orleans.

Jackson returned to New Orleans in triumph. January 23 was declared an official day of celebration, the *Te Deum* was sung in St. Louis Cathedral, and a arch of triumph was erected in the Place d'Armes (later in the century renamed Jackson Square in the general's honor). Local public opinion soon turned against Jackson, because he was determined to maintain martial law as long as the British fleet remained along the Gulf Coast. Reports reached the city that the United States and Great Britain had signed a peace treaty at Ghent, Belgium, on December 24, two weeks before the battle on January 8. Jackson maintained he would continue martial law and keep the local militia in service until he received official word of the treaty from Washington. On March 13 Jackson received word from Washington that the treaty had been signed. Martial law was suspended, and the following month Jackson returned to Nashville with his wife Rachel and his adopted son.

The war was over, and the Battle of New Orleans dispelled any fears held by other Americans that Louisianans might not make loyal citizens. People of diverse ethnic, social, political, and religious backgrounds had fought side-by-side against a common enemy of the United States.

The decades following statehood and the Battle of New Orleans were the golden years for Louisiana and its capital city, New Orleans. New Orleans was a boomtown, pulsating with energy—the energy of commerce, business, change and expansion. The great changes were hastened by the arrival of the steamboat *New Orleans* in 1812, which would greatly expedite the economic expansion of the upper and lower Mississippi Valley and, especially, New Orleans. The Mississippi and Ohio rivers and their hundreds, even thousands, of miles of tributaries, became highways for steamboats loaded with cotton, sugar, and other agricultural and manufactured goods en route to their point of export in New Orleans. The rivers also became the return highways for imported goods from Europe and South and Central America passing through the city's port. New Orleans quickly ranked among the largest and most prosperous cities in the nation. Louisiana was unquestionably a member of the United States.

NOTES

1. Thomas Jefferson to Robert Livingston, April 18, 1802, The Thomas Jefferson Papers at the Library of Congress, Thomas Jefferson Papers Series 1, General Correspondence 1651–1827, available at http://lcweb2.loc.gov.

2. Ibid.

3. Jon Kukla, *A Wilderness So Immense: The Louisiana Purchase and the Destiny of America* (New York: Alfred A. Knopf, 2003), pp. 234, 240.

4. Thomas Jefferson to James Monroe, January 13, 1803, Thomas Jefferson Papers.

5. Kukla, *A Wilderness So Immense*, pp. 218–225.

6. Ibid., p. 281.

7. Ibid., pp. 281, 335.

8. "Louisiana Purchase Treaty; April 30, 1803," The Avalon Project at Yale University Law School, www.yale.edu/lawweb/avalon.

9. *Annals of Congress*, 8th Cong., 1st Sess., pp. 33–34, www.loc.gov.

10. John R. Kemp, *New Orleans: An Illustrated History* (Sun Valley, CA: American Historical Press, 1997), pp. 58–60.

11. Gerard J. Toups, "The Provincial, Territorial, and State Administrations of William C. C. Claiborne, Governor of Louisiana, 1803–1806" (Ph.D. dissertation, University of Southwestern Louisiana, 1979), pp. 27–28.

12. Bennett H. Wall, ed., *Louisiana: A History* (Wheeling, IL: Harlan Davidson, 1997), pp. 89–91.

13. Toups, "The Provincial, Territorial, and State Administrations of William C. C. Claiborne," pp. 7–15, 26.

14. Dunbar Rowland, ed., *Official Letter Books of W. C. C. Claiborne, 1801–1816* (Jackson, MS: Mississippi State Department of Archives and History, 1917), 1: 322–328.

15. Ibid.

16. Ibid.

17. Ursuline Convent Museum and Archives, New Orleans.

18. Toups, "The Provincial, Territorial, and State Administrations of William C. C. Claiborne," pp. 25–27.

19. Marietta Marie LeBreton, "A History of the Territory of Orleans, 1803–1812" (Ph.D. dissertation, Louisiana State University, 1969), pp. 67–92.

20. Ibid., pp. 111–113; Bennett, ed., *Louisiana: A History*, pp. 91–94; Benjamin Wall Dart, ed., *Constitution of the State of Louisiana and Selected Federal Laws* (Indianapolis: The Bobbs-Merrill Company, 1932), pp. 414–421.

21. LeBreton, "A History of the Territory of Orleans, 1803–1812," p. 140.

22. Ibid.

23. Rowland, *Official Letter Books of W. C. C. Claiborne*, pp. 352–360.

24. Ibid.

25. LeBreton, "A History of the Territory of Orleans, 1803–1812," pp. 116–138.

26. Bennett, ed., *Louisiana: A History*, pp. 89–91.

27. Jared William Bradley, ed., *Interim Appointment: W.C.C. Claiborne Letterbook, 1804–1805* (Baton Rouge: Louisiana State University Press, 2002), pp. 121–122.

28. LeBreton, "A History of the Territory of Orleans, 1803–1812," pp. 149–164, 172–174; Bennett, ed., *Louisiana: A History*, pp. 91–94; Lawrence M. Friedman, *The History of American Law*, 2nd ed. (New York: Simon and Schuster, 1985), p.174.

29. John G. Clark, *New Orleans, 1718–1812: An Economic History* (Baton Rouge: Louisiana State University Press, 1970), p. 359.

30. Nathaniel Cox Papers, Louisiana State Museum, New Orleans, LA.

31. Ibid.

32. Toups, "The Provincial, Territorial, and State Administrations of William C. C. Claiborne," p. 178.

33. Rowland, *Official Letter Books of W. C. C. Claiborne* 4:360–361.

34. *West's Louisiana Statutes Annotated*, pp. 20–23.

35. LeBreton, "A History of the Territory of Orleans, 1803–1812," pp. 475–479.

36. Ibid., pp. 476–481; *West's Louisiana Statutes Annotated*, pp. 22–27.

37. *West's Louisiana Statutes Annotated*, pp. 22–23.

38. Toups, "The Provincial, Territorial, and State Administrations of William C. C. Claiborne," p. 180; LeBreton, "A History of the Territory of Orleans, 1803–1812," p. 483; Warren Billings, "From This Seed: The Constitution of 1812," in Dolores Egger Labbe, ed., *The Louisiana Purchase and its Aftermath: 1800–1830*, vol. 3, *The Louisiana Purchase Bicentennial Series in Louisiana History* (Lafayette, LA: Center for Louisiana Studies, University of Southwestern Louisiana, 1998), pp. 349–352.

39. Billings, "From This Seed: The Constitution of 1812," pp. 352–354; LeBreton, "A History of the Territory of Orleans, 1803–1812," p. 488.

40. LeBreton, "A History of the Territory of Orleans, 1803–1812," p. 490; Billings, "From This Seed: The Constitution of 1812," p. 355.

41. Billings, "From This Seed: The Constitution of 1812," pp. 357–359; LeBreton, "A History of the Territory of Orleans, 1803–1812," p. 491; "Constitution of 1812," in *West's Louisiana Statutes Annotated*, pp. 31–33.

42. *West's Louisiana Statutes Annotated*, pp. 33–39.

43. LeBreton, "A History of the Territory of Orleans, 1803–1812," pp. 492–494; Toups, "The Provincial, Territorial, and State Administrations of William C. C. Claiborne," p. 205; Billings, "From This Seed: The Constitution of 1812," p. 360; *Annals of Congress*, 8th Cong., 1st Sess.

44. The events leading up to, during, and after the Battle of New Orleans are drawn from Samuel Carter III, *Blaze of Glory: The Fight for New Orleans, 1814–1815* (New York: St. Martin's Press, 1971).

BIBLIOGRAPHY

Billings, Warren. "From This Seed: The Constitution of 1812." *The Louisiana Purchase and its Aftermath: 1800–1830*, vol. 3 in *The Louisiana Purchase Bicentennial Series in Louisiana History*, edited by Dolores Egger Labbe. Lafayette, LA: Center for Louisiana Studies, University of Southwestern Louisiana, 1998.

Bradley, Jared William, ed. *Interim Appointment: W.C.C. Claiborne Letterbook, 1804–1805*. Baton Rouge: Louisiana State University Press, 2002.

Carter, Samuel III. *Blaze of Glory: The Fight for New Orleans, 1814–1815*. New York: St. Martin's Press, 1971.

Clark, John G. *New Orleans, 1718–1812: An Economic History*. Baton Rouge: Louisiana State University Press, 1970.

Ford, Paul Leicester, ed. *The Works of Thomas Jefferson in Twelve Editions*. Federal Edition. The Thomas Jefferson Papers at the Library of Congress.

Friedman, Lawrence M. *The History of American Law*. 2nd ed. New York: Simon and Schuster, 1985.

Kemp, John R. *New Orleans: An Illustrated History*. Sun Valley, CA: American Historical Press, 1997.

Kukla, Jon. *A Wilderness so Immense: The Louisiana Purchase and the Destiny of America*. New York: Alfred A. Knopf, 2003.

LeBreton, Marietta Marie. "A History of the Territory of Orleans, 1803–1812." Ph.D. dissertation, Louisiana State University, 1969.

Rowland, Dunbar, ed. *Official Letter Books of W. C. C. Claiborne, 1801–1816*. Jackson, MS: Mississippi State Department of Archives and History, 1917.

Toups, Gerard. "The Provincial, Territorial, and State Administrations of William C. C. Claiborne, Governor of Louisiana, 1803–1806." Ph.D. dissertation, University of Southwestern Louisiana, 1979.

Wall, Bennett H., ed. *Louisiana: A History*. Wheeling, IL: Harlan Davidson, 1997.

THE STATE OF MAINE

Admitted to the Union as a State: March 15, 1820

J. Chris Arndt

INTRODUCTION

On March 14, 1820, the Portland *Eastern Argus* rejoiced. As the champion of the statehood movement, its banner headline announced an "*Independence Ball!*" to celebrate Maine's admission to the Union "as a FREE SOVEREIGN AND INDEPENDENT STATE."[1] The *Argus*'s headline capped one of the longest and most complex statehood stories in American history. For more than a century, Maine had been a northern appendage of Massachusetts. Many considered it a desolate, lightly settled frontier far removed from the capital city of Boston. Conflict with the Native American Wabenaki and a series of wars for empire had left much of the region inhospitable to English settlement. The ebb and flow of settlers and refugees in and out of Maine was a hallmark of the period and highlighted the region's dependence on Massachusetts. The removal of Native American and French threats opened the Maine frontier to a flood of settlers, but the region remained vulnerable to the ravages of war. The American Revolution and the War of 1812 brought conquest and suffering to the District of Maine and forced many of those living "downeast" to reconsider their relationship with the Bay State. Despite the emergence of a separation movement in the immediate aftermath of the Revolution, social, economic, and political issues kept Maine appended to Massachusetts for another generation. Two issues invigorated the drive for an independent Maine. The first was the War of 1812. The Bay State's refusal to take significant action after the British had occupied the eastern half of Maine, coupled with growing political differences between Republican Maine and Federalist Massachusetts, made the drive for statehood almost irresistible. A second issue, a coasting

Maine

Territorial Development:

- The Council for New England gives Ferdinando Gorges and John Mason land including Maine and New Hampshire, 1622
- Mason and Gorges divide the land; Gorge receives Maine portions, 1629
- Settlers in Kennebunk, Saco, Scarborough, and Casco Bay agree to become part of the Massachusetts Bay Colony, 1652–1658
- Heirs of Ferdinando Gorges claim Maine for themselves and dispute the ownership of the Massachusetts Bay Colony; Maine is restored to the Gorges family, 1664
- Massachusetts purchases Maine from the Gorges family, 1677
- Continental Congress approves Declaration of Independence from Great Britain, July 4, 1776
- Great Britain formally recognizes American independence through the Treaty of Paris, September 3, 1783
- Maine citizens vote for independence from Massachusetts, July 26, 1819
- Maine admitted into the Union as the twenty-third state, March 15, 1820

Capitals Prior to Statehood:

- Boston, capital of the commonwealth and state of Massachusetts, 1630–1819

State Capitals:

- Portland, 1820–1832
- Augusta, 1832–present

Origin of State Name: "Main" was a term that early explorers used to distinguish the mainland from the offshore islands. The state name may actually have come about in honor of Henrietta Maria, queen of Charles I of England, who was reported to have owned the French province of Mayne.

First Governor: William King
Governmental Organization: Bicameral
Population at Statehood: 298,335
Geographical Size: 30,862 square miles

law that favored Maine traders if they remained a part of the Bay State, ceased to be a factor after it was amended in the Congress. This amendment removed the last roadblock to Maine's voters accepting separation. The Missouri issue, however, delayed Maine's entry into the Union until a suitable compromise could be worked out.

IMPEDIMENTS TO INDEPENDENCE

Maine was an appendage of Massachusetts until 1819. Maine's colonial status began in the seventeenth century when the failure to establish a colony in Maine enabled the Massachusetts Bay Colony gradually to extend its authority over the region. In 1691, the Massachusetts Bay charter recognized Maine as a part of the Bay Colony. Resistance from the Wabenaki, coupled with the French threat to the north, left Maine dependent on Massachusetts throughout the colonial period. The British victory in the Seven Years' War spurred growing numbers of settlers to move to Maine.

Maine's status before statehood began not as a territory, nor as an independent colony of Great Britain, but as an appendage of Massachusetts. This status was not foreordained. One of the earliest English efforts to colonize North America occurred in 1607–1608, when a group led by Sir John Popham and supported by Sir Ferninando Gorges reconnoitered the mid-Maine coast and built a fort near the mouth of the Kennebec River. The failure of this expedition and the inability of Gorges to exercise any authority over the region left it open to exploration and settlement by others.

The region's bounty of fish and fur-bearing animals quickly attracted competitors. By the middle of the seventeenth century, Maine contained a few tiny villages south of Casco Bay, but mid-Maine, particularly the lower Penobscot region, was the scene of rivalry between Puritans from Massachusetts Bay, mercantile interests from the Plymouth Colony, and French traders making their way down from Acadia. All were interested in the lucrative fur trade centered at what is now Castine at the mouth of Penobscot Bay. By the mid-seventeenth century, the aggressive Puritan colony centered in Boston was winning control of the region. Strengthened by the Puritan control of government in Britain, the Massachusetts Bay Colony cited the lack of order on its undefined northern frontier to lay claim to the Maine coast. In 1652, Massachusetts extended its authority over the Kittery settlement in southern Maine even though many living in the frontier outpost opposed being governed by the Bay Colony. The following year, the Massachusetts General Court admitted two representatives, one from Kittery and another from York. In the following year, inhabitants of these communities voted to accept Massachusetts's jurisdiction.

By 1658, the Bay Colony had extended its authority east to the Casco Bay area. If some in Maine resented the extension of Puritan authority over their remote villages, the events of the 1670s underscored their dependence on Boston. King Philip's (Metacomet's) War in 1676 devastated the Maine frontier and led to the virtual depopulation of the Kennebec region and some areas further west. The flood of Maine refugees into Massachusetts proper, a scene that was repeated on several occasions during the early eighteenth century, made clear that these settlements could not stand alone. Massachusetts's 1691 charter officially recognized what was becoming fact and officially designated Maine as a part of the Bay Colony.[2]

Maine's exposed position as a frontier appendage of Massachusetts hindered settlement and kept the region dependent upon Boston. Wabenaki resistance to white encroachment coupled with Franco-British rivalry in the wars for empire discouraged the movement of settlers into the eastern frontier. In 1689 English settlers abandoned all settlements north of Wells. Early in the eighteenth century, a series of raids by primarily French forces from the St. Lawrence Valley threatened every community in the region. Dummer's War in the 1720s weakened Wabenaki power in the Kennebec region, but it was not until the Seven Years' War that Native American power was eliminated, and the French threat was removed.

Victory in the Seven Years' War secured the eastern frontier. At war's end, Maine contained a population of approximately 23,000 white settlers, primarily located in coastal communities in the far western portion of the state. Within a decade that figure doubled, with much of the growth occurring in the Kennebec region. Although Massachusetts's hold over the region had always been tenuous, Maine provided a huge area for land speculation. As early as the 1630s, huge tracts of land had been granted to groups of entrepreneurs who hoped some day to make good on their holdings. Proprietors like those of the Kennebec Company included many of the leading citizens of Boston. In addition to trying to promote settlement on their lands, they also fought other land companies for the shadowy rights outlined in their respective grants. Although the proprietors of these huge chunks of uncharted real estate sought wealth through speculation, most of the settlers coming into Maine in the 1760s were individuals of humbler means.

Most settlers tried to make a living through various combinations of farming, fishing, and lumbering. Some farmers worked the land during the season and supplemented their income in the winter and early spring by bringing readily available wood to nearby market towns. Most settlers were subsistence farmers with little contact with outside markets. Many were squatters who lacked title to the land they had cleared. Maine's small merchant elite, located primarily in Falmouth, looked to Boston for most of their needs. Nearly all finished goods, money, and news from abroad came from the capital of the Bay State. Most of Maine's raw materials, in turn, went to supply the leading city in New England. The poor, frontier nature of Maine prevented it from having much political clout in Massachusetts. Other than coastal communities that had commercial ties with the outside and had the wealth and desire to send representatives, most Maine communities saw no real need for representation in Boston. Maine's dependent status at the edge of the British Empire made it a colony of a colony.[3]

THE AMERICAN REVOLUTION

Maine had little disagreement with Great Britain following the Seven Years' War and, indeed, in most ways benefited from its connection. Maine, however, followed Massachusetts into the Revolutionary War, with disastrous consequences downeast. Early in the conflict the British burned Falmouth (Portland), Maine's leading commercial center and in 1779 successfully occupied Castine at the mouth of the Penobscot. A Massachusetts expedition to drive out the British met with failure and gave rise to efforts to create a Loyalist colony east of the Penobscot. The war's end brought a flood of settlers, many without land titles in the district, and made evident the Bay State's inability to protect its eastern frontier.

Mainers experienced some irritants but had no serious disagreements with Britain in the 1760s. Britain's insistence on saving the best white pines for masts to supply the Royal Navy irked many Mainers involved in the lumber business. Imperial policy also led to confusion over land grants. Some in Britain wanted to limit settlement to territory east of the Penobscot, a concept that particularly grated Boston merchants who sought to speculate in the region. Religious tensions between the established Congregationalists in Massachusetts and the Church of England further fueled the tension. According to James Leamon, the leading authority on revolutionary Maine, Maine's support for independence was largely the result of the proselytizing of Boston radicals. Towns in the interior tended to support resistance to British rule enthusiastically. Coastal merchants who benefited from economic connections with Britain were more tepid in their support.

The Revolution proved devastating to the district. Maine's exposed position and Boston's neglect of its eastern dominion contributed to these difficulties. Situated between Boston and Halifax, Maine's coastal communities were at the fringe of the commonwealth and within easy reach of the enemy. British forces were able to exert power in Maine while the Bay State did little to alleviate the suffering of settlers living downeast. At the outset of the war, British forces first dismantled Fort Pownal on the Penobscot. In October 1775, the British burned Falmouth (now Portland), the most important town in the district, resulting in the destruction of 130 houses and 230 stores and warehouses.[4]

Massachusetts's inability to defend its eastern frontier was made particularly obvious during the 1779 Penobscot expedition. British forces had occupied Castine at the mouth of the Penobscot River. Officials in Boston dispatched a fleet of eighteen ships with 2,000 men and 200 guns to evict the British, but despite its size the expedition was ill equipped for the task. The ships, primarily privateers designed for raiding, were poorly suited for laying siege and stood little chance in an engagement with vessels of the Royal Navy. When the British learned that Castine was under siege, they responded by sending seven ships to Penobscot Bay. The Massachusetts force quickly disbanded, all the American ships were destroyed, and survivors did their best to make their way overland to Massachusetts. In the ensuing conquest of the lower Penobscot Valley, the British demanded loyalty oaths from the inhabitants, a demand that most locals accepted. Before the debacle at York-town, British officials considered annexing land east of the Penobscot as the "New Ireland" colony, to be a province for Loyalists resettled from other colonies.

The war left Maine's economy in a shambles. Heavy taxes to pay for the war left many near destitution. Debtors found little relief from officials in Boston, because Massachusetts demanded that debts be paid in specie, such as gold or silver, rather than inflationary paper notes favored by creditors.[5]

The American Revolution was largely responsible for three important changes that contributed to the long, slow drive to statehood in Maine. The war demonstrated Massachusetts's inability to defend its eastern appendage from British privation and occupation. Second, the war exposed and intensified a rift between creditors, primarily entrepreneurs in Maine's coastal towns or in Boston, and frontier debtors. Finally, the Revolution accelerated a demographic shift that was already underway in the region. With much of New England becoming increasingly crowded by the agrarian standards of the eighteenth century, and with Massachusetts officials unable to pay soldiers to fight during the Revolution, a popular means to encourage enlistment was through the issuing of land grants. Veterans with three years of service in the Revolution received 200-acre grants from the commonwealth. Anyone who improved land could also receive a grant of 150 acres.

Such inducements attracted volunteers who headed for their claims at the conflict's end. Massachusetts also sought to dispose of land through a lottery. William Bingham of Philadelphia picked up approximately one million acres of Penobscot Valley land for 12.5 cents per acre. The flux and uncertainty that coincided with the war's end led some of New England's more destitute residents to dispense with the formality of a grant. They simply moved east and squatted on available land. Maine's population, which had stood at only 10,000 non–Native American inhabitants in 1750, had risen to 42,241 by 1777 and more than doubled over the next thirteen years, to 96,540. The era of the American Revolution had made Maine safe and available for settlement. Settlers responded by pouring into the region.[6]

ORIGINS OF THE SEPARATION MOVEMENT

The separation movement began as a result of the American Revolution. Downeast commercial interests initially championed the movement, arguing that Maine's remote location and Massachusetts's inability to protect the region made separation necessary. Resistance to the separation movement was powerful, in part because Shays's Rebellion brought any sort of challenge or change into question.

In the 1790s and early nineteenth century, separation proponents failed in several attempts to pry Maine from Massachusetts. Demographic changes in the state began to affect the political environment during this period and, by extension, to impact the separation movement. The flood of settlers from old New England challenged the position of proprietary interests who controlled huge tracts of land in Maine. The differences between proprietors and settlers culminated in a series of conflicts, sometimes violent. The landowners, and indeed most commercial interests within the region, were solidly behind the conservative policies championed by the Federalists. Their control of the courts and local politics gave the proprietors great power initially. Settlers ultimately sought to redress their grievances through the Jeffersonian or Republican Party. By 1805, the Republicans, as champions of the settler interest, had become the majority party in Maine.

The initial impetus for separation from Massachusetts came from the *Falmouth Gazette*, Maine's first newspaper. In the fall of 1785, it called for a convention to consider the question of separation. A small group dominated by the leaders of Maine's mercantile community met in Falmouth on October 5, 1785. Concern over unfair trade regulations in Boston, high taxes, and Maine's lack of political representation led them to draft a circular letter, which invited representatives to attend a convention in early 1786 to consider the separation question. They soon encountered considerable opposition within the district, with some opponents questioning the constitutionality of such a convention. Massachusetts officials, already concerned about backcountry discontent that would soon burst into Shays's Rebellion, considered the meeting seditious. The convention met in January, produced a report that cited Maine's concerns, and scheduled another convention for September to consider what steps to take.

By the fall of 1786, events in western Massachusetts dominated the news. The specter of social conflict unleashed by Shays's Rebellion had a chilling effect on the September convention. Fearful of social unrest and keenly aware that their own backcountry farmers nursed similar grievances, the convention closed ranks with officials in Boston. The supporters of separation reiterated their concerns over the relationship with the Bay State but avoided a more inflammatory statement on the need for separation. Concerns over social unrest gathered strength during the fall and early winter of 1786–1787. Pro-separation forces held a series of meetings over the next two years but lacked the support for statehood.[7]

The supporters of statehood kept the flame of separation alive over the next generation but enjoyed little success in rousing Mainers to the cause. Efforts to agitate for statehood met resistance on a variety of fronts. By comparison with Massachusetts, Maine was poor. Many Maine residents believed that it could not afford its own government and could not provide the necessary goods and services citizens expected from a state government. An even greater stumbling block was the existence of a federal coasting law passed by Congress in 1789. It required ships from noncontiguous states to clear local customs houses. As a part of Massachusetts, Maine vessels could claim borders with New Hampshire, Massachusetts, New York, Rhode Island, and Connecticut, but as a separate state Maine would border only New Hampshire. More important, the vital trade conducted with Boston would be subject to clearance for ships traveling in either direction. A separation vote in 1792 was rejected by 2,438 to 2,084. The results revealed that the seacoast towns were increasingly hostile to separation. Another referendum in 1797 reified the growing opposition to separation among those involved in trade. Although Mainers supported separation by a narrow margin, the Massachusetts General Court ignored the result.

The separation votes in 1792 and 1797 revealed a shift in the source of support for statehood. Although the leadership of the movement remained primarily Federalist and came from seaport towns like Portland (formerly Falmouth), most of the pro-separation votes came from the interior. Important social and economic changes in Maine led to this shift. Following the Revolution, major social fault lines began to develop within the district. Although much of Maine had been awarded to land speculators in the period before the Revolution, many of those who came to the area before, during, and after the Revolution were squatters who lacked title to the land where they lived. Often they simply located a piece of land on the frontier that they could develop for themselves and their families, cleared enough trees to put in a crop, built a cabin, and got on with their lives. Great landowners, like those in many other areas, were eager to enforce their own claims to the land.[8]

The first evidence of tension between the settlers and landlords occurred before the Revolution, but these differences intensified in the late eighteenth and early nineteenth centuries. Indeed, this contest in Maine and elsewhere contrasted two competing visions of the American Revolution. The great proprietors may have desired separation from Great Britain, but they certainly did not want any sort of social equality. Instead, they envisioned a hierarchical society in which their social inferiors deferred to their leadership. Settlers' vision of the American future was egalitarian and democratic. For them, the Revolution implied greater social and political equality, which included greater access to land and political rights. In the immediate aftermath of the Revolution, the Massachusetts General Court confirmed the title of the great landowners to their land, and the proprietors immediately brought lawsuits against squatters. This division pitted a mercantile elite against individuals with at best limited connections to the marketplace and virtually no access to the wheels of power.

The conflict of interest between landowners and settlers, common to many of the American colonies and states before and after the Revolution, had political implications as well. By the 1790s, political partisanship, which had been common on the local level during the colonial period, began to take on national characteristics. The Federalist Party came to represent the attitudes of those Americans who resisted democratization, who had strong ties to outside markets, and who wanted to see an orderly and hierarchical society with themselves at the pinnacle. Their opponents were Democratic-Republicans, sometimes known as Jeffersonians for their leader Thomas Jefferson, or simply as Republicans. They sought less-centralized political power, favored greater access to land and political rights, and in general, desired a more democratic society. Many of those who supported the Republicans were only slowly realizing their potential political power.[9]

In Maine, the division between Federalists and Republicans could be roughly drawn between the coastal trading towns and their immediate hinterlands, on the one hand, and the backcountry, on the other. Settler resistance to proprietary authority was organized and occasionally violent. Arguing that they were the true heirs of the Revolution, settlers believed that the proprietors threatened the hard-earned liberty of the Revolution. Coinciding with this proprietor/market-versus-backcountry division was the emergence of evangelical Christianity in the backcountry. Baptists and Methodists challenged the traditional dominance enjoyed by the Congregationalists. These divisions became manifest in the early nineteenth century. A "White Indian" movement that sought to resist the power of Maine's elite violently had simmered for years. Using the Native American as a symbol of liberty, they initiated a series of attacks against representatives of established authority between 1807 and 1809.

Maine Republican leaders saw an opportunity both to calm the enraged backcountry and to collect political support by championing the plight of the settlers. One of the most important Republican leaders was William King. He had established himself in Bath where he became one of the town's most important shipbuilders. Like many Maine entrepreneurs, he maintained interests in the lumber business, dabbled in land speculation, and became involved in local politics. The son of wealthy Scarborough merchant Richard King, he initially followed his father and brother Rufus into the Federalist Party, but he bolted to the Republican camp early in the century. He became one of the leading figures in the statehood movement and was elected Maine's first governor in April 1820. King successfully shepherded a "Betterment Act" through the Massachusetts legislature in 1808 that enabled settlers to pay landlords for lands they had improved at their "state of nature" value. The act helped to settle differences over land in the state and simultaneously made the Republicans the emerging political force in the district.

The growing divisions between urban, trade-centered Federalists and backcountry Republican yeomanry had a dramatic impact on the separation movement. Federalists, who had originally championed the movement, now reasoned that independence would place them in a permanent political minority in which their social inferiors held power. Federalist wavering on the separation question had been evident early in the century but accelerated after the Republicans emerged as the dominant party in the District of Maine in 1805. Conversely, Maine Republicans had not yet espoused separation. The result was decisive defeat for the separation forces in 1807. On April 6, Mainers voted once again on the question of separation. The anti-separationists swamped those who supported independence, by a 9,404 to 3,370 margin. Coastal towns in particular were opposed to statehood. Separation seemed to be a dead issue in Maine.[10]

THE IMPACT OF THE WAR OF 1812

The War of 1812 marked a turning point in the separation movement. Great Britain generally ignored the New England coast until 1814, when British forces occupied Castine and Bangor on the Penobscot River. British control of eastern Maine brought no response from Boston, and Maine was again left basically to fend for itself. Maine Republicans saw opportunity in Massachusetts's inaction. The inaction of Federalist leaders in Massachusetts provided political fodder for the Republicans, who now made a renewed case for separation. Maine statehood would also make them the majority party of a new state, rather than part of a disorganized minority in Massachusetts. Republicans used the occupation to argue in favor of separation. The pro-separation leadership, known as the "Junto," agitated for independence from the Bay State and secured a statewide vote on the issue in 1816.

The catalyst for the renewal of the separation movement was the War of 1812. New England opposition to the war caused the British to leave the northern coast unmolested during the first two years of the conflict. Despite this policy, Maine's coast was the scene of privateer activity throughout the conflict. Tensions increased in 1814, when the British brought the campaign directly to Maine. In July of that year, British forces occupied Eastport. On September 1, a British force of sixteen ships carrying 2,500 troops arrived at Castine. Two days later, British forces scattered the local militia at Hampden and soon advanced upriver to Bangor. Despite promises to leave the community unmolested, British forces took up residence in two schools, a courthouse, and a private residence, feasted on produce and liquor provided by the conquered community, and soon began to loot and ransack the town. Before leaving for Castine, the British burned the local fleet in the Penobscot River and demanded that all ships being built in Bangor be delivered to Castine upon their completion. The frontier community of Bangor faced ruin. Maine's leaders asked the General Court for aid in driving out the British, but Massachusetts officials did nothing.

The British occupation of eastern Maine seemed further proof of Boston's negligence. The war, and in particular the legacy of neglect at the hands of Massachusetts, had important ramifications for the statehood movement. Massachusetts's inaction could be blamed on Federalist leadership, and the convening of the Federalist-dominated Hartford convention and its threats of disunion further undermined Federalist credibility downeast. The post-war "Era of Good Feelings" was dominated by the Republicans. Even a local Federalist remarked, at the news of the war's end, "the days of festivity and mirth are universal." The time was ripe for a new effort toward separation.[11]

The group that ultimately led the fight for statehood included John Holmes, William King, William Pitt Preble, Albion Keith Parris, Ashur Ware, and John Chandler. They became known as the "Junto" and propagandized through their newspaper, the Portland *Eastern Argus*. The motives of many of these leaders were often personal. One of the two most important leaders of the movement, John Holmes, had made a name for himself as a young lawyer in the district by defending proprietor claims against the squatters. His legal acumen quickly made him an important figure in the local Federalist Party, and he served in the Massachusetts legislature in 1802 and 1803. He switched his allegiance to the Republican Party in 1811, a change many critics attributed to opportunism and ambition. He soon became a member of the Massachusetts General Court and was elected to the U.S. House of Representatives in 1816 and again in 1818.

Holmes and his colleagues began to implement their plan for separation before the end of 1815. They offered many reasons for Maine statehood. They argued that Massachusetts had left them to their own fate during the recent war, leading to the occupation and potential dismemberment of the eastern half of the state. Maine felt it had been neglected, and many of its citizens believed they no longer needed the connection with Massachusetts. With a population of well over 200,000, Maine was far larger and had a much more developed economy than most other prospective states and was larger in territory than many existing states. For John Holmes and other leading Maine politicians, statehood represented greater power. The Federalist Party remained dominant in Massachusetts, but an independent Maine would be heavily Republican. Statehood offered individuals like John Holmes greater access to political power than they could achieve through continued union with the Bay State.[12]

Federalists held mixed views. Many Massachusetts Federalists bemoaned the loss of valuable land in its eastern territory and demanded the Bay State receive some sort of compensation. Others feared that the loss of Maine would reduce Massachusetts's standing in the Union. In addition, an independent Maine would add to Republican strength in the U.S. Senate and House of Representatives. Ridding Massachusetts of Maine's mostly Republican representatives, however, would guarantee continued Federalist dominance in the Bay State. Maine's Federalists were aghast at the prospect. They feared that, if separated from the Bay State, they would become a small speck of respectable gentlemen in a sea of unwashed democracy. The Federalist *Portland Gazette* led the fight against separation in Maine. It argued that separation would be expensive, that the district lacked individuals of appropriate talent to lead the infant state, and, most important, that the coasting law would impoverish the merchants in an independent Maine.

The first post-war vote over the separation issue occurred on May 20, 1816. The General Court agreed to the vote but would respond only to an overwhelming vote in favor of separation. In addition to pointing out the benefits to be accrued by statehood, Maine Republicans also blamed wartime woes on Federalist leadership, a charge that resonated with particular strength in eastern Maine. Bangor resident Mark Trafton lambasted the "fatal policy which then gave direction to this section of our country" and warned Mainers to "supply yourselves once more with arms and swear never again to surrender them, upon the cowardly and traitorous spirit that the safety of life and property is dearer than liberty."

Mainers supported separation from Massachusetts by a margin of 10,584 to 6,941. The breakdown was both political and regional. Republicans tended to support statehood; Federalists opposed it. Citizens living in coastal communities often opposed separation, whereas those in the interior favored independence from Massachusetts. Opponents of statehood successfully argued that, because most voters had stayed home on May 20, (only 17,000 of 38,000 eligible voters appeared at the polls), the vote did not represent the wishes of the majority of Maine citizens. The Federalist-controlled General Court, bowing to pressure from Maine Federalists, concluded that the low turnout did not constitute a vote in favor of separation. Instead, the Massachusetts legislature authorized Maine to hold a separation vote in early September that would also select delegates to a constitutional convention to be held in Brunswick later that fall. According to the General Court, Maine could proceed with the Brunswick convention only if five-ninths (55.6 percent) of the vote favored separation.

The vote in early September brought out far more voters than the earlier plebiscite, largely because of the extensive press coverage. Although many of those who supported separation assumed an easy victory, Maine's Federalists bitterly criticized the terms of separation spelled out by the General Court. Under the terms of the agreement, Massachusetts would retain title to half of Maine's public lands, and Maine would receive no recompense for taxes paid to build public buildings in Massachusetts. These issues, Federalists argued, were an affront to Maine's sovereignty. The election was a victory for the foes of statehood. Although a slight majority of voters supported separation (11,927 to 10,539), it fell short of the five-ninths majority required for a convention to meet in Brunswick to draw up a constitution for the state. Again, seaport towns tended to oppose separation, whereas the interior was more generally in favor.[13]

THE BRUNSWICK CONVENTION, SEPARATION, AND THE MAINE CONSTITUTION

Although a slim majority of Maine voters favored separation from Massachusetts in September 1816, the margin failed to meet the five-ninths majority required by the Massachusetts General Court. Pro-separation forces ignored this stipulation, citing their slim majority as proof that Maine's citizens supported statehood, met at Brunswick, and proceeded to draft a constitution in the hopes that Bay State officials might ignore the five-ninths requirement. The General Court ignored the convention results and dissolved the convention late in 1816. Following the failure at Brunswick, Republican leaders who championed the separation movement used their political clout to strike down the coasting law. The existing law required that ships pass customs when in ports of non-contiguous states. An independent Maine would only be contiguous to New Hampshire, placing its merchants at a great disadvantage. With the demise of the coasting law, separation became a foregone conclusion and was overwhelmingly approved at the polls in the spring of 1819. The ensuing constitutional convention would approve one of the most democratic documents to date.

Despite the loss at the polls, separationists cited their slim majority as proof that Maine's citizens supported statehood. They held their convention in Brunswick anyway, hopeful that the General Court might waive the five-ninths requirement if Maine produced a constitution. One hundred eighty-five delegates met in Brunswick on September 30, 1816, to determine the district's future. By all accounts, chaos ruled the day. Pro-separation forces, with a majority of twelve, succeeded in selecting statehood proponent William King as convention president. The proponents of separation succeeded in forcing through the convention a set of resolutions that essentially ignored the five-ninths requirement, arguing that a majority of Maine's citizens supported statehood. The pro-separation *Eastern Argus* disingenuously argued that:

> It is said in a revolution of this kind, something *more* than a *majority* ought to be required. Who ever heard of doctrine so ridiculous before? Where will you stop? Once depart for the great and immutable principle of freedom, that a MAJORITY SHALL RULE, and a unanimous vote may be required.... Revolutions of more consequence than the erection of Maine into an independent State, have been affected up a single *majority*. The *old confederation* of the U.S. was *dissolved*, and the present Constitution *adopted*, upon a *simple majority*. The several State constitutions have all been adopted upon *this principle*.... Massachusetts having NO RIGHT to require a greater number than a *majority* to assent to her terms; the Convention was not *bound* by the majority of five to four.[14]

Opponents of separation had a different response to the convention, terming the decision to go ahead with separation as an act of "outrage, profligacy, wickedness and crime." Supporters of separation would later resort to charges that "a very large proportion of those [opposition] votes were incorrectly or illegally returned." The members at the convention decided not to postpone action but to present the results to the General Court. The *Eastern Argus* reasoned:

> This course appeared to them the more proper and expedient, inasmuch as the fact was unquestionable, that what ever the correct and sound construction of the Act, there was a large majority of the People of Maine in favor of the separation upon the terms and conditions proposed by the Legislature.[15]

Despite the intellectual gymnastics of the pro-separation forces, the Massachusetts General Court rejected this claim in early December and dissolved the Brunswick convention.

The Brunswick convention's failure to realize the cherished goal of separation coincided with plunging Republican fortunes in Massachusetts. Although the Republicans remained the majority party downeast, their disorganized and dispirited brethren in Massachusetts were in disarray. Separation had increasingly become a Republican issue in Maine, but it was not until the Brunswick convention that it emerged as a major political issue for Maine Republicans. The usefulness of this issue coupled with declining Republican fortunes in Massachusetts ultimately led to its adoption as the primary rallying cry for Maine Republicans.

In the meantime, a sense of foreboding hung over pro-separation forces in Maine. In December 1818, the *Eastern Argus* lamented that whereas western territories such as Illinois and Alabama "seem fully apprised of the advantage of having a local government of their own,…Why we are often asked, does not Maine derive the same advantages from a local government—a legislature of our own?" The supporters of separation recognized that the main stumbling block to independence from Massachusetts was the coasting law. Toward this end, William King went to Washington to lobby his close political ally, Secretary of the Treasury William Crawford. As the leader of the "Old Republican" faction of the national party, Crawford's support carried considerable weight in Washington.[16]

With pro-separation agitation building in Maine, the Junto determined to try again. Led by William King, Maine's representatives to the General Court caucused in Boston in February to consider the separation issue. Federalists fumed over the meeting, charging, "Separation or office-seekers are at their dirty work again." Supporters of statehood denied that separation was a partisan issue and observed "that sooner or later the district must be separated from Massachusetts. The only difference of opinion is whether the time for it has yet arrived." On the last day that the General Court was in session, news arrived that the U.S. Senate had amended the coasting law. The entire Atlantic seaboard was now one shipping district open to Maine vessels. Maine's legislators immediately selected a standing provisional committee to "take such measures, as they shall judge most efficacious for bringing before the people of Maine, the separation of the district from Massachusetts, and for erecting it into an independent State."[17]

The change of the coasting law removed a major stumbling block to separation. The editorialist "Independence" observed, "By the patriotic and persevering efforts of one of our distinguished fellow citizens, Congress have been induced to modify the *Coasting Law*, and thus prepare the way for our emancipation from the thralldom of Old Massachusetts." The campaign for separation and statehood began in earnest during the spring of 1819. On April 20, 1819, the *Eastern Argus* published a circular letter from leading supporters of separation. It urged those who supported statehood to elect pro-separation delegates to the state legislature and suggested the "propriety of forwarding petitions to the Legislature, at the next session, soliciting the passage of a law authorizing the sense of the inhabitants of this District to be again taken." It sought to blunt Federalist opposition by disavowing "party feelings as having any influence on this question."[18]

The Republican-organized drive for a petition in favor of statehood flooded the Massachusetts General Court. The General Court responded by creating committees to explore separation on May 27, just two days after convening. By June 9, a bill providing for terms of separation was reported. It provided that Massachusetts retain half of all title to public lands within Maine, that Maine receive one-third of federal reimbursements owed Massachusetts for its expenditures in the War of 1812, and added that Maine's future was probably best safeguarded by having its own independent government. It provided that Maine voters convene in July to determine whether Maine should become a "separate and independent State." A 1,500-vote majority in favor of separation was required for Maine to call a constitutional convention for October. Maine Republicans disliked the requirement for a 1,500-vote majority, but, believing that this was the best deal they could strike, they accepted it. Both houses of the legislature approved the bill by overwhelming margins.

The ensuing debate over separation from Massachusetts placed the Federalists in a political quandary. Recognizing themselves as a minority party in Maine, they sought to oppose statehood without alienating voters. Initially, Federalists had argued that separation would carry heavy financial costs resulting in depressed shipping and higher taxes, but Congress's passage of the revised coasting law removed the threat of higher costs to Maine. With their contentions of economic ruin now irrelevant, the Federalists turned to other arguments. They portrayed the supporters of separation as "ambitious, designing men, office seekers" who sought to use statehood for their own selfish advantage. Aware of the strong pro-statehood sentiments downeast, the Federalist *Portland Gazette* sought to rouse local pride by bitterly criticizing Maine's negotiators for allowing Massachusetts to keep half of the unsold public lands in the state, a total of roughly eight million acres. It observed that "the OLD STATE [Massachusetts] appear[s] to be MOST AMPLY PROVIDED FOR" and questioned Maine's junior status in the separation. It concluded, "if Maine is to be separate, she ought also to be independent."[19]

Republicans eagerly supported separation from Massachusetts and statehood. Portland's *Eastern Argus* rebutted Federalist attacks against the separation agreement, observing that the deal was a fair one for Maine and was the best that could be obtained given the Bay State's reluctance to lose her eastern frontier. Statehood supporters also appealed to local pride. They claimed that Maine's citizens had been mistreated by "the political and mercantile coxcombs of Boston" who viewed the state's residents as "ignorant, vicious, half civilized and incapable of self government." They reasoned that statehood would help Maine's economy by keeping money at home, rather than sending "streams of money flowing from Maine to Massachusetts." Maine statehood would put the Republicans in charge of local affairs.

Republicans were also able to play upon local religious divisions during the statehood campaign. The growing community of dissenters in Maine, primarily Baptists and Methodists, desired an institution of higher education to meet their needs. The Maine Theological and Literary Institute in Waterville had been chartered in 1813 but lacked support from the state. At the same time, Congregationalist Bowdoin College had received grants of land and benefited from tax monies, because the Congregational Church was the established church in Massachusetts. William King, a staunch supporter of Maine dissenters and leader of the statehood movement, capitalized on this split, pointing out that Bowdoin discriminated against dissenters and that fairness demanded support for both institutions. Republicans also rallied backcountry farmers. The pro-separationists argued that absentee landlords, similar to those who had sought to block settlers' title to land in previous decades, opposed statehood. With the voters appropriately aroused, the turnout for the July 26 vote was heavy, and Maine's voters overwhelmingly approved the agreement by a margin of 17,091 to 7,132, carrying every county in the state. The *Eastern Argus* jubilantly observed that the result was "gratifying beyond our most sanguine expectations.... Having atchieved [sic] our independence, we have now to complete the work by framing a good constitution and organizing a prudent and discrete government."[20]

The resounding victory for the pro-statehood forces triggered the meeting of a constitutional convention in Portland in October, where 274 delegates from across the state met to hammer out a new government. The convention selected William King as the nearly unanimous choice to preside over the convention and then got down to the business of drafting a constitution. The resulting document, one of the most democratic documents to date, revealed the Republican political dominance of Maine and represented a departure from the Massachusetts constitution of 1780.

Maine's new constitution marked the trajectory of change in American political and constitutional thinking since the American Revolution. The founding generation consisted of classical republicans who distrusted democracy. They believed that an orderly republican society could exist only if a community's wealthiest and best-educated men served as its leaders. These men, to whom their social inferiors would naturally defer, were expected to make disinterested decisions that favored community, not individual, interests. Few lived up to the ideal. Classical republican theorists accepted mass participation but feared its excesses. Property qualifications for voting and office holding, the indirect election of officials, and apportionment of political power according to wealth were among the means for diluting the voice of the democracy. By 1815, this attitude had begun to change dramatically. The federal Constitution embraced a more liberal form of republicanism, which eschewed a communitarian vision in favor of individualism regulated by law and political processes. Such individualism quickly undermined notions of deference and encouraged democratic impulses that had been unleashed during the American Revolution. Federalists still clung to belief in a hierarchical and deferential society, but they were being swamped by a democratic tide.

Maine Republicans represented the new, more democratic approach to constitution making. On the issue of religion, Maine refused to establish any single church and guaranteed freedom of religion, citing men's "natural and inalienable right to worship Almighty God according to the dictates of their own consciences." Maine also provided for universal suffrage for adult males, including African Americans, rejecting property qualifications for electors because they "have been of little benefit—sometimes of injustice." And unlike Massachusetts, where representation in the state Senate was determined by wealth, Maine apportioned its state senators according to population. Maine's governor was also not subject to a property qualification or a religious test. Annual elections, to be held every September, would keep Maine's representatives in close touch with their constituents' wishes. Their democratic rhetoric to the contrary, however, the Republican-controlled convention pursued a fairly moderate course. It promised a fairer, more democratic political system but shied away from any condemnation of accumulating wealth in a capitalist society. The convention completed its business on October 29, 1819, with 236 of the 274 delegates signing. Most of those who refused to sign came from Federalist-dominated communities that had resisted separation. The constitution was submitted to the people of Maine on December 6, 1819, and was overwhelmingly accepted, 9,040 to 797.[21] Supporters of separation seemed to have finally won. Only the formality of congressional approval stood between Maine and statehood.

THE MISSOURI ISSUE

The Missouri crisis was the final hurdle in Maine's quest to become a state. Maine's petition for statehood arrived while Congress was split over whether to admit Missouri as a slave or free state. With the question of the future of slavery in the western territories in the balance, southern congressmen held Maine's statehood bid hostage in an effort to force their northern compatriots to admit Missouri as a slave state and preserve the sectional balance. Many

Mainers were so appalled at being party to the expansion of slavery that they were willing to eschew statehood. Federalists, who were a dwindling minority in Maine, made the most of this argument. Despite concerns downeast and the opposition of several Maine legislators, Congress approved a compromise agreement that resulted in Maine becoming a state in March 1820.

Maine statehood seemed a foregone conclusion once it had received the approval of the people in late 1819, but more impediments remained. While Maine's citizens rejoiced over their new constitution and savored their upcoming independence, the U.S. Senate was embroiled in a heated debate over the status of Missouri. The Founders had largely avoided discussion of slavery in the U.S. Constitution, but most generally assumed that the institution would eventually wither away. The economic realities of 1787 no longer existed by 1815. An industrial revolution in textile manufacturing centered in Great Britain had created an enormous demand for cotton. Southerners, armed with the cotton gin and availing themselves of lands recently conquered from the southern Native American tribes during the War of 1812, rushed into Alabama and Mississippi, both of which became states in the war's immediate aftermath. In the South, cotton invigorated an agricultural economy and made slavery and territorial expansion essentials for the region's economic well-being. For many Northerners, the westward march of the "peculiar institution" seemed a violation of a sacred understanding. In February 1819, a bill for Missouri statehood reached the floor of the House of Representatives. There, James Tallmadge of New York offered an amendment to the bill that would prohibit "the further introduction of slavery or involuntary servitude" and furthermore would free all slaves already in Missouri at the age of twenty-five. The bill passed the House in a strictly sectional vote but was rejected in the Senate two days before the closing of the session.

When Congress reconvened in December, the debate moved from the simple admission of Missouri to the fate of the Union. The issue dominated debate in both houses from December 1819 until the following March. Congressman John Holmes submitted Maine's request for statehood to the House of Representatives on December 8, 1819. Its fate quickly became entangled with that of Missouri when House Speaker Henry Clay of Kentucky fused the issues in a December 30 speech before the Congress. Despite Clay's opposition, the House passed the bill and sent it on to the Senate. When the upper house began to debate the bill on January 13, 1820, the issue had become more than merely whether Maine and Missouri would be admitted to the Union. The question increasingly seemed to be whether the Union would survive.

Maine's application for statehood further complicated the matter. Southern congressmen, determined to prevent an imbalance between free and slave states in the Senate, cited the precedent of Kentucky's waiting for Vermont in 1791 as an example of maintaining regional balance. They tied Maine's admission to that of Missouri entering the Union as a slave state. Although Northerners might argue that there was no justice in tying the statehood of the two territories together, Southerners cited the first clause of the third section of the fourth article of the Constitution that prohibited creating a state from the territory of another state. Some Southerners went so far as to suggest that Congress had as much right to demand that Maine admit slaves as it did to attempt to prohibit them from Missouri. In the House, similar debates raged, with northern congressmen questioning the expansion of slavery as well as the constitutional clause that counted each slave as three-fifths of a person. Southerners countered arguments that slavery was incompatible with a nation built on liberty.[22]

The Missouri controversy nearly doomed Maine statehood. Initially, five of the seven representatives from Maine supported separation, but the debate quickly took a turn for the worse. Like many in the North, Mainers grudgingly accepted slavery where it existed but believed that its extension was wrong. Many in Maine were appalled that Maine's and Missouri's statehood had become linked.

> The injustice of such a proceeding as it regards Maine, is so palpable, that we still believe that body [The U.S. Senate] will separate those two subjects.... To combine our case with one of doubtful right and doubtful expediency, and thus compel the house to admit both or reject both, is a most gross piece of injustice.[23]

Most appalling was the fact that Maine's admission might lead to the spread of slavery. Pro-statehood Republican leaders initially split on the issue; Congressman John Holmes worked feverishly to fashion a compromise that would admit Maine, while William King remained ambivalent to such an agreement. Eventually, King and many other Republicans came around to Holmes's point of view that Maine had to go forward with statehood.

Holmes played a leading role in helping to fashion the compromise but in the process lost the support of all but one of his Maine colleagues. In the meantime, the *Portland Gazette* charged that Holmes and his colleagues were allied with southern slaveholders. The champions of separation had a ready answer. The *Eastern Argus* contended that Maine's admission was so important that its citizens should overlook the tragic expansion of slavery. The resulting Missouri Compromise resolved the crisis and brought Maine into the Union on March 15, 1820.

Even after the statehood had been achieved, supporters of the compromise had some explaining to do. According to the *Eastern Argus*, the compromise restricted slavery from much of the Louisiana Purchase. Without the compromise, the nation would have become more bitterly divided, with section pitted against section. It concluded, "However earnest we may feel to prevent southern planters from emigrating with their slaves to Missouri, was it polite to hazard everything for the purpose of gaining perhaps nothing?" John Holmes and Mark L. Hill, the only two congressmen from Maine to support the compromise, wrote open letters to their constituents seeking reconciliation and understanding. Holmes concluded, "In reviewing, however, my course, since the question has been decided, I find no cause of regret, but much felicitation." He noted that slavery had been limited from much of the territory and concluded, "The framers of the Constitution were obliged to yield much for the sake of the union.... Those who saw, in this contest, an approaching storm with devastation and ruin in its wake, may rejoice 'with joy unspeakable.'"[24]

THE TWENTY-THIRD STATE

When Maine became a state in 1820, it was far larger than any of the other territories that had recently become states. Its population of nearly 300,000 was larger than that of many existing states. Most of Maine's citizens were farmers, the majority of whom had limited connection with distant markets and who produced most of their own food. Primarily Congregationalists and Baptists, these small farmers had made the Republican Party the most powerful in the state. Maine's seacoast communities, led by Portland, were centers of commercial activity that included shipbuilding, lumber milling, and some banking. Most commercial connections remained with Boston.

The new state, with a population of 298,335, blended an odd mix of old New England and raw frontier. It contained few population centers. Portland was the state's largest town with 8,581 inhabitants, followed by North Yarmouth (3,646), York (3,224), and Bath (3,026), all located in the southwestern part of the state. Most of the state's inhabitants, if not native to Maine, had come from elsewhere in New England, especially Massachusetts and New Hampshire. Excluding a few Native Americans uncounted by the census, the region displayed little ethnic diversity. Indeed, this uniformity was best observed in the state's churches. The overwhelming majority of the population was either Congregationalist or Baptist; the numbers of congregations of the two denominations were roughly equal, and together they accounted for nearly 90 percent of the state's churches. There was also a scattering of Methodists, Quakers, and Episcopalians. The *Maine Register* reported just one Roman Catholic Church.

Most Mainers were farmers. The 1820 census reported that 55,031 of the state's nearly 300,000 residents were engaged in agriculture. Because nearly all of those counted were heads of households, farming was by far the most common occupation in the state. The interior counties of Somerset and Oxford contained the largest percentage of residents who worked in agriculture (27.1 percent and 25.2 percent, respectively), and Kennebec County contained the largest number of farmers, 9,785. Newspapers from the state's market towns revealed that most had limited participation in a market economy. Stores throughout the 1820s advertised for agricultural products that could be bartered for goods such as tools, seed, fabric, and the like. Such stores served as sources of credit for farmers, offering short-term advances to cover the costs for farm implements, seed, and other necessities. Self-sufficient farmers preferred to be as free from outside constraints as possible, valuing independence and self-reliance. Their political behavior tended to manifest itself close to home through participation in town meetings. State and national politics had less relevance for them. The few surpluses that did make their way to outside markets included cattle driven to Massachusetts and foodstuffs produced for sale to lumbermen and in the state's few towns. Most of this commerce occurred in the winter, when farmers had more free time and when snow covered the state's wretched roads and made movement by sleigh easier than by wagons traversing deeply rutted roads. As the backbone of the Jeffersonian republic, Republicans sought to promote agriculture as a means of developing a prosperous independent yeomanry and, in Maine, to prevent out-migration to the West. These hopes were dashed by the "Ohio fever" following the War of 1812. Partly as a result of a succession of unusually cool summers, many left the state and potential settlers looked west rather than north for their future.[25]

Manufacturing also played an important economic role. Several Maine towns boasted of their manufacturing establishments, but most activities were conducted on a small scale, generally within the home. Cumberland County, for example, contained 422 workshops but only two cotton or woolen factories. Textile production was particularly important. Historian Paul Rivard argues that in 1810 the domestic production of textiles constituted the largest manufactured product in the District of Maine. Moses Greenleaf noted that there were "comparatively few factories in the State" for the production of textiles and concluded "that this important manufacture is conducted chiefly in private families; and it is well known that it is confined almost wholly to the female part of the families." According to Bidwell and Falconer, this form of production was a hallmark of the self-sufficient farm family.

Lumber, shipbuilding, and commerce generated most of the state's great fortunes and were considered the most important commercial activities in the state. These enterprises were closely interconnected. In the eighteenth century, lumbermen had foraged the coastal waters of Maine in search of the white pine used for ship masts. Moses Greenleaf saw the extensive forests as the "most important native production of the State." Although timber cutting occurred throughout the settled portions of Maine, the industry centered on the Presumpscot, but soon moved east to the Androscoggin. In 1820, Maine's 746 sawmills contained only 826 saws, clear evidence that most milling operations were conducted on a small scale.[26]

By the early nineteenth century, the ready quantity of available lumber and the low cost of labor had made the region a major shipbuilding center. The industry had initially been centered in the western ports of Kennebunk and Portland, but by 1820, the Kennebec region, especially Bath, had become the state's most important shipbuilding center. Local farmers hoping to supplement their incomes often provided the necessary labor. Local shipbuilders had provided the state with a fleet of more than 140,000 tons in 1820, most of it engaged in commerce. Small fishing boats also made up a substantial portion of the fleet.

Maine's economic relationship with the outside world was colonial. The leading trade items tended to be raw materials such as lumber and fish, especially cod. Maine also exported significant quantities of potash, lime, beef, pork, corn cider, and other agricultural products. Most of these products went to Massachusetts and other nearby states. Imports included West Indian molasses and sugar, manufactured goods, salt, iron, and hemp.[27]

Fifteen banks and one institution for savings met the credit needs of the state's manufacturers and merchants. The largest bank was the Wiscasset Bank in Lincoln County with a capital of $250,000, followed by the two major Portland banks, the Cumberland Bank and the Bank of Portland, each with $200,000. Although no specific town or region dominated banking within the state, nearly all of the banks were east of the Penobscot, and all but one were in port towns. Despite the relative dispersion of banks, residents of Cumberland County owned more than half the bank stock in the state.

Maine, like much of America, contained two economies. Most of the population remained in a traditional economy of subsistence and barter and had limited contact with the outside market. The towns of seaboard Maine, in contrast, responded to more distant market forces. The dual economy created disparities in outlook and in income. Maine households on the average were wealthier in the areas where market forces were at work. Cumberland County, which reported the highest average wealth ($463.59) in the state, showed marked discrepancies between market towns and interior villages. The average poll in Portland, the state's largest city, was worth $977.62. Bridgton and Gray, two nearby interior towns with less connection to the market, displayed far less average wealth, $292.65 and $328.07, respectively. Other commercial centers displayed similar disparities when compared with interior towns. The average of Bath's 541 polls was $436.91. The typical head of household in the interior Lincoln County town of Litchfield was worth only $259.44. The average wealth of a poll living in Bangor at the head of navigation on the Penobscot River was $498.12. His counterpart to the west in the small town of Dexter averaged $288.32.[28]

Maine statehood was a clear victory for the Republicans, and their successful struggle for separation from Massachusetts left an indelible imprint on the state. The Federalists denied unconvincingly that the vote on statehood was a referendum on the parties. Their opposition to statehood damaged a party that was already fading in Maine and in much of the rest of the country. The Republicans now constituted the clearly ascendant party in an increasingly egalitarian state. Another residue of the separation campaign was the appeal to state pride. Both sides found that popular appeals to the voters' state loyalty could reap important results at the polls, but it was the Republicans' view that an independent state was the best means to safeguard liberties.

In his initial message to the state legislature, Governor William King rebutted Federalist criticism of the settlement, commenting that Massachusetts had dealt fairly with Maine. Addressing Maine's future, the governor considered one of the most criticized aspects of the settlement. Under the terms of separation, the state of Massachusetts maintained title to one-half the public lands in Maine. King was eager to develop a coherent policy for the disposal of land that would enrich the state, but he was eager to keep the land out of the hands of speculators. He favored buying Massachusetts's holdings, which the new state government could turn into a profit later.[29]

SUMMARY

For more than a century, Maine was a northern appendage of Massachusetts, a desolate, lightly settled frontier far removed from the capital city of Boston. Conflict with the Native American Wabenaki and a series of wars for empire left much of the region inhospitable to English settlement. The ebb and flow of settlers and refugees in and out of Maine was a hallmark of the period and highlighted the region's dependence on Massachusetts. The removal of Native American and French threats opened the Maine frontier to a flood of settlers, but the region remained vulnerable to the ravages of war. The American Revolution and the War of 1812 brought conquest and suffering to the District of Maine and forced many of those living downeast to reconsider their relationship with the Bay State. Despite the emergence of a separation movement in the immediate aftermath of the Revolution, social, economic, and political issues kept Maine appended to Massachusetts for another generation. Two issues invigorated the drive for an independent Maine. The first was the War of 1812. The Bay State's refusal to take significant action after the British had occupied the eastern half of Maine, coupled with growing political differences between Republican Maine and Federalist Massachusetts, made the drive for statehood almost irresistible. A second issue, the existence of a coasting law that favored Maine traders if they remained a part of the Bay State, ceased to be a factor after the law was amended in Congress. The change in the coasting law removed the last roadblock to Maine's voters' accepting separation. The Missouri issue, however, delayed Maine's entry into the Union until a suitable compromise could be worked out.

Statehood left the Republican Party as the dominant force in the state's politics. Nonetheless, Maine did not experience political harmony, because factions of Republicans fought for power and patronage in the ensuing years. The dramatic growth of the state's population continued into the 1820s, fueled by the availability of cheap land and the growing need for lumber in the expanding cities of the Northeast. Maine, however, experienced difficulty in escaping the Bay State's shadow. The Pine Tree State's inability to settle the issue of public landownership as provided by the state's separation agreement left Massachusetts with title to half of the state's lands. Maine's few banks remained under the influence of Boston financiers. Finally, the failure to resolve Maine's northern boundary with Canada continued the region's exposure to external threats.

NOTES

1. (Portland) *Eastern Argus*, March 14, 1820, p. 2.
2. Henry S. Burrage, *The Beginnings of Colonial Maine, 1600–1658* (Printed for the State, 1914); Edwin A. Churchill, "The European Discovery of Maine" and "English Beachheads in Seventeenth Century Maine," in *Maine: The Pine Tree State from Prehistory to the Present*, ed. Richard W. Judd, Edwin A. Churchill, and Joel W. Eastman (Orono: University of Maine Press, 1995).
3. Harald E. L. Prins, "Turmoil on the Wabenaki Frontier," and David L. Ghere, "Diplomacy and War on the Maine Frontier, 1678–1759," in *Maine: The Pine Tree State*; James S. Leamon, *Revolution Downeast: The War for American Independence in Maine* (Amherst: University of Massachusetts Press, 1993), chap. 1.
4. Leamon, *Revolution Downeast*, chap. 2, 3.
5. Ibid., chap. 4–6; John Calef, *The Siege of Penobscot* (London: G. Kearsley, Ashby, and Neale, 1781), pp. 18, 24, 26–27; Gardner W. Allen, *A Naval History of the American Revolution* (Boston: Houghton Mifflin Co., 1913), 2:419–438.
6. Frederick S. Allis, Jr., "The Maine Frontier," in *A Collection of Readings on the History of Maine*, ed. Ronald F. Banks (Dubuque, IA: Kendall-Hunt Publishing Co., 1976); Ronald F. Banks, *Maine Becomes a State: The Movement to Separate Maine from Massachusetts, 1785–1820* (Middletown, CT: Wesleyan University Press, 1970), chap. 1; Leamon, *Revolution Downeast*, chap. 5–7; Alan Taylor, *Liberty Men and Great Proprietors: The Revolutionary Settlement on the Maine Frontier, 1760–1820* , introduction (Chapel Hill: University of North Carolina Press, 1990).
7. Banks, *Maine Becomes a State*, chap. 1–2; Leamon, *Revolution Downeast*, chap. 7; William D. Williamson, *The History of the State of Maine* (Hallowell: Glazier, Masters and Smith, 1839), chap. 19–20.
8. Taylor, *Liberty Men and Great Proprietors*, introduction, chap. 1–3; Banks, *Maine Becomes a State*, chap. 2.
9. Taylor, *Liberty Men and Great Proprietors*, introduction, chap. 1–3; James R. Sharp, *American Politics in the Early Republic: The New Nation in Crisis* (New Haven: Yale University Press, 1993).
10. Taylor, *Liberty Men and Great Proprietors*, chap. 4; Banks, *Maine Becomes a State*, chap. 3; Joel Eastman, "William King," in *American National Biography* (New York: Oxford University Press, 1999).
11. Journal of Joseph Leavitt, July 1813–March 1815, Bangor Public Library, Bangor, Maine; Barry J. Lohnes, "A New Look at the Invasion of Eastern Maine, 1814," in *Maine Historical Society Quarterly* 15 (1975): 8–9; Williamson, *History of Maine*, 2: chap. 25–26; Banks, *Maine Becomes a State*, chap. 4.
12. J. Chris Arndt, "John Holmes," in *American National Biography* (New York: Oxford University Press, 1999); (Portland) *Eastern Argus*, 1815–1816; Banks, *Maine Becomes a State*, chap. 5.
13. Banks, *Maine Becomes a State*, chap. 5–6; (Portland) *Eastern Argus*, 1815–1816; *Portland Gazette*, 1815–1816; *Bangor Weekly Register*, 1815–1816.

14. (Portland) *Eastern Argus*, October 30, 1816, p. 2.

15. *Portland Gazette*, October 15, 1816, p. 2; (Portland) *Eastern Argus*, November 23, 1816.

16. Banks, *Maine Becomes a State*, chap. 7; (Portland) *Eastern Argus*, 1817–1818.

17. (Portland) *Eastern Argus*, February 1819.

18. Ibid., March–April 1819.

19. Banks, *Maine Becomes a State*, chap. 7; *Portland Gazette*, June–July 1819.

20. Banks, *Maine Becomes a State*, chap. 7; (Portland) *Eastern Argus* June–August 1819; *Portland Gazette*, August 3, 1819, p. 2.

21. (Portland) *Eastern Argus*, November 1819; Banks, *Maine Becomes a State*, chap. 8; Louis C. Hatch, ed. *Maine: A History* (New York: American Historical Society, 1919), 1: chap. 7.

22. George Dangerfield, "The Politics of Slavery," in *The Era of Good Feelings* (New York: Harcourt, Brace and Co., Inc., 1952); *Annals of Congress*, House of Representatives, 16th Cong., 1st Sess., pp. 841–846; Senate, 16th Cong., 1st Sess., pp. 85–100; *Statutes at Large*, 16th Cong., 1st Sess., *Public Acts of the 16th Congress*, p. 544; Banks, *Maine Becomes a State*, chap. 9; Hatch, *Maine*, chap. 7.

23. (Portland) *Eastern Argus*, January 18, 1820, p. 2.

24. W. King to R. King, February 6, 1820, in *Rufus King: Life and Correspondence*, ed. Charles R. King (New York: G.P. Putnam's Sons, 1894–1900), 6:265; (Portland) *Eastern Argus*, March 14, 1820, p. 3; (Portland) *Eastern Argus*, May 1820, p. 2.

25. *The Maine Register and U.S. Calendar, 1820* (Portland: Douglas and Shirley, 1820), pp. 113–121; Moses Greenleaf, *A Statistical View of the District of Maine* (Boston: Cummings and Hilliard, 1816), pp. 33–35, 55–56; Percy W. Bidwell, John I. Falconer, *History of Agriculture in the Northern U.S., 1820–1860* (Washington, DC: Carnegie Institution, 1925), pp. 247–249, 252; Clarence A. Day, "A History of Maine Agriculture," *University of Maine Bulletin* 56 (11) (April 1954), (Orono, Maine: University of Maine Studies, Second Series, no. 68, 1954), pp. 127–128, 146, 147–150.

26. Moses Greenleaf, *A Survey of the State of Maine* (Portland: Shirley and Hyde, 1829; reprint, Augusta, ME: Maine State Museum, 1971), pp. 110, 276–277; Richard W. Judd, "Maine's Lumber Industry," *Maine: The Pine Tree State*, pp. 268–270; Richard G. Wood, *A History of Lumbering in Maine, 1820–1861*, introd. David C. Smith, (Orono: University of Maine Press, 1971), p. 28.

27. John G. B. Hutchins, *The American Maritime Industries and Public Policy, 1789–1914: An Economic History* (Cambridge, MA: Harvard University Press, 1941), pp. 100, 177, 180; William H. Rowe, *The Maritime History of Maine: Three Centuries of Shipbuilding and Seafaring* (New York: W. W. Norton and Co., 1948), pp. 148–153; James E. Defebaugh, *History of the Lumber Industry of America* (Chicago: The American Lumberman, 1906), 2:22; *Hazard's U.S. Commercial and Statistical Register*, 1 (13) (September 18, 1839): 206; Greenleaf, *Survey of Maine*, pp. 218–220.

28. *The Maine Register and U.S. Calendar, 1820*, pp. 153–156; Moses Greenleaf, *A Survey of the State of Maine*, p. 453.

29. Robert H. Ferrell, *American Diplomacy: A History*, 3rd ed. (New York: W. W Norton and Co., 1975), p. 209; Hatch, *Maine* 2:114–122; *Portland Gazette*, June 6, 1820, p. 2; (Hallowell) *American Advocate and Kennebec Advertiser*, June 20, 1820, pp. 2–3.

BIBLIOGRAPHY

Banks, Ronald F. *Maine Becomes a State: The Movement to Separate Maine from Massachusetts, 1785–1820*. Middletown, CT: Wesleyan University Press, 1970.

Greenleaf, Moses. *A Survey of the State of Maine*. Portland: Shirley and Hyde, 1829; reprint, Augusta, ME: Maine State Museum, 1971.

Hatch, Louis C., ed. *Maine: A History*. 4 vols. New York: American Historical Society, 1919.

Judd, Richard W., Edwin A. Churchill, and Joel W. Eastman, eds. *Maine: The Pine Tree State from Prehistory to Present*. Orono: University of Maine Press, 1995.

Leamon, James S. *Revolution Downeast: The War for American Independence in Maine*. Amherst: University of Massachusetts Press, 1993.

The Maine Register and U.S. Calendar, 1820. Portland, ME: Douglas and Shirley, 1820.

Taylor, Alan. *Liberty Men and Great Proprietors: The Revolutionary Settlement on the Maine Frontier, 1760–1820*. Chapel Hill: University of North Carolina Press, 1990.

Williamson, William D. *The History of the State of Maine*. Hallowell, ME: Glazier, Masters and Smith, 1839.

THE STATE OF MARYLAND

Ratified the Constitution of the United States: April 28, 1788

Peter Heyrman

INTRODUCTION: MAY 1, 1788

In Annapolis on April 28, 1788, after a week of bitter debate, Maryland's convention on the Constitution ratified the new federal Constitution by a vote of 63-11. The vote was not as lopsided as it looked. The previous year, Maryland had sent five delegates to the Philadelphia convention. Luther Martin, the Marylander who had worked hardest and had the most influence on the finished document, had refused to vote "yes" on its submission to the states. Martin had always opposed a central government strong enough to dominate the state governments. He had poured his heart into an effort to defeat the Constitution or, failing that, to weaken its final form. In succeeding at the latter task, Martin had probably done as much as any American, save James Madison, to shape the new government. Despite this partial victory, he voted against submitting the document to the states. He then returned to Maryland and fought its ratification in Annapolis. Although Martin had labored knowing the nation would approve the new government, he had hoped for better from his fellow Marylanders. Their readiness to accept federal authority cut him deeply.

Martin came to Annapolis representing Harford County. A fellow Harford representative, William Paca, voted for the Constitution but, along with a committee of doubters, submitted a minority report. In it Paca is reported as having declared that he "gave his assent to the government, in the firm persuasion and full confidence, that such amendments would be peaceably obtained as to enable the people to live happy under the government."[1] The report recommended a dozen amendments creating limitations on this new seat of power.

Maryland

Territorial Development:

- Charles I grants the Colony of Maryland to Lord Baltimore, June 20, 1632
- Continental Congress approves Declaration of Independence from Great Britain, July 4, 1776
- Great Britain formally recognizes American independence through the Treaty of Paris, September 3, 1783
- Maryland becomes the seventh state to ratify the U.S. Constitution, April 28, 1788

Capitals Prior to Statehood:

- St. Mary's City, colonial times–1694
- Annapolis, originally named Ann Arundel Town, 1694–1788

State Capitals:

- Annapolis, 1788–present

Origin of State Name: Maryland was named in honor of Henrietta Maria, in accordance with a proviso contained in the charter that Lord Baltimore received from Charles I, husband of Queen Henrietta Maria

First Governor: John Eager Howard
Governmental Organization: Bicameral
Population at Statehood: 319,728
Geographical Size: 9,774 square miles

Massachusetts had been the last state to ratify the Constitution before Maryland. Its February vote had been a narrow victory, with 187 votes for ratification and 168 votes against. Only the full weight of John Hancock's influence had saved it from defeat. Dissenters in New England had many of the same objections as Martin and Paca. They distrusted the power of the proposed government. There, too, many votes had been won only by the proposal of amendments guaranteeing the peoples' rights. With Massachusetts's affirmative vote, six of the thirteen states had ratified in less than ten weeks. Since then nearly three months had passed without a single state taking positive action. In March tiny Rhode Island had rejected the charter, feeling that it cheated the small states while throwing them bones in the Senate. As the weeks went by, it became clear that North Carolina and perhaps other states were tilting the same way.

Maryland's vote gave the ratification forces a bare majority, seven of thirteen. By the terms laid down in Philadelphia, this majority was not enough. Two-thirds, or nine states, were required. Creating a majority for ratification, however thin, had its effect. Within a few weeks South Carolina and New Hampshire voted "yes," making the document into effective law. Virginia and New York quickly followed, and eventually even Rhode Island approved, although not without coercion. Luther Martin's concerns were not forgotten: his voice split his state, but this was nothing new for Maryland.

COLONIAL MARYLAND: THE RULE OF THE LORDS BALTIMORE

Just as George Calvert, the first Lord Baltimore, was the founder of the proprietary Colony of Maryland, one might consider his descendant, Frederick Calvert, the last of the proprietors, to be a founder of the State of Maryland. This proclivity for playing a role in creation may be the only quality the first Lord Baltimore shared with the last. Large as the last Lord Baltimore's part was in the birthing of a state, it was also purely coincidental. Frederick never meant to lose the lucrative family holding.

Through hard work, persistence, and the principle of religious tolerance, the first Lord Baltimore brought about a colony on the upper Chesapeake. He pressed the advantage of his friendship with two English kings, overcoming the handicap of his Catholicism in an Anglican court. Calvert died without ever seeing his colony. It was two years after his death, well into the proprietorship of his son, Cecil, that the first settlers landed on a Maryland shore.

Cecil and his son, Charles, exhibited the same strength of character that typified George Calvert. This family trait began to deteriorate, however, as the Lords Baltimore became ever more distant from their province. Charles, the last of the stronger Lords Baltimore, was the last proprietor to give Maryland his full attention. He served as governor for more than two decades, starting in 1661. In the early 1680s Charles returned to England in a desperate bid to defend the colony's interests in a boundary dispute with William Penn to the north. Penn had a surer touch in Court, and Charles lost thousands of square miles to Pennsylvania. Before Charles could return to his diminished colony, the Glorious Revolution broke out. Sadly for Charles, its glory was not his. Taking the wrong side at the wrong time, he forfeited control of the colony. Charles made several petitions for restoration of the family's proprietorship, but never got it back.[2] The fourth Lord Baltimore, Leonard Calvert, made a similar petition on assumption of his father's title. Leonard died within two months of inheriting the lordship and was never Maryland's proprietor, but the petition was granted to his sixteen-year-old son, Charles, the fifth Lord Baltimore, a few months later.

With the colony restored to the family's hands, this younger Charles went on to a life of travel, writing, and occasional administering. He visited Maryland once, in 1732. Opinions about his abilities varied greatly. Prussia's Frederick the Great wrote about him to Voltaire: "This is a very sensible man, who possesses a great deal of knowledge and thinks like us that sciences can be no disparagement to nobility nor deride an illustrious rank." Perhaps Charles did have the intellect the Prussian king claimed for him, but the sharp-eyed Horace Walpole described Charles as having "a good deal of jumbled knowledge." A fellow baron's doubts about Charles went beyond intellect. Lord Hervey wrote: "Lord Baltimore...thinks he understands everything and understands nothing.... [He] is a little mad."

A mad or jumbled Lord meant little to Maryland. The third Lord Baltimore's loss of colonial rule had come in 1689. By the time the younger Charles regained the proprietorship in 1715, conditions in Maryland had changed. Although the terms of restoration assured that the original 1632 charter still applied, much of the Lord's real authority was gone. In its quarter century without a proprietor, the Maryland assembly had redefined itself along the lines of England's House of Commons. The legitimacy of the assembly arose from a clause that George Calvert had inserted in Maryland's charter nearly a century before: "that all and singular the Subjects and Liege-Men of Us, our Heirs and Successors... [be] Natives...of our Kingdom of England and Ireland; and in all Things shall be held, treated, reputed, and esteemed as...born within our Kingdom of England."[3] Citizens of Maryland and their descendants were to be regarded, first and foremost, as subjects of the Crown, with all the rights therein. The rights of a British subject had expanded in the decades following the Glorious Revolution. The inherent link between taxes and representation had become more firmly established in the mother country.

In the years since the third Lord Baltimore had lost the colony, the lower house of the Maryland assembly had come to take the charter's clause literally. With no proprietor to rule them and the status of their colony in flux, these elected representatives had formed the habit of running Maryland on their own. They were glad to have the stability of a proprietor again, but they were not about to relinquish their new-found rights as Englishmen, rights that implied an increasing degree of autonomy. As long as Charles got his quitrents from the family lands, he made no objection. Whatever his other abilities, he had no urge to rule.

THE LAST LORD BALTIMORE: MARYLAND'S SHIFT TO SELF-GOVERNMENT

The sixth and last Lord Baltimore, Frederick, was a dilettante who spent the sum of his life trying to buy pleasure. No one will ever know whether he got what he paid for. The colony's last Lord died five years before the Declaration of Independence, leaving no record of his passions. Although he craved all things sensual, he did not seem to enjoy them. One Maryland historian has said that Frederick "lacked his father's modest ability." A reviewer of the time dismissed one of Frederick's many literary efforts, observing, "It is to be regretted that in this book there is not one event, description, or remark worth recording."

Frederick was a man of great appetites but of narrow personality. He was spoiled, conceited, and showed only limited intelligence. He had little empathy for those around him. In 1753 he married Diana Eggerton. They separated in 1756, and the Lady Baltimore died in 1758. She had gone through a period as an invalid as the result of back injuries suffered when she fell from a carriage during an outing with Frederick. Not long after her death, Frederick left England for travels across the Continent. Although few of Frederick's own travelogues survive, he did appear in Laurence Sterne's famous account *A Sentimental Journey* under the pseudonym "Mundungus," a term used for Maryland's lowest-quality tobacco.

> Mundungus, with an immense fortune, made the whole tour; going on from Rome to Naples—from Naples to Venice—from Venice to Vienna—to Dresden, to Berlin, without one generous connection or pleasurable anecdote to tell of; but he had travell'd straight on, looking neither to his right hand or his left lest Love or Pity should seduce him out of his road.

Sterne pitied the rich, young Lord who seemed so impoverished in the area of normal human compassion:

> Peace be to [him] if it is to be found; but heaven itself, was it possible to get there with such temper…[he has] brought up no faculties for this work; and was the happiest mansion in heaven to be allotted to Mundungus, [he] would be so far from being happy, that [he] would do penance there to all eternity.

Cold, selfish, but with oddly unbridled desires, Frederick developed a reputation for sensual excesses that eventually caused him to leave England, cutting the last tenuous bonds between the Lords Baltimore and their colony. This estrangement, as much as any other event, helped peel Maryland away from its mother country.[4]

In his two decades as Maryland's proprietor, Frederick neither visited his property nor expressed any desire to visit it. He appointed relatives and in-laws to govern the colony. He had no time for such tasks: he was busy writing his travelogues and fathering illegitimate children. At the same time, he refused to allow his colony to have an agent representing its interests in London, as most colonies had, and he refused to be taxed for or to allow his income from the colony to go toward the war with France. Much of the burden eventually fell on Marylanders in the form of new fees and taxes and contributed greatly to their disaffection from Mother England.

Frederick's attentions to Maryland were paid to profit alone. He liked the money but cared nothing about its source. In this he was an extreme example of England's attitude in the reign of King George III. The Crown had armies and navies to pay for and became increasingly deaf to voices from the opposite side of the Atlantic.

With an apathetic proprietor an ocean's distance away, Maryland's governors were on their own. They could represent the Calverts' interests, and they had the authority to hire others to collect various fees and taxes, but their ability to enforce the will of England was limited. They had no armies and little in the way of police presence. As long as Marylanders were willing to accept royal rule, this lack of ability to enforce British rule was not a problem. But what do people do in the face of neglect? As the last Lord Baltimore's descendants have written: "[Frederick] was himself a contributing factor in Maryland's willingness to join the rest of the colonies in throwing off British rule." Maryland did join the other colonies, but not speedily.

On October 3, 1771, before news of Frederick's death had reached the colony, the following passage found its way into the Maryland assembly's resolutions:

> [B]eing [that Maryland is] a Colony of the English Nation, encouraged by the Crown for the Sake of Improving and Enlarging its Dominions; which...at their own Expense and Labour, has been in a great measure obtained: ...'tis unanimously resolved, that whosoever shall advance that His Majesty's Subjects ...have forfeited any Part of their English Liberties, are not well-wishers to the country, and mistake its happy constitution.

This resolve was in response to a call for more funds, this time from the Crown.

Maryland had borne the burden of the Stamp Act and the subsequent Intolerable Acts along with the rest of the colonies. The protests of Marylanders had been dwarfed by those of Bostonians and Virginians, but Marylanders sympathized with their fellow colonists. Duties on tobacco had risen along with those on other exports to England. Maryland was still paying duties in the fall of 1771, but in the last years before independence the colony was becoming more and more disaffected. Maryland's planters and merchants were questioning the value of the Crown's rule. After all, Maryland was a state that already ran itself.

There were plenty of resources to run it. In the mid-1700s, Maryland was a thriving land with a bright future. The colony was rich in tobacco, which the whole world craved. Tobacco was such a Maryland mainstay that it was accepted as currency. Ministers and public officials were paid by the hogshead or pound of tobacco. Tobacco was accepted in lieu of taxes, duties, or proprietary fees. In 1771, Church of England clergymen petitioned the assembly for their fair share of tobacco. Their ration had been "40 [pounds] per poll," but their parishioners had cut them back to thirty. The assembly prevailed upon both sides to compromise. They reached agreement at thirty-two.

Slavery fueled the tobacco economy, and the slaves provided well for their masters.

> One hand could till with ease 6,000 hills of tobacco and five acres of corn, and many driving planters got double this much from their slaves. One pound of tobacco would buy three pounds of beef; two pounds would buy a fat pullet; a hogshead would purchase all the luxuries of a family needed in the course of a year, and the net and the gun covered every deficiency.[5]

On the strength of demand for tobacco, ports had sprung up along both the Chesapeake's shores. By the 1750s, Baltimore rivaled and then surpassed Annapolis and Port Deposit. African slaves bore the brunt of the labor in tobacco, while white planters drew the profits, part of which flowed into Lord Baltimore's coffers. Young Frederick's habits were already bleeding the family fortune.

Maryland's growth began primarily along its Eastern Shore. The flat, rich land with its winding rivers was perfect for both tobacco farming and shipping. As the prime river acreage filled up, more and more settlers looked west. Annapolis on the western shore of the Chesapeake Bay became the colony's capital in 1694. From there population spread north and further west, creating farms out of forests. Farms were the first necessity in any newly settled area, and in the colonies this necessity was enforced by legal restraints. England did not allow the colonies to export any manufactured goods. The colonists did, however, need goods for themselves, and in the towns and villages trades were growing. Baltimore was known for cabinetmaking, and the area's first mills were opening on the Patapsco and the Jones Falls. The possibilities for self-sufficiency were fast evolving. Nonetheless, there was little or no questioning of the Crown's policies.

Although Maryland society was changing quickly, its surface structure seemed unaltered. At bottom were the three classes of laborers: slave, indentured, and freeborn. Slaves were Africans brought to America by force, owned for life, with little or no hope of freedom for themselves or their children. Indentured laborers were those who had been compelled by circumstance to sell themselves into a limited form of servitude. They were bound to their masters for a period of years. Some were convicts, whereas others had fallen so far into poverty that indenture seemed to be the only way out. Freeborn laborers had the hope of rising in the world, although few did. Some small farmers worked their own plots, but by the end of the colonial period the majority did not. Most were renters, paying with crops for the use of their land. Above these groups was the managerial class, often called overseers. Overseers did the day-to-day work of running operations in the fields. These managers served the landed gentry. In a little more than a century, Maryland had developed a genteel upper stratum. Most were related to one another, and all were planets revolving around the sun of the Calvert family at varying removes. Although Frederick never visited his lands, many of his kin had settled in Maryland. Frederick and his family were landlords of much of the best tobacco land throughout the colony.

As noted, ultimate allegiance stretched across the ocean to the Crown. The strands of this tether were of a complex weave, some stretching back to the principles of toleration laid down by George Calvert; others were the bonds of subject to king. Allegiance could be religious, although if one were a Catholic or a Jew, this loyalty would be strained by the narrowing of religious toleration in 1692. Economic ties bound colonists to king, but a merchant paying higher taxes might find his loyalty fraying. Politics was a link, but this too was tested as fees piled on duties and stories of British atrocities in Boston made the rounds. All bonds were weakened by Frederick's inattention. By the time he died, the forces that would lead to independence were already being felt. Maryland was hardly a leader in the revolutionary movement but, with its history of self-rule, was well situated to join it.

Three years before Frederick Calvert's death, as the conflict between England and its colonies simmered, the Lord's legal problems in England came to a boil. As the Crown imposed the Intolerable Acts upon the colonies, the sixth Lord Baltimore found himself fighting for his life. It was 1768 in London, and the charge was rape. It came from Sarah Woodcock, a milliner. Sarah charged that Frederick and two accomplices (both females) had held her against her will, and that she had suffered unwanted advances from Lord Baltimore.

The trial went against her. An examining doctor testified that, although indications pointed to rough physical relations with a man, it had not necessarily been rape. Witnesses pointed out that she had had the chance to flee or communicate her imprisoned status to outsiders several times during her supposed confinement. Although Frederick was acquitted of the charge, his debauchery brought such public ridicule that he felt obliged to leave his home. Once again he journeyed to the Continent, where he continued his entertainments until his death. Frederick died in Naples in 1771. Four months later, his body was returned to England, where it lay in state before being interred. There the people subjected Frederick Calvert to one last indignity. According to *Gentleman's Magazine*, "His Lordship had injured his character in his life by seduction, so that the populace paid no regard to his memory when dead, but plundered the room where his body lay the moment it was removed."

His will named one of his bastard heirs to be his successor as proprietor of Maryland, but the claim was suspect. Although Maryland's assembly accepted the heir, Henry Harford, he was not a legitimate Calvert and certainly had no claim on the title of Lord Baltimore. George Calvert of Deep Hole Farm in Virginia, the one descendant of the original Lord Baltimore who might have taken up the standard, declined the honor. Ten years later, in the Revolution's last year, George Calvert accepted an honorary captaincy in the Virginia State Militia. At eighty years of age there was no thought of his actually fighting. The governor who honored him was Thomas Jefferson. Like their fellow colonists, the Calverts had become Americans.

Besides his title, Frederick left behind legal squabbles concerning his Maryland estates. *Benedict Calvert's Lessee v. Sir Robert Eden et al.* was the largest case. Luther Martin, one of the lawyers for the defendants, initiated the case in 1772, but it was not concluded until 1789.[6] The case, resulting from one of Frederick's ploys for money, concerned a huge parcel of land, almost twenty square miles, which Frederick's father had tried to give to his illegitimate son, Frederick's half-brother, Benedict. It was prime tobacco acreage in what is now Ann Arundel County, home to Annapolis, with shoreline on the Chesapeake Bay and navigable creeks. Frederick wanted the land for himself, feeling that, as Lord Baltimore, he deserved it. He engaged his friends in a scheme to get it, enlisting his brother-in-law, Robert Eden, and several other Maryland residents to buy the land from his father's estate. Frederick was going to bleed his colony in any way he could.

Frederick's behavior showed the hyperactive side of English indifference to America. The changes of the previous decades were now being felt in the social fabric. Although they hardly knew it, the colonies were growing away from their roots and becoming their own nation. Many colonists felt they did not need King George III any more than Maryland needed another Lord Baltimore.

THE EVOLUTION OF INDEPENDENCE

Frederick's last major appointment for his colony was that of his brother-in-law, Robert Eden, as Maryland's governor. When Eden came from London in 1769, he brought with him a young Londoner named William Eddis as his surveyor and searcher of His Majesty's customs in the Port of Annapolis. Eddis kept a diary that gives a picture of the Annapolis they found. With only 1,400 residents, the provincial capital was little more than a village, but it was also the center of commerce, politics, and an unusually developed upper caste.

On arrival Eddis thought these developments had little application to public affairs. He wrote of Annapolis's courthouse: "This building has nothing in its appearance expressive of the great purposes to which it is appropriated; and by strange neglect is suffered to fall into decay; being both without and within, an emblem of public poverty, and at the same time a severe reflection on the governments of this country."

Yet he also noted the potential of the place: "[Maryland's] inhabitants are enterprising and industrious; commerce and agriculture are encouraged; and every circumstance clearly evinces that the colony is making rapid progress to wealth, power, and population."[7]

Eddis and his patron, Governor Eden, were typical of representatives from England in that they did not recognize how quickly the bonds were breaking. This lack of awareness and their blindness to the emergence of an effective self-government caused a huge underestimate of Maryland's disaffection.

Marylanders themselves, in fact, had no idea how close they were to revolution. What could later be seen as active steps toward separation were far ahead of any conscious intent. The notion of independent states had few adherents in the first years of the 1770s. Even after the Boston Massacre none of the major colonial leaders called for total independence. Most colonists, including those of Maryland, would not take that step until the shooting had already started. The predominant idea in the early 1770s was autonomy within the British Empire. The protesters wanted to rule themselves. The propertied men of the colonies felt that only under such an arrangement could they be guaranteed their rights as English citizens.

As the rift widened between America and England, Maryland stumbled further into self-rule, filling vacuums that had developed over decades. With the lower house of the assembly running the day-to-day affairs of the colony for most of a century, the process was already well underway. As long as relations with England were calm, few noticed. But as differences developed, Maryland found itself unable to back away from real autonomy. Marylanders had already developed a great measure of self-rule without asking. Were they now supposed to give it back?

As England demanded more fees, duties, and taxes, Marylanders began to act. Their motives varied. For Maryland's Catholic Carroll family, rich but barred from political life because of their religion, the promise of independence included freedom of faith. Others, like Luther Martin, were increasingly incensed by the Crown's treatment of all colonists. He had been espousing a complete break for more than a year when he heard the news of Lexington and Concord and wrote of his "abhorrence of being any longer connected with a nation whose rulers had thus inhumanly stained their hands with the blood of their innocent subjects."

As a lawyer, Martin had an American's view of the law. He liked things spelled out clearly. Marylanders were like-minded with other colonists in their view toward written law. Whereas Englishmen tended to think of their legal system as a vague assemblage of acts, precedents, and commonly accepted notions, the colonists had come to believe in written codes.[8] England prided itself in its "unwritten constitution," yet each American colony began with a charter.

Lord Baltimore's original charter for Maryland was not exceptional in this sense. It was a specific document, guaranteeing rights. Since its issuance, other laws had amended and superseded portions of the charter, including its grant of a degree of religious freedom, but Marylanders still clung to ink and parchment. This feeling infused the founding documents with far more power than they would have had in England.

By late 1774, Annapolis colonists were following Boston's Tea Party with their own, forcing the owner of the brig *Peggy Stewart* to burn its cargo of tea. When British soldiers occupied Boston that fall, a group of Baltimoreans sent that city's beleaguered citizens three thousand bushels of corn, twenty barrels of flour, two barrels of pork, and twenty barrels of bread. Maryland had already sent representatives to the Continental Congress, and in 1774 they held elections for a convention to meet in Annapolis. The convention effectively governed the colony, acting as proprietor, governor, and assembly. It enforced restrictions against imports and exports in protest against the Crown's demands but tactfully waited until one last tobacco crop had been shipped and paid for. The convention did not overthrow Governor Eden.

To the chagrin of the radicals from other colonies, Maryland's representatives at the Continental Congress leaned toward moderation. They were not closet revolutionists. John Adams of Massachusetts admitted his respect for the legal abilities of Maryland's William Paca and Samuel Chase, but he and other militants grew impatient with the colony's reticence. Maryland straddled the line, caught between patriots and Tories.

As revolutionary fervor spilled south from New England, Maryland acted but did not shout. It governed itself but made no violent moves. No Lexingtons and Concords occurred in the villages of Maryland.

REVOLUTION AND CONFEDERATION: THE WESTERN QUESTION

On a sun-baked July 4th, 1828, on the western edge of Baltimore, Charles Carroll of Carrollton turned the first shovelful of soil for the nation's first railroad, the Baltimore & Ohio. The ninety-one-year-old Carroll told a friend that day: "I consider this among the most important acts of my life, second only to my signing the Declaration of Independence, if even second to that."

Two years before, Carroll's friend, William Baer, had interested him in the proposed railroad line, saying: "It will unite the East and West, [and] will commemorate an Epoch in our History." Baer had no need to preach to Carroll. The old revolutionary's interests in America's West preceded nationhood. In the early 1770s he and several other Marylanders had invested in the Illinois-Wabash Company, which laid claim to vast tracts in the Ohio Valley. Title to these lands had been recognized by agents of the Crown but not by the Virginia Commonwealth. Virginia's claims under its charter had stretched all the way to "the South Sea."

Carroll was the richest man in the Maryland colony and perhaps the richest in British America. He owned plantations and many slaves. A businessman and declared Catholic, Carroll supported revolution in both roles. England was taxing him without giving him a voice in Parliament, and the Crown's colonial rulers barred anyone of his faith from public service. A free Maryland promised both representation and religious freedom.[9]

Carroll came home from the Continental Congress in 1776 and helped to write Maryland's constitution. The document stated its "opposition to the British plan...to enslave America." Carroll's hand was in that statement, as it was in the wording: "That all government of right originates from the people, is founded in compact only, and instituted for the good of the whole." The delegates went on to say:

> As America will be strengthened by a union of all ranks of men, we do most earnestly recommend that all former differences about religion or politics, and all private animosities and quarrels of every kind, from henceforth cease and be forever buried in oblivion, and we intreat...every man...to unite in defence of our common rights and liberties.

The rhetoric was fresh enough, but Carroll was no radical. The document proceeded to guarantee that "the inhabitants of Maryland are entitled to the common law of England, and the trial by Jury, according that law, and to the benefit of such of the English statutes, as existed at the time of their first emigration." The break with the mother country was not as clean as some liked to think. For all the talk of bonds breaking, English customs and manners still held sway over Maryland's courts. The state began as England's child, no matter how wayward.

After its initial rhetorical shot, Maryland became a quiet rebel. Throughout the revolution the state was often a pathway for traveling armies but was seldom the site of real action. Washington and Lafayette both led armies through Maryland but fought their battles elsewhere. Although the port of Baltimore proved indispensable to the Tidewater economy, and Maryland cut right through the center of the new United States, the British overlooked its value. Maryland's comparative calm prolonged this inattention. Although Carroll and three other Marylanders signed the Declaration of Independence, the state kept its profile low.

Britain blundered into paying the most heed to the loudest voices. The Crown saw the colonies as separate entities, a notion that the newly sovereign states often encouraged. Yet despite their independent notions, those states signed the Declaration together, formed a common army, and fought the war as one. If the British Army fought them piecemeal, that was its mistake. When the Crown heard shouts from Massachusetts, it sent troops to Boston. When New York raged, General Howe went there. When the Carolinas and Virginia protested, British troops marched to silence them. Maryland sat quietly. The colony that might have split America in two was no more than a highway for armies marching elsewhere.

Although the new states had declared independence and were fighting a war together, they were early in the process of defining themselves. Maryland, always a split personality, was having a harder time than most. During the debates leading to independence John Adams wrote to James Warren: "Maryland…is so eccentric a Colony—sometimes so hot, sometimes so cold; now so high, then so low—that I know not what to say about it, or expect from it.…When they get agoing, I expect some wild or extravagant flight or other from it. To be sure they must go beyond everybody else when they begin to go."

Baltimore was Maryland's jewel. The channels in the Patapsco were deep enough to accommodate the world's largest ships. Baltimore ships would soon be carrying 60,000 tons per year. But much of what would bring Baltimore its boom was not yet obvious. The National Road, predecessor to Carroll's Baltimore & Ohio, was barely a vision. The development of America's West fell somewhere between imagining and planning. Without a view beyond the mountains, Maryland was almost invisible. Yet in the nation's first years, the West was where Maryland would make its mark. With the independence of 1776, Maryland officially became a state amid a dozen other sovereign entities. They had declared themselves independent of their ruler, but were they also independent of each other? The pressures for union were there, but the Continental Congress had to make up the rules as it went along. Thirteen states watched, each one jealous of its own prerogatives.

Although union was essential to fight England, each colony had its own ideas about the future. With union undefined, geographical disputes sharpened. The most obvious of these concerned western boundaries. It was in this context that Maryland raised the issue of how the United States would develop. In doing so Maryland wagered the fate of the small states against that of the large. It expressed high principles, but beneath those lay the bedrock of money.

The West was the great unknown, a concept in movement, rather than a definite place. In 1776 the West was anything past central Maryland. Once one reached the higher foothills of the Appalachians, colonial civilization faded along with population. Only a few colonists had been there. In 1775, Daniel Boone and his men blazed a trail to Boonesborough. Once there they built a fort, which they successfully defended against attacks by Native Americans in 1779. But this was one outpost. A young George Washington had surveyed more than 80,000 acres of western land for Lord Fairfax in the early 1750s. In 1755 Washington, serving under English General Benjamin Braddock, guided an army from Fort Cumberland to Fort Duquesne.[10] During these expeditions Washington saw the future of America's West. He and his regiment in Braddock's army received large western tracts for their services. Washington, like many of his prosperous brethren, wanted land with a future. Later he bought more acreage in areas that are now western Virginia, West Virginia, Maryland, Pennsylvania, and Kentucky. Most of these holdings remained unimproved even at Washington's death in 1799, but by then the West was already playing a significant role in American affairs.

Carroll's interest in the Illinois-Wabash Company was shared by Maryland office holders William Paca, Daniel of St. Thomas Jenifer, and Thomas Johnson. When Virginia contested the company's title to many of these lands, the Marylanders realized that only a strong central government could protect them. In the next decade they became ardent Federalists. Maryland's rich had every intention of becoming richer.

Maryland's only western land lay in the Glades country, now known as Garrett County, less than two hundred miles from the Chesapeake. It is a narrow band of mountainous country. The first recorded colonial settlers arrived in the early 1760s, when a man named Tomlinson bought one hundred acres on the Braddock Road. Within five years, the Friend family had purchased lots from local Native Americans. By the time of the Revolution there were beginnings of real settlement in the Glades country, but the area accounted for little in the day-to-day life of the state. With Virginia on its far western border, Maryland could not make a claim for more land.

Great obstacles of wilderness geography stymied efforts at western exploration. The necessities of politics and population were not yet present. Yet there was movement. One hundred twenty thousand Americans, or nearly 3 percent of the population, lived beyond the mountains by 1790. These people often settled on the lands claimed by companies like the Illinois-Wabash. Virginia and other states with claims to western territory were prone to give the land to those who lived there. This was Thomas Jefferson's suggestion.

Numerous other states called western lands their own. New York claimed title to some of the same territory as Virginia as well as land in the northwest. Connecticut claimed tracts as well. In the southwest, Georgia and South Carolina staked out thousands of square miles in what are now Alabama and Mississippi. These lands could spark conflict between claimants, but that was not Maryland's concern. With no western lands of its own, Maryland foresaw a different danger in America's West: the probability that a few huge states with an inexhaustible supply of cheap land would come to dominate the small ones. The little states would be left with nothing to offer new settlers, and their influence in the confederation would drain away. In addition, there were those holdings of Charles Carroll of Carrollton.

In the fall of 1776, Congress called for each state to offer its soldiers a bounty of land. Enlisted men would get one hundred acres, and officers might be given considerably more. This call woke up Maryland's elite. What lands would it give? There was only so much land in Maryland, and the best of the disputed western lands were titled to the companies owned by the elite. On October 30, 1776, Maryland's provincial convention de-clared that

> the very extensive claims of the State of Virginia to the back lands hath no
> foundation in justice, and if the same or any like claim is admitted, the freedom
> of the smaller states, and the liberties of America may be greatly endangered,
> this convention being firmly persuaded that, if the dominion over these lands
> be established by the blood and treasure of the United States, such lands ought
> to be considered common stock to be parcelled [sic] out at any time into conve-
> nient, free and independent governments.

Maryland added to arguments of blood, treasure, and lost liberty by pointing out that, without western lands to give, smaller states would be "so weakened and impoverished, that they can hold their civil liberties only at the will of their more powerful neighbours." Maryland made its point within the contexts of that revolutionary time. Safeguarding civil liberties was considered the responsibility of each state, not of a central government. It was up to the small states to defend their liberties against threats from the larger ones. This attitude made sense when the central government did not even have a constitution.

Charles Carroll wanted title to his western lands and wanted a central government. "Congress is anxious for Confederacy," he wrote, "being sensible that [it] will certainly add much weight and consequence to the United States collectively." Carroll expected that government to solve the problem of Virginia's western claims. Maryland stood its ground, assuring that principle would line up with profit. In 1777, when the Articles of Confederation were submitted for approval, Maryland refused to ratify them. Maryland pro-posed that Congress have jurisdiction over the western territories. Under the plan Congress would gradually create new states from these lands, as population and political organization demanded. At first Maryland stood alone, but soon other territory-poor states joined it.

The lands became the primary issue in the states' approval of the Articles of Confederation. North Carolina, New Jersey, and Rhode Island all spoke out in opposition to western claims, but they also capitulated, one by one, giving their approval to the Articles. After New Hampshire's approval in 1779, only two states held out. New Hampshire's General William Whipple wrote a friend that all but "Froward Maryland, and Her little Crooked Neighbour" had approved. "Her little Crooked Neighbour," Delaware, gave in that summer. Maryland held out and did as long as the nation's gentry were divided.

The West was not opening yet anyway, not with a war being fought by an ill-clad, underfed army. The small states had people, coastline, tilled farms, and other resources. The war could not be won without them. Washington had one of his greatest (and one of his few) victories in Trenton, New Jersey. Washington's army was peopled by soldiers from Maryland, Rhode Island, Delaware, and every other state. The nation needed every one of them. The young nation also needed money. It had to listen to Charles Carroll of Carrollton who, when he'd pledged his life, fortune, and sacred honor to the cause, could easily put the emphasis on "fortune." Those who had paid for property should have it.

In February 1780, New York instructed its delegates in Congress to make whatever cessions necessary on its western claims. Connecticut began the process of giving up land claims in October of that year. Virginia lagged but finally voted to give up a huge stake northwest of the Ohio under a number of conditions. These triumphs were not complete, but once these states began the process they could not stop it. The New York and Virginia cessions had some relation to a French offer to protect the Chesapeake from a flotilla commanded by Benedict Arnold. The French held back at first but then suggested that they would send in their navy if the Articles could finally be ratified. Under this coercion Maryland finally approved the Articles of Confederation in 1781. One opponent who held out to the end was Luther Martin. In fights between haves and have-nots, Maryland's Attorney General almost always sided with the former.

FROM A NORTHWEST ORDINANCE TO A CONSTITUTION

In the course of the debate about the Articles of Confederation, Maryland had made another, related point. In it lay a further argument for cession of the land. In these years Maryland made it plain that it did not regard the confederation as permanent. The Union was a product of the move for independence and the need for war. Once the emergency was over, Maryland said, "the states which have acceded to the Confederation will consider it no longer binding." At that point Virginia, New York, and any other state with land stretching across the continent would have the potential to become powerful nations and would certainly dominate their tiny neighbors. This assumption of impermanence was felt throughout the colonies even after ratification of the Articles and the American victory at Yorktown. The confederation's powers were so slight in peacetime that no state bothered to oppose it. There was barely any government to oppose.

Six years after Yorktown, Congress ended lingering controversies over western land claims with the Northwest Ordinance. It was a surprising show of power. This "compact between the original States and the people and States in the said territory" greatly exceeded the Confederation's congressional authority. The Articles strictly defined the powers of the central government, and taking over a vast tract of unclaimed land was not among them. Also, acts of Congress were to be ratified by all thirteen states. In March of 1784, a congressional committee reported an ordinance for this takeover of the western domain. It was not adopted, but it became a defining factor in the debate about the Northwest Territories. By July 1787, while the Constitutional Convention met in Philadelphia, Congress passed the ordinance. It was, in itself, almost as contradictory to the Articles of Confederation as the new Constitution would be. The Northwest Ordinance was the single great step toward nationhood under the Articles.

The Northwest Ordinance provided a means for territories to have legislatures. It defined the method of gaining statehood and the formation of new congressional districts. Many of these provisions were written into the Constitution. The ordinance also guaranteed certain religious freedoms, the right to jury trial, and prohibition of cruel and unusual punishment. These provisions foreshadowed the Bill of Rights. Finally, it provided that states formed from its lands would be territories free of slavery. Maryland, a slave state, had made a stand, resulting in a huge victory for non-slave interests.

Maryland's voice had forced the strongest single move toward central government during the period of Confederation. The law governing western lands pushed the government into a position of central authority. The government had not asked for this authority. Congress sent the ordinance to the states for their approval. Opposition might have been greater, but Anti-Federalists had something larger to fight. At the end of the summer, the Philadelphia convention presented the states with a new Constitution.

Once again Maryland's leaders failed to play a significant role in the call for a Constitutional Convention. Ever since 1776, some colonists had argued for a stronger federal government. John Adams and Alexander Hamilton never tired of stating this as their goal, although each man had his own thoughts as to its nature. These colonies, however, had just thrown off the yoke of a king. Few wanted to replace the monarchy with any authority as great, but some kind of central authority was necessary. The Articles' mechanisms for finance could not fund the governing of a nation. America was in debt. Congress had no effective way of raising money. All it could do was ask each colony to pay its fair share. The colonies were short of funds and mired in depression. Men like Charles Carroll of Carrollton, who had lent his fortune to the cause, were not being repaid. For the most powerful interests in the country the Articles simply were not working, although there was no groundswell for change among the common folk. In the fall of 1786, the French chargé d'affaires, Louis-Guillaume Otto, described the situation this way:

> [I]n America, there is a class of men denominated "gentlemen," who by reason of their wealth, their talents, their education, their families, or the offices they hold, aspire to pre-eminence which the people refuse to grant them...moreover they are creditors, and are therefore interested in strengthening the government...[but by] proposing a new organization of the federal government all minds would have been revolted; circumstances ruinous to the commerce of America have happily arisen to furnish the reformers with a pretext for introducing innovations.

James Madison and John Tyler proposed to Virginia's legislature in 1786 that a meeting be held to discuss ways to strengthen the Confederation's role in commerce. That year a convention was held in Annapolis. Only five states attended. Maryland sent no one. State leaders spoke of not wanting to undermine the Congress in New York by participating in what foreign powers might see as a competing body, a flimsy excuse with the convention sitting in Maryland's own State House.

The Annapolis convention issued a call for a more wide-ranging convention the following year. It would be held in Philadelphia, and its purpose would be to amend the Articles of Confederation. Marylanders were forced to act. Over the winter, Maryland selected five representatives for the Philadelphia convention: Daniel Carroll, Luther Martin, Daniel of St. Thomas Jenifer, James McHenry, and John Francis Mercer. Daniel of St. Thomas Jenifer, one of the nation's most prominent lawyers, was probably the best known of these men at the convention's start. He had long been a proponent of a stronger central government. Jenifer, however, was an old man whose health was failing, and his influence would be slim. Jenifer and Daniel Carroll were the only native Marylanders of the five. Carroll came from one of the state's most prominent families. His cousin was Charles Carroll of Carrollton. Another cousin, John, would soon be America's first Catholic bishop. At twenty-eight, Mercer was the youngest. This would be his first public office. McHenry had emigrated from Ireland just before the Revolution. He had fought the British and had been secretary to General Washington. His would be the voice of compromise, but within the delegation he would often go unheard. Nonetheless, McHenry's letters provide one of the most complete accounts of the workings of the Maryland delegation. Luther Martin, then far more suspicious of centralized power than he would become in later years, was the state's most active participant at Philadelphia. Of the five, Martin had the most fully formed ideas about the relationship between state and central government. He was ready to fight for those ideas. Some thought McHenry had been chosen to temper Martin's most pugnacious instincts. He would only partially succeed.

MARYLAND'S LUTHER MARTIN: FRAMER OF THE CONSTITUTION

Although the Northwest Ordinance's strictures on slavery had not gone unnoticed, there was no great outcry from Southerners. They had been mollified by the absence of provisions covering the southern lands extending to the Mississippi River and beyond. Also, although slavery was banned, escaped slaves in the new territories would still be seen as property and would be returned to their masters. National leaders saw the shadow of slavery but were not yet focused on it. On August 6, 1787, near the end of their summer of deliberations on the Constitution, Luther Martin proposed a tax on the importation of slaves. In doing so he called into question much of the foundation of the new Union.

Martin had been born in New Jersey, studied at Princeton (then The College of New Jersey), and settled in Maryland in 1770. Starting as a teacher, he had turned to law. In 1778, a few days short of his thirtieth birthday, he had become Maryland's attorney general. One of the finest lawyers of the period, Martin suffered from an inability to economize when speaking. Martin himself admitted to an "endless garrulity." He was as contentious as he was brilliant, and his temper often got the better of him. A later historian wrote: "Luther Martin [had] fighting proclivities. In the case of *Martin v. State, 1ˢᵗ H. & J. 420*, there is the following statement: 'That the defendant, Martin had been presented [in] Dorchester County Court in one hundred and one cases for assault and battery.... [T]hat the defendant appeared, confessed the charges and was fined in each case.' "[11] Perhaps such a record was inevitable in a man as mercurial as Martin.

Martin was famous for his drinking. Once, when defending a teetotaler, he promised not to drink a drop until the trial was done. On the trial's first morning, Martin fumbled his way through opening arguments. At lunch he felt great need of libation, but he had made his pledge, so he went to an inn and ordered a full loaf of bread, soaked in brandy. He ate with relish and went back to court, confident in the knowledge that he had not drunk a drop. He won the case on this diet.

Throughout the Revolution and the years under the Articles of Confederation, Martin had remained leery of strong central government. Less of a democrat than many of his contemporaries, he was no Federalist either. He believed each state should rule itself. His views could not be changed by any of the arguments put forth at Philadelphia.

In many ways he was the perfect representative for his ever-split state. Martin opposed nearly every measure to strengthen the proposed central government, and in his opposition he became a rallying point on question after question. He opposed the Virginia Plan and helped frame the New Jersey response. He considered the preemptive tactics of the Virginians to be a conspiracy. In his report to the Maryland's General Assembly the following spring, Martin noted:

> Before I arrived [at the convention], a number of rules had been adopted…by one of which, seven States might proceed to business, and consequently four States, the majority of that number, might eventually have agreed upon a system, which was to affect the whole Union. By another, the doors were to be shut, and the whole proceedings were to be kept secret.

It was this secrecy, and Martin's outspoken opposition to it, that convinced many Marylanders to listen to him.

As the convention wore on, the Federalists made concessions to Martin's views on slavery, representation in the Senate, and the division of powers between the two branches of Congress. If Martin is almost forgotten today, it is because, while winning battles, he lost his war. He diluted but did not destroy the strong central government. After having more influence on the Constitution's final form than any other Marylander, he saw it as his duty to return home to lead the fight against ratification.

Luther Martin seldom stood in the middle. He only felt comfortable when firmly advocating a position, often one at odds with his state. At Philadelphia, his proposal of an importation tax on slaves was an effort to contain slavery in hopes that it would eventually wither. This hope seemed possible in 1787. With Whitney's invention of the cotton gin and the subsequent explosion of King Cotton several years in the future, there had been some small progress against the institution of slavery. In the North, where its hold was weakest, most of the states had passed laws phasing out the practice. It would be decades before slavery completely vanished from the North, but these laws were a step.

Martin's proposed tax on the slave trade threatened to open freshly healed wounds, coming a month after the convention's Great Compromise that provided a solution to the problem of representation. Once it was determined that each state's membership in the House of Representatives would be according to population, the delegates had to decide how African American slaves would be enumerated. Underlying this question was the white man's view of the nature of African Americans. Were they people? If so, were they not endowed with those inalienable rights championed in the Declaration of Independence? Without ever saying so, the convention showed that it did not consider them so. If they were people they would have the rights, and no slave had the right to liberty.

The southern states, where slaves sometimes outnumbered whites, wanted them counted as people. The South wanted as much representation as it could get. Northerners pointed out that if slaves were not true citizens, they should not be counted at all. What were slaves worth in terms of representation? They could not vote, yet they were there. Not only that, but the slave states wanted more of them. Slave ships from Africa were still unloading their cargoes at American ports. Amid debates that threatened to bring down the convention, a compromise was reached. The slave population could be counted, but not as "free persons," or "persons bound to service for a term of years." They would be labeled "all other persons."

Most of the white opponents of slavery had no great love for African Americans. Thomas Jefferson could not attend the Philadelphia convention, but his views were represented. A few years before, in his *Notes on Virginia*, Jefferson had written a lengthy argument for an end to slavery. Writing of a proposal in the Virginia legislature to end slavery, Jefferson contended: "they [African Americans] should be colonized to such a place as the circumstances of the time should render most proper, [and provided] the handicraft arts, seeds, pairs of useful domestic animals, &c., to declare them a free and independent people, and extend to them our alliance and protection, till they have acquired strength." Further on in the same passage Jefferson gives as part of a rationale for the ultimate separation of white and black: "I advance it, therefore, as a suspicion only, that the blacks, whether originally a distinct race, or made distinct by time and circumstances, are inferior to the white in the endowments both of body and of mind."[12] Jefferson also noted historical reasons to separate the races:

> Deep-rooted prejudices entertained by the whites; ten thousand recollections, by the blacks of the injuries they have sustained; new provocations; the real distinctions which nature has made; and many other circumstances, will divide us into parties, and produce convulsions, which will probably never end but in the extermination of the one or the other race.

The idea of ending slavery was advanced, almost radical, among white Americans at the time. But Jefferson never went beyond the written word. Those at Philadelphia who were in sympathy with his views accepted the three-fifths compromise. They avoided direct confrontation with the question of whether an African American was a man (women had limitations on their liberty anyway), allowing that the black slaves, as a whole could count as three-fifths of themselves in the census. This resulted in their white owners gaining greater representation for themselves.

Luther Martin was no ally of Jefferson, but he agreed that slavery was an evil. Although Martin had lived for years on Maryland's Eastern Shore—tobacco and slave country—he opposed the three-fifths compromise. In his report to Maryland's General Assembly Martin wrote:

> It was said…that we had appealed to the Supreme Being for his assistance, as the God of freedom, who could not but approve our efforts to preserve the right that he had thus imparted to his creatures; that now, when we had scarcely risen from our knees from supplicating his aid and protection, in forming our government over a free people, a government formed pretendedly on the principles of liberty, and for its preservation,—in that government to have a provision, not only putting it out of its power to restrain and prevent the slave-trade, even encouraging that most infamous traffic, by giving the States power and influence in the Union, in proportion as they cruelly and wantonly sport with the rights of their fellow creatures, ought to be considered as a solemn mockery of, and insult to that God whose protection we had then implored.

The Great Compromise had been proposed on July 12. Both sides grasped it as a road to peace. Anti-slavery men could live with it, as could the South. Although Martin opposed the settlement, in the end he voted for it "rather than do nothing." Beaten on the issue of representation, Martin waited nearly a month to offer his tax on importation. Placing the slavery issue back on the table put the compromise in jeopardy along with the whole Constitution. John Rutledge of South Carolina took the floor, declaring that slavery was not a moral issue. "Religion and humanity have nothing to do with this question," he said, adding: "If the Northern states consult their interest, they will not oppose the increase in slaves, which will increase the commodities of which they will become carriers." When others raised their voice against this reasoning, Rhode Island's Roger Sherman suggested that the whole matter be dropped.[13] This was not the last time that supporters of the Union would wish the whole issue of slavery would just go away. As tempers flared, southern negotiators dealt with New England delegates. They agreed to accept a compromise on the passage of navigation laws in return for continued importation of slaves through 1808.

Maryland's voice on slavery was contradictory at the founding. Slaveholders and anti-slavery men both represented the state. Its economy was still based on tobacco, and the profitable production of tobacco relied on extremely cheap labor. Black slavery, with its basic premise that an African was no more than a fraction of a person, was the simplest source for that labor. As the northern states gradually outlawed slavery in the years after independence, Maryland's Quakers and Methodists spoke out against the practice. Public meetings in a half-dozen Maryland counties issued calls for its abolition. In 1789, a House committee led by William Pinckney recommended emancipation by "silent and gradual steps with the consent of the owner." In the same session the Senate considered an abolition bill introduced by Nicholas Hammond. In one of many such ironies, Hammond himself was a slaveholder. His bill failed.

As a slave state Maryland generally sided with the South, but it had led the fight that had resulted in a settlement of western land claims that included a ban on slavery. In that same fight it had championed the rights of individual states against the dominance of a few states. Yet the Northwest Ordinance was the first effective use of central government, bypassing state legislatures. These actions followed a decades-long practice of balancing between two competing realities: functioning in practical independence from its proprietor, while holding fast to allegiance to the Crown. Now Maryland teetered once again, with its most powerful voice opposing its entrenched interests. At its founding it was a state of conflicts.

MARYLAND'S LUTHER MARTIN: OPPONENT OF THE CONSTITUTION

By the beginning of August 1787 the delegates in Philadelphia had cobbled together a working draft of the Constitution. James McHenry had been away, visiting his sick brother in Maryland and did not return to the convention until August 4. Copies of the working draft were in the delegates' hands by August 6. Meeting with the other four Marylanders that evening in Daniel Carroll's lodgings, McHenry said: "[We] must act in unison."

Mercer asked McHenry whether Marylanders would back the proposed national charter. "I presume the people would not object," McHenry told him. But when Mercer, who had his own reservations, canvassed the other three delegates, Luther Martin disagreed. He said he would reject it, as would their fellow citizens. McHenry later wrote: "[He] was against the system. [He said] that only compromise enabled its abettors to bring it to its present stage, that had Mr. Jenifer voted with him things might have taken a different turn. Mr. Jenifer said he voted with him until he saw it was in vain to oppose its progress."

At this point Martin and Jenifer were so at odds that McHenry feared they might come to blows. He "begged the gentlemen to observe some order to enable us to do some business we had convened upon." McHenry tried to broker a compromise, hoping still that the delegation might act as one. He suggested that they might get the convention to postpone action on this draft and come up with a new draft that would officially be amendments to the Articles of Confederation. Martin was not so concerned with one draft or another. He was on record as opposing any draft. He said they had been charged with amending the Articles, not creating a whole new government, and doing the latter would not work.

Daniel Carroll did not agree with Martin's stand, but he did admit, "the Confederation could [not] be amended to answer [the convention's] intentions." Mercer and Jenifer agreed.[14] None of the five was without concerns. McHenry later wrote: "We had taken an oath to support our state constitution. We had been empowered by the legislature to amend the Confederation.... I feared we could not...[but] Carroll hoped we should be able to get over this difficulty." McHenry, Jenifer, and Carroll managed to climb over this hurdle. Mercer finally joined the opposition. Martin left no question that he would fight the document. He kept the clang of cacophony in Maryland's voice. In late August he reiterated his disgust with the three-fifths clause, repeating over and over that slavery weakened the whole of the nation.

In early September, on hearing Jenifer declare that the people of Maryland would accept the Constitution, Martin said: "I'll be hanged if ever the people of Maryland agree to it." "Then I advise you to stay in Philadelphia, lest you be hanged," Jenifer replied. Although Jenifer would have preferred that Martin heed his advice, Martin returned home.

In 1788, Martin reported to Maryland's General Assembly that the proponents of a strong central authority had come to Philadelphia with a view toward establishing "a national, not a federal government, as calculated and designed not to preserve and protect, but to abolish and annihilate the State governments." In a speech he reiterated the other aspect of this view, saying of those who had approached the convention as he had: "We had not been sent to form a Government over the inhabitants of America considered as individuals. The system of government we were intending to prepare was a Government of Thirteen States." J. B. Cutting wrote to Thomas Jefferson: "So far did Luther Martin proceed in his avowed hostility as even to detail, in the face of decency, before the assembled legislature of Maryland, the petty dialogues...and private conversations [at] the convention in Philadelphia." Martin's call went unheeded. In May 1788, by a vote of 63-11, Maryland became the seventh of the thirteen states to ratify the Constitution. As in all things, Maryland stayed resolutely in the middle.

MARYLAND AND SLAVERY

The new nation had written and fought its way into existence with professions of liberties far greater than any practiced in the countries across the Atlantic. As it came to see that its success depended on union, America felt torn between liberty and slavery. Although South Carolina's Rutledge might contend that "interest alone is the governing principle of nations," the Declaration of Independence stated otherwise. In that first official document of the United States "all men" are created equal. This statement left out women and forced persons on both sides of the slavery issue to ask, "What is a person?" The humanity of more than half a million Americans was granted to their white owners in the form of greater representation in Congress. African Americans were rewarded with property status.

The first slaves to arrive on the Chesapeake (or in British North America) were probably a group of twenty who landed in Port Comfort in 1619. They were followed by others who totaled no more than a few hundred by the 1650s. Europeans regarded Africans as fit to be slaves, and the practice was hardly questioned. Some Africans learned English and European ways quickly, and a number of these were freed. There were areas in the Tidewater country where free blacks and whites lived in conditions of near equality. With further settlement and the growth of tobacco culture, this situation had to end.

Tobacco planters needed a consistent source of labor at the cheapest price possible. Tobacco farming was harsh work, with Maryland's summer heat, and a rough, resinous plant that scraped and stuck to the skin. Most white English-born colonists were free to leave a farm whenever they had a mind to, and they often did. Even those who had fallen into indentured servitude rebelled against tobacco's regimen. Most of these were bound over for only a given number of years and could see a future. In those first years, enslavement of the Africans had no place in written law, but whites saw them as ignorant and one step away from savagery at best. When a colonist took possession of a black man or woman, he tended to think of it as ownership, pure and simple. By such subtleties black slavery was institutionalized *de facto*. Slavery entered Maryland law in 1664.[15] With this legal sanction, African American life deteriorated quickly. Some freed slaves found themselves thrown back into an even more brutal slave status, now enforced by law. Slave importation increased. In the eighteenth century, African men, women, and children were sold singly and in groups on the wharves of Annapolis, Baltimore, and Port Deposit. As Europe and the rest of the world demanded more tobacco, African slavery increased.

By the time of the Revolution nearly 70,000 slaves lived in Maryland, a third of the state's population. As with whites, almost all African American slaves lived on farms where they did the work no one else wanted to do. Their lives were strictly controlled. Broken families were the rule. It was normal practice for a child to be taken from his or her mother, typically between the ages of seven and fifteen. Although courtship and marriage were practiced, many white owners ignored the marriages. The law did the same.

The status of slaves was seldom questioned openly in colonial days—certainly not in Maryland or any of the major slaveholding states—and, as we have seen, by the end of the following decade debates about slavery in the halls of government had taken the form of arguments about importation or how to count slaves as pawns in federal power arrangements. Washington, Jefferson, and some other Southerners privately questioned the institution, but their ideas about its diminution were vague possibilities involving generations to come, much as people today speak of the death of the internal combustion engine.

Once again on this issue, Maryland's uniqueness lay in its conflict. Slavery was as clear and present a fact in Maryland as it was in any state. By the brutal nature of its cultivation, Maryland's primary crop depended on involuntary servitude. There were, however, whites such as Luther Martin who publicly questioned justifications for slavery's existence.

In the years between the Declaration of Independence and the passage of the Constitution, slavery ebbed in the North. One by one northern states passed legal measures banning or phasing out the practice. In these states slavery was less a part of the culture and was rather the odd convenience. Life was hard on northern farms, but the nature of the work was different. Tilling, planting, tending, and harvest were part of everyone's life. There was no single cash crop like cotton or tobacco that could support a whole economy, nor was there a single crop whose farming required such a dedication of onerous labor.

Tobacco wedded Maryland to slavery just as cotton would bind the deep South to the institution. The culture of subjugation had already taken hold, pitting white prosperity against white conscience. Although Maryland was split on this issue, too, in the end its leaders chose to be prosperous.

SUMMARY: A STATE ON THE BORDER

In 1789, Luther Martin was still serving as a lawyer to the defendants, the last Lord Baltimore's allies, in *Benedict Calvert's Lessee v. Robert Eden et al.* The case still involved the 12,600-acre parcel in Anne Arundel County. Judge Alexander Contee Hanson heard the case in Maryland's General Court. Martin's clients, the friends of Frederick Calvert, won their case. As part of the settlement Hanson directed the plaintiffs to pay the last Lord Baltimore's grantees "the sum of Fifteen thousand six hundred and ninety one pounds and two-fifths of a pound of tobacco."

The late Lord Baltimore won his point at last in the Maryland of the new Union. Part of the payoff was made in the traditional currency of Lord Baltimore's former colony, tobacco. The tobacco crop came from fields harvested by African American slaves. The tobacco leaf would aid and abet slavery through the next seven decades.

Yet Maryland also held the seeds of northern urban life. Baltimore was the fourth-largest city in the nation in 1790 and passed Boston, to become third, within a decade. The beginnings of industry were arising in mills along Jones Falls. Industrialization had begun. Even as Maryland approved the new national charter that came out of Philadelphia, affirming its place within the national design, the contradictions of previous decades nurtured the seedlings of fresh conflicts. As it entered the United States Maryland was, and ever would be, a state on the border.

NOTES

1. Quotations from the various Maryland conventions and assemblies taken from The Archives of Maryland, www.mdarchives.state.md.us.

2. Information about the Lords Baltimore comes from Matthew Page Andrews, *History of Maryland* (Baltimore: The Norman Remington Company, 1926), pp. 568–571; Clayton Coleman Hall, ed., *The Lords Baltimore and the Maryland Palatinate* (Baltimore: Nunn & Company, 1904), pp. 144–171; Wallace Shugg, "The Baron and the Milliner: Lord Baltimore's Rape Trial as a Mirror of Class Tensions in Mid-Georgian London," *Maryland Historical Magazine* 83 (Winter 1988), pp. 310–330; Shirley Calvert-Faoro and Peter Faoro, *The Calvert Chronicles*, available at: http://home.insightbb.com/ ~pfaoro/CHRONICLES.HTM; Peter Faoro, personal communication.

3. All quotations from Maryland's 1776 constitution and the Maryland Charter come from The Avalon Project of The Yale Law School, available at: http://www.yale.edu/lawweb/avalon.

4. Robert J. Brugger, *Maryland: A Middle Temperament, 1634–1980* (Baltimore: The Johns Hopkins University Press in association with the Maryland Historical Society, 1988), pp. 108–110. General background on Maryland life and social development comes from Robert J. Brugger and J. Thomas Scharf, *History of Maryland, From the Earliest Period to the Present Day* (1879; reprint, Hatboro, PA: Tradition Press, 1967); Aubrey C. Land, Lois Green Carr, and Edward C. Papenfuse, eds., *Law, Society, and Politics in Early Maryland*, in *Proceedings from the First Conference on Maryland History*, June 14–15, 1974 (Baltimore and London: The Johns Hopkins University Press, 1974); Ira Berlin, *Many Thousands Gone: The First Two Centuries of Slavery in North America* (Cambridge, MA: The Belknap Press of Harvard University Press, 1998).

5. Scharf, *History of Maryland*, p. 13.

6. Paul S. Clarkson and R. Samuel Jett, *Luther Martin of Maryland* (Baltimore and London: The Johns Hopkins Press, 1970), pp. 155–158. Unless otherwise noted, information about Luther Martin comes from Clarkson and Jett and from *Luther Martin, The Genuine Information Laid before the Legislature of Maryland*, reprinted in *Secret Proceedings and Debates of the Constitutional Convention 1787* (Hawthorne, CA: Omni Publications, 1986).

7. Aubrey C. Land, ed., *Letters from America: William Eddis* (Cambridge, MA: Belknap Press of Harvard University Press, 1969), diary entry from October 1, 1769, p. 31.

8. T. Harry Williams, Richard N. Current, and Frank Freidel, *A History of the United States* [*To 1877*] (New York: Alfred A. Knopf, 1967), p. 131. Most quotations

and information concerning the Revolution, the western lands question, and the Articles of Confederation come from Williams et al., and from Henry Steele Commager and Richard B. Morris, *The Sprit of 'Seventy Six'* (New York, Evanston, and London: Harper & Row, 1958); Allan Nevins, *The American States During and After the Revolution, 1775–1789* (New York: The Macmillan Company, 1927); and from Richard B. Morris, *The Forging of the Union, 1781–1789* (New York: Harper & Row, 1987). Quotations from the actual documents come from The Avalon Project of the Yale Law School.

9. Ellen Hart Smith, *Charles Carroll of Carrollton* (New York: Russell & Russell, 1942). References to Carroll and his western interests come from Smith and from Merrill Jensen, *The New Nation: A History of the United States During the Confederation 1781–1789* (New York: Alfred A. Knopf, 1950); Thomas O'Brien Hanley, *Revolutionary Statesman: Charles Carroll and the War* (Chicago: Loyola University Press, 1983).

10. From records of The Garrett County Historical Society.

11. John E. Semmes, *John H.B. Latrobe, His Life and Times* (Baltimore: The Norman Remington Company, 1917), pp. 204–205.

12. Adrienne Koch and William Peden, eds., *The Life and Selected Writings of Thomas Jefferson* (New York: Random House, The Modern Library, 1944), pp. 255–261.

13. *A More Perfect Union: The Creation of the United States Constitution*, introduction by Roger A. Bruns (Washington, DC: Published for the National Archives and Records Administration by the National Archives Trust Fund Board, 1986).

14. Bernard C. Steiner, ed., *Life and Correspondence of James McHenry* (Cleveland: The Burrow Company, 1907), pp. 100–111. Information on meetings at Philadelphia and subsequent debates comes from Steiner; Ralph Ketcham, ed., *The Anti-Federalist Papers and Constitutional Convention Debates* (New York: New American Library, 1986); Sydney Howard Gay, *James Madison* (Boston: Houghton Mifflin Company, 1898).

15. *The History of Caroline County from Its Beginning: Material Largely Contributed by the Teachers and Children of the County*, rev. and supplemented by Laura C. Cochrane, Lavinia R. Crouse, Mrs. Wilsie S. Gibson et al. (Federalsburg, MD: Printed by the J.W. Stowell Co., 1920), pp. 123–125.

BIBLIOGRAPHY

Andrews, Matthew Page. *History of Maryland*. Baltimore: The Norman Remington Company, 1926.

Brugger, Robert J. *Maryland: A Middle Temperament, 1634–1980*. Baltimore: The Johns Hopkins University Press in association with the Maryland Historical Society, 1988.

————, and J. Thomas Scharf. *History of Maryland, From the Earliest Period to the Present Day*. Reprint. Hatboro, PA: Tradition Press, 1967.

Clarkson, Paul S., and R. Samuel Jett. *Luther Martin of Maryland*. Baltimore and London: The Johns Hopkins Press, 1970.

Hall, Clayton Coleman, ed. *The Lords Baltimore and the Maryland Palatinate*. Baltimore: Nunn & Company, 1904.

Land, Aubrey C., Lois Green Carr, and Edward C. Papenfuse, eds. *Law, Society, and Politics in Early Maryland. Proceedings from the First Conference on Maryland History, June 14–15, 1974*. Baltimore and London: The Johns Hopkins University Press, 1974.

Massachusetts

Territorial Development:

- The Plymouth Colony and the Massachusetts Bay Colony are united to form the Massachusetts Bay Colony, 1691
- Continental Congress approves Declaration of Independence from Great Britain, July 4, 1776
- Great Britain formally recognizes American independence through the Treaty of Paris, September 3, 1783
- Massachusetts becomes the sixth state to ratify the U.S. Constitution, February 6, 1788
- Massachusetts is deprived of substantial northern lands when Maine votes for independence on July 26, 1819, and is admitted into the Union on March 15, 1820

Capitals Prior to Statehood:

- Boston, 1630–1788

State Capitals:

- Boston, 1788–present

Origin of State Name: The name "Massachusetts" comes from the Massachusetts tribe of Native Americans, meaning "large hill place."

First Governor: John Hancock
Governmental Organization: Bicameral
Population at Statehood: 378,556
Geographical Size: 7,840 square miles

THE COMMONWEALTH OF MASSACHUSETTS

Ratified the Constitution of the United States: February 6, 1788

Roland Marden

INTRODUCTION

As one of the thirteen North American colonies, the path to statehood for Massachusetts was part of the common experience of Revolution and nation building. Each colony, however, approached independence, confederation, and nationhood in distinctive ways. The Bay Colony's distinct heritage rooted in its Puritan origins made it especially protective of its traditions of self-government. When Britain attempted to undermine that autonomy beginning in the 1760s, no colony was more vigorous in its resistance. Massachusetts played the leading role in making independence a reality for the North American colonies. This tradition of self-government, however, tempered Massachusetts's support for the federal Constitution. More than any other state, Massachusetts was suspicious of transferring political power from the states to a distant and seemingly less accountable central government. Just as the people of Massachusetts had championed rights during the Revolution, so they demanded those same rights be protected under the federal government by the addition of a bill of rights. Responding to this pressure, the federal Bill of Rights was drawn up and ratified in 1791. The Bill of Rights drew largely from the Declaration of Rights in the Massachusetts Constitution. In this complex fashion, the distinctive character of the Bay State became part of the broader heritage of the American people and the new republic that had been created.

COLONIAL SETTLEMENT

The character of the community that settled in Massachusetts Bay had a lasting impact on its development as a colony and its later establishment as an independent state. Its singular dedication to creating a religious community free from outside interference gave it a fiercely independent character. This characteristic made the colony particularly eager to stake out its own path of development and to resist efforts to impose control on its activities.

The nature of Massachusetts as a settlement also bore an imprint on the form in which the colony became a state. Government by consent was a deeply ingrained tradition in Massachusetts that had its roots in the early history of the colony. The idea that authority should be subject to the consent of the members of the community was central to the political system practiced by the Puritan settlement in New England. This deeply rooted commitment to the principle of government by consent was dramatically expressed in deliberations concerning the appropriate way to establish a constitution to replace the royal charter in the late 1770s. The insistence that the original source of political authority, the people, be actively consulted in the constitution-making process was more pronounced in Massachusetts than in any other state.

The legacy of the Bay Colony's Puritan heritage was also evident in the constitutional provision that maintained a religious establishment for the new state. Government support for the Congregational Church had been in place since the original Puritan settlement, and it remained a part of the new political system in Massachusetts even as other states were beginning to move toward formally separating church from state. Even as the people of Massachusetts, like their fellow Americans in other states, began to articulate political grievances in terms of individual rights, many of them remained supportive of at least one aspect of their heritage that gave precedence to community norms.

Settlement in Massachusetts Bay followed hard on the heels of the Pilgrim settlement of Plymouth in 1620. Seeking to establish a new Christian community away from the perceived corruption of Church of England, the Pilgrims negotiated with the Virginia Company to set up a joint stock company that would allow them to settle in the northern coastal area known as New England. With this agreement in hand, the Pilgrims amassed a party of just over one hundred followers and set sail for America. Before disembarking, the Pilgrims drafted and signed the Mayflower Compact. The Compact declared that they "solemnly and mutually in the Presence of God and one another, covenant and combine ourselves together into a civil Body Politick." Under it they would "enact, constitute, and frame, such just and equal Laws, Ordinances, Acts, Constitutions, and Offices, from time to time, as shall be thought most meet and convenient for the general Good of the Colony; unto which we promise all due Submission and Obedience." Rather than being a blueprint for democracy, the Compact was intended to enforce religious orthodoxy on the community by making the decisions of the majority binding on the whole group. Accordingly, the religious stalwarts who constituted the majority of the group would be able to enforce their will on the less religious members of their party.

The *Mayflower* landed at the site the settlers named New Plymouth late in 1620, and the Pilgrims established a small settlement around the natural harbor. The Pilgrim venture encouraged other Separatist groups in England to consider settlement in New England. A group of Puritans led by John Winthrop secured a royal charter for "The Company of Massachusetts Bay," which gave that company title to all lands between the Merrimack River and the tip of Massachusetts Bay. The charter gave the company broad, mostly unspecified powers to govern the people in the colony with only two significant restrictions: the settlers and their descendants were to "have and enjoy all liberties and immunities of free and naturall subjects...as if they and everies of them were born within the realme of England," and any laws made by the company could not be "contraries or repugnant to the lawes and statutes of... England."[1] The charter contained no clause indicating where the company had to keep its headquarters. The Puritan leaders took advantage of the omission and decided to take the charter with them to America. In doing so, the Puritans took the first step in transforming the document from a stock company patent into a constitution for the colony.

Winthrop could have maintained the colony as a small, self-perpetuating corporation that excluded anyone other than original members from participation in decision making. The Puritan belief in the need for consent swept aside any such temptation. Drawing on the Puritan tradition, Winthrop held that the origin of any body politic lay in "The consent of a certaine companie of people, to cohabite together, under one government for their mutual safety and welfare." After the first wave of settlers scattered around the bay during the summer of 1630, Winthrop convened a General Court in October. It agreed that shareholders or "freemen" would choose the "assistants," that assistants would select the governor and deputy governor from among themselves, and that the assistants would make laws and appoint other officials. "This was fully assented unto by the generall vote of the people, and erection of hands," and then 108 colonists were admitted to the company as freemen. The arrangement of government put into practice the Puritan idea that political authority should be subject to popular consent.

From 1632 to 1634 the freemen greatly enlarged their role in the government. In 1632 they won the power to elect the governor and deputy governor directly and to vote on taxation issues. In the spring of 1634, after demanding to see the text of the charter, they claimed a share in the passage of all legislation. During the next decade the General Court evolved into a genuine bicameral legislature. As mandated by the charter, the freemen elected the governor, the deputy governor, and a slate of assistants every spring. Instead of meeting together four times a year in the General Court, however, the freemen gathered in their towns to choose representatives. These representatives then traveled to Boston and convened as the House of Deputies.

The notion that government should be subject to popular control was given dramatic expression with the framing of the Body of Liberties in 1641. Many of the Puritan settlers felt that it was necessary to spell out the terms of their "covenant of grace" between each settler and God, among themselves, and with the government of the colony. As John Cotton, one of the leaders put it, "it is therefore fit for every man to be studious of the bounds which the Lord hath set: and for the People, in whom fundamentally all power lyes, to give as much power as God in his word gives to men.... So let there be due bounds set." The people's representatives accordingly drafted and enacted the Body of Liberties that in ninety-eight articles specified what their government must and must not do to fulfill its contract. The liberties that were to be protected included many of the civil liberties laid out in the Magna Carta. Many of these liberties, for example, equality before the law, judicial rights of due process, and the right of petition, have since become familiar to us as modern rights. If the liberties listed in the Body of Liberties had not quite reached the status of rights in the modern sense, the document remained a significant precursor of the bills of rights framed in the following century. Most of the specific rights guaranteed in the Bill of Rights in the federal Constitution were also protected in the Massachusetts Body of Liberties.

The adoption of powers of self-government was made possible largely because the attentions of the home government were directed toward other matters. The distant affairs of Massachusetts Bay were on so small a scale and affected so few people as to appear of minor importance compared to the political challenges faced closer to home. In these early years there was practically no administrative supervision for the colony, and the development of an imperial policy was only begun with the Navigation Act of 1651. The early settlers thus gained a great deal of ground in the direction of self-government in a deceptively easy manner. Much of this ground had to be fought for again in the eighteenth century once the imperial authority had began to rein in its American colonies.

THE RESTORATION AND THE GLORIOUS REVOLUTION

The Charter of 1691

The Restoration led to an aggressive attempt to impose a measure of order on the empire in America after the instability of two decades of civil war. In 1684, Charles II revoked the Massachusetts charter and merged the colony first with its New England neighbors and then with New York and the Jerseys in an enlarged Dominion of New England, ruled by a hostile governor, Edmund Andros. The governor and an appointed council were given sweeping powers that allowed them to make all laws and raise taxes. To ensure the laws passed were conformable to English practice, they were to be sent to London for approval within three months.

The imposition of the dominion was a bitter blow to all the colonies affected, but to none more so than Massachusetts. Practically all the autonomy that the Bay Colony had experienced was abolished, including the General Court and the privileged position of the Congregational Church. Although the dominion lasted for only a few years, the initiative opened the door to a more enduring reorganization of Britain's North American colonies.

The English Glorious Revolution of 1688, in which the Catholic James II was deposed by William and Mary, prompted the overthrow of James's unpopular colonial government.[2] After lengthy negotiations with London, Massachusetts was re-established as a separate colony in 1691. The new charter laid out a governing framework that attempted to tighten imperial control over the colony. Among the most significant changes were to the office of governor. Under the new charter the governor was appointed by the Crown rather than elected locally, and his powers were significantly strengthened. The governor's enhanced legislative role included the power to veto acts of the Assembly, and as the principal executive officer he appointed all judicial officials. Unique among the offices of government in the provincial structure, the governor was intended to act as a direct link between the internal government of the colony and the British government.

The legislature, known as the General Court, consisted of two chambers, a House of Representatives, elected by the towns, and a Governor's Council, elected by the representatives and the outgoing councilors with the governor's consent. The competence of the legislature was not precisely stipulated, but certain prescribed limits provided both the governor and the Crown with veto power and required all laws to be consistent with those of England. The council acted both as an auxiliary to the governor's office and as an upper house of the legislature. Reflecting William III's preference for religious toleration, the charter also secularized the requirements of citizenship in the colony. Church membership was abolished as a qualification for suffrage and was replaced with a property requirement. Finally, the charter confirmed the Bay Colony's claim to the province of Maine and gave to it the islands of Nantucket, Martha's Vineyard, and the Elizabeths off Cape Cod. The charter also incorporated the settlement of Plymouth into the territory of Massachusetts.

The overall intention of the charter was to curtail the colony's autonomous tendencies and bring it into line with the other members of Britain's reorganized empire. Although the charter attempted to placate the colony by conceding the place of the locally elected legislature in the political process, it also attempted to strengthen imperial control. The appointed governor had the right to review all acts passed by the General Court, and he enjoyed a free hand in the management of judicial matters in the colony.

EIGHTEENTH-CENTURY POLITICAL DEVELOPMENT

The Rise of the Assembly

The Crown's attempt to secure more effective imperial control of the colonies was not entirely successful. In significant respects the new charter laid out an institutional framework that could be exploited to the advantage of home rule. By accepting a locally elected legislature alongside a Crown-appointed governor, the new charter gave a secure foothold to the local assembly. The endorsement by Britain of a locally elected assembly proved difficult to reconcile with an executive appointed from the distant mother country. In practical terms it was extremely difficult for the governor to implement imperial policy against the wishes of the locally elected legislature. Furthermore, the ideological climate in the wake of the Glorious Revolution gave added legitimacy to the status of the assembly. The principles associated with the Glorious Revolution championed the elected assembly as an independent source of political authority. As Massachusetts prospered economically and leaders gained self-confidence through the eighteenth century, colonists were increasingly willing to draw on these ideas to defend the colony's autonomy against British incursions.

The institutional arrangements established by the new charter quickly proved amenable to an authoritative local assembly. The emergence of a politically able colonial elite that maintained a close relationship with its local constituents often gave the assembly the edge over the governor in working the political system. In contrast, the governor was hampered in his actions by his subservience to royal edicts issued from three thousand miles away. The governor's problems were compounded because, unlike the practice in other colonies, the Governor's Council was selected by the assembly rather than by the governor himself. Lamenting this feature, Governor Thomas Pownall wrote that the council was "little other than an annually elected committee of the General Court." The governor, therefore, was denied the type of patronage that could be used to wield influence in the legislature. Buoyed by the popular support it enjoyed, the assembly quickly established itself at the focal point of governmental power. Claiming a status analogous to the British House of Commons, representatives in the assembly claimed comparable powers for their representative institution. On this basis they asserted a formidable list of legislative powers that included the sole right to impose taxes and to control the expenditure of public funds and the right to initiate almost all legislation affecting the inhabitants of Massachusetts. The assembly also adopted considerable judicial and executive powers, settling boundary disputes, appointing officers, and occasionally hearing civil cases. Although the statutes enacted by the legislators were subject to the governor's veto and the royal disallowance from London, the assembly did its best to protect its activities from such action by putting many of its decisions in the form of resolutions and orders not subject to review.[3]

One of the major factors that encouraged assembly politicians to assert their institutional power with such vigor was an intense awareness of English constitutional rights. The inhabitants of Massachusetts warmly embraced the principles that were believed to have been triumphant in the Glorious Revolution. Most importantly, these principles declared the cherished liberties of

Englishmen such as the right to representation, to trial by jury, and to security of property. These rights, the residents of Massachusetts believed, could be safeguarded only by an alert and vigilant representative body that curbed executive excess. Representative assemblies were understood to exist to secure popular rights against arbitrary rule. Assemblies were synonymous with the rights of the people and thus had to be defended without qualification.

This consciousness of rights had particular urgency within the context of colonial government. The particular manner in which the imperial authority could overrule colonial government meant that the colonial assembly was subject to powers of executive prerogative that had been swept away in England in the wake of the Glorious Revolution. Royal powers that were no longer wielded over Parliament remained a feature of government for the colonies. The colonial assemblies remained subject to the governor's power of prerogative that allowed him unfettered power to prorogue, dissolve, and indefinitely extend the life of the assembly, to veto laws or suspend their operation, and to appoint judges to serve at pleasure rather than good behavior. In addition to the governor's power, the Privy Council had the right to disallow colonial acts upon their review in London. Even if these powers were rarely actually used, the possibility of their use was enough to convince Massachusetts politicians that popular liberties were insecure under colonial government. Responding to the perceived threat, representatives augmented the institutional power of the assembly at every opportunity. By the early eighteenth century, the Massachusetts assembly had consolidated its power so that its control of the provincial political agenda virtually excluded the influence of the governor and British government. The constraints of the new royal charter had done little to curb the assertion of popular powers grounded in a half century of Puritan corporate autonomy.

Path to Revolution

With a self-confident assembly keen to protect its control of provincial affairs, any attempt by the British to redress the balance of power was certain to be met with resistance. The accumulated experience of holding political power within the colony coupled with the firmly held belief that representative legislatures were the preeminent guarantors of English liberties ensured that Massachusetts politicians were loath to accept any change in the political status quo. This overwhelming sense of legitimacy encouraged them to oppose British authority when imperial policy changed during the third quarter of the century.

The Stamp Act Crisis

The spiraling costs of maintaining a far-flung and extensive empire finally prompted the British to make a concerted effort to reform administration of the American colonies. Victory over France in the Seven Years' War (1756–1763) had incurred massive debt, and public opinion in Britain was impatient to shift some of this burden onto the provincials whose borders British troops had successfully defended. The British government began its program of reform with a series of measures that sought to extend the reach of imperial authority into colonial society. The Sugar Act of 1763 and the Stamp Act of 1764 were the first initiatives of this program. Both acts were new tax measures that sought to raise much-needed revenue by imposing taxes on the importation of sugar and on all published and legal documents used in the colonies.

The introduction of the measures aroused opposition throughout the colonies, but indignation was particularly intense in Massachusetts. Colonists argued that the imposition of taxes by Parliament violated the right of British subjects to be taxed only by their own representative assemblies. The instructions of the town of Braintree to its representatives in the General Court, written by a then largely unknown young lawyer, John Adams, became a rallying call for opposition throughout the colony. "We have always understood it to be a grand & fundamental principal of the British Constitution," Adams wrote, "that no Freeman should be subjected to any Tax to which he has not given his own consent in person or by proxy."[4]

Words of protest were quickly followed by deeds of resistance in which Boston led the way. Protesters hanged the Massachusetts stamp distributor in effigy and then attacked his house causing him to resign his post the next day. A few days later an angry crowd marched on the house of Thomas Hutchinson, the lieutenant governor, and ransacked the property. The threat of violence ensured the resignation of enough stamp distributors to make the act unworkable. Meanwhile widespread smuggling had led to the failure of the Sugar Act to raise more than a small portion of the anticipated revenue.

From Resistance to Revolution

The failure of these measures only made the British government more determined to overcome local resistance and to find effective ways of securing colonial revenue. By challenging the scope of Britain's sovereignty over the colonies, American opposition significantly raised the stakes of the effort to reform imperial administration. Clarifying the imperial subordination of the American colonies to Britain became as important an objective as raising tax revenue. British opinion was virtually unanimous in believing that the mother country had the right to tax the colonies. Colonial resistance to the measures was widely perceived as an embarrassing rebuff to the legitimate authority of Parliament. Reflecting this sentiment, Parliament was resolved to demonstrate its power over the colonies. It certainly was not about to yield to what seemed like a handful of precocious offspring who had forgotten the gratitude rightly owed their mother country.

The tax measures introduced in the Townshend Acts of 1767 sought to rectify the situation. The acts imposed taxes on goods imported into the American colonies and reorganized the system of enforcement and collection. The acts aggravated an already tense situation in the colonies. To provincials already suspicious of imperial authority, the policy seemed to confirm the intent of the British to undermine their rights. The Massachusetts assembly prepared a circular letter to register its opposition. Written by Samuel Adams, the letter urged other colonies to resist the acts and declared that Parliament had no legal right to tax the colonies for the sole purpose of raising revenue. The British response to these activities further heightened tensions. The Massachusetts governor, Francis Bernard, was ordered to require that the assembly rescind the letter, and troops were dispatched from New York to Boston in anticipation of resistance. Faced with increasingly strident opposition from the assembly, Bernard dismissed it and had troops assembled in Boston in October 1768.

The combination of resentful citizens and hostile soldiers made for a volatile atmosphere on the streets of Boston. "The madness of mobs or the insolence of soldiers, or both, should, when too near each other occasion some mischief difficult to be prevented or repaired," Benjamin Franklin observed upon learning that the government had ordered troops for Boston in 1768. Franklin's fears were confirmed when simmering tensions produced a clash between soldiers and civilians. The incident that later became known as the Boston Massacre arose when soldiers protecting a customs house against a hostile mob opened fire on the crowd. Although the casualties from the melee were small—five civilians were killed—the incident became a dramatic symbol of an oppressive regime attempting to enslave a free people.

Boston again undertook a dramatic act of resistance to the British measures when its Sons of Liberty organized the now-famous Tea Party of December 1773.[5] The British government had allowed the East India Company to export a large shipment of tea to the colonies at a very low price while maintaining the colonial tax. Bostonians were determined to prevent the tea from being landed because they feared that paying taxes on it would establish a precedent that would encourage the colonists to accept the taxes. Disguised as Native Americans, the group boarded three vessels and threw the cargo of tea into the harbor. Colonial observers were quick to recognize the significance of the event. Considering the entire period "since the Controversy, with Britain, opened," John Adams concluded ominously, now "the Dye is cast." "The People have passed the River and cutt away the Bridge:... This is the grandest Event, which has ever yet happened."

This brazen act of destruction was taken by the British as an open flaunting of imperial authority that demanded decisive action. The British government responded by taking immediate steps to restore its authority in the American colonies. The Coercive Acts of 1774, or Intolerable Acts as the Americans called them, closed the port of Boston, stipulated that the upper house or council in the General Court be appointed by the King, required that town meetings occur only annually and discuss only local matters, and provided for trials of Massachusetts residents in other colonies or in England. In one sweeping act the reach of imperial authority was extended, and long-cherished practices of self-government in the colony were abolished or drastically curtailed.

The aggressive display of authority shown by the Coercive Acts provided seemingly irrefutable evidence for the colonists that the British were engaged in a conspiracy to deny them their liberties. The Boston Committee of Correspondence portrayed the unfolding events as a "Plan of *Despotism*, rapidly hastening to completion."

The measures served to galvanize opposition both within Massachusetts and across the colonies. Political leaders outside the Bay Colony expressed their support for Massachusetts's defiance. Following the proposal of the Boston committee of correspondence it was agreed that a Continental Congress consisting of delegates from all the colonies meet in Philadelphia to coordinate opposition. The First Continental Congress met in Philadelphia in September 1774. Within Massachusetts steps were taken to coordinate resistance across the colony. Country conventions were held comprised of town delegates to deliberate on an appropriate course of resistance. The conventions were united in declaring that the townspeople of Massachusetts were not going to acquiesce in the destruction of their liberty and took steps to nullify the governmental changes enacted by the Coercive Acts. Appointees under the Government Act were pressed to resign their positions, and mass gatherings were called to prevent any courts from sitting under the new law. Furthermore, the conventions went on to recommend that town militia companies be readied for combat. "We have hitherto employed lenient measures *more* than enough," one writer claimed in the *Boston Gazette*.

The Beginnings of an Alternative Government

As conflict seemed increasingly inevitable, extralegal organizations began to take the first steps toward establishing a new political order in defiance of the British. When the new governor, Thomas Gage, dissolved the General Court in June 1774, representatives met illegally in Concord and invited the pre–Government Act Council to resume business as if they were still operating under the 1691 charter. After the Continental Congress promised aid in the event of an attack, the representatives of the General Court meeting in Salem declared the General Court to be a Provincial Congress.

This tentative step toward independence was more firmly established the following summer. With outbreak of armed conflict at Lexington and Concord in April 1775, the Provincial Congress in Massachusetts turned to the Continental Congress for advice. The Massachusetts political leaders requested support for the establishment of "Civil Government, which we think absolutely necessary for the salvation of our country," and agreed to submit to such "a general plan as congress might direct for the colonies." The Continental Congress replied on June 2 suggesting that Massachusetts consider its charter of 1691 as still in force and the offices of governor and lieutenant governor as temporarily vacated. It also recommended that new elections be held and a new Governor's Council be elected by the Provincial Congress. On June 19, 1775, the Massachusetts congress elected a 28-member council that replaced the governor as executive. With this one alteration, the replacement of the governor with an executive council, the Massachusetts charter of 1691 became the first state constitution. Although it was replaced in 1780, it constituted, along with the Connecticut and Rhode Island charters, the first concrete step taken to bridge colonial and new state political institutions.[6]

Framing the New Constitution

Although the Provisional Government of 1775 represented a vital step toward establishing statehood, in several respects it was a compromised arrangement that was not designed to establish a permanent system of government. As a foundation document it was rather short and incomplete, written and adopted by a sitting legislature in a manner indistinguishable from normal legislation and bearing the marks of compromise between proponents for independence and supporters of reconciliation. It could in truth be viewed either as a temporary expedient implying no significant alteration in colonial status or as a manifestation of the intent to break with Britain. If the American Revolution had not been successful, perhaps history would have recorded it as the former. Because the Revolution did succeed and no other constitutional action was necessary for Massachusetts to assert its independence, we can view the Provisional Government as the constitution that actually established statehood. Still, its transitional status is clearly reflected in the fact that once independence had become unequivocal, the people of Massachusetts were in wide agreement that the charter of 1691 and the Provisional Government were not acceptable as a permanent system of government. Reflecting this sentiment, a process of wholesale remodeling of the constitution was initiated the following year in September 1776. This process was eventually concluded with the ratification of a new constitution in 1780.

On June 16, 1780, Massachusetts, after a lengthy and painstaking process of public debate, finally adopted a constitution that provided a permanent replacement to the 1691 charter. No state constitution up to this point had been subject to such thorough debate and popular consultation. The close scrutiny to which the constitutional remodeling was subjected by citizens across the state ensured a well-refined final product. Indeed the prudent design of the Massachusetts Constitution was so widely acknowledged that it was emulated by many other states in their constitutional remodeling and was arguably an influential example in the framing of the U.S. Constitution in 1787.

The Provisional Government Challenged

The process of establishing a secure constitutional basis for the new government began with the rejection of the revised 1691 charter. Despite efforts to rejuvenate the charter, it was clear that the document had shortcomings as a constitutional framework. The legislature's removal of all references to the British Crown in May 1776 did little to alleviate the sense that the government needed a fresh legal basis that should be established by direct consent of the people. Now that the sovereignty of the political system lay exclusively in the people, it was only fitting that the people of Massachusetts be able to give their actual consent to the form of government under which they were to live. The petition from the town of Pittsfield expressed this concern while explaining the alleged deficiencies of the current arrangement. "We have always been persuaded that the people are the fountain of power. That since the Dissolution of the power of Great Britain over these Colonies they have fallen into a state of Nature. That the first step to be taken by a people in such a state…is the formation of a fundamental Constitution as the Basis & ground work of Legislation."[7] The status of the constitution as a fundamental framework for legislation, the petition continued, therefore limits the role of the legislature in its formation:

> That a Representative Body may form, but cannot impose the said fundamental Constitution upon a people. They being but servants of the people cannot be greater than their Masters, & must be responsible to them. If this fundamental Constitution is above the whole Legislature, the Legislature cannot certainly make it, it must be the Approbation of the Majority which gives Live & being to it.

On the basis of this careful reasoning, it was clear that the current constitution was deficient. "That said fundamental Constitution has not been formed for this Province," the petition concluded. "The Corner stone is not yet laid & whatever Building is reared without a foundation must fall into Ruins." Well versed in the principles of natural rights and popular sovereignty, many people in Massachusetts shared Pittsfield's concern that the current situation compromised the distinction between ordinary legislation and constitutional law.

After July 4, 1776, and the formal declaration of independence from Britain, it was obvious to most observers that a fresh constitutional start was needed. Independence removed any lingering hope of reconciliation and thus removed the rationale for retaining a charter that was specifically designed for a colonial government. It was commonly argued that the new circumstances required a new design of government that vested all authority in the consent of the people. It nonetheless remained unclear how popular sovereignty would actually be exercised in the process of framing a constitution. Could a newly elected assembly deem itself authorized to perform this task? Or did a special constitutional convention have to be elected for the purpose? And once a constitution was formulated, did it have to be ratified by the people before it came into effect, or was the authority of the elected framers sufficient?

Responding to calls for a new constitution the House of Representatives asked the towns to approve a method of adoption whereby the inhabitants would have an opportunity to examine the proposed constitution written by the General Court before the legislature also approved it. Seventy-four towns, a clear majority, replied in the affirmative, but twenty-three towns said no with enough vigor to force reconsideration.

Not surprisingly considering earlier sentiment, many towns made spirited objections to the legislature's writing and adopting a constitution that was supposed to limit that very body. The town of Lexington, for example, reiterated the position earlier made by Pittsfield. Lexington complained that allowing an assembly elected as a legislative body to frame a constitution usurped the authority of the people. "Proposing themselves to the People, and asking their Consent as Candidates for this Service," they wrote, "appears to Us to be a Clog to that Freedom of Election which ought always to be exercised, by a free People, in Matters of Importance, more especially in an affair of such lasting Concernment as this." Arguing along similar lines, the town of Concord complained that this mixing of roles posed a risk to the rights of the people, "[b]ecause a Constitution alterable by the Supreme Legislative is no Security at all to the Subject against any Encroachment of the Governing part on any, or on all of their Rights and privileges."

After some debate, the General Court nonetheless decided to move forward with their initial proposal and on May 5 proposed that the towns authorize their representatives to draft a constitution, which would be referred back to the towns for ratification. After reviewing the town returns, the assembly and the council voted "to proceed in one body with the Council to form a constitution...agreeable to the resolve...of the 5th of May." The house and council then resolved themselves on June 15 into Massachusetts's first constitutional convention.

The proposed constitution produced by the convention in February 1778 received a decidedly mixed reception in the towns. A substantial majority of townspeople rejected the constitution—some 10,000 against 2,000—and many of the complaints raised at town meetings were noted in the returns. As might have been anticipated, the dissatisfaction with the constitution was as much related to the manner by which it had been framed as to its actual content. Many towns reiterated their earlier grievance, complaining that the legislature was not qualified to act as a constitutional convention. Other common objections focused on the alleged inequities of the suffrage clause relating to the burden of the property qualification imposed and the exclusion of "Negroes, Indians, and molattoes." Objections also noted the absence of a bill of rights. Westminster citizens, for example, declared their opinion "that no Constitution Whatsoever ought to be Established, till previous theirto the bill of Rights be Set forth, and the Constitution formed their-from."

The most sophisticated explanation of grievances came from the *Essex Result*, written on behalf of the county of Essex by Theophilus Parsons. In it, Parsons provided an elaborate sketch of the theoretical basis of legitimate government, detailing the natural rights held by individuals in the state of nature and the reasons for forming a government to act on its behalf. In highlighting "those principles, upon which all republican governments…are founded," he echoed the words of the Declaration of Independence. "All men are born equally free. The rights they possess at their births are equal, and of the same kind."

Significantly, however, Parsons also proposed a certain design of government that he argued flowed from these principles. Among the most prescient of his points was the importance he placed on a strict separation of powers. Parsons insisted, "That the legislative, judicial, and executive powers, are to be lodged in different hands, that each branch is to be independent, and further, to be so balanced, and be able to exert such checks upon the others, as will preserve it from a dependence on, or an union with them." In his discussion Parsons warned of the danger of any of the three branches of government assuming powers beyond its specific function. At a time at which many of the newly established states had made the executive branch entirely subservient to the legislature, Parsons went against the grain of current Revolutionary thinking. He deftly illustrated his point by examining republican government in Holland. "The assembly or representatives of the united states of Holland, exercise the executive and legislative powers, and the government there is absolute." The legislature, as much as any other branch, he suggested, had to be restricted to its appropriate function.

Parsons's model of independent branches of government that checked each other's authority constituted an early statement of the type of political thinking that came to the fore in the post-Revolutionary period. When states began to revisit their constitutions after the heated activity of 1776–1777, many enacted changes that created more institutional independence for the different branches of government and, in particular, established a stricter separation between the legislature and the executive. Such a model of separation of powers was, of course, also a prominent feature of the U.S. Constitution framed in 1787.

Taking stock of these events, the General Court yielded to the demand for a proper constitutional convention in February 1779. The General Court requested that the towns consider whether they would like to proceed with a new constitution if it were written by a constitutional convention instead of the legislature. Returns indicated a two-to-one majority in favor of the resolution. In June 1779 the General Court issued the call for the election of a state constitutional convention, stipulating that each town choose the same number of delegates as it elected representatives to the assembly. The franchise for electing delegates was generous by contemporary standards. All freemen over twenty-one could vote, irrespective of property owned. The work of the convention had to have the approval of two-thirds of those voting before the constitution could become effective. A ratifying convention would examine the returns and count the votes.

Elections were held for delegates, and the first such body in Western history elected solely for the purpose of writing a constitution convened on September 1, 1779. Samuel Adams, James Bowdoin, and especially John Adams were the delegates most prominent in the framing process. The final version was approved on March 2, 1780, and was sent to the voters. The returns from the towns were complex, and for a while no one could figure out how to count the votes. Finally, the convention simply declared that the draft had been accepted in its entirety by at least two-thirds of the voters even when taking into account reservations about specific passages, and the constitution went into effect on October 25, 1780. The constitution implemented many of the recommendations that had been put forward by the townspeople, including the protection of certain individual liberties in the form of a bill of rights and a strengthened separation of powers.

The Massachusetts Constitution

The framework of government proposed a system that balanced power with restraint. "A Government without Power to exert itself, is at best, but an useless Piece of Machinery.... And, a Power without any restraint is Tyranny," declared the address issued by the constitutional convention to accompany the draft constitution. Accordingly, the branches of government were made independent of each other, and each house of the bicameral legislature and the executive were separately elected by the people. The "due Proportion of Weight" granted to each institution was to be balanced with "such *Checks*... as maybe sufficient to prevent its becoming formidable and injurious to the Common wealth." These checks included the power of each house to negate the acts of the other. Most significantly, they also included the power of the governor to veto legislation passed by the legislature. Strengthened in its powers and elected directly by the people, the executive created by the 1780 constitution was a far cry from the creature of the legislature that had been the norm for the Revolutionary state constitutions. In sum, this constitution introduced a system of government by which independent branches charged with distinct functions shared the exercise of political power. Such a system of checks and balances between strong and independent institutions set a precedent that shortly became the norm for constitutionalism in the new republic. The design was widely admired for its apparent judicious balancing of power and restraint. Many states emulated it in their later constitutional remodeling. Similarly, the Massachusetts Constitution provided an influential model in the framing of the federal Constitution in 1787. Madison's advocacy of an institutional design for the federal Constitution by which political power is dispersed among independent institutions that check each other is testimony to the influence of Massachusetts's precedent.

The Declaration of Rights that prefaced the constitution was in many ways a fuller and more sophisticated Bill of Rights than the earlier versions adopted by other states.[8] Not all the clauses, however, were unequivocal about protecting individuals from the reach of government. The treatment of religion was conspicuous in this respect. Although the Declaration of Rights stated that an individual was free to worship as he chose, and the government was prohibited from compelling people to attend the public worship of God, Article 3 permitted the legislature to mandate public support for Protestant denominations. The new state of Massachusetts was willing to practice religious toleration in this age of natural rights, but it would not go so far as to permit a complete severance of the connection between church and state. The religious establishment remained in place in Massachusetts until 1833.

The other civil liberties listed were more consistent with the type of rights protected in other bills of rights. Article 19 affirmed standard political rights: the right to assemble, to instruct representatives, and to present petitions to the legislature. A related issue, freedom of press, was given strong protection in Article 16, which proclaimed that "The liberty of the press is essential to the security of freedom in a state; it ought not, therefore, to be restrained in this commonwealth." Defendants were given the rights not to be compelled to accuse or furnish evidence against themselves, to confront witnesses, and to trial by jury. Other articles required that reasonable compensation be given for property taken for public use and prohibited bills of attainder. Cruel and unusual punishments, ex post facto laws, excessive fines and bail, the quartering of troops in a private house without the owner's consent, and unreasonable searches and seizures were made unlawful.

The final two of these protections drew directly upon the experience of colonial Massachusetts and anticipated the language of the Third and Fourth Amendments to the federal Constitution. Concerns regarding the unwarranted quartering of soldiers had grown out of quarrels in Massachusetts between the colonists and the Crown. In the first instance this grievance arose in 1757 during the Seven Years' War when General John Campbell demanded quarters for his army in Boston taverns. Bostonians were indignant that the General attempted to impose such an order despite the availability of sufficient barracks at Castle William in Boston harbor. These tensions were revived during the imperial crisis when the British army imposed quartering in the town in an effort to enforce the Townshend Acts and other imperial measures. Patriots considered the imposition of quartering without the owner's consent to be an abridgement of the right to personal liberty.

Concerns regarding unreasonable search and seizures had grown out of the celebrated writs of assistance case of 1761. At the outbreak of the Seven Years' War in 1755, Massachusetts's customs officials had successfully petitioned the Superior Court to issue such writs, which were, in effect, general search warrants that remained valid for the life of the monarch. The writs attracted little resistance during the years of active warfare, but in late 1760 the fall of

Montreal effectively ended the struggle on the North American continent. At the same time George II died and was succeeded by his grandson, George III. When customs officials requested a new set of writs of assistance there was no longer any military urgency. Moreover, the probable long life of these documents once they were issued in the name of the new king made many merchants uneasy, especially those engaged in various forms of smuggling. James Otis, Jr., made a legal challenge to the writs on behalf of the merchants, arguing that such a broad power of search and seizure was illegal because it violated the natural right of men to personal liberty. Although his challenge was unsuccessful, and the writs were issued, the issue became a cause célèbre as an example of tyrannical government. The writs were an example of the ever-present possibility of unbounded political power, a prospect that required constant vigilance from colonists.

Evaluating the significance of the writs of assistance case some decades later, John Adams wrote, "Then and there the child Independence was born." If Adams's claim was exaggerated, it was certainly true that the case gave rise to Article 14 of the Declaration of Rights. The article read, "Every subject has a right to be secure from all unreasonable searches, and seizures of his person, his houses, his papers, and his possessions." The provision ensured that any such warrant would have to supported by oath or affirmation and would have to be specific in identifying the persons, places, and things to be searched. The Fourth Amendment of the federal Constitution followed the lead established by Massachusetts in words that barely deviated from the original.

The final point to note about the Declaration of Rights in the Massachusetts Constitution is its application to the institution of slavery. Common to bills of rights in other state constitutions, the Massachusetts Declaration made an opening statement regarding the equality of men and their possession of natural rights. In the Declaration this statement was worded, "All men are born free and equal, and have certain natural, essential, and unalienable rights." What was exceptional in the case of Massachusetts was not what was said, but how the courts interpreted this statement.

Although slavery was always a peripheral institution in Massachusetts, about five thousand slaves resided in the state at the time of the Revolution. More literate than African Americans in most other parts of North America, slaves followed the Anglo-American debate over natural rights with great interest. In 1773 and 1774 "a Grate Number of Blacks" made a series of petitions to the governor and the General Court, objecting that they were being "held in a state of slavery within the bowels of a free and christian Country." Paraphrasing the natural rights theorist John Locke, they claimed to be a freeborn people who had never forfeited that blessing by compact. They not only demanded their emancipation, but they also asked the government to grant them land. The legislature debated the subject but took no action. Nonetheless, opinion in favor of emancipation gained ground in the aftermath of the Revolution. Prompted by the state supreme court's interpretation of the equality clause of the Declaration of Rights, Massachusetts's judges and juries in 1781 and 1783 found slavery incompatible with the state constitution. In 1790 the census reported that there were no longer any slaves in the state.

MASSACHUSETTS AND THE FEDERAL CONSTITUTION

If the ratification of the 1780 constitution finalized the form of internal government for the fledgling state, much work was still to be done to clarify the political arrangement among the states. Both the politicians of Massachusetts and the events that unfolded within the state during the 1780s contributed to the process that led to the federal convention and the framing of the Constitution itself.

Economic Crisis and Social Unrest

As the war continued through the early 1780s, the strains of supporting a protracted military effort began to take their toll. Confronted with the massive financial demands of mobilizing resources and manpower for battle, Massachusetts's legislators were forced to implement a host of economic restraints and financial measures. Almost every segment of society found cause to feel aggrieved by the policies that the government was forced to pursue or by its inability to control the severe economic consequences of war: rising prices, a depreciating paper currency, and shortages of goods.[9]

Governor Bowdoin attempted to address the deteriorating situation by raising taxes. This approach appealed to creditors and merchants but promised to deal a severe blow to farmers and those in debt. Farmers, who were already having trouble meeting their taxes because of the slump in farm prices, were particularly alarmed at the prospect of increased taxes. The policy seemed to favor the interests of eastern merchants and tradesmen over farmers in the western communities. With tensions rising, the farmers began to organize resistance in 1786. In August farmers in Hampshire County drew up a petition complaining of the intolerable tax burden and requested that paper money be issued, court fees be reduced, and home and farm foreclosures be suspended. A few weeks later resistance became violent. Farmers armed with guns prevented a court from sitting at Northampton, and other court sessions were broken up at Worcester, Concord, and Great Barrington in an attempt to block further foreclosures.

Shays's Rebellion

Governor James Bowdoin responded to the unrest by ordering six hundred militiamen under General William Shepard to protect the sitting of the Supreme Judicial Court at Springfield. On September 26 these troops were confronted by five hundred insurgents, led by former Revolutionary War captain,

Daniel Shays, who were trying to prevent indictments from being issued for previous court disruptions. The standoff made it impossible for proceedings to take place, and the court was adjourned.[10]

To the contemporary observer, the unrest in Massachusetts was a dramatic illustration of the weaknesses of the fledgling state governments. Local assemblies tried in vain to contain the strains of war-torn societies, but the inevitable hardship caused by economic policy aroused intense indignation. The explosion of these tensions into armed confrontation in Massachusetts conveyed the gravity of the problem at hand. If a state that supposedly benefited from such a stable and well-governed political system could not contain these pressures, what hope had other states?

Sensing the wider significance of the events, Congress dispatched General Henry Knox, a veteran of Washington's army, to investigate the rebellion. Knox's report sent a chilling message to those assembled in Congress. The insurgents numbered 12,000 to15,000, he wrote, and were intent on redistributing property. "They see the weakness of government," he wrote, "they feel at once their own poverty, compared with the opulent, and their own force, and they are determined to make use of the latter, to remedy the former." Congress responded on October 20 by authorizing Knox to raise 1,340 troops and to protect the federal arsenal at Springfield from the rebels. Despite the presence of federal troops, the rebels continued to block court sittings.

With no sign of any abatement of the disturbances, Governor Bowdoin dispatched 4,400 militia under General Benjamin Lincoln to suppress Shays's rebels. When Shays and his followers attempted to seize the Springfield arsenal on January 25, 1787, the assembled militia opened fire and killed four rebels. Skirmishes continued as the insurgents fled, but the militia's triumph at Springfield effectively ended the insurrection. Shays and other leaders ended up fleeing to Vermont, and as punishment the Massachusetts passed a disqualification act that barred the rebels from political privileges in the state. Despite the defeat of the insurrection, the cause of the farmers was in some ways vindicated. The Massachusetts legislature chose not to levy a direct tax in 1787, as Bowdoin had proposed, and adopted measures that gave some relief to debtors.

The political and psychological wounds of the conflict were slow in healing, and the memories of the rebellion exercised a profound influence on Massachusetts public life for a generation. For many people in western Massachusetts, Shays's Rebellion generated an enduring distrust of government. The memory of repression at the hands of the state government made many particularly fearful of the power of government.

For those who saw the specter of anarchy in the events of 1786 and 1787, the obvious lesson learned was the fragility of republican government. Many of Boston's political elite drew this conclusion, but this perspective was not limited to residents of the Bay State. A number of national leaders were alarmed at what had happened in Massachusetts and saw these events as part of a wider malaise that afflicted state governments. Having won independence at great cost, Americans seemed incapable of managing their affairs wisely or peacefully. The need to allow central government the proper authority to manage continental affairs seemed more pressing than ever. Delegates at the Continental Congress were suddenly more supportive of the proposal to hold a constitutional convention to increase the powers of the Confederation than they had been previously. Rufus King from Massachusetts, for example, was one of many delegates who had become convinced of the need for action. King conveyed his new sense of conviction in a letter to Elbridge Gerry, a fellow delegate from the Bay State. "Events are hurrying to a crisis," King wrote. "Prudent and sagacious men should ready to seize the most favourable circumstances to establish a more permanent and vigorous government." As James Madison, one of the principal architects of the federal Constitution, observed, "the evils issuing" from the states "contributed more to that uneasiness which produced the Convention, and prepared the public mind for a general reform, than those which accrued to our national character and interest from the inadequacy of the Confederation to it immediate objects."

Spurred in part by events in Massachusetts, Madison proposed a solution to the apparent fragility of republican government in America in his "Vices of the Political System of the United States." Madison's diagnosis of the ills that beset government focused squarely on the economic policy that had been produced by state legislatures.[11] Madison concluded that the injustice of the various laws that had been passed called "into question the fundamental principles of republican government, that the majority who rule in such Governments are the safest Guardians both of public good and of private rights." His concerns about the security of private rights were rooted in his fear that fundamental rights of property were being jeopardized by the rise of populist forces in the states. Madison's solution, which he vigorously promoted at the Philadelphia convention later that year, was a wholesale revision of republican government at the national level. National government should be strengthened, he argued, but also should be redesigned to ensure that the rights of minorities would be protected against the "vicious" designs of majorities.

Madison's ideas about the benefits of representation in an extended republic and the importance of separated powers that could check and balance each other struck a chord with delegates at Philadelphia and ended up having considerable influence on the final document. Madison's line of defense for the proposed Constitution was a telling indication of the type of priorities that were salient in the aftermath of Shays's Rebellion. Without apology, Madison, writing in Federalist Paper 51, dismissed the republican idea that a virtuous people would sustain a republican government. "But what is government itself but the greatest of all reflections on human nature? If men were angels no government would be necessary." If the weaknesses of men made government necessary, it followed that the abuses of government could not be controlled by relying on "a dependence on the people" alone. "In framing a government which is to be administered by men over men," Madison concluded, "you must first enable the government to control the governed; and in the next place oblige it to control itself." For Madison it was clear that the harsh realities of political governance demanded an attenuation of republicanism if the American experiment were to survive.

Massachusetts at the Federal Constitutional Convention

The Massachusetts legislature sent a delegation of four to the Constitutional Convention in Philadelphia: Nathaniel Gorham, Elbridge Gerry, Rufus King, and Caleb Strong. All the delegates except for Strong had been members of the Continental Congress and so were familiar with the difficulties that the Confederation had faced as a result of its limited powers. The Massachusetts delegates arrived at the convention united in their support of a stronger central government and for limitations on the powers of the states. They firmly believed that a new federal system was necessary to protect Americans from foreign invasion and domestic unrest. Despite their endorsement of the aims of the convention, the Massachusetts delegates were divided over whether to approve the final document. Of the three delegates who remained at the end of the convention (Strong left before August 27 because of an illness in his family), King and Gorham signed the Constitution, whereas Gerry did not.

Gerry's behavior at the convention was particularly interesting because he seemed to harbor conflicting feelings toward the creation of a strong national government. At the start of the convention, Gerry expressed strong support for the convention's stated aim. Shays's Rebellion had shaken his faith in the republican ideology that had shaped his long public career. He had "been too republican heretofore," Gerry admitted. His commitment to the revolutionary ideology was now tempered, having been "taught by experience the danger of the levilling spirit." "The evils we experience," he said, "flow from the excess of democracy." On this basis Gerry firmly supported strengthening national government at the expense of the states and creating only indirect election of the national legislature and executive. Gerry seemed to reverse his staunch antipopulism in the last month of the convention. He took issue with Congress's power over the state militias, the creation of a federal standing army in peacetime, federal intervention in rebellions without the application for assistance by the state legislatures, and the power to pass laws deemed necessary and proper. Gerry ultimately rejected and refused to sign the Constitution because it lacked a bill of rights and because he deemed it a threat to republicanism.

Gerry's inconsistency infuriated other delegates. According to a colleague, he "objected to everything he did not propose." Although the views he presented may have been ultimately inconsistent, they nonetheless captured some of the ambivalence toward government that remained in Massachusetts in the wake of Shays's Rebellion. Like many other Massachusetts residents, Gerry was profoundly concerned about the extent of power that would be transferred to the national government under the new Constitution. He left Philadelphia worried that ratification would lead to civil strife in Massachusetts and the rest of the country.

On the other hand, King and Gorham's strong support for the new Constitution articulated the sentiment that political order had to be restored. King worried "that an extreme caution in favor of liberty might enervate the Government" that the convention was framing. Gorham similarly favored union and a strengthened national government. He favored giving Congress the power to create inferior courts, to regulate federal elections, to guarantee a republican form of government in each state, and to suppress rebellions in them. King and Gorham returned to Massachusetts as staunch advocates of the new form of government.

The Ratification Convention in Massachusetts

The work of the Philadelphia convention received a decidedly mixed reception in the Bay Colony.[12] Nowhere was the ratification of the federal Constitution more in doubt than in Massachusetts. Support for a stronger national government had been thin before the rebellion. The events of 1786–1787 had to the cause converted many who feared an excess of democracy and who hoped for a federal assumption of state debts. Supporters of the new federal Constitution, however, were in a decided minority when the ratifying convention met in Boston on January 9, 1788. By one estimate, the Anti-Federalists opposing ratification had a lead of roughly forty delegates out of the total body of 355. Delegates from the west of the state were united in opposition. One contemporary observer commented that the delegates from Worcester County "entertain such a dread of arbitrary power, that they are afraid even of limited authority."

Debates at the convention reiterated many of the concerns that had been expressed during the Revolutionary crisis. Would liberty be secure if a distant national authority was created with the power to tax or establish a standing army? Could liberty be safe if officials were elected for two six-year terms of office instead of being subject to annual elections? Would the people of Massachusetts retain the autonomy that was a legacy from their ancestors as well as from their own recent past?

Gerry led the drive against ratification and denounced the document as "full of vices." Among the vices, he listed inadequate representation of the people, dangerously ambiguous legislative powers, the blending of the executive and the legislative, and the danger of an oppressive judiciary. John Taylor complained about the lack of a bill of rights and the federal government's powers to suspend *habeas corpus*, issues that were of explosive importance given the events of 1786–1787. In perhaps the most famous speech opposing the Constitution, Amos Singletary addressed the issue of taxation as one of "those who had stood forth in 1775." Singletary saw a profound threat to household property in the taxing powers granted by the Constitution. He was sure that the new government would never "be able to raise enough money by impost, and then they will lay it on the land and take all that we have got." From his concern about taxation, Singletary moved directly into the thorny issue of social power that lay behind the Anti-Federalists' fears.

> These lawyers, and men of learning, and moneyed men that talk so finely, and gloss over matters so smoothly, to make us poor illiterate people, swallow down the pill, expect to get into Congress themselves; they expect to be managers of this Constitution, and get all the power and all the money into their own hands, and then they will swallow up all us little folks, like the great leviathan, Mr. President; yes, just as the whale swallowed Jonah.

Early in the convention Anti-Federalists sensed that they had enough support in the convention to defeat the Constitution outright rather than proceed by a clause-by-clause debate. They proposed a straight vote on the entire Constitution. Samuel Adams declared that although he had reservations about some parts of the Constitution, he thought it should be fully considered. The motion for an immediate vote was defeated. Convinced that ratification without amendments of some kind was impossible, Federalist leaders reached agreement with the president of the convention, Governor John Hancock, on a compromise proposal. On January 31 Hancock addressed the convention, supporting ratification and recommending nine amendments for adoption by Congress and the states after the Constitution went into effect. Samuel Adams declared support for Hancock's proposal and suggested that it would set an example for other states that were yet to ratify. On February 4 a committee of the convention reported on a revised form of the amendments proposed by Hancock. On February 6 Hancock called for conciliation in his final speech to the convention, which then voted, 187 to 168, to ratify the Constitution and recommend nine subsequent amendments.

The concession that proved decisive in securing ratification in Massachusetts caught on elsewhere. South Carolina, New Hampshire, Virginia, New York, and North Carolina followed the Bay State's example and ratified an amended version of the Constitution with a bill of rights attached. Without this concession, ratification by the necessary minimum of nine states would have been impossible. The recommended changes that had secured a Massachusetts majority were heeded in the first federal Congress the following year when Madison introduced a bill tabling the amendments. Ratified in 1791, the Federal Bill of Rights drew largely from the Declaration of Rights in the Massachusetts Constitution. Most telling, considering the Bay State's particular concern for the preservation of local government, the Ninth Amendment seems to have been particularly influenced by Article 4 of the Massachusetts Declaration of Rights. The pledge of the Ninth Amendment, that "the enumeration in the Constitution, of certain rights, shall not be construed to deny or disparage others retained by the people," mirrored closely Article 4's guarantee that the people of the commonwealth "do, and forever hereafter shall, exercise and enjoy every power, jurisdiction, and right, which is not...expresly delegated to the United States of America."

SUMMARY

The stormy passage of the Constitution through the ratification convention was perhaps a fitting way for Massachusetts to become a part of the new Union. Throughout its colonial history the Bay Colony had jealously guarded its independence. In the contest with Britain after 1763, beginning with the Stamp Act riots of August 1765 and continuing through Bunker Hill a decade later, Massachusetts had set the pace of resistance. It was with mixed feelings then that the delegates at the convention acquiesced to demands to limit the powers of their state and accept a strong national government. With the ratification of the federal Constitution and its hastily added Bill of Rights, however, the distinctive but provincial history became part of the broader heritage of the American people and the republic they had just created.

NOTES

1. All early seventeenth-century Massachusetts quotations are taken from Edmund S. Morgan, ed., *The Founding of Massachusetts: Historians and the Sources* (Indianapolis: Bobbs-Merrill, 1964); and Edmund S. Morgan, ed., *Puritan Political Ideas, 1558–1794* (Indianapolis: Bobbs-Merrill, 1965).

2. See David S. Lovejoy, *The Glorious Revolution in America* (New York: Harper & Row, 1972); and Richard R. Johnson, *Adjustment to Empire: The New England Colonies, 1676–1715* (New Brunswick, NJ: Rutgers University Press, 1981).

3. See Benjamin W. Labaree, *Colonial Massachusetts: A History* (Millwood, NY: KTO Press, 1979), chap. 8.

4. For original sources and background to the Stamp Act crisis, see Edmund S. Morgan, *Prologue to Revolution: Sources and Documents on the Stamp Act Crisis, 1764–1766* (Chapel Hill: University of North Carolina Press, 1959); and P.D.G. Thomas, *British Politics and the Stamp Act Crisis: the First Phase of the American Revolution, 1763–1767* (Oxford: Clarendon Press, 1975).

5. See Benjamin Woods Labaree, *The Boston Tea Party* (New York: Oxford University Press, 1964).

6. For a wider perspective on Revolutionary constitution-making, see Willi Paul Adams, *The First American Constitutions: Republican Ideology and the Making of the State Constitutions in the Revolutionary Era* (Chapel Hill: University of North Carolina Press, 1980); and Donald S. Lutz, *Popular Consent and Popular Control: Whig Political Theory in the Early Constitutions* (Baton Rouge: Louisiana State University Press, 1980).

7. All quotations relating to the Massachusetts constitution are taken from Robert J. Taylor, ed., *Massachusetts, Colony to Commonwealth: Documents on the Formation of Its Constitution, 1775–1780* (Chapel Hill: University of North Carolina Press, 1961). See also Oscar and Mary Handlin, eds., *The Popular Sources of Political Authority: Documents on the Massachusetts Constitution of 1780* (Cambridge, MA: Belknap Press of Harvard University Press, 1966).

8. For more detailed discussion of the Declaration of Rights, see John M. Murrin, "From Liberties to Rights: The Struggle in Colonial Massachusetts," in *The Bill of Rights and the States: The Colonial and Revolutionary Origins of American Liberties*, ed. Patrick T. Conley and John P. Kaminiski (Madison, WI: Madison House,1992), pp. 63–99.

9. See Christopher Clark *The Roots of Rural Capitalism: Western Massachusetts, 1780–1869* (Ithaca: Cornell University Press, 1990); and Conrad Edick Wright, ed., *Massachusetts and the New Nation* (Boston: Massachusetts Historical Society; distributed by Northeastern University Press, 1992).

10. On Shays's Rebellion, see David P. Szatmary, *Shays's Rebellion: The Making of an Agrarian Insurrection* (Amherst: University of Massachusetts Press, 1980); and Robert A. Feer, *Shays's Rebellion* (New York: Garland, 1988).

11. See Jack N. Rakove, *Original Meanings: Politics and Ideas in the Making of the Constitution* (New York: Knopf, 1996).

12. See Thomas H. O'Connor and Alan Rogers, *This Momentous Affair: Massachusetts and the Ratification of the Constitution of the United States* (Boston: Boston Public Library, 1987).

BIBLIOGRAPHY

Bailyn, Bernard. *The Ordeal of Thomas Hutchinson*. Cambridge, MA: Belknap Press of Harvard University Press, 1974.

Brown, Robert E. *Middle-class Democracy and the Revolution in Massachusetts, 1691–1780*. Ithaca, NY: Published for the American Historical Association by Cornell University Press, 1955.

Bushman, Richard L. *King and People in Provincial Massachusetts*. Chapel Hill: University of North Carolina Press, 1985.

Hall, Van Beck. *Politics without Parties: Massachusetts, 1780–1791*. Pittsburgh: University of Pittsburgh Press, 1972.

Handlin, Oscar, and Mary Handlin, eds. *The Popular Sources of Political Authority: Documents on the Massachusetts Constitution of 1780*. Cambridge, MA: Belknap Press of Harvard University Press, 1966.

Labaree, Benjamin W. *Colonial Massachusetts: A History*. Millwood, NY: KTO Press, 1979.

Murrin, John M. "From Liberties to Rights: The Struggle in Colonial Massachusetts." In *The Bill of Rights and the States: The Colonial and Revolutionary Origins of American Liberties*, edited by Patrick T. Conley and John P. Kaminski. Madison, WI: Madison House, 1992.

Patterson, Stephen E. *Political Parties in Revolutionary Massachusetts*. Madison: University of Wisconsin Press, 1973.

Pencak, William. *War, Politics and Revolution in Provincial Massachusetts*. Boston: Northeastern University Press, 1981.

Peters, Ronald M. *The Massachusetts Constitution of 1780: A Social Compact*. Amherst: University of Massachusetts Press, 1978.

Taylor, Robert J., ed. *Massachusetts, Colony to Commonwealth: Documents on the Formation of Its Constitution, 1775–1780*. Chapel Hill: University of North Carolina Press, 1961.

Michigan

Territorial Development:

- Great Britain cedes future territory of Michigan to the United States through the Treaty of Paris, September 3, 1783
- The United States passes the Northwest Ordinance: territorial claims inherited from colonial charters ceded to the public domain; future territory of Michigan organized as a part of the Northwest Territory, July 13, 1787
- Reorganized as a part of the Indiana Territory, May 7, 1800
- Reorganized as the Michigan Territory, January 11, 1805
- Michigan admitted to the Union as the twenty-sixth state, January 26, 1837

Territorial Capitals:

- Detroit, 1805–1837

State Capitals:

- Detroit, 1837–1847
- Lansing, 1847–present

Origin of State Name: "Michigan" comes from the Chippewa word "majigan," meaning "clearing." The Great Lake of Michigan was named after the clearing.

First Governor: Stevens Thomas Mason
Governmental Organization: Bicameral
Population at Statehood: 212,267
Geographical Size: 56,804 square miles

THE STATE OF MICHIGAN

Admitted to the Union as a State: January 26, 1837

Jim Schwartz

INTRODUCTION

After the Missouri Compromise of 1820, Congress sought to maintain parity between the North and South in the U.S. Senate by permitting one slave and one free state to enter the Union at the same time. In keeping with this policy, Michigan gained admission to the Union in January 1837, approximately six months after Arkansas. Becoming a state, however, proved to be no easy task for Michigan. Its entry into the Union was complicated by a long and bitter boundary dispute with Ohio, its southern neighbor. The conflict stemmed from competing claims to a tract of potentially valuable land encompassing current-day Toledo, Ohio, on Michigan's southern border. The dispute with Ohio not only delayed Michigan's entry into the Union by several years but also led to a brief armed confrontation between the two states that became known as the Toledo War.

Michigan's quest for statehood, however, began long before the Toledo War and occurred in four phases. Each involved efforts to establish the rule of law, limit the power of local and federal officials, and protect the rights established by the Northwest Ordinance, which Michiganians believed served as their constitution. They also concerned efforts to establish boundaries that would protect Michigan from the wildness and lawlessness of their neighbors in Ohio, immigrants, and other cultural outsiders. Phase one, which took place between the 1810s and 1823, involved efforts to impose legal and constitutional limitations on the power of territorial officials appointed by the federal government. Reformers hoped that such limitations would secure property rights and quell a spirit of wildness and anarchy stemming from doubts about the legitimacy of laws enacted by a legislature that did not represent the will of the people. The second, third, and fourth phases of the campaign to achieve political independence took place during the 1830s, as Michigan sought to become a state.

Phases two and three revolved around questions concerning the proper balance of power between states and Congress's role in helping to shape states. Phase two began with Michiganians debating the merits of entering the Union, after which they struggled to establish a boundary that would protect them from the rapacity and greed of Ohio officials who, like Philip the Great, seemed bent on conquering their smaller and weaker neighbors. Fearing that Ohio's large congressional delegation could induce federal lawmakers to give Toledo to the Buckeye State, Michiganians asserted that the Northwest Ordinance was a constitutional document and that Congress, therefore, lacked the authority to change its provisions. Phase three centered on debates over issues involved in creating a state government. Despite opposition from the Whigs, the Democrats, who controlled Michigan politics, insisted that the Northwest Ordinance gave Michigan the right to enter the Union and form a state government without first obtaining enabling legislation from Congress. The two parties also disagreed on whether Michigan's new constitution should permit immigrants, blacks, or Native Americans to vote.

The fourth phase occurred in the second half of 1836, after Congress hammered out a compromise to settle the boundary dispute with Ohio and permit Michigan to become a state. Before entering the Union, however, a Michigan convention elected by the people had to assent to the terms offered by Congress. In the campaign to elect delegates to the convention, Democrats and Whigs strongly disagreed on whether to accept the congressional compromise. Democrats recommended that Michiganians accept the terms offered by Congress, whereas Whigs and dissident Democrats urged that they reject the proposed settlement and hold out for a more favorable settlement. Michigan's four-phase campaign to become a state thus raised important questions about the proper balance of power between states, Congress's power to admit new states, the Northwest Ordinance's status as a constitutional document, and the wisdom of permitting immigrants or other cultural outsiders to vote.

TERRITORIAL GOVERNMENT

During the first two decades of the nineteenth century, Michigan settlers focused primarily on issues concerning their territorial government. At the turn of the century they broke away from Indiana and established their own territory. After the War of 1812, they initiated a campaign to win the right to an elected legislature. Establishing such a legislature would limit the power of territorial officials, help establish the rule of law, and enable many of the territory's white men to enjoy some of the rights that their counterparts possessed in the states.

Origins of Territorial Government

Occupied by the French and the British in the seventeenth and eighteenth centuries, Michigan became part of the United States after the American Revolution. Eventually it was incorporated into the Northwest Territory, the lands north of the Ohio River ceded to the confederacy during the Revolution. Because of dramatic population growth, Congress in 1800 created the Indiana Territory in the western portion of the Old Northwest and split Michigan in two, with the western portion of the peninsula joining Indiana and the eastern section remaining in the Northwest Territory. After Ohio became a state in 1803, the eastern section of Michigan was also placed under the jurisdiction of the Indiana Territory.

This change stirred unrest because Vincennes, the capital of Indiana, was remote from Michigan; settlers complained that mail service was poor, and they lacked easy access to the territory's legal system. Nor did Michiganians have a voice in the administration of the Indiana Territory, which was sparsely populated and, unlike the Northwest Territory, lacked an elected assembly. To remedy these problems, Congress established the Michigan Territory in 1805. As specified in the Northwest Ordinance, the federal government appointed a governor and three judges to govern the territory.[1]

Campaign to Reform Territorial Government

After the War of 1812, many settlers began to complain about their territorial officials and lobbied for the right to elect their own legislature. Michigan lacked the population of five thousand free white males that the Northwest Ordinance established as prerequisite for gaining an elected assembly, but Congress eliminated this requirement after Indiana became a territory. The effort to obtain an elected assembly occurred in two phases. The first phase began in 1817 with a series of articles in the *Detroit Gazette*, the territory's only newspaper at the time. It ended in 1818 when voters rejected a proposal to petition Congress for an elected legislature. Washington, however, did permit Michigan to send a non-voting delegate to Congress in 1819. The second stage began in 1820 with a new round of attacks on the territorial government published in the *Gazette*. At the time, residents also memorialized Congress for an elected legislature.[2]

One of the most common complaints reformers voiced was that Michigan's legislature frequently violated the provisions of the Northwest Ordinance when drafting legislation. Under the ordinance, the legislators were required to adopt laws enacted by the original states rather than draft statutes of their own creation. A writer in the *Gazette*, who called himself "Xenos," charged in 1820 that the legislature frequently violated this rule: "The Ordinance of '87, which is our constitution, ever has been, and still is continually violated in the making instead of adopting the law." The legislature often enacted laws "without referring to the statutes of the states from whence they purport to be adopted—and where in fact many of the provisions do not exist."

The transgressions of the legislature paled in comparison to those of Michigan's Supreme Court, which failed to give criminals the punishment that they deserved. To illustrate the latter point, critics recalled a number of cases in which the courts had let criminals off lightly. One of the most notorious involved a Native American named Petobig. In 1817, a *Gazette* writer named "Rousseau" looked back on the years before the War of 1812 and recalled that Michigan judges had refused to sentence Petobig to death, even though he had committed a "most atrocious" murder and been "convicted by a...jury." Critics also charged judges with abusing their power, claiming that Justice William B. Woodward, in particular, failed to recuse himself from cases in which he had an interest. A correspondent calling himself "Michigan" reported that in one case Justice Woodward had "acted as an accuser, a prosecutor or party, as a witness and as judge!"

The effects of such official misconduct by Michigan's judiciary and legislature were devastating, inciting a spirit of wildness, lawlessness, and "anarchy" in the territory, critics declared. After making this claim in 1817, "Rousseau" stated in the *Gazette* that Michigan had descended into a state of "anarchy" because residents questioned "the legitimacy of some of its rulers" and the need to obey the law that they created. Republics were "sustained by the virtue and good opinion of the people, by confidence in their rulers and sacred regard for, and implicit obedience the laws." Only by displaying an "exemplary assiduity" in performing "their official duties," could officials expect residents to "respect and obey the law." A few weeks later, "Rousseau" asserted that in Michigan the misdeeds of the legislature had rendered "property insecure" and created "confusion everywhere" because of the "doubtful obligations of the law."

To remedy these problems, Michiganians sought the right to elect their own legislature. This change would give white men in Michigan the right to vote and would reduce the power of Michigan justices by eliminating their dual role as judges and legislators. "Rousseau" insisted that, because Michigan judges served in both roles, they wielded an inordinate amount of power. "The concentration of legislative and judicial powers in the same body" was the "most abhorrent despotism," because few, if any, judges would deem the laws, which they had enacted as legislators, unconstitutional.

The campaign to win an elected assembly ended successfully in 1823 when Congress responded to Michigan petitioners with legislation that permitted the president to designate nine legislators from a list of eighteen candidates chosen by Michigan voters. As a result, Michigan's governor and three Michigan Supreme Court judges relinquished their legislative duties. The governor retained his veto power, however, and Congress continued to review all legislation passed by the council. In 1827, federal lawmakers granted Michigan more autonomy, permitting the territory's voters to elect their own thirteen-member legislature.[3]

THE DEBATE OVER STATEHOOD

After the reform of territorial government, Michigan's population grew rapidly, and in the early 1830s territorial officials began considering the possibility of joining the Union. Debate on whether to become a state crystallized around a referendum held in 1832 to gauge popular sentiment on the question. Much of the discussion turned on whether the economic and political benefits of becoming a state would outweigh the additional costs that such a move entailed. Voters narrowly approved the referendum in the fall of 1832, and Michigan asked Congress for permission to enter the Union the following year.

Referendum of 1832

Prompting the debate over statehood was a dramatic surge in Michigan's population during the 1820s and 1830s, resulting largely from the completion of the Erie Canal in 1826 and the arrival of steam-powered ships on the Great Lakes. These improvements in transportation made it much easier and less expensive for Easterners, many of whom came from New England and western New York, to migrate to Michigan. As a result, Michigan became "the most popular destination for westward-moving pioneers" during much of the 1830s. In 1830, Michigan's population had climbed to 31,640, and by 1834 it had risen to 87,278.[4]

The dramatic rise in population sparked growing interest in statehood. In the fall of 1831, the *Detroit Free Press*, for instance, observed that immigration to Michigan was continuing to grow and that soon the territory's population could climb "to upwards of sixty thousand." It was time, therefore, for settlers to "direct their attention to the subject of forming" a state government. At the beginning of 1832, the *Detroit Journal and Michigan Advertiser* echoed these sentiments, predicting that because of its growing population, Michigan soon would be "entitled…to demand admission to the Union."[5]

Opposition to Statehood

Responding to such concerns, Michigan's territorial legislature organized a referendum in October 1832 to determine whether voters wanted to create

597

a state government. Opponents of statehood argued that Michigan was prospering as a territory and that becoming a state would only increase taxes. One of the most outspoken critics of statehood was a writer in the *St. Joseph Beacon* who, according to the *Detroit Journal*, argued in 1832 against entering the Union because the cost of "supporting State Government" was "greater than could be conveniently borne by the people." After Michigan became a state, the federal government would no longer pay the cost of running its government, and tax payers would have to assume these expenses, which were likely to cost between $20,000 and $30,000 a year. It made more sense, therefore, to postpone statehood until Michigan's population grew, and such expenses could be spread over a larger number of taxpayers.

Advocates of Statehood

In challenging these claims, advocates of statehood usually began by refuting opponents' predictions about the costs of running a state government. In September 1832, the editors of the *Detroit Journal* observed that the *St. Joseph Beacon* writer who had so staunchly opposed joining the Union estimated that it would cost between $20,000 and $30,000 annually to operate a state government. The *Journal* editors, however, insisted that this figure was greatly inflated. They estimated that it cost "about ten thousand" annually to run Michigan's territorial government and saw no reason why the change to a state government would significantly increase those costs.

Even if state government were more expensive than a territorial regime, advocates of statehood insisted that it would be worth paying a few extra dollars to obtain the right to self-rule. As a territory, the *Detroit Journal* concluded in 1832, Michigan was nearly in the same situation as a "conquered Roman province." Assuming that the highest estimate of the *St. Joseph Beacon* writer was accurate, the *Detroit Journal* found nothing "very alarming" in this figure. Under a state government, landholders would pay $3 more per year, and few farmers would "think it a hardship to appropriate three bushels of wheat a year for the support of a Government" in which they had a "direct agency and a controlling voice."[6]

Advocates of statehood also predicted that Michiganians would reap other benefits from joining the Union. The *Detroit Journal* recalled in September 1832 that Congress had almost passed legislation that would have distributed revenue from the sale of public lands to the states. As a state, Michigan would receive a share in the distribution of those revenues. The *Free Press* agreed, estimating that any increase in taxes needed to establish a state government would be "more than repaid to the people" by the money accrued from the sale of public lands. Advocates of statehood also predicted that joining the Union would boost immigration to Michigan, give residents a more powerful voice in Washington, and increase federal funds for the construction of canals, turnpikes, railroads, and other internal improvements. These arguments proved persuasive, convincing a narrow majority of voters to approve efforts to become a state.[7]

CONFLICT WITH OHIO

Backed by Michigan voters, territorial officials sought enabling legislation from Congress in 1833 that would permit them to form a state government and to enter the Union. Their efforts, however, were complicated by a long-standing boundary dispute with Ohio. Ohio's powerful congressional delegation was concerned about losing the valuable tract of land on Lake Erie and in early 1834 blocked Michigan's efforts to become a state. During the next two years, Michigan officials fought two battles. The first was a war of words with Ohio, in which Michigan officials sought to convince the public and federal officials that Ohio was a rapacious state that threatened Michigan and also menaced other small states. The second was a brief, but nearly bloodless, clash with Ohio over the disputed tract, which soon became known as the Toledo War.

Leading Michigan in both battles was its fiery young governor, Stevens Thomson Mason. The scion of an old Virginia family that had played a significant role in the American Revolution, Mason was popularly known as the "Boy Governor" because President Jackson named him secretary of the territory when he was only nineteen years old. When Governor George Porter, who had succeeded Lewis Cass, died of cholera in 1834, Mason became Michigan's acting governor. Although settlers initially objected to his youth, scholars report that Mason became increasingly popular in Michigan. President Jackson was said to have nicknamed Mason "Young Hotspur" because of his "belligerent spirit," and that spirit was much in evidence during the Toledo War.[8]

The Dispute over Toledo

The roots of the conflict with Ohio grew out of uncertainty about the precise location of Michigan's southern border. The Northwest Ordinance had given Congress the option to create three or more states in the Northwest Territory. If Congress chose to create only three states, their northern boundary would be the Canadian border. If federal lawmakers decided to create one or more additional states in the northern portion of the territory, the northern boundary of Ohio, Indiana, and Illinois was to be a line running due east from the southernmost tip of Lake Michigan to Lake Erie. The ordinance, however, was silent on one key question: whether Congress could alter the east-west line that was to serve as the northern border of Ohio, Indiana, and Illinois.

To make matters worse, early maps of the region were sketchy, and no one knew exactly where the southern tip of Lake Michigan was situated. This point was important, because it might determine whether Toledo and its potentially valuable harbor on Lake Erie belonged to Ohio or Michigan. According to several scholars, a fur trapper who attended Ohio's constitutional convention of 1802 told delegates that Lake Michigan might extend farther south than the drafters of the ordinance had realized. Ohio noted this fact in its 1802 constitution and, pending congressional approval, claimed the land surrounding current-day Toledo, if the tract fell outside the line designated in the ordinance as Ohio's northern border. Congress had never explicitly endorsed Ohio's claim to Toledo, but because Congress accepted its constitution, Ohio officials asserted that federal lawmakers implicitly had agreed to award it Toledo. In 1805, however, Congress placed Toledo in the newly created Michigan Territory, and Michigan officials claimed this action proved that Congress intended to make Toledo a part of Michigan.

Over the next three decades, Ohio's congressional delegation sought and failed several times to win federal approval for its right to the land. Additionally, Congress ordered two surveys to mark the border between Michigan and Ohio, but neither proved to be conclusive. The first, conducted in 1817 by William Harris, placed the disputed tract within Ohio, and the second, performed a year later by Robert A. Fulton, located the land in Michigan. The Harris and Fulton lines thus became the informal borders of the nearly 470-square-mile disputed tract, which became known as the Toledo Strip.[9]

The battle over Toledo escalated dramatically after Michigan formally initiated efforts to join the Union in 1833. Worried about the loss of Toledo, Ohio officials used their influence in Congress to block Michigan from becoming a state unless it relinquished claims to the disputed land. In January 1834, the *Free Press* printed a letter from Lucius Lyon, Michigan's non-voting delegate to Congress, stating that the House Committee on Territories was considering Michigan's request for statehood but added that Michigan's efforts to enter the Union had encountered stiff opposition. "There is a good deal of difficulties about boundaries," he wrote. Ohio "has arrayed all her strength against us." Its delegation seemed "determined to take this opportunity to compel us to submit to her claims, and to induce the Committee to report a bill fixing the boundary between us according to her wishes." A few months later, the *Free Press* informed its readers that Congress had tabled Michigan's motion on statehood, reporting that Lyon had been "unable to procure the passage of a law for our admission into the Union." Ohio and its allies would continue to oppose Michigan's statehood unless Lyon agreed to "yield the question of boundary."[10]

The Toledo War

Congress's apparent inability to resolve the boundary dispute led Michigan and Ohio to take matters into their own hands. At the beginning of 1835, each of the two sides enacted legislation to break the deadlock over Toledo. As tensions heightened, federal efforts to mediate the conflict failed, and the two sides engaged in a series of armed confrontations. These confrontations ended in late 1835, after federal officials removed Michigan Governor Stevens T. Mason from office.

Before the two sides came to blows, however, Michigan and Ohio both passed legislation to strengthen their holds on the disputed tract. Ohio Governor Lucas sent a message to the state legislature at the beginning of 1835 asserting Ohio's right to the Toledo Strip and recommending that lawmakers pass "legislation to possess and control it." After learning of Ohio's plans, Michigan enacted a law seeking to prevent Ohio officials from taking jurisdiction of the disputed tract by imposing a one thousand dollar fine or five years in prison on anyone other than Michigan or federal officials who "should accept or exercise any public office" in the territory.

On February 23, Ohio's legislature responded defiantly. Without waiting for federal approval, the Buckeye State enacted legislation taking control of the Toledo Strip. The *Michigan Sentinel* informed its readers in March that "this powerful and arrogant state" seemed bent on the "forcible possession" of Michigan's "soil—regardless alike of the justice of her claim or of the consequences which must inevitably follow." In addition to extending Ohio's jurisdiction over the Toledo Strip, the legislation authorized residents in the disputed tract to elect justices of the peace, constables, and other officials.[11]

Ohio's new law soon became a source of growing tension between Michigan and the Buckeye State. In early 1835, both sides ordered their militias to the Toledo Strip, and Ohio Governor Lucas dispatched surveyors equipped with an armed escort to establish the Harris line as Ohio's permanent northern border. Michigan Governor Mason, meanwhile, ordered Michigan's militia to shoot any Ohio surveyors or militia who entered Michigan. The *Michigan Sentinel* also reported in March 1832 that Mason had "removed from office" all those in the Toledo Strip "favorably disposed to the claims of Ohio."[12]

Fearing that such moves might result in violence, the federal government sought to resolve the dispute peacefully. By late March President Jackson had named two U.S. commissioners, Richard Rush and Benjamin W. Howard, to find a peaceful solution to the conflict. The commissioners, who traveled to Toledo in April, were unable to work out an agreement, and fighting broke out in the spring of 1835. In April, a Michigan posse arrested most of the Ohioans re-marking the Harris line after they entered Michigan.[13] Lawlessness and rioting also erupted in Toledo during the next few months as Ohio loyalists rebelled against Michigan authorities. The *Michigan Sentinel* reported, a deputy sheriff had arrested several Irishmen and was escorting them to the magistrate when two Toledo residents helped the prisoners escape.[14]

A more dramatic instance of rebellion and violence occurred in July of that year after Michigan officials executed a debt against Toledo resident Jeremiah Odel, Jr. Trouble began shortly thereafter, the *Free Press* noted, when Truman Heminway, a Michigan constable, held an auction to sell Odel's wagon and horses. After bidding opened on Odel's steeds, J. B. Davis, a local tavern keeper, struck the officer, while others in the crowd "seized the horses," stopped the sale, and threatened to take the life of plaintiff, Henry Clark, Jr., of Toledo, if he insisted on collecting his debt. Michigan authorities then obtained a warrant to arrest Two Stickney, one of the leaders of the Toledo riot. Stickney and his family were among the strangest characters to appear in the Toledo War. Stickney's father was "an ardent Buckeye who fancied himself a military genius" and who had named "his two sons, respectively, One and Two." After finding Stickney at a local tavern a number of days after the riot, the *Free Press* stated, Deputy Sheriff Joseph Wood sought to arrest him, but the suspect wounded the deputy, stabbing him with "a large dirk knife." Although Michigan sheriffs were unable to bring Stickney to justice, they did capture others alleged to have instigated the riot.[15]

As Michigan authorities sought to quell lawlessness in Toledo, federal mediators continued their efforts to end the Toledo War. In the spring of 1835, Rush and Howard worked out an agreement with Governor Lucas after they agreed to his demand that Ohio and Michigan be given concurrent jurisdiction of the disputed tract, meaning that residents in the area could choose to be governed by either Ohio or Michigan. Ohio's legislature agreed to the proposal in June.[16] Michigan's lawmakers, however, rejected the proposal because they refused to accept concurrent jurisdiction in Toledo.[17]

Michigan's rejection of the compromise prompted President Jackson to remove Governor Mason from office, an action that helped end the Toledo War. Jackson, who dismissed Mason in September and replaced him with John S. Horner, evidently believed that Mason's confrontational style was obstructing efforts to end the conflict. Several scholars have cited a letter to this effect from Jackson's secretary of state, John Forsyth, stating that Mason's "zeal" for what he considered "the rights of Michigan" had "overcome that spirit of moderation and forbearance" that was needed to preserve the peace. This move had little effect on Mason's career. Michigan formed its new state government in the fall of 1835, and Mason was elected to his old post just a few weeks after he had been dismissed. Mason's dismissal, however, seemed to ease tensions between Michigan and Ohio. In September, Michigan's militia tried to stop Ohio from holding a session of the Court of Common Pleas in Toledo, but the confrontation never really materialized. Governor Lucas, who wanted nothing more than "an official record that the court" had met, fooled the Michiganians by sneaking the judges into town in the wee hours of the morning.[18]

The War of Words

The Toledo War was not the only battle Michigan and Ohio fought. They also engaged in a heated war of words, in which each side sought to convince Congress and the nation at large of the justice of their cause. Michiganians relied on several arguments to make this case. Pointing to Ohio's lawless conduct during the Toledo War, Michigan officials emphasized the need to establish boundaries that would curb this aggressive, power-hungry state. They also insisted that the Northwest Ordinance was a constitutional document and that Congress lacked the authority to change the boundaries that it established. In making this case, they insisted that the drafters of the ordinance had realized the importance of maintaining a rough parity between states. If some states became overly large and powerful, they could devour their smaller, weaker neighbors. The federal government, therefore, should permit Michigan to retain Toledo, because Ohio was already too large and powerful; if Washington let the Buckeye State grow even larger, it might destroy other states in the region.

This argument dated to the earliest days of the Republic and arose from concerns about equality among the states. Such fears arose from the belief that large states had a propensity to become predatory and "devour" smaller ones. A balance among states was therefore needed to protect small states and to guarantee the Union's survival. Just as a balance of power among nations was the key to world peace, the "same principle applied to American states." To maintain this balance, drafters of the ordinance sought to ensure that none of the new western states was too large. Otherwise, they could become "dangerous new centers of power" and jeopardize the Union.[19]

Applying this doctrine to the conflict over Toledo, Michigan officials noted that Ohio was already larger than Michigan and warned that if Congress gave the disputed tract to Ohio, it would undermine the balance of power between the states sought by the drafters of the ordinance. The *Michigan Sentinel*, a Democratic newspaper located in Monroe, Michigan, near Toledo, observed in September 1834 that the Buckeye State "was already sufficiently extensive, as it regards extent of country, resources, and natural agricultural and commercial advantages." Taking "from our soil an additional district" would "weaken us in point of numbers as well as in natural advantages." Michigan's congressional delegate Lyon seconded this view. In a speech to the Senate, which the *Free Press* reprinted, Lyon predicted that Toledo was likely to become a valuable port on Lake Erie once the Wabash and Erie Canal was completed. As a result, the town would "grow up a place of considerable commercial importance." Ohio was already larger and more powerful than Michigan. If federal lawmakers bowed to Ohio's demands, it would increase the disparity between the two.

Lyon then enlarged on this point, observing that once Michigan became a state, it would be small compared to Ohio. Michigan contained about half as much arable land as did its southern neighbor. Michigan's climate was more "unfavorable," and its population much smaller than Ohio's. Taking land from Michigan and giving it to Ohio would "only increase the present disparity in population and advantages and tend to make the "weak weaker and the strong stronger." Such a move would contravene the "ends of political justice, as well as the intention of Congress and the state of Virginia at the adoption of the ordinance." Both Congress and Virginia sought "to equalize the size and apportion the advantages of the different states to be formed in the North-west Territory."[20]

Because of its great size, Michigan pundits also insisted that Ohio already had become one of these menacing "new centers of powers" that the drafters of the ordinance feared. Pointing to Ohio's recent efforts to seize Toledo without federal approval, they portrayed the Buckeye State as wildly barbaric, avaricious, an invader determined to conquer smaller, weaker neighbors, and a threat to the federal system. One *Detroit Journal* correspondent in 1836 compared Ohio's behavior to Philip of Macedon's "encroachments upon weaker but smaller neighbors." The writer compared Ohio's behavior to "the lust of power which distinguished the whole history of the Roman commonwealth." The *Journal* also reprinted an address made that year which portrayed Ohio as wild, asserting that logic no longer could restrain it. The Buckeye State, said one, "exhibits to the world a lively specimen of the actings of our nature, when uncontrolled by reason, justice and morality." Its greed "keeps pace with her growth in wealth and resources. Not content with a large and fruitful territory and with a great proportion of the southern coast of Lake Erie…she also has laid her insatiable grasp upon a proportion of our comparatively small territory, and right or wrong seems determined to cling to it."[21]

Delegates to Michigan's constitutional convention in 1835 emphasized the importance of the federal government in enforcing the rule of law and controlling large and rapacious states, which threatened not only smaller and weaker states but also the Republic. The past demonstrated "that ambition is not the infirmity of monarchies alone, but that it frequently operates with decisive energy in republican governments." How would the nation protect the political rights and even the political existence of "the smaller states of this union…if the principle is once practically established that each member of the confederacy may, at any time, proceed without obstruction to its forcible possession?" Such developments could endanger the very existence of the federal system. "It is not difficult to foresee" that states would fall one after the other, and that "consummation would be found in the establishment of one single consolidated government."[22] The language here is not just of military, but also of sexual conquest, with large states taking "forcible possession" of smaller ones and finding "consummation" in the destruction of the federal system. In this analogy, Ohio was portrayed as a reckless and savage sexual predator who would stop at nothing to satisfy its lust for power.

To thwart Ohio's aggressive designs, Michigan officials urged Congress to obey the rule of law and enforce the boundaries established by the Northwest Ordinance. They insisted that the ordinance was a constitutional document and that Congress could not change it without the consent of the people. Michigan Governor Mason stated this position in a letter to the governor of Virginia in 1834, recalling that "the Ordinance fixed unalterably the southern boundary or boundaries of the state or states to be formed by Congress, north of an east-west line drawn through the southerly bend of Lake Michigan." Once approved by Virginia, which had ceded the land that constituted the Northwest Territory, "the ordinance became a fixed and fundamental law of the land" and could only be changed "by all the contracting parties." After Congress decided to form additional states north of the line established by the ordinance, "the rights of the people of Michigan" became "absolute and vested." Only through "common consent" could the federal government "alter the boundaries of this territory as prescribed" and not violate "an instrument as sacred and inviolable as the Federal Constitution itself."[23]

Other Michiganians also viewed the ordinance as a constitution that could thwart Ohio's claim to the Toledo Strip. The *Free Press* in 1834 said that the ordinance was "our constitution—our only peculiar constitution." It provided Michigan with "certain rights—among them the establishment of a Southern boundary" which had been "plainly marked out and defined." Delegates to Michigan's constitutional convention reiterated this argument in 1835 in their appeal to the people of the United States, which was later reprinted in the *Michigan Sentinel*. "Congress has no power to act upon this subject." The ordinance "prescribed" Michigan's boundaries, and the "national faith" put "the matter beyond the reach of the federal legislature." Congress's "power has been spent, and the most important political and territorial rights acquired by another party." Federal lawmakers could as well "change the boundaries of any state of the Union as those of this Territory." Similarly, in an 1835 letter to Congress, Michigan's territorial legislature insisted that the ordinance represented "articles of compact between the people of the original states, and the people and states in the ceded territory." The ordinance "was forever to remain unalterable, except by common consent." The government could not repeal it, and Congress had "no right to tamper with its provisions."[24]

In refuting these arguments, Ohio officials insisted that Congress had agreed to give the Buckeye State jurisdiction of the Toledo Strip when it approved its 1802 constitution. Ohio Governor Robert Lucas said that Congress had agreed to this change "when they adopted our constitution and admitted Ohio into the Union." Nor was the border that the ordinance created unalterable, as Michigan officials claimed. The Northwest Ordinance granted Congress "discretionary power" in forming states. Lawmakers were not confined "to this line, as the special boundary or one or two states to be formed north of it." Had this line "been intended as the permanent boundary" of the three southern states in the Northwest Territory, "there would certainly have been some expressions in the Ordinance that would have indicated such intentions." Instead, "we find no expressions of this character in the ordinance."

What is more, Governor Lucas continued, Congress provided a precedent on this question. Federal lawmakers had changed the boundary, which Michigan insisted was unalterable, when the states of Illinois and Indiana were admitted. The boundaries for both these states extended well beyond the southern extremity of Lake Michigan. If Illinois and Indiana had the right to extend their boundaries north of the line established by the ordinance, "Ohio undoubtedly had an equal right."

In Congress, meanwhile, Ohio Representative Thomas J. Hamer denied that the Northwest Ordinance had the weight of a constitutional document. Unlike a constitution, the ordinance was simply a law that Congress had passed. It was ridiculous to believe that "one Congress" could pass a law capable of binding "their successor and their country through all time," although this was the notion that Michigan put forward. "The ordinance is an act of Congress. It is no compact, as to the country north of the line named, whatever it may be, as to the rest." Compacts required "two parties," but in this case, "there was but one."[25]

POLITICS

Although the Toledo War sparked intense conflict between Michigan and Ohio, it stirred few battles between Michigan's two political parties. Michigan Democrats and Whigs largely agreed that the Toledo Strip belonged to Michigan. The two parties, however, did vehemently disagree on other issues. Most arose from Michigan's decision to form a state government without waiting to receive enabling legislation from Congress. Michigan officials had taken a census in 1834 and found that the territory contained more than 60,000 free men. Early the next year Michigan's Democratic legislature passed legislation, which came to be known as the Doty Bill after one of its creators, enabling the territory to draft a constitution and establish a state government.

This effort to create a state government sparked two debates. In one, Democrats and Whigs disagreed about voting rights. Most Democrats favored alien suffrage but opposed permitting blacks and other non-white groups to vote. Whigs, however, backed black suffrage and sought to prevent aliens from voting. In the second debate, the parties disagreed on whether Michigan had the right to form a state government without first obtaining congressional approval. Whigs denied that such a right existed, but Democrats insisted that it did.

FORMING A STATE GOVERNMENT

The Debate over State Government

The battle over Michigan's right to create a state government was a classic contest between those asserting the claims of national power and those claiming states' rights, with Whigs defending and Democrats opposing Congress's authority to admit new states. Citing Tennessee's entry into the Union in 1796 as precedent, Democratic officials asserted that Michigan did not need Congress's permission to become a state. Instead, the Northwest Ordinance granted Michigan the right to become a state once its population contained more than

60,000 free men. Michigan Governor Mason contended in 1834 that the ordinance required "only 60,000 free inhabitants, to entitle Michigan to admission into the Union as an independent state." Once the requisite population was achieved, the "only discretion left for Congress to exercise, is to determine that our constitution is 'Republican.'" Similarly, "A Friend of the West," writing in the *Free Press* that year, insisted that all Michigan needed to do to become a state was to draft "a constitution…and demand admittance into the Union."[26]

Whigs, however, charged that creating a state government without congressional approval was unconstitutional. They stated that the Constitution, which superseded the Northwest Ordinance, granted Congress the authority to regulate the territories and admit new states. The *Detroit Journal* said that if the ordinance "contained any provisions that were repugnant" to the constitution, they "were of course superseded and rendered void."

Whigs also alleged that, in ignoring Congress, Michigan officials were acting lawlessly and endangering the Union, as had South Carolinians, who a few years earlier had claimed that states possessed the power to nullify or overturn federal laws. In early 1836, the *Journal* opined that Democratic officials were offering a "new and refined system of nullification…to the favorable consideration of the people of Michigan." Violently, they were "severing" ties between the "territory and the general government, precipitating the people of Michigan into a state of revolution." Such a policy would not "give any greater security in the settlement of the boundary question."

Democratic officials ignored such views, in part because they believed that becoming a state as quickly as possible gave them the best chance of retaining Toledo. Governor Mason contended that once Michigan entered the Union, it could remove its dispute with Ohio from Congress, where the Buckeye State with its large congressional delegation had much greater power than Michigan, and place it before the U.S. Supreme Court. The governor complained, "As a Territory, we have but little weight in the deliberations of Congress, on subjects connected with our vital and permanent political rights." In Congress, these questions were "decided upon principles of expediency, with a view to other interests" than those of Michigan.[27]

THE CONSTITUTION

Creating a state government also sparked a long and bitter debate on alien suffrage and whether foreign or non-white voters represented a greater threat to Michigan's new republic. Most Democrats claimed that the violence and barbarism of non-whites posed a much graver threat to the polity than did foreigners. Their opponents, Whigs and dissident Democrats, took the opposite view, alleging that aliens lacked knowledge of republican institutions and could be manipulated by foreign powers. This battle over voting rights, however, was not based solely on notions of racial and cultural purity. Self-interest was also involved, with each party seeking to enfranchise groups that were likely to vote for its candidates.

The conflict over voting rights began when Whigs objected to a provision in the Doty Bill, which was approved in 1835, that permitted many aliens to vote in elections for delegates to the constitutional convention, and concluded with the battle in Congress in 1837 over Michigan's new constitution. The debate turned on two related questions: first, whether foreigners or non-white races—mostly blacks and Native Americans—posed a greater threat to the polity, and second, what stipulations were needed to protect the Republic from these cultural outsiders. At the time, foreigners accounted for roughly 4 percent of Michigan's population, many of whom were Catholics from Ireland or Germany. The Doty Bill allowed any white man who had lived in Michigan for three months to vote. Although aliens had voted in the 1832 referendum on statehood, the Doty Bill represented a much more important break with tradition. Whigs feared that Democrats would use the alien suffrage section of the Doty Bill to get their delegates elected to the constitutional convention and would then include a similar provision for alien voting in Michigan's new constitution, a provision that would help the Democrats maintain their dominance. The *Journal* stated that the bill would enable Democrats "to get such a delegation" as they wished, so that they could "form such a constitution as the interests of the party requires."[28]

Whigs, however, could not prevent this outcome. The Democrats won a stunning victory in the election for delegates to the convention. Whigs "succeeded in electing not more than ten or twelve of the eighty-five delegates." Despite this defeat, Whigs fought hard to prevent Michigan's new constitution from enfranchising aliens.

In opposing alien suffrage, Whigs warned of the danger of enfranchising foreigners, especially Catholics, who lacked knowledge of republican institutions, and who might be under the influence of foreign tyrants. Permitting such individuals to vote might well produce despotism, violence, and instability. William Woodbridge, a prominent Whig delegate, for instance, asserted that enfranchising such aliens would create the same kind of violence and instability that plagued Latin America. Like the United States, nations on that continent had hoisted "the standard of liberty and independence." During the past decade or two, however, these republics had been "drenched in blood—in human blood." Their "political features" had "changed incessantly, with the seasons and with the flowers!" These republics were in constant turmoil because their people were "strangers to the habits of freemen." Their transition "from despotism to liberty was too sudden." They did not possess and "could not acquire the habits of freedom."

Opponents of alien suffrage also expressed fear that foreign tyrants could use aliens to take control of Michigan's new republic. These rulers could easily manipulate foreign voters, because they often lacked two "masculine" qualities that were vital to citizens—independence and loyalty to their adopted country.

Woodbridge pointed out that Michigan might someday need to consider a "highly important measure," in which "some foreign power might take a deep interest...[and] send among us a mass of voters whose casting might control the decision."

Although mainstream Democrats dismissed Whigs' concerns about alien suffrage, they insisted on the need for racial barriers to protect the Republic from non-white people. Democrats who opposed black suffrage predicted that enfranchising non-whites would produce social disorder and political instability. Permitting blacks to vote would increase black migration to Michigan and dramatically boost the group's political power, predicted Isaac Crary. This increased migration would lead to chaos, because blacks by nature supposedly were prone to crime, violence, and disorder. John Williams reminded fellow delegates that a black community, which consisted of "renegades and runaways," already existed near Detroit. Enfranchising blacks would increase the size of this community and boost the rate of crime in the area. Almost "every gentleman" was aware of "the frequent disturbances and murders committed by blacks." If Michigan were to be "overrun" by blacks, "the consequences would be dangerous," resulting in increased violence, wildness, and social instability. Michigan residents would be threatened by growing numbers of black criminals. Worse, such criminals would have the power to elect officials who bowed to their lawless views.

After debating black suffrage, delegates briefly considered granting Native Americans the right to vote. At issue in this debate was whether Native American savagery was rooted in race or culture. If the latter were true, those who gave up their native ways and became civilized could be considered white and permitted to vote. This argument was made by delegates who favored enfranchising tax-paying Native Americans. John McDonell, for instance, introduced an amendment allowing Native Americans to vote, if they paid "a State, County or Township tax." Those supporting the amendment contended that what distinguished Native Americans from settlers were cultural rather than racial differences and that the convention should enfranchise Native Americans who had adopted white ways. There were, Williams said, "were many of this race, who were employed in agriculture, had excellent farms, and were identified with the very soil of Michigan. To such he was in favor of extending the privileges of citizens."

Although efforts to enfranchise blacks and Native Americans were defeated, Whigs succeeded in amending the alien suffrage provision initially proposed at the convention and placing some limits on the number of foreign immigrants who could vote. Mainstream Democrats initially sought to provide the "same generous suffrage qualifications" in the constitution as they had in the Doty Bill, permitting white males who were twenty-one years of age to vote after residing in Michigan for three months. Even though all white males over twenty-one and living in Michigan when the constitution was approved were enfranchised, the constitution imposed a six-month residency requirement on those who came to Michigan in subsequent years.[29]

FEDERAL APPROVAL

In the fall of 1835, voters approved Michigan's new constitution and elected the first state government. Less than a year later, Congress hammered out a compromise that awarded Toledo to Ohio, permitted Michigan to enter the Union, and gave the new state a large piece of the Upper Peninsula. Federal lawmakers also required Michigan to assemble a new convention to agree to the compromise. The proposed settlement sparked a fierce debate between Democrats, who mostly urged Michiganians to accept the compromise, and a coalition of Whigs and dissident Democrats, who recommended that they reject it. After months of fierce debate, a convention convened in September 1836 and rejected the compromise. Democrats, however, refused to accept this verdict. They organized a second convention that met in Ann Arbor at the end of 1836 and accepted the compromise, paving the way for Michigan to join the Union in 1837.

The Compromise

The final phase of Michigan's quest for statehood began in late 1835, when Congress began seriously considering legislation that would end the standoff over Toledo and allow Michigan to become a state. As details of what became known as the "admissions bill" began to emerge in early 1836, Michiganians were shocked to learn that Congress was planning to award Toledo to Ohio. In March of that year, the *Free Press* reported that federal lawmakers had decided in Ohio's favor on this question. In ignoring the Ordinance of 1787, Congress had based its decision on "expediency, that great innovator of the day, which threatens to undermine all the existing safeguards of popular rights."

At the time, the *Free Press* also reprinted a congressional report on the boundary dispute that explained why Congress planned to give Toledo to Ohio. Written by the Senate Judiciary Committee, it dismissed Michigan's assertions that Congress lacked the authority to rearrange boundaries in the Northwest Territories. In the act ceding the Old Northwest to the United States, Congress had insisted that Virginia grant it this power to ensure that states in the region had access to resources needed for economic development. Lawmakers also found that Congress originally had intended Ohio to have Toledo. They arrived at this conclusion after perusing maps from the late eighteenth century, which placed the southern tip of Lake Michigan much farther north than it was actually located. "Mitchell's map...so lays down this lake and the adjacent country, that a line drawn due east from this point" stretched "north, far north" of Toledo. Both Congress and the people of Ohio thought "that the new state of Ohio, would comprehend not only the territory in controversy, but a much larger tract of country lying north of it." As a result, "the intention of both...parties to this compact has been defeated by a mere mistake as to a single fact" of geography.

Rather than simply giving Toledo to Ohio, however, Congress worked out a compromise to make the decision more acceptable to Michigan. In return for relinquishing its claims to the disputed tract, Michigan could enter the Union and annex a sizable portion of the Upper Peninsula, a large tract of land that was situated on the south shore of Lake Superior and north of Michigan's Lower Peninsula. Initially, the *Free Press* reported the compromise was to become final after the "authorities of Michigan" gave their "assent" to the "altered boundaries." Some in Congress, however, insisted that Michigan's legislature lacked the authority to agree to such a change, because it altered Michigan's constitution. John Tipton, an Indiana Democrat, for instance, asserted that Congress could not "clothe the legislature of any state or territory with authority to alter or amend any portion of its constitution." Consequently, federal lawmakers amended the bill to require a "convention of delegates" elected by the people of Michigan to "assent" to the compromise, which President Jackson signed on June 15, 1836. In July, a special session of the Michigan legislature enacted a law enabling voters to elect delegates in September to a convention that was to assemble later that month in Ann Arbor and decide whether to "assent to" Congress's proposed compromise.[30]

The Convention of Dissent

Initially, both Democrats and Whigs denounced the settlement proposed by Congress. In March 1836, a Whig meeting in Detroit condemned Congress for "dismembering this territory" and manifesting "an extraordinary disregard of the dictates of wise policy." Michigan's Democratic Governor, Stevens T. Mason, expressed similar sentiments in July 1836, asserting federal lawmakers who awarded Toledo to Ohio had violated "every principle of justice" and had established a precedent that would "work evil of the utmost magnitude" to the nation's "civil institutions." Despite this criticism, Democrats eventually backed the compromise.[31]

In doing so, Democrats asserted that Michiganians could not hope to regain Toledo by rejecting the congressional compromise. A writer with the pseudonym "Common Sense" pointed out in a series of articles in the *Free Press* in August that Michiganians were not voting on whether to surrender the Toledo Strip to Ohio. The federal government already had told Michigan residents that they "must give up the disputed ground to Ohio." Congress did "not ask" Michigan residents "to assent to this surrender of territory." Michiganians, therefore, could not "expect to retain, against the laws and power of the United States, the disputed ground which those laws" had given to Ohio. No "enlightened man" could "anticipate any such result from a rejection of the proffered terms." Other Democrats reiterated this point, noting, in the words of the *Tecumseh Democrat*, that voting against the settlement "restores not the boundary and yields not the slightest glimmering of a hope of a future restoration."[32]

Instead, Democrats predicted that spurning the compromise could foster "anarchy," "bloodshed," and disorder. "Common Sense" forecasted "by their rejection, the people of Michigan would incur the odium…of a fruitless opposition to the laws of the Union." Rejecting the compromise might even encourage Michiganians to defy Washington in an effort "to maintain possession of the usurped portion of their soil." In this event, bloodshed would, in all likelihood, follow. In addition, "a deep stain would be inflicted" on republican institutions, and the "union of the states would be endangered." Similarly, the *Constantine Republican* prophesied, in an article reprinted in the *Free Press*, that rejecting the compromise would be "little short of political suicide" and could well lead to "anarchy, confusion, treason, and bloodshed." It was "humiliating and degrading" to lose Toledo, "but because our hair is scorched and our garments smell of fire, it would be extreme madness to plunge into a furnace."[33]

Democrats also reminded Michiganians of the benefits to be gained by agreeing to the compromise. "Common Sense" contended that the only chance Michiganians had of recovering the Toledo Strip was to approve the compromise and take their case to the Supreme Court. "As a state, we may possibly… be enabled to bring the subject" before the U.S. Supreme Court. If, however, Michiganians remained "out of the Union," they would not "be recognized by that court as a legitimate party" in any suit.[34] Democrats also emphasized the economic rewards that statehood would bestow upon Michiganians. The *Constantine Republican*, for instance, reminded its readers that once it entered the Union, Michigan would receive 5 percent of the revenue that the federal government earned from the sale of public land within its borders. A further inducement would be Michigan's share of the federal government's surplus revenue as well as the land it would obtain from Washington to construct public buildings, schools, and a university. This assistance, the *Free Press* predicted, would reduce taxes and increase immigration to Michigan. Democrats also argued that the Upper Peninsula might turn out to be quite valuable. The *Free Press* in August 1836 printed a letter from H. R. Schoolcraft, Michigan's Indian agent, who reported that although the Upper Peninsula had "little or no value" for farming, it might provide a rich source of minerals and other natural resources.[35]

Whigs, however, rejected these arguments, insisting that any loss of federal largesse would only be temporary. Writing in the *Detroit Journal* that August, "Amicus Republicae" doubted that Michigan would lose its share of surplus revenue from Washington. "Its reception may be retarded; we may be disappointed the present year, but we will eventually receive it." Even if rejecting the compromise meant losing federal revenue, however, the "highminded citizens of Michigan" were not "prepared to barter their birthright for a mess of pottage." Nor were they willing to agree to "their own dismemberment and humiliation for any sum which Congress might" offer. "Every patriot in Michigan, every citizen in whose veins flows the blood a free American will indignantly answer no."[36]

In addition, foes of the compromise denied that Congress had the authority to change Michigan's boundaries and asserted that by rejecting the settlement, Michiganians could cause federal lawmakers to reverse their decision. The *Michigan Sentinel* argued in June that, in giving Michiganians the power to veto their decision, Congress demonstrated that its resolution of the boundary dispute was not final. If Congress had given Michiganians no "redress but by force of arms," there would be no point in trying to retain Toledo. But federal lawmakers had "only" proposed to give Toledo to Ohio "with our consent." Michiganians, therefore, were not obliged "to sign [their own] death warrant," and anyone who did so "must be a traitor to our laws and institutions." Agreeing to the compromise, predicted the *Detroit Journal*, would make Congress's mistaken policy permanent, "forever" fixing Michigan's "boundaries to the inconvenient shape" that federal lawmakers had proposed. Even if federal lawmakers refused to restore Toledo to Michigan, voting against the compromise would probably induce them to reward the new state with land in the newly organized Wisconsin Territory that was more valuable than the Upper Peninsula.[37]

These arguments seem to have been persuasive. When voters went to the polls on September 12, 1836, most of the delegates they elected opposed the compromise. The *Free Press* reported in September that although returns were coming in slowly, it seemed certain that a "majority of the candidates supported by dissenters" had prevailed. Many dissenting delegates, however, were Democrats, and if enough of these delegates joined with their fellow party members, they would constitute "a decided majority in the convention." It still was possible, therefore, that the convention might give the "necessary assent" and permit Michigan to enter the Union.[38] Shortly after delegates assembled in Ann Arbor, however, these Democratic hopes were dashed. On September 27 delegates elected a "known dissenter" as president, and three days later the convention rejected the congressional settlement by a seven-vote margin.[39]

The Convention of Assent

After the Ann Arbor convention adjourned, Democrats began criticizing its decision to reject the compromise and calling for a second assembly that would agree to the terms that Congress had established for entering the Union. The *Free Press* in late September printed a letter from "A Gentleman at the West" who asserted that "darkness and gloom" pervaded Michigan's future and insisted that the convention's decision was not final because the "great body of the people" had "been deceived." They had voted for opponents of the compromise because they had been tricked into believing that Michiganians would "be received" into the Union "without opposition" and that they would "retain possession of the disputed territory by rejecting the terms proposed." Governor Mason echoed these sentiments, suggesting that the people might have been "represented by unfaithful agents" and "misled by the distorted representations of designing men."[40]

In late October, the Democratic Party of Wayne County recommended that a new convention be called and charged the delegates in Ann Arbor with acting wildly, contending that the actions of the Ann Arbor convention were "little short of nullification and incipient steps towards an illegal and violent resistance of the laws of the United States." The Wayne County Democrats also helped launch a campaign for a second convention that would agree to the terms offered by Congress. They expressed concern about the "spreading evils and dangers which a refusal to go into the Union" had "brought upon the people of Michigan" and urged other Democrats to convene meetings "in every county of the state" to call for "another convention" that would give the "assent required by Congress."[41]

Soon other Democrats followed the lead of their Wayne County compatriots and began calling for a new convention. The party made the elections for the state legislature that November into a referendum on the compromise, insisting that the overwhelming victory of "assenters" in those contests demonstrated that the people were behind them. The *Free Press* observed in December that the recent election indicated that a "large majority of the citizens of Michigan" were "dissatisfied with decision of the Ann Arbor Convention." Those opposing the compromise had nominated candidates to the Michigan Senate "in every district," and, "with but one solitary exception," they all had been defeated. Even worse, dissenters had elected only twelve of their candidates to Michigan's fifty-member House of Representatives. Democrats also reminded Michiganians of the federal funds and land that Ann Arbor delegates had relinquished by rejecting the compromise.[42]

Despite calls for a second convention, Governor Mason declined in November to convene the state legislature and pass another bill authorizing such an assembly. Nor, said Mason, did he possess the authority to "issue a proclamation recommending the election of delegates to another convention." Instead, the governor invited Michigan residents to "take the measure into their own hands" and, without state authorization, to elect delegates to a second convention. In making this case, he pointed to the example of Pennsylvania during the American Revolution, which relied on county committees to draft a constitution after breaking with Great Britain.[43]

Heeding Mason's advice, Michigan Democrats began organizing a second convention. They sent a circular to all the counties calling for delegates to be elected in early December and for a second convention to meet in Ann Arbor on December 14. The election for delegates took place in most, but not all, counties, and assenters won a huge victory. The second convention that assembled in Ann Arbor that December agreed to the compromise. Despite Whig protests that these proceedings were illegal, Congress approved, and President Jackson signed a bill on January 27, 1837, permitting Michigan to join the Union.[44]

SUMMARY

Michigan's effort to become a state thus demonstrates the faith that Michiganians placed in the Northwest Ordinance as a boundary-setting document that could establish the rule of law, limit the power of Congress, determine the proper balance of power between states, and tame the lawlessness and rapacity of local officials and their neighbors in Ohio. This reverence for the ordinance emerged in the first part of Michigan's four-phase campaign for self-rule. In the second decade of the nineteenth century, Michiganians accused territorial officials of violating the ordinance, which served as their constitution, and began clamoring for an elected assembly, which would end the spirit of "anarchy" and disorder in Michigan that arose from doubts about the legitimacy of laws that territorial government officials created. This campaign ended in 1823, after Congress granted white men in Michigan the right to elect their own legislature. The second, third, and fourth phases of this campaign for statehood took place in the 1830s, as Michigan officials sought entry into the Union and struggled with Ohio for control of Toledo.

In phases two and three, which occurred simultaneously, Michiganians asserted that the ordinance established boundaries that not only limited the power of Congress to shape new states but that also helped maintain a balance of power in the Old Northwest, preventing some states from becoming so large and powerful that they posed a threat to their neighbors. Phase two began when voters narrowly approved a resolution to apply for statehood in 1832 and Michiganians discovered the following year that Ohio would prevent them from joining the Union unless they relinquished their claims to Toledo. In their battle to retain the disputed land, Michigan officials repeatedly noted that the ordinance placed Toledo in Michigan. They also insisted that the ordinance was a constitution and that Congress, therefore, lacked the authority to change the boundaries that it established. Additionally, Michigan officials argued that Ohio's decision to take control of the Toledo Strip without federal approval indicated that it already had become one of those aggressive states that the drafters of the ordinance had feared.

Phase three involved two debates between Democrats and Whigs over the formation of a state government. In one, the two parties debated voting rights, with Democrats defending and Whigs opposing alien suffrage. In the second, Whigs and Democrats debated whether Michigan could form a state government without receiving enabling legislation from Congress. Democrats insisted that the ordinance established boundaries that limited Congress's authority to admit new states, contending that the document granted territories the right to become states once they contained 60,000 white men. Whigs, however, dismissed this argument, insisting that the U.S. Constitution superseded the ordinance and gave Congress the power to establish the terms on which new states could enter the Union.

The final step in Michigan's campaign to join the Union occurred in the second half of 1836, beginning in June when Congress hammered out a compromise that awarded the Toledo Strip to Ohio. In exchange, federal lawmakers gave Michiganians a sizable portion of the Upper Peninsula and agreed to let them enter the Union, if a convention elected by the people agreed to the conditions established by Congress. The compromise soon became the source of a heated debate, with Democrats supporting and Whigs opposing approval of the compromise. The Northwest Ordinance once again played a central role in these discussions, but now Democrats and Whigs reversed roles. Democrats, who had steadfastly defied Congress, suddenly urged Michiganians to accept the compromise, insisting that the only way Michiganians could retain Toledo was to become a state and take their case to the U.S. Supreme Court. Whigs, who had criticized Democrats for their states' rights position, invited Michiganians to defy federal authority, reiterating the notion that Congress lacked the authority to alter the boundaries established in the Northwest Ordinance. Initially, this view of the compromise prevailed, and in September 1836 a convention in Ann Arbor rejected the settlement offered by Congress. Over the next two months, however, the opinion of many Michiganians seems to have shifted. In December, a second convention, of questionable legality, assembled in Ann Arbor and agreed to the terms proposed by Congress. This acceptance ended Michigan's quest for statehood and established that Congress's power to admit new states and establish their borders took precedence over rights the Northwest Ordinance might have granted settlers.

NOTES

1. The material in this section comes from Willis F. Dunbar and George S. May, *Michigan: A History of the Wolverine State*, 3rd rev. ed. (Grand Rapids, MI: William B. Eerdmans Publishing Company, 1995), pp. 106–107; Alec Gilpin, *The Territory of Michigan, 1805–1837* (Lansing, MI: Michigan State University Press, 1970), pp. 4–6.

2. Gilpin, *The Territory of Michigan*, p. 74; Dunbar and May, *Michigan*, pp. 183–184.

3. Quotations are from the following issues of the *Detroit Gazette*: August 11, 1820, November 28, 1817, November 8, 1822, and December 5, 1817. Material on the change in Michigan's territorial government comes from Dunbar and May, *Michigan*, pp. 183–184.

4. Information is from Hon. Byron M. Cutcheon, "Fifty Years of Growth in Michigan, an Address Delivered in 1892 before the Michigan State Congregational Association," *Michigan Pioneer and Historical Collections* (Lansing, MI: Robert Smith & Co., 1894), 22:483; Dunbar and May, *Michigan*, pp. 163, 165.

5. Quotations come from the *Detroit Free Press*, September 8, 1831; the *Detroit Journal and Michigan Advertiser*, January 25, 1832.

6. *The Detroit Journal*, September 12, 1832.

7. Ibid., September 12, 1832, September 26, 1832, and January 25, 1832; the *Detroit Free Press*, August 16, 1832. Results of the referendum come from George N. Fuller, ed., *Messages of the Governors of Michigan* (Lansing, MI: The Michigan Historical Commission, 1925), pp. 91–92.

8. Peter S. Onuf, *Statehood and Union: A History of the Northwest Ordinance* (Bloomington: Indiana University Press, 1987), pp. 88–89; Dunbar and May, *Michigan*, pp. 187, 204–205, 211–213; Fuller, *Messages of the Governors of Michigan*, p. 115.

9. Background on the boundary dispute comes from Onuf, *Statehood and Union*, pp. 88–89; Dunbar and May, *Michigan*, pp. 204, 211–213.

10. *Detroit Free Press*, January 22, 1834, and April 23, 1834.

11. Background on the Toledo War comes from Gilpin, *The Territory of Michigan*, pp. 173–182; Dunbar and May, *Michigan*, p. 205; Frank E. Robson, "The Michigan and Ohio Boundary Line," *Michigan Historical Collections* (Lansing, MI: Wynkoop Hallenbeck Crawford Company, 1908), 11:223–224; *Michigan Sentinel*, March 17, 1835.

12. Robson, "The Michigan and Ohio Boundary," pp. 223–224; *Michigan Sentinel*, March 17, 1835.

13. Gilpin, *The Territory of Michigan*, pp. 177–178; Dunbar and May, *Michigan*, p. 214.

14. *Michigan Sentinel*, April 11, 1835.

15. *Detroit Free Press*, July 22, 1835; Dunbar and May, *Michigan*, p. 215; Gilpin, *The Territory of Michigan*, p. 181.

16. Gilpin, *The Territory of Michigan*, pp. 178–179.

17. Ibid.; Fuller, *Messages of the Governors of Michigan*, p. 151.

18. Fuller, *Messages of the Governors of Michigan*, p. 116; Henry M. Utley, Byron M. Cutcheon, and Clarence M. Burton, *Michigan as a Province, Territory and State, the Twenty-Sixth Member of the Federal Union* (New York: The Publishing Society of Michigan, 1906), p. 35; Gilpin, *The Territory of Michigan*, pp. 159, 181–182.

19. Onuf, *Statehood and Union*, pp. 89–90; Peter S. Onuf, *The Origins of the Federal Republic: Jurisdictional Controversies in the United States, 1775-1787* (Philadelphia: University of Pennsylvania Press, 1983), pp. 194–196.

20. Quotations come from the *Michigan Sentinel*, September 27, 1834; the *Detroit Free Press*, June 18, 1834.

21. The first quotation comes from Onuf, *Statehood and Union*, pp. 89–90; the other two quotations come from the *Detroit Journal*, April 12, 1836, and November 1, 1836.

22. *Michigan Sentinel*, July 11, 1835.

23. *Detroit Free Press*, December 24, 1834.

24. Quotations come from the *Detroit Free Press*, June 18, 1834; the *Michigan Sentinel*, July 11, 1835; the *Free Press*, February 18, 1835.

25. Quotations from Ohio Governor Lucas and Congressman Hamer come the *Michigan Sentinel*, March 7, 1835, and February 28, 1835.

26. Fuller, *Messages of the Governors*, pp. 125–126; *Detroit Free Press*, July 19, 1834.

27. Quotations come from Fuller, *Messages of the Governors*, p. 122.

28. Ronald P. Formisano, *The Birth of Mass Political Parties: Michigan, 1827-1861* (Princeton, NJ: Princeton University Press, 1971), pp. 80–84; *Detroit Journal*, January 14, 1835.

29. Quotations from Michigan's constitutional convention come from Harold M. Dorr, *The Michigan Constitutional Conventions of 1835-36: Debates and Proceeding s* (Ann Arbor: University of Michigan Press, 1940), pp. 30, 163, 164, 228, 229, 232,

246, 247; *Michigan Sentinel*, June 6, 1836; Dunbar and May, *History of the Wolverine State*, p. 207.

30. Quotations come from the *Free Press*, March 16, 1836, March 23, 1836, April 13, 1836; *Register of Debates in Congress*, p. 1010; Lawton T. Hemans, *The Life and Times of Stevens Thompson Mason* (Lansing: Michigan State Historical Commission, 1920), p. 199.

31. Fuller, *Messages of the Governors of Michigan*, p. 180; *Detroit Journal*, March 19, 1836.

32. *Detroit Free Press*, August 3, 1836, August 10, 1836, August 24, 1836.

33. Ibid., August 10, 1836, August 24, 1836.

34. Ibid., August 10, 1836.

35. Ibid., August 24, 1836, August 31, 1826, August 17, 1835.

36. Ibid., August 30, 1836.

37. *Michigan Sentinel*, June 25, 1836; *Detroit Journal*, August 23, 1836.

38. *Detroit Free Press*, September 21, 1836.

39. Gilpin, *The Territory of Michigan*, p. 191; Harold Dorr, *Michigan Constitutional Conventions*, pp. 543–544.

40. *Detroit Free Press*, September 28, 1836; Dorr, *Michigan Constitutional Conventions*, p. 569.

41. *Detroit Free Press*, November 2, 1836.

42. Ibid., December 17, 1836, November 9, 1836.

43. Dorr, *Michigan Constitutional Conventions*, pp. 568–571, 1835–1836.

44. Gilpin, *The Territory of Michigan*, p. 192.

BIBLIOGRAPHY

Dorr, Harold M. *The Michigan Constitutional Conventions of 1835-36: Debates and Proceedings*. Ann Arbor: University of Michigan Press, 1940.

Dunbar, Willis F., and George S. May. *Michigan: A History of the Wolverine State*. 3rd rev. ed. Grand Rapids, MI: William B. Eerdmans Publishing Company, 1995.

Formisano, Ronald P. *The Birth of Mass Political Parties: Michigan, 1827-1861*. Princeton, NJ: Princeton University Press, 1971.

Gilpin, Alec. *The Territory of Michigan, 1805-1837*. Lansing: Michigan State University Press, 1970.

Onuf, Peter S. *The Origins of the Federal Republic: Jurisdictional Controversies in the United States, 1775-1787*. Philadelphia: University of Pennsylvania Press, 1983.

———. *Statehood and Union: A History of the Northwest Ordinance*. Bloomington: Indiana University Press, 1987.

Utley, Henry M., Byron M. Cutcheon, and Clarence M. Burton. *Michigan as a Province, Territory and State, the Twenty-Sixth Member of the Federal Union*. New York: The Publishing Society of Michigan, 1906.

☆☆☆

THE STATE OF MINNESOTA

Admitted to the Union as a State: May 11, 1858

Jonathan Kasparek

INTRODUCTION

By the time of California's admission in 1850, incorporating territories into the Union had become a bitter sectional issue. California's admission as a free state required significant negotiation and compromise to overcome the opposition of slave states, whose leaders saw their political power waning. Only the maneuvering of Senators Henry Clay and Stephen A. Douglas secured its place in the Union. Their Compromise of 1850 infuriated many Northerners because it included a draconian fugitive slave law and left the territories acquired from Mexico open to slavery under the doctrine of popular sovereignty. Conflict between the North and South over the development of western territories only increased with the passage of the Kansas-Nebraska Act of 1854, which allowed slavery in the territory west of the Missouri River, and the crisis in Kansas Territory, in which two rival governments, one pro-slavery and one anti-slavery, were formed. Both of these events spurred the growth of the Republican Party, which began to challenge Democratic hegemony in the western states and territories.

Against this backdrop of sectional crisis and political turmoil, Congress admitted Minnesota to the Union in 1858. In the territory, competition between Democrats and Republicans produced fraudulent elections, a divided constitutional convention, and some doubt as to whether Minnesotans could actually govern themselves. The balance in the Union stood at fifteen slave and sixteen free states. Southern congressmen and senators were hostile toward the admission of another free state while Kansas's admission as a slave state was delayed. Although the Minnesota Territory developed quickly, its tumultuous transition to statehood jeopardized its admission to the Union.

Minnesota

Territorial Development:

- Great Britain cedes future Minnesotan territory to the United States through the Treaty of Paris, September 3, 1783
- The United States passes the Northwest Ordinance: territorial claims inherited from colonial charters ceded to the public domain, July 13, 1787
- The United States obtains more lands containing future Minnesotan territory from France through the Louisiana Purchase, April 30, 1803, and from Great Britain through the Joint-Occupancy Treaty, October 20, 1818
- Portions of the future Territory of Minnesota organized under the Louisiana Territory, 1804
- Reorganized as a part of the Indiana Territory, 1804; as a part of the Orleans Territory, 1805–1812; and as a part of the Missouri Territory, 1812–1821
- Becomes an unorganized territory, 1821–1834
- Organized as a part of the Michigan Territory, 1834–1836; reorganized as a part of the Wisconsin Territory, 1836–1849; reorganized as the Minnesota Territory, March 3, 1849
- Minnesota admitted into the Union as the thirty-second state, May 11, 1858

Territorial Capitals:

- Saint Paul, 1849–1858

State Capitals:

- Saint Paul, 1858–present

Origin of State Name: "Minnesota" is taken from a Dakota word, "mnishota," which means "cloudy" or "milky" water.

First Governor: Henry H. Sibley
Governmental Organization: Bicameral
Population at Statehood: 172,014
Geographical Size: 79,610 square miles

DEFINING BOUNDARIES

The Mississippi River gave the area that would become Minnesota almost mystical significance to Americans determined to find the source of the Father of Waters. This quest became the principal motivation for early exploration of the area. In 1805 the governor of Louisiana Territory, General James Wilkinson, authorized the first American military expedition to the region under the command of Lieutenant Zebulon Pike. Pike's orders were to travel up the Mississippi River to its source and ally the Native American tribes in the region to the United States. In September, Pike's party encamped at the mouth of the Minnesota River and held a council with the Lakota. Pike urged them to maintain peace with the Ojibwa tribe to the north and to abandon their trade with the British. He also negotiated a treaty securing two tracts of land for military posts. Moving north, he warned British traders to abandon their commerce with the Lakota and Ojibwa and encountered Leech Lake, which he mistakenly dubbed the main source of the Mississippi River. He returned to St. Louis in April 1806, but American presence in Minnesota remained virtually nonexistent.[1]

Pike's expedition, however, provided an important foothold for future exploration. In 1819, the army established Fort Snelling at the juncture of the Minnesota and Mississippi rivers as part of a national policy of increasing American military presence in the west following the War of 1812. A detachment of troops commanded by Lieutenant Colonel Henry Leavenworth arrived in August 1819, but the permanent structure of the fort was not begun until 1820, when Leavenworth was replaced by Colonel Josiah Snelling. The fort was completed in 1824 and, after passing inspection by Major General Winfield Scott, was renamed in honor of its commander in 1825. Fort Snelling marked American military presence and also spurred commercial and economic development of the area immediately surrounding it. The fur trade flourished under military supervision. More than two hundred acres of land were under cultivation by 1823. The fort even became the social and cultural center of the region; plays, dances, and martial entertainment were regular events.[2]

For the next decade, the area attracted explorers as harbingers of American settlement. In 1820, Michigan governor Lewis Cass led an expedition to the farthest reaches of his territory, setting out from Detroit and proceeding across Lake Superior to Cass Lake, which the governor regarded as the source of the Mississippi. A second expedition commanded by Major Stephen A. Long in 1823 traveled through the country via the Mississippi and Minnesota rivers to the Red River of the North into Canada. Additional expeditions explored the area, the most significant of which occurred in 1832 under the leadership of Henry Rowe Schoolcraft, a veteran of Cass's 1820 expedition. Schoolcraft at last ascertained the actual source of the Mississippi River, which he dubbed Lake Itasca, a clumsy combination of two Latin words, *veritas* and *caput*: "true head."[3]

Reasons for exploring Minnesota Country transcended scientific curiosity. The northern boundary remained unclear, in part because of geographic uncertainties. These expeditions did much to fix the boundary between Minnesota and Canada. The 1783 Treaty of Paris fixed the boundary between the United States and Canada as a water route between the intersection of the 45th parallel and the St. Lawrence River and the Lake of the Woods. This decision, however, was marred by a lack of geographic knowledge west of the Great Lakes. The best available map, drawn by Dr. John Mitchell in 1755, showed the Lake of the Woods draining into Lake Superior at what he dubbed "Long Lake." In reality, "Long Lake" was the mouth of the Pigeon River, which was unconnected to the Lake of the Woods. The western border of the United States was to be the Mississippi River, and the northern border was to be a line due west to the river from the Lake of the Woods. By the 1820s it was clear that such a line was a geographic impossibility, and in 1818 negotiations between Great Britain and the United States arrived at a seemingly simple solution: a line due south of the northwest point of the Lake of the Woods to the 49th parallel. This decision settled the question, but the United States gained possession of a bit of land known as the Northwest Angle that was separated from the rest of American territory by Buffalo Bay, a southwestern projection of Lake of the Woods. The boundary east of Lake of the Woods was not settled until 1842, when the Webster-Ashburton Treaty specified the boundary as the Rainy River between the lake and Lake Superior. Thus the first border of what would become Minnesota was settled.[4]

Civil government remained nominal throughout the 1830s and 1840s. The portion of Minnesota east of the Mississippi (approximately one-third of the present state) had been ceded to the United States by Great Britain in 1783. The territory west of the Mississippi was part of the Louisiana Purchase. The eastern portion, therefore, formed part of the territory governed by the Northwest Ordinance and administered as part of Indiana Territory from 1800 to 1809, part of Illinois Territory from 1809 to 1818, and part of Michigan Territory from 1818 to 1836. The western portion was part of Louisiana Territory from 1803 to 1812 and part of Missouri Territory from 1812 to 1821. After Missouri statehood, the area was "unorganized." The two portions of Minnesota were united and separated multiple times and were attached variously to the Territories of Michigan, Wisconsin, and Iowa.

ESTABLISHING THE TERRITORY

On August 6, 1846, President James K. Polk signed legislation authorizing the citizens of Wisconsin to write a constitution and form a state government. At this time, Wisconsin Territory included Minnesota East. The Wisconsin Enabling Act, however, defined the northwestern boundary of the future state as the St. Louis River to its rapids, then a line due south, the St. Croix River, and the Mississippi River. This decision had profound implications for the future Minnesota, because it left Minnesota East without any civil government whatsoever. A few months later, Wisconsin's congressional delegate, Morgan L. Martin, introduced a bill for the incorporation of this area into a new territory bounded by the St. Croix River on the east and the Red River of the North on the west. The House Committee on Territories changed its name from "Minasota" to "Itasca" before reporting the bill favorably to the House, which changed the name to "Minnesota" after considering "Chippewa," "Jackson," and "Washington." The House passed the bill on February 17, 1847, but it was tabled in the Senate on March 3. Senator William Woodbridge of Michigan led the opposition, arguing that the population of the proposed territory was too small, composed mostly of fur company employees at the head of Lake Superior. Furthermore, the area had not been surveyed, and the people themselves had not petitioned for a territorial government. Thus died Minnesota's first attempt to become a territory.[5]

That same day Congress, agreeing to the preference expressed in Wisconsin's first constitution, passed a law allowing Wisconsin to adjust its western boundary. The persons living in the St. Croix Valley wished to become part of Minnesota with a boundary at the Chippewa River, some eighty miles to the east. These residents of St. Croix County dreamed of a separate state to be united with the eastern portion of Minnesota Country, believing that the whole of the St. Croix Valley was too far removed from, and had different economic interests than, the residents of the centers of population in Wisconsin. The leader of this movement, William Holcombe, managed to secure from Congress acquiescence to a more easterly boundary. The Wisconsin constitution of 1846 specified the western boundary as a line south from the rapids of the St. Louis River to Lake Pepin, leaving the entire St. Croix River Valley out of the state. The defeat of the constitution of 1846, however, dashed the hopes of St. Croix dreamers and left the Wisconsin/Minnesota boundary uncertain.[6]

Citizens of Wisconsin confronted this boundary question again when a convention drafted another constitution in 1847, but the St. Croix separation movement was decisively rebuffed; instead, the convention adopted, and the people ratified, a constitution that included a western boundary at the Rum River, which included much of the settled areas of eastern Minnesota, including Fort Snelling. While Wisconsin struggled to draft a constitution, define boundaries, and apply for statehood, residents of the Minnesota Country again petitioned Congress for the creation of a separate territory. On February 3, 1848, Senator Stephen A. Douglas introduced a bill to create the "Territory of Minesota." Over the next few months, the bill was reported from and sent back to the Committee on Territories before coming to the floor of the Senate on August 8. Once again, the aspiring leaders of a new territory were disappointed when Congress adjourned before taking any action.[7]

Wisconsin was finally admitted as a state on May 29, 1848, with the boundaries first established by Congress in its 1846 Enabling Act. This measure gave renewed hope to the residents of the Minnesota Country. Their first two efforts to secure an organized territory had failed, and now both Minnesota West and Minnesota East were cast off from the states of Iowa and Wisconsin and left without government. That summer, eighteen men issued a call for a convention to be held in Stillwater on August 26. Sixty-two delegates attended and drafted memorials to President Polk and Congress demanding that residents of both sides of the Mississippi River be organized into a new territory and represented in Congress:

> Whereas, by the omission of Congress to organize a separate Territorial Government for the region of country which we inhabit, we are placed in the unparalleled position of being disfranchised of the rights and privileges which we were guaranteed to us under the Ordinance of 1787; and without any fault of our own, and with every desire to be governed by laws, are in fact without adequate legal protection for our lives or property.

The memorial to the president asserted that a population of "nearly 5,000 persons" was "without fault or blame of their own, virtually disfranchised."[8]

Henry Hastings Sibley delivered these memorials and acted as an unofficial delegate. Sibley had been born in Detroit in 1812. His Massachusetts-born father had been one of the early settlers in the Northwest and a member of the first Legislative Assembly of the Northwest Territory, later serving as delegate to Congress and Justice of the supreme court of Michigan. Sibley moved to Minnesota as an agent of the American Fur Company, continuing in that capacity even after the firm's 1842 bankruptcy until he was selected delegate to Congress.[9]

Promoters of the Minnesota Territory did not stop at merely urging congressional action. John Catlin, former secretary of Wisconsin Territory, suggested that the admission of Wisconsin as a state with reduced boundaries did not mean that the Territory of Wisconsin ceased to exist; rather, he suggested that the leftover portion of Wisconsin was still legally the Territory of Wisconsin. Moreover, because the former governor of Wisconsin Territory, Henry Dodge, had been elected U.S. senator from the State of Wisconsin, he himself was acting governor of the Territory of Wisconsin. He therefore saw no reason why he could not call a special election to elect a new delegate to replace the recently resigned delegate, John Tweedy. Catlin moved to Stillwater and issued a call for such an election to be held on October 30; the winner was Sibley. Sibley thereby went to Washington to represent the people of Minnesota as an informal delegate chosen at the Stillwater convention and as a formally elected delegate of the Territory of Wisconsin.[10]

Sibley arrived in Washington to attend the second session of the thirtieth Congress "convinced that my admission as delegate was extremely uncertain, in fact I may say absolutely improbable."[11] Sibley's claim was referred to the Committee on Elections, and on December 22 he testified before the committee. Congress, he argued persuasively, must surely not have meant to disfranchise thousands of citizens by depriving them of a functional territorial government when it admitted the State of Wisconsin. The committee reported the matter favorably, and on January 15, 1849, the House voted 124-63 to admit him as the territorial delegate from Wisconsin. The House did, however, by a vote of 76-35, refuse to appropriate $10,500 for territorial officers. The entire incident brought into question Congress's policy toward territorial development and raised questions about what happened to territorial remnants left by new states and whether funding civil government was de facto organic legislation. One member argued convincingly that when Wisconsin was admitted to statehood, the territory ceased to exist, even though the house had seated Sibley as delegate from this now nonexistent territory.[12]

Shortly after he took his seat, Senator Douglas again introduced a bill to the Senate creating Minnesota Territory. Here Sibley's influence was critical. He persuaded Douglas to amend the bill to make St. Paul the capital and to set aside not one, but two sections of public land in every township for schools, a precedent recently set when Oregon Territory was established. The only objection raised on the floor of the Senate was that the proposed territory would be too sparsely settled for civil government; in response, Douglas noted that similar provisions had been made for Iowa, which had a smaller population. When Douglas assured his colleagues that the population was "now somewhere between eight and ten thousand people," the Senate passed the bill on January 19.[13]

The political situation in the House of Representatives, however, threatened passage of the Minnesota bill. A small Whig majority was determined to postpone the bill until after March 4, when Zachary Taylor would take office, to forestall Democratic President James K. Polk from appointing Democrats to important territorial positions. The bill was reported from committee on February 8, and on February 22 Sibley used some astute parliamentary maneuvering to bring the bill to the floor. The committee had added twelve amendments to the bill, all of which were quickly disposed. One amendment, however, reflected the Whig determination to secure the territorial spoils. The wording of the Senate bill included the customary provision that "this act shall take effect upon its passage." The committee changed it so that the bill would take effect on March 10, 1849, when Taylor would be in office. The House disagreed to this amendment by a vote of 97-101, but an identical amendment was offered from the floor and passed 99-95, and the bill passed as well. Because his sole motivation was in passing the bill, Sibley was content with this political chicanery, but opposition arose in the Senate, which refused to concur in the amendment. Once again it seemed that creation of Minnesota Territory would be delayed.[14]

At this point Douglas intervened. A bill to establish the Department of the Interior, which would have created a vast number of positions to be filled by

President Taylor, was pending before the Senate. Douglas had Sibley report to the opponents of the Minnesota bill in the House that unless the House abandoned its amendment, the Senate would kill the Interior bill. Douglas's bluff worked, and on the last day of the session, Sibley moved that the House concur in the Senate version of the Minnesota bill, which was voted in the affirmative, 107-70.[15] On April 9, 1849, word reached the settlers at Lake Pepin of the creation of Minnesota Territory despite inter-party feuding and by urging from a delegate from a territory that did not actually exist.[16]

The Minnesota Organic Act closely followed earlier precedents. The land area included in the new territory was much larger than would eventually be included in the state. Minnesota Territory was bounded by Wisconsin on the east, Iowa on the south, and Canada on the north. Its western boundary was formed by the White Earth River (in present North Dakota), the Missouri River, and the Sioux River (the present western border of Iowa). The governor, secretary, marshal, attorney, and supreme court justices were appointed by the president with the advice and consent of the Senate. The legislature was elective with a council and house of representatives. All laws had to be submitted to Congress and would be valid unless specifically rejected. The laws of Wisconsin Territory, which had applied to approximately one-fourth of the new territory that lay east of the Mississippi, were applied to the entire territory.[17]

Despite the Whigs' eagerness to use the new offices of Minnesota Territory for political rewards, President Taylor at first had a difficult time finding a governor. After three others refused the office, Taylor offered it to Alexander Ramsey of Pennsylvania. Ramsey, then thirty-four years old, had been born near Harrisburg, Pennsylvania, educated at Lafayette College, and served in the U.S. House of Representatives from 1843 to 1847. He was not a great public speaker, but he cut an imposing figure nonetheless, shrewd but good-humored.[18] On the June 1, 1849, Governor Ramsey declared the territory organized. The other territorial officers had been chosen by the president: Charles K. Smith of Ohio as territorial secretary; Joshua Taylor as marshal; Henry L. Moss as attorney; Aaron Goodrich of Tennessee as chief justice; and Bradley B. Meeker of Kentucky and David Cooper of Pennsylvania as associate justices. Judicial circuits were established ten days later, and on July 7 Ramsey apportioned council districts and ordered the election of councilors, representatives, and a delegate to Congress. On August 1, Minnesotans elected their first territorial legislature and re-elected Sibley to Congress, rewarding him for his service and finally giving him an actual political entity to represent.[19]

On September 3, 1849, the first Legislative Assembly convened in the "Central House," a building in St. Paul that served as both hotel and capitol. Ramsey perhaps exceeded expectations in his address and spoke of a grand future for the territory, which, he reminded the legislators, was 166,000 square miles. In typical frontier fashion, he urged the legislature to memorialize Congress to acquire quickly the vast lands owned by the Lakota to make available the land that he predicted would be "peopled with a rapidity exceeding anything in the history of western colonization." He also urged internal improvements to facilitate transportation and restrictions on land speculation. Minnesota was a land of the future. Informality was the hallmark of the assembly, but the first session was productive. The Legislative Assembly created nine counties, recommended a territorial seal, incorporated the Minnesota Historical Society, and established a system of common schools.[20]

The second Legislative Assembly convened on January 1, 1851, and was quickly made rancorous by political developments both local and national. The major questions to be decided were the locations of the capital and the prison. The Organic Act specified St. Paul as the temporary capital, and some members attempted to relocate it. Eventually a bill to locate the capital permanently at St. Paul received enough support when a provision to establish the prison at Stillwater was attached. Soon thereafter another major boon was dispensed when the university was chartered and located at St. Anthony. More significant was the revision of the laws of Wisconsin Territory still in force. Three lawyers were brought in to assist a joint committee in its work, but the entire legislature, composed largely of fur traders and lumbermen, made numerous alterations on the floor. Charters were granted liberally, often to companies in which the legislators held some financial interest.[21]

NATIVE AMERICAN AFFAIRS

Governor Ramsey envisioned rapid growth for the territory, but white settlement depended on the federal government's acquiring title to the land owned by the Lakota and Ojibwa tribes. In 1837, the government secured a triangular-shaped piece of land between the Mississippi and St. Croix rivers, but no additional land had been acquired. In 1847, the Ojibwa ceded another parcel of land west of the Mississippi, just less than half the size of the 1837 cession, for a reservation for the Ho-Chunk (or Winnebago) tribe who were being moved west from their Wisconsin homeland. This land was later exchanged for another reservation along the upper Missouri River and was opened to settlement after statehood. That most of the territory was still owned by the Lakota and Ojibwa nations was not lost on the governor nor on members of the legislature, all of whom foresaw a rapid influx of white settlers if only the land were available. In his first message to the legislature, Ramsey urged that body to memorialize Congress for treaty negotiations with the Lakota, and delegate Sibley convinced the Commissioner of Indian Affairs, Orlando Brown, that negotiations were urgent. Traders representing fur companies also anxiously looked to treaties ceding the land, because treaties entailed cash payments that the traders could claim against accumulated inflated debt owed them by individual Indians.[22]

Secretary of the Interior Thomas Ewing immediately appointed Ramsey (*ex officio* superintendent of Indian affairs) and John Chambers, former governor of

Iowa, to conduct negotiations to obtain as much Lakota territory between the Mississippi and the Big Sioux and Wild Rice rivers as they could at a price of no more than two and one-half cents per acre. Payments, both lump sums and annuities, were to be primarily in goods rather than in cash. Attempts to begin negotiations in 1849 failed when most bands of Lakota refused to attend them.[23]

Beginning in December 1849, Sibley made a second attempt to initiate negotiations to occur in 1850, but Congress made no appropriation for a general cession, and the president did not appoint treaty commissioners to carry out the task. In the summer of 1851, President Fillmore appointed Luke Lea, commissioner of Indian affairs, and Ramsey to negotiate a treaty with the Lakota. The commissioners and their party arrived at Traverse des Sioux on June 29, 1851, and within a few days several hundred Lakota had gathered. After extensive negotiations, those present agreed to the terms presented by the commissioners. Under the terms of the Treaty of Traverse des Sioux, the Lakota bands ceded to the United States their land lying east of the Red River, Lake Traverse, and the Big Sioux River, a total of about 24 million acres (19 million in Minnesota, 3 million in Iowa, and about 2 million in South Dakota). The Lakota retained a reservation stretching ten miles wide on each side of the Minnesota River from Lake Traverse to the Yellow Medicine River. For this empire, the United States agreed to pay $1,665,000, most of which was set in trust with annual interest payments in cash and supplies. A group of traders attending the treaty council secured the approval of another document in which the Lakota promised to pay debts to traders. As a result, the traders came away with most of the money. A second treaty with the lower bands of Lakota was negotiated at Mendota in July and August. These bands also gave up their claims to the "Suland," but with a reservation along the Minnesota River from the Yellow Medicine River to the Little Rock River. The U.S. Senate approved both treaties in June 1852 with an amendment, subsequently approved by the Lakota, which removed the reservation provision and empowered the president to select reservation land.[24]

With the "Suland" purchased, Ramsey immediately traveled north to begin negotiations with the Pembina and Red Lake bands of Ojibwa for cession of the Red River country. Ramsey easily reached a treaty whereby these bands ceded 5 million acres at about five cents an acre. The Senate, however, refused to approve this treaty. Frustrated, Ramsey continued his efforts to negotiate purchase of the northern portion of Minnesota, rich in timber and ore and with fertile agricultural land to the west. Treaties in 1854 and 1855 ceded to the United States a swath of territory stretching from the Red River to Lake Superior. A treaty negotiated at La Pointe, Wisconsin, with the Lake Superior Ojibwa ceded the triangular "arrowhead" region. A second treaty negotiated in Washington with the Mississippi Ojibwa ceded another vast stretch of land around the headwaters of the Mississippi River, stretching west to the Red River.

In exchange the Ojibwa received reservations at Sandy Lake, Mille Lacs, Cass Lake, Leech Lake, and elsewhere, as well as annuities. The Red River area was finally obtained in 1863, and additional parcels of land were acquired in 1866 and 1889, the year in which Native American land titles were finally extinguished in Minnesota.

AMERICAN SETTLEMENT

The land cessions by the Lakota and Ojibwa opened the way for American settlement. An act of Congress in 1854 granting Minnesota settlers preemption rights on unsurveyed tracts of public land hastened settlement and the filing of land claims. By the time the Panic of 1857 cooled frontier land purchases, there were eight land offices in the territory. Between 1854 and 1857 over 5.25 million acres of public land had been sold. By 1860, one year after statehood, the census revealed a total population of 172,023. Of these, more than 113,000 were native-born and were part of the great westward migration that began in New England in the 1820s. Forty thousand people came from either New England or New York. Minnesota's population in 1860 was about 30 percent foreign-born. More than 18,000 had migrated from the German-speaking states of Europe, and another 12,800 from Ireland. Smaller numbers came from Norway, Canada, Sweden, Switzerland, and Wales.[25]

Beyond mere numbers of people, Minnesota Territory developed other hallmarks of a settled country. On April 28, 1849, the first newspaper, the *Minnesota Pioneer*, was published in St. Paul by New England native James Madison Goodhue. Goodhue's paper was only one of eighty-nine published during the territorial period but was certainly the best. All vigorously promoted the territory and glorified its natural beauty and dramatic future. Ramsey referred to these newspapers as the "day-books of history," and he served as the first president of the Minnesota Historical Society, chartered by the legislature in 1849. Such was the interest in the history of the young Territory that the secretary of the Society published the first history of Minnesota that went through five editions within twenty-five years.[26]

Transportation, too, was critical to settlement and to fulfillment of Minnesotans' determination to bring civilization to the frontier. At first, transportation was almost exclusively on foot or in canoe. By the 1850s the upper Mississippi hosted regular steamboat traffic, and when Lake Pepin was clear of ice, enthusiastic throngs welcomed the boats to the docks of St. Paul. After the Lakota ceded their territory, the Minnesota River became a major artery for steamboat traffic. Nearly four hundred arrivals from the river occurred at St. Paul by 1858. Even the windy Red River of the North carried steamboats by the late 1850s. Despite this advance in steamboat transportation, the most critical territorial infrastructure was roads. Congress authorized military roads connecting St. Paul to various points west and north. The territorial legislature also authorized a network of roads in southern Minnesota. Stagecoaches carried well-to-do passengers and the mail. Immigrants arrived in bumpy, ox-drawn wagons.[27]

However primitive the transportation network was during territorial days, it did convey settlers to the interior. By 1859, more than 500,000 acres were in cultivation with a total of some 18,000 farms. Subsistence farming began to give way to export by the 1850s. Boats that brought passengers to St. Paul and points north usually returned with loads of wheat and barley. In 1859 Minnesota produced nearly three million bushels of corn and just over two million bushels each of wheat and oats.[28]

POLITICAL LIFE

Politics in territorial Minnesota came into being during the calamitous 1850s, when political discourse ran hot over issues of slavery and states' rights. As congressional delegate, Henry Sibley was the most visible official and the only one elected by the whole territory. His position in Congress was both secure and untenable: reelected continuously, but without a vote, he could only make requests. Much depended on his personality and force of character. When reprimanded to keep silent except on matters that directly affected Minnesota, he responded that Minnesota, even if not a state, was part of the nation, and he had the right to be heard. No one has since challenged a territorial delegate's ability or duty to speak. Ultimately Sibley procured nearly $300,000 of federal money for the territory.[29]

Although closely allied with Stephen Douglas of Illinois, Sibley tried to remain aloof from political parties. In 1850, he ran for reelection but without party affiliation. His opponents, however, were quick to organize behind Colonel Alexander M. Mitchell, the territorial marshal, who ran as a Whig. Democrats unwilling to abandon their affiliation and back Sibley tarried and eventually nominated David Olmsted, who withdrew a week before the election. A hot and rancorous campaign ensued with surprising results: Sibley was reelected, but by a majority of only ninety votes. In 1853, Sibley declined to run again, and the contest pitted Democrat Henry M. Rice against Whig Alexander Wilkin. This time, the Democratic candidate won a thumping majority of more than 1,400 votes. This abrupt switch in political leanings indicated that change was in the air.[30]

The sectional animosities created by the Mexican War and the Compromise of 1850 had profound political implications for Minnesota and for the whole of the Northwest. The Kansas-Nebraska Act, allowing slavery in the western territories as far north as the Canadian border under the doctrine of popular sovereignty, spurred free-soil Northerners to action. In Michigan, Wisconsin, and other western states, new parties organized to oppose the extension of slavery into the territories and adopted the name "Republican." The first of these meetings to take place in Minnesota occurred on March 29, 1855, when some two hundred men gathered at St. Anthony and issued a call for a territorial convention, which met on July 25 in St. Paul. The convention denounced the Kansas-Nebraska Act and the Fugitive Slave Law, endorsed internal improvements for rivers and harbors, and came out in favor of prohibition, thus combining elements of the old Free-Soil, Whig, and Know-Nothing parties. The Republicans nominated William Rainey Marshall for territorial delegate.

In the meantime, the Democratic Party was divided between supporters of Rice and Sibley. The party convention, held in St. Paul on July 25, 1855, nominated Rice, but a large minority bolted and nominated David Olmsted. In this three-way race, Rice won with a plurality, probably due in no small part to the prohibitionist platform of the Republicans, which alienated German and Irish immigrants.[31]

The change in national administration with the election of Franklin Pierce in 1852 brought changes to Minnesota politics as well. Many lobbied Pierce to appoint Sibley to the governorship. He was an obvious choice, well respected in Congress and at home, but a large portion of Minnesota Democrats opposed him. Rather than increase intra-party strife, Pierce nominated an outsider, former Congressman William A. Gorman of Indiana, in 1853. Whig officials were swept aside, and Democrats were placed in territorial offices.[32]

TOWARD STATEHOOD

The rapid settlement of Minnesota Territory boded well for early admission to the Union. After the railroad reached Rock Island, immigration increased quickly, and during 1855 some 50,000 people entered the territory. By 1857, territorial leaders and public sentiment favored quick statehood. In Congress, too, there was support for Minnesota statehood driven by financial reasons. The expenses of the territorial legislature and the courts regularly exceeded congressional appropriations, and territorial officials continued to draw their salaries even when outside of the territory. In 1856, during debate on the Minnesota appropriation bill, one congressman said in committee that he desired "to give a gentle hint to the delegate from Minnesota Territory, that with a population of one hundred and fifty thousand or one hundred and sixty thousand, it is time that the territory should make application to come into the Union as a state, and pay its own expenses."[33]

One of the first issues to be decided before statehood was the division of the territory. In 1856, Minnesota Territory extended west to the Missouri and White Earth rivers, making an area of about 166,000 square miles, or roughly twice the size of the present state. Such a large state would never be admitted. Northern politicians wanted to create as many free states as possible to maintain parity with slave states, and such a large state would also be out of proportion to its neighbors. Wisconsin was approximately 54,000 square miles in area, Iowa was 56,000, and Illinois was 56,000. Clearly Minnesota had to be split in half, but where to divide it?

In 1856, some Democratic leaders, including Governor Gorman, hatched a plan to divide the territory along an east-west line around 45° north latitude. Behind this idea was a growing sectional rift between the old settled area between the St. Croix and Mississippi rivers, which maintained the largest population and the important territorial facilities, and the rapidly growing southern counties, which were isolated from the capital for several months of the year and had considerably less political power. Such a memorial was introduced into the territorial legislature that year, requesting Congress to divide Minnesota at 45°10' north latitude, thus creating a northern and southern territory and greatly diminishing St. Paul's influence. In the end, the Rice-dominated St. Paul faction of the Democratic Party maintained control and defeated efforts to divide the territory. A proposal to hold a referendum on statehood also failed.[34]

The 1856 session did, however, spur politicians to action. On Christmas Eve 1856, Delegate Rice introduced an Enabling Act in the House of Representatives. His bill specified a western boundary for the new state along the Red River of the North, Lake Traverse, and the Big Sioux River, thus depriving southern Minnesotans of their desire for increased political autonomy. Rice did include a measure to encourage their support: a railroad land-grant bill for five railroad lines, one of which was centered at Winona. Rice's actions were well planned. His bill created a state that would not be merely agricultural and dependent on an outside commercial and industrial center, but rather a state that encompassed farming areas, a vast timber region, and a future mining area in the northeast. The entire state would be centered on the St. Paul area, its political and economic capital as well as the state transportation hub.

The Enabling Bill was immediately referred to the House Committee on Territories, which made a minor adjustment to the boundaries. The western boundary was altered to run from the foot of Lake Traverse through Big Stone Lake and then due south to the Iowa boundary, rather than along the Big Sioux River. The committee also included a provision, omitted by Rice, providing for concurrent jurisdiction of boundary waters with other states, a convention that originated in the Northwest Ordinance. Representative Galusha Grow of Pennsylvania reported the bill back to the House on January 31. At this point, sectional animosity overtook the proceedings, because Southerners opposed the bill that created another free state. John S. Phelps of Missouri mocked Grow's and other Northerners' willingness to violate the Northwest Ordinance and create a sixth state out of the Old Northwest. To this, Grow retorted that "no one proposes to make any more, but only to take a gore of land left outside of all the organized states, and incorporate it with other territory never under the Ordinance of 1787." The bill was approved 90-75.[35]

The Minnesota Enabling Act had a much more difficult time in the Senate. Although Stephen Douglas's Committee on Territories reported the bill without amendment, the debate was hot when the bill came to the floor on February 21. Senator Asa Biggs of North Carolina assailed Minnesota's liberal suffrage provisions, which allowed non-citizens to vote. Douglas reported that the Minnesota Organic Act had allowed the legislature to set voting qualifications and the Enabling Act merely continued this precedent. The legislature had provided that aliens who had resided in the territory for two years and had declared their intention to become citizens were allowed to vote. An amendment was proposed to restrict voting for delegates and statehood to citizens, which was adopted 27-24. All but three senators in favor of the amendment were from the South. It seems that Southern senators used the suffrage provisions as a means of forming an alliance with northern Know-Nothings to defeat the bill.[36]

With only a few days left in the congressional session, Rice had to lobby assiduously to reconcile the two bills. On February 24, Senator John P. Hale successfully moved reconsideration, and two days of intense debate occurred, again on the subject of alien suffrage. John B. Thompson of Kentucky and John Bell of Tennessee both argued that citizenship was a congressional matter and refused to allow any state to undermine congressional authority. Reconsideration of the bill passed by a vote of 35-21, the suffrage amendment was rejected, and the bill passed by a vote of 31-22. The debate was ostensibly on the suffrage provisions, but the sectional conflict was not far below the surface. One southern senator remarked that he opposed the bill because it would skew the balance of free and slave states, and many of his southern colleagues undoubtedly shared this view.[37] President Buchanan signed the Enabling Act on February 26 and the Railroad Grant on March 3.[38]

The Enabling Act called for the election of delegates to frame a constitution and authorized, subject to congressional approval, the formation of a state government. As a financial incentive, Congress made several grants of land: two sections in each township for schools, seventy-two for the state university, ten to fund state buildings, up to twelve "salt springs," and 5 percent of the proceeds from sales of public land in the state. This was the most generous package of grants yet made to a new state. The act called on the voters of Minnesota to elect two delegates from each legislative district to meet on July 13 to vote on whether to seek admission to the Union and, if so, to frame a constitution.[39]

At the same time that Congress debated the Enabling Bill, the territorial legislature convened in January 1857. By now, sentiment had shifted decisively toward statehood. In his address, Governor Gorman made a strong case for admission to the Union. First, he outlined the financial advantages that would come with statehood. The annual congressional appropriation was only $30,000, a sum that could easily be raised by a property tax of ten cents on every $100 of property. Congressional appropriations were made grudgingly and encouraged waste, he declared, and the government would mind its pocketbook more closely if it raised its own funds from taxpayers. Second, he foresaw vast federal land grants that would aid in the development of the state. These lands now lay idle, but once Minnesota became a state, they could be used to finance schools and internal improvements. Finally, Gorman reminded the legislators of the political principle at stake: people would be able to elect their own officials and send a full delegation to Congress, where Minnesota would at last have a full say over the issues of the day, most important of which was the location of a railroad to the Pacific.[40]

Gorman's abrupt turnabout—a year earlier he had urged delay—resulted from Rice's bill. Gorman had favored an east-west division of the territory, and he wanted to act fast to procure a dividing line that ran in that direction. The legislature sent memorials to Congress demanding the right of the convention to define Minnesota's boundaries, and some in Winona had petitioned Congress for an east-west division. Rice, however, had the upper hand, and his bill dashed the hopes of the southern counties. Southern Minnesotans received another defeat when a measure to relocate the capital to St. Peter, to the south of St. Paul, was signed by Gorman but was overturned by the Supreme Court, which decided that the bill had not been properly passed by the council.

Governor Gorman left Minnesota after the legislature adjourned in February, apparently unaware of the exact provisions of the Enabling Act or of Congress's refusal to appropriate enough money for the territorial courts. Upon learning of the congressional action, he called for a special session of the legislature on March 16, 1857, even though the Organic Act did not give him authority to do so and, in fact, specified that the governor's duties devolved upon the territorial secretary when the governor was out of the territory. Under his call, the legislature was to convene on April 27 to deal with the lack of congressional funding for the courts, arrange for the constitutional convention, and dispose of the lands under the terms of the railroad land grant. When the legislature convened, it took several weeks to pass a bill conferring the federal lands on four corporations. The provision for the convention was more troublesome because of some vague wording in the Enabling Act. The act called for "two delegates for each representative," which strictly read meant a total of seventy-eight, or twice the number of seats in the territorial House of Representatives. In the council, however, a committee decided that "representative" was a generic term and that the act required two delegates for every representative and two delegates for every councilor, making a total of 108 delegates. The Democratic majority in the council believed that increasing the number of delegates would increase the number of Democrats elected to the convention. This advantage was most likely offset by an amendment added by the Republican House, which disqualified holders of federal appointments or commissions, thereby eliminating some of the territory's leading Democrats. This provision did not affect Gorman, whose term had expired. Governor

Samuel Medary, appointed by President Buchanan to replace Gorman, signed the bill on May 25, just one week before elections were to be held. Thus, some argued, an illegal meeting of the legislature called by a governor without authority had now passed a bill that was itself invalid because it contradicted the apparent provisions of the congressional act.[41]

Further conflict occurred over the legislative apportionment that dictated House and council districts. The election was carried out under the 1855 apportionment even though a significant shift in population had since occurred. The southern counties had become the most populous portion of the territory and were strongly Republican. Furthermore a Democratic district, Pembina County, had been cut in half, with most of its population west of the proposed state boundary, but it retained its old apportionment of one councilor and two representatives. As a result, the Democrats went into the convention elections with a distinct advantage. Based on a federal census carried out in 1857, the Democratic districts contained an approximate population of 49,600 and elected fifty-six delegates; the Republican districts contained a population of approximately 90,000 but elected only fifty-two delegates. A more representative distribution would have been thirty-eight delegates from the Democratic districts and seventy for Republican districts.[42]

Both Democrats, badly divided, and Republicans, only recently organized, scrambled to nominate candidates and campaign. Little public debate accompanied the rush to election, both parties apparently emphasizing the need to win Minnesota for their own camp. Voter turnout throughout the territory was light; only half the legal voters participated according to the *St. Paul Pioneer and Democrat*. Irregularities abounded, and both sides charged fraud. Some counties were tortuously divided among "council candidates" and "house candidates," and some communities abandoned party labels altogether and nominated "citizen tickets" composed of locals from both parties. In other counties, local officials awarded certificates of election to candidates who had lost their race. The vote totals were unclear, but the Democrats claimed to have won a majority of 1,600, resulting in part from the heavy turnout in large towns and relatively light turnout in agricultural areas. Despite Democratic advantages, the Republicans succeeded in electing more delegates, although the final count remained clouded in controversy.

With the delegates to the convention closely divided between Republicans and Democrats and several seats disputed, both sides prepared for a battle to gain control over the proceedings.[43] Anticipating continued shenanigans from the Democrats, Republican delegates began arriving in St. Paul several days before the convention was to meet and held a caucus on July 11. Democratic delegates arrived more slowly, but a sufficient number had arrived by July 12 to begin negotiations with their Republican counterparts. The Democrats were fewer in number but included some of the most experienced politicians in the territory, including former Governor Gorman and former Delegate Sibley. They used their greater knowledge of political processes in an attempt to wrest control of the convention from the Republicans. When the Republican caucus proposed calling the convention to order at noon on July 13, Democrats delayed before cryptically responding that they would "meet at the usual hour for the assembling of parliamentary bodies in the United States." Because most of the Republicans were inexperienced with government, this vague reply alarmed them—was there indeed a "usual hour," or were the Democrats trying to manipulate the Republicans into arriving late and organizing the convention to their own advantage? To forestall the Democrats' getting a head start and organizing the convention, Republican delegates camped out in the council chamber of the capitol all night, expecting the Democrats to arrive at any moment.

Even stranger to the Republicans was the situation they confronted the next morning as they awaited the Democrats' arrival in the House chamber. The Democrats failed to appear until just before noon, when forty-five delegates entered, led by Territorial Secretary Charles L. Chase, who quickly mounted the speaker's platform and called the convention to order. The Republican leader scurried to the platform and did likewise, quickly nominating Thomas Galbraith as president pro tem. At the same time, Chase called the question on a motion made by former Governor Gorman to adjourn until noon the next day. All the Democrats (and some confused Republicans) voted to adjourn and marched from the hall, leaving the Republicans to carry out their own organization, swearing in fifty-six members and taking up business. The next day at noon, the Democrats returned to the House chamber and demanded it be turned over to the territorial convention. Those within the chamber refused, and Gorman thereupon led the Democrats to the council chamber and proceeded to organize a separate convention. For six weeks, the Minnesota constitutional convention never sat as one body—Republicans and Democrats met separately, each refusing to recognize the other's legitimacy.

The Republican convention had begun business immediately on July 13 and appointed committees to draft portions of the constitution. The proceedings reflected a group of intelligent people all wanting to express their opinion on matters, but they were not well organized. There were too many Committees with somewhat overlapping assignments. Much work was done in the Committee of the Whole, where committee reports were often rewritten extensively. At first aiming to write a brief constitution, the Republicans ended up drafting one that included far too many detailed descriptions of the intricacies of government instead of leaving minutia to the legislature.

The Democrats were slower in getting underway, mainly because they had only fifty-four members, short of the number needed to claim a legitimate majority. Not until the ninth day did the Committee on Credentials report firmly on fifty-four delegates and reported "unofficial evidence" toward a fifty-fifth. Even though this last delegate did not arrive until August 11, the Democratic body proceeded to claim a majority and acted as if it were the sole constitutional convention, denouncing the Republicans as "without the authority of law or of parliamentary usage." Because many of the Democratic delegates were better versed in governance, their work was done in committees that were fewer in number, smaller in membership, and with clearly defined authority. Proceedings as Committee of the Whole were considerably briefer and better led than those of the Republicans.

At first both parties were smug with what they had done and confident in eventual vindication. The eastern press, however, ridiculed the convention, and some predicted another "Bleeding Kansas." Would rival factions adopt separate constitutions? Would Congress have to choose between them? Some of the more responsible leaders realized that the reputation and commercial credit of the territory were at stake and began to suggest compromise. On August 8, the Democrats considered a resolution calling for a joint committee of five from each party to plan for a single constitution. Hotter heads prevailed, and the Democrats rejected the motion 23-19. Two days later, however, the Republicans adopted a nearly identical proposal unanimously. Flummoxed, the Democrats refused to accept a proposal they had themselves rejected, and the Republicans refused to enter into the behind-the-scenes negotiations proposed by the Democrats.

Finally, on August 18 Democrats relented, and a conference committee composed of five delegates from each party began piecing together a single constitution from the Republican and Democratic versions. Each day the committee received engrossed reports from the two conventions on various articles. Working from the two versions, they harmonized conflicting proposals, occasionally rejecting the less workable version. Sometimes the committee reworked whole sections or omitted ideas altogether. For a week, all went smoothly. But on August 24 the committee encountered what threatened to be an impasse, for a moment abandoned the task of forming one constitution, and began considering ways to submit two different versions to the people. The issue was African American suffrage. Republicans proposed submitting to the people the constitution and the question of voting rights for African Americans at the same time. Democrats opposed the idea. After several days of frustrating debate and a physical encounter in which Gorman broke his cane over the head of a Republican delegate, a compromise was reached whereby the legislature could, in the future, extend suffrage, provided that the people ratified its actions in a referendum.

A second issue that caused much bitterness was the provision for creating electoral districts. Republicans, still angry at their lack of proportionate representation, proposed a plan that would change the apportionment to their own benefit, to secure both a majority in the legislature and at least two congressional seats. The Democrats likewise developed a scheme to ensure their control of the legislature, the judiciary, and the congressional delegation. In the end, the committee's version of the constitution favored the Democrats. The Democrats won a major victory by calling for three congressmen to be elected at-large. Believing they had a majority in the territory, they preferred this plan to the Republicans' two-district plan, which would have probably given one seat in the House to each party. The legislative apportionment also gave a slight edge to the Democrats. The committee in addition created six judicial circuits, as the Republicans had proposed, but drew them in so as to ensure that four would be solidly Democratic.

On August 27 the compromise committee delivered its report to both conventions. The Republicans immediately approved the constitution 42-8, with only a few members vigorously denouncing the document as being too much of a compromise. No amendments were proposed. The Democrats, however, took longer. Several amendments were proposed to alter articles on the elective franchise, the legislative apportionment, and the judicial districts. On August 28 the Democratic convention finally approved the document 38-13. Two complete copies of the constitution were written, because Sibley, the president of the Democratic convention, refused to sign the same document as the Republican president. A hasty job of copying divided among several copyists resulted in two documents with 299 small differences in punctuation. A final act of partisanship marred the final days of the conventions when the secretary of the territory, despite promises made by Democrats, refused to honor the certificates of the Republican members and pay their expenses.

Despite the partisan rancor in the bifurcated constitutional convention, on October 13 the voters of Minnesota adopted the constitution almost unanimously. The canvassers' returns indicated 30,055 for and only 571 against. The overwhelmingly positive response resulted largely from yet another Democratic maneuver. According to the schedule, elections for congressmen and state officers were held on the same ballot as the constitutional referendum. As a result, the ballots printed by the parties and distributed among voters all read "for constitution" followed by candidates' names. Because no ballots reading "against constitution" were actually printed, to vote against the constitution, one had to cross out the word "for" and write "against." On December 2, as required by the schedule, the state legislature met for the first time. Democrats had a majority of both houses of the legislature and a full complement of state officers, although the vote for governor, between Democrat Sibley and Republican Ramsey, was fairly close.

There were questions from the outset as to the legislature's legality. Congress had not yet admitted Minnesota to the Union, and the new constitution forbade the executive and judicial officers from assuming their duties until Congress acted. Without a lieutenant governor, the senate elected both a president pro tem and a president of the senate, an office not even mentioned in the constitution. Republicans protested vigorously that the state of Minnesota could not be administered by an appointed territorial governor, but their arguments fell on deaf ears as the legislature continued in session for four months, passing thirty-two general and ninety-two special laws, electing two U.S. senators, and approving two constitutional amendments (one authorizing a loan on state credit, the other authorizing state officials to take office on May

1, 1858). Making the situation even more absurd was the fact that Governor Medary had left the territory, so territorial secretary Chase signed all laws twice, once as secretary and once as acting governor, all while the state governor-elect waited impatiently in St. Paul.[44]

On January 11, 1858, President Buchanan submitted Minnesota's constitution to the Senate, informing the House of his action. Senator Douglas reported the bill out of committee on January 26 but was unable to bring it to a vote then or on February 1. Both times his efforts were blocked by southern senators who believed that the Minnesota congressional delegation opposed the recognition of the pro-slavery government of Kansas. Albert G. Brown of Georgia warned that if the Senate were to "admit Minnesota and exclude Kansas, the spirit of our revolutionary fathers is utterly extinct [,] if the Government can last for one short twelvemonth." Once the Kansas issue had been decided, a major sticking point was the number of representatives to which Minnesota was entitled. The constitution just approved called for three, clearly too many. Under the Census of 1850, the apportionment under which the rest of Congress had been elected, Minnesota was probably entitled to only one. Eventually Minnesota was allowed two representatives. Not until April 7 did the Senate finally vote to admit Minnesota to the Union, 49-3.[45]

In the House, committee chairman Alexander Stephens had an equally difficult time bringing the Minnesota bill to the floor. After failing on April 15, he managed to make the bill a special order for May 4. The bill was debated for three days. The chief opponent of the bill was John Sherman of Ohio, who derided the irregularities that occurred in the convention. On May 11, the House at last passed the bill, 157-38. Opposition in the House came from several sources.[46] Twelve Republicans voted against the bill, knowing that the state had elected a Democratic administration and congressional delegation and eleven Know-Nothings who opposed the state's liberal alien suffrage provision. Fifteen others objected to various provisions in the constitution. The same day, President Buchanan signed the bill, and Minnesota was at last admitted to the Union. News reached Minnesota on May 24, 1858, and Governor Sibley and others finally took up their duties as the North Star State became the thirty-second state.

NOTES

1. William Watts Folwell, *A History of Minnesota*, rev. ed., 4 vols. (St. Paul: Minnesota Historical Society, 1956), 1:90–101.

2. Theodore C. Blegen, *Minnesota: A History of the State* (Minneapolis: University of Minnesota Press, 1963), pp. 98–104.

3. Early explorations of the Minnesota Country are summarized in Folwell, *History of Minnesota*, pp. 102–130.

4. William E. Lass, "How the Forty-Ninth Parallel Became the International Boundary," *Minnesota History* 44 (Summer 1975): 209–219.

5. *Congressional Globe*, 29th Cong., 2d Sess., pp. 445, 572.

6. William E. Lass, "Minnesota's Separation from Wisconsin: Boundary Making on the Upper Mississippi Frontier," *Minnesota History* 50 (Winter 1987): 309–316.

7. *Congressional Globe*, 30th Cong. 1st Sess., pp. 136, 656, 772, 1052.

8. "Organization of Minnesota Territory," in *Minnesota Historical Society Collections* (Minneapolis: Minnesota Historical Society, 1902), 1:35–40 (hereafter cited as "Organization of Minnesota").

9. Edward D. Neil, *The History of Minnesota from the Earliest French Explorations to the Present Time*, 4th ed. (Minneapolis: Minnesota Historical Company, 1882), pp. 32, 497–498.

10. Blegen, *Minnesota: A History of the State*, pp. 161–162.

11. "Organization of Minnesota Territory," p. 41.

12. *Congressional Globe*, 30th Cong., 2d Sess., pp. 2, 259–260, 295–297.

13. Ibid., pp. 298–99.

14. Ibid., pp. 485, 513, 581–583.

15. Ibid., pp. 635–637, 666, 681, 698.

16. Folwell, *History of Minnesota*, pp. 244–246. The House clearly did not expect the territory to be established and earlier had failed to pass any appropriation for the territorial government. On the last day of the session, an amendment to an unrelated pension bill provided $19,300 for this purpose.

17. "Minnesota Organic Act," reprinted in William Anderson in collaboration with Albert J. Lobb, *A History of the Constitution of Minnesota*, Research Publications of the University of Minnesota, Studies in the Social Sciences, No. 15 (Minneapolis: University of Minnesota Press, 1921), pp. 291–296.

18. For a description of Ramsey, see Neil, *History of Minnesota*, pp. 496–497.

19. Ibid., pp. 502–507.

20. Ibid., pp. 511–522.

21. Folwell, *History of Minnesota*, pp. 260–265.

22. Ibid., pp. 266–271.

23. Ibid., pp. 271–274.

24. Ibid., pp. 278–295.

25. Blegen, *Minnesota: A History of the State*, pp. 174–175.

26. Ibid., pp. 185–186.

27. Ibid., pp. 189–193.

28. Ibid., pp. 195–200.

29. Folwell, *History of Minnesota*, p. 365.

30. Ibid., pp. 369–373.

31. Ibid., pp. 375–377.

32. Ibid., pp. 377–378.

33. *St. Paul Pioneer and Democrat*, August 19, 1856, quoted in Anderson and Lobb, *History of the Constitution of Minnesota*, p. 43.

34. Anderson and Lobb, pp. 44–50.

35. *Congressional Globe*, 34th Cong., 3d Sess., pp. 201, 517–520.

36. Ibid., pp. 734, 807–813.

37. Ibid., pp. 849–865, 872–877.

38. Anderson and Lobb, *History of the Constitution of Minnesota*, pp. 54–55, 59–60.

39. The Enabling Act appears in *U. S. Statues at Large*, pp. 166–167; 34th Cong., 2d Sess., chap. 60, and is reprinted in Anderson and Lobb, *History of the Constitution of Minnesota*, pp. 297–298.

40. *St. Paul Pioneer and Democrat*, January 15, 1857.

41. The progress of the bill can be followed in the *House Journal* and *Council Journal* for 1857, special session.

42. Anderson and Lobb, *History of the Constitution of Minnesota*, pp. 69–71.

43. The proceedings of the Minnesota constitutional convention are described fully in Anderson and Lobb, *History of the Constitution of Minnesota*, pp. 69–114.

44. Theodore C. Blegen, *Minnesota: A History of the State*, pp. 225–228.

45. *Congressional Globe*, 35th Cong., 1st Sess., pp. 405, 462, 497–505, 1299–1302, 1322–1330, 1402–1411, 1417–1423, 1487–1492, 1511–1516.

46. Ibid., pp. 1978–1981, 2004–2012, 2057–2061.

BIBLIOGRAPHY

Anderson, William, in collaboration with Albert J. Lobb. *A History of the Constitution of Minnesota*. Research Publications of the University of Minnesota, Studies in the Social Sciences No. 15. Minneapolis: University of Minnesota Press, 1921.

Blegen, Theodore C. *Minnesota: A History of the State*. St. Paul: University of Minnesota Press, 1963.

Folwell, William Watts. *A History of Minnesota*, rev. ed., 4 vols. St. Paul: Minnesota Historical Society, 1956.

Lass, William E. "How the Forty-Ninth Parallel Became the International Boundary." *Minnesota History* 44 (Summer 1975): 209–219.

———. "Minnesota's Separation from Wisconsin: Boundary Making on the Upper Mississippi Frontier." *Minnesota History* 50 (Winter 1987): 309–320.

Neil, Edward D. *The History of Minnesota from the Earliest French Explorations to the Present Time*. 4th ed. Minneapolis: Minnesota Historical Company, 1882.

Mississippi

Territorial Development:

- Great Britain cedes future Mississippian territory to the United States through the Treaty of Paris, September 3, 1783
- The United States passes the Northwest Ordinance: territorial claims inherited from colonial charters ceded to the public domain, July 13, 1787
- Mississippi organized as a United States territory, April 7, 1798
- Mississippi admitted into the Union as the twentieth state, December 10, 1817

Territorial Capitals:

- Natchez, 1798–1802
- Washington, 1802–1817

State Capitals:

- Natchez, 1817–1821
- Columbia, 1821–1822
- Jackson, 1822–present, with Macon and Columbus serving as temporary capitals during the Civil War

Origin of State Name: "Mississippi" is derived from a Chippewa word meaning "large river."

First Governor: David Holmes
Governmental Organization: Bicameral
Population at Statehood: 75,448
Geographical Size: 46,907 square miles

THE STATE OF MISSISSIPPI

Admitted to the Union as a State: December 10, 1817

Deanne Stephens Nuwer

INTRODUCTION

When England and the United States negotiated the Treaty of Ghent in December 1814, the War of 1812 officially ended. With its victory, the once loosely organized United States experienced a strengthened national spirit and a keener sense of union. Common sympathies bound the states together in this new spirit of nationalism, and emerging states quickly applied to Congress for admission into the Union. As a result, the U.S. Congress welcomed two new states into the republic during James Madison's presidency, Louisiana on April 8, 1812, and Indiana on December 11, 1816. Mississippi, another territory poised on statehood, entered the Union on December 10, 1817, as the twentieth state. The unfolding of that event revealed almost two centuries of intrigue and political maneuvering.

The story of Mississippi's evolution from an unexplored region into statehood commenced in 1540 when Hernando de Soto and his expeditionary forces, exploring for Charles V, sovereign of Spain, crossed the Tombigbee River and entered what would become the northern portion of that state. On May 5, 1541, de Soto and the other Spaniards gazed for the first time upon the "Father of Waters," the Mississippi River. From that year until 1798, when the region became a U.S. territory, three European powers, Spain, France, and England, each sought wealth in the New World and vied for control of the rich resources in the Mississippi region as well as navigational rights of the mighty Mississippi River.

The history of Mississippi's march to statehood intimately involved the competition of these three colonial powers for domination in the New World.

Each of these nations recognized that the one that controlled the Mississippi River would ultimately control the entire hinterland east of that waterway. Thus, were conflicts born.

Spain began its exploration in the Gulf of Mexico's Central and South American lands after Christopher Columbus landed on San Salvador on October 12, 1492. Subsequent Spanish explorers claimed vast stretches of land to enrich Spain's coffers and establish trade routes. These claims ultimately included the Gulf Coast region and portions of Mississippi. In the 1540s de Soto did not discover the anticipated riches in Mississippi that other Spaniards had found in Central and South America. The Spanish left that region and did not return as a colonial power for more than two hundred years. The Spaniards, however, left behind unseen agents of death, European diseases such as smallpox and measles. Between 1540 and 1670, it is estimated the Native American population in the Mississippi region was reduced by 80 percent because of introduced diseases. That drastic decrease in the Native American population may have made the colonization of the next European power, France, easier than it would otherwise have been.[1]

France began its exploration of the Mississippi lands when Father Marquette and Louis Joliet paddled their way from Quebec, Canada, and the Great Lakes region down the Mississippi River to present-day Arkansas, proving that this river flowed in a southerly direction. Later, Louis XIV, monarch of Bourbon France, engaged Robert Cavalier de La Salle to explore the western portion of New France in 1692. La Salle hoped to discover the mouth of the Mississippi River, thus completing French claims for that entire waterway. Accomplishing his task, La Salle claimed the river, its delta, and all of the lands that it drained for France. Although an attempt to establish a French colony in the Gulf Coast area failed, the French maintained a claim to the region as a result of La Salle's expeditions.[2]

The third European nation to vie for Mississippi were the English, who wished to protect their Atlantic seaboard colonies that had been permanently established as early as 1607. The English began forays into the Mississippi River Valley to establish boundaries against encroaching French and Spanish and to seek rich furs for trade. The fate of the Mississippi Valley supposedly had been decided in the Treaty of Ryswick, which ended the War of the League of Augsburg, a conflict beginning in 1689 between France and the combined allies, England and Spain. In the Mississippi region, as in many instances, events in Europe controlled the destiny of land claims in the New World. That treaty stipulated that all New World claims were to remain as they had been when the war began. In the Mississippi region, however, France and Great Britain soon became rivals for trade with the Chickasaw, Choctaw, and Natchez who represented the largest Native American markets for these two European countries. By 1754, France and England engaged in yet another conflict to determine dominance in the New World and to resolve European conflicts. When this conflagration, the French and Indian War, ended in 1763, the treaty of the Peace of Paris stripped France of its vast New World holdings. England then assumed control of Canada and all lands east of the Mississippi River, including, of course, the Mississippi territory.[3]

These three European nations settled and fought over Mississippi from 1540 until 1798, when the area officially became a territory of the newly forged United States. Each European nation contributed to the present-day culture of the twentieth state in the Union.

MISSISSIPPI UNDER THE FRENCH FLAG

Intense rivalry between France, England, and Spain involved the Gulf of Mexico shoreline and Mississippi regions early in its history, but it was the French who succeeded in establishing the first permanent settlement in that region. After the Treaty of Ryswick in 1697, which ended European hostilities between England and France, England and Spain were not satisfied with its stipulation that pre-war colonial claims remain intact. In fact, those two nations began actions to thwart the treaty's tenets because of France's vast New World holdings. Spain began to fortify its claims along the Gulf Coast shoreline to protect its trade routes. Pensacola, Florida, a fine harbor site for the Spanish, was quickly prepared for any action. France, responding to growing tension among the three nations, organized an expedition to colonize the Gulf Coast area. Pierre LeMoyne, Sieur d'Iberville, a soldier who had distinguished himself against the English and who had already settled colonies in Acadia and Cape Breton Island, organized an expedition of about two hundred settlers, left Brest, France, on October 21, 1698, and sailed on *La Marin* and *La Badine*, thirty-gun frigates, to the Gulf of Mexico. Marquis de Chateaumerant, commandant of a fifty-gun frigate, *Le Francois*, rendezvoused with Iberville at Santo Domingo before they headed north to explore the shoreline of present-day Mississippi and Louisiana. Iberville's two-pronged plan was to locate a site for a permanent French settlement and to pinpoint the mouth of the Mississippi River once again for France. Although claimed by La Salle, the exact location of the river's terminus had become unclear, because no marker remained from that earlier expedition; the Mississippi River delta is intermingled with numerous bayous and swamps, making the mouth of the river elusive.[4]

Iberville and his expedition sailed the coastal waters of the northern rim of the Gulf of Mexico in search of a suitable location for settlement. He arrived first in Spanish-held Pensacola, on January 20, 1699. The Spanish there indicated to Iberville that he would not be allowed to drop anchor in that location, so he was forced to move westward along the coast. The French forayed into Mobile Bay in present-day Alabama but continued on to Ship Island, twelve miles offshore from Mississippi, when soundings revealed that Mobile Bay was too shallow to serve as a safe harbor. They reached Ship Island on February 10. Iberville stated that he chose this place for "the sheltered bay, or roadstead, where small vessels can come and go safely at all times." From that anchorage point, the French were able to begin preparations for selecting a permanent settlement location.[5]

Setting forth in long boats, the French approached the shore and encountered the Biloxi, a Native American tribe. Iberville named the Bay of Biloxi after this group and quickly befriended them to learn where the Mississippi River spilled into the Gulf of Mexico. With their information, he then began explorations to the west to reestablish French claims to the Mississippi River's mouth.

On February 28, Iberville set out to find the Mississippi delta. Accompanying him was Father Anatasius Douay, who had traveled with La Salle on previous explorations and who carried a copy of La Salle's earlier account to be used as a reference. Approaching what originally appeared to be an inlet into the coastline, Iberville discovered that the party was paddling into a much larger waterway. By chance, he had entered the Mississippi River's North Pass. Father Douay assured him he was on the great river, but Iberville decided to continue the journey northward for verification. Traveling north as far as present-day Baton Rouge, Louisiana, or "Istrouma" in the native language, Iberville and his party, low on supplies, decided to head back down the river. As they paddled downstream, putting into the shore at various locations, they learned of a tribe called the Mongoulachas that apparently had in its possession a "speaking bark" or letter written by Henri de Tonty, an associate of La Salle. The correspondence had been written to La Salle fourteen years earlier. Furthermore, de Soto, on his original expedition, had left behind a coat of mail with the tribe. The existence of these items proved to Iberville that he was on the Mississippi River, and thus he reclaimed the waterway and its delta for France.[6]

Returning to their Mississippi camp, the French began building a wooden fort on the Back Bay area of the Biloxi peninsula and named it Fort Maurepas, in honor of Jean Phellyppeaux, Count Maurepas, minister and secretary of foreign affairs for King Louis XIV. Mechanics, carpenters, and masons finished the fort by May 4. This fort represented the first fortification and seat of French sovereignty in Mississippi that would last until 1763.[7]

After completing his two goals in the Mississippi region, Iberville returned to France to report to Louis XIV. He left Sauvole de la Villantry in command of seventy-six men, with Francois de Bienville, Iberville's younger brother, second in command. The French continued to explore the Gulf Coast as far east as Pensacola and west to the Mississippi River. On one expedition, Bienville encountered an English ship, the *Carolina Galley* commanded by a Captain Barr, on the great river. It is unclear whether the French deceived the English with false information regarding their location on the river or ordered the interlopers to leave the area claimed by the French. Whatever the reason, the English did leave, and Bienville realized the need to redouble his efforts to maintain French holdings. He would make that goal his lifework.[8]

Unfortunately, for the next sixty-three years the Louisiana/Mississippi territory did not produce the expected boon to the French economy, even though the

French controlled the Gulf Coast and a majority of the Mississippi River. During this time, the capital of Louisiana, the territory that included present-day Mississippi and Alabama, shifted from Biloxi to Mobile and finally, by 1723, to New Orleans. The French settled northward on the Mississippi River as high as the territory controlled by the Natchez, another Native American tribe. The French named this settlement on the waterway after the natives. Bienville eventually built a French fortification there, Fort Rosalie.

During the period of French control, the territory was not profitable, so the French government authorized two men to organize, promote, and commercialize the southern French holdings. First, in 1713, Louis XIV granted Anthony Crozat exclusive control of the Louisiana colony. Crozat appointed Governor Antoine de la Mothe Cadillac to govern Louisiana. Cadillac, however, believed the region to be "a very wretched country, good for nothing, and incapable of producing tobacco, wheat, or vegetables, even as high as Natchez." This opinion seemed to be the common attitude toward the Louisiana colony; after losing much capital attempting to promote the region, Crozat willingly relinquished his entrepreneurial monopoly to the Louisiana colony by 1717.[9]

Next, John Law, a native of Edinburgh, Scotland, received an exclusive monopoly for Louisiana's commercial development from the king of France, Louis XV, on November 26, 1719, through the Company of the Indies, with the Mississippi Company specifically addressing that region. The company, however, had been selling stocks since 1715. The king's monopoly stated that the company could operate the government of the colony by "appointing the governors of the colony, and the other officers commanding the troops," make land grants, raise a militia, negotiate treaties with Native Americans and "build ships of war and cast cannon" or wage war. In return, with its twenty-five year lease, the Company was also to advertise and promote settlement in the Louisiana colony. According to the stipulations of the agreement between the French Crown and the company, six thousand settlers and three thousand slaves, none of whom could be from other French colonies, were to be transported to Louisiana during the period of the lease.[10]

By 1723, during the Mississippi Bubble, as Law's promotional activities came to be known, Bienville established New Orleans as the last capital of French Louisiana. During this time, prominent people received large land grants in the hope that they would encourage settlement. In Mississippi, Yazoo River grants were made to several lesser nobles, including Count de Belleville, the Marquis D'Auleck, and LeBlond. Around Natchez, the company made a substantial grant to Louis XV's *commissaire ordonnateur* and several merchants of St. Malo, whereas Madame de Mezieres received lands on the Bay of St. Louis and at Old Biloxi. In present-day Jackson County, Madame de Chaumont accepted grants on the Pascagoula Bay, and Madame Paris Duvernet's grants included the Native American village of Pascagoula.[11] These absentee landlords encouraged colonial settlement by inviting French immigrants to their

New World holdings. The labor force of French settlers was not adequate for profitable agricultural endeavors, however, so the company, already bound by its charter to provide laborers, imported African slaves. According to the company rules,

> These slaves were sold to the *old* settlers; those who had been two or more years in the colony, at one-half the price, in cash, and the remainder on one year's credit. The *new* inhabitants, those less than two years in the colony, were authorized to purchase slaves on a credit of one and two years.[12]

The slaves were valued by age and health. A male or female slave between the ages of seventeen and thirty was worth 660 livres. Children were grouped for sale in twos or threes. A grouping of three slaves between the ages of eight and ten cost 660 livres, and a pair between the ages of ten and fifteen was the same price. The French had imported slaves into the Louisiana colony in significant numbers by 1719, but even earlier historical records in French Louisiana reveal that Native Americans were held as slaves at the inception of the colony. Because of the growing slave population, Governor Bienville issued the Black Code in 1724 to address legal and moral issues regarding slave ownership. This code transferred complete control to owners and stipulated that slaves should be converted to Catholicism. It also enumerated regulations concerning matters such as slave marriage arrangements, commercial activity, housing, and clothing allotments. With slave labor, the Louisiana colony began to export lumber, navel stores, tobacco, silk, rice, and indigo. Tobacco became the chief export by 1726. In 1728, Governor Boucher de la Perier ended the practice of enslaving Native Americans, and the settlers in the regions thereafter relied chiefly on African or other black imported slaves. By 1763, at the end of France's proprietorship, estimates place the number of slaves in the Louisiana colony at about 6,000.[13]

Law's plans to sell stock in Mississippi burst by 1723. He fled France to avoid arrest for his unsuccessful land promotions. The company, however, continued moderate operations for approximately ten years. Even though Crozat's and Law's financial plans were not profitable, the Louisiana colony had grown economically. Because of this growth, England increased its overtures toward the Native Americans in the Mississippi Valley to secure some of the financial opportunities in the region. Using trade items to entice Native Americans, the English from the Atlantic colonies made inroads on the trade with the Natchez and the Chickasaw, facilitating growing tensions between the Native Americans and French by befriending groups who resented the expansion of the French into their lands. The massacre at Fort Rosalie exemplified those animosities.

Governor Perier, a successor to Bienville, appointed a Frenchman named Chopart as commander of Fort Rosalie. By all accounts, Chopart was abusive toward the Natchez, and tension developed between the two groups . The commander intensified problems when he demanded that the Natchez abandon their village called White Apple and turn the area, which occupied a beautiful area on a bluff and which he apparently coveted, over to him. The Natchez chief known as the Great Sun decided then that he would plot to overthrow the French and expel them from Natchez lands.[14]

On November 28, 1729, the Natchez feigned that they needed to exchange corn and poultry with the French for guns, powder, and lead. One native contingency entered Fort Rosalie, while two other groups positioned themselves near the French housing area and farms, both of which were outside the palisades of the fort. At the appointed hour, the three groups simultaneously attacked the French. At the end of the assault, the Natchez had killed 138 men, 35 women, and 56 children. When the attack commenced, the Great Sun "took his place under the tobacco shed of the Company and the heads of the victims were piled at his feet. Their bodies, after being mutilated, were left to the dogs and buzzards." Commander Chopart was beaten to death by the lowest class of the Natchez tribe, the Stinkards, because "no warrior would soil his hands with such a wretch." French revenge against the Natchez was severe. Within approximately two years after the attack, the French had destroyed the Natchez nation.[15]

Native American problems, however, continued to plague the French. The Chickasaw, a tribe located in the northeastern part of Mississippi, maintained continuous warfare with them. Bienville organized two campaigns against that tribe, one in 1736 and another in 1740, but both were complete failures. There was, moreover, intertribal warfare between the Choctaws and the Chickasaws; the Choctaws joined the French in expeditions against the Chickasaws, and the Chickasaws allied with the British, who were a growing hostile presence in the Mississippi frontier. These hostilities created an environment that few settlers wished to chance, and Louisiana therefore experienced great difficulty in encouraging settlement. Moreover, Bienville, after approximately forty years in the service of the French monarchy, left Louisiana in 1743. Bienville's two successors had little success; French control of the region had begun to unravel because of difficulties with Native Americans, English interference, financial problems, and growing European conflicts. A 1744 census by the French revealed startling population numbers: there were only eight white males in Natchez and ten white males and sixty African Americans in Pascagoula. The population of Bay St. Louis, Biloxi, and Pass Christian was not recorded.[16] Certainly, the French had problems in Mississippi.

In 1754, tensions between England and France existed on multiple fronts in the New World, including Louisiana and the ambiguous borders in the Ohio River Valley. Seeking to establish more control and to survey French strength, a British expedition under the command of Virginian George Washington headed toward the Ohio River Valley through Pennsylvania. The British met the French in that colony's western wilderness at Ft. Duquesne. As the result of a skirmish there, the French and Indian War began. This conflict was the final confrontation between these two colonial powers for domination in North America.

When the war ended in 1763, the Treaty of Paris awarded the entire eastern portion of North America, all of Canada, and Spanish Florida to England. Spain, having entered the conflict when Louis XV secretly ceded Louisiana to her in 1762, received the remaining Louisiana territory, the trans-Mississippi West, that began west of the Mississippi River and ended at the Rocky Mountains. The Isle of New Orleans also was awarded to Spain. As a result, after 1763, the French no longer played a role in shaping the development of Mississippi. Since 1699, France had established colonies along the Mississippi River, the Gulf Coast, and inland. Settlers established inroads to rich agricultural lands and left behind place names familiar today. When England assumed control of the region, some charted areas existed, but the region was largely still unknown and controlled by Native Americans. Intrigue continued then between the two remaining colonial powers in the region, Spain and England.[17]

MISSISSIPPI UNDER THE ENGLISH FLAG

When the British assumed control of the former French lands, the initial northern boundary for Mississippi was 31° north latitude. Realizing that rich lands east of the Mississippi River around Natchez and the Yazoo River were not included in these boundaries, the British revised the treaty through a supplementary codicil extending the northern boundary to 32°28'. The British called the area of its new Gulf Coast holdings West Florida; the area east of Pensacola was designated East Florida. Captain George Johnstone became West Florida's first governor.[18] Johnstone arrived in West Florida in 1764, quickly established his seat of government at Pensacola, and began organizing British colonial rule. He created a civil government council by appointing James McPherson as provincial secretary, John Stuart as superintendent of Indian affairs, and Robert MacKinen as commander of the local garrison. James Bruce and William Struthers were put in charge of customs collections and Native American trade relations.[19]

Governor Johnstone also established a Superior Court at Pensacola that had jurisdiction over the entire territory. For local cases, twenty-eight justices of the peace were to try cases in which English common law was the precedent. Cases involving capital crimes, however, were to be heard by the Superior Court. Johnstone also included a court of pleas in Pensacola as part of the judicial infrastructure of the colony. This court convened on Tuesday in January, April, July, and October. Arthur Gordon was appointed attorney general. Johnstone effectively had installed the judicial structure for West Florida by 1765.[20]

To encourage settlement, Johnstone had liberal license to make land grants, especially to British veterans of the French and Indian War. For instance, a field officer was entitled to five thousand acres, a captain to three thousand acres, a staff officer to two thousand acres, noncommissioned officers to three hundred acres, and privates to one hundred acres. At first slow to respond, many settlers eventually took advantage of these land grants. With an influx of immigrants seeking rich West Florida land, Johnson also recognized local assemblies' right to convene and to address colonial problems, including licensing taverns, governing slaves and indentured servants, and the increasing problems with Native Americans. Growing tension in the Atlantic colonies probably precipitated this pioneering West Florida assembly convention.[21]

Unfortunately for Johnstone, overwhelming problems with Native Americans consumed most of his energies. The British hosted two meetings in attempts to resolve problems regarding trade and boundaries and to establish friendly relations with the natives. The first meeting convened in Mobile in 1765. Attending were Chickasaw and Choctaw chiefs, including Paya Mattaha from the Chickasaw nation and Alibamon Mingo, Nashuba Mingo, Tomatle Mingo, and Chulustamastable from the Choctaw nation. The second meeting convened in Pensacola later in 1765. The notable chief of the Upper and Lower Creeks, The Mortar, attended. The Creeks occupied much of what is present-day Alabama. In both meetings Johnstone attempted to establish safe routes of passage for persons coming from the Atlantic seaboard colonies through native-held lands. The congress with the Choctaw and Chickasaw nations was more successful than the one with the Creeks, but the Native American question continued to plague Johnstone and his successors in West Florida.[22]

As settlers moved into West Florida, Johnstone also had to address a growing problem regarding cattle. To protect the private ownership of cattle, he issued a decree that required all those who butchered beef to display publicly "the green hide with the hair out, on his stockade fronting the street for four hours in the day." Johnson also mandated that cattle's brands be registered with the provincial secretary of West Florida. Herding had been a lucrative enterprise since French colonization, with colonists from European nations introducing a variety of breeds into the Mississippi Valley. Reports in 1746 indicated that cattle were raised in significant numbers on Deer Island off of the coast of Biloxi. Observers traveling in West Florida during the 1770s consistently described huge herds of cattle roaming the region from Natchez to the Florida Panhandle. Cattle raising continued to expand as more settlers received land grants and immigrated into the region.[23]

Because of the multiple problems plaguing Johnstone, particularly the conflicts with the Creeks, the British government replaced him with John Eliot in 1769. Lieutenant Governor Montfort Browne, who had assisted Johnstone in West Florida since 1766, had been acting as chief executive officer of the region. One month after Eliot's arrival in Pensacola, however, Browne was accused of embezzlement. Charges indicated that he had misappropriated public funds.[24]

The chain of command in West Florida was disrupted when Eliot hanged himself shortly after proceedings against Browne began. Because of that tragic incident, Browne remained in charge of West Florida. Elias Durnford, the colonial surveyor, soon replaced the accused as lieutenant governor in West Florida while embezzlement charges against Browne remained pending. Apparently, those charges were later resolved at Durnford's urging, because Browne was promoted to the government of the Bahamas in 1777. During his brief administration, Durnford, distinguished himself in handling colonial matters such as Native American affairs and colonization. In 1770 Durnford and the West Florida assembly passed a law that more equitably regulated trade with Native Americans. He also advocated establishing a town at Fort Bute, present-day Baton Rouge, Louisiana, in an effort to encourage more trade on the Mississippi River. Durnford's proposal was not executed, however, because more English troops would have been needed to protect the proposed settlement from Native Americans and the Spanish. Durnford's brief tenure ended in August 1770 when Governor Peter Chester arrived in Pensacola as Eliot's replacement.[25]

During the administration of Governor Chester, settlement and Native American issues again took center stage. Lands in the vicinity of Walnut Hills (Vicksburg), Bayou Pierre (Claiborne County), and Natchez were prime locations for settlement. Chester praised the stands of timber in the region and encouraged development at Fort Bute and Natchez. When Chester assumed control of West Florida, approximately one hundred land claims had been filed. The number of claims had more than doubled by 1773 and continued to increase throughout the American Revolution. Settlers from the Atlantic colonies, seeking fertile acreage and safety from growing tensions along the Eastern Seaboard flocked into the region. Governor Chester even offered free transportation and an added incentive of rations to persons migrating to West Florida. According to records from the 1770s, most settlers migrated to the Mississippi territory, with approximately three thousand people living there by 1774.[26]

In the Natchez district, Samuel Swayze, a Congregationalist minister, settled on the Homochtto River in 1772. He was credited with being the first Protestant minister in the Natchez district. Swayze, from New Jersey, and his brother had purchased nineteen thousand acres to settle upon from Captain Amos Ogden for twenty cents per acre. Eventually, this area became known as Jersey settlement because of the settlers from the New Jersey colony who established homes there. Other land grants in the district included one to the Earl of Eglinton for twenty thousand acres, one to Admiral Bentinck for ten thousand acres, and several large tracts, including the White Apple village of the Natchez, to Colonel Anthony Hutchins. Obviously, fertile land was abundant in the Mississippi territory. Natchez grew into an agricultural center producing and raising tobacco, beeswax, honey, leather, cattle, and indigo. As recorded in one account, the district maintained "good order."[27]

To address problems with Native Americans, Chester convened two meetings, one in Pensacola and the other in Mobile, in 1771 and 1772. As with earlier congresses, the convocation in Pensacola included the Creeks, and the one in Mobile was for the Choctaw and Chickasaw nations. Even though the meetings did not establish complete harmony between the Native Americans and the settlers, they did ameliorate relations so that no major confrontation occurred during the British period.[28]

Governor Chester, despite his efforts to increase settlement and negotiate with the Native Americans, apparently was not popular with West Floridians because he did not convene the assembly for six years of his governorship. From 1771 until 1778, the assembly did not meet. Chester angered the elected assemblymen by not stipulating the length of service for the elected representatives; he, on the other hand, believed the assemblymen occupied themselves too much with personal privileges and methods of proceedings and did not adequately address the problems of West Florida. Therefore, in 1778, when the assembly had spent thirty-four days without productive activity, Governor Chester adjourned the meeting on November 24 and stated that he had no plans to reconvene it. Nevertheless, the seeds of representation and self-government were planted in West Florida.[29]

In the thirteen colonies along the Atlantic seaboard, meanwhile, the first Continental Congress had met in 1774, Lexington and Concord resounded with "the shot heard 'round the world" on April 19, 1775, and the Declaration of Independence was adopted on July 4, 1776. As a result of the colonies' successes in 1777, Louis XVI of France negotiated the Franco-American Alliance with the newly formed United States, pledging men, money, warships, and supplies to the struggling nation. By 1779, Spain joined France against England in the American Revolution.

Until 1778, the American Revolution had little impact on Mississippi. Settlers loyal to King George III of England moved to the Southeast to avoid the conflict, but no military action had occurred there. In March of that year, James Willing, who had lived in Natchez as a merchant, landed at the mouth of the Big Black River, north of Natchez, with an expedition from the second Continental Congress to secure the neutrality of the inhabitants in the Natchez district and to seek supplies from the Spanish in New Orleans. More than one hundred men took the oath of neutrality. Willing, however, was dissatisfied because not all of the district's citizens took the oath of neutrality. Breaking into the home of Colonel Anthony Hutchins, a retired British army officer, Willing seized Hutchins as a prisoner. Apparently looting slaves and other valuables along the way, Willing and his men made their way southward to Spanish New Orleans, where they hoped to make arrangements for supplies from the Spanish commander, Governor Bernardo de Galvez, for the American cause.[30]

Galvez, seizing the opportunity to attack British West Florida, launched an attack against Fort Bute (Baton Rouge). On September 21, 1779, Lieutenant Colonel Alexander Dickinson surrendered his British force and the entire Natchez district to Galvez. In 1780, Galvez seized Mobile, and with reinforcements from Havana, Cuba, his forces were able to capture Pensacola in 1781. Governor Chester and other British officials were allowed to leave for England. Although the citizenry of Natchez attempted a revolt while Galvez was in Pensacola, the movement was ineffectual, and West Florida, including the Mississippi region, became a Spanish colony.[31]

MISSISSIPPI UNDER THE SPANISH FLAG

Following the American Revolution, settlers poured into the Natchez district seeking fertile land. The Spanish governors in Natchez during its colonial period generally exercised their authority mildly. Galvez was the governor-general of both Louisiana and West Florida until 1786, when a series of other supreme commandants assumed control of the vast area. Don Esteban Miro, who replaced Galvez, governed until 1792; then Francois Lois Hector de Carondelet was in charge until 1797. The last commander of the large region, Don Manuel de Gayoso de Lemos, remained as commandant until 1798, when the Americans took control. Gayoso, however, also served as the first governor of Spanish Natchez in 1789 because he was fluent in English and had an American wife.

The governor of the Natchez district was subordinate to the governor-general of Louisiana and West Florida. That seat of government was in New Orleans. The governor-general, in turn, answered to the captain-general of Cuba, whose capital was in Havana. All these officers received orders from the secretary of war in Spain regarding military matters and from the Council of the Indies in other affairs. The king of Spain ultimately had supreme control over this entire colonial system. The legal code under which all the Louisiana lands and now West Florida operated was the Code O'Reilly, originally established in 1769 for Louisiana. Gayoso issued laws with the advice of leading citizenry in Natchez, and even though Spanish courts did not have the English jury system, the citizens seemed to accept willingly the tribunal judgment of the more prominent men in the district, whom Gayoso included in judicial proceedings. All told, the Spanish in Natchez administered easily and with clemency. One prominent citizen, William Dunbar, noted, "British property is in perfect security. An Englishman may come here and recover his debts, and obtain justice as soon as in Westminster Hall."[32]

Lands in Spanish Natchez were easily acquired. A settler only had to select an unoccupied parcel and then request a survey. If no legal problems existed, the settler paid the surveyor's fee, and the land was then registered to him. On these lands, tobacco was one of the chief export crops. In 1789, the district produced almost 1.5 million pounds bound for Spain through the port of New Orleans. Indigo was also a major export of the region. The plant produced a blue dye popular for military uniforms of the time and reached a high price of $2.50 a pound. Indigo cultivation, however, produced waste products that growers channeled into local streams. The cattle industry suffered in

Natchez when this contamination fouled creeks and other waterways. As a result, a Natchez law in 1793 forbade the polluting of creeks with indigo by-products.

The most important agricultural endeavor in Natchez was cotton production. In 1793, Eli Whitney assembled a cotton gin to separate the seeds from the valuable fiber. The Krebs family, however, had been using a gin in the East Pascagoula region since 1722. Because the cotton gin was a simple invention, many areas copied the concept. David Greenleaf and John Barclay adapted one in the Natchez district, and the cotton industry commenced. Around 1799 Dunbar, who had become a major cotton grower by 1797, invented the square bale that facilitated better storage and shipping. By the end of the eighteenth century, Natchez exported approximately 3 million pounds of cotton.[33]

The Spanish government required census reports from Gayoso. In 1784 the tabulation revealed a population of 619 people, including 498 black slaves. By 1798, reports indicated that 4,500 whites and 2,400 blacks lived in Natchez. Obviously, as agricultural productivity increased, so did the population, including the slave labor force. In fact, the Spanish government encouraged settlers from other regions to come to Natchez with their slaves by offering additional land opportunities for slave owners. Slavery was an embedded institution in the Natchez district.[34]

Militarily, the Spanish were never strong in Natchez and the Mississippi region. The Spanish tried to strengthen old Fort Rosalie, but eventually erosion took its toll. They also constructed fortifications near present-day Vicksburg, Grand Gulf, and Memphis, Tennessee. The Chickasaw Bluff fort (Memphis) controlled traffic on the lower Mississippi River. Manning the fortifications was also a problem for the Spanish. Local militia forces supplemented Spanish troops when needed, particularly against Native Americans and small colonial revolts throughout the region.

Perhaps the most significant problem Spain encountered as the colonial power in Mississippi was boundary disputes. When the colony of Georgia was established, its boundaries extended deep into Mississippi territory. Georgia's boundaries, if interpreted as originally chartered, included the Natchez district. On that basis, the legislature of Georgia created the County of Bourbon in 1785, which included part of the Natchez district. Georgia forged ahead with its plan of settlement even though the area included Spanish lands and subjects. Mississippi was carved up into huge grants, and land companies began selling smaller divisions. Eventually, this plan failed because no military force was available to enforce Georgia's claims and schemes. In 1795 four companies attempted to buy the entire area of the present-day state of Mississippi from the Georgia legislature, this time working with the Spanish government. Again, the land companies were not able to realize their plans.[35]

All these proceedings greatly affected the Spanish government. Settlers streamed into Mississippi with land sales receipts, and agents from the land companies arrived in Natchez reasserting Georgia's claims. Additionally, the

U.S. government had been emphasizing to the Spanish that the official boundary between the two nations should be the line of 31° north latitude. The Spanish, pressured by settlers, negotiating with the U.S. government, and fighting a war against France and England, were in no position militarily and economically to maintain their hold on Mississippi. On October 27, 1795, the Treaty of San Lorenzo el Real ended Spain's tenure in Mississippi north of 31° north latitude. The treaty, signed in Madrid, stipulated that all Spanish posts north of that line were to become American within six months. Free navigation of the Mississippi River was to exist for commerce of both nations, both nations would continue to promote peace with the Native Americans, and a joint commission would establish the boundary between Spain and the United States. Andrew Ellicott was appointed to be the American boundary commissioner. By March 30, 1798, the Spanish flag was lowered in Natchez, and the American flag was raised. Mississippi, north of 31° north latitude, was now American.[36]

MISSISSIPPI AS A U.S. TERRITORY AND STATE

On April 7, 1798, the U.S. Congress decreed that the lands "bounded on the west by the Mississippi; on the north by a line to drawn due east from the mouth of the Yazoo to the Chattahoochie River; and on the south by the thirty-first degree of north latitude, shall be and is hereby constituted one district, to be called the Mississippi Territory." Natchez became the capital of the newly created territory, and Mississippi was assigned the status of territory of the first grade. In 1787 the U.S. Congress had passed a law classifying territories according to population numbers; territories with five thousand free male inhabitants were designated as first grade; territories with lower populations had second-grade status. When the Mississippi Territory was established, its population was about five thousand, but approximately two thousand of those inhabitants were slaves.[37]

When Andrew Ellicott, the boundary commissioner for the new territory, arrived in February 1797, he discovered that there were two factions of citizenry in Natchez. One group consisted largely of creditors, the other of debtors. On several occasions Ellicott overstepped his authority regarding political control in Natchez. As a result, after much political tension between the two sides and with Ellicott intimately involved in the dissention, Captain Issac Guion arrived in Natchez with orders to quell all problems. Guion issued a deadline to the Spanish for evacuating Natchez and quickly calmed the divisive Natchez citizenry. Ellicott observed on March 30, 1798, "from the parapet, the pleasing prospect of the galleys and boats leaving the shore."[38] The last of Gayoso's Spanish troops had evacuated the city. The way was clear for Ellicott to survey and establish boundary lines in the new territory and for a new government to commence.

Because Mississippi was a territory of the first grade, the president of the United States had the power to appoint a governor, a secretary, and three judges. Therefore, President John Adams appointed Governor Winthrop Sargent of Massachusetts, Secretary John Steele of Virginia, and Judges Peter Bryan Burin of the Mississippi Territory, Daniel Tilton of New Hampshire, and William McGuire of Virginia. Sargent had served as a major in the Continental Army and was ready for the appointment. President Adams confided to Sargent that his appointment was essential for American success in the area because of the territory's factious background. In a correspondence, Adams wrote, "It is at this time peculiarly important that a man of energy, of application to business, and a <u>military</u> character, should be charged with this new government." Sargent predicted the tone of his tenure when he stated, "The footing on which Governor Gayoso lived with the inhabitants may not be equally in my power to observe, It shall be my study to conciliate and attach all parties to the United States." Sargent arrived in Natchez on August 6, 1798, and assumed his duties.[39]

In 1799, Governor Sargent created Adams County, which included Natchez, and Pickering County. Later, in 1800, Washington County became the third Mississippi county in the region and included lands east of the Pearl River. Sargent was not a popular governor, because he openly exhibited contempt for the Natchezians of "refractory and turbulent spirit" and issued unfavorable laws. He taxed the citizens for expenditures such as road maintenance and prisoner upkeep. Many citizens, particularly those in Pickering County, responded with cries of "no taxation without representation." Moreover, problems with Native Americans continued to plague the territory. The Choctaws near Natchez feared that American support would not be equal to that they enjoyed under the Spanish, so they began stealing and attacking outposts. Under Sargent's administration, settlers apparently had to resort to bribery to keep their homes safe from Native American attacks. In a letter to the secretary of state on May 29, 1798, Sargent admitted, "I have not competant [sic] Knowledge of the Expenses of the Southern Indian Department."[40]

In 1800, two important events adversely affected Sargent's already troubled governorship. Narsworthy Hunter and Cato West organized a committee for governmental reform that criticized Sargent's administration. Hunter carried a petition to the U.S. Congress stating that the citizens of Natchez were "against the improper and oppressive measures to the Territorial government." As a result of this group's campaigning, Mississippi's territorial status was raised to grade two, which bestowed increased representation and status. Also, Thomas Jefferson was elected the third president of the United States.

President Jefferson replaced Governor Sargent with William Charles Cole Claiborne, a twenty-six year old lawyer from Tennessee. On May 25, 1801, Claiborne became the second governor of the Mississippi Territory. Claiborne at once initiated changes. He stressed the need for political harmony. He created two new counties, Wilkinson and Claiborne, and renamed Pickering County, which was henceforth to be called Jefferson County. To help maintain order, Fort Dearborn was erected in Washington, a town to the east of Natchez. In that same town, the Mississippi legislature provided for construction of Jefferson College.[41] Claiborne also repealed all of Sargent's 1799 legal code. Natchez and the Mississippi Territory were changing.

The partisanship of its citizens, however, was one aspect of territorial life that did not change. Claiborne governed an area containing factions that wished to return to Sargent's more federalist type of territorial government as well as factions that desired universal manhood suffrage. James Madison, the secretary of state, wrote to Claiborne about the discord in the territory on May 11, 1802: "It is to be regretted that so much violence and vicisitude [sic] as you describe should afflict the inhabitants of a settlement, which both in its infant and frontier character more particularly needs the advantages of concord and stability." Offering no solution to the problems, Madison closed his correspondence by expressing his confidence in Claiborne's abilities.[42]

Claiborne met with some success regarding land claims. In 1802, Georgia ceded its western claims for $1,250,000 and proceeds from the first land transactions in the once-disputed region. By March 1803, at Claiborne's urging, Congress passed the first comprehensive land law for the Mississippi Territory. With this act, the path was cleared for purchasing lands and validating previous land grant titles. Two surveyors offices were established, one east of the Pearl River at St. Stephens and one west of that river at Washington, where the seat of territorial government was then located.

During 1802, as political factions and land questions continued, Mississippians experienced another incident beyond their control. Spain closed the port of New Orleans to Americans. This action violated the Pinckney Treaty of 1795 that granted Americans navigation rights on the Mississippi River and the free right of deposit in New Orleans. Hostile feelings toward the Spanish resulted in harsh correspondence and armed men urging the capture of New Orleans. Claiborne wrote to the Secretary of State on December 18, 1802:

> The people of this Territory are greatly agitated by the suspension of the right of deposite [sic] (secured to us by the treaty) and by a recent order prohibiting intercourse between the citizens of the United States and the subjects of Spain.... We have in the Territory of Mississippi about two thousand militia, well organized, and we can easily take possession of New Orleans now.[43]

President Jefferson, however, preferred to settle the Mississippi River question and right of free deposit dispute diplomatically. Sending James Monroe to France to join forces with Robert Livingston, the American minister to France, they negotiated with Emperor Napoleon Bonaparte, who now owned the land after secret diplomacy with Spain, to purchase New Orleans and West Florida. The result of those proceedings was the Louisiana Purchase on April 30, 1803. Napoleon sold Louisiana to the United States for $15 million. That single act more than doubled the size of the country. Mississippians and all other Americans living in the Mississippi Valley and Ohio River Valley again had free access to that mighty river.

Governor Claiborne was appointed by President Jefferson as one of three commissioners to receive Louisiana from French officials. Therefore, he left Natchez on December 2, 1803. He was allowed to retain his office as governor of the Mississippi Territory until Congress created the Orleans Territory, of which he was to be appointed governor. The Mississippi territorial secretary, Cato West, acted as interim governor until March 1805. At that time, a new executive for the territory, Robert Williams of North Carolina, assumed office.

Cato West was a popular figure in Mississippi and, therefore, Williams had a difficult tenure as governor. The complicated border at 31° north latitude, with Americans living on both sides, created many intriguing situations, particularly those events involving three Kemper brothers. Rueben, Nathan, and Samuel Kemper, originally from Virginia, involved themselves in several overt actions against the Spanish along the border frontier for a number of years. To compound Williams's problems, in January 1807 ex-Vice President Aaron Burr arrived in the area under extremely suspicious circumstances. Burr had killed Alexander Hamilton in a duel, so his position in Washington, D.C., had ended ignominiously. When Burr arrived in Claiborne County, rumors were already rife that the Spanish from West Florida were planning to take over the Mississippi territory. Burr's presence most certainly fueled the rumors, and the citizens of Mississippi were agitated. Governor Williams was in North Carolina, so acting governor Cowles Mead dealt with the Burr crisis. Burr was arrested by the Mississippi militia, but he was exonerated of any charges at his trial in Richmond, Virginia. As acting governor, Mead believed throughout this incident that he did not receive enough credit, or perhaps compensation, for his accomplishment. He wrote to the secretary of state on April 13, 1807, asking, "Who arrested Burr and his associates, and brought them to the pedestal of an offended Country—Who marched twenty-four hours without food and lay the same length of time, without blanket or tent?"[44] The tense situation resulting from Burr's secret activities and the apparent lawlessness along the border highlighted the need for better leadership in Mississippi.

In 1808, after the Burr crisis and numerous border incidents, Mississippians lobbied to abolish the property qualification for voting. George Poindexter was the chairman of a committee of prominent Natchez and Mississippi Territory citizens who lobbied for reforms in the region. The group was not successful in abolishing the property qualification, but it did make some significant strides. It extended suffrage to include every white male twenty-one years of age or over who owned fifty acres of land or possessed town property worth $100. The number of delegates for the territorial House of Representatives was also increased to twelve, and voters could elect the territorial delegate to the U.S. Congress. Mississippians were moving toward statehood.

Faced with the many political problems and a growing lack of support, Governor Williams decided to resign on March 3, 1809. Before his resignation, some Mississippians had openly attempted to thwart his decisions and had plotted his dismissal. Apparently, members of the Mississippi General Assembly were extremely satisfied with his decision, because many marched through the streets celebrating the news.[45]

Upon Williams's resignation President Jefferson offered the Mississippi territorial governorship to David Holmes of Virginia. Holmes had been endorsed by several senators who signed a letter addressed to President James Madison claiming that Holmes was a man "possessing Talents & capacity to see & promote the Happiness of the people and Firmness to make the Laws respected" and someone who has a "conciliating Character." Governor Holmes, who began his tenure of office on March 7, 1809, was determined to avoid political wrangles, or the "little collisions," as he called them, that had plagued Williams's administration. The territory was prospering, and Holmes seemed ready to reconcile disaffected Mississippians. A January 1809 Mississippi Territory census submitted to Secretary of the Treasury Albert Gallatin by Thomas Freeman revealed that Madison County had a white population of 2,223 and a slave population of 322. The territory was expanding and growing.[46]

The first crisis for Governor Holmes was the West Florida revolution in 1810. Rebels organized a militia and captured Spanish Baton Rouge. The fort there was in disrepair, and there were not enough soldiers to defend it effectively. The border between Spanish territory and American holdings had continuously been a hotbed of conflict, and this revolt simply epitomized the growing tension. Pensacola, Florida, another Spanish-held fortification, was no more defensible. On September 23, approximately eighty men armed with weapons from Mississippi captured Baton Rouge and hoisted the Lone Star Flag of the independent Republic of West Florida. Governor Holmes had dispatched two companies of troops to Pickneyville, located on the border of West Florida, in case problems erupted from the revolt. On October 27, President Madison recognized the captured territory as being part of the Louisiana Purchase, and Governor Claiborne in Louisiana assumed control of the region, now a part of the United States. The Pascagoula District in the easternmost portion of the Mississippi Territory supported the insurrection. Two years after the West Florida rebellion, the Spanish evacuated Mobile, Alabama, as revolutionary action spread eastward. Mississippi now possessed a coastal frontage. In 1812, the Pearl River was set as the dividing line between Louisiana and Mississippi on the Gulf Coast, thus ending much controversy between the Spanish and Americans about southern boundaries for the Mississippi Territory.[47]

Spanish conflicts, however, were not the only troubles that plagued Holmes. Problems with Native Americans had continued to threaten Mississippians, and trade restrictions resulting from embargoes during Jefferson's administration had created commercial difficulties, as had British attempts to halt the United States' trade with France. Political intrigue developed in France when Napoleon attempted to place his brother Joseph Bonaparte on the Spanish throne in 1808, and European affairs again spilled over into North America, including Mississippi.

England had been supporting Native Americans and supplying them with war material from many different fortifications, including Pensacola. Specifically, they encouraged the Prophet and Tecumseh, two Shawnee brothers in the Ohio River Valley, in their attempts to organize the Choctaws, Chickasaws, and Creeks and rid the Mississippi Valley of Americans.

As a result of continuing problems with the British on the western U.S. frontier and on the high seas, the United States declared war on England on June 18, 1812. The Mississippi Territory braced for troubles with Native Americans, who would support the British against the Mississippians. On July 27, the Creeks defeated an American force at the Battle of Burnt Corn. Chiefs William Weatherford and Peter McQueen led the assault by the Upper Creeks. Continuing their hostilities, the Creeks attacked Fort Mims and killed more than two hundred Americans. These two encounters created great panic on the Mississippi frontier throughout 1813.

In September 1813, Holmes called for two hundred cavalry from Adams, Amite, Jefferson, and Madison counties. Major Thomas Hinds commanded these Mississippi Dragoons. That same month, Chief Pushmataha, a Choctaw, pledged five thousand of his tribesmen to support the Americans. With the Choctaw and some Chickasaw help, the Americans attacked the Creeks on December 23 at the Battle of the Holy Ground. Although this encounter was a victory for the combined forces, the Americans had few supplies and had not been paid in months. Therefore, there were no follow-up encounters to administer the *coup de grace* against the natives, and one more battle was necessary in this theater of the War of 1812.[48]

General Andrew Jackson was the general who administered the final blow to the Creek nation in the Mississippi Territory's struggles. Jackson had past ties with Mississippi; he had married his wife Rachel in Natchez when they traveled down the Natchez Trace from their homeland in Tennessee. Jackson had acquired the nickname "Sharp Knife" among the Native Americans because of his fierce fighting methods. On March 27, 1813, with approximately 3,000 soldiers, including friendly Creeks and Cherokees, he attacked the hostile Creeks, or Red Sticks as they were known, at the Battle of Horseshoe Bend. It was a decisive victory for the Americans. Jackson commented on the fierceness of the battle and the mutilations that occurred afterward. The timing was fortuitous for the Americans, because the British were marching toward New Orleans. Colonel Hinds joined Jackson's forces to capture Pensacola in November before the Americans headed to New Orleans to thwart the English naval advance along the Gulf Coast.[49]

Jackson and his force met the British on January 8, 1815, in a rousing victory on the Chalmette Battlefield. Hinds and the Mississippi Dragoons were prominent in the decisive battle. The Treaty of Ghent, however, had already ended the War of 1812 on December 24, 1814. The Battle of New Orleans, although needless, propelled Jackson to political victories and the Mississippi Territory to new prominence.

America's victory in the War of 1812 was a boon to the Mississippi Territory. The Mississippi River remained free for navigational purposes, new feelings of patriotism flooded across the territory, and the problems with the Creeks that had plagued the region were resolved. Creek lands were now available for settlement by whites seeking fertile lands for agriculture. A postwar boom occurred in the thirteen counties that now composed the Mississippi Territory. After the war, William Lattimore, the territory's congressional delegate, proposed that the entire Mississippi region, comprising present-day Mississippi and Alabama, be admitted as a state. The War of 1812 illustrated the strengths of the area, and settlers were pouring into the newly opened Native American lands. Mississippians, however, were not unified in their views of which lands should be included in the state of Mississippi.

Natchez had been the leading district in the Mississippi Territory since its inception, establishing the hegemony for the district. Settlers in the Pearl River region did not necessarily believe they had common interests with the Natchez district. Meeting at John Ford's home on the Pearl River, the citizens in that area created the Pearl River convention. This group urged a separation movement for statehood. Harry Toulmin went to Washington, D.C., in an attempt to secure congressional support for the Pearl River convention's proposal, but Lattimore was already there campaigning for statehood, including the Pearl River district in his plan.[50]

Land grant problems still hampered the Mississippi Territory. Grants of land near the Yazoo River made to people who did not live in Mississippi created tension because settlers now occupied that land. The same problem involved British land claims. Until those problems could be resolved, statehood was delayed. After much haranguing and bargaining, Congress, in 1814 compensated individuals who possessed controversial grants with $5 million from the proceeds of land sales in the territory. British claims remained unresolved, however, and Lattimore stated that those claims should also be cleared before another statehood bid was presented.[51]

As momentum for Mississippi statehood increased, conflicts such as moving the Adams county seat from Washington back to Natchez were resolved either by elections or arbitration. The issue of the boundaries for Mississippi and Alabama was also addressed. The population of Mississippi, according to an 1816 census, totaled approximately 47,000 people, of which 45.73 percent were non-white. The Natchez district comprised Adams, Amite, Claiborne, Franklin, Jefferson, Warren, and Wilkinson counties. Between 1810 and 1820, the white population declined in Adams and Amite counties but not in the other counties in the district. Census figures indicated that the population of Mississippi proper was increasing, and therefore statehood for Mississippi, exclusive of Alabama, seemed plausible.[52]

William Lattimore, an open advocate of dividing the Mississippi Territory into western and the eastern portions, was from Adams County. Perhaps the counties in the Natchez district realized that an undivided territory could result in their losing political and economic domination. In 1817 Lattimore suggested a division into a western government (Mississippi) and an eastern one. Judge Toulmin, as a compromise for the Pearl River convention, negotiated with Lattimore to include Wayne, Green, and Jackson counties in the eastern government.[53]

Regardless of Lattimore and Toulmin's maneuvers, the U.S. Congress began procedures to admit Mississippi as a state, separate from Alabama. On March 1, 1817, President Madison signed the Enabling Act that outlined Mississippi's admittance into the Union. The eastern portion of the old Mississippi Territory became the Alabama Territory. As the Mississippi territorial representative, Lattimore agreed to the congressional suggestion. A compromise designated the district of Mississippi as including Pascagoula or Hancock and Jackson counties; Pearl River or Pike county, Lawrence, Marion, Wayne, and Green counties; and the Old Natchez district of Warren, Claiborne, Jefferson, Adams, Wilkinson, Franklin, and Amite counties. Even though some in the western portion were unhappy about losing Mobile, and some in the eastern portion were unhappy about being separated from Mobile, Mississippi's march to statehood continued.[54]

THE CONSTITUTIONAL CONVENTION

A constitutional convention met during July and August 1817 at Jefferson College in Washington, Mississippi, with forty-eight delegates attending from fourteen counties. The Mississippi River counties were best represented as proceedings opened at the Washington Methodist Church. David Holmes of Adams County was elected president of the convention, and Louis Winston of Pike County was chosen as secretary.[55]

The convention illustrated the tension between the Mississippi River delegates and those from the Pearl River region. In fact, because of these conflicts, on July 15, the delegates called for a vote to reconsider the territory's bid for statehood.[56] The motion failed, and the convention continued. The delegates decided that "All laws and parts of laws, now in force in the territory, and not repugnant to the constitution, shall remain in force until they expire by limitation, or be altered or repealed by law."[57] George Poindexter was elected chairman of the drafting committee, and on August 15 a final draft of Mississippi's constitution was approved. Signing the document were forty-four members. Cato West refused to do so.

Mississippi's 1817 constitution was patterned after the constitutions of Tennessee, Louisiana, and Kentucky. It reflected the conservative cultural, economic, and political interests of the era. The most difficult challenge was determining representation in the General Assembly. The delegates from the Mississippi River counties wanted slaves and other property to count toward representation in both houses, whereas the delegates from the "piney woods" counties wanted all counties to have an equal number of senators.[58] A compromise between the two regions provided that representation in the lower house would be determined by the population of free, white males in each county, with each county guaranteed one representative. The population of free, white, taxable residents would determine the number of senators with no minimum guarantee. Every free, white male twenty-one or older who was a citizen of the United States and who had resided in Mississippi for at least one year and in his precinct for the last six months was an elector, as long as he also had served in the state militia, was exempt by law from military service, or had paid a state or county tax.[59]

To qualify for the General Assembly, as outlined in Article 3, a representative had to be a free, white male, at least twenty-two years old, a resident of Mississippi for two years, a U.S. citizen, and a property owner holding a minimum of 150 acres of land or an interest in real estate worth $500. Representatives were to serve a one-year term. Senators were to serve a three-year term and had to be at least twenty-six years old, a U.S. citizen, a four-year resident of Mississippi, and own either 300 acres of land or possess interest in real estate worth at least $1,000. Prescribed in Article 4, the requirements for governor were that a man have been a resident of the state for five years, be at least thirty years old, and own a minimum of 600 acres or real estate valued at $2000. The qualifications for lieutenant governor were the same. This article also stipulated that each county could elect a sheriff and coroner for a two-year term. The General Assembly would appoint the state treasurer and auditor.[60]

Article 5 provided that the General Assembly would elect judges under the age of sixty-five to hold office contingent upon good behavior. The General Assembly could also create a Supreme Court and lesser "superior courts," probate courts, and justice of the peace courts. The legislature would appoint the attorney general and district attorneys.[61]

The last article of the constitution contained an assortment of provisions. Candidates for office had to profess a belief in God, and no minister or priest of any denomination was eligible for the office of governor, lieutenant governor, or either branch in the General Assembly. Divorce could be granted only by a two-thirds vote in the General Assembly. New counties had to be at least 576 square miles in area, and no slave could be freed without the consent of the owner. Also, the General Assembly had the power "to oblige the owners of slaves to treat them with humanity." Slaves were also denied an inquest by a grand jury in criminal proceedings, except for capital cases.[62]

In September, the voters of Mississippi elected David Holmes the first governor of the state and Cowles Mead the first lieutenant governor. George Poindexter was the first elected congressman. The first General Assembly of the state chose Walter Leake and Thomas H. Williams as Mississippi's first senators. After congressional approval in early December, President James Monroe, signed the resolution admitting Mississippi as the twentieth state in the Union on December 10, 1817.[63]

SUMMARY

The story of Mississippi's statehood unfolds a tale of colonial intrigue, Native American encounters, and personality conflicts. All these themes, however, have contributed to the culture and character of Mississippi. French, English, and Spanish colonial influences are still apparent in the state. African American history was intertwined with the state's earliest development. Native American culture has left its indelible overlay on a multilayered cultural fabric. Individuals of all socioeconomic levels struggled to shape Mississippi into the twentieth state. Personalities like David Holmes and George Poindexter helped Mississippi evolve from a colonial possession to statehood. Mississippi's history embodies the saga of past challenges and fascinating tales of individuals whose perseverance created a state.

NOTES

1. Martha M. Bigelow, "Conquistadors, Voyageurs and Mississippi," in *A History of Mississippi*, ed. Richard Aubrey McLemore (Jackson, MS: University & College Press of Mississippi, 1973), 1:101–102; John W. Monette, *History of the Discovery and Settlement of the Valley of the Mississippi, by the Three Great European Powers, Spain, France and Great Britain* (New York: Harper & Brothers, 1846; reprint, New York: Arno Press, 1971), pp. 33–47.

2. For further information concerning the early French in the Mississippi region, see Benjamin Franklin French, *Historical Collections of Louisiana* (New York: J. Sabin & Sons, 1869); and Patricia Kay Galloway, ed., *Mississippi Provincial Archives: French Dominion* (Baton Rouge, LA: Louisiana State University Press, 1984).

3. For further information concerning Britain early in the Mississippi region, see Clarence Walworth Alvord, *The Mississippi Valley in British Politics* (New York: Russell & Russell, 1959); and Cecil Johnson, *British West Florida* (Hamden Coon: Archon Books, 1971).

4. Nellis M. Crouse, *LeMoyne d'Iberville, Soldier of New France* (Ithaca, NY: Cornell University Press, 1954), pp. 1–154, 161–162; Robert Lowry and William H. McCardle, *A History of Mississippi from the Discovery of the Great River by Hernando DeSoto including the Earliest Settlement Made by the French under Iberville to The Death of Jefferson Davis* (Jackson, MS: R. H. Henry & Co., 1891), pp. 20–21; Walter G. Howell, "The French Period 1699–1763," in McLemore, *A History of Mississippi*, 1:110–115.

5. Henry Folmer, *Franco-Spanish Rivalry in North America, 1524–1763* (Glendale, CA: A. H. Clark, 1953), pp. 190–194; Lowry and McCardle, *A History of Mississippi*, p. 21.

6. Howell, "The French Period, 1699–1763"; John K. Bettersworth, *Mississippi: A History* (Austin, TX: The Steck Company Publishers, 1959), pp. 62–63.

7. Lowry and McCardle, *A History of Mississippi*, pp. 21–22.

8. Jean Baptiste B'enard de La Harpe, *The Historical Journal of the Establishment of the French in Louisiana*, trans. Joan Cain and Virginia Koenig, ed. Glenn R. Conrad (Lafayette, LA: Center for Louisiana Studies, University of Southwestern Louisiana, 1971), pp. 21–26. Even today, the place where the French and English met on the Mississippi River is called *Detour des Anglais* or English Turn.

9. Lowery and McCardle, *History of Mississippi*, pp. 31–45; Howell, "The French Period, 1699–1763," pp. 122–125.

10. Charles Gayarre, *Louisiana: Its Colonial History and Romance* (New York: J. Wiley, 1852), pp. 208–210.

11. Lowry and McCardle, *A History of Mississippi*, p. 52.

12. Ibid.

13. Nancy Maria Miller Surrey, *The Commerce of Louisiana during the French Regime, 1699–1763* (New York: AMS Press, 1968), pp. 245–246; Howell, "The French Period, 1699–1763," pp. 127–128. The Black Code, in its entirety, is located in Gayarre, *Louisiana: Its Colonial History and Romance*, pp. 537–546.

14. Various historians spell the name Chopart, the commander of Fort Rosalie, in different ways. Howell, in "The French Period, 1699–1763," spells it Chepart. In Lowry and McCardle, *History of Mississippi*, it is spelled as Chopart. In Pearl Vivian Guyton's *Our Mississippi* (Austin, TX: The Steck Company, 1952), Chopard is the preferred spelling.

15. Howell, "A History of Mississippi," pp. 129–130; Patricia Kay Galloway, ed., *Mississippi Provincial Archives, French Dominion* (Baton Rouge, LA: Louisiana State University Press, 1984), 1:54–56, 56–60, and 122–126; J. F. H. Claiborne, *Mississippi, as a Province, Territory and State* (Jackson, MS: Power & Barksdale, 1880; reprint, Spartanburg, SC: The Reprint Company, 1978), pp. 43–44.

16. Lowry and McCardle, *History of Mississippi*, p. 97.

17. Fowler, *Franco-Spanish Rivalry*, pp. 303–309; Howell, "The French Period, 1699–1763," pp. 132–133.

18. Byrle A. Kynerd, "British West Florida," in McLemore, ed., *A History of Mississippi*, pp. 134–135; Claiborne, *Mississippi as a Province, Territory, and State*, p. 102.

19. Cecil Johnson, *British West Florida, 1763–1783* (North Haven, CT: Shoe String Press, 1971), pp. 25–26.

20. Kynerd, "British West Florida," p. 138.

21. Claiborne, *Mississippi as a Province, Territory, and State*, p. 103; Kynerd, "British West Florida," pp. 142–143.

22. Kynerd, "British West Florida," pp. 140–142; Johnson, *British West Florida*, p. 43; Claiborne, *Mississippi as a Province, Territory, and State*, p. 105.

23. Kynerd, "British West Florida," p. 139; Johnson, *British West Florida*, p. 28; Thomas D. Clark and John D. W. Guice, *Frontiers in Conflict: The Old Southwest, 1795–1830* (Albuquerque, NM: University of New Mexico Press, 1989), pp. 101–103. See "Rough Riders in the Old Southwest," chapter 6 in Clark and Guice, eds., *Frontiers in Conflict*, pp. 99–116, for detailed information regarding cattle herding in colonial Mississippi.

24. Kynerd, "British West Florida," pp. 145–146; Dunbar Rowland, ed., *Mississippi Provincial Archives, English Dominion*, vol. 3 (Nashville, TN: Press of Brandon Printing Co., 1911), pp. 91–102, 323–329, 331–332, 377–378.

25. Kynerd, "British West Florida," pp. 146–149; Clinton N. Howard, *The British Development of West Florida, 1763–1769* (Los Angeles, CA: University of California Press, 1947); Cecil Johnson, "The Distribution of Land in British West Florida," *Louisiana Historical Quarterly* 16 (October 1933): 539–553.

26. *Mississippi Provincial Archives, English,* 4:697–761; Claiborne, *Mississippi as a Province, Territory, and State,* p. 106.

27. Lowry and McCardle, *History of Mississippi,* pp. 116, 121.

28. *Mississippi Provincial Archives, English,* 4: 805–818, 827–836; Ibid., 5:17–23, 95.

29. Ibid., 8:185–190.

30. Lowry and McCardle, *History of Mississippi,* pp. 121–124; Guyton, *Our Mississippi,* pp. 66–67; Claiborne, *Mississippi as a Province, Territory, and State,* pp. 117–122; Bettersworth, *Mississippi: A History,* pp. 97–98.

31. *Mississippi Provincial Archives, English,* 9:137–174; Johnson, *British West Florida,* pp. 201–119; Claiborne, *Mississippi as a Province, Territory, and State,* pp. 125–134.

32. Jack D. L. Holmes, "A Spanish Province, 1779–1798," in McLemore, ed., *A History of Mississippi,* p. 160; Claiborne, *Mississippi as a Province, Territory, and State,* p. 137.

33. Holmes, "A Spanish Province," pp. 161, 166–167; Claiborne, *Mississippi as a Province, Territory, and State,* pp. 140–144; Jack D. L. Holmes, *Gayoso, the Life of a Spanish Governor in the Mississippi Valley, 1789–1799,* p. 16; Jack D. L. Holmes, "Cotton Gins in the Spanish Natchez District, 1795–1800," *Journal of Mississippi History* 31 (August 1969): 159–171.

34. Holmes, "A Spanish Province, 1779–1798," p. 169.

35. Holmes, *Gayoso,* p. 145; Lowry and McCardle, *History of Mississippi,* pp. 140–150.

36. Lowry and McCardle, *History of Mississippi,* pp. 146–162; Holmes, "A Spanish Province, 1779–1798," pp. 17–173.

37. Guyton, *Our Mississippi,* p. 92; Robert V. Haynes, "The Formation of the Territory," in McLemore, ed., *A History of Mississippi,* p. 174. Descriptions of the Natchez territory can be found in Laura D. S. Harrell, "Horse Racing in the Old Natchez District," *Journal of Mississippi History,* 13 (July 1951): 123–137; Clarence E. Carter, ed., *The Territorial Papers of the United States,* 5:18–22; and D. Clayton James, *Antebellum Natchez* (Baton Rouge, LA: Louisiana State University Press, 1993). See Francis Newton Thorpe, ed., *The Federal and State Constitutions, Colonial Charters, and other Organic Laws of the States, Territories, and Colonies Now or Heretofore Forming The United States of America* (Washington, DC: Government Printing Office, 1909) for complete copies of government documents relating to Mississippi, especially pp. 2025–2048.

38. Andrew Ellicott, *The Journal of Andrew Ellicott* (Philadelphia: Printed by Budd & Bartram for Thomas Dobson, 1803), pp. 162–167.

39. Clarence Edwin Carter, ed., *The Territorial Papers of the United States,* vol. 5, *The Territory of Mississippi, 1798–1817* (Washington, DC: United States Government Printing Office, 1937), p. 27; Lowry and McCardle, *History of Mississippi,* p. 165.

40. *Mississippi Territorial Papers,* p. 37; Claiborne, *Mississippi, as a Province, Territory and State,* p. 210; Bettersworth, *Mississippi: A History,* p. 123.

41. See Guy B. Braden, "A Jeffersonian Village: Washington, Mississippi," *Journal of Mississippi History,* 30 (May 1968): 135–144.

42. *Mississippi Territorial Papers*, p. 150.

43. Claiborne, *Mississippi as a Province, Territory, and State*, p. 243; quoted in Lowry and McCardle, *History of Mississippi*, p. 190.

44. Claiborne, *Mississippi Territorial Papers*, p. 545.

45. Carter, *The Territorial Papers of the United States*, 5: 661, 674, 682–683, 713–714. Williams's saga unfolds in a series of letters to and from President Jefferson in these citations.

46. J. F. H. Claiborne Papers, Mississippi Department of Archives and History, Jackson, MS; Carter, *Mississippi Territorial Papers*, pp. 697–698.

47. Carter, *Territorial Papers of Mississippi*, 6:120–122; Clark and Guice, *Frontiers in Conflict*, pp. 52–56.

48. Haynes, "The Road to Statehood," in *A History of Mississippi*, ed. Richard Aubrey McLemore (Hattiesburg: University & College Press of Mississippi, 1973), pp. 228–233, Clark and Guice, *Frontiers in Conflict*, pp. 133–150.

49. Frank Lawrence Owsley, *Struggle for the Gulf Borderlands: The Creek War and the Battle of New Orleans, 1812–1815* (Gainesville, FL: University Press of Florida, 1981).

50. Bettersworth, *Mississippi: A History*, pp. 162–164.

51. Carter, *Territorial Papers of Mississippi*, 6:636–637.

52. United States Census, series A, vol. 25. This may also be found in Carter, *The Territorial Papers of Mississippi*, 6:730.

53. Charles D. Lowery, "The Great Migration," in *A Mississippi Reader*, ed. John Edmond Gonzales (Jackson, MS: Mississippi Historical Society, 1980), pp. 69–84.

54. *Annals of Congress* (Washington, DC: Gales and Seaton, 1855), 14th Cong., 2d Sess., 1:282–284. The Enabling Act was also printed in the *Natchez Intelligencer*, April 16, 1817.

55. Claiborne lists the delegates in *Mississippi as a Province, Territory and State*, p. 352.

56. Bettersworth, *Mississippi: A History*, p. 164.

57. Claiborne, *Mississippi As a Province, Territory, and State*, p. 486.

58. Robert V. Haynes, "The Road to Statehood," 1:247.

59. William H. Hatcher, "Mississippi Constitutions," in *Politics in Mississippi*, ed. Joseph B. Parker (Salem, WI: Sheffield Publishing Company, 2001), pp. 35–38.

60. Ibid.; Lowery and McCardle, *History of Mississippi*, pp. 236–245.

61. Ibid.

62. Ibid.; Thorpe, *The Federal and State Constitutions*, 4:2032–2048.

63. Thorpe, *The Federal and State Constitutions*, 4:2032. The Enabling Act is also located on p. 2029, and the Mississippi State constitution of 1817 can be found on pp. 2032–2048.

BIBLIOGRAPHY

Akin, Edward N., and Charles C. Bolton. *Mississippi: An Illustrated History*. Northridge, CA: Windsor Publications, 2002.

Claiborne, J. F. H. *Mississippi, as a Province, Territory and State*. Jackson: Power & Barksdale, 1880; reprint, Spartanburg, SC: The Reprint Company, 1978.

Clark, Thomas D., and John D. W. Guice. *Frontiers in Conflict: The Old Southwest, 1795–1830*. Albuquerque, NM: University of New Mexico Press, 1989.

Crouse, Nellis Maynard. *Lemoyne d'Iberville: Soldier of New France*. Ithaca, NY: Cornell University Press, 1954.

Hyde, Harford Montgomery. *John Law: The History of an Honest Adventurer*. London: Home & Van Thal, 1948.

Loewan, James W., and Charles Sallis, eds. *Mississippi; Conflict & Change*. New York: Pantheon Books, 1974.

McLemore, Richard Aubrey, ed. *A History of Mississippi*. 2 vols. Hattiesburg, MI: University & College Press of Mississippi, 1973.

Skates, John Ray. *Mississippi: A Bicentennial History*. New York: Norton, 1979.

Sullivan, Charles L. *The Mississippi Gulf Coast: Portrait of a People*. Northridge, CA: Windsor Publications, 1985.

Missouri

Territorial Development:

- The United States obtains future territory of Missouri from France through the Louisiana Purchase, April 30, 1803
- Future territory of Missouri organized as part of the Louisiana Territory (or, the District of Louisiana for a time in 1804), 1804–1812
- Reorganized as the Missouri Territory, June 4, 1812
- Missouri admitted into the Union as the twenty-fourth state, August 10, 1821

Capitals Prior to Statehood:

- St. Louis, 1805–1821

State Capitals:

- Saint Charles, 1821–1825
- Jefferson City, 1825–present

Origin of State Name: Named after the Missouri River, which itself was named after the Missouri tribe; "Missouri" means "town of the large canoes."

First Governor: Alexander McNair
Governmental Organization: Bicameral
Population at Statehood: 66,586 (figure taken from the 1820 Census)
Geographical Size: 68,886 square miles

———————————— ☆☆☆ ————————————

THE STATE OF MISSOURI

Admitted to the Union as a State: August 10, 1821

William L. Olbrich, Jr.

INTRODUCTION

Missouri celebrates two different dates for admission to the United States. The state government celebrates July 19, 1820, when the Missouri territorial legislature accepted the newly written state constitution. The federal government, however, celebrates August 10, 1821, when President James Monroe, adhering to a congressional resolution, proclaimed Missouri a state. This conundrum resulted from the four years of legislative combat to make Missouri a state, 1818–1821.

The controversies revealed and compromises reached in the admission of Missouri to full statehood remained prominent in the political agenda of the United States until after Reconstruction in 1877. The issues of states' rights versus federal controls, cultural wars between the North and the South, strict versus loose construction of the U.S. Constitution, and the definition of "citizen" obscured the path for Missouri's admission to the Union as much as the emotional issue of black slavery. Indeed, these issues still lace current policy matters.

BOUNDARY ISSUES

Missouri became a part of the United States in 1803 by a treaty with France. The United States purchased the Province of Louisiana for $15 million, gaining the crucial port of New Orleans near the mouth of the Mississippi River and more than 800,000 square miles of land bordered by the Mississippi River, the Rocky Mountains, Spanish Texas, and the British Canadas.

Article III of the treaty signed on April 30, 1803, stipulated that inhabitants of this Louisiana Purchase would become full citizens of the United States, and "they shall be maintained and protected in the free enjoyment of their liberty, property, and the Religion which they profess." The inhabitants did indeed become full citizens in due course, but protecting their property ownership meant settling endless land title disputes, dealing with recalcitrant Native American tribes, and coping with the issue of black slavery. The Senate ratified the treaty, and on October 31, 1803, federal officials began American administration.[1]

Congress required its written permission be given to President Thomas Jefferson to send U.S. government agents into the new territories. Captain Amos Stoddard took civil and military control of St. Louis and "Upper Louisiana" on March 9 and 10, 1804. The territorial governor of Indiana, William Henry Harrison, then acted as the interim administrator for all lands west of the Mississippi.[2] People living in what became Missouri immediately began to petition Congress. They prefaced all their complaints with the unfilled promise of full citizenship. They took strong exception to being administered by the Indiana Territory, whose capital at Vincennes lay 130 miles to the east. On March 26, 1804, Congress divided the Louisiana Purchase into the District of Orleans, with its capital at New Orleans, and the District of Louisiana, with its capital at St. Louis. The latter had as its southern boundary 33° north latitude from the Mississippi River to the Spanish land claims and included the bulk of the Louisiana Purchase.

Both new territories received governments more or less according to the provisions and practices employed under the Northwest Ordinance of 1787 for Ohio, Indiana, and Illinois by 1818. The ordinance's provisions for levels of territorial status and statehood were never followed to the letter, but the differences of adherence never varied enough from state to state to make much difference.[3] On April 8, 1812, the District of Orleans became the State of Louisiana without any official explanation for the choice of names. Another six weeks passed before Congress re-named the remaining territory "Missouri." Again, no official records explaining the choice of name seem to exist, but Clarence Carter claimed the name "Missouri" originated in the U.S. Senate.[4] Missouri's boundaries actually remained in flux until present times.

The state's first petition for statehood in 1817 drew the first complete set of boundaries for a manageable jurisdiction. The Mississippi River formed the eastern boundary. The northern border was 40° north latitude, and 36°30' north latitude became the southern boundary. The Osage treaty line, at 95°30' west longitude, crossing the Missouri at the mouth of the Kansas River, formed the western boundary. Peter Chouteau and Meriwether Lewis secured this boundary line between U.S. land controlled by the Osage on its west and U.S. land controlled by Washington to the east in 1808.[5] During 1818, several proposals for the new state circulated through both the U.S. Congress and the Missouri populace. An example of these unofficial proposals retained the southern and western boundaries of the 1817 proposal but made the Missouri River the northern boundary.

The second statehood petition printed in the fall of 1819 sought to push the northern, western, and southern boundaries out another thirty-seven miles in each of these directions. These proposed borders ignored the already established southern border with the new Arkansas Territory and the treaties with the Osages. Congress separated the Arkansas Territory south of 36°30' north latitude from the Missouri Territory in 1819. The state boundaries that emerged from Congress between 1819 and 1821 kept the boundaries of the 1817 petition with the addition of the southeast corner, known today as "the boot heel."[6]

Outdated survey methods and meandering rivers kept the Missouri boundaries from becoming exact until the 1980s. In 1837 Missouri successfully negotiated with the Osage tribe and the federal government for the purchase of land known as the "Platte Purchase." This new boundary followed the Missouri River upstream from the mouth of the Kansas River, on the west bank of the Missouri, to the point where the 40°30' north latitude line intersects the Missouri River. In 1849 the state of Iowa and the state of Missouri argued over their common border. Iowa wished the boundary moved further south, claiming that the westward line from the Des Moines River forming the northeast boundary was closer to its point of merging with the Mississippi River. The U.S. Supreme Court, however, sided with Missouri, and the common border with Iowa remained 40°30' north latitude. In 1870, Kentucky and Missouri disputed ownership of Wolf Island in the Mississippi River. In 1820 the statutory border between the two states was the middle of the main channel of the Mississippi, but since that time, the main channel had moved east of Wolf Island. The Supreme Court awarded the island to Kentucky.

In 1937, Iowa and Missouri again argued over the Des Moines River boundary. By mutual agreement, Iowa included all lands north and east of the Des Moines River from its mouth to the 40°30' north latitude intersection, and Missouri included all lands south and west of the river from the mouth to the same point. In 1981, in the Missouri-Nebraska Boundary Compact, Nebraska and Missouri finally accepted the middle of the main channel of the Missouri River as their mutual boundary, and both states shared control of the river commerce.[7] The U.S. Corps of Engineers currently keeps the river boundaries of Missouri static. Further changes in the boundaries are not likely.

TERRITORIAL GOVERNMENT AND POLITICAL ISSUES

Territorial Governors

Captain Amos Stoddard acted as the first American governor of Upper Louisiana. This captain of artillery had been a Maine lawyer in civilian life. He arrived in St. Louis in February 1804 and prepared for the formal transfer of military authority from the Spanish in early March 1804. In May, he witnessed the departure of Lewis and Clark on the expedition of discovery. During his eight months as interim civil governor, Stoddard faced the perennial problems of the territory: Native Americans, land, and slaves. Attempting to placate the Osage to the south and west of St. Louis, he unintentionally encouraged the northern Sac tribes to begin predations on outlying homesteads north of the Missouri River. In writing to his superiors about his suspicions of fraudulent land deals, he alienated most of the French population, who had acquired many of the Spanish land grants. Being told that the local slaves thought American control meant automatic manumission, Stoddard rigidly enforced the Spanish Black Code curtailing the use of slaves to fetch and carry outside their owner's lands.

William Henry Harrison, as governor of the Indiana Territory, was given control of Upper Louisiana in October 1804. He immediately set out to create entirely new legal systems for the whites and trans-Mississippi homelands for Native American tribes then in the Indiana territories. Secretary of State James Madison quickly curtailed these efforts, having Harrison instead establish militia, court circuits, and civil districts. Governor Harrison visited St. Louis in October 1804 and offered civilian government posts to many of its local citizens. He also bought off the Sac and Fox Indian tribes for $1,000 a year. Harrison later served as a military general in the Native American wars, winning fame for his victory at Tippecanoe, and was elected president in 1840.

With the passage of the 1805 law formally dividing the Louisiana Purchase into the District of Orleans and the District of Louisiana, President Jefferson appointed General James A. Wilkinson as governor. Wilkinson arrived in St. Louis in July 1805, but his short term was forever stained by his association with Aaron Burr's grandiose plots. Jefferson transferred Wilkinson to New Orleans in August 1806 to avoid disgracing him. His territorial secretary, Joseph Browne, became acting governor. Browne, however, was Aaron Burr's brother-in-law, and Jefferson replaced him as territorial secretary with Frederick Bates in February 1807. Frederick Bates served as acting governor from February 1807 until William Clark's appointment in 1813. Bates theoretically served under two governors—Meriwether Lewis and Benjamin Howard—but neither man chose to spend much time in St. Louis or the Louisiana Territory.

William Clark served as governor of the Missouri Territory from 1813 until it became a state in 1821. He was the only governor during Missouri's time as a second-class territory. The intense emotional and political excitement involved in Missouri's admission as a state left Clark with little to do except keep an eye on the Native American tribes. Clark also served as the superintendent of Indian affairs for the War Department. He was more successful with his Native American relations than with his civilian ones. Gossip said he led the political faction known as the "St. Louis Junto." When Clark wrote President Monroe in 1821 about disposing of the Missouri territorial materials still in his possession and receiving his back pay, the answer came that the budget made no allowances for paying him as governor after 1820, and his pay as Indian superintendent would end soon. Clark remained in St. Louis until his death in 1838.[8]

Congressional Delegates

One of the provisions of the 1812 law making Missouri a "second-class" territory entitled it to send a non-voting delegate to the House of Representatives. The first delegate elected was Edward Hempstead of St. Louis. Born into a well-respected family in New London, Connecticut, in 1780, Hempstead moved to St. Louis as a lawyer in 1805. He held several appointed and elected posts in the territory before being elected as a delegate to Congress in 1812. Hempstead took his oath of office and was seated in the House on June 13, 1813. For most of his term, he submitted petitions for monetary support and resolutions on settling public land claims. He made three inquiries into funding a trans-Mississippi military force to be called the "Rangers." He also made inquiries into federal laws concerning the government of Missouri and the location of a state capital. Hempstead took a leave of absence for the remainder of the Thirteenth Congress on March 29, 1814. He declined a second term, preferring to superintend the resettlement of several Hempstead families from Connecticut to St. Louis after the War of 1812.

Rufus Easton, postmaster of St. Louis, was elected to replace Hempstead in 1814. Easton came to St. Louis via Litchfield, Connecticut, and Vincennes, then capital of the Indiana Territory. Almost as soon as he took his seat on December 11, 1815, he faced a challenge to his election. John Scott, his opponent during the previous August's election, claimed fraudulent votes put Easton in office. Seventeen of Easton's forty-three appearances in the *Annals of Congress* concerned this problem; in August 1816 he was forced by the House to vacate his seat to Scott. Easton's work as delegate included eight resolutions on public land issues and four on the lead mines in Washington County. He even sponsored an unsuccessful bill giving wounded war veterans large tracts of Missouri public land as rewards for service. Easton returned to St. Louis to practice law and dabble in real estate.

John Scott was born in Hanover County, Virginia, and graduated from Princeton. He moved to Ste. Genevieve on the Mississippi River in southeastern Missouri in 1806. His first political outing was his election against Rufus Easton for the office of territorial delegate. Scott was considered an ally of the St. Louis Junto, so it is not surprising that its ex-officio leader, Governor William Clark, discovered the miscast votes after Easton left for Washington. Scott assumed the office of territorial delegate one day after Rufus Easton vacated it. Scott served as delegate from August 1817 until March 1821. He was then elected the state of Missouri's first representative to Congress, a post he held until 1827. In the second session of the Fourteenth Congress (1817), Scott produced nine separate petitions and resolutions concerning the public lands in Missouri. He made two resolutions concerning the same lead mines Rufus Easton sought to aid. During the next two Congresses, the Fifteenth (1818–1819) and the Sixteenth (1820–1821), Scott spent most of his time on Missouri's admission to the Union.[9]

TERRITORIAL ISSUES: RIGHTS, NATIVE AMERICANS, AND LAND

The inhabitants of Missouri continually worried their federal administrators with three large issues: the legal status of the inhabitants in the territory, land title disputes, and Native American relations. Congress continually received petitions from groups in Missouri reminding it of the treaty promise to make them full citizens of the United States. Petitioners protested their status as a first-class territory in which all administrators were appointed by the federal executive on the Atlantic coast. They repeatedly begged for second-class territorial status so they could elect at least one chamber of the General Assembly and have a delegate in Congress.[10] Relations with Native American tribes on both sides of the Mississippi vexed the European settlers. They reacted strongly against Governor Wilkinson's plan to remove tribes living east of the Mississippi to the western lands. The inhabitants continually pleaded for army troops and trading goods to keep the tribes mollified. They also criticized the agents and traders working with the tribes. The Missouri Baptist Association of St. Charles County, for example, claimed the European traders cheated and defrauded the Native Americans, causing them to seek revenge on outlying settlements.[11]

Land disputes undoubtedly caused American officials the most problems. Toward the end of the Spanish rule, the process for awarding grants of land became extremely slipshod. Many land grants around Ste. Genevieve were never registered with the viceroy in New Orleans. American settlers found they had purchased land in good faith from fraudulent land dealers. Other settlers simply moved onto land without securing ownership. Some of the first officials sent to the territories were judges to sort out the various claims, a process that took years to settle. Territorial Delegate John Scott in Washington, D.C., found occasion to remind one of the judges in Missouri of the laws to be enforced in an upcoming public land auction. Especially at risk, in Scott's opinion, were the people eligible for public land under the concept of preemption. Preemption allowed persons who had settled on public lands without first securing title to it to be given a first chance at purchasing the land when it came up for sale.[12]

TERRITORIAL ISSUE: SLAVERY

The statutory nonexistence of slavery in the Northwest Territory caused some consternation in Missouri soon after the Louisiana Purchase. William

C. Carr, the second American lawyer to arrive in Missouri after the Louisiana Purchase, wrote to his friend Senator John Breckinridge, in Lexington, Kentucky, that the citizens of Ste. Genevieve voiced concerns about their slave properties. Carr, originally from Virginia, came to the Louisiana Purchase after similar territorial experiences in Kentucky and Indiana. Fellow Virginian John Breckinridge, senator from Kentucky from 1801 to 1805, was also a confident of President Thomas Jefferson and later became Jefferson's attorney general. Carr claimed slavery continued unabated in New Orleans after the Purchase only under certain unnamed political conditions, and the American settlers in Missouri feared they would face worse: gradual abolition and manumission. These American settler concerns, he said, came from the illiterate, the ignorant, the villains, and the fugitives who previously fled the United States. The local French settlers, Carr claimed, were indifferent to the issue. These concerns about possible federal anti-slavery action planted the first seeds of slavery as a political issue in the new state of Missouri.[13]

PROCESS OF BECOMING A STATE

The 1817 Petition

Territorial Delegate John Scott presented the first surviving petition for Missouri statehood to the House of Representatives on March 18, 1818. The petition carried sixty-eight signatures, nearly all from members of the grand jury for Washington County, Missouri, located southwest of St. Louis. The petition presented arguments justifying the admission and suggesting boundaries for the proposed state.

The boundaries it recommended were the Mississippi River to the east, the Osage treaty line of 1808 to the west, latitude 40° to the north, and 36°30' to the south. The petition stated that such boundaries allowed the creation of future states to the north and south of the proposed state of Missouri. The Northwest Ordinance of 1787 thus appeared in spirit if not in the actual words. The proposed state of Illinois, to the east of Missouri, also at this time requested 40° north latitude as its northern boundary. The petition argued that such a state put the Missouri River—whose name the state later carried–at the center of the state, rather than its northern boundary. The Missouri River boundary appeared occasionally in the talk of the few anti-slavery adherents in St. Louis as well as several Spanish land grant hustlers in Ste. Genevieve on the Mississippi River and Potosi (county seat of Washington County). By keeping the Mississippi and Missouri rivers as its foci, the petitioners wrote, the proposed state avoided what they considered to be the sterile plains to the west of the Osage treaty line that stretched hundreds of miles to the "Shining Mountains" (the Rocky Mountains). Within these proposed borders lived around 40,000 people, a population greater than Tennessee, Ohio, or Mississippi possessed

677

when they were admitted to the Union. The petition again brought up the third section of the treaty with France that guaranteed full citizenship to the inhabitants of the Louisiana Purchase as soon as possible.

The petition also included a list of grievances Missouri citizens suffered because of their lack of the promised full citizenship. They were taxed by Congress and the federal government without possessing any meaningful representation. The territorial assembly was limited to passing laws of a local nature only. Also, the appointed governor held the power of absolute veto over its acts without recourse. Last, and somewhat surprisingly from the members of a county grand jury, the territorial courts held too much power over civil and criminal matters. Missourians wished to establish the state's boundaries as they saw fit, not as eastern map-readers might fancy. The petition ended with the note that its printer in St. Louis was Sergeant Hall. Hall also published *The Emigrant and General Advertiser*, a St. Louis newspaper controlled by a political faction that strongly endorsed statehood as a means of making money through land dealings.[14]

The 1819 Petition

On November 13, 1819, the territorial legislature of Missouri adopted a memorial to Congress applying for statehood. This memorial consisted of three separate documents: the formal request for statehood, a document listing donations and appropriations, and the summary page for the territorial census of August–September 1817. The census showed a white male adult population of more than 19,000 in nine counties. No white women, white children, blacks, or Native Americans were included in the count.

The donations and appropriations document consisted of six detailed requests for sections of public lands the territorial legislature wanted given to the state government to provide an economic infrastructure. Each request stated the amount and type of land requested and its intended use for the state. The first request was for lands containing one lead mine and lands surrounding salt springs to provide revenue for the state government. The second request was for one township of land to sell in support of a state college. The third request sought one township to sell in support of public buildings in the capital city, and the fourth request sought all vacant lands within existing towns and villages to sell in support of public schools. The fifth request was for 9 percent of monies gained from the sale of U.S. public lands to support a canal from the Illinois River to Lake Michigan, an extension of the National Road from Wheeling (now West Virginia) to St. Louis, and a new road from St. Louis to New Orleans. The sixth request was for another 5 percent of public land sales to support education and transportation in the state. These requests occupied Congress for some time during the admission process.[15]

CONGRESSIONAL DEBATES OVER STATEHOOD

The formal debate in Congress to make Missouri a state consumed four years and two Congresses. The final product, known in history books as the Missouri Compromise, actually required four separate roll-call votes in the Fifteenth Congress (1818–1819) and the Sixteenth Congress (1819–1821) to accomplish.

During the Fifteenth Congress (1818–1819), Missouri territorial delegate John Scott introduced H.R. 177 to the full House on April 3, 1818. This bill, using language that had become standard for admission of new states, "to enable" the state of Missouri, went to the Committee of the Whole; that is, all representatives participated in free debate on the admission. The bill moved steadily through the committee, mostly receiving amendments and changes to the donations and appropriations list included with the memorial from the territorial legislature.

On Saturday, February 13, 1819, Representative James Tallmadge, elected as a Jeffersonian Republican from New York State to fill a vacancy caused by the previous incumbent's death, submitted an amendment forbidding new slaves from entering the state of Missouri. The amendment also required manumission for existing slaves when they reached age twenty-five years. Although most observers expressed surprise over this totally unexpected turn of events, Tallmadge was already on record as attempting to deny slavery in the Arkansas and Alabama admissions. (A native New Yorker from Duchess County, James Tallmadge had graduated from Brown University and was a protégé of New York Governor DeWitt Clinton. After his one partial term in the House, he returned to New York state politics before becoming president of New York University from 1830 to 1846.)[16] The wording of the Tallmadge amendment closely resembled New York state's recent law prescribing gradual emancipation of slaves within the state. (The practice of slavery continued to exist in New York, albeit in diminishing conditions, until 1840.) During the heated discussion that followed the announcement of his amendment, Representative Tallmadge gave a speech typifying the vehement attitudes of northern and southern members in the ensuing years' debates: "Sir, if a dissolution of the Union must take place, let it be so! If civil war, which gentlemen so much threaten, must come, I can only say, let it come!" After long hours of speeches, the House voted to accept H.R. 177, as amended, by a vote of 97-56.

H.R. 177, as amended, went to the Senate on February 17. The Senate returned the bill on March 2 without the section restricting slavery, now dubbed the "Tallmadge amendment." The two chambers deadlocked over the addition of the Tallmadge amendment, and the bill enabling Missouri's statehood died for the remainder of the Fifteenth Congress.

James Tallmadge refused a second term as a representative, so the Sixteenth Congress (1819–1821) convened on December 6, 1819, without him. Other members of Congress quickly took his place. Territorial Delegate John Scott again presented the petition of the Missouri territorial legislature on December 8 as H.R. 1, and Senator William Smith from South Carolina offered the identical Senate version on December 29. (This legislative technique, today known as "companion bills," was relatively new in 1820. The rationale for this technique is that both chambers of Congress discuss the same matter at the same time, thereby reducing the time for passage.) Senator Jonathan Roberts of Pennsylvania amended the Senate bill to restrict slavery, as in the previous Tallmadge amendment, and Representative John Taylor of New York did the same in the House. In the Sixteenth Congress, the section restricting slavery in Missouri was dubbed the "Taylor amendment." Representative Taylor would be heard from again on the subject of Missouri.

The debates on Missouri's statehood dominated the first session of the Sixteenth Congress from December 1819 until March 1820. With more than two hundred speeches delivered by more than sixty different members of Congress, these debates occupied more than eight hundred pages of text in the *Annals of Congress*. Massachusetts alone provided twelve different speakers, on both sides of the question. Kentucky, Pennsylvania, and Virginia each provided eleven. Territorial Delegate John Scott spoke once for three hours, calling for his state's admission. Representative John Sergeant of Pennsylvania held forth on abolition of slavery for forty-seven pages of text and another three hours of time on February 9, 1820, after Representative Henry Clay of Kentucky spoke for four hours arguing against the constitutionality of the Taylor amendment. Finally, on March 2, 1820, Representatives Charles Kinsey of New Jersey and James Stevens of Connecticut begged their colleagues to accept compromises allowing Missouri to become a state.

The three issues at stake were Missouri statehood, slavery in Missouri, and slavery in the remaining unorganized territories. Each issue required its own separate vote for the Missouri Compromise to be successful. The House finally accepted the Senate version of Missouri statehood—without mention of slavery—by a vote of 90-87. The House then voted on prohibiting slavery in the unorganized territory north of 36°30' latitude by a vote of 134-42. The next day, March 3, 1820, the Senate accepted the House compromises, and H.R. 1 was signed into law by President James Monroe on March 6, 1820.

The editors of the *Annals of Congress*, which was not compiled until thirty years after the Missouri debates, described the speeches on Missouri as addressing four subjects: the evils of slavery, the politics of New England and the South involving the lands of the Louisiana Purchase, the balance of power between the national government and the state governments, and the obligations and benefits of the current union of states.[17] The members of Congress spoke of their deep beliefs on these topics, continually stating that the precedents set during this admission process would greatly affect the nation's future. Most speakers focused on the issue of black slavery, which seemed to outweigh all other political considerations concerning Missouri's statehood. Indeed, the fate of Missouri often disappeared in the heat of the arguments. Between 1819 and 1821, more than twenty petitions to forbid slavery in either Missouri or the Louisiana Purchase went to Congress from northern state legislatures, citizens of counties in northern states, and citizens of cities in northern states. Members of Congress from New York, Rhode Island, and Pennsylvania presented these petitions directly on their chamber floors as their own speeches, without the usual courtesy of allowing the presiding officer to announce the petition first.

In the Senate debates, anti-slavery and pro-slavery speakers alternated; in the House no such courtesies appeared. Examples of the congressional speeches condemning slavery, especially in Missouri, are those by Representatives Daniel Pope Cook of Illinois and Joseph Hemphill of Pennsylvania. Hemphill claimed slavery to be the forcible oppression of otherwise powerless people and asked, "[H]ow can this be claimed to be a right?" Cook went so far as offering to give the entire Louisiana Purchase to current slaveowners in exchange for the abolition of slavery. (Daniel Cook, born, in Kentucky in 1794, moved to the early state capital of Kaskaskia, Illinois, in 1815. For the next three years, Glover Moore wrote, he promised voters he would agitate against slavery and would represent the interests of Illinois, and not those of Missouri. His speech on Missouri was only his second time to speak on the floor.)

Senator William Smith of South Carolina proved a fierce defender of slavery. Born in North Carolina, he entered state politics at the age of forty and held elective offices in South Carolina and, in later life, in Alabama. In the course of his twelve speeches on the subject of Missouri, he claimed that American black slaves fared much better than their multiracial counterparts in Naples, Asia, and Brazil. His southern colleague Senator Alexander Smyth of Virginia theorized that slavery was the natural state of African blacks because they enslaved each other in their African kingdoms, and free blacks were slaveholders in the southern states. Furthermore, Smith claimed, when northern states abolished slavery within their borders, slaveowners often sold their property to Southerners rather than manumit them. Smith found such actions extremely hypocritical and often voiced his opinion on the floor of the House.

In their debates and petitions over slavery, members of Congress and American citizens exposed several issues of contention among the states during this so-called "Era of Good Feelings." Sectionalism, seeing either the northeastern states ("the North") or the southeastern states ("the South") as victim of the other section's lust for national hegemony, produced grave doubts for the future of the Union. Senator Jonathan Roberts of Pennsylvania claimed that Missouri was only a test case for southern expansion through the colonization of the western territories. (Roberts had been apprenticed to a wheelwright before becoming a career state politician, and afterward, like a good Republican, he retired to his small Pennsylvania farm.) Senator William Smith of South

Carolina countered with the reminder that the New England states had almost seceded from the Union in 1815 at the infamous Hartford convention rather than lose their control of American trade with Great Britain. Now, Smith said, New England wanted to continue its hold on the Congress by creating the otherwise fictitious state of Maine out of Massachusetts to gain two additional Senate seats. In vain did Representative Henry Meigs of New York warn that such arguments made the Congress act more like teenage gangs than wise statesmen. (A Connecticut Yankee with a degree from Yale, Meigs was a career state-level politician who served one term in the House for the Sixteenth Congress before returning to New York City.)

The political theory of states' rights in America argues that individual states have rights over which the other states and the federal government have no control. Senator Walter Lowrie of Pennsylvania first broached the states' rights issue during the Missouri debates. (Another career politician, born in Scotland, Lowrie served two terms in the Senate before moving to New York City to be on the Board of Missions for the Presbyterian Church.) Lowrie claimed to be anti-slavery, but he also believed Missouri had the right as a state to decide for itself on slavery within its borders, and Congress had no constitutional authority to stop the state. His anti-slavery stance, he said, meant he preferred that Pennsylvania secede from the Union rather than share it with slaveholding states. Senator William Pinckney of Maryland considered the individual states sovereign and independent of the Union and of each other, as Missouri's constitution would later declare. (William Pinkney [1764–1822] served as a high-ranking diplomat for presidents from Washington to Monroe. He accepted a term in the Senate as a favor and died in Washington, D.C., shortly after making his speech on Missouri.)

In their search for authoritative statements, some members of Congress turned to the Bible. Senator William Smith of South Carolina claimed that the Bible approved of slavery. Senator David L. Morrill of New Hampshire retorted that the book of Leviticus, Smith's chief source, was written for an ancient Jewish theocracy, not a modern American democracy. Moreover, asserted Senator Roberts of Pennsylvania, had Senator Smith read further into Leviticus, he would have found the fifty-year celebration of the jubilee, whereby all enslaved persons became free.

With a touch of prescience, Senator H. Gray Otis of Massachusetts told his colleagues about the New England Shakers, who were good honest Christian people except for their unusual marriage practices. Should such a religious sect occupy a portion of the unorganized territories and populate it sufficiently to request statehood, what would the Congress do? Otis answered himself by saying the Congress could certainly require restrictions on unacceptable behaviors in areas wishing to become states. Otis thus accurately and unknowingly foretold the problem of Mormon polygamy, which kept Utah a territory for several years. (A Harvard graduate and a staunch Federalist, Otis was politically tainted because he was a delegate to the controversial Hartford convention in 1814.)

The issue of Missouri statehood was finally settled by compromise but not until the members of Congress had exhausted themselves. Early in the Sixteenth Congress, Senator Jesse B. Thomas of Illinois had introduced a bill containing the elements of the eventual compromises, but the Senate vote squashed it soundly and immediately. (Senator Thomas was a career politician, first in the Indiana Territory [1803–1809] and then in the southern half of the Illinois Territory [1809–1818]. Elected to the Senate from Illinois in 1818, he served until 1829. The southern half of Illinois had the nickname of "Little Egypt" because of its pro-slavery and pro-southern sentiments. Senator Thomas consistently voted with the senators of the southeastern states.) By March 2, 1820, more than fourteen representatives, although reluctant and unrepentant, called for compromise. "For," asked Representative Benjamin Hardin of Kentucky, "of what benefits is abolition if at a sacrifice to your constitution?"

ENABLING LEGISLATION

The law only enabled the citizens of Missouri to form a state constitution. The law consisted of eight sections, of which seven were concerned with the proposed state. Section 8 prohibited slavery and involuntary servitude from the unorganized territories north of 36°30' north latitude, the extension of Missouri's southern border. No other mention of slavery appeared in the text. The first section did not require congressional approval of that constitution before making Missouri a full-fledged state in the Union, but the northern members of Congress later interpreted it that way. Section 2 defined some of the borders but failed to include the lines of longitude and latitude for the other borders, an omission that would trouble the state for another 150 years. Section 3 made all free, white males over the age of twenty-one with at least three months of state residency eligible to vote and to be elected to office. Section 3 also portioned out the seats in the lower chamber of the General Assembly. Section 4 enabled the electors to choose representation and establish a state government, which was to "be republican, and not repugnant to the Constitution of the United States." Sections 5 and 6 enabled the new state's electors to sell and tax public lands more or less in accordance with the 1820 Ordinance. Section 7 required the new state to provide a "true and attested copy of such constitution, or frame of State government" to the Congress but, once again, made no mention of congressional approval being required for implementing it. Throughout the text of the law, the state's name is never mentioned; it is described as "that portion of the Missouri Territory included." This point became important later.[18]

THE STATE CONSTITUTION

Fifty elected delegates and staff met in Bennett's Mansion House hotel in St. Louis on June 12, 1820, to compose a constitution for Missouri. The delegates came from the fourteen counties of the state, as apportioned by the territorial legislature. Although the restriction of slavery was the chief issue during the election, no delegate favoring the restriction or abolition of slavery in Missouri came remotely close to being elected to the constitutional convention.

The convention elected David Barton as its moderator and broke up into committees. Historian Floyd Shoemaker reports the principal authors of the constitution were David Barton, Edward Bates, John Cook, John R. Jones, Jonathan Findlay, and John Scott. The committee on style—Edward Bates of St. Louis, John Cook of Ste. Genevieve, and John R. Smith of Washington County—is credited with crafting the final draft. The convention completed its task in thirty-eight days on July 19, 1820.

In the fall of 1820, the Missouri territorial assembly sent a memorial to Congress that consisted of a package of four documents in its quest for statehood. David Barton, as president of the territorial legislature, certified the text of the constitution, a schedule for the establishment of state agencies, an ordinance on the sale of public lands in Missouri, and an accompanying certifying letter from David Barton as president of the constitutional convention. The constitution itself consisted of thirteen articles for the governing of the state. The schedule gave the procedure for the election of state legislators and a schedule for the first meeting of the state legislature in St. Louis. The ordinance requested that the federal Congress adjust the percentage of tax on the sale of public lands to aid the building of roads, canals, and schools. According to the preamble of the 1820 constitution, Missouri was a "free and independent republic."[19]

Article 1, "Of Boundaries," traces the lines with the southeastern boot heel of the New Madrid District and without the Platte Purchase of 1836–1837. As noted previously, the state's exact boundary lines remained in contention for another 150 years. Article 2, "Of the Distribution of Power," provided for three separate and distinct departments of government, "each of which shall be confined to a single magistracy." This constitution, however, later made both the supreme court and the equity court justices the equal of the governor in terms of civil authority (see Article 5).

Article 3, "Of the Legislative Power," named and described the first department, the state legislature. At thirty-six sections, it was the longest article. Sections 1 through 25 covered the General Assembly, which the constitution divided into two chambers, the House of Representatives and the Senate. Legislators were to be elected by vote of all qualified, free, white males (called "electors") on the first Monday in August of even-numbered years. Article 3 required the state to conduct a census of free, white males every four years for the reapportionment of seats in the General Assembly. Electors' requirements were a minimum age of twenty-one, U.S. citizenship, and state residence of at least one year. State and local executive branch officials, judiciary officials, the clergy, members of the federal government and military, and persons convicted of infamous crimes were not eligible to hold office in the General Assembly. Blacks, Native Americans, and white females received no notice in these qualifications. Voters were exempt from arrest for all save capital crimes while traveling to and from the election sites.

Article 3, Section 2 granted each county at least one representative, with a maximum of one hundred representatives in the House. Representatives were elected every two years. Requirements for representative were a minimum age of twenty-four years, U.S. citizenship, state residence for at least two years, county residence of at least one year, and paid-up taxes. The state was to be apportioned into fourteen to thirty-three senatorial districts composed of several adjacent counties according to the last census. These districts could be created or dissolved as needed. Senators were elected every four years. Requirements for senator were a minimum age of thirty years, U.S. citizenship, state residence of four years, district membership of one year, and paid-up taxes.

Each of the two chambers set its own rules for procedure and behavior. After the August elections, the General Assembly was to meet for one session, commencing on the first Monday of November of even-numbered years and continuing until the members voted to adjourn. Public attendance was to be allowed at all meetings, and a public journal of proceedings was mandatory for both chambers, except by a two-thirds vote of the members. Neither chamber could adjourn without first notifying the other. Public and private bills could originate in either chamber. The House was responsible for the impeachments of all state officials, and the Senate was to act as judge and jury for the same. Statute laws of civil and criminal import were to be revised, digested, and printed for public access every ten years. Nothing in this constitution limited the legislative powers of the General Assembly. The requirements to revise and digest the public statutes put Missouri in the forefront of U.S. legal thinking at the time.

Slavery received special attention in Sections 26, 27, and 28. Section 26 forbade the General Assembly the power to manumit slaves without the owner's permission and further denied the General Assembly the power to prohibit emigrants from bringing slaves with them. Section 26 instructed the state legislature to pass laws excluding free blacks or mulattos from living in the state. Section 26 also instructed the legislature to pass laws cautioning owners to treat their slaves humanely. Section 27 gave slaves the right to trial and to legal counsel. Section 28 made killing a slave murder and required that those convicted of crimes against slaves receive the same punishment as for similar crimes against whites. Why did the 1820 constitution add these three sections to the state framework? The proposed constitution gave few instructions for future legislation other than these three sections, and, given the pro-slavery attitudes of the majority of Missourians, any legislation concerning slavery could have been passed after statehood had been achieved. Could the adherents of strict construction of the U.S. Constitution and pro-slavery advocates have pushed these sections through the convention to provoke a fight on the floors of Congress? Shoemaker noted that John Rice Jones, Benjamin Emmons, and Robert P. Clark had the prime responsibility for composing Article 3 but assigned no authorship to these three sections. Section 26 would be the final stumbling block on Missouri's path to statehood.

Section 31 made the office of state treasurer a joint appointment of the two chambers of the General Assembly. The treasurer was required to reside in the capital city and could not distribute state funds without the prior authority of the General Assembly. Section 31 also required the treasurer to publish an annual accounting of receipts and expenditures of state money.

Article 4, "Of the Executive Power," contained twenty-five sections establishing the second of the three departments of government. The duties of the governor were covered in the first eleven sections. The governor served a four-year term and was not eligible to succeed himself. He received a salary of not less than $2,000 annually, as voted by the General Assembly. The state voters chose the governor by ballot during the general election. Run-offs for tie votes and contested elections were settled by a joint vote of both chambers of the General Assembly. Candidates for governor needed to be native-born Americans with a minimum age of thirty-five years and a four-year residence in Missouri prior to the election.

The governor received all bills passed by the General Assembly. He could sign them into law or veto them. The governor was to give the General Assembly an occasional state-of-the-state report, his recommendations for necessary legislation, and reasons for special sessions. The governor also possessed the pocket veto whereby bills passed less than ten days before the General Assembly adjourned could be ignored and not become law. The governor ensured the state's compliance with the laws and kept the peace. He served as ex officio commander-in-chief of the state militia and could issue remissions from fines, pardons, and reprieves.

Article 4, Section 12 made the office of state auditor of public accounts a four-year gubernatorial appointment, with the advice and consent of the General Assembly. He must keep office in the capital city, and his duties were to be mandated by statute law. The lengthy absences of territorial governors had borne stern fruit.

The duties of lieutenant-governor were listed in Sections 14 through 20. Candidates had to meet the same qualifications and be elected in the same manner as the governor. The lieutenant-governor served as president of the Senate and replaced the governor in cases of death, resignation, or impeachment. The secretary of state, in Sections 19, 21, and 22, was a four-year gubernatorial appointment, with the advice and consent of the Senate. He kept all election returns, General Assembly journals, gubernatorial proceedings, and signed laws. Section 22 required him to procure and keep safe the Great

Seal of the State of Missouri for official use. This constitution allowed governors to use their personal seals until the manufacture of the official state seal. The offices of county sheriff and county coroner took up the remaining Sections 23 through 25. They were elected for two-year terms, could not succeed themselves, and could serve no more than four of any eight years. Their duties were to be prescribed by statute laws.

Article 5, "Of the Judicial Power," had nineteen sections on the state supreme court, its circuit courts, the office of chancellor, and the offices of attorney general and county justice of the peace. The constitution also enabled the General Assembly to create any other inferior courts it deemed necessary. Supreme court and circuit court justices and the chancellor needed to be older than thirty and less than sixty-five years of age. No other requirements, such as residence or education, were made in the constitution. All these judges were appointed by the governor, with the advice and consent of the Senate, for lifetime tenures. Nothing in the constitution required these judges to retire at age sixty-five.

For the supreme court sessions, four districts were to be established in the state by the General Assembly. At least two of the supreme court judges were to hold two court sessions a year in each district. The supreme court served as the last court of appeal and also had the right to determine, hear, and issue original writs of *habeas corpus*, *mandamus*, *quo warranto*, and *certiorari*. That is to say, the supreme court judges dealt with situations in which the circuit courts, lower courts, justices of the peace, and county sheriffs may have acted improperly. *Habeas corpus* required local jails to produce prisoners on demand. *Mandamus* required state and local government to follow its own laws fairly and completely. *Quo warranto* did the same for corporations. The first case before the Missouri Supreme Court used such a writ to decide if the city of St. Louis could legally incorporate itself (it could). *Certiorari* required circuit and lower courts to produce all legal documents on a case, the obverse of *habeas corpus* for people. The constitution held the supreme court to be the equal of the General Assembly and the governor in keeping the peace.

The other courts received less constitutional attention. Circuit court judges had jurisdiction over all criminal cases and original civil cases. Circuit courts would also oversee the inferior courts to be established later by the General Assembly. The constitution was silent on how their circuits were to be created or how often circuit courts were to meet.

The court of chancery involved inheritances, wills, and custody of minors. Because of the importance of landownership, the chancellor of the court of equity held a position equal to that of governor and supreme court justice. All the courts selected their own clerks, but only the state supreme court could impeach them. Local plebiscite would determine how many justices of the peace a county would have, and their duties would be established later by statute law. The attorney general was a gubernatorial four-year appointment, with the advice and consent of the Senate. The barebones outline of the judicial system in Article 5 was more than adequate for state needs. Enabling legislation, such as this section, should not be confused with instructional legislation, as in the sections dealing with slavery. Enabling legislation allows legislative action; instructional legislation demands it.

Article 6, "Of Education," discussed the improvement and sale of public lands for public schools in two sections. Section 1 provided that the sale of U.S. public land in each township would support a township school "where the poor would be taught gratis." Section 2 outlined the plans for a state university, called both "a seminary of learning" and "a university." The constitution strongly urged the General Assembly to collect money from the sale and rent of public land for a university endowment. This school of higher education was mandated to teach literature, arts, and sciences.

Article 7, "Of Internal Improvement," stated in a single section that the General Assembly must provide funds for roads and navigable waters. The enabling legislation gave the state concurrent jurisdiction over the Mississippi River but said nothing about the Missouri River or its tributaries. This article clarifies the admission memorial's document on donations and appropriations.

Article 8, "Of Banks," established the Bank of Missouri and its five branches as the only banks in the state. Moreover, this bank could not sell more than $5 million in capital stock. Despite its conservative allowance for banking, this article proved controversial in the congressional ratification process.

Article 9, "Of the Militia," covered only the selection of officers. Militia units in America traditionally elected their noncommissioned and commissioned officers. The governor served as the ex officio commander-in-chief, and he also appointed the state's adjutant general and other staff officers. The military titles used by many southern and western gentlemen came from these sources instead of the national military.

Article 10, "Of Miscellaneous Provisions," contained two sections. Missouri gave itself jurisdiction over all non-boundary waters. Later concurrent jurisdiction over those parts of the Missouri bordering Kansas and Nebraska took another century to determine. Missouri denied itself the right to tax federal public lands or navigation in the Mississippi River, as per existing laws and constitutions of Illinois and Kentucky.

Article 11, "Of the Permanent Seat of Government," required the General Assembly to appoint commissioners to choose any site for the capital, as long as it sat on the banks of the Missouri River and within forty miles of the Osage River. The capital would thus be close to the geographic center of the state. St. Louis hoped to become the capital, but the out-state residents would not abide this. Besides, the largest concentration of inhabitants in the state of Missouri at this time lived along the Missouri River 150 miles west of St. Louis. St. Charles, thirty miles west of St. Louis on the banks of the Missouri, became the temporary capital after the territorial legislature accepted the new constitution. These instructions concerning the new capital city were the only other instance of instructional legislation in the constitution.

Article 12, "Mode of Amending the Constitution," required one-year prior notification in the state's newspapers before any vote. A two-thirds majority in both houses was also necessary to amend the constitution. Moreover, during this one-year notification period, the state's newspapers must run the proposed amendments three times on different calendar dates.

Article 13, "Declaration of Rights," contained twenty-two sections. They mostly repeated the federal Bill of Rights, except that the rights to religion and freedom of conscience appeared in four separate sections. Section 15 made specific several points of law. As in the U.S. Constitution, the only crime defined was that of treason: levying war against Missouri or giving aid and comfort to state enemies. Moreover, two witnesses were required to convict a person of the charge of treason. Treason, suicide, and miscegenation did not cause forfeit of a person's property to the state; instead property went to the assigned heirs, as in natural death.

The Schedule and the Ordinance

Following Article 13 in the proposed Missouri Constitution came a schedule of twelve sections for the establishment of the legislative and executive branches of the government. Sections 1 through 5 covered the executive branches by having all laws, regulations, and procedures of the territory continue unchanged by the state until lawfully changed by the new General Assembly. Sections 6 through 8 set the protocol for choosing the new state bicameral legislature. Each county received at least one representative; St. Louis received six; and Howard County in the west, had eight. The total for the first session of the new House was forty-three representatives from fifteen counties. For the Senate, these same counties were grouped into nine districts for a total of fourteen senators. Sections 9 through 11 made the fourth Monday in August 1821, the date for the election of the fifty-seven state legislators, state executives (governor and lieutenant-governor), and federal legislators (one representative, two senators). The ballots were to be collected by the county sheriffs and coroners and delivered to the territorial House for counting and validation. Any judge or justice of the peace was enabled to swear in any of these officials. Last, the governor was allowed to use his personal seal for all correspondence until the secretary of state had one made for the state. Forty-two signatures of the delegates to the constitutional convention followed the schedule.

After the signatures, the convention added a two-paragraph ordinance listing the taxation rates on the sale of public lands in the state. Most of these listings were added by the U.S. Congress during the Committee of the Whole discussions in the Fifteenth Congress. Thus, the donations and appropriations document of the admission's memorial becomes clear. The territorial legislature adopted this constitution on July 19, 1820. It is from this date that the state of Missouri celebrates its statehood.

FEDERAL APPROVAL OF THE CONSTITUTION

In statewide elections that August, Missouri voters sent David Barton and Thomas Hart Benton to the Senate and John Scott to the House to present the constitution for approval. Both the new senators were born in North Carolina, and both studied law in Tennessee. David Barton moved to St. Louis in 1809 and became a career politician. He was elected territorial attorney general in 1813 and rose in the territorial judicial hierarchy until his election to the territorial House of Representatives in 1818. In 1820 Barton was elected first to the constitutional convention and then to the convention presidency. He was next elected to the U.S. Senate, where he remained until 1831. Barton was elected to the Missouri Senate for a term (1834–1835) before retiring to Boonville, Missouri, where he died in 1837.

Thomas Hart Benton practiced law in Tennessee and was elected to the state Senate (1809–1811) before taking up a military career. He served as an assistant to General Andrew Jackson, was elected colonel in a regiment of Tennessee volunteers, and was appointed lieutenant in the U.S. regular army. After an almost fatal pistol duel with Andrew Jackson, Benton headed west to St. Louis in 1815. He purchased a newspaper in St. Louis, which he quickly made the mouthpiece for the St. Louis Junto. Benton's editorials promoted business development and increased public land sales. He backed preemption (that is, allowing land squatters the first right of purchase of undeveloped land, whether or not it was part of a large Spanish land grant). Benton tirelessly promoted trading expeditions to Spanish New Mexico, where quantities of silver were mined. Elected to the U.S. Senate in 1821, he remained there until 1851. After several failed attempts to gain election to a state position, Benton retired to Washington, D.C., to write his memoirs and support his son-in-law, John C. Frémont. After his death in 1858, Benton's body was returned to St. Louis for burial. Both Benton and Barton exemplified the political life in frontier America.

In the second session of the Sixteenth Congress (1820–1821), the final Senate discussion for Missouri's admission to the Union produced forty-three speeches, eight roll-call votes, and ninety pages of text in the *Annals of Congress*. Exhausting its own resources for a solution, the Senate gladly accepted the ones worked out by a joint Senate-House committee.

Senate Floor Actions

Senator John Gaillard of South Carolina, president pro tempore, presented the proposed Missouri Constitution to the Senate on November 11, 1820, without mentioning either the House version or that the Senate had denied seats to the new senators from Missouri, David Barton and Thomas Hart Benton. Gaillard, who was well respected both at home (he served as senator for 22 years) and in Washington (the Senate elected him president pro tempore seven times), appointed a select committee to study the documents and to report their findings to the entire Senate. This select committee consisted of veterans of the floor fight over Missouri's admission the previous session: Senators William Smith of South Carolina, James Burrill of Rhode Island, and Nathaniel Macon of North Carolina. These choices displayed Gaillard's political acumen. Smith and Burrill fiercely promoted their views on slavery, whereas Macon believed that the Congress lacked the constitutional authority to argue slavery as an issue for Missouri's admission. Indeed, Macon had voted against Missouri's admission during the Fifteenth Congress on just that point. Although the committee was seemingly balanced, Gaillard also knew the two southern votes would defeat the lone Northerner and move the admission process along.

On November 23, 1821, Senator Smith, speaking as the chair of the select committee, reported that the committee accepted the proposed Missouri Constitution as written. Senator John Eaton of Tennessee asked that the issue be postponed for several days. After a short, sharp debate between Senator Eaton, requesting the postponement, and Senators Smith, Barbour of Virginia, and Johnson of Kentucky, who demanded the report's acceptance, the discussion on Missouri was postponed for two weeks.

On December 6, 1820, Senator Eaton offered a proviso to Missouri's constitution that amended Article 3, Section 25, the section forbidding free blacks and mulattos residence in the state. The next day, December 7, 1820, Senator Eaton's initial proviso failed by a vote of 24-21. On December 11, 1820, a rewritten Eaton proviso passed the Senate by a vote of 26-18, and the Missouri Constitution was sent to the House. On December 16, the House rejected the Senate version.

The same day, Senator Jonathan Roberts of Pennsylvania moved that Missouri be admitted to the Union only if the exclusionary clause were amended to ensure the full rights of citizens of any state while in Missouri. Thus, the Missouri Constitution would comply with the federal Constitution. The Senate quickly rejected Roberts's amendment by a vote of 24-19. The Senate, which seemed to be as hopelessly split as it was during the Fifteenth Congress, ceased any further deliberation of its own regarding Missouri.

After word reached the Senate on February 24, 1821, that the House wanted to form a joint Senate-House committee to pass its version for accepting Missouri into the Union, Senator John Holmes of Maine moved that the Senate agree to do so. Senators Smith and Barbour attempted to table this motion, but it passed by a vote of 29-7. By February 28, the Senate accepted the joint compromise resolution for the admission of Missouri by a vote of

28-14. The Senate then sent the new law to President James Monroe, who signed it on March 2, 1821.

Prominent Speakers in the Senate

Between November 11, 1820, and February 27, 1821, the Senate speeches on the admission of Missouri mostly concerned the question of citizenship. This question arose from Article 3, Section 26 of the proposed constitution, instructing the new General Assembly to forbid residency to free blacks and mulattos. Citizenship by right of birth and legal naturalization seemed straightforward enough, but what about the often-disenfranchised groups in American society: free blacks, free mulattos (those of white and black parentage), paupers, and vagabonds? Discussions of women and children were totally lacking, because they either were not male or were not twenty-one years of age. Neither enslaved blacks nor Native Americans were considered by the Senate.

Senator Nathan Sanford of New York kept the anti-slavery drums beating by reading aloud a blanket anti-slavery petition signed by all the members of the New York state legislature on November 23, 1820. Sanford's timing helped postpone discussion of Missouri statehood for two weeks. Such petitions appeared regularly during the session, even after Missouri was admitted as a slave state.

Senator William Smith gave a major speech on December 8, 1820, listing the free black and mulatto exclusion or discrimination laws then current in northern localities. His list included townships, counties, and cities in every northern state. He also read into the official record a tremendous list of slave ships legally operating in the United States up until 1808, when the federal Constitution ceased their operations. Smith noted that South Carolina and Rhode Island tied for the largest number of registered slave ships. Armed with his lists, names, and statistics, Smith again derided the New England states as hypocrites, much as he had in the previous session, for allowing the anti-slavery agitation within their borders.

Following Smith on the same day, armed with his Harvard degree and training as a Boston lawyer, H. Gray Otis gave the Senate a thorough lecture on the issue of citizenship in the United States. In his native Massachusetts, people were either citizens or aliens. No separate class for undesirable inhabitants existed. He carefully explained that distinctions for women and minors were not really relevant to the discussion of citizenship. He also believed that emancipated slaves would not flock to a few free states to become a social and economic liability but would disperse throughout the Union.

Senator John Holmes of Maine gave more measured consideration to the citizenship question. He found the federal Constitution provided no legal definition of citizen. He noted that historical precedent showed republics contained several classes of male inhabitants, of which citizens were but one. Without a national decision on citizenship, he felt it best to leave the matters to the states. He expressed concern about the status and situations of enslaved blacks were they to be emancipated all at once. Again, Holmes sided with the states' rights theory. He was a good Jeffersonian Republican who had been the Representative from the District of Maine during the Fifteenth Congress, and he felt he owed Missouri's supporters his allegiance for their aid in making Maine a separate state in 1819.

Senator William Trimble of Ohio delivered a seemingly supercilious speech on December 11, 1820. He and unnamed others protested the inclusion of a state bank in the Missouri Constitution. Trimble said he and his constituents believed banks to be an unnecessary evil and inconsistent with the federal Constitution's demand that state constitutions create a republican form of government. Only gold and silver specie was money, he insisted, not the printed promissory notes from banks, whether national, state, or private. The principles of hard currency ran deep in the United States, and Trimble's speech showed just how staunchly the legislators could hold to their principles. Also, the economic panic of 1819 worsened as paper promissory notes collapsed to worthlessness. Trimble was not mollified when John Holmes reminded him that Alabama's constitution also established a state bank and Alabama had entered the Union without opposition in 1819. After Trimble spoke, the Senate did not consider Missouri statehood again until the House requested a conference committee.

The House of Representatives

In the House of Representatives, the process of approving Missouri's full admission to the Union required at least fifty-eight speeches and sixteen roll-call votes. The recorded speeches occupied 307 pages of the *Annals of Congress*, and the unrecorded speeches were noted to have lasted an additional sixteen hours. Many of the more active speakers from the first session also spoke long and hard in the second.

House Floor Actions

The second session formally convened on November 13, 1820. Three days later, on November 16, John Scott presented a manuscript copy of Missouri's proposed constitution to the House. Newly elected Speaker John W. Taylor of New York (after whom the restriction amendment in the previous session of Congress had been named) turned the document over to a select committee to study its contents and report back to the House. Taylor selected William Lowndes of South Carolina, John Sergeant of Pennsylvania, and Samuel Smith of Maryland, for the committee. Taylor, a life-long Jeffersonian

Republican from up-state New York, must have known his choices for the committee assured a pro-admission report. Taylor also seated Scott in the House when Barton and Benton were denied their seats in the Senate. Taylor avoided further difficulties by addressing Scott as "the honorable gentleman from Missouri" without labeling him as either the representative of a state or the delegate from a territory. The new Speaker obviously went to great lengths to appear impartial, despite his opposition to slavery.

On November 23, 1820, Representative Lowndes reported that the committee had voted to accept Missouri's constitution. Delaware, Lowndes noted, had an exclusion law for free blacks and mulattos similar to that in Missouri's constitution. He also noted, for the record, that the committee's vote on approval was not unanimous. Obviously, the House members already knew that the contention over Missouri's admission lay in Article 3, Section 26, wherein the constitution instructed the new General Assembly to forbid residency to free blacks and mulattos. After two weeks of speeches, on December 9, 1820, the House voted 90-73 against recommitting the constitution to a committee for study. Then, on December 13, 1820, the House voted on the third reading and engrossment of the resolution to admit Missouri, and it failed by a vote of 93-79. Much as in the second session of the Fifteenth Congress two years before, the resolution on admitting Missouri died for lack of support.

On January 15, 1821, Representative William Eustis of Massachusetts introduced a resolution to admit Missouri if the exclusion law was deleted from the constitution. William Lowndes next moved that the House consider a Senate resolution to extend U.S. law throughout Missouri. The House quickly rejected the Senate resolution. Henry Clay next moved that both resolutions be brought to floor debate immediately.

In January 30, 1821, Clay also proposed an amendment to the two resolutions removing the offending exclusionary clause from Missouri's constitution. Two days later, Clay's proposed amendment failed to pass by a vote of 88-79. Clay hurriedly rewrote his failed amendment, but it too was defeated by a vote of 88-75. The House did agree to form a conference committee to work out the difficulties. This time Speaker Taylor placed eight representatives of northern states on the committee and only five from southern states.

On February 12, 1821, the House conference committee reported that it had failed to convince the southern members to agree to abolish slavery both in Missouri and in the remaining territories. Four different proposed compromises to admit Missouri without the exclusionary clause were introduced, debated, and voted on. They all failed. On February 13, 1821, a vote to reconsider Scott's original resolution failed by a vote of 73-51. A vote for the third reading and engrossment of the Eustis-Lowndes resolutions also failed by a vote of 88-82.

In utter frustration, Representative William Brown of Kentucky introduced a motion on February 21, 1821, to repeal all three measures of the proposed compromise. The motion failed by a vote of 79-43. Although none of the interested parties liked the situation in which they found themselves, the situation was still preferred to starting all over again on the Missouri question.

On February 22, 1821, Henry Clay proposed that a joint House and Senate committee work out a compromise that would both admit Missouri and negate the effects of the offending exclusionary section of Missouri's proposed constitution. This time enough members were in agreement, and the proposal for a joint committee passed by a vote of 101-55. The House members on this joint committee included thirteen representatives from the North and ten from the South. On February 26, 1821, the House members of the joint committee reported the compromise, whereby Missouri would be fully admitted to the Union by presidential decree, if and only if "a certain condition" was met in November of 1821. The House voted to accept this compromise by a vote of 87-81 on February 26, 1821. The Senate sent the new law to President James Monroe, who signed it on March 2, 1821.

Important Speeches in the House

During the second session, speeches in the House on admitting Missouri mostly used the same arguments as in the previous session. Tensions and tempers remained high throughout the session. As in the Senate, the speeches in the House emphasized the relationship between the rights of citizenship and the political standing of blacks rather than the regional and constitutional issues of the first session.

On December 6, 1820, William Lowndes of South Carolina told the House that free blacks were not always full citizens in the state of their residence. Their level of citizenship depended more upon local laws than on state laws. Moreover, Lowndes reminded the House that state constitutions from the time of the Revolution on varied significantly in their contents. No state constitution existed, he believed, in which every section would be universally accepted.

On December 7, 1820, John Sergeant of Pennsylvania restated his position of the last session: Congress had the right to reject Missouri's bid for statehood, especially with the proposed constitution now in doubt. Sergeant claimed that several states, including New York, Massachusetts, and North Carolina, gave free blacks full citizenship. Sergeant laid great emphasis on free blacks' citizenship in North Carolina.

On December 8, 1820, Henry Storrs of New York stated that he must reject the proposed Missouri Constitution because it contained "repugnant sections." Missouri was not an independent republic, as stated in the preamble, but a territory under the jurisdiction of the United States. During the late war with Britain, he told the House, U.S. law specifically protected black sailors from British impressments on the high seas.

On December 9, 1820, Phillip Barbour of Virginia spoke first to Missouri's current political status. He granted that legally Missouri was a U.S. dependency, but, at the same time, Missouri acted as if it were a state. Rhetorical hyperbole accounted for the claim that Missouri was a free and independent republic. He then provided more evidence on the questionable relationship between free blacks and citizenship. Free blacks in North Carolina could vote in elections. Those same free blacks could not obtain licenses to marry in Massachusetts. Federal and state laws generally allowed only free men to serve in militia units. The phrase, "We, the People," Barbour stated, specifically excluded Indians, blacks, and mulattos.

The next speaker that day, Alexander Smyth of Virginia, reiterated Barbour's statement that Missouri was already a state in the Union. Within the Union, he asserted, degrees of citizenship existed. Smyth listed local exclusion laws on vagabonds, paupers, and lepers in various northern cities. The city code for Washington, D.C., allowed free blacks and mulattos residence only under strict conditions. James Strong of New York answered both Barbour and Smyth, stating that Missouri remained a territory until Congress voted it otherwise. Missouri must have congressional approval before becoming a state. He emphatically stated his belief that free blacks were indeed citizens of both their state and their country.

For the rest of December and all of January 1821, the House speeches reverted to the sectional and constitutional arguments of the previous session. Typical in the *Annals of Congress* is the statement for February 1, 1821, "the whole day was spent in animated debate and interesting proceedings." Then, on February 2, the future president of the United States, Representative John Tyler, implored the House to cease this "unhallowed struggle" for power. He urged the members to think of the United States as a nation and not as bickering states and regions. Missouri, he demanded, must remove the repugnant section to become a full-fledged state. On February 15, as the House lurched toward its compromise, Representative Henry Meigs moved that the federal government quickly sell off approximately 500 million acres of the western territories to build a naval fleet capable of suppressing, once and for all, the Atlantic Ocean trade in African slaves. His motion was voted down without further recorded comment. Two weeks later, Henry Clay worked out the second Missouri Compromise, and the Congress sent its messages to the Missouri territorial legislature and President Monroe.

RESULTING LAW

The law resulting from the months of tirade displayed several conceded points of argument as well as expressions of compromise. Missouri was to be admitted as a full-fledged state in the Union "on an equal footing with the original states in all respects whatever." The North conceded that Congress could not dictate the specific contents of constitutions to the states. The South conceded that states could not forbid the citizens of other states the rights their own citizens enjoyed. The South also won the point that individual states otherwise possessed the power to determine their citizenship. If the state constitution could instruct the state to pass legislation on citizenship, however, then the Congress could instruct the state to pass legislation adhering to the federal Constitution. The North won a public show of state adherence to Congress and the Constitution. The law required that the Missouri General Assembly pass a law stating that it would never pass legislation barring citizens of other states from legal residence.[20]

'SOLEMN PUBLIC ACT"

Missouri passed just such a public law on June 26, 1821, while protesting it loudly. Henry S. Geyer, then a state legislator but later a U.S. senator, started a word-of-mouth report that the wording of the congressional resolution was incorrect. Congress, in avoiding mentioning free blacks and mulattos in the resolution, had miscounted the number of clauses in the sentences. The Missouri General Assembly considered this mistake a great insiders' joke that hastened their public assent to the demands of the congressional resolution. Furthermore, it was widely known that the law passed was of no real consequence, because the General Assembly had the power to ignore it in future legislation. Indeed, the General Assembly stated in the public law that its declaration "will neither restrain, or enlarge, limit, or extend" the operation of either the federal or the state government, now or in the future.[21] The matter of Missouri's admission to the Union now rested with President James Monroe.

PRESIDENTIAL DECREE

Why include the president in this matter? Several speakers on February 21, 1821, had called on President Monroe to take the lead in settling this interminable congressional argument, but neither James Monroe nor current political practice allowed the office of the president such a role in shaping public laws. President Monroe finally issued a presidential proclamation on August 10, 1821, that Missouri was finally a full state in the Union on an equal par with the other states.[22]

CONCLUSION

The Missouri Compromise prevented civil war for thirty-four years until its effective repeal by the Supreme Court in 1854. The issues surrounding the admission of Missouri to full statehood remained prominent in the political agenda of the United States until after Reconstruction in 1877. The state of Missouri broke its solemn word in 1847 when the legislature passed a law forbidding free blacks and mulattos residence in Missouri.[23] The law was fitfully obeyed, at best. According to the 1860 census of population, St. Louis's population contained more free blacks than enslaved blacks.[24] The abolition of chattel slavery of African Americans then required four years of bloodshed, as predicted by Senator Thomas of Illinois, and others. Largely because of the northern routes taken by the first transcontinental railroads and the diaspora of New England sons and daughters to the upper midwestern states, the northeast mostly won the political struggle between the northeast and the southeast for the allegiance of the western states.

The southeast, however, spawned a hybrid culture in the southwestern states mixing Hispanic and Anglo traditions centered on ranching rather than on agricultural plantations. Missouri today sits surrounded by these regional cultures—east, south, and west—unsure of her own position in the middle of the middle. States' rights, also seemingly buried by the Civil War, returned in the late twentieth century. Congressional powers to mandate new states' actions based on territorial statutes lost out in a Supreme Court decision.[25] The Bible retains political potency to this day. In a letter written to Representative John Holmes, thanking him for copies of his congressional speech against the restriction of slaves in Missouri, Thomas Jefferson called the Missouri Compromise "a firebell in the night."[26] Did Jefferson mean the curse of slavery, the perils of sectionalism, or the emotional preference for higher law over the tranquility of a harmonious republic?

NOTES

1. For the text of the treaty with France, see Charles Bevans, comp., *Treaties and other International Agreements of the United States of America, 1776–1949* , Doc. #28 (Washington, DC: Government Printing Office, 1968–1976), 2:502.

2. *An Act to Enable the President of the United States to Take Possession of the Territories Ceded by France to the United States, By the Treaty Concluded at Paris, on the Thirtieth of April Last, and for the Temporary Government thereof.* 8th Cong., 1803, chap. 1; *Statutes at Large of the United States of America* 2:24 (October 31, 1803).

3. *An Act Erecting Louisiana into Two Territories, and Providing for the Temporary Government thereof,* 8th Cong., chap. 38; *Statutes at Large of the USA* 2:283 (March 26, 1804). The text of the Northwest Ordinance of 1787 is readily available. See, for example, "House Document No. 398," in Charles C. Tansill, ed., *Documents Illustrative of the Formation of the Union of the American States* (Washington, DC: Government Printing Office, 1927). It is available on-line through the The Avalon Project at Yale Law School, www.yale.edu/lawweb/avalon/avalon.htm.

4. *An Act for the Admission of the State of Louisiana into the Union, and to Extend the Laws of the United States to the Said State,* 12th Cong., chap. 50; *Statutes at Large of USA* 2:701 (April 8, 1812); *An Act Providing for the Government of the Territory of*

Missouri, 12 Cong., chap. 95; *Statutes at Large of USA* 2:743 (June 4, 1812). For the designation of the territory as "Missouri," see Clarence Carter, comp., *Territorial Papers of the United States: The Territory of Louisiana-Missouri, 1803-1821*, vols. 13–15 (Washington, DC: Government Printing Office, 1951), 14:552, footnote 24.

5. *Treaty with the Big and Little Osages, Statutes at Large of USA* 7:107 (November 10, 1808).

6. *An Act Establishing a Separate Territorial Government in the Southern Part of the Territory of Missouri,* 15th Cong., chap. 49; *Statutes at Large of USA* 3:493 (March. 2, 1819).

7. The information on historical boundaries was taken from *Revised Statutes of the State of Missouri, 2000: Comprising All Statute Laws of a General and Permanent Nature, the Constitution of the United States, and the Constitution of Missouri and Appendices* (Jefferson City, MO: The Committee, 2000) (hereafter cited as *Revised Statutes of the State of Missouri*), chap. 7.

8. The biographical data on the territorial governors came from William Foley, *A History of Missouri,* vol. 1, *1673 to 1820* (Columbia, MO: University of Missouri Press, 1971).

9. The biographical information on the territorial delegates came from Floyd Shoemaker, *Missouri's Struggle for Statehood, 1804-1821* (Jefferson City, MO: The Hugh Stephens Printing Co., 1916) and the *Biographical Directory of the United State Congress, 1774 to Present.* The directory is available on-line at http://bioguide.congress.gov/biosearch/biosearch.asp.

10. See, for example, "Petition to Congress by Inhabitants of the Territory" (January 6, 1810) reprinted in Carter, 13:357–360. This particular petition contains 143 signatures.

11. "Memorial to Congress from the Missouri Baptist Association" (October 24, 1818), reprinted in Carter, 13:448–450.

12. John Scott to Josiah Meigs, January 27, 1817, in Carter, 15:236–239.

13. William C. Carr to John Breckenridge, July 7, 1804, in Carter, 13:29–30.

14. *Memorial of the Citizens of Missouri Territory to the Senate and the House* (St. Louis, MO: S. Hall printer, 1817). The 1817 petition is reprinted in full in Shoemaker, *Missouri's Struggle for Statehood, 1804-1821*, pp. 321–323.

15. *Memorial and Resolutions of the Legislature of the Missouri Territory, and a Copy of the Census* (Washington, DC: Gales and Seaton, 1819). The full text is available in Shoemaker *Missouri's Struggle for Statehood, 1804-1821*, pp. 324–328.

16. All discussion of congressional actions in this paper came from the *Annals of Congress* (Washington, DC: Gales and Seaton, 1855), readily available in most academic libraries and on-line at www.loc.gov. All biographical information on the members of Congress participating in Missouri's admission came from the *Biographical Directory of the United States Congress, 1774 to the Present,* available at http://bioguide.congress.gov.

17. *Annals of Congress,* 16th Cong., 2d Sess. (February 2, 1821), p. 1007.

18. *Statutes at Large of USA* 3:545 (March 4, 1820).

19. Missouri's 1820 constitution is reprinted in full in Shoemaker, *Missouri's Struggle for Statehood, 1804-1821*, pp. 329–358.

20. *Statutes at Large of USA* 4:645 (March 2, 1821). The law is reprinted in full in Shoemaker, *Missouri's Struggle for Statehood, 1804-1821*, p. 300.

21. *A Solemn Public Act, Declaring the Assent of this State...*, in *Laws of a Public and General Nature, of the District of Louisiana, of the Territory of Louisiana, of the Territory of Missouri, and of the State of Missouri, up to the Year 1824* [i.e. 1836] (Jefferson City, MO: Printed by W. Lusk, 1842), 1:758–759. The law is reprinted in full in Shoemaker, *Missouri's Struggle for Statehood, 1804–1821* , pp. 360–362.

22. The full text of Monroe's proclamation is found in James Richardson, comp., *A Compilation of the Messages and Papers of the Presidents, 1789–1897* , 10 vols. (Washington, DC: Government Printing Office, 1896–1899), 2:95.

23. *Revised Statutes of the State of Missouri*, 2:101.

24. *Population of the United States in 1860* (Washington, DC: Government Printing Office, 1864), pp. 545 et. seq.

25. *Escanaba v. Chicago*, 107 U.S. 678 (1883). Cited in Glover Moore, *Missouri Controversy, 1819–1821* (Lexington, KY: University of Kentucky Press, 1966), p. 122, footnote 135.

26. Jefferson's letter to John Holmes is reprinted in full in Thomas Jefferson Randolph, ed., *Memoirs, Correspondence, and Private Papers of Thomas Jefferson*, 4 vols. (London: H. Colburn & R. Bentley, 1829; Charlottesville, VA: F. Carr & Co., 1829), 4:232–233.

BIBLIOGRAPHY

American State Papers. Available through the U.S. Library of Congress, "A Century of Lawmaking for a New Nation: U.S. Congressional Documents and Debates, 1774–1875." www.loc.gov. *Biographical Directory of the U.S. Congress, 1774–Present*. Available at http://bioguide.congress.gov.

A Compilation of the Messages and Papers of the Presidents, 1789–1897 . James Richardson, comp. 10 vols. Washington, DC: Government Printing Office, 1896–1899.

Debates and Procedures in the Congress of the United States, with an Appendix Containing Complete State Papers and Public Documents, and all the Laws of a Public Nature, with a Copious Index. Washington, DC: Gales and Seaton, 1855 (also known as *Annals of Congress*). Available through the U.S. Library of Congress, "A Century of Lawmaking for a New Nation: U.S. Congressional Documents and Debates, 1774–1875." Available at http://memory.loc.gov/ammem/amlaw/lawhome.html.

Foley, William E. *A History of Missouri. Volume I: 1673 to 1820*. Columbia: University of Missouri Press, 1971.

Laws of a Public and General Nature, of the District of Louisiana, of the Territory of Louisiana, of the Territory of Missouri, and of the State of Missouri, up to the Year 1824 [i.e. 1836]. Jefferson City, MO: W. Lusk, 1842.

Moore, Glover. *Missouri Controversy, 1819–1821* . Lexington: University of Kentucky Press, 1966.

Revised Statutes of the State of Missouri, 2000: Comprising All Statute Laws of a General and Permanent Nature, the Constitution of the United States, and the Constitution of Missouri and Appendices. Jefferson City, MO: The Committee, 2000.

Shoemaker, Floyd. *Missouri's Struggle for Statehood, 18041821*. Jefferson City, MO: The Hugh Stephens Printing Co., 1916.

Territorial Papers of the United States: The Territory of Louisiana-Missouri, 1803–1821, vols. 13–15. Clarence Carter, comp. Washington, DC: Government Printing Office, 1951.

Treaties and other International Agreements of the United States of America, 1776–1949. Charles Bevans, comp. Washington, DC: Government Printing Office, 1968–1976.

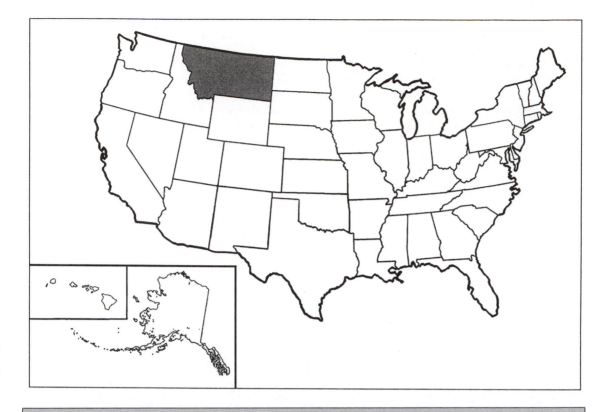

Montana

Territorial Development:

- Louisiana Purchase, April 30, 1803, gives United States future Montana territory east of Rockies
- The United States and Great Britain agree to joint tenancy of the Oregon Country, October 20, 1818
- The United States obtains formal title to all land in the Oregon Territory south of the 49th parallel from Great Britain through the Oregon Treaty, June 15, 1846
- Future Montana territory east of the Rockies organized as a part of the Louisiana Territory, 1804–1812
- Future Montana territory east of the Rockies organized as part of the Missouri Territory, 1812–1854
- Future Montana territory west of the Rockies enters the United States as a part of the Oregon Territory, 1846–1853
- Future Montana territory west of the Rockies reorganized as part of the Washington Territory, 1853–1863
- Future Montana territory east of the Rockies reorganized as part of the Nebraska Territory, 1854–1861
- Future Montana territory east of the Rockies reorganized as part of the Dakota Territory, 1861–1863
- The entire future territory of Montana is consolidated and organized into the Idaho Territory, 1863–1864
- Reorganized as the Montana Territory, May 26, 1864
- Montana admitted into the Union as the forty-first state, November 8, 1889

Territorial Capitals:

- Bannack, 1864
- Virginia City, 1864–1875
- Helena, 1875–1889

State Capitals:

- Helena, 1889–present

Origin of State Name: "Montana" was taken from the Latinized Spanish word *montaanus* ("mountainous").

First Governor: Joseph K. Toole
Governmental Organization: Bicameral
Population at Statehood: 132,159
Geographical Size: 145,552 square miles

THE STATE OF MONTANA

Admitted to the Union as a State: November 8, 1889

Harry W. Fritz

INTRODUCTION

The vast state of Montana was acquired in pieces by the United States beginning with the Louisiana Purchase in 1803. Its eventual geographic definition, therefore, owed more to political haggling and the vagaries of surveyors than to any historical circumstance. Before becoming a state in 1889, Montana found itself part of numerous territories, even designated for a time as an Indian territory. Although Montana Territory came into existence in 1864, it remained isolated until united by railroads in the 1880s. Gold discoveries from the 1860s onward helped to populate Montana, bringing many Democrats to a territory ruled by Republicans from the U.S. capital. The discovery of copper at the Anaconda Mine served to associate Montana forever with mining. It took Montanans three tries to attain statehood, but statehood seemed only to exacerbate the rivalry between Democrats and Republicans and to create a constitution that ultimately did not work.

NINETEENTH-CENTURY EXPLORATION
OF MONTANA

At the beginning of the nineteenth century, the vast area now called "Montana" existed without political definition in west-central North America. Geographers, mainly British, had identified a range of mountains running north and south and serving as a continental divide. Maybe, the Spanish learned, there was more than one range. Presumably, both the Missouri and Columbia rivers headed in these mountains, perhaps with interconnected drainage. It ought to be possible, therefore, to ascend the Missouri to its source, find an easily traversed portage, and descend the Columbia. All else was conjecture.[1]

The United States acquired about two-thirds of modern Montana with Thomas Jefferson's purchase of Louisiana in 1803. Louisiana consisted of all western tributaries of the Mississippi River. The most important western drainage was the Missouri. Also included was the Milk River, which, with its forks and feeders, reached almost as high as 50° north latitude.

The transfer of Louisiana from Spain to France in 1800, the Spanish removal of the right of deposit at New Orleans in October 1802, and the revelation that Alexander Mackenzie, a Scotsman working for the North West Company in 1793, had already crossed Canada to the Pacific impelled President Jefferson to send out an exploring party of his own. The Lewis and Clark expedition (1803–1806) first put the main geographical features of modern Montana on the map.

The Lewis and Clark Expedition

Lewis and Clark crossed the line of 104° west longitude—the eastern border of present-day Montana—on April 28, 1805. The expedition headed up the Missouri River past the Marias River and the Great Falls to the headwaters of the Missouri at Three Forks. Continuing up the Jefferson and Beaverhead rivers and Horse Prairie Creek, Meriwether Lewis crossed the continental divide at Lemhi Pass on August 12. Led by a Shoshone guide, "Toby," the explorers re-entered Montana at Lost Trail Pass on September 3 and proceeded down the Bitterroot River to the spot they called "Traveler's Rest" (modern Lolo).

At Traveler's Rest Toby informed the explorers of a shortcut to the Missouri River, across the top of the circuitous U-shaped river-and-mountain route they had just traversed. He recommended following the Clark Fork and Little Blackfoot Rivers, crossing Mullan Pass, and striking the Missouri just east of modern Helena. The geography of the northern Rockies was coming into focus. On the return trip in 1806, Lewis followed a revised route up the Blackfoot River and across Lewis and Clark Pass to the Sun River and Great Falls. Clark floated down the Yellowstone River to its confluence with the Missouri. The two men had led a remarkably thorough exploration of the main transportation routes of modern Montana. Today, nearly 75 percent of all Montanans live on or near the Lewis and Clark trail.

When Meriwether Lewis arrived back in St. Louis on September 23, 1806, he immediately wrote the president, "[W]e have discovered the most practicable rout which dose exist across the continent by means of the navigable branches of the Missouri and Columbia Rivers." Lewis's northwest passage described modern Montana up the Missouri and over the Rockies. A "passage by land of 340 miles from the Missouri to the Kooskooske [Clearwater River]" ran from the Great Falls over Lewis and Clark Pass and down the Blackfoot Valley through Missoula to Lolo, precisely his return route in 1806. Today, ironically, the

"200 miles…along a good road" is Montana Highway 200. Highway 12 crosses Lolo Pass and the Bitterroot Mountains.[2]

Lewis's "most practicable rout" makes today's Montanans proud, but he was spectacularly wrong. Already in 1814, when his directions reached the public, shorter and faster routes to the Pacific had been discovered. When the first generation of American settlers came to the Northwest, they followed the Platte River, not the Missouri, and crossed South Pass in Wyoming on the Oregon Trail. The northern Rockies were not easily traversed until the arrival of the transcontinental railroads in the 1880s. A paved road over Lolo Pass opened in 1962.

In truth, the Lewis and Clark expedition had little immediate impact on the future Montana. The first recognized historical and economic epoch in Montana history, the era of the fur trade, would have occurred anyway. On their return trip down the Missouri River in 1806, the explorers met no fewer than eleven parties of fur traders coming the other way. Two traders from Illinois, Joseph Dickson and Forest Hancock, persuaded Lewis to discharge John Colter, who returned to Montana for another winter. Two other members of the Corps of Discovery, George Drouillard and John Potts, returned to the Three Forks area as fur traders in 1810 and died there at the hands of the Blackfeet. Meanwhile, the British Hudson's Bay Company controlled the fur trade west of the continental divide for the first half of the nineteenth century.

MONTANA BOUNDARIES AND TERRITORIAL STATUS

Montana's northern border first appeared on the map in 1818, when the United States and Great Britain extended the 49th parallel of north latitude from the Lake of the Woods in Minnesota to the continental divide in the Rocky Mountains. By this transaction Canada gained a loop of the Milk River north of Montana, but the United States picked up the much larger Red River Valley in the Dakotas and Minnesota. By the same treaty western Montana became part of the expansive Oregon Country, stretching from north latitude 42° to 54°40' and running from the divide to the Pacific. Another treaty in 1846 divided the Oregon Country at the 49th parallel, providing a common northern border for the future Montana.

Before 1863 the continental divide provided a natural boundary irresistible to mapmakers. Eastern and western Montana had separate territorial histories from the time of their acquisition by the United States until the creation of Idaho Territory in that year. Eastern Montana was part of the Louisiana Purchase of 1803. Successively, it was part of the District of Louisiana (governed by Indiana Territory, 1804), Louisiana Territory (1805), Missouri Territory (1812), unorganized Indian country (1821), Nebraska Territory (1854), and Dakota Territory (1861). Western Montana, once claimed tenuously by four European nations (Spain, France, Russia, and Great Britain), became part of

Oregon Country in 1818, then Oregon Territory (1848), Oregon and Washington Territories (1853), and Washington Territory (1859).

Idaho Territory (1863) consisted of the present states of Idaho, Montana, and most of Wyoming. Its creation established the eastern border of modern Montana at the 104° west longitude. If the intent of the mapmakers was to hit the confluence of the Missouri and Yellowstone rivers, they missed their target by five miles. Perhaps their compass point fell on Fort Union, a trading post of the American Fur Company five miles west of the confluence. Today, visiting the reconstructed Fort Union, one parks in Montana, walks into North Dakota, and pays a sales tax at the gift shop. Or perhaps they just wanted to set the boundary at an even-numbered degree of longitude.

Immediately a huge problem arose. Miners in the Jefferson River watershed of present-day Montana faced a long, and in wintertime impassable, journey to the capital of Idaho Territory at Lewiston. One delegation, returning home from Lewiston, went west to Portland, south to San Francisco, east to Salt Lake City, and finally north to Bannack. It was a journey of some 2,500 miles to cover a distance of less than 200. Idaho Territory was a mistake.

Montana's pioneer history begins with the discovery of gold on Grasshopper Creek in the summer of 1862. An even bigger strike on nearby Alden Gulch in May 1863 attracted ten thousand people. These early gold camps provide the setting for one of the West's most spectacular instances of popular justice. In the winter of 1863–1864 the vigilantes of Montana identified, tracked down, and strung up twenty-two members of the notorious Henry Plummer gang of robbers and murderers. Watching (and probably abetting) this exercise in lawless lawfulness was the chief justice of Idaho Territory, Sidney Edgerton, unable to proceed from Virginia City to Lewiston because of winter snows.

Soon Edgerton, with considerable local good will and money, was on his way to the nation's capital to broker the creation of Montana. The parent Idaho Territory approved, provided, as seemed reasonable, that the western border of the new entity be the continental divide. Edgerton, and his close friend James M. Ashley, the powerful chairman of the House Committee on Territories, had other ideas. Ashley liked the name "Montana"; he had wanted to bestow it upon Idaho the previous year. With the connivance of Idaho's territorial delegate, William H. Wallace, Ashley and Edgerton moved the border of the new Montana Territory from the continental divide about 130 miles to the west, to the crest of the Bitterroot Mountains. Idaho complained (and Wallace lost his job at the next election), but Ashley got his new Montana, with Edgerton its first governor. President Abraham Lincoln signed Montana Territory into existence on May 26, 1864.

The Ashley-Edgerton-Wallace boundaries of Montana have since remained unchanged. The southern border is 45° north latitude, a line under previous territorial consideration, to 111°03' west longitude. There it turns south for thirty-six miles to the continental divide. Montana's rugged southwestern profile is defined by the crest of the Centennial and Bitterroot mountains.

This line neatly enfolds the gold fields and commercial settlements of 1864. At 116° west longitude the border runs straight north for 70.7 miles to Canada at the 49th parallel. This last was probably a sop to Idaho, allowing it to retain rich gold fields in its new panhandle.

MONTANA TERRITORY

When Montana became an official territory of the United States, statehood was inevitable. Twenty-four other states, all except the original thirteen, Vermont, Texas, and California, had already jumped the hurdles of territorial status and become full-fledged members of the American Union. Few would have predicted that more than a quarter century would elapse before Montana took the final step. On November 8, 1889, by proclamation of President Benjamin Harrison, Montana became the forty-first of the United States of America.

Explaining Montana statehood, therefore, involves issues of timing and politics.[3] Both involve demography. Montana's population grew more slowly than expected in the 1860s, as easy placer gold diggings ran out and the territory remained isolated from the rest of America. Although the population doubled in the 1870s, it was still three-to-one male, and the Panic of 1873 had hindered development. The 1880s, the decade that culminated in statehood, was the most significant period in the entire history of Montana. Population more than trebled, from 39,159 to 142,924, and the male-to-female ratio narrowed to two-to-one.

Montana's territorial population was overwhelmingly Democratic. Migration up the Missouri from the upper South and hard rock miners from Ireland insured the party's supremacy. The Democratic Party won all but two of the fourteen at-large elections for delegate to Congress. Martin Maginnis of Helena won six consecutive terms, beginning in 1872. Maginnis was second-generation Irish, a Civil War veteran, and editor of the Helena *Independent*, the leading Democratic newspaper in the territory.[4]

Montana territorial politics in the 1860s conform to the pattern of "chaotic factionalism" analyzed by Kenneth M. Owens.[5] Two factors buttress this interpretation. First, the timing of Montana's creation in 1864 meant that its politics were immediately caught up in the issues of Civil War and Reconstruction. Second, a set of Republican territorial officials presided uneasily over a heavily Democratic population. Montana was a tinderbox where everybody smoked.

Democratic majorities gave rise to the enduring myth of Confederate supremacy in early Montana. Spirited contests during the territory's first elections in October 1864 suggest the use of bullets, not ballots. The "pseudo-Democrats," claimed Thomas Dimsdale's *Montana Post*, "oppose the government of the United States." Governor Edgerton fanned the flames by blaming the Civil War on "the defiant attitude of treason" and "the imbecile administration of

James Buchanan."[6] This first territorial legislature, however, passed a resolution of support for the Union and left a creditable record of achievement.

Montana politics turned topsy-turvy in the 1860s with the arrival of an authentic but eccentric Irish and Civil War hero, Thomas Francis Meagher. Meagher, a Democrat appointed by Andrew Johnson, was the territory's official secretary and, on two occasions, acting governor. His bizarre actions—convening two illegal legislative sessions and an unauthorized constitutional convention, and recruiting troops for an unprovoked war against Native Americans—can only be explained by his perennial quest for fame and fortune.[7]

The territory's stiff-necked Republican governors did not help matters. The intemperate Sidney Edgerton took unauthorized leave in 1865 and was relieved by President Johnson. Green Clay Smith (1866–1868) cleaned up Meagher's mess but took long vacations. James M. Ashley (1868–1869), who had designed and named Montana, already had an unfavorable reputation as a Radical Republican. He treated Democrats shabbily, alienating even President Ulysses S. Grant, who relieved him. "Montana is Democratic," wrote Martin Maginnis, "and no governor, clique, faction or 'sorehead' can make it otherwise."[8]

Few predicted anything different when yet another Ohio Republican, Benjamin Franklin Potts, became governor in 1870. Times, however, were changing. The explosive issues of war and race were fading. Potts proved a conciliator. He fashioned informal, behind-the-scenes, cross-party ties with legislative Democrats in Helena (the territorial capital after 1874) and with Maginnis in Washington. His long and judicious leadership, which lasted until 1883, united Montana's partisan energies behind universal issues like economic development, removal of Native Americans, and statehood.[9]

The "Big Four" of territorial politics—William A. Clark, C. A. Broadwater, Marcus Daly, and Samuel T. Hauser—were all Democratic businessmen and millionaires. Clark, born in Pennsylvania, escaped the Civil War in Missouri and arrived in Bannack in 1863. He quickly demonstrated an inordinate ability to make money in trade, banking, and mining. When he acquired mineral claims in Butte in 1872, he went off to Columbia University to study mining. By 1876, when he delivered Montana's centennial oration at the Philadelphia Exposition, he was the most prominent man in the territory. Broadwater, a freighter, rancher, and Montana Central railroad man, operated a luxuriant natatorium in Helena. Daly (1841–1900), an Irish immigrant, was "undoubtedly one of the greatest practical miners and mine developers who ever lived." Hauser (1833–1914), from Kentucky, came to Montana as early as 1862 and made his fortune mining gold and smelting silver before branching out into banking, railroads, and the hydro-generation of electricity. President Grover Cleveland appointed Hauser territorial governor in 1885, a sign, perhaps, that statehood was imminent. He served for less than two years.[10]

In December 1880, when the thermometer read thirty degrees below zero, the first regional railroad, the Utah and Northern, reached Butte from the south. Less than three years later, on September 8, 1883, with former President

Grant presiding, a golden spike linked the eastern and western approaches of the Northern Pacific Railroad, Montana's first transcontinental link. Later, in 1887, James J. Hill's Great Northern line cut across the northern tier, then southwesterly, via the Montana Central, to Great Falls, Helena, and Butte. The Territory now boasted three interconnected, competitive rail lines.

The coming of the railroads constituted, individually, collectively, and beyond dispute, the most important chapter, in the history of Montana. The railroads made possible all that followed in the tumultuous 1880s and beyond. They were as important to economic growth and development as statehood was to politics—even more so, for without the railroads Montana would remain an isolated territory. The railroads linked Montana for the first time to the outside world and wrought changes beyond the hopes, even beyond the desires, of contemporaries who eagerly abetted their construction. William G. Conrad caught their essence:

> The railroad changed all the channels of business and many who had ardently prayed for it and longed for it, were ruined by its advent, because they were unable to adjust themselves to the new conditions it brought. The coming of the railroad annihilated time and distance...and annexed the country to the commercial territory of the great eastern merchant princes.

The Helena *Daily Herald* said it all: "We all long for statehood, but of the two, rail connection is the greatest blessing, whose beneficence we feel every moment."[11]

In 1880, after four years in Montana, Marcus Daly bought the Anaconda Gold and Silver Mine in Butte. Soon, however, the mine ran short of precious metals, only to expose the richest deposits of copper sulfide anywhere on earth. The mine was reorganized as the Anaconda Copper Mining Company, destined to become by the 1920s the fourth-largest corporation in the world. The red metal soon challenged Lake Superior copper for primacy in America and for the first time gave Montana a lasting industrial and economic base. Until the mid-twentieth century, "Anaconda" and "Montana" described the same entity.

Other productive industries arose in 1880s Montana. The open-range cattle kingdom peaked early in the decade, was devastated by the hard winter of 1886–1887, and then metamorphosed into a more stable farming and ranching economy. The first trickle of a twentieth-century flood of farmers began to arrive on the central and eastern plains. A booming logging industry met the demands of railroads, mines, and town builders. Underground coalmines in Belt and Red Lodge produced fuel for locomotives and smelters. Banking, printing and publishing, bottling, milling, textiles, and contracting added to the economic mix. Although Montana's economy was based on the extraction of natural resources, was dependent on outside investment, and was subject to national and international financial fluctuations, it was dynamic, diversified, and heavily labor intensive. Economically Montana was ready for statehood.

Montana was already occupied territory in the early nineteenth century. Plateau peoples—the Shoshone, Flatheads, Pend d'Oreille, Kalispel and Kutenai—occupied the mountain valleys and spoke Salishan dialects. They ventured onto the plains on seasonal buffalo hunts. Plains tribes—the Blackfeet, Atsina or Gros Ventre, Assiniboine, Cheyenne, and Crow—were mobile hunters who spoke Algonquian or Siouan languages. As early as 1851, reservations for these peoples were established by treaty. At first these assigned territories covered all Montana. White settlement after 1862 quickly reduced the size of Native American holdings. Military operations against the Blackfeet in 1870 and the Sioux and Cheyenne in 1875–1876 destroyed their power. The organized slaughter of the great buffalo herds in the 1870s left Native Americans helpless. By the 1880s they were confined to ever-shrinking reservations. No prominent white Montanan acted on their behalf. Territorial sentiment for the takeover of Native American lands was nearly unanimous. Statehood would add powerful voices in Washington for the dismemberment and allotment of Native American domains.[12]

In the 1880s the partisan division in Montana Territory came into balance, because many new arrivals were Republican. Cornish hard rock miners in Butte were not naturally Republican but often voted that way for personal and religious reasons. Democrat Marcus Daly was Irish and Catholic; Democrat William A. Clark was Scotch-Irish and Protestant. When Clark ran for the office of territorial delegate in 1888, many Daly Democrats voted for his opponent, Republican Thomas H. Carter.[13] At the same time the transcontinental railroads were bringing in Republican settlers from the upper Midwest. For both parties, the decade was a race against time. Democrats wanted statehood while they still formed a majority. Two Democratic U.S. senators was the prize. Republicans counseled delay until the tide of population turned in their favor. Ultimately the Republicans won, but only by changing the rules of the game.

A national Republican administration had no interest in admitting a state that undoubtedly would send two Democratic senators to Washington. Throughout the 1880s, while Montana waited at the door, and even under the presidency of the Democrat Grover Cleveland, Republicans controlled the Senate, Democrats the House. The Republican plan called for dividing the vast Dakota Territory at the 7th standard parallel (45°56'07" north latitude), adding Washington, and bringing in three Republican states with six senators. Democrats countered with Montana, New Mexico, and perhaps Idaho. Each House of Congress, unfortunately, vetoed the other's plan. The U.S. Congress sacrificed the interests of the western territories for partisan political advantage. No new state entered the Union in the 1880s. Only one, Colorado in 1876, entered the Union between the admission of Nebraska in 1867 and the four omnibus states, including Montana, in 1889.

Montana tried for statehood three times and failed twice. The first effort was comedic. Acting Governor Thomas Francis Meagher presided over a rump convention in Helena in March 1866. There was no call for statehood, no chance of admission, and not enough people to qualify. Meagher's ambition to serve in the U.S. Senate explains his unauthorized actions. The convention deliberated for a full week and produced a document that was immediately lost. There are no proceedings and no description of Montana's first constitution. It perished somehow, in a fire or in transit to St. Louis for engraving. The best account reports the St. Louis printer throwing it in the trash when Meagher could not pay his bill.

The territorial legislature authorized a call for a constitutional convention late in 1869, but neither the census numbers in 1870 nor new Governor B. F. Potts cooperated. Agitation abated during the depressed 1870s. Only the Helena *Herald*, a Republican paper, kept the issue alive. Its editor, Robert Fisk, argued ingeniously that, because the U.S. Constitution described only state and national forms, territorial government was unconstitutional!

Railroads, population growth, and a silver boom forced the statehood issue in 1883. The legislature set the first Monday in November for an election of constitutional convention delegates. Forty-five men, duly chosen, assembled in Helena on January 14, 1884. They completed their work on February 9. Their document was approved by the people at the November general election by a vote of 15,506 to 4,226.[14] The vote, by county, was as follows:[15]

County	For	Against
Beaverhead	727	160
Choteau	785	123
Custer	1,103	52
Dawson	34	379
Deer Lodge	1,887	425
Gallatin	1,260	879
Jefferson	446	217
Lewis and Clark	1,387	386
Madison	911	397
Meagher	646	979
Missoula	1,222	137
Silver Bow	4,650	90
Yellowstone	448	42
Totals	15,506	4,266
Plurality	11,240	

Off it went to Washington, with an explanatory memorial.

RATIFICATION OF THE CONSTITUTION OF 1884

Unfortunately, the U.S. Congress had not authorized this action, nor did statehood for Democratic Montana have much of a chance in Republican

Washington. Nonetheless, the stillborn constitution of 1884 offers a snapshot of territorial Montana, its personalities, issues, and politics.

The delegates were chosen by proportional representation, which weighted the convention in favor of western mining interests. A built-in east-west hostility accounted for minority opposition. Capitalists from the western part of the territory dominated the proceedings, with William A. Clark, the richest man in the territory, as president, and Marcus Daly and financier Thomas C. Power in attendance. The most explosive issue concerned the taxation of mines. States like Nevada and Colorado exempted bodies of ore from appraisal and taxation. To most western Montanans this policy seemed the best way to encourage economic growth and development. To most eastern Montanans, led by stockman James Fergus, it seemed like blatant favoritism and discrimination. The westerners won. Montana was mining country. All did agree that the proposed state could, as the territory could not, tax the property of the Northern Pacific Railroad. Free railroad passes were prohibited.

The constitution of 1884 went to Washington and died, but its authors had done well. Fully 90 percent of the 1884 document appears in the 1889 constitution. The real founding fathers of Montana are the forty-five men who worked for twenty-seven days in the winter of 1884, not the seventy-five delegates who labored for forty-five days in the summer of 1889. And the issues remained. Five years of gestation meant that the issues would be handled more dexterously in the next attempt. The constitution of 1889 is no worse and may be marginally better than its predecessor of 1884.

The national political upheaval of 1888 augured well for Montana. The president-elect, Benjamin Harrison, had a son, Russell B., working in Montana as a publisher and stockman. Democrats in Republican territories suffered from the opposition of their national party to statehood and complained. William A. Clark lost a race for territorial delegate to Republican Thomas H. Carter, an indication, perhaps, that Montana was no longer safely Democratic. Pressure across the entire Northwest was immense. The national Democratic Party threw in the towel. It abandoned its opposition to the division of Dakota and its support of New Mexico. An omnibus Enabling Act, sponsored by Democratic Representative William Springer of Illinois, and authorizing North Dakota, South Dakota, Montana, and Washington to draft constitutions and apply for admission to the Union, passed the lame-duck session of the Fiftieth Congress and was signed by President Cleveland on George Washington's birthday, February 22, 1889. Montana would enter the Union not on its own merits, but as the result of a national political balancing act.

THE CONSTITUTION OF 1889

The Enabling Act's instructions were straightforward: design a republican government on the basis of racial equality (except for Native Americans not taxed); mandate religious toleration; leave intact U.S. public lands and native American reservations except for lands granted specifically for education; tax non-Montana-owned land equitably; pay government debts; establish public schools.[16]

Accordingly, the last territorial governor, Benjamin F. White, set an election date of May 7, 1889, for delegates to Montana's third constitutional convention. This time the territory was divided into twenty-five equitable districts of approximately 5,300 residents each. Three delegates from each district were elected on a partisan basis. Democrats held a slight majority, 39-35, with one Independent, Leopold Schmidt of Butte.

The "Big County" bloc—Silver Bow, Deer Lodge, Lewis and Clark, and Missoula—sent forty-one delegates, a controlling faction. Thirty-three of the framers were connected to the mining industry. The seventy-five-member convention represented populous, western mining interests. Nonetheless, eastern interests fared well in 1889.

The convention assembled in Helena on the Fourth of July. Once again William A. Clark, the mining magnate, became presiding officer. Other prominent members included Hiram Knowles, former territorial supreme court justice; William W. Dixon and Charles S. Hartman, future congressmen; John R. Toole, Marcus Daly's right-hand man; Paris Gibson, founder of Great Falls and a future senator; Conrad Kohrs, Montana's cattle king; Martin Maginnis, longtime delegate to Congress; and, perhaps the most influential delegate, Joseph K. Toole, son-in-law of Union General William S. Rosecrans, recent territorial delegate, and future three-term governor. Toole was Montana's most magnetic orator, with a gift for organization and administration. His "The Right Kind of Nail" speech before Congress on January 15, 1889, greased the wheels for the Enabling Act. The convention featured the most prominent personages Montana had to offer. This time, everyone knew, it was for real.

The convention organized itself into twenty-three standing committees and referred the entire 1884 constitution for review. The proceedings were recorded and, thirty years later, printed. C. P. Connolly, later a muckraking journalist, was the convention's official stenographer. Most major daily newspapers covered the convention, especially its sporadic cat fights. Weekly coverage was more muted.

The Montana Constitution of 1889 consists of 21 articles (the federal Constitution has seven), plus two ordinances. The preamble expresses gratitude "to Almighty God for the blessings of liberty." Article 1 traces boundaries, unchanged since creation of the territory. Article 2 lists military reservations: Forts Assinaboine [sic], Custer, Keogh, Maginnis, Missoula, and Shaw.

Article 3 is a declaration of rights. Western constitutions far exceed the federal Constitution's ten items. The Montana Constitution of 1889 lists thirty-one rights; the 1972 revision contains thirty-five. Most of these are standard recitations of traditional American liberties. Only a few items engendered debate. William A. Clark wanted to abolish the grand jury, a medieval hangover, but it was retained. The right "to keep or bear arms" was added almost as an afterthought. The Australian ballot form, printed by government and arranged by offices, not parties, was adopted.

In the arid West, water is a precious commodity. Nothing must interfere with its beneficial use. All water flowing "over the lands of others" in ditches, drains, flumes, canals, and aqueducts, and in reservoirs, was held to be a "public" use. Property was private except when it was wet.

Federal territorial law prohibited aliens from holding mining property. Few issues fueled the drive for statehood more than this prohibition. Montanans were eager to attract foreign investment in the mining economy. Therefore, the constitution provides that "aliens and denizens shall have the same right as citizens to acquire, purchase, possess, enjoy, convey, transmit, and inherit mines and mining property, and milling, reduction, concentrating, and other works."

Organized labor was still a nascent force in late territorial Montana. It is not surprising, therefore, that the constitution contains no protection for the right to organize, to bargain collectively, to seek a closed shop, or to strike. Labor delegate Peter Breen of Jefferson County was able to obtain only the thirty-first and last provision: "No armed person or persons or armed body of men shall be brought into this state for the preservation of the peace, or the suppression of domestic violence, except upon the application of the legislative assembly, or of the governor." This prohibition would not prevent Pinkertons and other private security forces from employment in Montana. Nor were later governors, in times of labor strife, hesitant about declaring martial law and calling out the National Guard and even detachments of the U.S. Army.

Article 4 is a one-sentence distribution of powers. Article 5 finally reaches the legislative department (Article 1 in the federal Constitution). The Montana delegates faithfully reflected the late-nineteenth-century conservative fear of popular power, of unrestrained democracy, of reform. The two-house legislature (a sixteen-member Senate and a fifty-five-member House) was placed in a tight straightjacket. It could meet for only sixty days every two years (some delegates probably wished for two days every sixty years). The heart of the Article is literally a manual of parliamentary procedure, telling future assemblies how to conduct their business. Most sections placed limits on legislative activity. Most incredible is Section 26, which opens: "The Legislative assembly shall not pass local or special laws in any of the following enumerated cases." There follow eighty specific prohibitions, most of which seem like logical arenas of normal legislative activity. Clearly the delegates, successful and prosperous businessmen and professionals, succeeded in putting the people in their place. Simply put, they did not believe in truly representative government. In the words of one student, "the effect of this clause was to tie the legislature in knots."[17]

A contemporary critic agreed: "With the eastern and western portions of the state differing remarkably in climate, productions and interests," elaborate prohibitions of special and local legislation seemed unwise. "The practical operation of this constitutional inhibition in Montana must produce a dexterity in legislation which even the legislatures of some Eastern States might envy."[18]

Article 6, "Appointment of Representation," occasioned the longest and most bitter debate of the entire convention. Contrary to apportionment procedures governing both the 1884 and 1889 conventions and the territorial legislature, a committee reported the "little federal" system, with a House based on population and a Senate representing counties. Each county would have one senator, regardless of population. Dawson County, with three hundred voters, had the same power as Silver Bow, with ten thousand citizens. The delegates accepted the committee's report. Why? Why did the representatives of the populous west, with a clear majority in the convention, yield to eastern clamors? Perhaps they were mesmerized by the federal example, desirous of accord, confidant that eastern populations would grow, or confident of their continued majority. Was area representation the price the eastern plains paid for the 1889 constitution? The provision empowered minorities in the state Senate and to a lesser degree in the state House, where each county had a least one representative. Montana began and remained one of the most malapportioned states in the nation until the U.S. Supreme Court rectified this damage in the 1960s.

Article 7, the "Executive Department," is a chapter of contradictions. Section 5 states bluntly that "The supreme executive power of the state shall be vested in the governor." The Article, however, had already created a plural executive in Section 1: "The executive department shall consist of a governor, lieutenant-governor, secretary of state, attorney general, state treasurer, state auditor, and superintendent of public instruction." The components of this seven-headed hydra might be elected by different political parties and by different pluralities yet were expected to cooperate. The governor's pardoning power was diffused into a board of pardons; his authority over prisons was diluted by a board of state prison commissioners; he was only one member of a board of examiners and a state land board. Other executive officers might be his rivals, scheming to supplant him at the next election. Only an amendatory line-item veto sharpened his power. The delegates clearly were as afraid of strong political leadership as they were of democratic despotism.

Article 8, "Judicial Departments," is the strongest section of the proposed constitution. Reflecting the Gilded Age's reliance on the judiciary as a bastion of fixed property rights, the delegates centralized the system into a three-man Supreme Court and eight district courts. The old county probate courts were abolished, and only four counties had district courts of their own. Justices of the peace and police and municipal courts handled local matters. The supreme court accepted all appeals and could issue numerous writs of obedience. "The plain intent of these provisions," one scholar observes, "was to take the judicial system out of the hands of the legislature."[19] All branches of government were equal, but one was more equal than the others.

The 1889 delegates altered the 1884 suffrage provisions in one important respect—they denied aliens the right to vote. The 1884 draft qualified "every male citizen over the age of twenty-one years if a citizen of the United States, or an alien who had declared his intention to become a citizen not less than four months before offering to vote." This provision reflected territorial law. The 1889 report (Article 9) omitted aliens and added residency requirements. An amendment restoring alien suffrage failed.

An unsuccessful effort to add a literacy test to the proposed constitution at least provided some comic relief. Good Republicans opposed "the Anarchists, the Nihilists and the Socialists of foreign nations." Most of these culprits were apparently Irish Democrats. A story circulated that in one election 300 men marched to the polls wearing signs that read, "I can neither read nor write the English language. Give me a straight Democratic ticket." The *Helena Journal* reported: "Though every Democrat is not unable to read and write, all who are unable are Democrats."[20]

Women's suffrage occasioned shrill debate. Delegate Walter Bickford of Missoula pressed the issue. In the end it failed for the standard chauvinist arguments: women did not want the vote; they could not join the army; they preferred domesticity; it was against "natural law." The polite but powerful rationale held that statehood was the top priority and should not be risked at the polls or in Congress with this controversial proposition. The widely respected James Calloway of Madison County expressed majority sentiments:

> I have studied this question for a good many years, and I am rather favorable to the proposition of woman suffrage, but I am a conservative man, and perhaps somewhat of a fogey. Perhaps I am not up with the times, but I do not want to see anything put in this constitution that is liable to endanger it. I sincerely believe that, if this provision goes in, you will endanger the adoption of this constitution.

Joseph K. Toole of Helena, soon to be Montana's first governor, echoed these feelings:

> We are just launching the ship of state. The primary and paramount consideration with us is admission to the Union. We have long cried and clamored for the supreme hour when we might formulate our fundamental law and be received into the family of States. The hour has arrived, and, in my judgment, it is neither wise nor expedient for us to load down our constitution with this much-mooted question. Our work must first be ratified by the people before it has any binding force. We should be circumspect and discreet if we desire it to meet with popular approval.[21]

A motion to extend the franchise to women failed, 43-25. A proposal to allow the legislature to grant women's suffrage at a later date went down on a tie vote, 33-33. In one respect, however, the 1889 constitution surpassed its 1884 predecessor, which had been silent on the question of women's suffrage. Section 12 allowed that "women who are taxpayers...shall equally with men have the right to vote" in school and bond elections. Women could also hold educational offices. Montana men finally voted for women's suffrage in 1914.

Another controversial issue, as in all new states, concerned the permanent location of the capital. The convention decided (Article 10) to hold an all-cities election in 1892 and a run-off, if necessary, in 1894. Helena, territorial capital since 1874, won a rousing, expensive, and close contest.

Article 11 established "a general, uniform and thorough system of public, free, common schools." In the most forward-looking section of the new document, all revenues derived from state lands were to be invested and the interest expended only on education.

In Article 12 of the 1889 constitution, mine bodies remained exempt from taxation (only machinery, surface improvements, and net proceeds were subject), but the issue produced far less acrimony than in 1884. Frenzied financial conflict, both national and international, had reduced the price of copper below profit-making margins, and all agreed that the industry needed encouragement. Eastern Montana acceded without much of a fight, in large part because some thought irrigation ditches and equipment should also be exempt. Irrigators could even build ditches across the private land of others with compensation. In such a compromising manner, then and thereafter, did industrial and agricultural Montanans live in the same house.

Joseph K. Toole, an ardent opponent of mine exemption in 1884, switched sides and took others with him in 1889. Time had shown him the error of his ways, he claimed. Cynics charged he was buying the support of the mining interests in his forthcoming race for governor. Montanans eagerly awaited the opportunity to tax the Northern Pacific Railroad, exempt from territorial taxation by the terms of its 1864 charter.

Other articles, as much legislative as constitutional, concerned public indebtedness (13), organizing the militia (14), incorporation (15), county structure and duties (16), public land (17), labor (18), the amendatory process (19), a timetable of implementation (20), and a trust fund for gifts and legacies (21). Montana prohibited convict labor and established an eight-hour day.

The delegates breathed a collective sigh of relief and congratulated themselves on a job well done when they finished with a flourish: "Done in open convention at the city of Helena, in the territory of Montana, this seventeenth day of August, in the year of our Lord one thousand eight hundred and eighty-nine."

On the first Tuesday in October of 1889 the expectant citizens of Montana voted overwhelmingly for the convention's handiwork. The count was 24,848 for, 2,276 against, 91.5 percent in favor, an eleven-to-one majority. The vote, by county, was as follows:[22]

County	For	Against
Beaverhead	1,187	102
Choteau	807	45
Custer	801	59
Cascade	973	80
Dawson	364	25
Deer Lodge	3,802	593
Fergus	854	92
Gallatin	1,296	86
Jefferson	1,514	121
Lewis and Clark	3,141	191
Madison	1,145	105
Meagher	989	90
Missoula	2,331	137
Park	1,053	60
Silver Bow	4,134	469
Yellowstone	457	21
Totals	24,848	2,276
Plurality	22,572	

Statehood was at hand; the details could come later.

ADOPTION OF THE CONSTITUTION

Governor Benjamin White forwarded these certified returns to President Benjamin Harrison, and on November 8, 1889, Harrison proclaimed Montana the forty-first state.

The Montana Constitution of 1889 broke no new theoretical or intellectual ground. To say it distilled conventional wisdom on the subject of state government would be in error. Better to say it elaborated such wisdom. It was four times as voluminous as the revered Constitution of 1787 with all its amendments. It contained long sections of boilerplate, provisions that should have been left to subsequent legislatures. It diffused executive power, restricted legislative power, and exalted judicial power. It was more conservative, and less far-reaching than the constitutions of the other omnibus states. It was a document for its time, but the times were changing rapidly, and parts of it were obsolete before the printer's ink was dry. It was amended in an ongoing but vain effort to bring it up-to-date. Most amendments, like the abolition of child labor in 1907, resolved issues debated but denied in 1889. Governor Joseph M. Dixon thought the state should start all over in 1921. The legislature first considered calling another convention in 1945. A legislative commission in 1969 reported that only half of the original document was salvageable. Montanans had had enough.

In 1971 they voted overwhelmingly (by 65 percent) for a new convention, and in 1972, after eighty-three years, they approved a replacement constitution.[23]

Two contemporary observers offered contradictory assessments of the Montana Constitution. The historian Hubert Howe Bancroft graciously termed it "perhaps the most complete and well-considered instrument of the kind ever perfected by a new state." Francis Thorpe, a political scientist, charged that Montana had "framed a legislative code rather than a body of fundamental law."[24]

ELECTIONS AND POLITICAL FACTIONALISM

Ratification of the constitution in 1889 was a foregone conclusion in Montana Territory. Far more dramatic were the elections, held the same day, in a now evenly divided political arena, for a full slate of state officers, headed by a governor, including a lone congressional representative, and topped by the partisan battle for control of the new state legislature, which would choose two U.S. senators from the new state of Montana.

In a spirited contest, Democrat Joseph K. Toole edged Republican Thomas C. Power for governor, 19,735 to 18,985, a plurality of just 740 votes (1.9 percent). Every other state office went to the Republicans: lieutenant-governor, secretary of state, attorney general, treasurer, auditor, superintendent of public instruction, the chief justice, two associate justices, and the clerk of the supreme court. Republican Thomas H. Carter defeated Democrat Martin Maginnis for a seat in the U.S. House of Representatives. The races were very close, but the Democratic supremacy of territorial Montana had vanished.

Even more incredible was the partisan balance in the first legislative assembly: eight Republicans and eight Democrats in the state Senate; twenty-five Republicans and twenty-five Democrats in the House. Five disputed representatives from Silver Bow County (Butte) held the key to control of the House, of the joint bodies, and of the senatorial selections. The story of the Silver Bow elections undoubtedly made many Montanans regret statehood.[25]

On election day, 1889, the Northern Pacific Railroad was driving Homestake Tunnel through the main range of the Rockies just east of Butte, in Silver Bow County. Precinct 34 had been established near the pass to accommodate 175 workers and a few residents on this Butte and Gallatin line. When the returns came in, they showed 171 votes for Democratic House candidates and only three for Republicans. If these votes were tallied, the Democrats would win five of Silver Bow County's ten House seats; Democrats would control the House 30-25 and the joint session 38-33; and Montana would send two Democratic senators to Washington. If these votes were rejected, Republicans would elect all ten Silver Bow representatives, control the House 30-25, and send two Republican senators to Washington. One contested precinct controlled the future.

The Silver Bow county clerk, obviously a Democrat, accepted the returns from Precinct 34 and forwarded them to the board of county commissioners. The three-man board consisted of two Republicans and one Democrat. The board rejected the Precinct 34 returns, but the clerk refused to send its report to the state board of canvassers in Helena. The state board canvassed the vote itself and threw out the returns from Precinct 34. Silver Bow Democrats then brought a case before the second judicial district, asking that the court order the returns from Precinct 34 counted and accepted. The judge, a Democrat, agreed and ordered the county commissioners to count the disputed votes. The county clerk then issued certificates of election to the five Democratic legislative candidates.

Thus the state board of canvassers had certified one election and the district court had certified another. Ten men, five Republicans and five Democrats, showed up in Helena, claiming five seats. A House is the judge of its own membership, but at a twenty-five to twenty-five impasse this House could seat no one.

Both sides had a case in this contretemps. Republicans claimed that the names in the poll book were not in the order of voting, as required by law, but in alphabetical order. The poll book had not been sent by registered mail to the county clerk. Democrats explained that the election judges had moved from a cold tent to a warm house to make out the returns without the actual ballots, only the polling list. There was no post office near Precinct 34. The commissioners had certified disputed returns that favored Republicans in two other precincts.

It was high noon on November 23, 1889. Legislators responded to Governor Toole's call for the first session of the Montana State Legislature. Democrats (including their "favored five") met in one place. Republicans (with their own quintet) met in another. Montana had two organized Houses of Representatives, and they remained separate bodies throughout the ninety days of the first legislative session.

Democratic senators boycotted their first meeting, fearful that Lieutenant-Governor John E. Rickards might help the Republicans organize the Senate without them. They did not attend until the twenty-fourth day, and then they refused to vote. Republicans proceeded with dubious legality to organize the Senate with only seven of sixteen members present.

On New Year's Day, 1890, Republicans and Democrats met in separate caucuses and each chose two men as U.S. senators. The Republicans selected Wilbur F. Sanders and Thomas C. Power; the Democrats offered William A. Clark and Martin Maginnis. The U.S. Senate, controlled by Republicans, seated Sanders and Power.

On the seventy-sixth day Senate Republicans authorized warrants for the arrest and forcible attendance of absentee Democrats. Forewarned, the Democrats fled to Idaho, with the exception of W. S. Becker of Glendive. Becker was arrested, fined, and transported to Helena before he, too, escaped to Idaho.

This dramatic standoff ensured that the first session of the Montana state legislature accomplished absolutely nothing. It was an inauspicious beginning for constitutional government. Were Montanans ready for statehood, as they claimed? Apparently not. Not until January of 1891, when the Democrats controlled the Senate legitimately, did a compromise end the deadlock: Republicans gained three of the five contested seats but allowed the Democrats to choose the speaker.

"Chaotic factionalism" describes territorial politics in the 1860s, but it is even more apt for the 1890s. The political wars of the copper kings roiled Montana for thirteen years, from 1888 to 1901. When they were over, Marcus Daly was dead, and William A. Clark was a U.S. senator.

Clark's overweening ambition to enter the Senate as the capstone of his political career explains much of what happened. Daly's equal determination to thwart Clark's designs kept the two men and their political factions at loggerheads. Contributing to Montana's acute political instability was the rise of the Peoples Party, or Populists. The Populists and the Copper Kings created a multiparty system in fin de siècle Montana: Republicans, Clark Democrats, Daly Democrats, and Populists.

Here are the highlights. A divided legislature in 1889 allowed two Republicans to serve as Montana's first two senators. A factional division in 1893 prevented any election, and the state went without one of its two constitutionally guaranteed senators for two years. Populist defections in 1895 again allowed the Republicans to fill two seats. A bribed legislature in 1899 selected Clark, but he was forced to resign after one year, and again the seat remained vacant. Two Democrats (one was Clark) won legitimately in 1901. Thereafter Republicans and Democrats divided four terms. The last Democrat won the popular vote in 1912, before the Seventeenth Amendment, and was rubber-stamped by the legislature.

Montana senators elected by the legislature between 1889 and 1913 were as follows:

16 Apr 1880	Thomas C. Power (R)
4 Mar 1895	Thomas H. Carter (R)
4 Mar 1901	William A. Clark (D)
4 Mar 1907	Joseph M. Dixon (R)
4 Mar 1913	Thomas J. Walsh (D)
16 Apr 1890	Wilbur Fisk Sanders (R)
4 Mar 1893	Vacancy
16 Jan 1895	Lee Mantle (R)
4 Mar 1899	William A. Clark (D)
15 May 1890	Vacancy
7 Mar 1901	Paris Gibson (D)
4 Mar 1905	Thomas H. Carter (R)
4 Mar 1911	Henry L. Myers (D)

None of these men had much influence in Washington. Republican or Democrat, they supported extractive industry and opposed progressive legislation, like Theodore Roosevelt's national forests. Montana's national influence for a generation after statehood remained marginal. Only Joseph M. Dixon made a mark. The representative from Missoula (1903–1907) and senator (1907–1913) served as national campaign manager of the Progressive Party in 1912. Not until the direct election of senators did Montana produce notable statesmen. With Thomas A. Walsh (1913–1933), Burton K. Wheeler (1923–1947), James E. Murray (1934–1961), Mike Mansfield (1953–1977), and Lee Metcalf (1961–1978), the state achieved national repute.

CONCLUSION

Montana statehood in 1889 was as much symbolic as substantive. It was a logical end to a period of territorial gestation that had already birthed twenty-four other American states. Statehood represented the political capstone to a decade of fundamental change and development in economics, demography, and attitude. It created a rather traditional and disembodied constitutional structure that permitted basic economic and social change to occur with minimal governmental supervision, direction, and restraint. As events immediately and dramatically demonstrated, the system was not immune to chicanery and naked partisan power politics. Within a decade, profiteering and outright corruption would be added to the mix. Statehood symbolized, if it did not entirely secure, the worthy goals of self-government and economic growth, home rule, and political independence. Representative government strives for these ideals yet.

NOTES

1. For early geographical knowledge and the assumptions of Lewis and Clark, see John Logan Allen, *Passage through the Garden: Lewis and Clark and the Image of the American Northwest* (Urbana: University of Illinois Press, 1975).

2. A comprehensive history of the expedition is David Lavender, *The Way to the Western Sea: Lewis and Clark Across the Continent* (New York: Harper & Row, 1988).

3. Montana Territory is discussed briefly in Harry W. Fritz, "Montana Territory," in *Abraham Lincoln and the Western Territories*, ed. Ralph Y. McGinnis and Calvin N. Smith, 159–168 (Chicago: Nelson-Hall, 1994); and exhaustively in Clark C. Spence, *Territorial Politics and Government in Montana, 1864-89* (Urbana: University of Illinois, 1975).

4. Dumas Malone, ed., *Dictionary of American Biography*, 11 vols. (Hereafter cited as *DAB*) (New York: Charles Scribner's Sons, 1961), 6:199.

5. Kenneth M. Owens, "Pattern and Structure in Western Territorial Politics," *Western Historical Quarterly* 1 (October 1970): 373–392.

6. Quoted in Spence, *Territorial Politics*, pp. 23, 24–25.

7. Gary R. Forney, *Thomas Francis Meagher: Irish Rebel, American Yankee, Montana Pioneer* (forthcoming).

8. Clark C. Spence, "James M. Ashley: Spoilsman in Montana," *Montana the Magazine of Western History* 28 (April 1968): 24–35; Spence, *Territorial Politics*, p. 72.

9. *DAB*, 8:135–136.

10. *DAB*, 2:144–146, 3:45–46; 4:402–403; Michael P. Malone, *The Battle for Butte: Mining and Politics on the Northern Frontier, 1864-1906* (Seattle: University of Washington Press, 1981), p. 18.

11. Quoted in Harry W. Fritz, *Montana: Land of Contrast* (Sun Valley, CA: American Historical Press, 2001), p. 50.

12. The best brief introduction is Carling I. Malouf, "Prehistoric Montanans," *The Montana Almanac* (Missoula: Montana State University Press, 1958), pp. 106–117.

13. David M. Emmons, "The Orange and the Green in Montana: A Reconsideration of the Clark-Daly Feud," *Arizona and the West* 28 (Autumn 1986): 225–245.

14. Margery H. Brown, "Metamorphosis and Revision: A Sketch of Constitution Writing in Montana," *Montana the Magazine of Western History* 20 (October 1970): 2–17.

15. Ellis H. Waldron, *Montana Politics since 1864: An Atlas of Elections* (Missoula: Montana State University Press, 1958), p. 44.

16. The Enabling Act is found in *Proceedings and Debates of the Constitutional Convention Held in the City of Helena, Montana, July 4th, 1889, August 17, 1889* (Helena: State Publishing Co., 1921), pp. 3–10. The ensuing convention is covered in Spence, *Territorial Politics*, chap. 12, pp. 290–311.

17. John Welling Smurr, "A Critical Study of the Montana Constitutional Convention of 1889" (M.A. thesis, Montana State University, 1951), p. 178.

18. Francis Thorpe, *Century Magazine* 39 (1890): 506.

19. Smurr, *Critical Study*, p. 108.

20. Smurr, *Critical Study*, p. 92; C. B. Glasscock, *The War of the Copper Kings* (New York: Grosset Dunlap, 1935), p. 98.

21. Lyndel Meikle, "Montana's 1889 Constitutional Convention: The Founding Fathers—The Floundering Fathers," in *Speaking Ill of the Dead*, ed. Dave Walter, 62–71, quotation on 69–70 (Helena: Falcon Publishing, 2000); see also Annick Smith, "Woman's Suffrage in the 1889 Constitutional Convention," *Montana Business Quarterly* 9 (Autumn 1971): 34–41.

22. Waldron, *Montana Politics since 1864*, p. 54.

23. Richard B. Roeder, "The 1972 Montana Constitution in Historical Context," *Montana Law Review* 51 (Summer 1990): 260–269.

24. Bancroft and Thorpe quoted in Ellis L. Waldron and Paul B. Wilson, *Atlas of Montana Elections, 1889-1976* (Missoula: University of Montana Publications in History, 1978), p. 10.

25. This legislative logjam is described at length in James McClellan Hamilton, *From Wilderness to Statehood: A History of Montana, 1805-1900* (Portland: Binfords & Mort, 1957), pp. 558–579.

BIBLIOGRAPHY

Brown, Margery H. "Metamorphosis and Revision: A Sketch of Constitution Writing in Montana." *Montana the Magazine of Western History* 20 (October 1970): 2–17.

Burlingame, Merrill G. *The Montana Frontier*. Helena: State Publishing Co., 1942.

Constitution of the State of Montana as Adopted by the Constitutional Convention of the Territory of Montana. Helena: Park Brothers, 1884.

Malone, Michael P. *The Battle for Butte: Mining and Politics on the Northern Frontier, 1864-1906*. Seattle: University of Washington Press, 1981.

———, Richard B. Roeder, and William L. Lang. *Montana: A History of Two Centuries*. Rev. ed. Seattle: University of Washington Press, 1991.

Proceedings and Debates of the Constitutional Convention Held in the City of Helena, Montana, July 4th, 1889, August 17th, 1889. Helena: State Publishing Company, 1921.

Roeder, Richard B. "Electing Montana's Territorial Delegates: The Beginnings of a Political System." *Montana the Magazine of Western History* 38 (Summer 1988): 58–68.

Smurr, John Welling. "A Critical Study of the Montana Constitutional Convention of 1889." M.A. thesis, Montana State University, 1951.

Spence, Clark C. *Territorial Politics and Government in Montana, 1864-89*. Urbana: University of Illinois Press, 1975.

———. *Montana: A Bicentennial History*. New York: W.W. Norton, 1978.

Toole, K. Ross. *Montana: An Uncommon Land*. Norman: University of Oklahoma Press, 1959.

Waldron, Ellis L. *Montana Politics since 1864: An Atlas of Elections*. Missoula: Montana State University Press, 1958.

——— and Paul B. Wilson. *Atlas of Montana Elections, 1889-1976*. Missoula: University of Montana Publications in History, 1978.

THE STATE OF NEBRASKA

Admitted to the Union as a State: March 1, 1867

Mark R. Ellis

INTRODUCTION

On March 1, 1867, after almost thirteen years as a federal territory, Nebraska was admitted to the Union as the thirty-seventh state. Although most states were admitted without much controversy or debate, the organization of Nebraska Territory and the statehood process were both linked to volatile national issues. Sectional disputes over the expansion of slavery and the route of the transcontinental railroad dominated the debate over the organization of Nebraska Territory for almost ten years. The Kansas-Nebraska Act, which opened Nebraska to settlement on May 30, 1854, ended all hope of compromise between free and slave states, impelling the nation into the Civil War. Highly charged national issues also surrounded Nebraska statehood. As the first state admitted after the Civil War, Nebraska's statehood became enmeshed in Reconstruction legislation and disputes between the legislative and executive branches.

Nebraska, along with Nevada and Colorado territories, was targeted for statehood by Republican lawmakers during the Civil War. Republicans at the federal and territorial levels hoped that the addition of three strong, loyal Republican states would help re-elect President Lincoln in 1864 and make post-war Reconstruction congressional legislation easier to attain. Thus, although none of the three had reached the population required for statehood, forces from the outside attempted to push statehood onto these three western territories. Nevada was admitted to the Union on October 31, 1864 (while the war was still being fought), but internal opposition within Colorado and Nebraska territories successfully blocked the statehood movements in 1864,

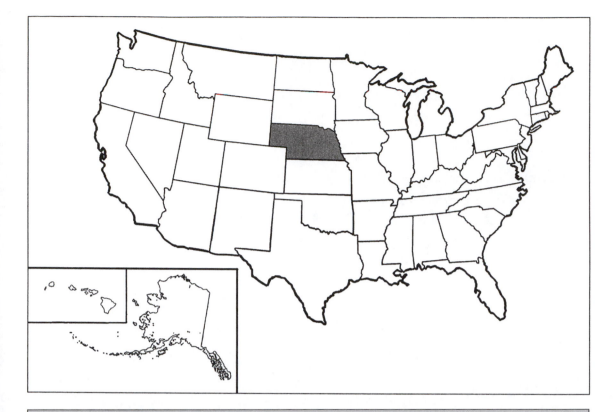

Nebraska

Territorial Development:

- The United States obtains future Nebraskan territory from France through the Louisiana Purchase, April 30, 1803
- Future territory of Nebraska organized as a part of the Louisiana Territory (or, the District of Louisiana for a time in 1804), 1804–1812
- Reorganized as a part of the Missouri Territory, 1812–1854
- Reorganized as the Nebraska territory, May 30, 1854
- Nebraska admitted into the Union as the thirty-seventh state, March 1, 1867

Territorial Capitals:

- Omaha City, 1855–1867

State Capitals:

- Lincoln, 1867–present

Origin of State Name: In 1842 John C. Frémont used the word "Nebraska," an Omaha word, in reference to the Platte River. The name was then applied to the territory when it was created in 1854.

First Governor: David Butler
Governmental Organization: Nebraska is the only state in the Union that presently operates with a unicameral governmental system. It is also the only state to switch from a bicameral to a unicameral system, which it did in 1934.
Population at Statehood: 122,993
Geographical Size: 76,872 square miles

thereby postponing statehood for both territories. In Nebraska a divided but determined Democratic Party, which convinced much of the population that statehood would bring higher taxes and turn the region into a "Negro State," led the opposition.[1]

PRE-TERRITORIAL NEBRASKA

Before 1844 few people, other than Native Americans, had heard of the word "Nebraska," which is derived from the Otoe word for the Platte River (Nebrathka), meaning "flat water." John C. Frémont, who explored and mapped the Platte Valley during the early 1840s, introduced the term to the nation when, in his popular journals and maps of the region, he labeled the Platte River as the Nebraska River. Borrowing from Frémont's journals, Stephen A. Douglas, a congressman from Illinois, forever linked the term Nebraska to the Platte Valley in 1844 when he introduced a bill in the House of Representatives to organize the Nebraska Territory.

The land that became the state of Nebraska was added to the United States through the Louisiana Purchase of 1803. For more than fifty years after its acquisition, however, it remained unorganized territory, largely because the federal government and the American populace viewed it as an uninhabitable region fit only for bison and Native Americans. Early nineteenth-century American explorers such as Zebulon Pike and Stephen Long fostered this unfavorable view of the Great Plains in their official reports. Long's map of the Great Plains, for example, labeled the region the "Great American Desert," a term that stuck until the 1840s. As a consequence, the federal government used the Great Plains as a dumping ground for eastern Native American tribes, and by the 1830s, the region was known officially as "Indian Country." Dozens of eastern tribes such as the Cherokees, Shawnees, and Wyandottes were removed to the region to make way for white settlers east of the Mississippi River.[2]

By the mid-1840s the image of the Great Plains as nothing more than inhospitable "Indian Country" began to change. Overland emigrants who traveled to Oregon, California, and Utah via the Oregon and Mormon trails, took notice of Nebraska's rich grasslands and the fertile Platte River Valley. More than 300,000 overland travelers trekked through Nebraska's Platte Valley between 1840 and 1860, and many wrote glowing descriptions of its rich soil and agricultural potential. The federal government also began its occupation of the Platte River Valley by establishing military posts such as Fort Kearny to protect overland travelers. No longer was the region described as a desert; according to Frémont's colorful reports, it was a "Garden of Eden" and ripe for American settlement.

While the popular image of the Great Plains was being transformed during the 1840s, international and national events brought Nebraska to the center of the national political debate. The acquisition of California and the Southwest through war with Mexico and the addition of the Oregon Country through treaty with Great Britain forced politicians to reconsider the purpose of the Great Plains. Because Oregon and California needed to be linked to the eastern United States by railroad, the Great Plains would have to be something more than uninhabitable "Indian Country." Territories and eventually states needed to be carved out of this region so that the nation could be linked as one. Beginning with Stephen Douglas's first Nebraska Territory bill in 1844 and gaining momentum after the admission of California in 1850, the "Nebraska Question," as the battle to create Nebraska Territory came to be known, was one of the most crucial and heated political debates of the nineteenth century.

THE KANSAS-NEBRASKA ACT: THE NEBRASKA QUESTION

Stephen A. Douglas was one of the first politicians to realize the importance of organizing the northern region of the Louisiana Purchase into a territory. As a representative and later as a senator from Illinois, Douglas understood that a transcontinental railroad via the Platte Valley would probably connect through to Chicago and make that city the transportation and commercial hub of the American interior. Before a railroad could be built across the Great Plains to the Pacific Coast, however, Native American tribes would have to be cleared from the land and a government established. Thus, in 1844 Douglas proposed his first Nebraska Territory bill in Congress. Although the bill never came up for debate, it served its purpose by bringing the idea of organizing Nebraska Territory before Congress and the nation. Douglas later commented that the intention of this bill was to notify the federal government not to relocate any more eastern Native American tribes to the region. During the late 1840s, war with Mexico and the conflict over acquiring full possession of Oregon shifted attention from debate about Nebraska Territory. California's admission to the Union in 1850, however, once again sparked interest in the railroad and the organization of Nebraska Territory.[3]

A major roadblock to territorial status for Nebraska was the conflict over slavery. Before 1820 the expansion of slavery had progressed westward. The Northwest Ordinance of 1787 prohibited slavery north of the Ohio River but made no mention of it elsewhere. Thus, the states of Ohio, Indiana, and Illinois entered the Union as free states, while Louisiana, Alabama, and Mississippi entered as slave states. To preserve the balance of free and slave states, a system was established whereby one free and one slave state were usually admitted in pairs: Indiana (1816) with Mississippi (1817); Illinois (1818) with Alabama (1819). When Missouri, a border territory that had been settled by slaveholders from Kentucky and Tennessee, applied for statehood as a slave state, it stirred controversy. No other territory was ready to be admitted as a free state, so Missouri's admission would tip the balance in favor of the slave states. To Northerners, especially in neighboring Illinois, the admission of Missouri as a slave state seemed to be an intrusion of slavery into traditionally free territory. Conflict was eventually avoided by compromise. The Missouri Compromise of 1820 admitted Missouri as a slave state and Maine (formerly part of Massachusetts) as a free state. To avoid future conflicts, the Missouri Compromise prohibited slavery in the region of the Louisiana Purchase north of Missouri's southern border. Legally, therefore, the Missouri Compromise would prohibit slavery in any state carved from a future Nebraska Territory.

This uneasy balance kept the nation tenuously united until California applied for statehood in 1850 as a free state, once again threatening the balance of free and slave states. To placate the worries of Southerners over the addition of another free state, lawmakers created New Mexico and Utah territories out of the Mexican Cession and promoted the concept of popular sovereignty, which allowed the citizens of the territories to decide for themselves on the issue of slavery. This measure gave Southerners some hope that the expansion of slavery would not be completely blocked if the population of future territories demanded it. With California's statehood settled by the Compromise of 1850, the nation's political focus turned to the transcontinental railroad and the Nebraska Question.

California statehood and the creation of New Mexico and Utah territories set off a flurry of discussion over the transcontinental railroad. Californians demanded connection to the eastern states by railroad, and the federal government was willing to help build it. Because only one railroad would be built, politicians began a heated battle over the proposed route. The Platte Valley was well known, well traveled, and with its fertile lands would make an excellent corridor of settlement across the Great Plains to the Pacific Coast. A southern route through Texas and the Southwest, however, made the most sense. There were fewer mountains to cross, the weather was less severe, and, because the region had recently been organized as New Mexico Territory, the railroad could be built without delay. Few politicians, however, could compete with the tenacity of Stephen Douglas, now a senator and a member of the Committee on Territories, who was determined to drive the railroad through the more northerly route of the Platte River Valley. Although Douglas had introduced several Nebraska bills as a member of the House of Representatives during the 1840s, he did not introduce any new bills as a senator. Instead he worked behind the scenes as the chairman of the Senate's Committee on Territories while other lawmakers from Illinois, Iowa, and Missouri introduced the legislation. On February 2, 1853, Illinois Representative William A. Richardson, who was Douglas's close friend and the chairman of the House's Committee on Territories, introduced a Nebraska territory bill. Although the bill passed in the House, Southern Democrats defeated it in the Senate. Unlike New Mexico and Utah territories, the bill did not mention slavery and, therefore the prohibition set forth in the Missouri Compromise would have applied to the territory. Looking at a map of the proposed Nebraska Territory, which extended from the southern border of present-day Kansas in the south to the Canadian border on the north, and west to the crest of the Rocky Mountains, Southerners realized that six to ten free states would eventually be carved out of the territory. These states would upset the precarious balance between free and slave states and threaten the existence of slavery and the southern way of life. Nebraska Territory, as it was proposed in Richardson's bill, was unacceptable to southern lawmakers.

Douglas and his supporters refused to surrender and continued to draft legislation in favor of territorial status. If Chicago were to become the transportation hub of the continent, then the railroad route would have to follow the Platte Valley. Senator Augustus Dodge of Iowa introduced yet another Nebraska territorial bill in December 1853. Again, the bill ignored the issue of slavery, and thus Southern Democrats in the Senate presumably would kill it. Not wanting to see another Nebraska Territory bill rejected, Senator Douglas worked behind the scenes with the Committee on Territories and revised Dodge's bill so that Southerners would accept it.

This bill, introduced on January 4, 1854, and debated for several months, catered to the worries of southern politicians who feared that Nebraska Territory would produce numerous free states. Rather than a single, massive Nebraska Territory, the new bill created two territories: Kansas Territory and Nebraska Territory. Carving two territories out of the northern plains really did not cause much concern. What really sparked controversy, however, was the provision that allowed the population to decide for themselves the issue of slavery. Borrowing the concept of popular sovereignty from New Mexico and Utah territories, Douglas's proposed bill effectively nullified the prohibition of slavery delineated in the Missouri Compromise.

Over the next five months the nation was drawn into an intense debate over the proposed Nebraska-Kansas Act (the original bill listed Nebraska first). New Englanders howled in protest, and hundreds of "anti-Nebraska" rallies broke out in northern states to oppose the proposed legislation. At the same time, the Missouri River towns in Iowa and Missouri cheered for the passage of the bill. Although most southern lawmakers supported the bill, congressmen from Texas allied with New York lawmakers in an effort to defeat the bill. Texans still hoped for a southern railroad route through their state, whereas New Yorkers feared that a northern route would end their monopoly on the maritime trade with the Pacific coast. Strangely, the opposition used the argument of Native American rights to block the bill, claiming that the federal government had no right to extinguish title to Native American lands and open the territory to settlement. In the end, however, Douglas made enough concessions to southern Congressmen to get the bill through both houses of Congress, and on May 30, 1854, President Franklin Pierce signed it into law.

Most Southerners hailed the Kansas-Nebraska Act. It repealed the hated Missouri Compromise and provided some hope that Kansas and possibly other future states might adopt slavery, thereby strengthening the South's position within the Union. Many Northerners, particularly New Englanders, despised the act and held mass meetings in protest. Douglas was vilified by many

Northerners and blamed for selling out to the slave interests to advance his own political career. He later commented that his own burning effigy lit every northern city between Chicago and Boston.

The Kansas-Nebraska Act had far-reaching ramifications. The act, for example, opened the Great Plains to settlement and within thirty-five years yielded all or parts of seven new states, including Nebraska. The act also ended the idea of a permanent Indian Country. If the Great Plains was to be opened to settlement by Americans and European immigrants, the native inhabitants would have to surrender their lands. The dispossession of Nebraska's Native Americans, therefore, was quickened as a result of the Kansas-Nebraska Act. Although most tribes, like Nebraska's tribes with an agrarian culture, signed away their lands with little violence, others such as the Lakota and Cheyenne, fought against white encroachment in conflicts such as the Sand Creek Massacre (1864), Red Cloud's War (1866–1867), and the Battle of the Little Bighorn (1876). Although few battles were fought specifically in present-day Nebraska, the organization of Nebraska Territory sparked the Native American wars on the northern plains.

The American political system was shattered and reconfigured as a result of the Kansas-Nebraska Act. Although Douglas had hoped that the Kansas-Nebraska Act would unite and strengthen the Democratic Party, it did just the opposite. Many northern Democrats, bitter over the repeal of the Missouri Compromise, abandoned the party. The Democrats were so fractured that in the presidential election of 1860 four Democratic candidates, including Douglas, vied for the presidency. The Whigs also suffered a devastating blow in the aftermath of the Kansas-Nebraska Act. Unable to protect the sanctity of the Missouri Compromise, the party withered away within a few years. In its place rose the Republican Party, the first national party to take a stance against slavery and a serious threat to the South.

Finally, the Kansas-Nebraska Act sparked the Civil War. Bloodshed immediately broke out in Kansas as free-state supporters and slave-state supporters killed one another over the expansion of slavery into that territory. The rise of the Republican Party and the election of Abraham Lincoln in 1860 finally ended all possibility of further compromise, and southern states began seceding from the Union, throwing the Untied States into four years of bloody warfare. The creation of Nebraska Territory, unlike most territories, created a maelstrom of controversy that impacted the lives of all Americans.

NEBRASKA TERRITORY

The original Nebraska Territory comprised more than 350,000 square miles, including all or parts of six states: Colorado, Montana, Nebraska, North Dakota, South Dakota, and Wyoming. South to north it stretched from the present-day southern boundary of Nebraska to the Canadian border. The Missouri

River marked its eastern border, and the Rocky Mountains delineated its western boundary. The territory was later reduced to approximately 77,000 square miles by the creation of Colorado, Dakota, Montana, and Wyoming territories. When the territory was opened to settlement perhaps ten thousand Native Americans and only a few hundred whites lived within the present-day boundaries. The only community resembling a town was at Bellevue, an old fur trading post and Indian agency along the Missouri River south of present-day Omaha. Soldiers at Fort Kearny, located along the Platte River in central Nebraska, and the residents of several dozen road ranches on the Oregon Trail comprised Nebraska's white population.[4]

The opening of the territory set off a flurry of entrepreneurial activity that increased the population and led to the founding of dozens of towns along the western bank of the Missouri River during the first few months. Not only had politicians such as Stephen Douglas been interested in Nebraska Territory, but also the citizens of Iowa and Missouri had been clamoring for years to open Nebraska to settlement. An organized Nebraska would provide opportunities in land speculation, town building, and commercial activities, especially if the federal government chose the Platte Valley for the railroad route. Even before President Pierce signed the Kansas-Nebraska Act into law, Iowans and Missourians who anticipated the organization of Nebraska Territory illegally crossed the Missouri River to survey and choose choice pieces of land. By the fall of 1854 some 2,372 people resided in Nebraska, and by 1860 the population numbered around 30,000.

Town building was a frenzied activity during the early territorial period. Dozens of groups of investors, mostly from Iowa and Missouri, formed companies or associations and by using the Federal Townsites Act, acquired 320 acres of land to be developed into a community. Townsites were expanded by pre-empting adjoining sections of land. The Sulphur Springs Land Company, for example, claimed 320 acres under the Townsites Act, and then its members took out 160-acre adjoining claims under the Pre-emption Act. In all, they claimed 2,300 acres and set out to build and promote the nascent community of Saratoga, located between present-day Florence and Omaha. Other companies included the Bellevue Town Company, which promoted Bellevue, and the Council Bluffs and Nebraska Ferry Company, which promoted Omaha. Once a site was selected and claims were filed, the company had the land surveyed, laid out streets, and divided the paper town into lots. Several buildings were usually erected to give the illusion of prosperity, newspapers were published to promote the community, and speakers were sent out to neighboring states to encourage settlers. To attract settlers, town companies often donated lots for public buildings, churches, and schools. The Council Bluffs and Nebraska Ferry Company, for example, donated a two-story brick building in 1855 to the fledgling community of Omaha for use as the territorial capitol building. The Sulphur Springs Land Company set aside 256 lots for churches, schools, and for settlers who began building houses or businesses by July 1, 1857.[5]

Those involved in town building obviously hoped to become wealthy by selling lots to new settlers. For each share purchased in a land company, investors received ten to fifteen lots. The more people who settled in a community, the more the lots would be worth. The ultimate goal for most Nebraska town builders was to become the site of the territorial capital, because the capital city was almost certain to become the terminus of the transcontinental railroad. Town companies, therefore, worked feverishly to build and promote their communities, and competition between early Nebraska towns was fierce.

During the first five to six years of the territorial period Nebraska was largely an urban society. Most residents lived in one of the dozens of Missouri River port towns: Bellevue, Brownville, Florence, Nebraska City, Omaha, or Plattsmouth. Unlike the settlers of the 1870s and 1880s, who moved to Nebraska as farmers, the early territorial population came to the region to make money in commercial activities, land speculation, and town building. In 1860, for example, about 60 percent of Nebraska's population worked in an urban-related occupation.

Those who did take out land claims often claimed land that had not been surveyed by the federal government. Land could be squatted on and then claimed under the Pre-emption Act once it was surveyed. It took three years, however, for eastern Nebraska to be surveyed, and conflicts often ignited between settlers who claimed all or part of the same section of land. To protect land claims, Nebraska's early settlers formed extralegal associations known as claims clubs. Groups such as the Omaha Township Claim Associations, the Saratoga Claims Club, and the Belleview Settlers Club drafted their own extralegal codes that protected land claims from squatters and administered retribution on transgressors. In one incident in 1857, the Saratoga Claims Club forced a claim jumper to relinquish his claim by tying a rope around his leg, throwing him into the Missouri River, and, just as he neared death by drowning, pulling him back to shore. After being tossed in the river three times, the claim jumper agreed to withdraw his claim to land held by the Sulphur Springs Land Company. The first territorial legislature legitimized the activities of claims clubs.[6]

Although Nebraska has been a Republican Party stronghold since the late 1860s, Democrats dominated the early territorial period. Democrats such as Stephen Douglas and William Richardson of Illinois had engineered the Kansas-Nebraska Act, and a Democratic president, Franklin Pierce, signed the territorial bill into law. Six of the eight original counties were named after Democrats who supported the Kansas-Nebraska Act: Pierce (President Franklin Pierce), Burt (Governor Francis Burt), Douglas (Senator Stephen Douglas), Cass (Senator Lewis Cass), Dodge (Senator Augustus Dodge), and Richardson (Representative William A. Richardson). Because the president appointed all the territorial officials, Democrats who supported President Pierce and the Kansas-Nebraska Act held all the early positions: Francis Burt of South Carolina (governor), Thomas Cuming of Michigan (secretary), Experience Estabrook of Wisconsin (district attorney), Fenner Ferguson of Michigan (judge), James

Bradley of Indiana (judge), Edward R. Harden of Georgia (judge), and Mark Izard of Arkansas (marshal).

The Organic Act creating Nebraska Territory provided for a bicameral legislature. The Council (upper house) comprised thirteen members elected to two-year terms; the House of Representatives (lower house), depending on population, had between twenty-six and thirty-nine members who served one-year terms. Once a census was taken, the territorial governor was given the power to divide the territory into counties and voting districts. Once a legislature was elected, the governor was to call a meeting of the territorial government to choose a site for the territorial capital.[7]

President Pierce appointed Francis Burt of South Carolina as the first territorial governor. Burt was a lawyer and editor who had served more than twenty years in the South Carolina legislature and at the time of his appointment was an official in the U.S. Treasury. At forty-seven years old, however, Burt's health was not good, and he was ill prepared for the four-week journey to Nebraska. After traveling by railroad, stage, steamboat, wagon, and on foot, Burt arrived in Bellevue, Nebraska, on October 7, 1854, and immediately sought the care of a physician. Although he was still quite sick, the oath of office was administered to Burt on October 16 while he sat infirm in his bed. Two days later Nebraska's first territorial governor died, most likely from a stomach ailment contracted during his arduous journey.[8]

Although he had been governor for only two days, Burt's death threw Nebraska into a bitter sectional dispute over the location of the territorial capital that would not be resolved until Nebraska became a state in 1867. The Platte River creates a natural boundary in Nebraska and divided the territory into two feuding sections. Both sections hoped to become the terminus of the transcontinental railroad, and territorial Nebraskans were sure that the honor would go to the capital city. Omaha dominated north-of-the-Platte Nebraska and was able to put together an effective and united voting block throughout the territorial period. No single community, however, dominated south-of-the-Platte Nebraska. Brownville, Nebraska City, and Plattsmouth all vied for power, sometimes uniting against Omaha but often working against one another. To make things more complicated, Bellevue, although it sat north of the Platte River, was overshadowed by neighboring Omaha and, therefore, allied with the south-of-the-Platte communities.

Evidence suggests that Governor Burt intended to make Bellevue the territorial capital, which would have made the community a prime candidate for the location of the future transcontinental railroad terminus. Burt's successor, Thomas B. Cuming, the first territorial secretary, shocked the citizens of Bellevue when he announced that the first session of the territorial legislature would be held at Omaha. Cuming was closely tied to investors of Council Bluffs, Iowa, directly across the river from Omaha. In fact, Cuming's primary residence was in Council Bluffs. At the time of his appointment as territorial secretary, Cuming was a twenty-five-year-old newspaper editor in Keokuk, Iowa.

He owed his territorial appointment to Iowa Democrats who had worked with Stephen Douglas to push the Kansas-Nebraska Act through Congress. Cuming was apparently determined to repay his debt by supporting Omaha over Bellevue.

Cuming's actions as the acting territorial governor clearly indicate that he was determined to do whatever was needed to ensure that Omaha became and remained the territorial capital. He cleverly manipulated the organization of counties, voting districts, and the assignment of political representation to benefit Omaha. The first territorial census taken in the fall of 1854 indicated that only 914 people lived north of the Platte River, whereas almost twice as many, 1,818, lived in the region south of the divide. Given their numerical majority, those who lived south of the Platte River expected their region to benefit from the creation of more counties providing greater political representation. Instead, Governor Cuming carved four counties out of the northern section (Burt, Dodge, Douglas, and Washington) and four counties out of the south (Cass, Forney, Pierce, and Richardson), raising concern among the South Platters. What Governor Cuming did next set off universal protest in the southern counties. Despite the numerical superiority of the southern section, Cuming assigned north-of-the-Platte counties seven councilmen and fourteen representatives to the territorial legislature, whereas south-of-the-Platte counties received only six councilmen and twelve representatives. If the northern counties united, they could block any legislation to remove the capital south of the Platte. To limit Bellevue's potential power, Cuming placed that city in the same county and voting district with the more populous Omaha.

Cuming's actions created a bitter conflict between the counties north and south of the Platte. Bellevue immediately rose up in protest and joined south-of-the-Platte counties against Omaha. Protest came in various forms. Mass meetings took place south of the Platte to protest the governor's actions, and legislators from the southern counties spent the entire first session of the territorial legislature investigating reports of Cuming's graft and attempting, to no avail, to undo what the governor had done. Out of the fires of protest rose J. Sterling Morton, a twenty-two-year-old Democrat who had migrated from Michigan. Morton quickly became the leading territorial (and later state) Democrat and spokesperson for the southern counties. Morton was so infuriated with Cuming and Omaha that during the second territorial legislature he, along with other south-of-the-Platte legislators, introduced a resolution that, had Congress agreed, would have moved the Kansas border northward to the Platte River and thereby added the southern counties to Kansas Territory. Although most South Platters supported the idea, Kansans, who had their own sectional dispute, were not interested in annexing the region. The territory's sectional dispute continued throughout the period and into statehood and often led to foul language, fistfights, and weapons being drawn during sessions of the territorial legislature.[9]

DISPOSSESSING THE NATIVE AMERICANS

In 1800 at least 14,000 Native Americans from four agrarian tribes lived in semi-permanent villages in what is today Nebraska: Pawnees (10,000), Omahas (2,000), Otoe-Missourias (1,000), and Poncas (900). Other tribes such as the Lakota, Cheyennes, and Arapahoes traveled through, traded, and lived part-time hunting bison herds on Nebraska's western plains. Nebraska's Native Americans, who grew corn, squash, and beans while living in large villages on bluffs overlooking the Platte, Loup, Republican, Nemaha, Niobrara, and Missouri rivers, stood in the way of territorial organization and settlement by whites. The opening of Nebraska Territory, therefore, had serious consequences for Nebraska's four permanent Native American tribes because it sped the process of land loss and cultural dispossession.[10]

Native Americans in Nebraska had suffered immensely from white contact long before the Kansas-Nebraska Act. Lack of immunity to diseases such as smallpox and cholera greatly reduced their population. Smallpox epidemics in 1800–1801, 1831–1832, and 1837–1838 decimated the native populations with each outbreak. The Pawnee population, for example, was cut in half during the 1800–1801 smallpox epidemic, from 10,000 people to approximately 4,800. Although by 1830 the Pawnees had rebounded to their 1800 population, another wave of smallpox hit in 1831–1832, once again reducing their population by half. The Pawnees never recovered after the 1831–1832 epidemic, and by 1900 their population fell to an all-time low of around 600 people.

In addition to disease, overland emigration through Nebraska's Platte Valley created difficulties for the native population. By the early 1860s more than 300,000 emigrants had traveled through the homeland of the Pawnees. Overland wagon trains cut straight through the heart of Nebraska Indian territory, consuming native grasses needed by Native Americans' livestock, cutting limited timber reserves, despoiling hunting campsites and water, and driving bison herds and other game farther from their villages. By the 1840s the virtual extinction of bison herds in eastern Nebraska triggered periodic famines and thereby further weakened resistance to European diseases. In turn, intertribal wars over the diminishing resources intensified, entangling the village tribes such as the Pawnees into multifront conflicts among themselves and with the Lakota, who raided semi-sedentary Nebraska tribes for horses, corn, and slaves, and who also tried to block access to the western bison herds by burning grasses needed for forage and attacking hunting parties.

Encroachment by whites and pressure from the federal government to free up large tracts of land forced some tribes to begin surrendering land in exchange for cash payments, annuities, and federal government protection. As early as the 1830s, the Otoe-Missourias and Pawnees ceded portions of their Nebraska homelands. In 1833, for example, the Pawnee signed away most of their land south of the Platte River, and in 1848 they surrendered an eighty-mile strip on the north side of the river to the military for use by Fort Kearny.

Opening Nebraska to settlement in 1854 required the federal government to negotiate further treaties with Nebraska's Native Americans. If Nebraska was to be organized and settled, the Native American tribes would have to surrender the bulk of their lands. Between 1854 and 1858, therefore, the federal government signed treaties with each of Nebraska's tribes: Otoe-Missourias (March 15, 1854), Omahas (March 16, 1854), Pawnees (September 24, 1857), and Poncas (March 12, 1858). In all, Nebraska's Native Americans assigned more than 17 million acres of land to the federal government for an average price of ten cents per acre. In exchange, they were paid cash, promised annuities, and given small reservations within the present-day borders of Nebraska. The Otoe-Missouria reservation, for example, straddled the Nebraska-Kansas border and measured ten miles wide by twenty-five miles long. The Pawnees, who before the 1830s controlled much of central Nebraska between the Loup and Republican rivers, were reduced to a fifteen-by-thirty-mile reservation on the Loup River in present-day Nance County. The bison-hunting tribes of the western plains were also pushed out of Nebraska by treaty. The Fort Laramie Treaty of 1851 assigned hunting lands to the Lakota, Cheyennes, and Arapahos, which opened a corridor through the Platte Valley for overland travelers. The Fort Laramie Treaty of 1868 effectively removed the Lakota from present-day Nebraska by creating the Great Sioux Reservation, which comprised all of present-day South Dakota west of the Missouri River.[11]

The treaties produced by the Kansas-Nebraska Act did not end the loss of Native Americans' land. Hemmed in by the borders of reservations, pressured on all sides by growing white settlement, suffering from the near extinction of the bison herds from their territory, and under constant attacks from Oglala and Brule Lakota, Nebraska's indigenous tribes suffered and surrendered more land. The Pawnees represent one of the most tragic cases of Native Americans' dispossession. They had lived in Nebraska since the 1200s and once controlled a significant portion of the central plains. Reduced by disease and unable to follow their traditional lifestyle, they moved onto a small reservation. After more than two decades of poor harvests, failing bison hunts, poor relations with their white neighbors, and constant death and destruction at the hands of the Lakota, they finally surrendered their last piece of homeland and relocated to Indian Territory in 1874–1875. One by one, Nebraska tribes gave up hope of surviving in their homelands and moved to Indian Territory. The Otoe-Missourias followed the Pawnees in two waves, in 1876 and 1882. The federal government forcefully removed the Poncas to Indian Territory in 1877. One group of Poncas later returned to Nebraska after the *Standing Bear v. Crook* case determined that an Indian is a person and can remove him/herself from their tribe. Only the Omaha managed to hold onto portions of their traditional homelands in Nebraska in present-day Thurston County. The Winnebago joined the Omaha on the reservation in 1865. Blessed with effective leadership and good relations with their white neighbors, the Omaha held out against removal and continue to live on their homelands in the twenty-first century.

STATEHOOD

Territorial status was intended to be a temporary stage on the path toward statehood, and as early as 1858, just four years after the organization of Nebraska Territory, the first discussion of statehood could be heard.[12] Nebraskans from south-of-the-Platte counties saw statehood as a way to gain power that Governor Cuming's graft had taken away. Statehood would bring reapportionment, and the southern counties would gain political power, the state capital, and possibly, the terminus of the transcontinental railroad. Many territorial newspapers during the late 1850s began a campaign for statehood. The *Omaha Times* suggested that the citizens of the territory deserved the right to vote on statehood. Politicians agreed, and on January 11, 1860, the territorial legislature called for a special election to elect delegates to draft a constitution. Although both Democrats and Republicans had supported a constitutional convention, as the March 5 election neared the sectional dispute between the northern and southern counties reared its head. North-of-the-Platte voters from both political parties realized that statehood could cost them the transcontinental railroad terminus. When Nebraska became a state, Omaha would almost certainly lose the capital, because legislative representation would be redistributed and give the more populous south-of-the-Platte counties the power that they rightly deserved. Led by voters from Omaha and Douglas County, a district that always voted as a solid bloc, the population rejected the legislature's call for a constitutional convention by a vote of 2,372 to 2,094. Only 569 north-of-the-Platte voters voted in favor of drafting a constitution.[13]

For the next three years there was little debate about statehood at either the territory or national level. All focus was on the Civil War, leaving little time to argue whether or not Nebraska should become a state. The territorial legislature did not even convene in 1862 or 1863, making it impossible to debate the issue. Nebraska Territory remained loyal to the Union and actively participated in the war effort by recruiting soldiers, paying wartime taxes, and producing crops for the war. Approximately 36.5 percent of all the territory's men between the ages of twenty and fifty served in the Union army. The territory also became a haven for war refugees from Missouri and Kansas.

The Civil War altered Nebraska's economy and population. With the transportation routes through Texas closed by that state's secession, government freighting and mail had to be rerouted through northern routes. Because Kansas was engulfed in a bitter guerilla war with Missourians, Nebraska cities such as Omaha and Nebraska City received government and private contracts. The transportation firm of Russell, Majors, and Waddell transformed Nebraska City into a commercial center by spending more than $300,000 on warehouses, boardinghouses, foundries, and livestock yards. Southern secession helped Omaha finally acquire the terminus of the transcontinental railroad. The Pacific Railway Act, passed along with the Homestead Act in 1862, created the legislation needed finally to begin building the long-awaited railroad. President

Lincoln originally ordered that Council Bluffs, Iowa, would be the terminus, but because the Missouri River was not bridged, Omaha earned the right by default. By the end of the Civil War, the Union Pacific was on its way westward, and by the end of 1867 it had pushed through the entire state.

The Homestead Act also altered the composition of the population and politics in the territory. Whereas before 1860 much of the Nebraska population was urban based, the Homestead Act brought in thousands of agricultural settlers. By the end of the Civil War Nebraska was transformed from an urban to a rural society. Republican supremacy in Nebraska began to take shape with the Homestead Act of 1862. Into Nebraska migrated thousands of Union soldiers, northern farming families, and European immigrants who supported President Lincoln and the Republican Party. Between 1860 and 1867 the population grew by more than twenty thousand people, most of whom were loyal to the Republican Party.[14]

As Nebraska was being transformed during the Civil War, mutterings about statehood could once again be heard in political conversations or read in the newspapers. At the national level, Republican supporters of President Lincoln realized that adding more loyal states to the Union would strengthen the party and help re-elect the president in 1864. The election of Abraham Lincoln in 1860 and the Civil War changed the political fabric of Nebraska Territory. Using his power of presidential appointments, Lincoln reduced the power of the Democrats by appointing Republicans as territorial officials, including the staunchly loyal Alvin Saunders of Iowa as territorial governor.

With Lincoln facing re-election in 1864, the president's supporters in Congress introduced enabling legislation in late 1863 for Nevada, Colorado, and Nebraska with the hope that each of these territories would achieve statehood by the election. The Nevada statehood process ran smoothly, and the territory was admitted in October 1864. Partisan politics, however, derailed and postponed Nebraska's bid for statehood.

In Nebraska, Governor Alvin Saunders was a staunch supporter of statehood. Probably under orders from the federal government, he began a campaign for statehood in early 1864. In his January 8, 1864, annual message to the territorial legislature, he delineated the advantages statehood would bring to Nebraska. As a state, Saunders pointed out, Nebraska would gain possession of large tracts of public lands needed for internal improvements, public schools, and state institutions such as the university and penitentiary. More immediately, Saunders pointed out that if Nevada and Colorado both achieved statehood and Nebraska did not, it could retard future economic and population growth because future emigrants would view the territory with suspicion and migrate elsewhere. The governor's prodding worked, and a majority of the territorial legislature, both Republican and Democrat, passed a bill to memorialize Congress for the enabling legislation needed to begin the statehood process. Congress granted Nebraska's request on April 19, 1864, authorizing the territory to draft a constitution and elect a state government.[15]

An election was scheduled for July 4, 1864, to elect delegates for a constitutional convention. At this point partisan politics began working against the statehood process. Republicans strongly supported statehood because with their majority they could control the organization of the state and the election of state officers. Most importantly, the Republicans would be able to send two senators and a representative to Washington, D.C., strengthening Republican Reconstruction policy. The Democrats, however, realized they were in a difficult position. They did not have the votes to put fellow Democrats into office and therefore would not have much power in the future state government. Further hurting the Democrats was the party's attachment to southern secession. Whereas the Republican Party could boast that it was the party of the Union and use patriotism to attract voters, Democrats had to walk carefully, being sure not to be too critical of President Lincoln or the effort to preserve the Union. Democratic leaders in the territory, therefore, began a campaign to sidetrack the statehood process. If statehood could be delayed long enough for the Democrats to regain some of the support lost during the Civil War, then they could participate in the organization of the state.

Led by the fiery J. Sterling Morton, the Democrats pointed out that statehood would only bring higher taxes. Rather than the federal government funding the territorial government, taxes would need to be raised to fund the new state government. Morton spoke throughout the territory, convincing the population to vote against forming a constitution. As the election for the constitutional convention election neared, two types of candidates entered the race: those who claimed that they would go to the convention and help draft a state constitution and those who would go to the convention and vote to adjourn without working on a constitution. The Democratic strategy worked well. Voters, with little time to understand fully what statehood would entail, listened to the Democratic argument and voted to protect their pocketbooks by electing delegates who would not draft a state constitution. On July 4, when the elected delegates met in Omaha, the majority voted to adjourn immediately without drafting a constitution, thereby ending the statehood process.

The supporters of statehood refused to surrender and continued to formulate plans to bring statehood to Nebraska. Governor Alvin Saunders was one of the strongest proponents of statehood and used his annual addresses to the legislature to challenge the territory to make another attempt. In his annual address in 1865, Governor Saunders called on the patriotism and loyalties of Nebraskans in an effort to push them toward statehood. In attempting to put aside the issue of increased taxes, Saunders instead called on Nebraskans to relieve the federal government from the burden of financing the territorial government. With the Civil War still being fought, Saunders pointed out that the federal government had more important bills to pay than to fund the territorial government, and that all "loyal and Union-loving people should be willing to assist in bearing their proper burdens."[16] Despite Saunders's plea the legislature failed to act.

In his January 1866 legislative address, Saunders once again called on Nebraska lawmakers to begin the process toward statehood. "Now that the great rebellion has been put down," Saunders stated, "the subject of a change of government from a Territory to a State is being freely discussed by our people." The governor pointed out that Nevada, with a much smaller population than Nebraska, had already been admitted and that Colorado would probably be admitted very soon. (President Johnson vetoed the Colorado bill, thereby postponing Colorado statehood until 1876.) Saunders then lectured the legislators on the benefits of statehood. Because the public had rejected previous statehood efforts over fears of increased taxes, Governor Saunders spelled out clearly that statehood would actually lower taxes. With statehood Nebraska would acquire land from the federal government that could be sold or leased to generate revenue: seventy-two sections of land to endow a state university, 50,000 acres of land for a penitentiary, 90,000 acres for the agricultural college, 46,000 acres of salt lands, and an appropriation for construction of the state capital and other public institutions. Saunders pointed out that the best lands were being taken by homesteaders, and the longer the territory waited for statehood, the poorer their land grants would be. In closing, the governor made it clear that the legislators themselves could draft a constitution. Although previous statehood efforts had included the public by allowing them to vote on delegates for a constitutional convention, Saunders suggested that the legislature bypass the public, draft a constitution, and then submit it to the people for approval, thereby streamlining the statehood process. Governor Saunders closed his address with clear language on the subject of Nebraska statehood: "I have no hesitancy in giving my opinion that the resources of Nebraska would be sooner developed, and her wealth and population increased by becoming a State."

Frustrated by a stubborn legislature that still refused to take any action, Governor Saunders and other leading territorial officials who supported statehood, including Secretary Algernon Paddock and Chief Justice William Pitt Kellogg, met secretly in early 1866 and drafted a constitution. The constitution drafted by Saunders and his committee was a hastily-thrown-together, barebones document. It simply provided for the formation of a minimal state government. Because the issues of taxes and expensive government had blocked previous statehood efforts, those who drafted the constitution focused on small government and economic thriftiness. Government officials were limited to a governor, secretary, auditor, and three supreme court justices who also served as district court trial judges. Immediate statehood was more important than a sound constitution to its drafters and to Republicans in Congress. A revised or entirely new constitution could always be drafted after Nebraska achieved statehood.

The constitutional committee then recruited John R. Porter, one of the few Democrats in the territorial legislature who supported statehood, to introduce the constitution to the legislature. Supporters of statehood pushed the bill through both houses of the territorial legislature without much debate. In fact, the constitution was not even printed for legislators to review. Although there was some opposition to the bill, it passed through both houses largely along party lines. On February 9, 1866, Governor Saunders signed it into law, and an election was set for June 9 so that voters could approve or reject the constitution and vote for state officers.

Nebraska Republicans universally supported statehood, and when they met in convention on April 12, 1866, they nominated a full ticket of candidates and approved a platform that supported the constitution. For governor, the Republicans nominated David Butler of Pawnee City (south of the Platte), a former territorial legislator who had lived in the territory since 1859. Republicans argued that statehood would promote rapid economic development of the region, put school lands under public control (thereby reducing taxes), allow Nebraska to select choice public lands before speculators filed on them, and provide political representation in Washington, D.C. Political representation was particularly crucial in 1866, because construction of the transcontinental railroad had already begun, and as a territory, Nebraska did not have a voting representative in Congress.

The Democrats were divided over the issue of statehood. One group, headed by J. Sterling Morton, still opposed statehood and hoped to stall the election by refusing to nominate candidates for office. Sterling and his supporters argued that the constitution had been illegally drafted and then forced through the legislature without debate. Another faction of the party, led by Dr. George L. Miller, editor of the staunchly Democratic *Omaha Herald*, realized that statehood could no longer be ignored. Rather than not fielding a ticket, as Morton had suggested, Miller and his supporters argued that the party should nominate candidates for state office but should oppose ratifying the state constitution. Under Miller's plan, Democrats might be elected to office, and if the constitution were defeated, then a new one would be drafted under the guidance of Democratic office holders. By the time the Democrats held their convention on April 19, 1866, they had worked out many of their disagreements and decided to participate in the election by nominating a full ticket with Morton as the candidate for governor. The Democratic platform, however, remained noncommittal on the issue of supporting statehood and approving the constitution. To attract moderate Republican voters, the Democratic platform announced its approval of President Andrew Johnson, who was involved in a bitter dispute with the Radical Republicans over Reconstruction legislation. The Democrats also chastised the Republicans for not supporting the president.[17]

The campaign during the spring 1866 was a heated and closely followed affair, punctuated by several debates between J. Sterling Morton and David Butler. Although Morton was widely known as the most skilled orator in the territory, Butler had the advantage as a member of the Republican Party. In post–Civil War elections, Republican candidates always reminded voters that they were the loyal political party who had stood up to the rebellious southern states. They were the party of the now-martyred President Lincoln who had saved the Union from Democratic secessionists. Not able to argue against Republican tactics, Morton and the Democrats still hammered on the taxation issue. Late in the campaign, however, the Democrats turned to the new issue of black civil rights and suffrage. At the national level, Congress was dealing with controversial issues such as the Civil Rights Act of 1866, as the citizens of Nebraska were well aware. Democrats, therefore, preyed on the fears of many citizens that statehood under the Republicans would turn Nebraska into a "Negro colony" where ex-slaves would have an equal voice with white citizens, something that many Americans, northern and southern, did not support.

The election results were much closer than expected. Although the Republican Party had greatly increased its numbers during the 1860s, many voters were apparently influenced by the Democrat's stance on taxation and fears of Nebraska becoming a haven for African Americans. The constitution was approved by a vote of 3,938 to 3,838—the margin of victory was only 100 votes. Butler also won the governorship by a margin of only 109 votes over Morton. Almost immediately the Democrats raised charges of election fraud. All of the votes from the largely Democratic precinct of Rock Bluffs in Cass County were disqualified on technical grounds. Apparently election officials had left the ballot box unattended while they went home for meals. The votes of soldiers at Fort Kearny, mostly Republican, also helped elect Butler and approve the constitution. These votes, according to Democrats, should have also been disqualified because the soldiers were residents of Iowa rather than Nebraska. Had the Rock Bluffs precinct votes been counted and the Fort Kearny soldiers' votes disallowed, the constitution would have been defeated, and J. Sterling Morton would have been elected governor. This would have created the awkward situation of having elected government officials but no state constitution. Although the Democratic press howled, and protests were made to Congress, the results were upheld, marking a Republican triumph. The disallowed Democrat votes from Rock Bluff's precinct also helped elect Republican legislators, giving that party a majority in the newly elected state legislature. With a majority in the new state legislature, the Republicans sent John M. Thayer and Thomas W. Tipton to the Senate to help formulate congressional Reconstruction legislation and battle President Johnson.

The next steps in the statehood process were to obtain congressional approval and President Johnson's signature. For most territories this step in the statehood process was a mere formality. The real battle was usually within the territory itself, and the proponents of statehood had won that battle, with some chicanery. The admission of Nebraska, however, proved to be a difficult battle because it became entangled in post–Civil War disagreements over Reconstruction policy. The Radical Republicans were locked in a bitter dispute with President Johnson over the treatment of the former Confederate states and the legal status of ex-slaves. The Nebraska statehood bill came before Congress in the middle of this dispute.[18]

On July 23, 1866, Senator Benjamin F. Wade (Ohio), chairman of the Committee on Territories, introduced the Nebraska statehood bill to the Senate. The bill was introduced in the wake of Congress's approval of the Fourteenth Amendment, which conferred citizenship on African Americans and gave Congress power to reduce the representation of any state that denied suffrage to males over the age of twenty-one. Almost immediately, opposition broke out over a clause in Nebraska's constitution that limited suffrage to white males. The drafters of the constitution had limited the suffrage to white males to suppress the arguments of territorial Democrats who believed Nebraska would become a black state. Although most Republicans in Congress favored Nebraska's immediate admission, even with the prohibition on black suffrage, a number of senators, primarily from New England, opposed the clause and argued against statehood. Led by Charles Sumner of Massachusetts, the Senate engaged in a lively debate. Senator Sumner objected to the Nebraska bill, asking supporters of the bill to explain to him how "a constitution which on its face disqualified citizens on account of color and disfranchises them can be republican in form."[19] Sumner moved to amend the constitution by striking out the word "white." There was urgency, however, surrounding the Nebraska statehood bill. Most Republican senators realized that the Senate desperately needed Nebraska's two senators in the battle against President Johnson and were willing to overlook the constitutional flaw. With the first session of Congress coming to a close on July 28, there was no time for amendments. The bill was passed by both the House and the Senate on July 27, and it was submitted to the president. President Johnson, who had no desire to see two additional senators and a representative voting against him, used a pocket veto to deny Nebraska statehood by not acting on the bill.

When the Senate reconvened in December, Senator Wade introduced a new bill for the admission of Nebraska. This bill would have still admitted Nebraska with its constitution that limited suffrage to white males. Opposition, once again led by Charles Sumner, led an attack on Nebraska's constitution, demanding that the prohibition on black suffrage be repealed. Senator B. Gratz Brown offered an amendment that would admit Nebraska as a state if a "fundamental condition" were met. The fundamental condition read, "[T]here shall be no denial of the elective franchise or of any other right on the account of color or race."[20] Brown's amendment also stipulated that the people of Nebraska would be required to approve or reject the "fundamental condition" in a special election. Realizing that the population was likely to vote against such a stipulation, another amendment was made to the bill that allowed the territorial legislature rather than the public to approve the condition for statehood. It would be easier to persuade the legislature to approve it than the entire electorate. Both the House and Senate debated whether the public or the legislature should approve the amendment. On January 15, the House passed the bill by a vote of 103-55, and the following day the Senate voted 28-14 to admit Nebraska with an amended provision known as the Edmunds Amendment after Senator George Edmunds of Vermont. The amendment read: "[T]his act shall take effect with the fundamental and perpetual condition that within said state of Nebraska there shall be no abridgement or denial of the exercise of the elective franchise or of any other right to any person by reason of race or color, excepting Indians not taxed."[21] The phrase "excepting Indians not taxed" was added at the last minute out of fear that Native Americans would be bribed or coerced to vote in elections. During the election of 1866 fifteen Native Americans of mixed-heritage—and therefore unclear citizenship status—from the Omaha reservation had voted. No Native Americans had yet been removed from Nebraska in 1867, and both parties feared that the other might use graft to increase their electorate with Native American voters during this tense period of national politics.

There was much more behind this attack on Nebraska's constitution than a desire to enfranchise African Americans. Radical Republicans such as Charles Sumner realized that if Nebraska could be forced to permit black suffrage, Congress could also force the former Confederate states to adopt similar constitutions. Nebraska essentially became a testing ground for the Reconstruction legislation that became the Fourteenth and Fifteenth Amendments. Congressional success in forcing the "fundamental condition" on Nebraska would indicate that the legislative rather than the executive branch could dictate Reconstruction policy.

The Nebraska statehood bill was now in the hands of President Johnson. Because Congress was in session, a pocket veto would not work this time. He had to act on the bill within ten days. On January 29, 1867, President Johnson formally vetoed the bill on the condition that the "fundamental condition" was unconstitutional and that the population rather than the territorial legislature had the right to approve or reject it. On February 8 the Senate passed the bill 31-9, and the House followed the next day with an overriding vote of 120-43, making Nebraska the only state to achieve statehood over a presidential veto.[22]

Although the president's veto was defeated, the Nebraska legislature still had to accept the conditions placed on it by Congress. To expedite the statehood process, Governor Saunders called a special session of the legislature to consider the "fundamental condition" imposed by the Edmunds Amendment. On February 20, 1867, the Nebraska legislature met in Omaha. Governor Saunders opened the session by reading to the legislature the bill to admit Nebraska as a state. Realizing that there would be criticism for not allowing the people of the territory to vote on the matter, Governor Saunders announced that he too believed that the citizens of Nebraska should be consulted. "But," the governor affirmed, "we must now meet the question as we find it, or as it has been presented by Congress." Before he left the legislature to debate the amended bill, Governor Saunders spoke about how attitudes concerning race and color had changed as a result of southern secession and the Civil War. "My opinion," stated the governor, "is that this liberal spirit is rapidly on the increase among the people of our own Territory, and if such is your belief, it would cause you to have much less hesitancy about accepting the conditions proposed than you otherwise might have."[23] After a two-day joint session, both the senate and house approved the amended bill. On March 1, 1867, President Andrew Johnson reluctantly signed the bill admitting Nebraska as the thirty-seventh state.

ESTABLISHING THE STATE GOVERNMENT

Nebraska as a state looked much different than it had when the Kansas-Nebraska Act first organized it in 1854. The organization of Colorado and Dakota territories in 1861 reduced Nebraska by almost 250,000 square miles. By the time Nebraska was admitted as a state, it had been whittled down from 351,558 square miles to 75,995 miles. Nebraska's population stood at approximately fifty thousand people at the time of statehood, including large numbers of European immigrants. The 1870 census indicated that 54 percent of the population was either foreign-born or had parents who were foreign-born, attracted to the state by railroad promotions and the promise of free land. Although many territorial boomtowns had disappeared by statehood, several, including Omaha and Nebraska City, had become thriving commercial centers. Omaha was finally named the terminus of the transcontinental railroad, guaranteeing that it would become the preeminent city in the state. Settlement had pushed well into the third and fourth tier of counties as farming families and Civil War veterans filed homestead claims. Between 1863 and 1867, 5,014 homestead claims were filed. At the time of statehood, the Union Pacific Railroad was being built across the Nebraska plains, and in its path a corridor of new communities sprang to life. Towns such as Grand Island, Kearney, Lexington (originally Plum Creek), North Platte, and Sidney grew up beside the tracks and attracted all types of settlers, including farming families, merchants, lawyers, and cattlemen. Within five years of statehood, Nebraska's population increased by 200,000 and thirty-seven new counties were added.[24]

The new state government had several important issues to deal with when the legislature met on May 16, 1867. Governor David Butler opened the session with a list of thirty-one topics for consideration. Some of the issues included the creation of new counties, locating sites for public buildings, internal improvements such as roads and bridges, encouraging emigration, and creating a free public school system. One of the most important items was the selection of state lands, which would generate revenues to help finance the new state government. The federal government granted the state more than 3.5 million acres of land to fund public schools, universities, and public buildings. Because much of Nebraska's best agricultural lands (in the eastern third of the state) had already been settled, government officials needed to identify the best available lands as soon as possible.

The most heated item debated by state legislators was removing the state capital from Omaha. The location of the capital had been a controversial issue ever since Acting Governor Thomas Cuming announced in 1854 that Omaha would be the capital. Omaha managed to hold onto the capital throughout the territorial period and eventually was made the terminus of the transcontinental railroad. Now that Nebraska was a state and political representation was redistributed so that the more populous counties south of the Platte River held power, Omaha was in danger of losing its position as capital. It hardly mattered to Omaha, because it had already been named the terminus for the railroad, and track stretched for more than 250 miles westward through the Platte Valley. Surrendering the capital was a small price to pay for acquiring the terminus of the railroad and becoming the commercial hub of the Great Plains.

On June 14, 1867, legislators from south-of-the-Platte counties succeeded in passing a removal bill. Rather than fighting over which established city should become the state capital, the removal bill specified that the capital would be built somewhere on state lands in the more sparsely settled counties of Seward, Saunders, Butler, or Lancaster (all south of the Platte River). In the original bill, the new capitol was to be named "Capitol City." North-of-the-Platte legislators, however, threw a parting shot at their long-time rivals and managed to change the name to Lincoln. As long as the capital was removed from Omaha, south-of-the-Platte lawmakers cared little about the name.[25]

A commission consisting of Governor Butler, Secretary of State Thomas P. Kennard, and State Auditor John Gillespie was assigned to survey and choose a site for the capital in the selected counties. On July 18, just four days after the bill passed, the commission left from Nebraska City to tour the region. Several areas were considered, including Ashland, Yankee Hill, and Saline City. The commissioners finally selected a site on Salt Creek near the tiny hamlet of Lancaster. The site was selected because of its central location (all of Nebraska's major cities or towns were within 110 miles) and because of its proximity to a large salt flats, which might help generate income for the state. The commissioners, however, ignored the stipulation that the capital must be on state lands and instead located it on land donated by the Lancaster Seminary Association. On July 29, at the house of W. T. Donavon of Lancaster, the commissioners decided on the site and changed the name of the village from Lancaster to Lincoln.

Lancaster was an odd choice. It had been founded in 1864 and had a population of about thirty people. Unlike almost every Nebraska community at the time, it was not situated on a river, nor did it have a rail connection. The site was widely criticized by Omaha and other established cities. "Nobody will ever go to Lincoln," the *Omaha Republican* sarcastically commented, "who does not go to the legislature, the lunatic asylum, the penitentiary, or some of the state institutions."[26] Despite the criticism, the new capital was immediately surveyed, platted, and divided into lots. Twelve lots each were set aside for the capitol grounds, state university, and city park. To facilitate the building of Lincoln and to attract settlers, additional lots were reserved for churches, a city hall, market place, the Lancaster County Courthouse, public schools, and fraternal orders such as the Odd Fellows, Good Templars, and Masons.

The first town lots went on sale on September 17, but problems arose immediately. The first day of sales looked bad for the capitol commission and supporters of Lincoln. Buyers were leery of investing money in a town that did not yet exist. The first lot, appraised at $40, sold for only twenty-five cents, and the net sales for the day comprised about 10 percent of the town builders' expectations. The commissioners realized that disaster loomed for the new capital city if the sale of town lots did not increase substantially. To ensure Lincoln's future, therefore, the commissioners coaxed a group of outside investors to come in and artificially inflate prices by bidding up to the appraised value on every lot that came up for auction. Bidding by the sham buyers instilled confidence in other buyers, and lot sales increased dramatically. Five days of auction produced more than $35,000 in sales, and some lots that sold for less than a dollar on the first day were going for $150. Lincoln developed slowly, but by 1870 it had a population of 2,500, and the arrival of the Burlington and Missouri Railroad connected the capital city to the Missouri River towns and to points west. Lincoln's survival was also helped by the fact that lawmakers located all of the state's institutions in the capital city. Unlike most states, which divvied out state institutions to various cities, Nebraska placed the capitol, state university (Nebraska combined the state and agricultural college into one), insane asylum, and penitentiary in Lincoln.

Within a few years of statehood, the inadequacies of the constitution of 1866 became apparent to Nebraskans. The constitution had been drafted with economic thriftiness in mind. Government officials were paid appallingly low salaries. Governor Butler, for example, earned only $1,000 per year, which may have influenced him to dip into the state's coffers. Butler was impeached in 1871 for appropriating school funds for his own use. If salaries could be raised, critics argued, honest and upright men would be attracted to government positions. A major problem with the constitution was that it could not be easily amended. To amend the document, a majority of the state legislature had to agree to a constitutional convention. In trying to attain statehood, its drafters tried to make it impossible to amend the constitution to streamline the statehood process. Amending the constitution essentially meant drafting an entirely new document. Other issues that concerned Nebraskans included railroad regulation, judicial reform, expanded political representation, prohibition, compulsory education, and women's suffrage. In June 1871, a constitutional convention was held in the state capitol building to draft a new, more workable document. The convention was characterized by bitter partisan politics, but after two months of debate, a new constitution modeled after the 1870 Illinois constitution was revealed to the public. Critics of the constitution appeared immediately. The railroads campaigned against the approval of the constitution because of its regulatory features. The Catholic Church opposed a section of the document that taxed church property valued over $5,000. The constitution also raised state salaries considerably and created the offices of lieutenant governor and attorney general, setting off fears once again about taxes and expensive government. In the end, opposition forces helped derail the 1871 constitution. In a special election Nebraskans rejected the document by a vote of 8,627 to 7,986.

For the next four years the state suffered under the original unwieldy constitution. The state's coffers, for example, were nearly empty because taxes went uncollected. Municipalities were heavily in debt because of railroad bonds. Public buildings such as the state capitol and state university were crumbling and in need of repair. The supreme court, which doubled as a district trial court, labored under a backlog of cases. Western counties clamored for additional political representation, but the constitution gave no way to acquiesce. Moreover, nearly every public official had been charged with graft, corruption, or bribery. David Butler was removed as governor in 1871, and the current governor, Robert Furnas, found himself involved in a widely publicized legal battle with the *Omaha Herald* over a charge of bribery.

In his 1873 annual message to the legislature, Governor Furnas called on lawmakers to pass a bill for a constitutional convention. "The present constitution," Furnas argued, "is not meeting either the present or growing wants of the state. The judiciary provisions are sadly deficient in supplying the demands of justice; the new counties filling up so rapidly...are without a voice; and the meager salaries of your state officers will not secure...efficiency."[27] The state legislature voted to hold a constitutional convention, and after the public voted in the affirmative, delegates met on May 11, 1875, in the decrepit capitol building to draft a constitution once again. After a month of work, the convention adjourned on June 12 with a new constitution that closely resembled the rejected 1871 document. The new document, however, was purged of some of the points that had produced heated opposition. The clause that would have taxed church property was dropped, appeasing the state's Catholic population, which totaled perhaps 25 percent of the population. The regulatory features aimed at the railroads were still in the document but were less severe. To modernize the legislative branch and give the western counties more representation, the legislature was greatly expanded. The offices of lieutenant governor and attorney general were added to strengthen the executive branch. Other new state officers included the superintendent of public schools and the commissioner of public lands. To assist the judicial branch, the supreme court was relieved of its onerous duty of traveling the state to hold sessions of the district court by the creation of five judicial districts staffed by judges and prosecuting attorneys. In short, the constitution of 1875, which was approved by an overwhelming vote of 30,332 to 5,474, stabilized the state government and restored confidence. The state still operates under a revised version of the constitution of 1875.

SUMMARY

When people think of Nebraska they often conjure up images of a dull agricultural state where nothing of significance happens outside of college football. As a staunchly Republican state, presidential candidates do not even bother to campaign in Nebraska because the outcome will be an overwhelming Republican victory. From 1844, when Stephen Douglas first introduced a bill to organize Nebraska Territory, through the attainment of statehood in 1867, however, Nebraska stood at the center of the some of the most important and controversial political debates of the nineteenth century. The Kansas-Nebraska Act, which opened Nebraska to settlement, set off a chain of events that eventually led to the Civil War. All or parts of seven states were carved from the original Nebraska Territory. Even though most of Nebraska's indigenous population died of disease or were removed to present-day Oklahoma, there is still a visible Native American presence in the state. The Omaha still reside on a portion of their ancestral grounds, and the Santee Sioux live on a reservation in Knox County. The Winnebagos joined the Omaha on their reservation in 1865.

The statehood process also threw Nebraska into the center of a national political debate. During the Civil War, local and national Republicans who wanted to strengthen the party and President Lincoln's post-war policy toward the South pushed statehood on Nebraska Territory. The statehood process was a long and arduous battle. Within the territory itself, partisan politics blocked the statehood process in 1860 and 1864, and only with some shady electoral technicalities did Nebraska finally approve a constitution and apply for statehood in 1866. When Nebraska, after several failed attempts, applied for statehood in 1866, Radical Republicans in Congress used Nebraska as a test case for Reconstruction legislation that became the Fourteenth and Fifteenth Amendment. After several failed attempts caused by internal political disputes and national political debates, Nebraska was granted statehood on March 1, 1867.

NOTES

1. For an overview of Nebraska Territory, the statehood process, and the establishment of the state government, see J. Sterling Morton and Albert Watkins, *Illustrated History of Nebraska*, 3 vols. (Lincoln: Jacob North & Co. and Western Publishing and Engraving, 1905 and 1913); James C. Olson and Ronald C. Naugle, *History of Nebraska* (Lincoln: University of Nebraska Press, 1997); Addison Sheldon, *Nebraska: The Land and the People*, 3 vols. (Chicago: Lewis Publishing Company, 1931).

2. For a survey of pre-territorial perceptions of Nebraska and the Great Plains, see Vernon Volpe, "Prairie Views," in *Prairie Mosaic* (Kearney, NE: University of Nebraska at Kearney, 2000), pp. 92–99.

3. On Stephen A. Douglas and the Kansas-Nebraska Act, see James C. Malin, *The Nebraska Question* (Lawrence, KS, 1953); James C. Malin, "The Nebraska Question:

A Ten Year Record, 1844–1854," *Nebraska History* 35 (March 1954): 1–16; Roy F. Nichols, "The Kansas-Nebraska Act: A Century of Historiography," *Mississippi Valley Historical Review* 43 (September 1956): 187–212.

4. For information on politics, economy, and society in territorial Nebraska, see Erastus F. Beadle, *Ham, Eggs, & Corn Cake: A Nebraska Territory Diary* (Lincoln: University of Nebraska Press, 2001); Norman A. Graebner, "Nebraska's Missouri River Frontier, 1854–1860," *Nebraska History* 42 (December 1961): 213–236; Donald R. Hickey, *Nebraska Moments: Glimpses of Nebraska's Past* (Lincoln: University of Nebraska Press, 1992), pp. 1–36.

5. For a first-hand account of town building during the early territorial period, see Beadle, *Ham, Eggs, & Corn Cake*; Olson and Naugle, *History of Nebraska*, pp. 78–130.

6. Beadle, *Ham, Eggs, & Corn Cake*, pp. xvi, 41.

7. For a discussion of the organizing the territorial government, see Olson and Naugle, *History of Nebraska*, pp. 78–86.

8. Hickey, *Nebraska Moments*, p. 4451; Olson and Naugle, *History of Nebraska*, pp. 80–86.

9. The work of the territorial legislature is meticulously reproduced in Morton, *Illustrated History of Nebraska*, pp. 194–573.

10. The best overview of Nebraska's agrarian Native Americans and the causes and consequences of dispossession is David J. Wishart, *An Unspeakable Sadness: The Dispossession of Nebraska Indians* (Lincoln: University of Nebraska Press, 1994).

11. On the Lakota (Sioux), see Robert Utley, *The Last Days of the Sioux Nation* (New Haven: Yale University Press, 1963).

12. Several detailed accounts of the Nebraska statehood process exist. Albert Watkins, "How Nebraska Was Brought into the Union," Nebraska State Historical Society, *Publications* 18 (1917): 375–434; Morton, *Illustrated History of Nebraska*, pp. 476–573.

13. Watkins, "How Nebraska Was Brought into the Union," pp. 375–434; Douglas Bakken, "Chronology of Nebraska Statehood," *Nebraska History* 48 (Spring 1967): 81–89.

14. On Nebraska during the Civil War, see Larry D. Duke, "Nebraska Territory," *Journal of the West* 16 (April 1977): 72–84.

15. For debates on Nebraska's enabling legislation, see *Congressional Globe*, 38th Cong., 1st Sess., pp. 19–20, 1176, 1166–1167, 1607.

16. All quotations from Governor Alvin Saunders's speeches and legislative addresses can be found in *Messages and Proclamations of the Governors of Nebraska: 1854–1942*, vol. 1 (Lincoln [?], 1941).

17. For a discussion of George Miller and the Democrats during the statehood process, see Wallace Brown, "George L. Miller and the Struggle Over Nebraska Statehood," *Nebraska History* 41 (December 1960): 299–318.

18. For debates on Nebraska statehood, see *Congressional Globe*, 39th Cong., 2d Sess., pp. 121–360.

19. *Congressional Globe*, 39th Cong., 1st Sess., p. 4207.

20. *Congressional Globe*, 39th Cong., 2d Sess., p. 125

21. Ibid., p. 360.

22. For the text of President Johnson's veto and the House and Senate's overrides, see Ibid., pp. 851–852, 1096, 1120.

23. *Messages and Proclamations of the Governors of Nebraska: 1854–1942* , 1:205–206.

24. On the early years of statehood see Olson and Naugle, *Nebraska History*, pp. 143–185; Hickey, *Nebraska Moments*, pp. 52–57.

25. The removal of the state capital to Lincoln has been widely, and colorfully told. See Don Hickey, *Nebraska Moments*, pp. 44–51; Olson and Naugle, *History of Nebraska*, pp. 147–151.

26. *Omaha Republican*, July 17, 1867.

27. *Messages and Proclamations of the Governors of Nebraska*, 1:387.

BIBLIOGRAPHY

Bakken, Douglas. "Chronology of Nebraska Statehood." *Nebraska History* 48 (Spring 1967): 81–89.

Brown, Wallace. "George L. Miller and the Struggle over Nebraska Statehood." *Nebraska History* 41 (December 1960): 299–318.

Duke, Larry D. "Nebraska Territory." *Journal of the West* 16 (April 1977): 72–84.

Graebner, Norman A. "Nebraska's Missouri River Frontier, 1854–1860." *Nebraska History* 42 (December 1961): 213–236.

Hickey, Donald R. *Nebraska Moments: Glimpses of Nebraska's Past.* Lincoln: University of Nebraska Press, 1992.

Homer, Michael W. "The Territorial Judiciary: A Overview of the Nebraska Experience, 1854–1867." *Nebraska History* 63 (Fall 1986): 349–380.

Malin, James C. "The Nebraska Question: A Ten Year Record, 1844–1854." *Nebraska History* 35 (March 1954): 1–16.

Morton, J. Sterling and Albert Watkins. *Illustrated History of Nebraska: A History of Nebraska from the Earliest Explorations of the Trans-Mississippi Region.* 3 vols. Lincoln: Jacob North and Co. and Western Publishing and Engraving, 1905 & 1913.

Olson, James C. and Ronald C. Naugle. *History of Nebraska.* Lincoln: University of Nebraska Press, 1997.

Potts, James B. "The Nebraska Capital Controversy, 1854–1859." *Great Plains Quarterly* 8 (1988): 172–182.

———. "Nebraska Statehood and Reconstruction." *Nebraska History* 69 (Summer 1988): 73–83.

Sheldon, Addison. *Nebraska: The Land and the People.* 2 vols. Chicago: Lewis Publishing Company, 1931.

Watkins, Albert. "How Nebraska Was Brought into the Union, Nebraska State Historical Society." *Publications* 18 (1917): 375–434

Webster, John Lee. "Controversy in the United States Senate over the Admission of Nebraska." *Nebraska State Historical Society Publications* 18 (1917): 345–374.

Wishart, David J. *An Unspeakable Sadness: The Dispossession of the Nebraska Indians.* Lincoln: University of Nebraska Press, 1994.

THE STATE OF NEVADA

Admitted to the Union as a State: October 31, 1864

Jeffrey M. Kintop

INTRODUCTION

Nevada was one of seven territories and one of two states created during the Civil War. It was created along with Dakota Territory and Colorado Territory in 1861 by a Republican Congress set on organizing the West as part of a plan to stop the spread of slavery to the territories, to create a system of patronage appointments, to assure the loyalty of Westerners to the Republican Party, to build a transcontinental railroad, and to enact a homestead act. Kansas became a state just before the attack on Fort Sumter in 1861, and Virginia's five western counties became West Virginia in 1863.

Nevada became a state on October 31, 1864, at a time of national crisis. From the passage and approval of its Organic Act to the presidential proclamation admitting it to the Union on, Nevada had the shortest territorial period of all the western states. Of all the states that existed as territories, only Alabama had a shorter territorial period. Nevada's short territorial history came at a major turning point in America's history. The Civil War raged in the East, and the very fabric of American society was changing. The sovereignty of the individual states was replaced by federalism, and the Gilded Age, when corporations became more powerful than governments, was beginning.

The federal government and national policies had more influence on the creation of western territories and new states in the nineteenth century than the actions of Westerners themselves. The U.S. Army explored and conquered the territory, Congress divided it up, and presidential appointees administered it. Local settlers petitioned Congress to organize their territories, wrote constitutions, and elected delegates to Congress, but their future was determined more by national politics than by local developments.

Nevada

Territorial Development:

- Mexico cedes future Nevadan territory to the United States through the Treaty of Guadalupe Hidalgo, February 2, 1848
- Nevada organized as a United States territory, March 2, 1861
- Nevada admitted into the Union as the thirty-sixth state, October 31, 1864

Territorial Capitals:

- Carson City, 1861–1864

State Capitals:
- Carson City, 1864–present

Origin of State Name: Spanish sailors originally gave the name "Sierra Nevada," or "snowy range," to the mountains that they beheld from their ship, and it was subsequently used in reference to the territory then being formed out of Utah.

First Governor: H. G. Blasdel
Governmental Organization: Bicameral
Population at Statehood: 28,841 (figure taken from the 1860 census)
Geographical Size: 109,826 square miles

EARLY SETTLEMENT

In the 1840s the region that would become Nevada was a great, arid sea of sand and sagebrush with islands of rugged mountains to be crossed by the fleets of wagons bound for the West Coast. Those who traveled across its expanse found it so demanding and troublesome that they never considered it a place to settle. Most of the emigrants avoided it altogether, choosing instead to go to California by ship. Those in the wagon trains saw it as an empty land, not as a place already settled by people who called themselves "Newe," "Nuwuvi," or "Washoe," and whom the migrants called "Shoshone," "Paiute," and "Washoe." When the California gold rush started the great overland migration in 1849, commerce became the driving force of settlement, and trading posts were established along the route on the eastern slope of the Sierra Nevada.

In the first year of the California gold rush, twenty-five thousand people traveled overland through what would become Nevada. The Mormon settlements in the Great Salt Lake Valley of Utah Territory survived in the Great Basin because of this trade. Their stores in Salt Lake City did a booming business, and they expanded their trade to the eastern slope of the Sierra Nevada, the last obstacle on the trail to California. The first U.S. citizens to claim land in Carson Valley in 1851 were placer miners from California, who sifted through alluvial and glacial deposits for gold, and merchants from Salt Lake City, who found they could dig more gold out of travelers' pockets than out of the ground. The merchants needed little capital for their ventures, because they did not have to buy a lot on the main street of a town or even rent business space.[1]

Those who had come overland knew the possibilities for profit because they had encountered such trading operations at Fort Hall or Fort Bridger farther east along the Overland Trail. Promoters and speculators followed, claiming large tracts of land and encouraging immigration to the region to create a market for their lands. Until the discovery of the Comstock Lode in 1859, the business of Nevada was the overland migration. The trails, with their obstacles and alternative routes, determined the locations; stations were set up at the entrance to the mountain passes and at fords on the Humboldt, Carson, and Truckee rivers. New passes were discovered, and new roads were promoted. In a couple of years, trading stations spread from Carson Valley north along the trail to Eagle Valley, the Truckee Meadows, and Honey Lake and east along the Carson and Humboldt rivers. During the 1850s Nevada was dotted with stations along the central route as the U.S. mail traveled by wagon, mule, and pony through the heart of the Great Basin.

Although these settlements were in western Utah Territory, California tried to claim them, and settlers who were not satisfied in either jurisdiction tried to form their own governments. In Carson Valley a handful of settlers led by Mormon Station owner John Reese and mail contractor Absalom Woodward set up a squatters' government and petitioned Congress for a new territory.

This government had no official standing among those who chose not to participate, and in 1853 those who disagreed with its actions petitioned the California legislature to annex their valley.[2] Not all the residents in western Utah were interested in living under an established government. They were there to profit from the wagon trains and, perhaps, to sell claims to land they did not own to somebody else.

In response to California's claims, Utah established Carson County in 1855 and sent probate judge and Mormon elder Orson Hyde to organize the county under Utah laws. There were courts, county officials, and law enforcement. Mormon Station in Carson Valley was renamed "Genoa" and became the county seat. Mormon rule was not always gentle, and Hyde found the local people difficult to govern. When the Mormon faithful were recalled to Salt Lake City in 1857 to prepare for the invasion of General Albert Sidney Johnston's army, those in western Utah were again left without government. Carson County was attached to Great Salt Lake County for judicial purposes, and the county seat moved hundreds of miles eastward.

In April 1857 rumors spread through Carson Valley that the Mormons would be recalled; in fact, the exodus of the Mormon faithful from Carson City began in July and continued until October. There were also rumors that Congress had approved the construction of an overland wagon road from the east to Honey Lake. The road was seen as an economic boon to the region soon to be abandoned by the Mormons. A wagon road convention held in Marysville advocated a road via Honey Lake, and one in Sacramento favored a Carson Valley route.

LOCAL ATTEMPTS TO ORGANIZE A NEW TERRITORY

Cut adrift from Utah Territory and with land prices declining, fifty men met in Gilbert's Saloon in Genoa on August 3 to form a committee to create a new territory. They invited representatives from Honey Lake, Carson, and Eagle valleys.

In Honey Lake Valley (which was actually in California), settlers led by Isaac Roop drafted a constitution and organized the Territory of Nataqua, laying claim to a great deal of land in western Utah. The proposed Nataqua Territory was not well received and was generally ignored by the valleys in the south including Carson Valley. These early efforts to create new territories in Carson Valley and Honey Lake Valley were fueled by speculation about the location of an overland wagon road being surveyed by the federal government and about the assignment of post roads through the Great Basin to California. Congress was also debating possible routes for a transcontinental railroad, and the U.S. Army Corps of Topographical Engineers explored the region for possible routes across the Great Basin. In 1856 a new road was being promoted from Placerville to Genoa, and in 1857 mail contracts were let for transporting mail from the Mississippi River to San Francisco. Mail transportation shifted from mule train to wagon.[3] New settlers speculating on these routes began to claim land near fords and mountain passes in anticipation of these new federally funded projects.

William M. Ormsby came to Carson Valley with the Pioneer Stage Company from Placerville, California, and saw the opportunity to create a new territory. Ormsby was a Pennsylvanian who came to California as a forty-niner by way of Kentucky, together with two brothers, John and Matthew, and his brother-in law, John K. Trumbo. He ran a stage line from Sacramento to Marysville, invested in Sacramento real estate, and served in a private army that invaded Nicaragua in 1856. His brother-in-law, John K. Trumbo, was already in the territory and had married John Reese's daughter. This marriage forged ties between the old settlers of the Carson Valley and the road promoters of Placerville. Ormsby was sent there to promote the road to Placerville through Carson Valley, but he soon shifted his gaze to Eagle Valley just a few miles north.

Ormsby allied himself with James Crane, who came to Utah in 1857 with a plan to create a territory lying between California and Utah. Crane spoke the language of popular sovereignty and independence the separatists wanted to hear. He was born in Richmond, Virginia, and came West in 1849 to start a Whig newspaper, the *Pacific Courier*, in California with eastern financing. Crane's editorials criticized the Washington government's administration of California. His views were well known on the Pacific Coast, and everyone knew he was an advocate of a Pacific republic, separate from the United States. Crane had compiled his beliefs in a book, *The Past, Present and Future of the Pacific*, which he published in San Francisco in 1856.[4]

Ormsby organized a meeting in August 1857. The group elected John Reese as president and named four vice presidents to represent the different valleys— Isaac Roop from Honey Lake, Dr. Benjamin L. King from Eagle Valley, Captain F. C. Smith from Carson Valley, and Solomon Perrin from Willow Town near Ragtown. That meeting created a crucial alliance between the northern and southern communities of the eastern slope. Ormsby may have been planning to create a new territory from the beginning, because he recruited James Crane, a man of similar opinions, as spokesman for his movement.

Crane, Ormsby, and others promoted their new territory in letters to California newspapers. They claimed credit for the Mormons' departure from western Utah. California newspapers took notice because they approved of the federal government's attempts to quash Mormon power and influence and firmly believed in popular sovereignty. Without organized government, the region became lawless. In Carson Valley Ormsby's territorial committee became a vigilance committee, modeled after its California predecessors, to restore order but also to control political activity in the region.

After the reports of Native American raids along the Humboldt River, Ormsby's committee investigated and blamed Mormons and their Native American allies. Crane went to Washington to lobby for the creation of a new territory, but at first he had trouble getting anyone in Congress to listen to him. He called on his friend Congressman William "Extra Billy" Smith to introduce a bill to organize Sierra Nevada Territory in 1858. Smith, who had been governor of Virginia and was a forty-niner who had returned to his home state in 1852, introduced the bill, but the violence in Kansas and the adoption of its pro-slavery Lecompton constitution raised heated debates in Congress and delayed the organization of territories in the West. The Kansas issue influenced every matter that came up in the House of Representatives, whether it was the proposed Homestead Act or the issuance of paper money. For all the talk and all the schemes of the territorial organizers, "bleeding Kansas" dominated that Congress. All territorial business was stalled, and no new territories were created.

The miners did not participate in the political activities of the traders and land speculators in the valleys. They were content to work their placer claims and to look for new claims. Early in 1858 many miners abandoned the Gold Canyon placers and began prospecting the Carson and Walker rivers. The Gold Hill miners organized the Columbia Quartz Mining District under the leadership of William Hickman Dolman. His small mining company was organized in Placerville, California. The district was modeled on the Placerville Quartz Mining District, and the organization was forgotten within a month of its creation.[5]

After Congress failed to establish a territory in 1858, the territorial organizers met again in July 1859 to create the Provisional Territory of Sierra Nevada, modeled after Oregon. This time the meeting included the miners from the Walker River country to the south and the traders and ranchers of Honey Lake and other areas of the eastern slope. It represented a merger of the ambitions of Ormsby, Crane, and Roop. Crane hoped to create a provisional government on the model of Oregon's government from 1843 to 1848. The need for government was universally acclaimed in the region, but opinion differed as to how it should be organized. The proposed constitution was modeled after California's constitution, and the boundaries of the new territory were ambitiously large.

The plans for the fledgling territory were brought to naught by the arrival of John Cradlebaugh, district judge for Western Utah. Cradlebaugh was an Ohioan, educated at Miami University and admitted to the bar in 1840. He practiced law, and from 1851 to 1858 he served in the Ohio Senate, where he supported President Buchanan. Buchanan appointed him an associate justice of Utah Territory when he appointed Cumming governor to replace Brigham Young. Cradlebaugh arrived shortly after General Albert Johnston's army. He began a relentless investigation and prosecution of those involved in the Mountain Meadows Massacre of 1857, but he was unable to organize a jury to convict those who had been indicted. The attorney general of the United States reprimanded him for exceeding his authority, and the Utah Legislature exiled him to western Utah with headquarters in Genoa. He arrived in Genoa in August of 1859 with a military escort, making a show of the arrival of a federal government appointee, as Hyde had before him. Because there was no courthouse in Carson County, he held court wherever possible.[6]

Crane died suddenly in Gold Hill shortly after the election, leaving the new government without a spokesman and without Washington connections. They hurriedly elected John J. Musser to represent them in Congress. In 1859 the Comstock Lode was discovered, and the "Rush to Washoe" began, bringing hundreds of California miners to the area. Utah tried again to maintain control over the region, and local residents pushed harder for separate status. The new discoveries of gold and silver on the Comstock Lode shifted the population center of the territory westward to Carson County. California withdrew its claim to any portion of western Utah that year, and three factions vied to organize a government in western Utah. One group wanted to retain the Carson County government. Another supported Ormsby's effort to create a new territory. A third group favored Cradlebaugh's proposal to reorganize Utah Territory and shift the capital to the western part of the territory, thus removing the Mormons from the seat of power.[7] In 1860 the bill to organize Nevada Territory again failed to pass Congress, and Native American problems in western Utah prevented further development of the provisional territory.

White ranchers moved large herds onto the Pyramid Lake reservation and began to torment Native American families, stealing their horses and killing members of their band.[8] On the Humboldt River an overland station keeper fled when Native Americans began to kill his cattle and threaten other stations.[9] On May 7, Paiutes killed Oscar and James Williams, who owned Williams's station on the Carson River. The Williams brothers had kidnapped and raped two young Paiute girls and hidden them in the cellar of the cabin. The girls' families gathered thirty men and retaliated, killed two of the brothers, burning the station, and causing a panic on the eastern slope. Ormsby wanted to deal with the matter immediately and decisively, thinking that by becoming a local hero he would gain support for his territorial plans. He organized the Carson Rangers, and other "militia" companies were organized in the other communities. Ormsby went to investigate the scene and arrived there the same time as Judge Cradlebaugh. Cradlebaugh was unwilling to pursue the Paiutes and refused to sanction the actions of Ormsby and his rangers. Ormsby gathered up his rag tag army of drunken miners and rode north.

The Paiutes had gathered in large numbers at Pyramid Lake for the spring fish run. Bannock and Pitt River Native Americans were also there, and they urged a more violent response to the outrage than the Paiutes had shown. Sarah Winnemucca, daughter of Chief Winnemucca, remembered that the tribes gathered to discuss the invasion of their lands by the white miners.[10] Earlier that spring, Governor Roop had asked Winnemucca for help in finding the Native Americans responsible for killing other white men. Winnemucca did not want to help him and protested against the encroachment of miners and ranchers on the reservation set aside for them by Major Frederick Dodge in 1858.

The Paiutes, Bannocks, and Pitt River Native Americans prepared an ambush much as they prepared for a rabbit drive, constructing barriers on both sides of the canyon with an opening in the center. As the rangers approached, a number of Paiutes retreated through the opening, drawing the rangers to their deaths. Sixty of the one hundred rangers were killed, and panic filled every town on the eastern slope. People from the countryside retreated to the towns, and the towns barricaded buildings and prepared for an attack that never came. Ormsby was one of the sixty who were killed. News of the Pyramid Lake defeat reached California, and almost seven hundred soldiers from Sacramento and the California mining towns rode to Pyramid Lake, scouring the countryside for unruly Native Americans. The Numa retreated to the Black Rock Desert, engaging the soldiers a couple of times. After a brief skirmish on May 31, the whites declared a victory and afterward referred to the incident as the Battle of Pyramid Lake.

The war was a turning point in Native American relations in the West. Military companies began to patrol the trails regularly and moved their operations closer to the problem areas on the Overland Trail. They also began construction of Fort Churchill, located at the junction of the overland mail route and the Emigrant Trail. After the battles in May, many people who had rushed to Washoe returned to California, leaving the Carson County "nearly depopulated."[11] For the next two years, the new miners coming into the territory congregated in Virginia City and Carson City. The provisional government was dead because of its inability to ward off the Native American problems, and the local residents were resigned to being part of Utah territory. Their Washington lobbyist Musser did not think that Congress would create another territory, and the *Territorial Enterprise* opined that to establish any form of government other than a state or territory was un-American.[12]

In 1860 the lure of the silver and gold claims and talk of separate territorial status attracted several former California state officials, including former Governor J. Neely Johnson, former Supreme Court Justice David S. Terry, and former Attorney General William M. Stewart. They were lawyers with lingering political ambitions, drawn to the region by the work of registering mining claims and litigating disputes. A new power also arrived in the territory in 1860 that would hold great influence in the future territory and state and control the lives of thousands of workers outside the state: the California mining corporation. The Ophir Silver Mining Company was the first to incorporate on April 28, 1860. By the end of the year thirty-seven companies had incorporated, all in San Francisco, California. The corporations became more important than the mining claims themselves, and the shares of stock were worth more than the gold and silver in the ground. The thirty-seven companies sold shares valued at $30 million.[13]

After the provisional government failed to protect the residents from the Native American battles in the spring of 1860, and with Crane and Ormsby dead, there was no real impetus to form a separate territory. Only Governor

Roop remained to blow on the embers of the fire that had raged the year before. For the time being, the residents of the eastern slope were resigned to being governed by Utah Territory.

In the elections of August 1860, the pro-Mormon faction elected John James to represent Carson County in the Utah legislative assembly in the following December. He worked hard to develop the region. The 1860–1861 session was almost exclusively devoted to the affairs of Carson County. Early in 1861 the county seat was moved from Genoa to Carson City. Virginia City was incorporated under Utah laws. The county jail was made a branch of the territorial prison, and a special act helped resolve the mining litigation in Carson County. The beginning of 1861 saw administration of the region divided among the provisional government now headquartered in Susanville, the Gold Hill Mining District, and Carson County, Utah Territory.[14]

CONGRESS CREATES NEVADA TERRITORY

After almost ten years of petitioning Congress for their own territory, the residents of the eastern slope of the Sierra Nevada finally received their territorial status. Governor Roop had left the West in the fall of 1860 to carry his petitions for a separate territory to Congress personally. He delivered his petitions to California's Congressman John L. Burch and Senators William M. Gwin and Milton S. Latham, who introduced them on February 11 in the Senate. The petition was signed by old settlers as well as by many new arrivals. It described the region's remoteness from the Utah capital at Salt Lake City and emphasized its mineral wealth and growing population.[15]

This time Congress was more receptive to territorial bills. Between President Abraham Lincoln's election and his inauguration, seven southern states led by South Carolina began withdrawing their representatives and senators from Congress. On February 14, Senator James Stephen Green of Missouri introduced a bill to create temporary governments for Nevada and Dakota as a compromise to the bill introduced by Latham and Gwin. It was part of a package of territorial bills that failed in the last several sessions. Congressman Galusha Grow of Pennsylvania had worked hard for their creation, hoping to tie them to his homestead bill. Senator Stephen Douglas of Illinois also supported the territorial organization of the West that was tied to his interest in a transcontinental railroad via the central route to California. When Congress was debating the Nevada Territory bill, it established the new post roads by the central route between St. Louis, Missouri, and Placerville and to other places in the region including Genoa, Washoe Valley, the Truckee Meadows, Carson City, and Virginia City.[16]

The Senate passed the bills to create Colorado, Nevada, and Dakota territories on February 26 and sent them to the House, where they were referred to the Committee on Territories and emerged without any reference to slavery.

The problem that had blocked the organization of the West for more than a decade was no longer a barrier. Congress rushed the new territories through the flurry of last-minute legislative business near the end of the session on March 2. Colorado Territory was created out of portions of Utah, Nebraska, and New Mexico territories, Nevada Territory out of Utah Territory, and Dakota Territory from what had been western Minnesota Territory. The bills passed out of the House with little opposition on March 1. The remaining southern senators tried one last time and failed to legalize slavery in the territories. President Buchanan approved the territorial bills on March 2. Two days later Abraham Lincoln was inaugurated as the sixteenth president of the United States and began his task of selecting the new federal officers to oversee the western territories. In the rush to pass the legislation no funds were appropriated for the territories' general government, for surveys, or for Native American affairs.

The Organic Act of a territory worked as a constitution did for a state. It set boundaries and assigned the powers of the executive, legislative, and judicial branches of territorial government. Terms of office were set at four years for each of the federally appointed officers.[17] The president appointed all the officers. The governor was the chief executive power in the district, commander in chief of the militia, and the superintendent of Indian affairs. He could approve or veto legislation, organize the territory into judicial and election districts, assign the judges to the districts, and set terms for the district courts. He could also appoint notaries public, commissioners of deeds, probate court judges, and district attorneys and make the initial appointments for county officers until elections could be held. Furthermore, the governor could select the place for the meeting of the first legislative assembly and appoint all territorial officers not specified in the Organic Act with the advice and consent of the council, the upper house of the legislature. As superintendent of Indian affairs, Nevada's governor reported to the U.S. commissioner for Indian affairs in the Department of the Interior.

The surveyor general served under the secretary of the interior and the superintendent of the government land office. His duties were defined in the act that created New Mexico Territory. The appointee was to oversee the surveying contracts in the territory, establish a land office for the sale of lands, and enforce the federal laws governing the public domain. The secretary of the territory was to preserve all laws and proceedings of the legislative assembly and all official acts of the governor. Every year in December, he was to send a copy of the executive and legislative acts and proceedings to the president and two copies of the legislative laws and proceedings to Congress, one to the president of the Senate and one to the speaker of the House. If the governor died, resigned or left the territory, the secretary would become acting governor.

Both the governor and a legislative assembly, composed of a nine-member council and a thirteen-member house of representatives, held legislative power. The legislature could meet the first time for sixty days and for no more than forty days at each subsequent meeting. It was to select the capital, create counties, and establish district courts. The governor could approve or veto legislative bills and send them to Washington, D.C., to be reviewed by Congress, which also had the power to veto them. Each house could expand its ranks as needed to a maximum of thirteen for the council and twenty-six for the house. No member of the legislature could hold any position created by its laws, nor could he receive any money under contract with the territorial government.

Congress set the boundaries of Nevada Territory. Three of the boundaries were straight lines, bordering Oregon on the north, Utah on the east, and New Mexico Territory to the south. On a map, these boundaries were well defined, but no one knew where they were on the ground. The California-Nevada border on the west was the crest of the Sierra Nevada. Some of the territory was in the state of California, which had set its own boundary as 120° west longitude from the Greenwich meridian, and was not to be included in the territory without California's consent. Isaac Roop had some success in keeping Honey Lake Valley out of California for a while longer. The lands of the Paiutes, Washoe, and Shoshone were not to be included in the territory unless those rights were given up under treaty or unless each tribe consented to being part of the territory. The local government could make no laws pertaining to Native Americans or their land.

The court system created under the Organic Act included three district court judges who held court individually in their respective jurisdictions and sat together as the appellate or supreme court. The court could act in cases involving territorial and federal laws. Its decisions could be appealed to the U.S. Supreme Court just as in U.S. circuit courts. The governor created the initial districts, assigned judges to them, and scheduled the terms of the courts until the first legislature met and assigned them by territorial law. The Organic Act also created the system of probate courts and justice courts and the office of attorney of the United States to act as prosecuting attorney in cases involving federal law and to provide legal opinions to the governor and legislature. There was also a U.S. marshal whose duties were to serve subpoenas for federal cases and guard prisoners held for federal trials.

THE NEW TERRITORIAL OFFICERS

The Republican Party's victory meant sweeping changes in the patronage appointments that until then had gone predominantly to Democrats. For those who supported Lincoln in the 1860 election, it was a boon to the political careers of both new and old politicians. President Lincoln appointed James Warren Nye as governor at the request of Secretary of State William Seward. Nye was born in DeRuyter, New York, in 1815, became an attorney in 1838, and served as district attorney in Madison County from 1841 to 1844. He was a probate judge from 1847 to 1851, ran for Congress in 1848 as a Free Soil Democrat, and was a general in the New York state militia. In 1857 he was appointed to the New York City police commission after the New York state legislature created the Metropolitan Police Department. New York City was predominantly Democratic, under the control of Mayor Fernando Wood and Tammany Hall. The Republican-dominated state legislature created a new state police force to remove control of the police force from the Tammany Hall machine. As president of the new Metropolitan Police, Nye made significant improvements that served as models to other metropolitan police forces until the end of the nineteenth century. Nye was suited for the position of territorial governor because of his experience in law, police work, and political organization. He was also an entertaining and effective speaker at rallies, political events, and almost any occasion. His most important attribute was an unbending loyalty to the new Republican Party and its view of a unified nation under a strong federal government.[18]

Orion Clemens of Missouri was appointed secretary of Nevada Territory after applying for the position in any territory except Utah. He was born in 1825 in Tennessee and was working as an attorney in Memphis, Missouri, looking for an appointment in the new presidential administration. Except for a brief acquaintance with Edward Bates when he was a judge in St. Louis, Clemens had no powerful political connections in the new Republican order and received his appointment through a friend of a friend. His brother Samuel obtained a letter recommending Orion for a clerk's position. Clemens then wrote to Bates directly, who then passed the letter and his recommendation along to Seward. Notice of his appointment arrived on March 27, and his commission arrived a month later.[19]

Ohioan George Enoch Turner was named chief justice. Born in Ohio in 1828, he attended Ohio Wesleyan and studied law under W. V. Peck, a prominent attorney and local politician in Portsmouth. Turner was an active politician and an energetic lawyer, specializing in land warrants. Secretary of the Treasury Salmon P. Chase and Senator Benjamin Franklin Wade of Ohio nominated Turner. Turner was thirty-three years old and was probably the least-experienced judge on the territorial bench.[20]

Lincoln picked Californian Gordon Newell Mott to be one of the associate justices. Mott was born in Zanesville, Ohio, in 1812, studied law, and was admitted to the bar in 1836. He served in the army of the Republic of Texas during its war of independence from Mexico and later served as a captain in the U.S. Army during the Mexican War. Following his honorable discharge he returned to his law practice in Miami County, Ohio. Mott had twenty-five years of legal experience before his appointment as associate justice for Nevada Territory. Following the other gold seekers in 1849, he went to California. In 1851 the California state legislature elected him as a county judge, and later the governor appointed him a district judge. Mott lost the 1855 nomination for California Supreme Court judge to David S. Terry, after which he became a law partner of General George Rowe and operated a stagecoach service and saddle train between Downieville and Virginia City. He made formal application for a justiceship in Nevada Territory to the U.S. attorney general on February 9, 1861, and was nominated and commissioned March 27, 1861. Nevada and California newspapers praised his appointment because he was familiar with western mining practices.[21]

Horatio M. Jones was another appointee from Missouri, recommended by Attorney General Bates. Born in Howellsville, Pennsylvania, in 1826, Jones was graduated from Oberlin College in 1849 and from Harvard Law School in 1853. He practiced law in St. Louis in 1854, and the Missouri Supreme Court appointed him its court reporter in 1856. He was the reporter of the supreme court until President Lincoln appointed him associate justice for Nevada Territory. The last appointment for the justice department was Benjamin B. Bunker of New Hampshire, who had applied for a consulate position in 1861 but whom Lincoln appointed U.S. attorney.[22]

For surveyor general President Lincoln appointed John Wesley North from Minnesota. Among Nevada's appointed officials, North was the only one who had experienced life in a territory and had been actively involved in the creation of a state. Born in New York in 1815, North had a seminary education and was graduated from Wesleyan University in Connecticut, where he became a vocal anti-slavery advocate. After college he studied law and was admitted to the bar in Syracuse in 1845. He attended the Democratic Party meeting in 1848 when the party split. He was also acquainted with Nye, because their political and legal careers brought them together, North as an attorney and Nye as a judge. Frustrated with New York politics, he and his family moved to Minnesota Territory in 1849, where he practiced law, engaged in business, and was active in politics. He was involved in land speculation, railroad planning, and town development, founding Fairibault and Northfield. North organized the Republican Party in Minnesota in his home in 1855, worked in the temperance movement, and in 1857 was elected to the Republican delegation to constitutional convention.[23]

THE NEW TERRITORIAL GOVERNMENT

Nevadans had to wait for their new government. Appointments were delayed by war and distance. One by one the new appointees were notified, and one by one they made their way to Nevada. Just before they began arriving, the new territory experienced its first taste of the Civil War. One month after the bombardment of Fort Sumter, the Department of the Pacific began suppressing secessionist activity in the West. Lincoln's victory in California came about because the Democratic Party's votes were split between Stephen Douglas and General George McClellan. Only a few months before, California's U.S. Senator Milton Latham had mentioned the possible secession of the West and the formation of a Pacific Republic, which was echoed in many newspapers. The western territories were not securely pro-Union, and the federal government had to protect the newly formed territories.[24]

Rumors of large secessionist organizations spread throughout California, particularly after General George A. Sumner replaced Albert Sidney Johnston as head of the Department of the Pacific and eight officers resigned their commissions and joined the Confederate Army. Once the Unionists were in control of the northern California cities, the search for secessionists moved into the southern part of the state and into sparsely populated Nevada. Whether the secessionist organizations actually existed did not matter, because even the possibility of their existence threatened the security of the Union and was taken seriously by the military. Southern sympathizers were considered as much of a threat as any real secessionist group. There was paranoia in the Far West, similar to the reaction against German immigrants during World War I, with neighbors spying and reporting on persons suspected of secessionist sympathies.

Major Don Carlos Buell, the assistant adjutant general at the Department of Pacific headquarters, knew that the territory had not yet been organized and that there were no federal officials there. He was confident that the troops at the fort could withstand any attempted takeover, but he sent reinforcements anyway. Rumors ran rampant through the territory. There were stories that Judge David S. Terry had been commissioned governor of Nevada Territory by President of the Confederacy Jefferson Davis and was on his way to the territory, waiting for the opportunity to take Nevada for the Confederacy. Major George A. H. Blake, the commander at Fort Churchill, placed no store in these rumors, but admitted that the fears existed and vouched for the loyalty of the committee of safety. Committee members echoed the rumors and swore to their veracity. The Union supporters were in the majority and were well organized but had no weapons. Blake reported that the Comstock's population were mostly from northern states, generally quiet citizens, and totally without guns, lacking even revolvers which were prevalent in many frontier towns.[25]

Major Buell ordered another infantry company to reinforce the fort. He then wrote to Judge Mott in Marysville, California, asking him to go to the territory as soon as possible because he believed there was sufficient evidence to issue writs for the arrest of treasonous offenders.[26] The army had no civil authority except when martial law had been declared, but neither did Mott, who reviewed the Organic Act for Nevada and admitted he had no power to act until Governor Nye organized the territory into judicial districts.[27] General Sumner ordered artillery to Fort Churchill on June 10 and withdrew troops from Oregon to help defend California and Nevada. At Fort Churchill, Major Blake ordered the quartermaster and twenty dragoons to Carson City, where he was to confiscate any guns of military issue he found there. Army muskets had been issued to Carson County residents during the Pyramid Lake battles with the Paiutes and Bannocks the year before, and the committee believed the secessionists intended to steal the muskets. The muskets were found and secured.[28]

Captain Moore reported that a Confederate flag had been raised in Virginia City as a rallying point for secessionists who planned to capture the fort, but, when questioned, the proprietor of the store where it was flown claimed that it was done as a joke. Moore searched the houses where guns were supposedly hidden. Finding none, he organized the local committee into two companies of fifty men each and recruited three hundred others, all of whom swore oaths to protect the Union. He left one hundred muskets with them, satisfied that they would preserve the peace, and returned to the fort. General Sumner was satisfied that the seizure of arms had checked the activities of Nevada secessionists. The crisis had passed, and the reinforcements were ordered to return to California on July 6, two days before Governor Nye arrived in the territory. Nevada's new government had been ushered in with military patrols and house-to-house searches, showing that the federal government would not allow free speech while it was at war.[29]

The new federal officers began arriving four months after Nevada's creation. John North was the first to arrive in the territory, followed by Governor Nye, who stopped in San Francisco to give speeches and meet politicians. Nye outlined his main objectives as governor of the new territory: to tame a remote and undisciplined corner of the country; to mold a Union coalition faithful to the federal government; to spur Nevada to admission as a state; and to fulfill his ambition to be a U.S. senator.

Celebrations in Genoa, Carson City, and Virginia City greeted Governor Nye when he arrived on July 10. Nye had been informed of the secessionist scare when he was in San Francisco and was aware of the territory's reputation for lawlessness, so he issued his first proclamation the next day, announcing that all territorial officers had assumed their duties and that the territory was officially organized, even though there were only three officers in the territory.[30] Later in July Nye issued two other proclamations, one calling for a census and the other dividing the territory into judicial districts and assigning the justices to these districts. Mott was the first judge to arrive and was assigned to the first judicial district that included Washoe Valley, Virginia City, and Gold Hill. Turner was assigned to the second and Jones to the third. Gordon Mott was recommended highly for the district that included Virginia City, Gold Hill, and Silver City by J. Neely Johnson, by William Stewart, and by other members of the self-proclaimed bar of Nevada territory. Mott was considered experienced in mining litigation and was familiar with California laws. They wanted him assigned to the district that would have the "largest class of that kind of litigation." With at least one judge in the territory, he was certain that any real problems could be controlled.[31]

According to the census 16,374 people were scattered among the valleys and towns of the territory, but there was not one town that met of the U.S. Census Bureau's criteria for a city. Virginia City was the largest town with a population of 2,704, followed by Carson City with 1,466, Gold Hill with 1,297, and Silver City with 1,022. The largest district was the Walker River District that had 3,286 people, two more than Virginia City and the Flowery Mining District. Susanville, the home of former provisional Governor Roop, had a population of 274. Nye had reviewed the census. He divided the territory into nine districts and assigned the number of nine councilmen and thirteen representatives. He gerrymandered the districts, combining Gold Hill and Virginia City to allow the Comstock interests more representation than the larger Walker River District because there was question as to whether the latter was in Nevada Territory or California. Virginia City had two councilmen and three representatives, whereas the Walker River District had one councilman and two representatives. Nye then issued his proclamation for elections and set the date of the first legislative session.[32]

NEVADANS ORGANIZE THEMSELVES

After Governor Nye had organized the territory by proclamation, he met with the business leaders, the military officers at Fort Churchill, and the Paiutes at the Pyramid and Walker Lake reserves. He then left for California to prepare his address to the upcoming legislature and to arrange for Nevada's mineral wealth to be exhibited at the London Exposition the next year. It was time for the residents of the territory to organize themselves. Electing legislators and local officials was the only real vestige of popular sovereignty allowed to the local residents of the territories, but despite all the petitions for self-government, very few men turned out for the election on August 31. Only 4,338 voters out of a potential of 16,374 Nevadans elected nine councilmen and thirteen members of the House of Representatives. John Cradlebaugh won the seat as the delegate to Congress.

A special session of Congress in July had approved funds for the administration of the government, but the money had not yet arrived by the time the legislature was to meet. The local population was not impressed by the federal administration of the territory. The people in the towns were not concerned with Native American threats or surveys; they were concerned about money. In the land of gold and silver, there was simply not enough hard currency. Nevada was in a peculiar situation by eastern standards, but one that was common among the territories: there was no local money to support its major business endeavors, primarily mining. The saying that it took a mine to work a mine was no exaggeration. The start-up costs for a quartz mine in equipment, shipping costs, and manpower were high. The residents expected the new government to bring government gold and contracts for construction, goods, and services, but it brought only greenbacks, which were worth half their face value in gold. Samuel Clemens summed up their feelings toward the new government:

> The new government was received with considerable coolness. It was not only
> a foreign intruder, but a poor one. It was not even worth plucking—except

by the smallest of small fry office seekers and such.... The Organic Act and the "Instructions" from the State Department commanded the legislature should be elected at such and such a time, and its sittings inaugurated at such and such a date. It was easy to get legislators, even at three dollars a day, although board was four dollars and fifty cents, for its distinction and charm in Nevada as elsewhere, and there were plenty of patriotic souls out of employment; but to get a legislative hall for them to meet in was another matter all together. Carson blandly refused to give a room rent free, or to let one to the government on credit.[33]

With only the promise of money, Clemens tried to find a suitable place for the assembly in Carson City. There were no large meeting rooms within the town limits, only boarding houses, saloons, and small hotels. Finally he found large rooms on the upper story of a lonely stone building called Abe Curry's Warm Springs Hotel nearly two miles east of Carson City. It had originally been built on speculation to be the territorial prison for western Utah Territory. When the new territory was created, Curry named it the Warm Springs Hotel and hoped it would entice invalids to recuperate in the nearby hot springs. He also operated a stone quarry there and built Nevada's first railroad to haul the stones from the quarry to town. Now his railroad, made from planks set on edge and with horse-drawn cars, would carry legislators, lobbyists, newspapermen, and curious onlookers to and from the makeshift legislative hall.

There were no political parties in the first session. Democratic and Republican political parties were not organized until 1863. Men were elected on popularity and influence. Each one came with a personal agenda and friends who wanted special franchises granted for monopolies on railroads, toll roads, and public utilities for the cities and towns. The most important issues of the first session were to create counties, locate county seats, locate a capital city, and create a body of law dealing with crimes and punishments, civil practice and criminal practice, and the collection of revenues. For some, the most important issues were the designation of judicial districts and the assignment of judges.

The most heated debate during the session was over the location of the capital. Citizens from every town of any size promoted their own as best location and offered free land and free buildings for the government's use. Virginia City promoters thought it logical for the mining and commercial center to be the capital of the territory. The residents of Chinatown had changed its name to Nevada City, then to Dayton, and offered its services as capital. Despite the many offers, only one bill was introduced. Stewart introduced the bill to make Carson City the capital on November 7, and it was read nine days later. Carson City residents offered to deed a two-block portion in the middle of town, known as the Plaza, for government buildings. Dividing the territory into counties, assigning county seats, and fixing the location of the capital were intimately related issues that were hotly debated throughout the session.

As a compromise, the final bill created nine counties, for each of the nine members of the council,[34] but it still occasioned much protest because it created Churchill County, which barely had 150 white inhabitants.

The major confrontation between the federal governor and legislature was over the creation of the positions of the territorial treasurer, auditor, and superintendent of public instruction. Nye returned the bill calling for the election of these territorial officials without his approval, pointing out that the Organic Act stated clearly that the governor should appoint all territorial officers not included in the act.

The first legislature met for sixty days, from October 5 to November 29, and introduced 309 bills, 84 in the council and 125 in the house. Most were borrowed from California, submitted as printed bills with the word "California" crossed out and "Nevada" written in red ink between lines. By the end of the session there were 104 chapters or statutes. A few patronage bills were passed for the creation of toll roads and bridges in the districts. Nine months after its creation, Nevada Territory was finally organized.[35]

While the legislature was still in session, Nye had to turn his attention to the welfare of the Native American population. Nye had not yet received instructions from Commissioner Smith. His own report did not arrive in Washington, D.C., until December.[36] By late November winter storms swelled the rivers, filled the valleys with snow, and mired the wagon trails in mud. The mountain passes connecting California and Nevada were impassable. By the late summer and fall of 1861, Nye's Indian agents reported that Native Americans were without food. The overland migration along the Humboldt Trail had depleted the grass and game along that route. The increasing traffic along the Overland Mail route and the station keepers' grazing their cattle and horses in the central territory depleted the bunch grass that grew in those valleys, and the winter staple of the Native Americans in the Great Basin, the pine-nut crop, was nonexistent. Bannock or Goose Creek Shoshone continued to raid wagon trains and drive off stock. The army officials thought that the mail route was in danger. Nye thought that the Native Americans would starve. Nye arranged with General Wright to use the extra provisions from Fort Churchill to feed the Native Americans.[37]

EVENTS IN NEVADA: 1862

Nevadans were filled with hope at the outset of 1862. The first legislature had located a capital, divided the territory into counties and judicial districts, created new officials to oversee the territorial treasury, militia and schools, and provided new laws to replace the ones imposed on them by the Mormon rule of Utah Territory. On January 14 they would go to the polls to elect the officers for the newly created counties. They hoped that new prosperity would come from their exhibit at the London World Exposition and that people from around the world would invest in their mines. Most important, they now had courts to settle their disputed mining claims and make them more attractive for investment. On December 9 Nye had appointed sheriffs to preserve law and order and surveyors to ascertain the boundaries of each county. They were to continue in office until the new officers assumed their offices on February 1. They were also able to run for election as incumbents. The district courts had been defined and judges assigned, and the courts were ready to hold their first sessions.

The new territory offered the promise of great possibilities to those that came there. On the Comstock Lode there were many internal improvements. With the operation of sawmills, brick works, and stone quarries, the tent villages of the year before gave way to cities. As one early settler remembered, "the settlements were thickening; discoveries of new gold and silver mines were daily occurrences. Mill-sites and waterpower were sought at for round prices, and new quartz mills for the reduction of ore were constantly planned. Town property was valuable and corner lots were in demand, and it was a matter of speculation as to how large and important the several towns and villages of the county would some day become."[38] The Ophir mine reached its highest production in 1862 and extended its sphere of influence. Mining districts were being formed every day in the eastern and southern parts of the territory.

From the top of Mount Davidson one could view the whole Comstock Lode. Andrew Jackson Marsh described it as villages somehow transported to the surface of the moon. Twenty-seven hundred people lived in three hundred to four hundred houses in Virginia City. Some houses had canvas roofs, and some had no roofs at all. Four miles to the east was Flowery with four hundred people. The narrow roads were crowded day and night with teamsters hauling ore to the mills, building materials for the towns, and food and supplies for the people. There were almost one hundred ore crushing mills in the region. The mines operated all day and all night, as did the mills. The noise was incessant, from the banging of the stamps, the traffic from the horse- and mule-drawn wagons, and the clang of ore cars and winches.[39]

Before the first term of the court in Virginia City, Judge Mott reviewed the laws enacted by the session just ended. He was concerned about several sections relating to grand juries and witnesses. He wrote to Nye asking for legal advice because Nye had once been a judge.[40] When the court opened in February in Virginia City, most of the litigation was not about the single-ledge versus multiledge theory of the composition of the Comstock Lode, but rather was a battle between the holders of valid claims and those who owned undefined "floating" claims. Mining notices had been written in vague terms, were unsurveyed, and often were unrecorded. Individual claimants and corporations waited for Nevada courts and Nevada laws to be in place before the onslaught of litigation because Utah law settled these matters with each claim's being surveyed and the location's being determined by the judge. Mott was familiar with mining litigation from his days on the California bench, but mining was different in Nevada, and he was not prepared for the cases that came before him.[41]

The *Chollar v. Potosi* case, which would make several appearances in the new courts, did not reach the district court until the May term, even though the original filing was made in January. There was no national mining law or even one for the territory. The legislature left the governing of mining districts to the rules created by the miners themselves, and these rules did not provide for adjudication of disputes.[42] The question in *Chollar v. Potosi* was whether a company with a "quartz and surface" claim could follow its vein into another company's adjacent claim, even if the former claim was made earlier. The trial lasted a week and was watched closely from inside the courtroom and as far away as San Francisco. The stock of the company that won the suit would increase in value, and its profits would soar faster than it could ever dig the gold and silver from the ground. The jury reported back that it was hopelessly deadlocked. Mott dismissed the jury and ordered a new trial for the October session.

In late fall of 1862, the legislature met again and spent most of its time granting exclusive franchises for toll roads, gas companies, and railroads rather than legislating for the public good. When Isaac Roop introduced "An act to frame a constitution for the state of Washoe," Nye was not surprised. Nye had considered how to get Nevadans to think about becoming a state ever since he arrived in the territory and especially since he heard that Utah drafted a constitution under a Utah legislative act. He planned to have the bill introduced this session and even confided his plan to Utah's Indian Superintendent James Doty when they discussed future treaties with the Shoshone.[43] Roop's bill proposed action similar to Utah's. In March 1862 Utahans met, wrote, and adopted a state constitution and submitted it to Congress for consideration during the current session. Among those in the Utah convention were John Reese and Orson Hyde. Nye may have known that enabling acts would be introduced in the present session of Congress because Republicans would want to increase their control in both houses.

Nye needed someone outside the clique of territorial legislators and lobbyists to introduce the bill and found Roop to be the best candidate because he was not interested in the Comstock doings and had few dealings with his fellow members in the legislature. He had always been considered the "Councilman from California" and was still referred to as "Governor Roop."[44] Nye and Roop had worked together in California as part of the boundary commission earlier that year when neither Governor Stanford nor the legislature would concede California's border claims. Statehood for Nevada was Roop's last hope to separate from California and to strengthen his position. He even introduced a bill to move the capital to Susanville.

If Nevada were a state, it would have a better chance to negotiate the crest of the Sierra Nevada as its western boundary, which was desirable to Aurorans and owners of toll road franchises for the Sierra Nevada. The bill took everyone else by surprise, because no lobbyists were promoting the idea, only Roop, Nye, and an Indian superintendent four hundred miles away. The legislative reporter Marsh wrote that when Roop introduced the bill and it passed both houses, it had blanks to be filled in later, but when it received Nye's signature on the last day, there were no blanks.[45]

Nye left Nevada after the session had ended. He sailed to Washington, D.C, where he intended to lobby Congress to pass an Enabling Act in response to the Nevada legislature's desire for a constitutional convention and to establish a branch of the U.S. mint in the territory. A mint in Nevada would mean that the final reduction of ore could be done locally, thereby increasing the yield per ton by decreasing the expenses drastically.[46] Nye also sought New York capital for his investment interests in the railroads to Aurora and the Truckee River, for a wagon road over the Sierra Nevada, and for mills. California newspapers speculated that he returned to Washington to obtain a military appointment, and Clemens and North were both hoping to be appointed the next governor of the territory.[47]

Before Nye left for Washington, Congressman James Mitchell Ashley of Ohio, the chairman of the House Committee on Territories, introduced bills to create the states of Nevada, Nebraska, Utah, and Colorado.[48] He also introduced the bill to create Montana Territory. Ashley's bills were setting the scene for the future policy of Radical Reconstruction; he intended to kill the idea of popular sovereignty once and for all by requiring each new state to include in their constitutions a clause pledging paramount allegiance to the federal government. The Senate's Enabling Act for Nevada was referred to the House, which had not acted on any of its territorial bills.[49]

BORDER TROUBLES

Early in 1863 Nevada Territory went to battle with California over Honey Lake. Roop's plans to include the area as a part of Nevada Territory began to fall apart even as Congress was considering the Enabling Act. The legislature changed the name of Lake County to Roop County and authorized its organization. Nye made the initial appointments before he left, and Judge Mott traveled to Susanville to swear in the officers. Thus Honey Lake was claimed by Nevada as part of Roop County and by California as part of Plumas County. Like Aurora farther south, the county held two elections to elect both California and Nevada officials.[50] Whereas Aurorans considered the situation farcical and were willing to accept their dual residency, Honey Lakers fought for their separation.

When the Honey Lakers refused to pay taxes in Plumas County, the local judge sent the sheriff and a posse of one hundred men to Susanville to arrest the Nevada justice of the peace. The protestors fortified a large barn they named Fort Defiance, and the sheriff's men took up positions in a barn one hundred yards from the fort. Fighting broke out when Pierce's deputies tried to pull a log back to fortify the barn. The shooting lasted four hours. One California man was killed, and two Nevadans were wounded before the shooting stopped. The rebels threatened to burn the town unless Pierce withdrew, but other citizens of Susanville arrived with a white flag, requesting a cease-fire to negotiate a peaceful settlement. Pierce agreed to a truce if the mob disband immediately and if all parties agree not to exercise their jurisdiction over the area until both the state and territorial governors had settled the matter. On March 5, 1863, Governor Stanford and Acting Governor Clemens agreed to let a boundary commission survey the boundary between state and territory. The boundary survey was completed in August, placing Honey Lake (and Isaac Roop) in California and Aurora in Nevada.

Things were also heating up in the territorial courts in 1863, particularly in Virginia City. Because William Stewart could not get Mott to rule in his favor, he and other attorneys tried to persuade Mott to run for Congress; if elected, Mott would leave the territory. Mott won the election but insisted on staying until the next session of Congress began in the fall of 1863, and he continued to preside on the supreme court even though his days in the first district were numbered. When the supreme court met for its February session, it heard the *Chollar v. Potosi* case. Mott and Turner upheld the jury's verdict; Jones dissented in the court's ruling because he thought that the judgment included claims that were not part of the original adjudication. Stewart was dealt another blow in the last case heard in Mott's court in Virginia City before he and Jones would exchange districts. The supreme court's term overlapped with the district court's term because of the protracted arguments in *Chollar v. Potosi*. Although Mott's term in the Virginia City court ended March 4, his case was not concluded.[51]

Late in 1862 Stewart also persuaded the legislature to have Mott and Jones exchange districts. Mott was leaving soon, and the exchange apparently did not bother him, but Jones was incensed, maintaining that the bill was invalid because it was signed after the legislature's adjournment. Jones refused to practice the kind of law the Virginia City attorneys practiced, walked out of his court, and refused to hear any more cases in the May term. On July 30, Jones unexpectedly resigned, saying he had enough of the plots and intrigues of the Storey County bar, left the bench, and went to Austin to open a law practice. President Lincoln appointed another Missourian, Powhatan Locke, to the court. Because Mott was soon leaving the territory to begin his term as territorial delegate, he appointed former Surveyor General John North as his replacement.[52]

Judge Locke was born in Kentucky in 1830 and moved to Missouri to practice law in 1850. Originally a Whig, he was active in political conventions in 1852 and 1854, was elected mayor of Sonora, Missouri, when the town incorporated, and was re-elected the following year. He organized the first anti-slavery group in St. Joseph and was the county judge in Buchanan County when he received his temporary appointment on August 31, 1863, one month after Jones's resignation. He arrived in Nevada on September 9, was sworn in as justice, and filed his oath with Secretary Clemens. Judge North opened his court in Virginia City on August 20, 1863, and cleared much of the business that had accumulated since Jones's departure. He was praised by many of the local newspapers.

By 1863 Nye had organized his Indian superintendency into four agencies, Walker River, Truckee or Pyramid Lake, Humboldt, and Ruby Valley. Although the Pyramid and Walker reservations were established in 1858, they had never been surveyed. Nye continually asked that they be surveyed but could not obtain the funding. Nye also opposed a toll road with its accompanying hotels and whiskey shops that had been authorized by the 1862 legislature through fifteen miles of the Pyramid reservation, because he was certain that this was the beginning of a movement to abolish the reservation. The Indian agencies were very large. The largest agency, the Humboldt, covered 15,000 square miles, almost one-third of the territory. There was no reservation or headquarters there, and the agent had to be continually on the road. Almost as large and considered the most important was the Ruby Valley agency, headquartered about twenty miles north of the Overland Mail road and Fort Ruby.

Nevada's Native Americans had been peaceful since the Pyramid Lake War. Nye kept them supplied with food and clothing, even if doing so meant using military supplies. In October 1863 Nye helped negotiate the first treaty with Native Americans in Nevada with the help of Utah's Indian superintendent James Duane Doty and funding from Congress. The funding for the negotiation of treaties had not arrived, and Doty accompanied the army on its patrols throughout the spring to promote formal peace treaties.[53] Several of the bands told him they were tired of fighting and wanted peace. The three large bands of Shoshone were independent of each other, so three treaties had to be negotiated. The first, with the Eastern Shoshone under Chief Washakie, was settled July 2, 1863. The second, the Treaty of Box Elder, was negotiated with nine bands of the Northwestern Shoshone on July 30, 1863. Doty then turned his attention to the Western Shoshone in Nevada Territory and contacted Nye to participate in the negotiations on October 1 in Ruby Valley.[54] Nye agreed because the Shoshone "never received much attention from the government." Nye and Doty agreed that boundary between their territories would be a line running north and south through a valley fifty miles east of Ruby Valley, and each would be responsible for Indians in their respective districts. Doty, accompanied by soldiers from Salt Lake City, and Nye, accompanied by troops from Fort Churchill, met with the Tosogowich, or White Knives, and the Unkoahs, representing about 2,500 Shoshone.

The treaty declared peace and friendship between the two races, assured the safety of the mail route, mail stations, and military posts, and permitted the operation of telegraph, stage, and railroad lines through the region. It allowed mineral exploration and use of timber, defined the boundaries of the Western

Shoshone lands, and set the stage for establishing a reservation for the wandering bands. Finally, the treaty granted the natives an annuity of $5,000 for twenty years and acknowledged the distribution of $5,000 of goods distributed during negotiation. Temoak was the first to sign the treaty, followed by twelve others.

THE 1863 CONSTITUTIONAL CONVENTION

On November 2, 1863, the thirty-nine delegates representing seven counties met in Carson City on the second floor of the courthouse. They elected Judge North as the president of the convention, started with California's constitution, and began crossing out the word "California." The first major debate was over the name of the new state. The act had called for the new state to be called "Washoe," but no one liked that name, and the delegates settled on "Nevada." During the convention, William Stewart, representing the largest mining companies, loudly criticized the section on taxation because it required mines to be taxed according to gross proceeds, that is, according to the value of their ore. Although most of the attention of the 1863 constitutional convention focused on the mining tax clause, the right-of-suffrage section was also hotly debated. It provided that no disloyal person or any person who, after arriving at the age of twenty-one years, had voluntarily borne arms against the United States or held civil or military office under the Confederate States, should be allowed to vote unless granted an amnesty by the federal government.[55] These major points of contention ended in compromise, with both the taxation clause and the limitation of right-of-suffrage section retained. Stewart conceded the tax clause because it would be open to the interpretation of the legislature, and, knowing that most representatives would be from the populous mining towns, he believed he would control the legislature. The convention passed the constitution.

The election day for the constitution and the state officers approached. Supporters of Nevada statehood paraded throughout the territory making speeches in its support. William Stewart, who for years was considered to be opposed to the document, was actually one of its staunchest supporters.[56] Stewart did fight against the taxation clause in the convention, but he changed his position after the document was approved. He had his own interpretation of the mining clause, namely, that legislature was free to define what the gross proceeds really were. Under the new constitution, Storey County would have had one-fourth of the senators and one-third of the assemblymen in the state legislature, so the legislature could easily define gross proceeds to their constituents' satisfaction.

When the Union Party met in Virginia City to assemble its list of candidates, Stewart took control of the nominating convention and handpicked all the state officers. A great majority of the delegates to the territorial convention in Carson City were from Storey County. When they met in Virginia City,

Stewart pushed through two resolutions to the platform that caused eight of the delegates to leave. The first one would allow the legislature to "leave free from taxation undeveloped mining claims of mere speculative value."[57] The second was aimed directly at Judge John North: to "oppose by all honorable means the nomination of J. W. North to office by said convention."[58] Because in *Chollar v. Potosi* North had ruled in favor of the many-ledge theory of the composition of the Comstock Lode, he was considered a hero among the small mining companies and a foe by the larger ones.

It was Stewart's handling of the candidate selection, however, that outraged those who bolted, and when the territorial convention met in Carson City three days later, both sets of delegates arrived to take their seats. Those who had bolted the convention were not admitted, leaving Stewart in control. Those barred from the convention began a campaign against statehood. No town was too small as they took their show on the road. The *Gold Hill Evening News* was the most avid supporter of the new constitution and referred to the opposition as "sore-headed and disappointed office seekers."[59] The editor even tried to explain the "Stewart construction" of the mining tax clause.[60] The *Virginia Daily Union* was the most vocal opponent of Stewart's movement. Stewart began to attack North before the nominating convention in the hope of discrediting him before the public. On December 28, 1863, North denied a permanent injunction requested by Stewart in the *Burning Moscow v. Ophir* case, dealing a tremendous blow to the single-ledge theory. North's popularity soared in the territory, particularly among those who were adherents of the multiledge theory, and people wanted to nominate him as governor. The Storey County delegation killed the nomination and spread stories of North's being bribed by James H. Hardy in the *Burning Moscow v. Ophir* case. North confronted Stewart and threatened to sue him for slander. Stewart knew that a pending lawsuit would not help his cause, and he retracted the accusations in a published card.[61]

When the election day for the new constitution came on January 19, 1864, it failed miserably. Samuel Clemens wrote to his mother in January, 1864, just before the election, "[T]the bill was a fraud—the Constitutional Convention was a fraud—the Constitution is born of a fraud—a State erected under it would be a fraudulent & impotent institution, & we should ultimately be kicked back to Territorial Status again on account of it. Wherefore, when men say 'let the Constitution slide,' I say Amen."[62] As the constitution was voted down in each city, Nye had the best communications network in the territory and received the news by telegram before the newspapers had the stories printed.

The failure of the 1863 constitution surprised no one. When Nye sent his report on the condition of the territory off to Washington, D.C., on January 25, after receiving the news of the Enabling Act, he mentioned the causes for its defeat. The stringent clause on suffrage united all "the disloyal or secession element against it." The mining tax did not please the miners. The Union representatives from Virginia City, making up more than one-third of the delegates to the state convention, "instructed their nominees for the legislature to vote against taxing the mines, thereby nullifying one of the plainest provisions of the constitution." The farmers and ranchers opposed the constitution because the burden of taxes would fall on them. There was dissatisfaction with the state ticket, also controlled by Virginia City delegates.[63] The defeat of this constitution was only a minor setback for Nye, and he began to mobilize the voters much as in a New York precinct. He appointed officeholders for the new counties of Nye and Churchill, notaries, and officers for the newly formed militia companies in the territory.

The failure of the constitution was soon followed by failure of the mines and failure of the stocks in the mines. In Aurora the Del Monte Mine's surface vein ended at the one hundred-foot level. When Montgomery Street brokerage houses received word, there was panic selling, and many brokers lost their fortunes. The Comstock mines had reached water in the lower levels, and their stocks declined. Smaller mines closed, and larger ones laid off their marginal employees and sought to reduce their expenses by lowering the miners' prevailing wage to $4 per hour. Nevadans were content with territorial status, and the legislature asked Congress to amend the Organic Act to increase the number of judges and district courts from three to four so judicial business could be handled more efficiently.[64]

THREE NEW STATES

Eighteen days after the 1863 constitution was voted down, Congress introduced bills to create three new states, Nebraska, Colorado, and Nevada. President Lincoln had already outlined his plan for presidential reconstruction, and he also planned to introduce the Thirteenth Amendment. He was looking toward his re-election campaign and wanted to bolster his chances of election by increasing the number of electoral votes. Radical congressmen had already begun to pave the way for Radical Reconstruction with the introduction of enabling acts the previous year, but the time was not right for them to act. On February 9, 1864, Senator James Rood Doolittle of Wisconsin introduced the Enabling Act for Nevada. It was the same bill that Congressman James Ashley introduced the year before to create new states that would vote favorably for Lincoln's re-election and to do away with the idea of popular sovereignty once and for all.

Each of the new states was required to prohibit slavery, guarantee religious freedom, and forever relinquish all unclaimed public land. A paramount allegiance clause that made each state subservient to the federal government was another irrevocable condition. The clause would end the discussions of the previous decade over popular sovereignty versus federal authority. If the territories were admitted as states, their constitutions would be models for all subsequent admissions, particularly for the southern states seeking readmission to the Union.[65]

On June 6, Nevadans again went to the polls to elect the delegates to represent them in the convention. In comparison with the excitement of the convention six months before, there was little interest now. The Union Party was the only one to hold meetings and nominate candidates, and their slates were elected. The lone Democrat elected was Francis M. Proctor, representing Nye County and receiving 118 votes. It only took 36 votes to be elected in Churchill, 99 in Washoe, 105 in Douglas, 214 in Esmeralda, 158 in Humboldt, 157 in Lyon, and 593 in Storey.[66] Ten of the delegates had been at the first convention; more significantly, fourteen were friends or business partners of Nye or had received political favors from him. Stewart was absent in San Francisco, and North was handling court business in the supreme court. Nye had no doubts that the convention would produce a constitution.

Thirty-six delegates came to Carson City; four delegates chose not to attend. The defeated constitution provided a sound basis for a beginning. Only two sections had been objectionable to the people six months before—the section on the taxation of mines and the requirement of the loyalty oaths as a condition of suffrage. The mining companies controlled most of the votes in Storey County, the territory's most populated area, and would have to be appeased, but unless mining was taxed the burden of paying for government would be borne by a small landowning group of ranchers and townspeople. Even the Virginia City newspapers thought the mines should be taxed, because Storey County's climbing debt almost equaled that of the territory. Territorial Treasurer Kinkead could not find any buyers for the territorial bonds. There was also a growing federal movement to tax the mines to pay for the war debt.[67]

In April 1864 the cloud of secessionist plots that lingered over Nevada since the war began became thicker and threatened a new storm. When the California state legislature passed a law requiring attorneys and all public officeholders in that state to take an oath of allegiance to the Union, there was a large migration eastward into Nevada Territory. Some of the largest property owners in the territory were from the South.[68]

The last cases introduced to the court, *The People v. Empire* and *The People v. Ophir*, were two cases from Storey County's first district. These were the test cases alluded to in the territorial auditor's report to the legislature in January 1864 concerning taxation on the gross proceeds of mines in the revenue bill from the second session. Lloyd Frizell, the Storey County assessor, took three companies to court for not paying their taxes. The juries upheld the law and ordered the mining companies to pay their taxes. Both cases were appealed to the supreme court. Baldwin and Stewart, the attorneys for the Gould & Curry Mining Company, argued that taxing mines was unconstitutional. Judges Turner, North, and Locke upheld the verdict. The court defeated Stewart time and again. He was incensed. He was not a man who liked to lose, and he began to fill the newspapers with stories of judicial corruption. He also filed his intent to appeal the decision to the Supreme Court of the United States.

By the time of the court's decision, Nevada Territory was suffering a severe depression. The Ophir's vein was declining in yield, stock prices fell, and the company paid out its last dividend to the stockholders in March. There was unemployment throughout the Comstock. The long year of depression on the Comstock Lode caused tension there that began with reaction to the Ophir case in May and continued until the September election. On August 6 vigilantes hanged an accused killer in Dayton. The news reached Nye quickly, and he acted immediately. The proximity of the hanging gave him an opportunity to avoid the embarrassment of the vigilante execution in Aurora in February. He telegraphed the commander of Fort Churchill and the provost marshall in Virginia City. By afternoon the provost guard arrived, and fifty cavalry rode into town, having covered the twenty-four miles from the fort in little more than two hours. Nye came personally and investigated the murder with the military officers. No action could be taken against the anonymous committee members, but Nye hoped that the immediate military response would discourage future vigilante activities in the territory. Nye saw any kind of violent group activity as having secessionist overtones.[69]

On August 22 William Stewart and his cronies attempted to take over the territorial judiciary by organizing their own vigilance committee of would-be members of the bar and threatening violence to the judges if they did not resign. At the morning session of court, only North and Turner were present, busily admitting attorneys to the bar and scheduling the next term of the court. Court adjourned until six o'clock in the evening when Turner reported that he had just been informed of North's resignation and that he would resign himself.

Judge North submitted his resignation to the president, saying he would continue to serve until the president appointed his successor. He told everyone his health was poor and that he was encouraged by friends to resign. He also said he wanted to take William Stewart and his private press, the *Territorial Enterprise*, to court to sue them for libel, which he could not do while he was sitting on the bench.

Judge Turner's letter of resignation was entered in the official record of the supreme court; it stated that the court had been emasculated by North's resignation. Two judges could not fairly address the cases before them, because each decision would require a unanimous decision. Because the next session of the court was scheduled to meet after the approval of statehood, he was resigning his seat on the supreme court and continue to serve the second district as their judge. When he telegraphed his resignation to President Lincoln, it too was conditional upon appointment and qualification of his successor. Powhatan Locke had arrived late for the session from holding court in Austin and was kidnapped by two men who brought him to a meeting of the so-called bar, where he was forced to resign for the "public good."

The newspapers reported the resignations the following day and opined "we put our trust in a State Government as our salvation.... They were at last *resigned* to their fate, and Stewart & Co. Triumphant."[70] The Storey County attorneys lost no time in selecting North's replacement. They recommended Richard S. Mesick for the first district. Mesick had been Esmeralda County's prosecuting attorney from 1862 to January 1864, when he resigned to represent large mining companies like the Real Del Monte in Aurora and the Ophir Gold and Silver Mining Company in Virginia City.[71] Stewart and his cronies learned they had been hoodwinked the next day, when the newspapers announced that neither North nor Turner had resigned. "If we understand this matter, John W. North is still Judge of the First district, and will remain so until State Government goes into operation in December—if no appointment is made sooner.... Judge Turner, we are also informed, did not resign as supposed. Somebody has been *sold* more than once in this resignation business."[72]

The *Territorial Enterprise*, Stewart's main tool for spreading propaganda against the court, continued to publish diatribes against the judges for their treachery and public deceit. "We have been sold," owner John T. Goodman wrote, much to the pleasure of its rival the *Union*.[73] It was fitting, continued the *Union*, that Stewart, "in his hour of triumph at his success in hounding down Judge North and compelling his resignation, to make room for a tool of his own, he finds himself checkmated by his victim and gives vent to his rage in the above prolonged shriek of agony and despair.... The people of this territory have not surrendered to Stewart & Co., nor do they intend to." The Carson City bar and citizens of Ormsby County met and had only praise for the manner in which Judge Turner had conducted his court during the past three years. Turner told them that if they wanted new judges they needed to vote for the constitution. Turner and North were heroes who had publicly embarrassed Stewart and company and were now using Stewart's plan to pack the court with his representatives as a means of promoting the new constitution and statehood for Nevada.[74]

The voters went to polls again in September and approved the constitution. Nye sent certified copies to Washington, D.C., and waited for the president's proclamation. Even after the election Nye was concerned. He did not want the presidential elections in the new state to be disrupted in any way. In Austin, local Nye appointees requested that federal troops be stationed at Austin until after the election. Nye requested guns and three howitzer cannon be issued to him from California and was forming companies of Union Guards to protect the territory.[75] Alf Doten wrote, "Things have been assuming more and more of a squally aspect of late. Secessionists and treasonable sympathizers are known to exist in abundance among us, but they are watched with vigilant eyes. Secret meetings are held by them and we have abundant evidence that they are thoroughly organized throughout the territory and California."

Nye requested and received a stay of troops that were being transferred out of Fort Churchill.[76]

Meanwhile President Lincoln met with his cabinet on September 30 to discuss Nevada's entry into the Union. Cabinet members were divided in opinion, because no one had yet seen a copy of the constitution. Seward wanted the proclamation issued immediately, but William Pitt Fessenden, secretary of the treasury, did not think Nevada should ever become a state. The cabinet convinced Lincoln to wait until he saw the Nevada's constitution before issuing his proclamation.[77]

On October 24 Nye received a telegram from Seward that he had not received a certified copy of the constitution and that the president would issue his proclamation only after he had received it. It was two weeks before the national elections, and there was not time to send a certified copy by land or by sea. The general superintendent of the Overland Telegraph Company's local office told Nye to telegraph the document to Washington, D.C. On October 26 James Guild, the California Telegraph Company's best telegrapher, sent the 16,543-word document to Washington in about seven hours. The telegram had to be transcribed and re-sent at Chicago and Philadelphia before the telegraph operator in the War Department transcribed the document in 175 pages and delivered it to President Lincoln. Lincoln received it two days after it was sent and issued his proclamation.

Nye was campaigning for the re-election of President Lincoln when the president's telegraphed proclamation was received at Carson City on October 30. The proclamation of statehood was to be official on October 31. After the celebrations, Nevadans went to the polls again and voted for the re-election of Abraham Lincoln. In December the new state officials took their offices and had to pick up the pieces left by the territory. They were left with a $360,000 debt and offices where they could find little or no information. Nye realized his goals and went to Washington as one of Nevada's senators. Stewart was also elected senator. They arrived too late to vote on the Thirteenth Amendment in the Senate, but Congressman Henry Gaither Worthington was able to vote for it in the House. Congress waited until the Nevada delegation was seated, and, together with the senators and congressmen of California, they wrote the Mining Law of 1866, the first national mining law in U.S. history; as amended in 1872, it survives to the present.

Nevada played an important role in the Reconstruction. By congressional decree, limits to its sovereignty and to its control over public lands were set as a condition of its entry to statehood. Slavery was forbidden, and religious tolerance was mandated. The federal government demanded paramount allegiance before granting statehood. All these crucial issues of national debate were passed by the Nevada citizenry without discussion or protest. Nevada's constitution became the model for all new territories seeking statehood and for every southern state seeking readmission.

CONCLUSION

Nevadans voted for statehood because of the depression of 1864. The debts of the territory and counties were increasing, and no one would buy the territorial bonds. Because of the stock market crash, there was no new investment for mining exploration or the development of new claims, and there was no new support for the Comstock mines. When Nevada became a territory with an organized government whose court decisions had some weight, investors and immigrants came to the territory. After Nevada became a state, the population of the state swelled to more than 40,000 in five years. Nevada became a state because of its failure as a territory but not because of the failure of the federal officers. Where local attempts to organize a territory failed, national politics prevailed. Nevada was born out of the Civil War and this birth is part of the Nevada mystique.

NOTES

1. John D. Unruh, *The Plains Across: The Overland Emigrants of the Transcontinental West, 1840–1860* (Urbana: University of Illinois Press, 1979), pp. 119–120. All numbers referring to overland migration are from this work.

2. *Journal of the Senate, Fourth Session of the Legislature of California* (San Francisco: George Kerr, State Printer, 1853), p. 90; appended document, p. 46.

3. U.S. Congress, 34th Cong., 1st Sess., *Statutes at Large of the United States of America, 1789–1873*, chap. 168, August 18, 1856, established a post road from Placerville to Genoa; 34th Cong., 3d Sess., chap. 96, March 3, 1857, allowed the postmaster to issue a six-year contract from the Mississippi River to San Francisco.

4. J. Wells Kelly, *First Directory of Nevada Territory*, introd. Richard Lingenfelter (reprint, Los Gatos, CA: The Talisman Press, 1962), pp. 29–31; Kent D. Richards, "Rudimentary Government in Washoe Territory," *Arizona and the West* 11 (Autumn, 1969): 220–223; Guy Louis Rocha, "Nevada's Emergence in the American Great Basin: Territory and State," *Nevada Historical Society Quarterly* 38 (Spring1995): 257.

5. Brigham D. Madsen, *The Shoshone Frontier and the Bear River Massacre* (Salt Lake City: University of Utah Press, 1985), p. 119.

6. Russell McDonald, "Biographies of Nevada's Territorial, District and Supreme Court Judges," unpublished mss., February 24, 1993, pp. 118–138, at John Cradlebaugh file, McDonald Collection, Nevada Historical Society, Reno.

7. Richard N. Allen, *The Tennessee Letters: From Carson Valley, 1857–1860*, comp. David Thompson (Reno: The Grace Dangberg Foundation, Inc., 1983), pp. 101–102.

8. *Sacramento Union*, May 21, 1860, quoted in Brigham D. Madsen, *The Shoshone Frontier and the Bear River Massacre* (Salt Lake City: University of Utah Press, 1985), p. 119.

9. Virginia City (Nevada) *Enterprise*, May 5, 1860.

10. Sarah Winnemucca Hopkins, *Life Among the Piutes: Their Wrongs and Claims*, ed. Mrs. Horace Man (reprint, Reno: University of Nevada Press, 1994), pp. 70–72.

11. Frederick Lander to the Commissioner on Indian Affairs, October 31, 1860, in National Archives, "Letters to the Commissioner on Indian Affairs from Utah," microfilm roll 899.

12. *Territorial Enterprise*, August 4, 1859, p. 2.

13. Maureen Bloomquist Jung, "The Comstocks and the California Mining Economy, 1848–1900: The Stock Market and the Modern Corporation" (Ph.D. dissertation, University of California, Santa Barbara, 1988), pp. 69–70.

14. Utah Territorial Legislature, *Laws of the Tenth Session* (Salt Lake City, UT: Territorial Printer, 1861).

15. *Senate Journal*, 36th Cong., 2d Sess., p. 213.

16. U.S. Congress, 36th Cong., 2d Sess., *Statutes at Large of USA*, chap. 57, February 27, 1861. For Senator Green's bill, see *Congressional Globe*, 36th Cong., 2d Sess., p. 897; for Senators Latham and Gwin's bill, see *Congressional Globe*, 36th Cong., 2d Sess., pp. 317, 374, 2668.

17. Frederick E. Hosen, *Unfolding Westward in Treaty and Law: Land Documents in United States History from the Appalachians to the Pacific, 1793–1934* (Jefferson, NC: McFarland & Company, Publishers, 1988) reprints all treaties, acts regarding public lands, organic acts, and enabling acts for U.S. territories.

18. Jud Burton Samon, "Sagebrush Falstaff: A Biographical Sketch of James Warren Nye" (Ph.D. dissertation, University of Maryland, 1979); James F. Richardson, *The New York Police: Colonial Times to 1901* (New York: Oxford University Press, 1970), pp. 109–123, describes the period from the time of the creation of the Metropolitan Police until Nye's resignation to work on Seward's presidential campaign.

19. Mark Twain, *Mark Twain's Letters*, ed. Edgar Marquess Branch et al. (Berkeley: University of California Press, 1988–2002), 1:114, n. 9; Andrew Jackson Marsh, *Letters from Nevada Territory, 1861–1862*, ed. William C. Miller et al. (Carson City: Legislative Counsel Bureau, 1972), p. 670, n. 38, quotes Bates's letter to Seward.

20. Russell McDonald, "Biographical Summaries about Nevada's Territorial, District, Supreme Court and Federal Judges, 1856–1993," unpublished mss, the Russell McDonald collection, Nevada Historical Society, 366A–424A; compiled from George Turner file in same collection.

21. McDonald, "Biographical Summaries," pp. 317–320; also see Gordon Mott file in McDonald collection.

22. Horatio M. Jones file in McDonald collection; Andrew J. Marsh, *Letters from Nevada Territory, 1861–62*, p. 695, n. 255.

23. Merlin Stonehouse, *John Wesley North and the Reform Frontier* (Minneapolis: University of Minnesota Press, 1965); Theodore C. Blegen, *Minnesota: A History of the State*, 2nd ed. (Minneapolis: University of Minnesota Press, 1975), pp. 188, 216, 223.

24. Robert J. Chandler, "The Velvet Glove: The Army During the Secession Crisis in California, 1860–1861," *Journal of the West* 20 (October 1981): 40.

25. George A. H. Blake to Don Carlos Buell, June 5, 1861, in U.S. War Department, *The War of the Rebellion: A Compilation of the Official Records of the Union and Confederate Armies* (Washington, DC: Government Printing Office, 1880–1900) (hereafter cited as *War of the Rebellion*), series 1, vol. 50, part 1, pp. 499–500.

26. Ibid., Buell to Gordon N. Mott, June 7, 1861, pp. 503–504.

27. Ibid., Mott to Buell, June 8, 1861, p. 506.

28. Ibid., E. V. Sumner to Governor J. G. Downey, June 7, 1861, pp. 502–503; Special Orders No. 97, June 7, 1861 commanded Company G, Sixth Infantry to leave Benicia for Fort Churchill.

29. Ibid., T. Moore to Buell, June 8, 1861; Buell to Moore, June 8, 1861; Blake to Buell, June 10, 1861, Moore to Blake, June 10, 1861, pp. 505–511. The removal of the troops was ordered by Richard C. Drum to Blake, July 6, 1861, p. 530.

30. *Official Record and Proclamations of Nevada Territory, 1861–1864*, in the Nevada State Library and Archives, Carson City, Nevada.

31. *Official Record and Proclamations of Nevada Territory*, pp. 16–20, in the Nevada State Library and Archives; the text of the proclamations were published in Angel, *History of Nevada*, p. 77.

32. Henry DeGroot, "Census Report of Nevada Territory," in Nevada Territorial Records at Nevada State Library and Archives, published in *Journal of the Council of the First Legislative Assembly of the Territory of Nevada* (San Francisco: Valentine & Co.: Commercial Steam Printing Establishment, 1862), pp. 397–403.

33. Samuel Clemens, *Roughing It* (reprint, New York: American Library, 1962), p. 47.

34. Marsh, *Letters from Nevada Territory*, pp. 292–293.

35. Nevada Territorial Legislature, "Council and House Bills Introduced 1861–1864," mss in Nevada State Library and Archives.

36. William Dole to James Warren Nye, December 5, 1861, in Governor James Warren Nye, Executive Records in the Nevada State Library and Archives, Carson City, NV (hereafter cited as Nye Executive Records).

37. *War of the Rebellion*, series 1, vol. 50, part 1, p. 667.

38. Beck, "Laying out of the Then Metropolis—A Little Poker Episode," in *Nevada State Journal* September 14, 1895 in McDonald, "Flush Times in Washoe," unpublished mss in the McDonald Collection.

39. Marsh, *Letters from Nevada Territory*, pp. 211–213.

40. Gordon Mott to James Warren Nye, January 26, 1862, in James W. Nye, Nye Executive Records.

41. *Minutes of the First District Court*, Storey County Clerk's Office, Virginia City, NV, 1:22; Eliot Lord, *Comstock Mining and Miners*, U.S. Geological Survey Monograph, No. 4 (Washington, DC: Government Printing Office, 1883; reprint, Berkeley, CA: Howell-North, 1959), p. 132.

42. Robert B. Murray, "The Supreme Court of Colorado Territory," *Colorado Magazine* 44 (Fall 1967): 20–34.

43. James McLean to James Warren Nye, May 18, 1862. Nye began thinking about statehood in May 1862. James D. Doty to James Warren Nye, November 29, 1862. McLean represented Genoa in the 1861 legislature.

44. Marsh, *Letters from Nevada Territory*, pp. 39, 369,

45. Ibid., pp. 565–566; Samuel Clemens to Jane Lampton Clemens, January 2, 1864 in *Mark Twain's Letters*, 1:267–268 and n. 1. The original bill and its printed version are available in *Nevada Territorial Legislature, Bills and Resolutions, 1862* in TERR-109, Council Bill 88. The printed version contains all the blanks, but William Gillespie, chief clerk of the House, later filled in the blanks in the original.

46. Henry A. Cheever to James Warren Nye, March 8, 1863; John H. Cheever to James Warren Nye, March 16, 1863; John Nye to James Warren Nye, March 16, 1863, Nye Executive Records.

47. North to Salmon Chase, December 25, 1862, in Salmon Portland Chase Papers, Library of Congress; Stonehouse, *John Wesley North*, pp. 154–155 and n. 18.

48. *Congressional Globe*, 1863, p. 166.

49. *Congressional Globe*, 1863, p. 1543.

50. Mono County Record, Board of Supervisors, 1:7, 26–27, 60–61, 82. Aurora was the largest precinct in the county.

51. Nevada Territory, Supreme Court Case Files, No. 21, *Chollar v. Potosi*, Nevada State Library and Archives.

52. *Humboldt Register*, May 2, 1863, 3:1; Horatio M. Jones to Abraham Lincoln July 30, 1864, in General Records of the Department of Justice, Appointment File–Nevada 1861–1865, in National Archives; copy in Horatio M. Jones file in McDonald Collection.

53. James D. Doty to W. P. Dole, July 18, 1864, in *Report of the Secretary of the Interior*, 1864, pp. 513–514; Edward P. Conner to R. C. Drum, July 18, 1863 in *War of Rebellion*, vol. 50, part 2, pp. 527–531.

54. James D. Doty to James Warren Nye, August 3, 1863; and James D. Doty to James Warren Nye, September 14, 1863, Nye Executive Records.

55. Andrew J. Marsh, Samuel L. Clemens, and Amos Bowen, *Reports of the 1863 Constitutional Convention of the Territory of Nevada*, ed. William C. Miller and Eleanor Bushnell (Carson City: Nevada Legislative Counsel Bureau, 1972), p. 111.

56. David A. Johnson, "A Case of Mistaken Identity: William M. Stewart and the Rejection of Nevada's First Constitution," *Nevada Historical Society Quarterly* 30 (2) (Summer 1987): 118–130.

57. *Sacramento Daily Union*, December 31, 1863.

58. Ibid.

59. *Gold Hill Evening News*, January 11, 1864, quoted in Johnson, "Mistaken Identity," p. 124.

60. "How to Tax Mining Claims," in *Gold Hill Evening News*, January 5, 1864; January 6, 1864; February 22, 1862; "Constitution and the Tax," in *Gold Hill Evening News*, January 5, 1864, and January 6, 1864.

61. North described the episode to his friend George Loomis in John Wesley North to George Loomis, February 7, 1864, in the John Wesley North Papers, the Huntington Library, San Marino, CA, quoted in Stonehouse, *John Wesley North*, p. 168.

62. Samuel Clemens to Jane Lampton Clemens, January 2(?), 1854, in *Mark Twain's Letters*, 1:267.

63. James Warren Nye to William H. Seward, March 25, 1864, referred to the U.S. Senate on April 29 by President Lincoln, read on May 2, and published as Ex. Doc No. 41, in *Index to the Senate Executive Documents for the First Session of the Thirty-eighth Congress of the United State of America, 1863–64* (Washington, DC: Government Printing Office, 1864), pp. 1–3.

64. Joseph L. King, *History of the San Francisco Stock and Exchange Board* (San Francisco: printed by the Stanley-Taylor Co. for the author, 1910), p. 21; "Memorial of the Legislature of Nevada Territory Asking for an Amendment of Their Organic Act," House Miscellaneous Document No. 74, in *Miscellaneous Documents of the House of Representatives Printed During the First Session of the Thirty-eighth Congress, 1863–64* (Washington, DC: Government Printing Office, 1864).

65. For a discussion of the paramount allegiance clause in Nevada and other states, see Michael J. Brodhead, "Accepting the Verdict: National Supremacy as Expressed in State Constitutions," *Nevada Historical Society Quarterly* 13 (2) (Summer, 1970): 3–18; Jerome E. Edwards, "Federalism and the Nevada Constitution," *Halcyon* 10 (1988): 41–48; for a more popular version, see Brodhead, "Union Made," *Nevada Magazine* (September/October, 1989): 43–47.

66. Myron Angel, ed., *History of Nevada, With Illustrations and Biographical Sketches of Prominent Men and Pioneers* (reprint, Berkeley, CA: Howell-North, 1958), p. 86.

67. "Mines Should be Taxed," *Virginia Evening Bulletin*, May 2, 1864; "County Treasurer's Report," *Virginia Evening Bulletin*, May 2, 1864. The Storey County debt was $182,543.96. *Virginia Evening Bulletin* May 4, 1864; Andrew Jackson Marsh, *Official Report of the Debates and Proceedings in the Constitutional Convention of the State of Nevada, Assembled at Carson City, July 4th, 1864, to Form a Constitution and State Government* (San Francisco: Frank Eastman Printer, 1866).

68. Robert J Chandler, "California's 1863 Loyalty Oaths: Another Look," *Arizona and the West* 21 (1979): 215–234.

69. Angel, *History of Nevada*, pp. 346, 358; Walter Van Tilburg Clark, ed., *The Journals of Alfred Doten, 1849–1903*, 3 vols. (Reno: University of Nevada Press, 1973), pp. 797–798; Van Bokkelen to James Warren Nye, August 9, 1864; and McDermit to James Warren Nye, August 9, 1864, Nye Executive Records.

70. *Virginia Daily Union*, August 23, 1864.

71. Angel, *History of Nevada, 1881*, pp. 335–340.

72. *Virginia Daily Union*, August 26, 1864. The article was copied by the San Francisco *Evening Bulletin*, August 29, 1864.

73. *Virginia Daily Union*, August 24, 1864, reprinting the article "The Cards Stacked Against Us Again," *Territorial Enterprise*, August 24, 1864.

74. *Virginia Daily Union*, August 25, 1864, contains the letters in support of North and North's reply; the proceedings of the Carson City meeting in support of Turner are in the *Virginia Daily Union*, August 27, 1864.

75. H. G. Worthington, et al., to Edward P. Conner, September 17, 1864; George A. Thurston to Edward P. Conner, September 18, 1864; Edward P. Conner to Headquarters, District of Utah, September 22, 1864; Edwin M. Stanton to James Warren Nye September 18, 1864, in *Records of the Rebellion*, series 1, vol. 50, part 2, pp. 979–981.

76. Clark, ed., *The Journals of Alfred Doten, 1849–1903*, pp. 802–803. James Warren Nye to Major-General Irvin McDowell, September 21, 1864, McDowell to James Warren Nye, September 21, 1864, Drum to Major Charles McDermit, September 21, 1864, in *Records of the Rebellion*, series 1, vol. 50, part 2, p. 982; McDermit to James Warren Nye, September 26, 1864, in Nye Executive Records.

77. Gideon Wells, *Diary of Gideon Wells*, ed. Howard K. Beale (New York: W.W. Norton, 1960), 2:164.

BIBLIOGRAPHY

Angel, Myron, ed. *History of Nevada, With Illustrations and Biographical Sketches of Prominent Men and Pioneers*. Reprint. Berkeley, CA: Howell-North, 1958.

Edwards, Jerome E. "Federalism and the Nevada Constitution." *Halcyon* 10 (1988): 41–48.

Johnson, David A. "A Case of Mistaken Identity: William M. Stewart and the Rejection of Nevada's First Constitution." *Nevada Historical Society Quarterly* 30 (2) (Summer 1987): 118–130.

Kelly, J. Wells. *First Directory of Nevada Territory*. Reprinted with introduction by Richard Lingenfelter, Los Gatos, CA: The Talisman Press, 1962.

Madsen, Brigham D. *The Shoshone Frontier and the Bear River Massacre*. Salt Lake City: University of Utah Press, 1985.

Marsh, Andrew Jackson. *Official Report of the Debates and Proceedings in the Constitutional Convention of the State of Nevada, Assembled at Carson City, July 4th, 1864, to Form a Constitution and State Government.* San Francisco: Frank Eastman Printer, 1866.

———, Samuel L. Clemens, and Amos Bowen. *Reports of the 1863 Constitutional Convention of the Territory of Nevada.* Edited by William C. Miller and Eleanor Bushnell. Carson City: Nevada Legislative Counsel Bureau, 1972.

Richards, Kent D, "Rudimentary Government in Washoe Territory." *Arizona and the West* 11 (Autumn, 1969): 220–223.

Unruh, John D. *The Plains Across: The Overland Emigrants of the Transcontinental West, 1840–1860.* Urbana: University of Illinois Press, 1979.

THE STATE OF NEW HAMPSHIRE

Ratified the Constitution of the United States:
June 21, 1788

Peter E. Carr

INTRODUCTION

"Live Free or Die": New Hampshire's famous motto epitomizes its history as a march toward freedom. Within ten years after the first European settlement was established in 1623, settlers were making compacts among themselves for self-government. New Hampshire fishermen, farmers, fur traders, and religious dissenters fought off border disputes with Massachusetts and New York. They were tossed around the political landscape as a new Massachusetts county in 1643, a separate royal colony in 1679, one of many colonies in the Dominion of New England from 1686 to 1689, and again a separate royal colony in 1691. Through all these political changes, hostilities with Native Americans were a constant element. On January 5, 1776, New Hampshire promulgated a new constitution that made it the first independent colony in New England. Then on June 21, 1788, New Hampshire became the ninth state to ratify the U.S. Constitution, thus assuring that the United States would go forward under the rule of this new law.

COLONIAL ERA

Martin Pring and forty-three crewmen sailed by the mouth of the Piscataqua River in 1603 in two small ships named the *Speedwell* and the *Discoverer*. Unable to trade his cargo of "clothing, spades, and axes, 'scissors and chisels,' bells, beads, bugles, and looking glasses, thimbles and needles" while sailing along the coast of New England, he returned to England. As did most early explorers, he wrote an account of the New England coastline.[1] By 1605,

New Hampshire

Territorial Development:

- The Council for New England gives Ferdinando Gorges and John Mason land including Maine and New Hampshire, 1622
- Mason and Gorges divide the land; Mason receives New Hampshire portions, 1629
- Future state of New Hampshire annexed by the Massachusetts Colony, 1641
- New Hampshire becomes a colony independent of Massachusetts, 1679
- Continental Congress approves Declaration of Independence from Great Britain, July 4, 1776
- Great Britain formally recognizes American independence through the Treaty of Paris, September 3, 1783
- New Hampshire becomes the ninth state to ratify the United States Constitution, June 21, 1788

Capitals Prior to Statehood:

- Portsmouth, 1679–1774
- Exeter, 1774–1783
- No definite capital, 1783–1788

State Capitals:

- No definite capital, 1788–1807
- Concord, 1807–present

Origin of State Name: John Mason named New Hampshire after the English county of Hampshire, where he had spent some time in his youth.

First Governor: John Langdon
Governmental Organization: Bicameral
Population at Statehood: 141,899
Geographical Size: 8,968 square miles

Samuel de Champlain sailed into the area. He discovered the Isles of Shoals. It was not until 1614, however, that Captain John Smith explored the area and gathered detailed information. In his *Description of New England*, Smith mentions the convenient harbor at the mouth of the Piscataqua. He named the new land "North Virginia," but King James I changed it to "New England."[2]

In 1620, Sir Ferdinando Gorges of Plymouth became the leader of the Council for New England. This group obtained a grant from King James I of all country from sea to sea between 40° and 48° north latitude. The Council for New England would later make nine grants that directly affected the future New Hampshire.

An April 18, 1635, document granting the province of New Hampshire to John Wollaston, a goldsmith of London, calls the bulk of the area "New Hampshire" and 10,000 acres of it "Masonia." This grant was based on letters patent dated November 3, 1632. Interestingly the term of the grant was for three thousand years. Wollaston's grant was described in this way:

> ye sd Councill hereunto especially moveing have demised granted & to farme letten & by these p'nts doe demise grant & to farme left unto ye sd John Woollaston his Executors & assignee all yt part purpart & porc'on of ye Maine Land in New England aforesd being from ye middle part of Naumkeck river & from thence to proceed Eastwards along ye Sea Coast to Cape Anne & round about ye same to Passcattaway harbour & soe forwards up wthin ye river of Newichewanock & to ye furthest head of ye sd River & from thence northwestward till Six miles be finished from ye first enterance of Passcattaway harbour & also from Naumkeci; through ye river therof up into ye land west Sixty miles from wch period to crose over land to ye Sixty Miles end accompted from Passcattawy though Newichewanock to ye land north westward aforesd & alsoe all yt ye South half of ye Isles of Shoulds together wth all other Islands & Isletts as well imbayed as wthin five leagues distance from ye premises or abutting upon ye same or any part thereof not otherwise granted to any by speciall name and together alsoe wth all ye woods & underwoods & trees now standing growing & being or web may stand growe to be upon ye sd demised premises or any part or pacell thereof wet porc'on of land and premises are from hence forth to be called by ye name of New Hampshire And alsoe ye sd Councill for ye considerac'ons aforesd have demised granted & to farme letten & by these p'nts doe demise grant & to farme lett unto ye si John Wallaston his Executors & assignee all yt other parcell of lands woods & wood grounds lying on ye South east part of ye river of Sagadahock in ye North east part of New England aforsd aft ye mouth & entrance therof containing & to contain tenn Thousand Acres together alsoe wth all ye woods under woods & trees of ye same other parcell of land & wood ground shall from hence forth be called by ye name of Masonia.[3]

Nevertheless, the first grant made by the Council of New England from the original royal grant was to Gorges and the man sometimes called the founder of New Hampshire, Captain John Mason. They received the first grant on March

9, 1622. On November 7, 1629, Mason received another grant for land located between the Merrimack and Piscataqua rivers. This latter grant is the first document that contained the name New Hampshire. After receiving his grant, John Wollaston, in turn, granted it to Captain John Mason on June 11, 1635.[4] Captain Mason died that same year in England and never saw his new land. His land investment at the time of his death had a value of £22,000.

The earliest colony for which unquestionable record exists is that of 1623, when, under the authority of another land grant, Captain John Mason and others sent David Thomson, a Scotsman, and Edward and Thomas Hilton, fish-merchants of London, with a number of other people in two companies to establish a fishing colony in what is now New Hampshire, at the mouth of the Piscataqua River.[5]

The first actual settler of New Hampshire was David Thompson (or Thomson). His father worked for Sir Ferdinando Gorges of Plymouth. David Thompson worked with four Abenaki Indians who had been kidnapped from the Cape Cod area during earlier British voyages. Another captured Indian, Sassacomoit, better known to history as Squanto, had befriended Thompson and had taught him many things about surviving in the wilds.

With another charter in hand, Gorges entrusted Thompson to set up a plantation at a spot on the mouth of the Piscataqua River now known as Odiorne's Point, near Portsmouth. The Isles of Shoals was made the home base of the fishing crew. At the Isles the fishermen constructed salt-drying fish racks and a factory to process the fish. Thompson built his house on the 6,000-acre Pannaway site, also called Little Harbor, in what is now Rye. His wife, Amais, and son, John, joined him there. On April 16, 1623, the Thompson family and the fishermen became the first New Hampshire colonists of European origin.

Edward and William Hilton have an equal claim to fame. Their settlement, also dated 1623, was farther down the Piscataqua at Northam, later Dover Point, where Pring had explored twenty years earlier. Although the Thompsons may have been the first to settle, they moved on; the Hilton family stayed, and their name is important throughout local history.[6]

Other colonists, this time sent by the Laconia Company, arrived in 1630. They had traveled to the new colony to establish an extensive fur trade with the Iroquois Indians. They had the mistaken impression that the Piscataqua River had its source in Lake Champlain. These colonists built their houses near the old Mason house in what became Portsmouth but was known as Strawbery Banke until 1653.[7]

Religious intolerance also brought settlers to New Hampshire. By 1638, an Antinomian leader named Reverend John Wheelwright founded Exeter on land supposedly purchased from the Indians. Wheelwright was a religious dissenter who had been banished from Massachusetts. Others from Massachusetts followed and formed the town of Hampton. In August of 1639, the colonists at Exeter made an agreement among themselves to form a government, to follow the laws of King Charles, and to live as Christians and, strangely enough, as part of the colony of Massachusetts. These settlers were taking steps to form the first government in New Hampshire:

> [we] do in the name of Christ and in the sight of God combine ourselves together to erect and set up among us such Government as shall be to our best discerning agreeable to the Will of God professing ourselves Subjects to our Sovereign Lord King Charles according to the Libertyes of our English Colony of Massachusetts, and binding of ourselves solemnly by the Grace and Help of Christ and in His Name and fear to submit ourselves to such Godly and Christian Lawes as are established in the realm of England to our best Knowledge, and to all other such Lawes which shall upon good grounds he made and enacted among us according to God that we may live quietly and peaceably together in all godliness.[8]

In 1641, the inhabitants on the Piscataqua River made a compact submitting themselves to royal laws because they had no government. This document, called the Combinations of the Inhabitants, was also an effort by the forty-one settlers to maintain some sort of identity independent of Massachusetts.[9] The compact was not enduring, because by 1643 Massachusetts had taken control.

> Whereas sundry Mischiefs and Inconveniences have befallen us, and more and greater may, in regard of want of Civill Government, his gracious Majesty haveing settled no order for us, to our knowledge wee chose names are underwritten, being Inhabitants upon the River of Pascataqua [sic] have voluntary agreed to combine ourselves into a body Politick, that wee may the more comfortably enjoy the Benefit of his Majesties Laws and doe hereby actually engage ourselves to submit to his Royall Majesties laws, together with all such Laws as shall be concluded by a major part of the Freemen of our Society, in Case they be not repugnant to the laws of England, and administered in behalf of his Majestie And this wee have mutually promised, and engaged to doe, an so to continue till his excellent Majestic shall give other orders concerning us. In witness whereof Wee have hereunto set our hands, October 22. In the 16 Year of the Reigne of our Sovereiglle lord, Charles by the grace of God, King of Great Brittaine, France and Ireland, Defender of the Faith, &c.[10]

Religious differences created friction between the Antinomians in Exeter, Puritans in Massachusetts, and Anglicans in Dover Neck and Strawbery Banke. This friction marked the start of the border dispute between Massachusetts and New Hampshire. Massachusetts's charter had been written under the impression that the Merrimack River flowed eastward for its entire length. Once its true course was discovered, Massachusetts decided to press its advantage. The Massachusetts charter read that its northern boundary was "three English miles north of the Merrimack River, or the northward of any and every part thereof."[11] Massachusetts claimed that Dover, Portsmouth, and Hampton fell within its patent, and in 1643 three of the four settlements in New Hampshire came under the control of Massachusetts. Exeter was the only holdout. Many Exeter townspeople were former Massachusetts colonists; they did not want to be part of that colony, and some left the area. In May 1643, a petition was sent to the Massachusetts General Court requesting that Exeter might be received within its jurisdiction. This petition has not survived, but the court answered that Exeter must accept the conditions imposed by Massachusetts.

Immediately after receiving the court's reply, Exeter sent another petition dated May 12, 1643, that stated:

> To the Right Worshipful the Governor, the Deputie Governor, and the Magistrates, with the assistance and deputyes of this honored Court at present assembled at Boston.
>
> The humble petition of the inhabitants of Exeter, who do humbly request that this honored Court would be pleased to appoint the bounds of our Towne to be layed out to us, both towards Hampton & also downe the River on that side which Capt. Wiggons his farm is on, for he doth Clame all the land from the towne downwards, on the one side, & Hampton on the other side doth clame to be neere us, that we shall not be able to subsist to be a Towne except this honored Court be pleased to releave us. And we suppose that Capt Wiggens his farme and a good way below it, may well be laid within our Township if this honored Court so please.
>
> Also we do humbly crave that the Court would be pleased to grant that we may still enjoy thouse small quantitie of meddows, which are at Lemperell river that Dover men now seeme to lay clame to, notwithstanding they know we long since purchased them & allao quietly possess them with their consent.
>
> Likewise we do humbly request that this Court would be please to establish three men among us to put an Ishew to small differences amongst us & one to be a Clarke of the writes, that so we might not be so troblesom to the Courts for every small matter.[12]

On September 7, 1643, the general court accepted Exeter's petition. The town was assigned to the newly formed county of Norfolk. The men who had petitioned for appointment as permanent town officers were rejected, however, and four others were named in their stead.

The terms of acceptance for Exeter were basically the same as those given to the other New Hampshire towns. Administration of justice and record keeping were to be the same as at Ipswich and Salem, Massachusetts. Exeter could continue to enjoy the lawful liberties of fishing, planting, and timber cutting in the Piscataqua River that had previously been enjoyed. Court cases were to be tried at one of three or four other towns in the new county of Norfolk, excluding Exeter.[13]

The heirs of John Mason attempted to have the boundary dispute settled. Nothing was resolved, however, until after the resignation of Richard Cromwell. At that point, Robert Tufton Mason, John's grandson, filed a petition with Parliament and then with the king seeking relief for this situation. The king appointed a commission in 1664 to hear the matter in New England. The leader of this commission was Colonel Richard Nichols, an acquaintance of Mason. Another member was Samuel Maverick who had interests in New Hampshire and various grievances and complaints against Massachusetts.

In July 1664 the commission landed at Piscataqua and soon found that Massachusetts had misdrawn its boundaries. The new boundary would be a line drawn east and west from a point three miles north of the mouth of the Merrimack River, not as the general court had declared. The commission's decision, its recommendations for the building of fortifications at Portsmouth, and its attempt to assert its authority proved disastrous. In the end nothing was accomplished, although Puritans tried to appease the Crown by making concessions.[14]

In 1671, Mason petitioned the Crown again. Charles II and the Privy Council renewed their interest in the case in 1672, but hostilities with the Dutch postponed any further investigation. In an effort to resolve the issue, the Crown abolished the Council of Trade and Plantations and replaced it with a standing committee of Privy Council members. Massachusetts was requested to send a delegation to England. The Massachusetts delegation arrived in England in December 1676. The case was tried before the Lords Chief Justices of the King's Bench and Common Pleas in April 1677.

Because Mason made no claim to the right of government, the court ruled that the title to the lands should be determined by the local court having jurisdiction over the matter. Mason seized the opportunity to have a separate governor appointed and in January 1679 petitioned the king to appoint a governor who should have jurisdiction over the lands that Mason claimed. On September 18, 1679, New Hampshire was made a separate colony or province with a government vested in a president and council appointed by the king. An assembly was to be chosen by the people. Thus New Hampshire became a royal province in 1679. John Cutt was its first president.[15]

In 1684, Charles II revoked the old Massachusetts Bay charter because he wanted to combine Connecticut, Maine, Massachusetts, New Hampshire, and Rhode Island into a single political unit. Charles II died before he could put his plan into action; it was left to King James II, after he became king in 1685, to establish the Dominion of New England.

From 1686 to 1689 New Hampshire formed part of the Dominion of New England. Its first governor general was Sir Edmund Andros. In 1688, New Jersey and New York were added to the dominion. This dominion was dissolved after James II fell from power. Because no provincial authority yet existed in New Hampshire, the local citizens attempted to form one. This attempt failed, so a nominal union was made with Massachusetts until 1691, when William and Mary made New Hampshire a separate royal province.[16]

Samuel Allen, the assign of Mason, formed a royal government in 1692. His son-in-law, John Usher, was lieutenant governor. For the remainder of the colonial era, New Hampshire was separate from Massachusetts. Their only remaining connection was having the same governor from 1699 until 1741, when Benning Wentworth was made the first governor of New Hampshire alone. Wentworth governed for nearly thirty years and died in 1770.[17]

Even after the separate governments were formed, the boundary disputes between the two colonies continued. Because both Massachusetts and New Hampshire had granted land in the disputed territories, both sought jurisdiction to levy and collect taxes. In an attempt to settle the dispute, New Hampshire appealed to the home government. In 1737 a commission of councilors from New York, Rhode Island, and Nova Scotia was established to settle the matter. The councilors agreed upon the eastern boundary but not on the southern one. Another appeal was then made to the king.

The king and council confirmed the decision of the councilors in 1741 and established a southern boundary more favorable to New Hampshire. The western boundary with New York, however, was not settled. Governor Benning Wentworth of New Hampshire, along with some friends and associates, purchased the rights to the Mason grants in 1746. This group became known as the Masonian Proprietors.

Governor Wentworth made grants in the name of the king of England, many of them to soldiers who had fought in the Native American wars. The terms of the grants were simple. The proprietors could convey only the soil. No taxes could be levied on these lands until improvements had been made by the new grantees. Roads, churches, and schools were to be built within a specified period of time. The fees charged were small and were often token, in many cases a shilling or an ear of corn each year.

By 1764, 138 townships had been chartered. Their establishment led to another boundary dispute with New York in 1749. By 1764, New York had procured a royal order declaring the western shore of the Connecticut River to be the western boundary of New Hampshire. This dispute arose again during the American Revolution and was not settled until Vermont became a state. New Hampshire's northern boundary was fixed in 1842 when the Webster-Ashburton Treaty set the international line between Canada and the United States.[18]

NATIVE AMERICAN CONFLICTS

The indigenous people of northern New England present at the time of the European arrival became known collectively as the Abenaki and Pennacook. These Algonquian-speaking people did not form one tribe but lived as several family groups joined together by family ties. They lived by hunting and gathering wild game, fruits, and seeds. They built canoes, trapped fish, and cleared land for limited maize agriculture. In fact, the first colonists' survival depended on the natives' knowledge of the land. Had it not been for their help, the colonists might have perished.

For the most part, the first fifty years of contact were peaceful. Even as the Europeans encroached more and more on native territory, leaders like Passaconnaway sought peace and coexistence. Other leaders distrusted the newcomers. The Europeans often used deception and trickery, along with guns and whiskey, to drive away or wipe out the natives. These tactics led to reprisals and counter-reprisals until the Cochecho Massacre.

Passaconaway's son, Wonalancet, assumed leadership of the tribe in 1665 and continued his father's peaceful ways. The leader of the colonists at Cochecho was Richard Waldron (originally Walderne), an Englishman who had emigrated in 1635. By 1642, Waldron owned a large tract of land at the Lower Falls of the Cochecho River, where he built a sawmill. This area was then settled by 41 to 43 families and became known as Cochecho. Waldron cared more for profit than for the law. Although it was illegal, he sold liquor and arms to the natives at the trading post he had established in town.

Meantime, in the colony of Massachusetts, a Wompanaug chief named Metacomet (nicknamed "King Philip") declared war on the English in 1675. He became sachem after his brother died from poisoning at the hands of the colonists. For a time some of the Native Americans from the south harassed, attacked, and killed people along the frontier areas of the Oyster River and in Exeter.[19]

Wonalancet kept his Pennacook members out of the fray until King Philip was defeated. King Philip's War, as it became known, ended with the natives losing about 3,000 people. Two hundred of the survivors fled to the Cochecho area. Waldron, who by now had the rank of major, was required to capture them and turn them over to the Massachusetts militia who had followed them. This action displeased the local natives, who saw it as a violation of the treaty they had just signed with Waldron. Waldron, however, did not want any of the locals harmed. As a subterfuge, Waldron suggested a mock battle or war games with the natives, who did not suspect what was about to happen. The natives, locals and outsiders alike, congregated outside the town. Four militia companies surrounded them, separated the local natives, and captured the 200 Native Americans from Massachusetts. These were taken back to Boston, where some were sold as slaves and some were hanged.

Chief Wonalancet was replaced by Kancamagus, who was more warlike than his two predecessors. He resented the injustices perpetrated by English settlers on his people. Natives had no right to travel in the woods east of the Merrimack without written permission from Major Waldron. The Pennacook natives were losing more and more territory from unfair payments or barter. Tensions between the settlers and locals were so high that in 1684 the governor ordered the meetinghouse at Dover be fortified. Every town or small settlement also established at least one fortified blockhouse to which people could flee if the Indians attacked.

Probably fifty garrisons existed within a radius of fifteen miles of Dover. At public expense, Major Waldron transformed five homes located on highest ground in the Cochecho settlement into garrisons. The homes on the north side of the river belonged to Richard Waldron, Richard Otis, and Elizabeth Heard. On the south side of the river, the homes of Peter Coffin and his son Tristam were fortified. The garrisons were built with foot-thick squared logs impenetrable to bullets. The second story projected over the lower story by two or three feet. A loose board in the overhang could be removed to pour boiling water on the attackers and to combat fires. The walls had narrow slits for firearms. An eight-foot palisade of logs surrounded the garrisons.[20]

Although Governor Bradford wrote Waldron on June 27 informing him of the impeding treachery, the letter arrived one day late. On the evening of June 27, several Native American women sought shelter at each garrison house. This was a common practice, and none of the settlers suspected anything amiss. After all the families in each house were asleep, the women quietly opened the gates. Several hundred Pennacook warriors stormed each house, and the massacre began.

The Indians poured into Major Waldron's garrison. Although he attempted to defend himself, he was overpowered. He was tied to a chair. Then in a fury usually unknown from the Pennacook natives, each cut Waldron across the chest using his own sword. As each Indian made the cut, he cried out, "I cross out my account." They then cut off Waldron's nose and ears, shoved them into his mouth, and forced Waldron to fall upon his own sword. After his death, they cut off his hand as a sign of protest against his cheating them on the scales in trades. They burned the house to the ground. Members of his family were either killed or taken captive.

Each garrison in turn suffered a similar fate. At the Richard Otis garrison, Stephen, his son, and daughter Hannah were killed. The Otis garrison was burned to the ground. His wife Grizel and his three-month old daughter Margaret were taken captive. Two of his grandchildren were also taken captive to Canada. Margaret, the daughter, would later be taken in by French nuns who raised her in Quebec and renamed her Christine. In 1735, at the age of forty-five, Christine and her husband returned to Dover and opened a tavern in Tuttle Square.[21]

Across the Cochecho River, the Native Americans quickly overwhelmed Peter Coffin's garrison. Because of his friendly relations with the Indians, they did not burn his house but merely looted it. He and his family were taken captive and brought to his son Tristam's garrison. Tristam's home was so well fortified that the Indians had not been able to penetrate it. Kancamagus's men forced him to surrender by holding Peter in front of the gates and threatening to kill him. Tristam's house was only pillaged, not burned. Both Coffin families escaped safely while their captors were busily plundering their homes. In the town of Conway, three of the Otis's daughters were recaptured.[22]

The Massacre at Cochecho was part of a wider war with the Native Americans known as King William's War. The wars ended after the Treaty of Ryswick between the French and English in 1697, but it took Cochecho many years to recover fully. A quarter of the population was lost, making recovery and growth much more difficult, but houses and mills were eventually rebuilt. By the beginning of the eighteenth century, Cochecho had fully recovered and was an important town in New Hampshire.

After a hiatus of about five years, Queen Anne's War started between France and England in the West Indies and on the New England frontiers from 1702 to 1713. The Native Americans were incited by the French in Canada to attack the frontier towns of New Hampshire. The Native Americans took the blame for the hostilities in the Portsmouth Indian Treaty of 1713 and promised to be loyal to the British:

> Wherefore, we whose names are hereunto subscribed, delegates for the several tribes of the Indians, belonging unto the River of Kenybeck, Amarascogen, St. Johns, Saco, Merrimac, and parts adjacent, being sensible of our great offence and folly in not complying with the aforsaid submission and agreements, and also of the sufferings and mischiefs that we have thereby exposed ourselves unto, do, in humble and submissive manner, cast ourselves upon Her Majesty's mercy for the pardon of our past rebellions, hostilities, and violations of our promises, praying to be received unto Her Majesty's grace and protections. And for and on behalfe of ourselves, and of all other the Indians belonging to the several rivers and places aforesaid, within the sovereignty of Her Majesty of Great Britain, do again acknowledge and profess our hearty and sinceer obedience unto the Crown of Great Britain, and do solemnly renew, ratify, and confirm all and every of the articles and agreements contained in the former and present submission.[23]

Major hostilities ended with the Portsmouth Indian Treaty of 1713, but for more than half a century Native American raids continued to plague many coastal towns. Other Native American conflicts of the eighteenth century were outgrowths of problems between European powers. The British wanted to add French Canada to their dominions, whereas the French were spreading further south and west in North America.

Native Americans were recruited to fight on one side or the other in most of these wars between the European powers. When Europeans were not engaged, Native Americans fought a hit-and-run type of warfare as opposed to the set battles of European armies. The French and Indian War, from 1754 to 1763, was largest of the wars, but its origins lay for the most part in European conflicts rather than in Native American hostilities. It resulted in France's losing Canada. By the middle of the eighteenth century, however, the Indian population of New Hampshire had been reduced to insignificant levels. Disease, famine, and the continual influx of Europeans decimated them. By 1770 few Indians remained in New Hampshire.

THE ROAD TO INDEPENDENCE

The French and Indian Wars had prevented colonization of the inland areas. With the end of the wars a land rush began. With so much waterpower available, lumber camps were set up, and sawmills were built along the streams. In 1719 Scotch settlers from Londonderry, Ireland, arrived. Most were Tories, or Loyalists. By 1722, they established a settlement called Londonderry just across the border from Haverhill, Massachusetts.

Benning Wentworth was the royal governor for almost thirty years during the time when the independence movement began. He was a very wealthy man because of his position and somewhat unscrupulous dealings. As surveyor general of the king's woods, he managed huge tracts of forests, a major source of wealth. After the enactment of the unpopular British Stamp Act in 1765, Wentworth decided to give up his office to his nephew John Wentworth II. This Wentworth was a native of Portsmouth, so his ties with England were lessened by distance and birthplace, and he opposed the Stamp Act. Shortly, the English Parliament passed the Revenue Act that taxed luxury items, including glass and tea. As more and more of the population became dissatisfied, acts of protest began to take place.

In 1773, Governor John Wentworth disbanded the local citizens' assembly. The citizens moved their meetings to a tavern in Exeter. There a provincial congress was taking place. The owner of the tavern, Nathaniel Folsom, and John Sullivan of Somersworth were elected to attend the Continental Congress in Philadelphia. Sullivan would later become New Hampshire's first president.[24]

After patriots stole 200 barrels of gunpowder from Fort William and Mary in New Castle Island, hostilities were inevitable. Within a few months the first shots would be fired at Lexington and Concord in Massachusetts. New Hampshire's revolutionary regiment was immediately sent to what would be the next skirmish at the Battle of Bunker Hill. New Hampshire had more than one thousand troops at this battle, more than the combined numbers from Massachusetts and Connecticut.

Because he was a Loyalist, Governor Wentworth removed his family first to Boston and later to Nova Scotia, where many other Loyalists had taken refuge. He became Nova Scotia's lieutenant governor, a post he held until his death in 1820.[25]

INDEPENDENCE AND CONSTITUTION

On the recommendation of the Continental Congress, the New Hampshire provincial congress assembled at Exeter on December 21, 1775. It adopted a temporary constitution on January 5, 1776. Thus it became the first colony to declare its independence from England. Because the constitution was not submitted to the people for their review or ratification, strong protests ensued from many parts of the state. The western towns, in particular, became so agitated that it was necessary to send a committee to assure everyone that the form of government adopted was temporary. On June 15, 1776, the first assembly elected under that government declared independence. New Hampshire's independent government functioned from its establishment on January 5, 1776, until June 2, 1784.[26]

THE 1776 NEW HAMPSHIRE CONSTITUTION

In the preamble to the temporary constitution adopted at Exeter on January 5, 1776, the members of the Congress of New Hampshire listed the grievances with Great Britain that had caused them to take up the business of forming a new government:

WE, the members of the Congress of New Hampshire...Have taken into our serious consideration the unhappy circumstances, into which this colony is involved by means of many grievous and oppressive acts of the British Parliament, depriving us of our natural and constitutional rights and privileges; to enforce obedience to which acts a powerful fleet and army have been sent to this country by the ministry of Great Britain, who have exercised a wanton and cruel abuse of their power, in destroying the lives and properties of the colonists in many places with fire and sword, taking the ships and lading from many of the honest and industrious inhabitants of this colony employed in commerce, agreeable to the laws and customs a long time used here.

The sudden and abrupt departure of his Excellency John Wentworth, Esq., our late Governor, and several of the Council, leaving us destitute of legislation, and no executive courts being open to punish criminal offenders; whereby the lives and properties of the honest people of this colony are liable to the machinations and evil designs of wicked men, Therefore, for the preservation of peace and good order, and for the security of the lives and properties of the inhabitants of this colony, we conceive ourselves reduced to the necessity of establishing A FORM OF GOVERNMENT to continue during the present unhappy and unnatural contest with Great Britain; PROTESTING and DECLARING that we neaver sought to throw off our dependence upon Great Britain, but felt ourselves happy under her protection, while we could enjoy our constitutional rights and privileges. And that we shall rejoice if such a reconciliation between us and our parent State can be effected as shall be approved by the CONTINENTAL CONGRESS, in whose prudence and wisdom we confide.

The congress assumed "the name, power and authority of a house of Representatives or Assembly for the Colony of New-Hampshire." It then proceeded to choose

twelve persons, being reputable freeholders and inhabitants within this colony, in the following manner, viz. five in the county of Rockingham, two in the county of Stratford, two in the county of Hillsborough, two in the county of

Cheshire, and one in the county of Grafton, to be a distinct and separate branch of the Legislature by the name of a COUNCIL for this colony, to continue as such until the third Wednesday in December next; any seven of whom to be a quorum to do business.

The council was to appoint its president, and in his absence the senior counselor was to preside. A secretary was to be appointed by both branches.

Acts and resolutions had to be passed by both branches of the legislature before they became effective. Public officers of the colony and of the counties were to have one-year joint appointments except for clerks of the executive courts, who would be appointed by the justices. General and field officers of the militia as well as army officers were to have joint appointments. Interestingly, "all bills, resolves, or votes for raising, levying, and collecting money" had to originate in the House of Representatives. There were also provisions for the appointment of civil officers for the colony and the counties, the duration of the appointments to be determined by both the branches. The people of the counties were to choose a treasurer and a recorder of deeds annually. And finally, taking nothing for granted, the Congress resolved

that if the present unhappy dispute with Great Britain should continue longer than this present year, and the Continental Congress give no instruction or direction to the contrary, the Council be chosen by the people of each respective county in such manner as the Council and house of Representatives shall order.[27]

After the national Declaration of Independence was read in public at Portsmouth, it became the rallying point for New Hampshire revolutionaries. New Hampshire's Josiah Bartlett, Matthew Thornton, and William Whipple were signatories of the Declaration. Two of the navy's first warships were built at Portsmouth shipyards. John Paul Jones, the father of the American Navy, lived in Portsmouth for a year and a half. Later he joined the fight.[28]

In June 1777, representatives from various New Hampshire towns met in Hanover. They adopted resolutions that any permanent form of independent government should be debated and constructed in a convention meeting strictly for that purpose. These resolutions may have been the result of the Concord Resolutions of October 21, 1776, which stated in part, "because a Constitution alterable by the Supreme Legislature is no Security at all to the Subject against Encroachment of the Governing part on any, or on all of their Rights and privileges." Subsequent constitutional procedure in New Hampshire followed those suggested lines.[29]

In 1777, the New Hampshire legislature asked the various representatives to verify with their particular towns whether it was appropriate to hold a convention. Because many of the towns approved, the legislature voted in February 1778 that a convention be scheduled in June of that year. New Hampshire was the first colony to hold a constitutional convention. The first constitution provided for a general court consisting of a senate and a house of representatives. The council was to be an advisory body to the president of the state. New Hampshire was also the first state to require that its constitution be referred to the people for approval, and the people, in fact rejected the constitution drafted by this convention.[30]

A second convention met on June 5, 1781. The constitution it drafted and sent to the town meetings for ratification in the spring of 1782 was also rejected. The same convention submitted a revised version in the fall of 1782 after reviewing all the amendments. This third draft, likewise containing a provision that the work of the conventions should be submitted to the voters for approval, was resubmitted in October 1783 and was finally adopted, becoming effective on June 2, 1784. The 1784 document was amended in 1792.[31]

THE FEDERAL CONSTITUTION

According to the House of Representatives, "in May 1785, a committee of Congress made a report recommending an alteration in the Articles of Confederation," but nothing was done. So, it was left to the state legislatures to initiate changes. In January 1786, the legislature of Virginia passed a resolution

> providing for the appointment of five commissioners, who, or any three of them, should meet such commissioners as might be appointed in the other States of the Union, at a time and place to be agreed upon, to take into consideration the trade of the United States; to consider how far a uniform system in their commercial regulations may be necessary to their common interest and their permanent harmony; and to report to the several States such an act, relative to this great object, as, when ratified by them, will enable the United States in Congress effectually to provide for the same.

The first Monday in September was fixed as the date for the meeting in Annapolis, Maryland. Besides Virginia, only four other states appeared—New York, New Jersey, Delaware, and Pennsylvania.

Based on a report prepared by Alexander Hamilton of New York, it was decided that the commissioners present would seek the attendance of the other commissioners at a meeting in Philadelphia on the second Monday of May 1787. Congress resolved on February 21, 1787, that

> it is expedient that on the second Monday in May next a Convention of delegates who shall have been appointed by the several states be held at Philadelphia for the sole and express purpose of revising the Articles of Confederation and reporting to Congress and the several legislatures such alterations and provisions therein as shall when agreed to in Congress and confirmed by the states render the federal constitution adequate to the exigencies of Government & the preservation of the Union.[32]

The states appointed delegates, and on May 25, seven states having convened, George Washington of Virginia was unanimously elected president. Consideration of the proposed constitution began. Besides John Langdon and Nicholas Gilman, the State of New Hampshire named two other delegates, John Pickering and Benjamin West. Although they did not arrive in Philadelphia until July, they then set about their task immediately. John Langdon became their leader and joined the debate many times.

The act that credentialed these four men to represent New Hampshire in Philadelphia made it clear that New Hampshire wanted change and that its delegates would not be restricted in any way from participating wherever the debate led. The "infant state of our Republic" was blamed for "a system which in the course of time and experience, would manifest imperfections that it would be necessary to reform." The Articles of Confederation, which limited congressional power, were "found far inadequate, to the enlarged purposes which they were intended to produce." The situation was "truly critical and alarming...unless timely measures be taken to enlarge the powers of Congress, that they may be thereby enabled to avert the dangers which threaten our existence as a free and independent People."

New Hampshire was prepared "to act upon the liberal system of the general good of the United States, without circumscribing its views, to the narrow and selfish objects of partial convenience; and has been at all times ready to make every concession to the safety and happiness of the whole, which justice and sound policy could vindicate." Thus, it empowered its delegates

> to confer with such Deputies, as are, or may be appointed by the other States for similar purposes; and with them to discuss and decide upon the most effectual means to remedy the defects of our federal Union; and to procure, and secure, the enlarged purposes which it was intended to effect, and to report such an Act, to the United States in Congress, as when agreed to by them, and duly confirmed by the several States, will effectually provide for the same.[33]

Of the four New Hampshire delegates, two were active participants. Nicholas Gilman, an Exeter merchant born on August 3, 1755, had taken part in the Revolutionary War. He was commissioned regimental adjutant in the Third New Hampshire Regiment of the Continental Line in November 1776 and became assistant adjutant general in January 1778. In January 1781 Gilman transferred to the First New Hampshire Regiment. He served in this unit until the end of the war.

From 1786 to 1788 he was a member of the Continental Congress, although his attendance record was poor. In 1787 he was sent as a representative of New Hampshire at the Constitutional Convention. He made no speeches and did not participate in the debates. He was, however, active in getting New Hampshire to ratify the Constitution.

Gilman served in the U.S. House of Representatives from 1789 until 1797, and in 1793 and 1797 he was a presidential elector. He was a member of the

New Hampshire legislature in 1795, 1802, and 1804. Gilman was state treasurer from 1805 to 1808 and again from 1811 until 1814. He was elected senator from New Hampshire in 1804 and served until his death in 1814.[34]

John Langdon was born near Portsmouth, New Hampshire, on June 26, 1741, the son of a farmer. He went into the mercantile business for himself and prospered. Langdon supported the Revolution. In 1774 he participated in the stealing of British munitions from the Portsmouth fort. He sat in the Continental Congress during 1775 and 1776. Also, he was speaker of the New Hampshire assembly. During the war, he accepted a commission as colonel in the militia of New Hampshire. In addition, he built ships for operations against the British, an occupation which made him rich.

Langdon participated actively in the conduct of the war, but he concentrated on politics. He was speaker of the New Hampshire legislature from 1777 to 1781. In 1783 Langdon was elected to the Continental Congress, at the same time serving in state senate. In 1784, he was elected president of New Hampshire. In 1786 and 1787 he served again as speaker of the legislature.

New Hampshire would not pay Langdon's expenses, as well as those of Nicholas Gilman, to attend the Constitutional Convention, so Langdon was forced to pay them himself. Arriving at Philadelphia in late July, Langdon became an active participant. He favored a strong national government and spoke more than twenty times during the debates. In 1788, he took part in the New Hampshire ratifying convention.

Langdon was the first acting vice president of the United States. From 1789 to 1801 Langdon sat in the U.S. Senate, serving as the first president pro tempore for several sessions. During these years, his political affiliations changed. Although at first he supported a strong central government, by 1801 he backed the Democratic-Republicans. That same year he declined Thomas Jefferson's offer to be secretary of the navy. He remained active in New Hampshire politics, serving in the legislature, as a speaker, and as governor. In 1812 Langdon refused the Democratic-Republican vice presidential nomination because of his age and health. He died at the age of 78.[35]

At the ratification convention in Exeter, New Hampshire, many delegates opposed the Constitution as it was written, and ratification was in danger of failing. Most of the opposition came from the central part of the state. The convention at Exeter was adjourned to allow those delegates to consult with their constituents.

The Portsmouth newspaper, the *New Hampshire Gazette* of April 16, 1788, published an article titled, "To Be or Not To Be? Is the Question." It began

> Can you, my fellow countrymen, on a question of existence as a nation hesitate in your decision whether to be united and powerful, each supporting the dignity of the other; or to be divided into petty States, each seeking and contending for its own local advantages; and like the bundle of twigs which separated, was easily destroyed by an old and infirm man?

It continued by arguing that shipbuilding, farming, and manufacturing would benefit from adoption of the Constitution. Although most of the arguments it presented for adoption were economic, protection of individual liberties and national dignity were also mentioned. It concluded that New Hampshire should adopt the conduct of neighboring states. It urged, "From the best information yet obtained, Maryland, Virginia, and South-Carolina are decidedly in favour: Accounts from New York are favourable. Let us then be cautious, that we do not stand alone in rejecting what every State in general convention has already approved, and in State Conventions, as far as it had been considered, adopted."[36]

When the convention was again gaveled into order, the final vote for ratification was fifty-seven in favor to forty-seven against.

As a result of the debate during New Hampshire's examination of the Constitution, twelve amendments were added to the ratification document, the delegates declaring "that certain amendments & alterations in the said Constitution would remove the fears & quiet the apprehensions of many of the good People of this State & more Effectually guard against an undue Administration of the Federal Government." Many of the amendments proposed by New Hampshire later appeared in the Constitution in the Bill of Rights.

The New Hampshire convention, like many other state conventions, feared a strong central government that would take away states' rights. It recommended, therefore that "it be Explicitly declared that all Powers not expressly & particularly Delegated by the aforesaid Constitution are reserved to the several States to be, by them Exercised." It was also concerned with representation, recommending that there should be one representative for every 30,000 persons until the number of representatives reached 200 and that Congress should not be permitted to "make regulations contrary to a free and equal Representation." Taxation was another concern. The convention wanted it stated explicitly that the federal government could not levy direct taxes unless funds from imposts, excise taxes, and other resources were insufficient; even then, the government should first make "a Requisition upon the States, to Assess, Levy, & pay their respective proportions, of such requisitions agreeably to the Census fixed in the said Constitution in such way & manner as the Legislature of the State shall think best." If a state should resist, it should be charged its proportional obligation along with six percent interest. Nor did the convention want the government to create monopolies.

Three of the recommended amendments dealt with citizens' rights in legal matters. One stated that no one should be tried for a high crime without having been indicted by a grand jury, with the exclusion of military matters. A second amendment recommended that state common law courts should try common-law cases between citizens of different states without appeal to federal courts "unless the sum or value of the thing in Controversy amount to three Thousand Dollars." Another suggested that jury trials, if requested by either party, should be required in civil actions at common law concerning disputes between citizens of different states.

Finally, the New Hampshire convention recommended four amendments that spoke to its recent revolutionary experience. The first would prohibit Congress from consenting to "any Person holding an Office of Trust or profit under the United States" accepting "any Title of Nobility or any other Title or Office from any King, Prince, or Foreign State." The second would prohibit a standing army in peacetime without the consent of 75 percent of both the House and the Senate as well as the quartering of soldiers in private homes in peacetime without the consent of the owners. The third would prohibit Congress from making laws "touching Religion, or to infringe the rights of Conscience." And last, Congress would be prohibited from disarming "any Citizen unless such as are or have been in Actual Rebellion."[37]

The Constitution was adopted by a convention of the states on September 17, 1787, and was subsequently ratified by the several states. New Hampshire ratified it on June 21, 1788. It was the ninth and binding state to ratify it. The Constitution was now binding on the eight other states that had ratified it.

THE 1792 NEW HAMPSHIRE CONSTITUTION

On September 7, 1791, New Hampshire held another constitutional convention to reform its own constitution. This convention proposed seventy-two amendments to the 1784 document. The delegates did not want to leave anything to chance. The constitution had to be redrafted into a new document. It was submitted for popular approval on February 8, 1792. Forty-six of the seventy-two amendments proposed by the convention were accepted by the towns on May 7, 1792. The constitution became effective on June 5, 1793. Officially, the 1784 constitution is the base document, and the 1792 constitution is considered an amendment of it. Although this priority may be a matter of some historical contention, the 1792 Bill of Rights is interesting in its own right. It echoed the amendments New Hampshire delegates wanted to see in the U.S. Constitution and retained much of the language of the 1784 version. Like the 1784 constitution, it was a remarkable statement of natural rights philosophy, but this time tempered by practical Protestant ethic.

The constitution declared that "all men are born equally free and independent." Government "originates from the people, is founded in consent, and instituted for the general good."[38] Among the "natural, essential, and inherent rights" possessed by all men are "enjoying and defending life and liberty, acquiring, possessing, and protecting property; and, in a word, of seeking an obtaining happiness." But "when men enter into a State of society they surrender up some of their natural rights to that society, in order to ensure the protection of others." The "rights of conscience," however, are among the natural rights that are "in their very nature unalienable, because no equivalent can be given or received for them."

The people of New Hampshire "have the sole and exclusive right of governing themselves as a free, sovereign and independent State," except for those rights not "expressly delegated to the United States of America, in Congress assembled." Because all power resides in the people, government employees remain always accountable to the people, and no government office can be hereditary. Government is to exist for "the common benefit," not for the "private interest or emolument of any one man, family, or class of men." Thus, if

> ends of government are perverted and public liberty manifestly endangered, and all other means of redress are ineffectual, the people of right ought and may to reform the old, or establish a new government. The doctrine of non-resistance against arbitrary power and oppression is absurd, slavish, and destructive of the good and happiness of mankind.

This reasoning guaranteed what might be called the right of revolution, but in return for government protection of "life, liberty, and property" the members of the community have an obligation to contribute their share "in the expense of such protection, and to yield his personal service, when necessary, or equivalent."

This constitution provided for a government of law, with executive, legislative, and judicial powers maintained as separately as humanly possible, in which every citizen was entitled to timely legal remedies for injuries and "to obtain right and justice freely, without being obliged to purchase it." Citizens could not be tried for the same crime once acquitted, jury trials were guaranteed for capital offenses as well as other cases when requested, and criminal trials were, in most cases, to be held in the county in which the crime occurred. The courts were to issue punishments that fit the crimes, "the true design of all punishment being to reform, not to exterminate, mankind." Citizens were protected from excessive bail and unreasonable searches and seizures as well as retrospective laws. Freedom of assembly, "liberty of the press," and a well-regulated military under civilian control were guaranteed. Perhaps of greatest concern to many citizens, the constitution clearly stated that "no subsidy, charge, tax, impost or duty shall be established, fixed, laid, or levied, under any pretext whatsoever, without the consent of the people or their representatives in the legislature, or authority derived from that body."

"A frequent recurrence to the fundamental principles of the constitution, and a constant adherence to justice, moderation, temperance, industry, frugality, and all the social virtues, are indispensably necessary to preserve the blessings of liberty and good government." This statement in the constitution inextricably entwines traditional Protestant values with liberty and good government. Article 5 provides for the freedom of worship: "no person shall be hurt, molested, or restrained in his person, liberty, or estate for worshipping God in the manner most agreeable to the dictates of his own conscience, or for his religious profession, sentiments, or persuasion." Yet even this statement of religious freedom was qualified by practical consideration. The exercise of worship could "not disturb the public peace or disturb others in their religious worship."

The next article of the state constitution in effect institutionalizes Protestant-ism as the state religion by empowering the legislature to promote "morality and piety" by authorizing "from time to time, the several towns, parishes, bodies corporate, or religious societies within this State, to make adequate provisions, at their own expense, for the support and maintenance of public protestant teachers of piety, religion, and morality."

Article 6 goes on seemingly to contradict the first section by stating that, "every denomination of Christians, demeaning themselves quietly and as good subjects of the State, shall be equally under the protection of the law; and no subordination of any one sect or denomination to another shall ever be established by law." In effect, Catholicism, although a Christian religion, is neatly removed from the mainstream because it is not a Protestant denomination. Other religions such as Judaism and Islam are also completely excluded. Additionally, Article 14 states that a person seeking office as a member of the House of Representatives "shall be of the Protestant religion." Article 29 states that "no person shall be capable of being elected a senator who is not of the Protestant religion." Without question, this provision was in violation of Article 5, granting freedom of worship. It was not until 1968 that any reference to Protestantism was removed by an amendment. Article 6 now reads, in part, "And every person, denomination or sect shall be equally under the protection of the law; and no subordination of any one sect, denomination or persuasion to another shall ever be established."[39]

Another most interesting provision of this Bill of Rights section is Article 13. It states: "No person who is conscientiously scrupulous about the lawfulness of bearing arms, shall be compelled thereto, provided he will pay an equivalent." This in effect allows for conscientious objectors to not participate in war as long as they pay the equivalent. The price of equivalency was not stated anywhere. This provision was later removed by amendment.

Finally, the New Hampshire Constitution of 1792 does not mention slaves or slavery. Through property requirements, it excluded anyone who was a slave from being a citizen and participating in the government. It also, of course, excluded women from political power.

CONCLUSION

The original colonial New Hampshire towns were given grants as money-making ventures by the British Council of New England. Without any natural luxurious wealth such as gold or spices, the seacoast settlers engaged in farming, salt production, fishing, and the timber trade. By the late 1600s there were fifty working sawmills. The Isles of Shoals were home to more than one thousand fishermen and their families. The New Hampshire tradition of personal freedom, hard work, and frugality inherited from these early settlers were inculcated into the state's political arena through its constitution. To the present day, New Hampshire's politically astute citizens are the first to express their opinions on U.S. presidential candidates by holding the first primary election in the country, a fitting place for the state that clinched the ratification of the U.S. Constitution.

NOTES

1. Ralph N. Hill, *Yankee Kingdom Vermont and New Hampshire*, rev. ed. (New York: Harper & Row, 1973), pp. 9–10.

2. Ibid., p. 10.

3. "Grant of the Province of New Hampshire to John Wollaston, Esq., AN. 1635," in *The Federal and State Constitutions Colonial Charters, and Other Organic Laws of the States, Territories, and Colonies Now or Heretofore Forming the United States of America, New Hampshire State Papers*, comp. and ed. Francis Newton Thorpe, 26, 6: 64–66 (Washington, DC: Government Printing Office, 1909) (hereafter cited as *New Hampshire State Papers*). The Avalon Project at Yale Law School, www.yale.edu/lawweb/avalon/avalon.html (hereafter cited as The Avalon Project) (accessed September 12, 2003).

4. Ibid., "Grant of the Province of New Hampshire From Mr. Wollaston to Mr. Mason, 11th June, 1635," pp. 66–69.

5. Jere R. Daniell, *Colonial New Hampshire: A History* (Millwood, NY: KTO Press, 1981), p. 21.

6. Ibid., pp. 26–29.

7. Hill, *Yankee Kingdom*, p. 19.

8. "Agreement of the Settlers at Exeter in New Hampshire, 1639," in *Federal and State Constitutions, Colonial Charters, and Other Organic Laws of the States*. The Avalon Project.

9. Ralph May, *Early Portsmouth History* (Boston: C.E. Goodspeed, 1926), p. 135.

10. "The Combinations of the Inhabitants Upon the Piscataqua River for Government, 1641," in *The Federal and State Constitutions, Colonial Charters, and Other Organic Laws of the States*. The Avalon Project.

11. Daniell, *Colonial New Hampshire, A History*, p. 69.

12. Charles H. Bell, *History of the Town of Exeter, New Hampshire* (Exeter, NH: J.E. Farwell, 1888), p. 45.

13. Ibid., p. 46.

14. Daniell, *Colonial New Hampshire, A History*, p. 71.

15. Ibid., p. 78.

16. Elizabeth Forbes Morison and Elting E Morison, *New Hampshire, A Bicentennial History* (New York: Norton and Co., 1976), p. 14.

17. Daniell, *Colonial New Hampshire, A History*, p. 135.

18. Morison, *New Hampshire*, pp. 18–20.

19. Bell, *History of the Town of Exeter*, p. 220.

20. "Cocheco Massacre," www.seacoastnh.com/history/colonial/massacre.html.

21. Ibid.

22. Ibid.

23. "Portsmouth Indian Treaty of 1713," www.seacoatnh.com/history/colonia/treaty.htm.

24. Nancy Coffey Heffernan and Ann Page Stecker, *New Hampshire: Crosscurrents in Its Development* (Graham, NH: Tompson & Potter, 1986), p. 53.

25. Ibid., p. 55.

26. Daniell, *Colonial New Hampshire, A History*, p. 242.

27. "Constitution of New Hampshire—1776," in *Federal and State Constitutions, Colonial Charters, and Other Organic Laws of the United States*. The Avalon Project

28. "Constitutions of the Several States," www.TheGreenPapers.com/slg/constitution.phtml.

29. Henry Steele Commager, *Documents of American History*, 2 vols, 8th ed. (New York: Appleton-Century-Crofts, 1968), 1:105.

30. Jeremy Belknap, *The History of New Hampshire*, 3 vols. (Boston: Belknap and Young, 1791–1792).

31. Heffernan, *New Hampshire: Crosscurrents in Its Development*, pp. 76–78.

32. Max Farrand, *The Records of the Federal Convention of 1787*, 3 vols. (New Haven: Yale University Press, 1911), 3:14, www.loc.gov.

33. "Credentials of the members of the Federal Convention: State of New Hampshire; June 27, 1787" (reprinted from *Documentary History of the Constitution*, [1894], 1:9–10) in *Documents Illustrative of the Formation of the Union of the American States*, selected, arranged, and indexed by Charles C. Tansill, House Document No. 398 (Washington, DC: Government Printing Office, 1927). The Avalon Project.

34. Founding Fathers Page, National Archives and Records Administration, http://www.nara.gov/exhall/charters/constitution/newhamp.html (accessed September 10, 2003).

35. Ibid.

36. *New Hampshire Gazette*, April 16, 1788.

37. "Ratification of the Constitution by the State of New Hampshire; June 21, 1788" (reprinted from *Documentary History of the Constitution*, [1894], 2:141–144), in *Documents Illustrative of the Formation of the Union of the American States*. The Avalon Project.

38. "New Hampshire Constitution of 1792," in Founder's Library, www.founding.com (accessed September 12, 2003). All quotations from the 1792 constitution are from this source.

39. "New Hampshire State Constitution," www.state.nh.us.

BIBLIOGRAPHY

Adams, Nathaniel. *Annals of Portsmouth*. Portsmouth, NH: Nathaniel Adams, publisher, 1825.

Belknap, Jeremy. *The History of New Hampshire*. 3 vols. Boston: Belknap and Young, 1791–1992.

Bell, Charles H. *History of the Town of Exeter, New Hampshire*. Exeter, NH: J.E. Farwell & Co., 1888.

Bouton, Nathaniel et al., ed. *Documents and Records Relating to the Province, Towns and State of New Hampshire*. 40 vols. Concord, Nashua, and Manchester, NH: Various Publishers, 1867–1943.

Commager, Henry Steele. *Documents of American History*. 2 vols. 8th ed. New York: Appleton-Century-Crofts, 1968.

Committee for a New England Bibliography. *New Hampshire: A Bibliography of Its History*. Boston: G.K. Hall, 1979.

Daniell, Jere R. *Colonial New Hampshire, A History*. Millwood, NY: KTO Press, 1981.

Goodwin, William F., ed. "Journal of the Congress of the Colony of New Hampshire Which Assembled at Exeter December 21st, 1775, and Adopted, January the 5th, the First Written Constitution in the United States." *Historical Magazine*, 2d Ser., 4 (October 1868): 145–154.

Heffernan, Nancy Coffey, and Ann Page Stecker. *New Hampshire: Crosscurrents in Its Development*. Grantham, NH: Tompson & Rutter Inc., 1986.

May, Ralph. *Early Portsmouth History*. Boston: C.E. Goodspeed & Co., 1926.

Mayo, Lawrence Shaw. *John Langdon of New Hampshire*. Concord, NH: Rumford Press, 1937.

McClintock, John Norris. *History of New Hampshire: Colony, Province, State, 1623–1888*. Boston: B.B. Russell, 1889.

Morison, Elizabeth Forbes, and Elting E. Morison. *New Hampshire, A Bicentennial History*. New York: W.W. Norton, 1976.

New Hampshire American Revolution Bicentennial Commission. *New Hampshire's Role in the American Revolution, 1763–1789: A Bibliography*. Concord: New Hampshire State Library, 1974.

Stackpole, Everett S. *History of New Hampshire*. 5 vols. New York: American Historical Society, 1916.

Stearns, Ezra S., William F. Witcher, and Edward E. Parker, eds. *Genealogical and Family History of the State of New Hampshire: A Record of the Achievements of Her People in the Making of a Commonwealth and the Founding of a Nation*. 4 vols. New York: Lewis Publishing Co., 1908.

Whittaker, Robert. *Land of Lost Content*. Dover, NH: Alan Sutton Publishing, 1994.

☆☆☆

THE STATE OF NEW JERSEY

Ratified the Constitution of the United States: December 18, 1787

Maxine N. Lurie

INTRODUCTION

It is easier to determine precisely how and when Ohio or California became a state than to answer this question for New Jersey. In fact there are actually three possible answers: on July 2, 1776, when it adopted its first state constitution; on July 18, 1776, when the provincial convention formally resolved that New Jersey was a state rather than a colony; or on December 18, 1787, when it became the third state to ratify the U.S. Constitution. As the three possible choices make clear, the road to statehood for New Jersey runs directly through the maelstrom of the American Revolution and then the Confederation period. On the way New Jersey residents had to make difficult decisions first on which fork to take (colony or state) and then on the form the Union should take (confederation or federation). Once the Constitutional Convention agreed to equal representation in the senate, the last decision, for ratification, was easy. For probably the only time in its history, New Jersey residents were unanimous on a political question—they favored the new Constitution.

Behind that decision is the story of how New Jersey became the place it was in 1776, why it supported the Revolution, and how it survived the war that followed. For context it is necessary to go back to the seventeenth-century colonial origins of the Garden State. New Jersey's complicated early history resulted in an unusually diverse population and a hard-to-classify political system, the consequence of myriad divisions. Because New Jersey had an overwhelmingly rural economy, often existed in the shadow of larger and more powerful neighbors (New York and Pennsylvania), and had relatively few direct contacts with England, it was slow to join the Revolution. In June 1776,

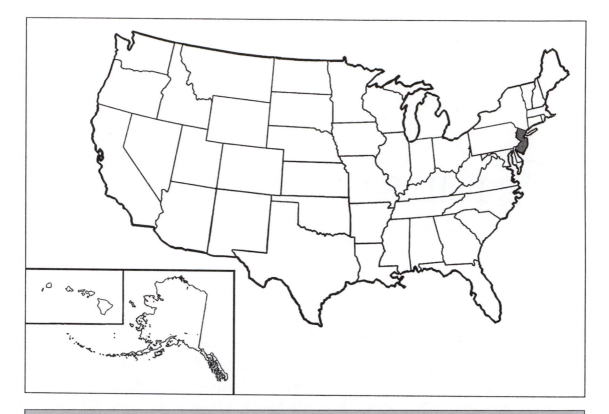

New Jersey

Territorial Development:

- Charles II grants New Jersey to James, the Duke of York, March 12, 1664
- Continental Congress approves Declaration of Independence from Great Britain, July 4, 1776
- Great Britain formally recognizes American independence through the Treaty of Paris, September 3, 1783
- New Jersey becomes the third state to ratify the U.S. Constitution, December 18, 1787

Capitals Prior to Statehood:

- Perth Amboy and Burlington, twin capitals, 1703–1775
- No fixed capital, 1775–1787

State Capitals:

- No fixed capital, 1787–1790
- Trenton, 1790–present

Origin of State Name: Sir John Berkeley and Sir George Carteret named New Jersey after the Island of Jersey in the English Channel.

First Governor: William Livingston
Governmental Organization: Bicameral
Population at Statehood: 184,139
Geographical Size: 7,417 square miles

however, the colony fell quickly into step with the supporters of independence. By the fall it had become the "cockpit of the revolution," and because of its location was the center of the war itself. Military incidents in the state continued until the peace treaty of 1783. The severe destruction wrought during the war directly influenced New Jersey's attitudes toward the Articles of Confederation and then the Constitution. Lacking resources such as taxable imports or land to sell and holding numerous state and continental debts from the war, residents overwhelmingly wanted a stronger national government that could help solve the problems they were experiencing. As a result New Jersey quickly ratified the Constitution and became the first state to approve the Bill of Rights in 1791.

THE COLONIAL PERIOD

During the seventeenth century New Jersey was, in succession, a Swedish, Dutch, and then a British colony. Starting in 1638, the New Sweden colony scattered settlements across both sides of the lower Delaware River (in part of the present-day states of Delaware, Pennsylvania, and New Jersey). From the beginning Swedish claims were contested by the Dutch who, starting in 1621, settled mostly to the north along the Hudson River but claimed the entire region. In 1655, after several confrontations, the Dutch took control, ending Sweden's colonial efforts. New Netherland stretched from Albany to the Delaware River and by 1660 included the fortified town of Bergen in what would become northern New Jersey. The Dutch, however, did not maintain their control for long, because New Netherland was bracketed by English colonies to the north and to the south. English mercantilists also viewed Dutch merchants as interlopers in the tobacco trade. In 1664 Charles II granted his brother, James, Duke of York, title to a region that ranged from Martha's Vineyard to Delaware Bay. When British warships appeared in New Amsterdam's harbor, Dutch authorities agreed to surrender, and most residents remained in the colony that was now New York.

While Richard Nicolls, the first proprietary governor of colonial New York, imposed his authority on the region and began to give out land grants, the Duke of York in England divided the province. He deeded the land south of 40°41' north latitude and between the Hudson and Delaware rivers to two men, Sir George Carteret and John, Lord Berkeley, both of whom had supported royal government during the English Civil War. In 1665 they wrote their "Concessions and Agreements" for New Jersey outlining the form of government and terms for potential colonists. Meanwhile settlers, primarily Puritans from New England, already had started moving into the region after obtaining land patents from Governor Nicolls. Their land claims, rejected by subsequent proprietors, became the source of land disputes that resulted in riots in the eighteenth century and were not resolved until the nineteenth century.

Because it had been the host to a succession of colonies, by 1670 New Jersey was home to Swedish Lutherans, members of the Dutch Reformed church, English Puritans, Baptists, Anglicans, and members of a few other religious groups. Some native Lenape remained, and the importation of African slaves slowly began. Both the government and composition of New Jersey soon became even more complex. In 1673 the Dutch, while at war with England, re-conquered the region. Peace and English rule returned in 1674, but Berkeley decided to sell his share of the colony to John Fenwick representing Edward Byllynge, a Quaker unable to act in his own name because of financial difficulties. Although Fenwick and Byllynge later disputed their personal arrangement, New Jersey was now two proprietary colonies, East New Jersey and West New Jersey. By the terms of the Quintipartite agreement of 1676, New Jersey was to be divided on a diagonal line that ran from Little Egg Harbor on the Atlantic northwest to the boundary line with New York on the Delaware River. While Fenwick left to start a settlement in West New Jersey called Salem, Byllynge remained in England, where William Penn and other Quaker leaders worked to settle the dispute between the two over who owned what. The settlement they devised divided the proprietorship into one hundred shares, of which Fenwick received ten. Byllynge sold off most of the remainder to Quaker investors in England, Ireland, Scotland, and Wales, some of whom migrated to the colony. West Jersey was now a Quaker province with members of the sect settling in Salem, Burlington, and other towns in the southwest along the Delaware River.

George Carteret retained East Jersey, along with Philip Carteret, a relative, who tried to govern the colony and get the Nicholls's patentees to take out new proprietary grants. In 1681, after his death, Carteret's widow sold East Jersey to a consortium of twelve (later twenty-four) investors led by William Penn. Most were Quakers, although the group also included several prominent non-Quaker Scots. Penn turned his attention to the newest refuge for Quakers, his Pennsylvania proprietorship, but the Scots became so involved in settling East Jersey and establishing the port town of Perth Amboy, that it has been called Scotland's "first colony."

By the 1690s the proprietors in both West and East Jersey were having difficulty maintaining their governments. There were disputes about the original grant from the Duke of York to Berkeley and Carteret (whether the right to govern could be given by the Duke or was reserved to the Crown alone), conflicts with the settlers over quit rents and the right to govern, and an effort by the English government to centralize the British Empire and, in the process, eliminate the proprietary colonies. Under pressure from all sides, the proprietors of both Jerseys agreed to surrender their claims to the governments of the Jerseys to the Crown in 1702. New Jersey was again one colony but was now under royal jurisdiction. From the arrival of Lord Cornbury, the first royal governor, in 1703 to 1738 the colony shared its governor with New York, but its legislature remained a separate body. From 1738 until 1776 English authorities appointed a separate governor for the colony.

The complex story of New Jersey's origins in the seventeenth century had important long-range consequences. First, by 1702, Scotch, Irish, and French settlers had been added to the already complex mix, and they were Presbyterian, Quaker, Huguenot, and Anglican. Germans who later followed added German Lutherans, German Reformed, and Moravian congregations. Second, the two proprietary groups gave up their claims to the government but not to the land of New Jersey. The West Jersey Council of Proprietors (1688) and the East Jersey Board of Proprietors (1685), both formed to handle land grants and records, continued in existence, and issued disputed land claims in the colony. Third, royal governors agreed to alternate meetings of the legislature between the two previous capitols, Burlington and Perth Amboy; to balance membership of the council between the two sections; and to appoint two treasurers in the colony, one for the eastern division and the other for the western. Thus the heritage of the early colonial period was a complex ethnic, religious, sectional, and political mix. New Jersey's early colonial history and heritage directly affected its actions during the Revolution and its aftermath.

Added to this complex heritage were several important developments. While original land disputes derived from the Nicolls patents remained unsettled, additional controversies over titles arose from grants made during Cornbury's tenure, claims based on purchases from Native Americans, and disagreements over the boundaries between New Jersey and New York as well as between East and West Jersey. These disagreements fueled by the uncertainty of land titles led, particularly in the period from 1735 to 1755, to a series of riots in the colony. At the same time there were the controversies that stemmed from the Great Awakening. The religious revivals that spread through the colonies in the wake of preaching by George Whitefield, the Tennents, and others divided New Jersey Presbyterians into "New Light" and "Old Light" factions and the Dutch Reformed into comparable "Coetus" (liberal) and "Conferentie" (conservative) groups. In the 1760s New Jersey's Anglican ministers, led by the Rev. Thomas Bradbury Chandler, called for the appointment of a bishop for the American colonies. This controversial proposal was opposed by many dissenting Protestants who, together, were an overwhelming majority in the colony. In addition, as in other colonies, the colonial legislature gradually acquired more power until it exerted a great deal of actual local control. This process was particularly marked in New Jersey, where royal appointees were rare.

NEW JERSEY BEFORE THE REVOLUTION

By the 1760s, New Jersey was characterized by its diverse population, its two-colony history, and the remaining proprietary groups. In terms of land it was tenth in size of the thirteen original states; in population it stood ninth, with about 130,000 residents. The population included approximately 10,000 blacks,

817

most of whom were slaves, but probably no more than a few hundred Lenape remained.

New Jersey was overwhelmingly rural and agricultural, producing a wide variety of livestock (cattle, sheep, and hogs), and crops (wheat and other grains, vegetables, and flax). The products of its farms were consumed locally or sent to nearby urban areas and the West Indies. Nascent industries included iron production from mines in the northern part of the state and the bogs in the south, copper, flour, lumber, glass, and leather goods. New Jersey had a number of relatively small towns and no significant cities or large ports. The largest town was Elizabethtown with an estimated 350 households. Few of its merchants were engaged in long-distance trade. Most of the colony's wares, particularly its imported goods, were routed through Philadelphia, which dominated West Jersey economically, and New York City, which dominated East Jersey. Many of the colony's leading merchants, lawyers, and large landowners had business and family ties to the two neighboring urban centers, which also served to distribute news to the colony. Not until after the Revolution started did New Jersey have a newspaper of its own.

New Jersey as a whole had been described by Governor Belcher in 1748 as "the best country I have seen for middling fortunes, and for people who have to live by the sweat of their brows."[1] Although there were a number of large landowners (more in East Jersey than in West Jersey), most farms were relatively small (though somewhat larger in the west than in the east). Also, reflecting the colony's origins, most Quakers lived in the western section of the colony. These differences proved important.

Thus, although New Jersey was united by its largely agricultural economy, it was divided historically into two sections and was splintered by a wide variety of religious groups. The numerous divisions had an impact on politics, leading historian Larry R. Gerlach to note that the "structure and operation of Jersey politics remain an enigma for scholars," because it was a place with "no easily identifiable, province-wide political groupings."[2] There were no obvious emerging "parties" like the DeLancey and Livingston factions in New York, nor clear-cut outstanding leaders, either radical like Sam Adams or conservative like Thomas Hutchinson in Massachusetts. Although the "Perth Amboy Group," consisting primarily of merchants, lawyers, and East Jersey proprietors, most of whom were Anglicans, was important, its power was countered by the West Jersey proprietors and by an antiproprietary faction in East Jersey. Significantly, from 1763 on, New Jersey enjoyed a popular royal governor who was a colonial by birth and an astute politician by training. William Franklin was the illegitimate son of Benjamin Franklin, who learned politics from his father while in Pennsylvania and studied law and the empire while in England with him. Appointed in 1763, Franklin tried from 1765 on to keep New Jersey in the empire and to retain his governorship. Although he ultimately failed, his administration survived longer than that of any other royal governor.

Small, complex in composition, a relative rural backwater, overshadowed by its neighbors who were reluctant to join the Revolution, New Jersey, not surprisingly, played no major role in the events leading up to it. When the English government passed the Sugar and then the Stamp Acts, there was little response from the colony. The assembly declined to appoint representatives to the Stamp Act congress. By the end of September members had second thoughts. To the consternation of Governor Franklin, who had reported proudly to England that the colony was "quiet," a rump session of legislature met on October 3, 1765. It appointed three men who attended the Stamp Act congress that started four days later in New York. In addition, lawyers in the colony held a meeting in which they agreed not to use any stamps, halting business and, in effect, "striking" until the law was repealed. When the assembly was next called into session, it adopted a series of resolutions that reiterated much of the discussions in the Stamp Act congress and then went further by labeling the British legislation "unconstitutional, contrary to the Rights of the Subject, and dangerous in its Consequences." In a colony with little long-distance trade and no newspapers, this strongly worded opposition was based on the principles of self-rule, "no taxation without representation," and "the Right of Trials by Jury."[3] Slow to act, in the end the colony declared its opposition to measures that most residents clearly considered British violations of their rights.

In the period that followed, from 1766 to 1774, New Jersey was more concerned with local issues than with imperial matters. Most important to its residents were the robbery of the East Jersey treasury, the need for paper money, the boundary disputes with New York and between the two sets of proprietors, and the high fees charged by some lawyers (the last produced several riots in 1770). The first two issues were important because they eroded Franklin's political stock with legislators, whereas the boundary issues set residents in the two sections against each other.

In 1768 the home of Stephen Skinner, the East Jersey treasurer, was robbed of more than £6,570 in colonial funds. The theft initiated a long-simmering dispute first over who should replace the money and then over whether the governor or the legislature had authority to appoint the colony's treasurers. Not resolved until 1774, the arguments engaged Franklin in a battle with the legislature that he ultimately lost, along with some of his good standing with that body. This difficulty was compounded by Franklin's inability to get British approval for colonial issues of paper money. New Jersey, usually chronically short of specie, had long been dependent on loan-office issues of paper money. Such measures, viewed with disfavor in England, became illegal after the passage of the Currency Act in 1764, which forbade the use of legal tender issues. Franklin worked to convince the British government to revise its policies, but changes made in 1774 came too late to help him politically.

The third important local issue involved the location of the northern boundary with New York and the dividing line between the two Jersey proprietorships.

Both questions dated back to the seventeenth century but became more important as settlement spread. In 1769 a royal boundary commission was created to settle the dispute between the two colonies. Although the proposed solution satisfied neither side, it became the basis for a boundary line that had been surveyed by 1774. The West Jersey proprietors used this line as the basis for a request that a corrected "province" line be surveyed between the two sections. The war intervened, however, and this question returned to impact politics in the 1780s.

NEW JERSEY AND THE REVOLUTION

Despite New Jersey's concern with its own affairs in this period, it did protest the Townshend duties and then the Tea Act. Students at the College of New Jersey (now Princeton University) symbolically burned tea, and in December 1773 a group of local rabble-rousers in Greenwich, down in Cumberland County on the Delaware River, reduced the cargo from a tea ship intended for Philadelphia to ashes. These events were relatively minor affairs because, although New Jersey residents protested the measures and boycotted British goods, the colony, without major shipping interests, was less directly affected by the new laws than other places. This situation started to change after the Boston Tea Party provoked the British government to pass the Intolerable Acts. New Jersey residents were slowly being caught up in an imperial controversy that involved far more than issues of taxation. The process took time, because New Jersey was rural and relatively conservative and because Governor William Franklin was determined to keep it in the empire. Because he refused to let go, and because there were no radical leaders or urban mobs to grab control, New Jersey ended up with two governments co-existing from 1774 to 1776. Royal rule continued even as a new provincial government was gradually created.[4] In the end, the extra-legal government that developed created the state of New Jersey.

In February 1774 the assembly established a formal committee of correspondence to remain in contact "with our Sister Colonies," making it the last colony to take this action.[5] County committees also were formed to help maintain contact in a time of growing crisis. In July, the Whigs led by James Kinsey (a Quaker, lawyer, and member of the assembly) were unable to get either Cortland Skinner, speaker of the assembly (and later, next to Franklin, New Jersey's most prominent Loyalist), or the governor to call the legislature into session to address the Intolerable Acts. The assembly then convened a provincial convention to which local committees of correspondence sent delegates. The meeting denounced the Intolerable Acts as "unconstitutional and oppressive," adopted a series of resolutions expressing its opposition, and began a campaign to show support for Boston (its port closed by the acts) by collecting money and goods for it gathered from across the colony. It also appointed five delegates to the Continental Congress: James Kinsey, William Livingston, John De Hart, Stephen Crane, and Richard Smith, all lawyers.

The following May (1775) the first of three provincial congresses met, with delegates sent by an assortment of groups throughout the colony. Meeting just after the incidents at Lexington and Concord, the congress authorized taxes and called out militia forces as it started to assume the powers of government. In August, to ensure its continued existence, this first provincial congress provided for annual elections to be held every September. It also created a committee of safety to act when the congress was not in session. The second provincial congress met in several sessions from October 1775 through March 1776. Its main efforts involved collecting revenues and military preparations, but it also issued paper money. Then in February 1776 it appointed delegates to the Second Continental Congress (William Livingston, Richard Smith, John De Hart, John Cooper, and Jonathan Dickinson Sergeant) and provided that they be paid for their expenses. The first three men had served in the First Continental Congress. Cooper was a Quaker, only Sergeant was known as a strong supporter of independence.

During this period royal government continued. The legislature met in March 1774, but after that Franklin deliberately avoided calling it back into session to prevent any action by the assembly that would support the growing intercolonial protest movement. He relented in January 1775, when he gambled that he could persuade New Jersey to break ranks with the First Continental Congress and send a separate conciliatory remonstrance to the king. He told the legislature it had a choice of "two Roads—one evidently leading to Peace, Happiness, and a Restoration of the publick Tranquility—the other inevitably conducting you to Anarchy, Misery, and all the Horrors of a Civil War," language making crystal clear which path he thought they should take.[6] Learning of Franklin's intentions, three Elizabethtown Whigs (William Livingston, John De Hart, and Elias Boudinot—the first two of whom represented the colony in the Continental Congress) hastily journeyed to Perth Amboy where they convinced the assembly to remain in step with the other colonies. The assembly then approved the resolutions of the First Continental Congress and reappointed to the Second Continental Congress the same five delegates that the provincial convention had appointed to the first. Although the assembly also sent its own remonstrance to the king, the wording defending the colonist's rights so infuriated Franklin that he refused to send it through official channels. Ironically the message was delivered by the colony's agent in London, his father Benjamin Franklin.

The old legislature met again in May 1775 just before the first provincial congress (with some members sitting in both bodies) but did little. It met once more starting in November of that year, when Franklin again tried to influence the proceedings. Conservatives in the legislature introduced three resolutions condemning the idea of independence. In early December the Second Continental Congress responded by sending several of its most persuasive speakers, John Dickinson of Pennsylvania, George Wythe of Virginia, and John Jay of New York, to urge New Jersey not to act separately. The legislature dropped the resolutions, agreeing instead to support the "common cause." The royal legislature never met again.

By January 1776 the tide had begun to change. Franklin was increasingly regarded with well-deserved suspicion, the idea of independence gained support, although slowly, and the provincial congress gained strength. The year began dramatically when, at 2 o'clock A.M., on January 7, colonial militia forces surrounded the Perth Amboy home of the governor, placing him under arrest and in the process terrifying his wife Elizabeth Downes Franklin. The subsequent negotiations of Chief Justice Frederick Smyth, a Loyalist and the lone British-born appointee in the government, led to Franklin's release. The arrest was intended as a warning to Franklin, but he failed to take heed, maintained his steady stream of reports to royal officials in England, and continued to work to hold New Jersey in the empire.

Before the month was out, Thomas Paine's *Common Sense* appeared in print encouraging the idea of independence, which increasingly appeared to be the only logical step as war continued and more American blood was shed. The Rev. John Witherspoon, leader of the Presbyterian Church in America and president of the College of New Jersey, became one of the earliest and most vocal advocates of independence. By April he was echoed by the Rev. Jacob Green of Hanover in Morris County, also a Presbyterian, who argued in a pamphlet called *Observations on the Reconciliation of Great-Britain and the Colonies* that it was time to separate. In March the second provincial congress called for the early election of new delegates to a third provincial congress. Held in May, this election was tacitly understood to be a referendum on independence.

From the Stamp Act on, New Jersey residents had agreed that British measures violated their rights but not on how to remedy the situation. As a result the move toward independence reflected some hesitation. The growing chorus in favor of separation was countered by the persistent arguments of Governor Franklin and other Loyalists, such as Anglican minister Thomas Bradbury Chandler, that such a step was unnecessary and would bring disaster. At the same time moderate Whigs, like Elias Boudinot, and New Jersey's Quakers counseled caution. Charles Petitt summed up the situation when he advised a friend in March 1776 that the Whigs in New Jersey needed to avoid "hasty" action, warning "An explicit Declaration [of independence]...now, would probably raise up such a Schism as would be more dreadful than any outward Enemy. Whereas a few Months, perhaps a few weeks may, like the Sun to ripening Fruit, make that pleasant and desirable, which appears sour and disgusting."[7]

Resolution came in May and June 1776 as New Jersey was pushed to act from two directions. First, on May 15, 1776, the Second Continental Congress sent a resolution to all the colonies stating that if they had not formed a government they should do so. Second, Franklin called for the royal legislature to hold a session at the end of June, forcing counter action. The final factor at this juncture was that Whigs who had come to support independence dominated the third provincial congress. Pettit's fruit had ripened. In June 1776 the provincial congress acted quickly, ordering the arrest of Franklin, prohibiting the old legislature from meeting, appointing a committee to write a constitution, and selecting new delegates to the Continental Congress to replace those who had either resigned or appeared too hesitant on the crucial question at hand.[8] At this point New Jersey moved more rapidly than its middle-colony neighbors, having taken a series of actions that, first, put it clearly in the rebel camp and, second, created the state of New Jersey.

On June 14 and 15 the provincial congress resolved that William Franklin, the "late Governor of New Jersey," was "an enemy to the liberties of this country," and stopped his salary.[9] At first he was offered a "parole," the opportunity to remain in New Jersey, but only if he remained quiet. After his refusal he was sent to Connecticut and placed in jail. While he was there, his wife, who had taken refuge in New York City, died. Later exchanged, Franklin headed the Associated Loyalists, a group that conducted raids into New Jersey and elsewhere during the war. After the war, he went to England where he lived as a bitter exile until 1813.

On June 21 the provincial congress voted 54-3 "That a government be formed for the regulating the internal police of this Colony, pursuant to the recommendation of the Continental Congress on the fifteenth of May last." On June 24 it appointed a committee of ten, headed by the Rev. Jacob Green and including Jonathan Dickinson Sergeant, which quickly wrote a constitution.

On June 22 five men were selected to represent the colony in Philadelphia: John Witherspoon, Abraham Clark, Richard Stockton, Francis Hopkinson, and John Hart. Clark, a surveyor, farmer, and politician, was, like Witherspoon, known as an early supporter of independence. Hopkinson and Stockton were former members of the royal council, lawyers who now agreed that independence was necessary. Hart a substantial farmer and former speaker of the assembly, was likewise convinced of the need for independence. John Adams later recalled that New Jersey had deliberately sent a "new sett [of delegates] on purpose to vote for Independence."[10] This was clearly the intention, because the instructions written the day they were selected empowered them to "join with the Delegates of the other Colonies…in the most vigorous measures for supporting the just rights and liberties of America. And if you shall judge it necessary and expedient for this purpose, we empower you to join with them in declaring the United Colonies independent of Great Britain."[11] Jonathan Dickerson Sergeant, a week earlier, was sure that whomever the provincial congress selected would vote for independence; he wrote Adams, "We are passing the Rubicon, and our delegates in Congress, on the first of July, will vote plump." He was off by one day. On July 2 New Jersey's delegates in Philadelphia voted for independence, while members of the third provincial congress in Burlington voted for a constitution that included its own declaration of independence.[12] Left in doubt was what they would call this new government.

COLONY OR STATE

New Jersey's 1776 constitution began with a preamble declaring the colony's independence. Government, it argued, was based on a "Compact, derived from the People." George III had broken the existing compact by refusing "Protection to the good People of these Colonies," consenting to "Sundry Acts of the British Parliament," and by making "War upon them in the most cruel and unnatural Manner, for no other Cause than asserting their just Rights." The result was that government was "at an end." To preserve order, "unite the People," and provide for their "Happiness and Safety," this constitution created a new government for the "Colony of New Jersey." This constitution provided a brief but clear statement of the compact theory of government and the right of revolution. Shorter than Jefferson's more famous declaration, it was based on the same eighteenth-century concepts.

The new government was to consist of a governor, council, and assembly. As in the initial constitutions written by other states, and as part of the general reaction against royal rule, power was concentrated in the legislature. The constitution provided for a weak governor who was selected annually by the two houses of the legislature meeting jointly and who had no veto. Each county annually elected one member of the council and three representatives for the assembly. There were property qualifications: £1,000 for the council, £500 for the assembly, and £50 to vote. Some stake in society was needed to participate in this government. The precise wording of who could vote, probably reflecting the haste of actions in this period, had unintended consequences. The document gave the suffrage to "all Inhabitants of this Colony of full Age who are worth Fifty Pounds proclamation Money." This restatement of a measure passed by the provincial congress in February 1776 widened the electorate by including all property; valued in local paper money, not just land. Under its vague statement of "all Inhabitants," blacks and women who owned property could vote in New Jersey until an 1807 law disqualified them. Finally, the constitution in effect continued the old judicial system under which the governor sat as chancery judge and the court of appeals consisted of the governor and members of the council. Powers were not separated among three branches, as they would be under the United States Constitution of 1787 or in later New Jersey constitutions in 1844 and 1947.

New Jersey's first constitution, also unlike later state documents, did not have a separate bill of rights. It did, however, include provisions clearly meant to protect those rights considered most crucial, even specifying that these were to be "without Repeal forever." Included were annual elections, the right to trial by jury, and religious freedom. No one was to be denied "the inestimable Privilege of worshipping Almighty God in a Manner agreeable to the Dictates of his own Conscience." A person could not be "compelled to attend any Place of Worship, contrary to his own Faith and Judgment" nor required to "pay Tithes, Taxes, or any other Rates" to support a church. There was also to be "no Establishment of any one religious Sect in this Province in Preference to another." The only limitation was that only Protestants could hold office, and, by implication, vote. The constitution also stated that those accused of a crime were to have "the same Privileges of Witnesses and Counsel, as their Prosecutors are or shall be entitled to," but this was included without the phrase "forever."

Under royal rule New Jersey had neither annual elections nor an established church. The diverse groups of Protestants in the colony, with the exception of the Anglicans, did not want the latter. Trial by jury clearly was regarded as a sacred right by the early Quaker settlers, who had provided protections for this in the 1676 Concessions of West Jersey. Concerns about protecting this particular right appear in New Jersey protests of British measures from the Stamp Act on. The new constitution protected what were seen as essential rights and included the requirement that future members of the legislature take an oath of office in which they promised not to abrogate them.

The New Jersey Constitution ends with a statement providing "that if a reconciliation [sic] between Great Britain and these Colonies should take Place...this Charter shall be null and void." This statement needs to be understood in its context. New Jersey was one of only four states to write a constitution before the Declaration of Independence; of the four, two others, New Hampshire and South Carolina, also hedged.[13] New Jersey had a large Quaker population, particularly in the western section, that was overwhelmingly in favor of a peaceful solution and that was represented in the third provincial congress. Finally, this statement was not accepted without a fight. On July 3, the day after the constitution was approved, a second vote was taken on a resolution not to publish the constitution until this last statement could be reconsidered by the full membership of the third provincial congress. At that time, British forces had been sighted off the coast of New Jersey, and nearly half the members were absent, preoccupied with other matters. Several New Jersey patriots, including Jonathan Dickerson Sergeant, switched their votes between July 2 and July 3. He and William Paterson, secretary of the third provincial congress, apparently wanted to wait for members to return and join them in voting to strike out this reservation. They failed, and it stayed in the document. If Sergeant failed to get the objectionable phrase deleted, he did manage to get for New Jersey the "republic" he had recently predicted it would choose.[14] Despite the hesitant note on which it ended, this document was a radical departure from the past. This government, created "by the People," had no king. Power rested in an annually elected legislature unchecked by any other body.

Although it established a republic, the 1776 constitution repeatedly used the term "colony," to the embarrassment in later years of some in New Jersey. Not until a new document was written in 1844 did this wording change. Although the old term remained in the constitution, it was not long used elsewhere. On July 17, 1776, the third provincial congress recorded in its minutes that it had received the Declaration of Independence from the Continental Congress. It acknowledged the declaration with a resolution to support "the said States with our lives and fortunes, and with the whole force of *New-Jersey*." The next day it "*Resolved*, That this house from henceforth, instead of the style and title of the Provincial Congress of *New-Jersey*, do adopt and assume the style and title of the Convention of the State of *New-Jersey*." All future documents were to refer to New Jersey as a "state," not a "colony." The new term appeared in the oath of office taken by members of the legislature when they first met under new constitution in August 1776. Each member pledged "that I do and will bear true Allegiance to the Government established in this State under the Authority of the People."[15]

New Jersey's road to independence was slow, whereas the change in the terminology used for its new government was made quickly, but both were far easier than maintaining the new state in the period that followed. As early as October 1774 a young woman named Jemima Condict, living near Newark, wrote in her diary: "It seems we have troublesome times a Coming for there is a great Disturbance a Broad in the earth & they say it is tea that caused it. So when if they will Quarel about such a trifling thing as that [,] What must we expect But war & I think or at least fear it will be so." She was right to be fearful. Aaron Harrison, the man she later married, served in the New Jersey militia with many men of her family, while she died after having their first child in 1779.[16] The war she had predicted started in Massachusetts on April 19, 1775, but it arrived at New Jersey's front door even as its constitution was being written. The British landed on Staten Island on July 2, 1776, and took Paulus Hook (now part of Jersey City across from Manhattan) in New Jersey on September 23. The capture of Fort Lee overlooking the Hudson River on November 20 and the subsequent retreat of General George Washington and his ragtag army across New Jersey threw the state and its government into disarray. Meanwhile, Loyalists caught their breath and began to organize.

While British forces followed Washington all the way to the Delaware River, but not across the river into Pennsylvania, and took control of much of New Jersey, the new state government moved from place to place until, by the end of December, it had disbanded. On December 22, 1776, patriot General McDougall wrote from Morristown that "This State is totally deranged, without Government, or officers, civil or military, in it, that will act with any spirit. Many of them have gone to the enemy for protection, others are out of the State, and the few that remain are mostly indecisive in their conduct."[17] In these "times that tried men's souls," to paraphrase Thomas Paine's *Crisis Papers*, some 2,700 New Jersey residents accepted the British offer of a pardon. Among them were patriot leaders Richard Stockton, signer of the Declaration of Independence, who had been captured and then imprisoned under terrible conditions in New York until released in ill health, and Samuel Tucker of Trenton, who had been president of the third provincial congress. William Livingston, governor of the new state from 1776 to his death in 1790, later claimed he had not slept in the same place twice during the war. Although this claim was exaggerated, Livingston did have a price on his head, and his home in Elizabethtown was raided in a narrowly failed effort to capture him.

After the battles of Trenton in December 1776 and Princeton in January 1777 turned the tide and resurrected the patriot cause, the British were restricted in the New Jersey territory they held, and the state government regrouped. A council of safety was organized to act when the legislature was not in session. Not until after the Battle of Monmouth in June 1778, however, was the state relatively secure. Until the end of the war New Jersey was subjected to raids and was the location of several minor battles. The new state government, although precarious, was the only civil government in New Jersey after July 1776. Loyalists might raid and rage, but they never gained control.

ARGUMENTS FOR AND AGAINST A STATEHOOD

No single pattern accurately describes who in New Jersey supported the Revolution and creation of a state government and who was opposed. This lack of sharp social, economic, and geographic demarcations is not surprising in a place historically noteworthy for its diversity, divided by sections as well as by religion and ethnicity, and subject to repeated military actions. It is clear, however, that the Revolution became a civil war in much of the state. In New Jersey John Adams's often discounted estimate that Americans were in equal thirds Loyalists, neutrals, and patriots came close to the mark. Although emphasized by some historians, neither social class nor occupation adequately explains the sides that individuals took. As John Pomfret observed in his history of early New Jersey "in either camp [Tory or Whig] one found rich and poor, landed and landless, farmers and merchants, high-ranking and lowly officials, ministers, lawyers, doctors."[18] Women and blacks (both free and slave) also had divided allegiances. Religion is a better predictor of allegiance, but even here there are exceptions. Looking at those who were Loyalist, neutral, or patriot in this diverse community during its time of grave "troubles" is important, not only because it indicates who favored statehood, but also because it shows the influences of the colony's past on its actions during the war and on the state's future.

Estimates of the number of Loyalists in New Jersey vary from 5,000 to 13,000 "active" individuals, meaning those who took up arms or otherwise directly aided the British. Cortlandt Skinner and William Franklin stand out because of their pre-war prominence (Skinner was an East Jersey proprietor, speaker of the assembly, and attorney general), and because they worked to create an organized military opposition. Skinner's New Jersey Volunteers was the largest royal American military unit. Another Loyalist was James Moody, a substantial Sussex county farmer, who later wrote in his *Narrative of his Exertions and Sufferings in the Cause of Government* (1783): "The general cry was, *Join or Die!*

... [but he] relished neither of these alternatives." Being "perpetually harassed" by patriot "committees" in 1777, he led seventy-three of his farmer neighbors off to fight with the Loyalists.[19] Both wealthy and poor New Jersey residents, conservatives unable or unwilling to foresee a different world, sided with their king. If those who sympathized more quietly are also counted the number is, by one estimate, possibly 51,000 or about 36 percent of the population.[20]

Among the Loyalists, two religious groups stand out. The first, not surprisingly, is the Anglicans. The Rev. Thomas Bradbury Chandler was joined by most other Anglican ministers in New Jersey in remaining loyal (a total of seven did). He became an exile during the war but returned at its end. John Odell of Burlington was equally vocal in opposition to the Revolution. He worked with William Franklin in New York during the war and moved to Nova Scotia afterward. Three Anglican ministers stayed and remained as quiet as possible, their churches usually closed because their ordination oaths and the liturgy included a pledge to defend the king. Only the Rev. Robert Blackwell, of Gloucester in south, sided with the patriots. In addition to the ministers, members of Anglican churches were most often Loyalist, although there were exceptions. Some of New Jersey's most prominent patriot leaders were Anglicans, including Francis Hopkinson, John Stevens, Sr., and William Alexander, known as "Lord Stirling" because of his claim to a Scotch title. All three resigned from the royal council. Hopkinson served in the Second Continental Congress and signed the Declaration of Independence. Stevens was state treasurer and later president of the state convention that ratified the U.S. Constitution, whereas Stirling became one of Washington's generals.

The second group is the "conferentie" faction of the Dutch Reformed Church. Conservative in reaction to the Great Awakening, preferring services in Dutch, insisting that ministers be ordained in Holland, this group opposed the Revolution. All but one of the ministers remained loyal to the Crown. The Hackensack Valley, in northeastern New Jersey, where many lived, became a no-mans-land torn apart as neighbors and relatives battled each other in the midst of both British and American raids.

Often counted by the patriots as Loyalists, the Quakers, who until the Revolution dominated politics in West Jersey, considered themselves neutral. They were both pacifists and conservatives. In 1775 the Philadelphia Yearly Meeting, which included Quaker leaders from New Jersey, issued a statement on the mounting crisis, stressing that they were "peaceable subjects" who opposed "every usurpation of power and authority, in opposition to the laws and government."[21] Quakers were directed to refuse military service, to decline to pay taxes to the extralegal government, and even not to use its paper money. Although most remained neutral, and their refusal to cooperate or serve the new government was a serious problem, not all did so. Some, like lawyer James Kinsey, were prominent in the protest movement against British policies but dropped out of politics after the Declaration of Independence. A few continued to participate, taking an affirmation rather than swearing the oath of allegiance to the state when they took office under the new constitution. A number of Quakers, perhaps 10 percent, even took up arms or in other ways more actively supported the state government. They were disowned by their Meetings; in response, some later formed the Free Quakers, a splinter group. Although the Quakers were by far the largest group that tried to remain neutral, they were not the only ones. So did the small number of Moravians in the state and others who had family members fighting on both sides in the war and were unable to make such a painful choice.

The largest group of patriots came from the Presbyterian churches, urged on by ministerial leaders such as Witherspoon, Green, and the Rev. James Caldwell of Elizabethtown. Caldwell, known as the "fighting parson," along with his wife, Hannah Ogden Caldwell, ultimately became martyrs to the cause, killed in separate actions toward the end of the war. Richard Stockton, Jonathan Dickinson Sergeant, William Livingston, Abraham Clark, members of the Dayton and Boudinot families, William Paterson, and many other Whigs were members of Presbyterian congregations. The College of New Jersey, a Presbyterian institution, was justifiably regarded by the British as a house of sedition. Witherspoon was its president, and his work in healing the divisions among Presbyterians caused by the Great Awakening enabled them to present a fairly united front in the war.

Presbyterians were often joined by Baptists and in the south by Swedish Lutherans, but the most important additional support for the Revolution came from the Coetus faction of the Dutch Reformed Church. Leading ministers such as Frederick Frelinghuysen, Jacob Hardenberg, and Dirck Romeyn advocated ordination in America, the use of English in the churches, and the establishment of Queen's College (now Rutgers University) to further their aims. They also became advocates of independence, bringing members of their congregations into the Revolution with them. Frelinghuysen and Hardenberg served in the government, Romeyn's Tory neighbors in the Hacksensack Valley called him the "rebel parson" and so resented his outspokenness that they led British raiders to his house and watched it being sacked.

Factors other than religion were also important in determining which side individuals supported during the Revolution. Sometimes family, political ties, or even location became relevant. Richard Stockton presents an interesting example of the ways in which cross-currents operated and how hard the decision could be for some persons under extraordinary circumstances. Stockton was one of New Jersey's most distinguished colonial lawyers, a judge, and a member of the royal council. A moderate, he slowly came to accept the need for independence. By June 1776 he was a committed patriot and signed the Declaration of Independence. At the end of November, as British forces approached Princeton, he fled with his family to Monmouth County, only to be captured the next day. He was imprisoned in New York City under deplorable conditions, apparently without heat and little food. By January, in precarious health, he accepted General Howe's offer of a pardon, took an oath of allegiance to the king, and promised to do nothing to help the American cause. In the wrong place at the wrong time, Stockton, although he was not the only signer captured by the British, had the dubious distinction of being the only one to recant.

Stockton returned to Princeton to find his house partially destroyed, his reputation shredded. Witherspoon wrote that he was "not well in health, and is much spoken against for his conduct. He signed Howe's Declaration and gave his word of Honor that he would not meddle in the least in American affairs during the war."[22] There is no evidence he "meddled." He died of cancer in 1781, before the war was over. His brother-in-law, Elias Boudinot, at Washington's request, became American commissioner for prisoners of war and later president of Congress. His son-in-law, Benjamin Rush of Pennsylvania, served the patriot cause as physician and politician. They and other patriot leaders apparently visited Morven, Stockton's home in Princeton, where his wife Annis Boudinot Stockton wrote poems praising Washington and the American cause. In 1781 she proudly wrote her brother "while female I was born a patriot."[23]

New Jersey had notorious Loyalists like James Moody, neutrals, and strong patriots like politician John Fell, who was captured by the British and refused a pardon.[24] It also had some who twisted in the wind, changing sides depending on who was standing at their front door. The Baroness von Riedesel, wife of a Prussian officer serving the British, noted in her diary three visits to the family of Philip Van Horne in Bound Brook. On the first visit her hosts praised the king. During the second the daughter joined patriot soldiers who were present in singing "God save great Washington! God Damn the King!" On the third visit she was asked to "give their regards to the King."[25]

These stories show how difficult it was to stand firmly for or against the Revolution and the creation of a state in New Jersey while the war swirled around. The state's diversity complicated the process by adding pre-existing cross-currents such as those that divided the Dutch. In this complex society, the Revolution shifted the political landscape. Anglican and Quaker power declined, and Presbyterian and Dutch influence increased as new men from these groups rose in prominence. These new men, and the devastation left by the war itself, played an important role in the period that followed.

NEW JERSEY IN THE CONFEDERATION PERIOD

New Jersey was a corridor between north and south, adjacent both to New York City, which the British controlled from 1776 to 1783, and to Philadelphia, which they held during 1777 and 1778. The state became a center for military action during the Revolutionary War because it produced food and iron. Three major battles—Trenton, Princeton, and Monmouth—and a number of smaller ones were fought in the state. New Jersey also served as the winter encampment for the Continental Army three times, twice at Morristown, where it was protected by the Watchung Mountains and local patriots, and once in Middlebrook near Somerville.[26] Loyalists, among them the notorious black Loyalist "Col. Tye," raided the Monmouth County coast while American privateers operated out of southern inlets, provoking British retaliation.[27]

The price for the war was high on all sides. Approximately five hundred Loyalist estates were confiscated. More than four hundred individuals later applied to the Royal Claims Commission for compensation. Several thousand Loyalists decamped, most for Canada. Patriot leaders, including the signers of the Declaration of Independence, and their property were targeted by the British. Witherspoon's, Stockton's, and Hart's estates were raided. Two of Clark's sons serving in the war were captured and apparently treated particularly harshly. Eight years of war left "ruined buildings, worthless money, and crippled men."[28] A state study of wartime incidents that had destroyed property ran to six volumes, five dealing with enemy actions. The costs were high, but they were not evenly distributed across the state. East Jersey, the scene of more fighting, suffered greater destruction than the pacifist, Quaker-dominated western section. East Jersey also contributed more men, wagons, grain, and other supplies to the war effort and as a result had a larger number of state and national certificates of debt at its end.

The main issues New Jersey faced in the post-war period were economic: depression, problems with the money supply, debtors who were hard-pressed to pay their loans, and creditors who wanted to be repaid full value for what they had loaned state and continental governments. Because of the pattern of the war and of support for it, settling the issues was more pressing and divisive in the east than the west. Further, the revival of the boundary dispute between the two proprietary groups affected local politics and the state's actions to solve its problems. Although they disagreed about how the state should solve local problems, New Jersey residents were united in their dislike of the Articles of Confederation and in their desire for a stronger national government.

When the Second Continental Congress appointed a committee to write a Declaration of Independence in 1776, it also appointed one to write a national constitution. The Articles of Confederation was completed in 1778 and was sent to the states for ratification. New Jersey, Delaware, and Maryland objected to the document and at first refused to ratify. In June 1778 the New Jersey legislature wrote Congress, listing its objections to the document.[29] The state suggested that the Articles require an oath of office "binding each Delegate" not to vote for anything that would "violate the general Confederation." The 1776 New Jersey constitution required just such an oath. There should be no "standing Army" in "Time of Peace" unless nine states agreed. Property and population of the states ought to be re-counted every five years before being used to assess requisitions and military forces, so these could be adjusted fairly. Most important were the requests that the national government regulate trade, collect import duties, and control western lands.

The New Jersey resolutions stated that the national government should have the "sole and exclusive Power of regulating the Trade of the United States, with foreign Nations." The national government also should be able to tax this trade and use the funds "for the Common Benefit of the States." Much of New Jersey's long-distance trade had always gone through the major ports of New York City and Philadelphia, with New York and Pennsylvania benefiting from the revenues collected on it. The legislature believed that the state would benefit if the power to regulate commerce and the right to tax were shifted to the central government.

As a land-locked state, New Jersey had no western land claims. The legislature argued "that the Property which existed in the Crown of Great-Britain, previous to the present Revolution, ought now to belong to the Congress in Trust for the Use and Benefit of the United States." This reasoning was supported, the resolutions continued, because "They have fought and bled for it in Proportion to their respective Abilities." It was not fair for states with no western land claims to "be left to sink under an enormous Debt, whilst others are enabled, in a short Period, to replace all their Expenditures from the hard Earnings of the whole Confederation." New Jersey wanted the western lands sold and the revenues used to pay the costs of the war. Some residents in New Jersey also wanted Congress to control lands west of the Appalachian Mountains because they had invested in land companies with claims there, such as the Indiana Company, that were not recognized by Virginia and other states.

Although New Jersey's objections to the Articles of Confederation remained consistent from 1778 to 1787, the state thought adoption of a formal government for the new nation sufficiently important that, despite its objections, the legislature ratified the document in November 1778. Not until 1781 did Maryland, the last holdout, ratify the Articles so that the document went into effect. New Jersey quickly approved proposed impost amendments both in 1781 and 1783 because they addressed some of the state's problems with the Articles. These amendments failed adoption because the required unanimous approval by all thirteen states was not forthcoming.

When the Articles of Confederation went into effect, paper money was worthless, and financial problems became increasingly important. The peace treaty did not resolve these problems. In the period that followed, New Jersey tried to deal with the economic difficulties of both its state government and its citizens. The interest in doing so was greater in the eastern section than in the west, but the proposed answers divided those in the east. At the same time, the issue of the proprietary boundary line came back to haunt the legislature and complicate the discussions.

In the initial years of the war, both the state and the central government had turned to paper money as a method of paying for what they needed. By 1780 the paper money had depreciated so that it was virtually worthless. New Jersey responded to a congressional request to issue new state funds and exchange them for old continentals at the rate of 1:20, but these depreciated as well, failing to solve the problem. After 1782 residents and politicians argued whether to redeem what remained at face (original) or actual (current) value. The first was preferred by creditors, the second by debtors and those in west Jersey holding little paper money or certificates of debt. In 1784 proponents of exchange at actual value prevailed; paper was exchanged for specie (coin) at the rate of 3:1. The paper money was accepted as payment for taxes and, when taken in, was destroyed. The result was an increasing shortage of money, high taxes, and a vigorous debate over issuing new paper money in 1785 and 1786.

Much of this debate took place in a pamphlet war waged between those opposed to paper money, led by William Livingston and William Paterson, and those in favor, headed by Abraham Clark. All three lived in east Jersey, entered New Jersey politics before the war, had been patriot leaders during it, but now found themselves on different sides. Livingston had a long-standing reputation as the author of biting satirical pieces, but they all used strong language and tied their comments on the issue to notions of republican virtue. Livingston and Paterson argued that if Americans lived simple lives, their economic problems would be resolved. The real source of difficulty, Livingston maintained, was those who lived beyond their means, such as farmers who wanted "French dancing masters" for their daughters. One of his essays, presented as a fictitious petition, was a request for paper money over the signatures of Amos Spendthrift, Josiah Workless, John Tippler, Peter Holiday, Simon Dreadwork, Hezekiah Dolittle, and David Neverpay.[30] Paterson, whose legal work in the period included attempts to collect debts for clients, argued that paper money would always deteriorate. The result took money from those who worked for it and gave it to "idle, extravagant Wretches" who "live upon the Earnings of others" and "run into Debt."[31] Clark's contribution to the debate appeared in a pamphlet called *The True Policy of New-Jersey Defined*, signed by "Willing to Learn." He argued that taxes were high and money scarce, causing difficulties for the honest farmers of the state. The real problem was "the moneyed-men" who were not "under the necessity of getting their bread by industry" and had an "avaricious thirst for gain."[32]

The New Jersey legislature was divided on this issue and failed to resolve it in its regular 1786 session, doing so only when it returned for a special session. By this time those in debt were adamant that something needed to be done. The legislature passed a paper-money bill providing for funds to be put into circulation via loans to residents backed by collateral, the method used to provide a needed circulating medium in the colonial period. One reason for the deadlock was that hard-money advocates in both eastern and western sections were divided over the boundary question. East Jersey politicians who were or had ties to the East Jersey Board of Proprietors could not afford to alienate members of the legislature from their section on the question of paper money, because they needed votes on the boundary issue.

The dividing line was an unresolved legacy of the pre-war period. During the Revolution the East Jersey Board had been in disarray because a number of its members were Loyalists, and John Smyth, the registrar and brother of Richard Smyth, took its records into New York City. The board met only once during the war and afterward was unable to retrieve the records until 1785. In the meantime the West Jersey Council of Proprietors moved to take advantage of the situation. It requested that the legislature approve the running of a new line connecting in the west to the boundary line with New York settled just before the war. This line would supplant the 1743 Lawrence line and give west Jersey more than 425,000 additional acres. Twice they failed, once by one vote. The results were to strengthen the political power of east Jersey but to remove the issue from the political arena and return it to the courts, where it lingered well into the nineteenth century.

After paper money and boundaries, the other significant issue was the repayment of state and national war debts owed New Jersey residents. Because so much of the war had been fought in New Jersey, its share of the national debt was proportionally quite high, most of it owed to residents in the eastern section. The state government tried to help creditors by attempting to pay off these debts, resulting in high taxes. The state even moved, beginning in 1783, to assume and repay directly the debts the national government owed New Jersey citizens. New Jersey expected that the costs for assumption would be deducted from its congressional requisitions. Because of the high costs involved, and because of a situation caused by the Articles of Confederation that they considered unfair, the legislature in 1784 decided not to pay any more money to Congress until an import tax had been adopted by amending the Articles. This action went unnoticed until 1785 when Congress requisitioned the states for money to pay its debts and specifically provided that it would not credit those states paying the national debts of their own citizens. At this point, in February 1786, the legislature refused to pay any more congressional requisitions. This action caught the attention of Congress, which quickly sent Charles Pinckney of South Carolina, Nathaniel Gorham of Massachusetts, and William Grayson of Virginia to reason with the legislature. They emphasized how serious this action was, because it "endangered" the central government and threatened to dissolve "those ties that bind us as a nation." After three days of debate the legislature rescinded its resolution, but "the capitulation was more one of form than substance," because the legislature sent no funds.[33]

This action came in the middle of the paper-money debate and Clark, in his pamphlet *The True Policy*, addressed this issue as well. He pointed out that New Jersey residents were paying double taxes: first to their state government, which paid requisitions to Congress to repay war debts, then to New York and Pennsylvania in the form of import taxes that those states used to pay their requisitions. If the central government had the power to tax, he argued, New Jersey residents would pay only once.

New Jersey's action at this point contributed to the growing crisis over government under the Articles. Strapped for money, finding it difficult to get a quorum at meetings, its situation was of increasing concern, particularly to those who had long wanted a stronger government. The events leading to change, however, came in response to more immediate problems of transportation and trade. A meeting was called to discuss these issues in Annapolis, Maryland, in September 1786. The New Jersey legislature quickly selected three delegates to attend: Abraham Clark; William Churchill Houston, a lawyer and politician who had served in Congress; and James Schureman, a New Brunswick merchant, hard-money advocate, and politician who had also served in Congress. It unanimously authorized them to discuss far more than trade. They were also "to consider how far a uniform System in their commercial Regulations and *other important Matters* may be necessary to their common Interests and permanent Harmony."[34]

With only five states represented at the Annapolis convention and all delegates except those from New Jersey saddled by restrictive instructions, the members issued a call for a wider meeting in Philadelphia the following May. Clark wrote the resolution that went with the request. It called for the states to empower delegates to decide "other objects than those of Commerce," as the New Jersey legislature had done for the Annapolis meeting. They should, it continued, be able to "make adjustments of other parts of the Federal System."[35]

Not surprisingly, New Jersey was the first state to appoint delegates to the Constitutional Convention. The state had never liked the Articles and saw an opportunity for change. In November 1786, the legislature appointed David Brearley, a former colonel, then chief justice of the state supreme court, and later a federal judge, William Paterson, William Churchill Houston, and John Neilson, a New Brunswick merchant and quartermaster during the war. When Neilson declined to serve as delegate, the legislature added William Livingston. Abraham Clark refused because he expected to attend the congress in New York and was replaced by Jonathan Dayton, a former captain and land speculator from a prominent family, who became one of the youngest members at the convention. All the men selected had served the patriot cause, and although they disagreed over paper money, they agreed that the Articles needed to be changed.

NEW JERSEY AND THE CONSTITUTION

The Constitutional Convention met from May to September 1787. Once enough delegates arrived and after the convention adopted rules of operation, the Virginia delegation presented a proposal for a new form of government. For the next two weeks the convention discussed this plan under which the states would elect delegates to a lower house proportional to their population and the lower house would then select a second house. It also provided for an executive and expanded the powers of the central government. Then Paterson stepped forward with an alternative proposal, closer to the Articles, in which each state retained equal representation. It also gave the central government additional powers, including the ability to tax and regulate commerce.

Several of New Jersey's delegates, most notably Paterson, played important roles in these debates. Houston, who was ill and would not live much longer, attended only briefly. Livingston lent his prestige but apparently spoke rarely. Brearley and Dayton participated and supported the small states' position. At one point Brearley suggested that the states should be abolished and the country divided into equal parts. There was too much history behind the existing configuration for this proposal to be taken seriously, and Brearley may have made it only to emphasize the seriousness of the issues. This suggestion, however, and Paterson's threat at one point to go home, with the implication that he would not return, helped James Madison from Virginia and other state representatives of large states realize the seriousness of the disagreement. A committee was appointed and came up with the "Great Compromise." It provided for a two-house legislature with representation in the House based on population and with the states equally represented in the Senate. The Constitution also specified that this provision could not be changed unless every state agreed, an event not likely ever to happen. Once this compromise was worked out, Paterson went home to attend to personal business, returning only in September to sign the document.

Paterson could leave because he and New Jersey got what they wanted in the Constitution—a stronger central government with the ability to regulate trade and tax and protection of the small states through equal representation in the Senate. As a result the state acted quickly to ratify, as many inside and outside of it had predicted it would do. The Constitutional Convention ended on September 17, 1787, and the legislature issued a call for elections on October 29. In November thirty-nine delegates were elected from across the state. A total of thirty-eight attended the state ratifying convention held at the Blazing Star tavern in Trenton from December 11 to 20.[36] John Stevens, Sr., served as the president of the convention, and virtually all its members, who included John Witherspoon and David Brearley, had served in some capacity during the Revolution. The minutes of the meeting are brief, indicating that the Constitution was read section by section, discussed, and then unanimously approved on December 18. There is no record of the discussion itself. The delegates signed the next day the document and on December 20 voted to offer Trenton as the national capital.

Although there is no record of the debate during the ratifying convention, it is clear that New Jersey residents were in agreement on the Constitution. There is only one Federalist essayist from the state and there are no Anti-Federalist publications or statements. The Federalist was Col. John Stevens, son of the ratifying convention's president, who wrote a series of seven articles that appeared in *The New York Daily Advertiser* from November 1787 to January 1788. Begun as an attempt to influence New Jersey delegates, they apparently continued to influence those from New York.[37] The essays were contemporaneous with *The Federalist* essays by John Jay, Alexander Hamilton, and James Madison, at times even appearing on the same newspaper page with them. The arguments were also similar. They emphasized the problems of the Articles of Confederation, discussed the ways the Constitution rectified them, and maintained that the extended republic created by the Constitution would be viable. The last point is of interest, because Stevens and his sons went on to design steam boats and railroads, means of transportation that later tied the republic together.

The closest thing to an Anti-Federalist in the state was Abraham Clark, and he denied that he was one during the election of 1788. Clark was silent during the debate over the Constitution, later saying he had reservations but they were resolved by proposed amendments that would become the Bill of Rights. He was certainly capable of writing in opposition, but apparently chose not to do so. The Constitution provided for the regulation of trade and the authority to tax, both of which Clark had previously said were needed. It answered his objections to the Articles of Confederation as well as those of others in the state. It also gave the central government the sole right to coin money, eliminating state-issued paper money. Although this measure surely pleased Livingston and Paterson rather than Clark, overall the document resolved the major problems with which he was concerned.

Less satisfactory for New Jersey was the ultimate location of the national capital. New Jersey had been discussed as the location several times early in the 1780s and had even been so designated at one point. The day after the state ratifying convention voted on the Constitution, it passed a resolution offering a piece of land "ten miles square" at Trenton for use by the national government. Congress, however, agreed first to meet in New York City, then moved to Philadelphia, and finally settled on the banks of the Potomac following a deal brokered in 1791. By that time New Jersey had decided to use the location for its own capital, ending the colonial tradition of alternating between Burlington and Perth Amboy and the Revolutionary practice of wandering from place to place.

On December 20, 1787, after passing the resolution on the capital, the delegates of the ratifying convention went to Vandergrift's Tavern in Trenton for a dinner that was followed by a symbolic thirteen toasts. Included were ones to "The new Constitution;" to Washington, who presided over the Constitutional Convention; to the governor of New Jersey; to the "states of Delaware and Pennsylvania" who had been first and second to ratify; and to America's allies and its daughters. Someone added two more: one to the new government with a "tattoo to anarchy and confusion," and a second, to "Universal liberty, justice, and peace."[38]

These toasts represented an appropriate sentiment with which to end a harmonious meeting. New Jersey, as colony and then state, divided into sections, by religious and ethnic groups, and by the Revolution itself, agreed on adopting the Constitution and on becoming a state under the new government. This was a rare moment of concord in state history. The election of representatives in 1789 to the First Congress that followed was among the most rancorous in New Jersey history. Eastern and western sections presented different slates of candidates, the election lasted for weeks, and the dispute over the results continued into the halls of the First Congress. New Jersey quickly divided into Federalists and Jeffersonian Republicans, and the two new parties competed for votes through the 1790s and beyond. Sectional, religious, and ethnic differences were again important, along with winning office, foreign policy, banking, and other issues. New Jersey faced its future tied to its past. It always was and still remains a small place with a great deal of diversity.

CONCLUSION

The story of how New Jersey became a state cannot be separated from its colonial past or experiences in the American Revolution. The question of statehood was the question of independence. Ratifying the Constitution was for this particular place a logical next step. In deciding for or against independence and hence statehood, New Jersey residents were influenced by religion, family ties, political friends, the war itself, and by their individual willingness to take risks and accept change. Most residents, even those who remained loyal to the king, agreed that British policies violated their rights. To them "no taxation without representation" and trial by jury were important. They differed on whether these rights could be obtained within the British Empire or only by separating from it and also on whether victory was possible. Those who hoped for victory declared the colony's independence on July 2, 1776, declared the colony a state on July 18, 1776, and unequivocally joined the Union under the Constitution on December 18, 1787.

NOTES

1. John E. Pomfret, *Colonial New Jersey: A History* (New York: Scribner, 1973), p. 205.

2. Larry R. Gerlach, *Prologue to Independence: New Jersey in the Coming of the American Revolution* (New Brunswick, NJ: Rutgers University Press, 1976), p. 19.

3. Larry R. Gerlach, *New Jersey in the American Revolution, 1763–1783: A Documentary History* (Trenton: New Jersey Historical Commission, 1975), pp. 22–24.

4. Of the old governments only the proprietary legislature in Pennsylvania survived longer than the royal legislature in New Jersey.

5. The best source for the series of actions is Gerlach, *Prologue to Independence*.

6. Sheila L. Skemp, *Benjamin and William Franklin: Father and Son, Patriot and Loyalist* (Boston: Bedford Books of St. Martin's Press, 1994), pp. 176–177.

7. Charles Pettit to Joseph Reed, March 26, 1776, in Gerlach, *New Jersey in the American Revolution*, pp. 181–182.

8. De Hart had resigned for family reasons, Smith because he was ill, Sergeant to attend the provincial congress in New Jersey. Cooper had never attended. Livingston, later one of the strongest patriots in New Jersey, at this point hesitated on independence. Gerlach, *Prologue to Independence*, p. 337.

9. Gerlach, *New Jersey in the American Revolution*, p. 210.

10. Gerlach, *Prologue to Independence*, p. 337.

11. Gerlach, *New Jersey in the American Revolution*, p. 211.

12. The third provincial congress ratified the 1776 constitution; it was not sent to the voters, because ratification by the voters was not yet seen as necessary. For the constitution see Julian P. Boyd, *Fundamental Laws and Constitutions of New Jersey* (Princeton: Van Nostrand, 1964), pp. 156–163.

13. The exception is Virginia.

14. Ruth Bogin, *Abraham Clark and the Quest for Equality in the Revolutionary Era, 1774–1794* (Rutherford, NJ: Fairleigh Dickinson University Press, 1982), p. 40.

15. Two signed copies of oaths, one taken by members of the assembly and the other by the council, are in the New Jersey State Archives.

16. Diary quoted in Gerlach, *New Jersey in the American Revolution*, pp. 134–135; "Jemina Condict Harrison," in Joan N. Burstyn, ed., *Past and Promise: Lives of New Jersey Women* (Syracuse, NY: Syracuse University Press, 1997), pp. 23–24.

17. Quoted in Leonard Lundin, *Cockpit of the Revolution: The War for Independence in New Jersey* (Princeton: Princeton University Press, 1940), p. 158.

18. Pomfret, *Colonial New Jersey*, pp. 270–271.

19. *Lieut. James Moody's Narrative* (reprint, New York: New York Times, 1968).

20. Paul H. Smith, "New Jersey Loyalists and the British 'Provincial' Corps in the War for Independence," *New Jersey History* 3 (1969): 67–78.

21. "The Testimony of the People Called Quakers," in Gerlach, *New Jersey in the American Revolution*, pp. 111–112.

22. Alfred Holt Bill, *A House Called Morven: Its Role in American History*, rev. ed. (Princeton: Princeton University Press, 1978), pp. 42–43.

23. Ibid., p. 53; Carola Mulford, ed., *Only for the Eye of a Friend: The Poems of Annis Boudinot Stockton* (Charlottesville: University Press of Virginia, 1995).

24. Donald W. Whisenhunt, ed., *Delegate from New Jersey: The Journal of John Fell* (Port Washington, NY: Kennikat Press, 1973).

25. Marvin L. Brown Jr., ed., *Baroness von Riedesel and the American Revolution* (Chapel Hill, NC: University of North Carolina Press, 1965), pp. 91–93, 95. She called the Van Horne's "turncoats" and "two-faced people."

26. The Continental Army encamped in Morristown in the winters of 1776–1777 and 1779–1780 and at Middlebrook in the winter of 1778–1779.

27. On Tye and other black Loyalists, free and slave, see Graham Russell Hodges, *Slavery and Freedom in the Rural North: African Americans in Monmouth County New Jersey, 1665–1865* (Madison, WI: Madison House, 1997), pp. 91–112.

28. Richard P. McCormick, *Experiment in Independence: New Jersey in the Critical Period 1781–1789* (New Brunswick, NJ: Rutgers University Press, 1950), p. 19.

29. Gerlach, *New Jersey in the American Revolution*, pp. 407–412.

30. Series of Primitive Whig essays in the *New Jersey Gazette*, 1786.

31. Essay on Paper Money (n.d., c. 1786), Special Collections, Rutgers University Library.

32. Abraham Clark, *True Policy Defined* (1786).

33. McCormick, *Experiment in Independence*, p. 242.

34. Ibid., p. 253.

35. Merrill Jensen, ed., *Documentary History of the Ratification of the Constitution* (Madison, WI: State Historical Society of Wisconsin, 1976), 1:182–185.

36. Ibid., 3:178–186.

37. Essays reprinted in Maxine N. Lurie, "Colonel John Stevens, The Forgotten Federalist," *New Jersey History* 27 (1993): 58–106.

38. Merrill, *Documentary History of the Ratification*, 3:189–190.

BIBLIOGRAPHY

Barbour, Hugh, and Frost, J. William. *The Quakers*. New York: Greenwood Press, 1988.

Bill, Alfred Holt. *A House Called Morven: Its Role in American History*. Rev. ed. Princeton: Princeton University Press, 1978.

Burr, Nelson. *The Anglican Church in New Jersey*. Philadelphia: Church Historical Society, 1954.

Burstyn, Joan N., ed. *Past and Promise: Lives of New Jersey Women*. Syracuse, NY: Syracuse University Press, 1997.

Cody, Edward J. *The Religious Issue in Revolutionary New Jersey*. Trenton: New Jersey Historical Commission, 1975.

Cunningham, John T. *New Jersey's Five Who Signed*. Trenton: New Jersey Historical Commission, 1975.

Gerlach, Larry R. *William Franklin: New Jersey's Last Royal Governor*. Trenton: New Jersey Historical Commission, 1975.

———. *Prologue to Independence: New Jersey in the Coming of the American Revolution*. New Brunswick, NJ: Rutgers University Press, 1976.

———, ed. *New Jersey in the American Revolution, 1763–1783: A Documentary History*. Trenton: New Jersey Historical Commission, 1975.

Hodges, Graham Russell. *Slavery and Freedom in the Rural North: African Americans in Monmouth County, New Jersey, 1665–1865*. Madison, WI: Madison House 1997.

Jones, E. Alfred. *The Loyalists of New Jersey: Their Memorials, Petition, Claims etc From English Records*. Reprint. Boston: Gregg Press, 1972.

Kemmerer, Donald Lorenzo. *Path to Freedom: The Struggle for Self-Government in Colonial New Jersey, 1703–1776*. Princeton, NJ: Princeton University Press, 1940.

Leiby, Adrian. *The Revolutionary War in the Hackensack Valley: The Jersey Dutch and the Neutral Ground*. New Brunswick, NJ: Rutgers University Press, 1962.

Lundin, Leonard. *Cockpit of the Revolution: The War for Independence in New Jersey*. Princeton, NJ: Princeton University Press, 1940.

McConville, Brendan. *These Daring Disturbers of the Public Peace: The Struggle for Property and Power in Early New Jersey*. Ithaca, NY: Cornell University Press, 1999.

McCormick, Richard P. *Experiment in Independence: New Jersey in the Critical Period 1781–1789*. New Brunswick, NJ: Rutgers University Press, 1950.

———. *New Jersey from Colony to State, 1609–1789*. Princeton, NJ: Van Nostrand, 1964.

Murrin, Mary R. *To Save this State From Ruin: New Jersey and the Creation of the United States Constitution.* Trenton: New Jersey Historical Commission, 1987.

O'Connor, John E. *William Paterson: Lawyer and Statesman, 1745–1806.* New Brunswick, NJ: Rutgers University Press, 1979.

Pomfret, John E. *Colonial New Jersey: A History.* New York: Scribner, 1973.

Price, Clement A. *Freedom Not Far Distant: A Documentary History of Afro-Americans in New Jersey.* New Brunswick: New Jersey Historical Society, 1980.

Sinclair, Donald A., and Grace W Schut. *The American Revolution and New Jersey: A Bibliography.* New Brunswick, NJ: Rutgers University Press, 1995.

Skemp, Sheila. *Benjamin and William Franklin: Father and Son, Patriot and Loyalist.* Boston: Bedford Books of St. Martin's Press, 1994.

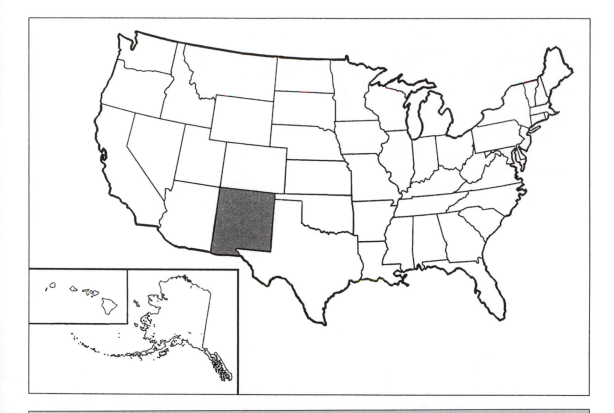

New Mexico

Territorial Development:

- The United States obtains future New Mexican territory through the annexation of Texas, December 29, 1845
- The United States obtains more lands containing future New Mexican territory from Mexico through the Treaty of Guadalupe Hidalgo, February 2, 1848
- The United States obtains more land containing future New Mexican territory through the Gadsden Purchase, April 25, 1854
- New Mexico organized as a U.S. territory, September 9, 1850
- New Mexico admitted into the Union as the forty-seventh state, January 6, 1912

Capitals Prior to Statehood:

- Santa Fe, 1609–1912

State Capitals:

- Santa Fe, 1912–present

Origin of State Name: New Mexico is named after the country of Mexico, which was named after the Aztec god Mexitli.

First Governor: William C. McDonald
Governmental Organization: Bicameral
Population at Statehood: 327,299 (figure taken from the 1910 census)
Geographical Size: 121,356 square miles

☆☆☆

THE STATE OF NEW MEXICO

Admitted to the Union as a State: January 6, 1912

Agnesa Reeve

INTRODUCTION: A LONG, BUMPY ROAD TO STATEHOOD

New Mexico's road to statehood was the longest of any state other than Alaska, covering the sixty-six years from 1846, when it was acquired from Mexico, to 1912, its year of admission. The road was rough and far from straight, winding through seventeen presidencies with the attendant detours in parties and policies. The road was also lengthened by suspicions concerning Hispanic culture, close church-state relationships, and Confederate sympathies as well as problems with Native Americans and unruly miners and veterans. Various national issues, framed in the Free Silver, Populist, Progressive, and Conservation movements, waxed and waned, but a wary attitude toward the Southwest continued throughout the period.

There were a few well-defined reasons for objecting to admitting states from the Southwest and New Mexico in particular. The publicly voiced arguments included their small populations, slow economic development, and difficult arid climate, but these conditions applied equally to other western states without blocking their admission. The real objections surfaced at intervals. A long-held and widespread prejudice against non-Protestant, non-English-speaking peoples was exacerbated by the Spanish-American War. Could these descendents of Hispanic tradition really be loyal to the Union? New Mexico's prompt response to a call for recruits to fight in the war helped allay this doubt, but imperialists, in favor of an empire with colonial holdings, believed these "foreign" peoples should not be a part of the core Union. Critics cited the different judicial system, scant parochial education, a *patrón*-based social organization, and inability to speak or read the language of the U.S. Constitution. Even the name was held to be a liability, fostering proposed names such as "Lincoln" and "Navajo" and, in 1889, "Montezuma," all angrily opposed by New Mexicans.

At various times during the long struggle, other issues worked against New Mexico. During the Civil War and Reconstruction, all of the territory was suspected of having harbored Confederate sympathies. Indeed some areas, notably the Mesilla Valley and Tucson, briefly enjoyed dreams of being part of a Confederacy stretching sea to sea. Mesilla felt estranged from Hispanic-controlled Santa Fe, and Tucson had become a society of miners and merchants ideologically far removed from the old capital. That center of the territory, however, was always firmly Union oriented.

After a Confederate effort to take over New Mexico failed, the enmity between Tucson and Santa Fe resulted in the creation of Arizona as a separate territory in 1863, a consummation greatly desired by both regions. Congress made the division north-to-south rather than east-to-west, a decision that left Mesilla in New Mexico despite its inclinations. Creating two territories did not separate the fates of New Mexico and Arizona. In fact, one of the battles in the last decade of the admission fight centered on a strong jointure movement to admit the two territories as one state, thereby limiting the number of representatives in Washington. The proposal, detested in Arizona and disliked in New Mexico, did not survive.

It seemed that for much of the entire waiting period New Mexico managed to be at cross-purposes with the prevailing national, or at least Washington, D.C., trends. Because of internal political strife, the territorial power structure changed from time to time, confusing Congress as to what motivations and which party was dominant and therefore which side could depend on its support if New Mexico were a state. Naturally, this uncertainty made politicians from the East and the South, both Republicans and Democrats, reluctant to support admission.

Free Silver and Populism

Usually conservative, and even reactionary in the matters of women's rights and public education, the territory sometimes adopted a new idea. The Free Silver debate was an example. Extensive deposits of silver had been discovered in a number of western states, New Mexico among them. In the 1890s, the western states were suffering a depression, and many people thought the answer was to permit coinage of silver up to the rate of $16 of silver for every gold dollar in circulation. The eastern Republican "money-men," conspiring against the common people in the latter's opinion, warned against inflation. Feelings ran high. The Free Silver movement was defeated, and New Mexico had temporarily lost its Republican support.

Associated with Free Silver was Populism, a controversial reform movement advocating women's suffrage and a federal income tax, among other things, and decrying the influence of moneyed interests and government corruption. Although there was no outspoken support for Populism in the territory, the movement was perceived as being part of the insurgency.

The Catholic Church and Education

Throughout the period there were unsolved problems. The lack of adequate public education was a continuing liability, because it ran counter to a basic tenet of U.S. policy. In a speech to Congress in 1890, territorial delegate Antonio Joseph stressed the improvements gained, citing 342 public schools with an enrollment of 16,803 pupils and, trying alleviate another sore point, stated, "in 143 of these schools nothing but English is taught."[1] The matter was further complicated because much of the education was supported by public money but provided through the Catholic Church, a practice in opposition to another U.S. policy, the separation of church and state.

Indian Hostilities and Violence

New Mexico suffered a reputation for disruption and disorder. The Native American menace threatened sporadic but continuous violence until 1886 when the Apache chief Victorio surrendered in southwestern New Mexico. Hostile Native Americans were not the only troublemakers. Following the discovery of gold in California in the 1840s, the territory became part of the road traveled by forty-niners, some of whom were rough men with little consideration for rules or residents. The post–Civil War period saw another influx, this time of discharged veterans and other unsettled vagrants who gathered in dangerous clusters until the situation erupted, as it did in the Lincoln County War of 1875.

New Mexico had continuing violent incidents and disturbances. Time after time federal troops were called into action to pursue villains and rescue their victims. These events were all too enthusiastically reported by eastern journalists and opposing politicians.

Always a Bridesmaid

At the turn of the twentieth century, only New Mexico, Arizona, and Oklahoma were still relegated to territorial status in the continental United States. The period between 1901 and 1912 brought its own controversies, none of which helped the cause of statehood. These last three territories approached Congress with several joint applications in the early years of the decade. They were all defeated until 1907, when the names of New Mexico and Arizona were deleted from an omnibus bill, allowing Oklahoma alone to be admitted. The discrimination largely resulted from the implacable position of Indiana Senator Albert J. Beveridge, chairman of the Committee on Territories. Beveridge considered Oklahoma "American," but was vehemently opposed to the other two as "frontier" or "alien."

The anti-Hispanic prejudice of Beveridge and others continued, but at least two other elements came into play. One was the successor to the Populist movement, Progressivism, a reform movement championed by Theodore Roosevelt that aimed at curbing the economic and political dominance of corrupt big-money interests. The notorious Santa Fe Ring, a confederation of greedy and unscrupulous men with powerful cohorts in other parts of the country, held New Mexico in its grip starting in the 1870s. When its influence declined in the 1890s, another political machine gained power. This widely known situation was read by Progressives, and most importantly by Senator Beveridge, as indicating that statehood was sought simply to further the ambitions of the clique in power.

President Roosevelt made conservation a national imperative, which struck at the roots of the Southwest economy by reserving previously open land to the federal government. More important, however, was the privatization of community land grants. Farmers accustomed to grazing their livestock on the village commons were suddenly excluded. The cutting of firewood in national forests was restricted or forbidden. Corporate speculators, their position already under fire from Progressives, found their schemes drastically curtailed by the conservation movement's removal of public domain lands from their grasp.

Altogether, at the end of the nineteenth century, the obstacles in the path of New Mexico's statehood were as formidable as they had ever been.

MILITARY TO CIVIL GOVERNMENT

New Mexico's first four years as a U.S. possession were not auspicious for early statehood. Military occupation gave way to a civilian government that was toppled quickly by revolt in 1847. Military occupation resumed until the territory was organized in 1850. If internal political strife and murder were not enough, the politics of the U.S. Senate made statehood nearly impossible. Since the Missouri Compromise of 1820, the Senate had achieved a balance in representation between free and slave states. With free California booming because of the gold rush and ready for statehood, a free state of New Mexico was not politically possible in 1850.

The Mexican War brought Brigadier General Stephen Watts Kearny into New Mexico in August of 1846 at the head of his occupying force. Although U.S. and Mexican forces were belligerently engaged farther south, Kearny's orders were to take over the area peacefully if possible, establish a temporary civil government, and try to leave the profitable Santa Fe trade undisturbed.

Military Occupation

Kearny proceeded to do all three. Starting as he entered foreign territory, he announced at every opportunity that the United States would protect the property and rights of New Mexican citizens and do them no harm. From Santa Fe he issued a proclamation that pulled no punches. It announced that he "has more troops than is necessary to put down any opposition that can be brought against him, and therefore it would be but folly or madness for any dissatisfied or discontented persons to think of resisting him," but "those who remain quiet and peaceable will be considered good citizens and receive protection."[2]

In addition to his efforts to reach the citizens by proclamations, Kearny played another card. Ahead of his army, he sent a small delegation to Santa Fe under a flag of truce to treat with the New Mexican governor, Manuel Armijo. The nine troopers who volunteered for the mission were led by a young officer on Kearny's staff, Major Phillip St. George Cooke, and were accompanied by James Magoffin, a well-known trader, and Juan de Gonzales, a merchant from Chihuahua. Magoffin and Gonzales both had caravans traveling the Santa Fe Trail and were widely respected in New Mexico. Much to the Americans' relief, Governor Armijo received them amiably. What was discussed at their meeting is unknown, but as he left the Palace of the Governors, Cooke told the Mexican sentry, "I'll call again next week." Diplomacy notwithstanding, Armijo with his troops awaited Kearny's force at Apache Canyon, the pass over the last range of mountains before Santa Fe. No battle ensued. Armijo dithered, and his army dispersed. Some of his lieutenants urged defense, but Armijo had interests in the Santa Fe trade and less interest in a fight. St. George Cooke later described the Kearny expedition as "Quixotic."

> A colonel's command, called an army, marches eight hundred miles beyond its base…mostly through a desert—the whole distance almost totally destitute of resources, to conquer a territory of 250,000 square miles;… [T]hey arrive without food before the capital—a city two hundred and forty years old, habitually garrisoned by regular troops! I much doubt if any officer of rank, but Stephen W. Kearny, would have undertaken the enterprise; or, if induced to do so, would have accomplished it successfully.[3]

Kearny issued the "Laws of the Territory of New Mexico," known as the Kearny Code. The code, written by lawyers in Kearny's command, incorporated laws of Mexico, the United States, Texas, and the Livingston Code of Louisiana. It was a common sense and practical set of laws that is still being cited.

He then set up a civil government, appointing Taos trader Charles Bent as governor and a distinguished native New Mexican, Donaciano Vigil, as secretary, as well as naming judges and lesser officials. These arrangements were not to stand, however. Congress believed that Kearny had taken too much authority into his own hands and had ignored the Northwest Ordinance of 1787, which made the creation of territories the task of Congress.[4] The disgruntled Congress appealed to President Polk, who repudiated portions of the code and Kearny's authority to set up a permanent government.

847

New Mexicans now did not know what rules applied or who was in charge, undermining any stability Kearny had established. A tear appeared in the fabric of the "peaceful" invasion. In December of 1846, Colonel Sterling Price, then in command of the Santa Fe garrison, received information that a widespread revolt was being planned. On investigation he learned that many influential people in the northern part of the territory were suspected of being involved. Arrests were made, but some leaders escaped.[5]

On January 19, 1847, northern New Mexico erupted in a bloody series of murders. In Taos, Governor Bent, the sheriff, the circuit attorney, the prefect, and two others were "murdered in the most inhuman manner that savages could devise." Seven Americans were killed at Arroyo Hondo, two others on the Rio Colorado. Turley's distillery was burned and its owner murdered.

In Santa Fe the rebels were foiled when the plot was discovered. Colonel Stirling Price with a force of 350 men, marched to Taos, skirmishing with several hostile bands on the way. He was joined by a small body of reinforcements and quelled the rebellion there in a two-day siege of the Pueblo. Price was impressed by the rebels' "remarkable aboriginal progress in the defensive art of war." He recounted a singular incident: "In the heat of the assault, a dragoon was in the act of killing a woman, unrecognized by dress, similar to the man's, and both sexes wearing the hair long; in this extremity she saved her life by an act of the most conclusive personal exposure!" Illustrating the changing positions in Native American warfare, Price added that seven years later, he "raised, in half a day, a company of irregulars in this same town, to serve against the Apaches, and efficient fine fellows they were."

The strength of the insurrection was broken by the Taos defeat, but until midsummer, roving outlaws who murdered and stole livestock harassed small U.S. Army camps and settlers' trains in northern and eastern New Mexico. Price asked for reinforcements, and by autumn there were more than 3,000 troops in the territory, "about double the number of those who made the first audacious invasion and apparent conquest." This bloody uprising ended the power of the civil government and put the military in charge for the next several years.

Expansion

During that period the United States expanded its southwestern possessions again. One of the mid-nineteenth-century obsessions was the desire for a transcontinental railroad. After the Mexican War, a survey proved that there still was not a favorable southern east-west route within the U.S. border and led to the Gadsden Purchase in 1853. With this treaty the United States paid $10 million for approximately 45,000 square miles along its southern border between the Colorado and Rio Grande rivers. Although Congress flinched at the steep price, there was general approval of the purchase.

Now New Mexico Territory was even larger, and the questions about her prospects remained. In every era a national issue stood in the way of easy acceptance of new states. When the Treaty of Guadalupe Hidalgo ended the Mexico War in 1846, the stumbling block was the slavery question, even though New Mexico did not have, and was not likely to have, a significant slave-based economy.[6] Practical issue or not, the additional 525,000 square miles aggravated the issue of slavery being permitted in states carved from the new region.

This vast area had constituted the Department of New Mexico under the Mexican government and included the present states of New Mexico, Arizona, and parts of Utah and Colorado. Southerners argued that a man from Virginia or Carolina had a right to move into this new Southwest with his property, including slaves. Anti-slavery arguments pointed out that the Treaty of Guadalupe Hidalgo stipulated that all existing Mexican laws would be continued, and the Republic of Mexico had afforded protection against slavery.

The application of California for admission as a free state further compounded the issue. The gold rush of 1849 had brought so many people to the West Coast, and the promise of wealth was so great, that this application could not be denied. Therefore, if the traditional practice of balancing the free and slave states were to be maintained, a system intended to keep the Senate evenly divided, New Mexico would have to be admitted as a slave state.

Also brought to a head was Texas's unresolved claim of the Rio Grande as its western boundary, from the Gulf north, including Santa Fe. To New Mexicans, citizens of a much older and, in their opinion, much more civilized community than Texas, the idea of being under the rule of Austin was abhorrent and unacceptable. In addition, they did not care to see sections of their lands chopped off and given to Texas or any other state.

Along with these concerns was the stipulation in the Treaty of Guadalupe Hidalgo that the United States "forcibly restrain" any Native American raids into Mexico. This restraint was not just difficult, it was impossible, because in 1849 the Native Americans were not under control in much of the West, and nowhere was there less control than in the western half of New Mexico (present-day Arizona).[7]

In spite of these difficulties, New Mexico's prompt admission to the Union seemed likely. The Treaty of Guadalupe Hidalgo stated that New Mexico "shall be admitted at the proper time (to be judged of by the Congress of the United States) according to the principles of the constitution." Equally important, President Zachary Taylor was strongly in favor of conferring statehood on New Mexico.

Some enthusiastic New Mexicans felt there was a good possibility of bypassing the territorial period and attaining statehood immediately. There seems never to have been a period when all New Mexicans agreed on the issue, but in the spring of 1850 the group advocating statehood organized a convention to draw up a state constitution for approval by the electorate. Before the constitution reached Washington, D.C., however, the request was rendered futile by the sudden death of President Taylor and the Compromise of 1850.

The Compromise of 1850

Vice President Millard Fillmore replaced Taylor. Fillmore did not have personal ties to the Southwest, as Taylor had, and preferred to settle several questions with one document, Senator Henry Clay's Compromise of 1850.[8] Included in the compromise were the admittance of California as a free state, the organization of New Mexico and Utah as territories, and the settlement of the Texas boundary. New Mexico, the western half of which would later become Arizona, and Utah were designated as territories with "popular sovereignty," that is, they would decide on the slavery matter themselves when they became states. Texas was not given all the land she demanded but was paid $10 million in settlement.

The most controversial segment of the compromise was the Fugitive Slave Act that required citizens to aid in returning runaway slaves to their owners. The uneasy truce created by the compromise did not last long, and within a few years the slavery controversy simmered again, aggravated by the Kansas-Nebraska Act (1854), which allowed new territories to make their own decisions about slavery. On September 9, 1850, Congress approved that portion of the compromise settling the Texas boundary and debt questions and accepted the Organic Act establishing the Territory of New Mexico.[9] On December 13, 1850, President Fillmore signed the compromise into law and declared the Organic Act to be in force. New Mexico had lost her chance for statehood for the time being but at least had achieved a definite status in the United States as the Territory of New Mexico.

The Organic Act

The Organic Act stipulated that the government of the territory follow a pattern set by other territories. The president of the United States, with the advice and consent of the Senate, would appoint the governor of the territory, the secretary of the territory, the chief justice and the two associate justices of the Supreme Court, the territorial attorney, and the territorial marshal. Qualified voters would elect a legislative assembly composed of a council and house of representatives. Also to be elected was a delegate to the U.S. House of Representatives. James S. Calhoun, formerly the territorial secretary of Indian affairs, was appointed the first governor, with William S. Allen as secretary of the territory. One of Calhoun's first responsibilities was the appointment of probate judges, posts for which he primarily chose conservative New Mexicans.

Because New Mexico had been under martial law for four years, with the commanding officer of the army in charge of the government, and because the problems with Native Americans necessitated the continuing presence of the army, there was a built-in rivalry between the governor and the commanding officer, a situation that put the governor at a handicap.

SOLDIERS AND NATIVE AMERICANS

The military commanders were implacably opposed to statehood, although to call them members of a territorial party would be misleading, because each commander believed that he alone should make decisions. Some rationale supports this view, because the Native American menace was continuing and severe, and feuds between other lawless factions caused intermittent violence, making military force necessary to protect citizens. Because of opposition from the military commander and a lack of resources, no governor or superintendent of Indian affairs was able to implement a continuing plan for controlling the Native Americans.

Governor James S. Calhoun and Colonel Edmund Vose Sumner

The first territorial governor, James S. Calhoun, came to New Mexico as superintendent of Indian affairs and also to lobby for statehood on behalf of President Zachary Taylor. In 1849, with Manual Alverez and Major Richard H. Weightman, Calhoun began the first real statehood movement with the establishment of the *Santa Fe New Mexican*, a voice for statehood.

Calhoun's first job in Indian affairs was to educate the federal government on the difference between the Pueblo and nomadic Native Americans, so that the Pueblos might enjoy property rights and the vote. They finally were allowed property rights but not the vote.

His program for the hostile Indians, "compulsory enlightenment," was not successful because Washington did not provide the goods and food he needed or the staff to carry out his plans and because he did not get the cooperation of the new military commander, Colonel Edwin Vose Sumner. Convinced that harsher measures were called for, Sumner totally disagreed with Calhoun's food-and-treaty philosophy, refusing to be a part of it. As a result, no coherent Native American policy was implemented, and raids and depredations continued.

Vermonter Sumner, who came to the territory in 1851, was not impressed with New Mexico and its inhabitants. He reported to Washington in 1852:

The New Mexicans are thoroughly debased and totally incapable of self-government, and there is no latent quality about them that can ever make them respectable.

They have more Indian blood than Spanish, and in some respects are below the Pueblo Indians, for they are not as honest or as industrious. No civil Government emanating from the Government of the United States can be maintained here without the aid of a military force; in fact, without its being virtually a military government.[10]

When this report was read aloud in the House of Representatives, New Mexico delegate Richard Weightman was understandably outraged. He termed it an "atrocious libel" and in rebuttal listed the abuses practiced by the military government in the territory. The damage was done, however, because the report was then a matter of record.

Sumner did institute a system of Native American control by establishing a number of outlying army posts, including Cantonment Burgwin near Taos, Fort Defiance in Navajo country west of Albuquerque, Fort Craig south of Albuquerque, and Fort Fillmore near El Paso. Disagreements continued under succeeding governors and military commanders. Comanche, Apache, and Navajo troubles increased to the point that some local militia organized for their own protection. With the outbreak of the Civil War, federal troops were called away to the East, hostile activity became even more frequent, and any progress made in Native American relations evaporated.

General James Henry Carleton

In 1862, after the Confederate invasion of New Mexico was repelled, General James Henry Carleton became commander of the Department of New Mexico. He had been trained under Sumner and admired him as a model, hardly a background promising for a temperate handling of the Native American situation.

Carleton's approach was not temperate. He stated that his aim was to kill or capture all Native Americans, transporting the survivors to a reservation to be "civilized" and taught agriculture. He succeeded in subduing the Native Americans, but the internment from 1863 to 1868 at Bosque Redondo reservation was a notorious mistake. The crucial problem for the five years of the camp's existence was lack of sufficient food. In spite of large federal expenditures, the Navajo were starving, but he refused to let them return to their land where they could feed themselves.

There were other problems. Bosque Redondo, "Round Grove," was named for a grove of tall cottonwood trees at the location on the Pecos River chosen by General Carleton for his reservation. When the army arrived, the cottonwoods were immediately cut down to use for firewood and building material, creating the site's second-most-dire shortage, firewood. Bitterly cold winters, inadequate housing, and a shortage of warm clothing and blankets took their toll of people already weakened by malnutrition.

For an old Indian hand Carleton used remarkably poor judgment in crowding Navajo and Apache, traditional enemies, together. In his nineteenth-century view of humanitarianism, Carleton believed it necessary to eliminate the Native

Americans' culture and teach them to "live like white men." To accomplish this goal, he decided the Navajo, and even the roaming Apache, must be removed from their hunting grounds, divested of their lifestyle (and livelihood), and turned into farmers and craftsmen. To some extent he succeeded with the Navajo, who were not totally averse to settling in one place and cultivating crops.[11]

The Apaches were another story. Although 1,500 Mescalero Apaches lived for a time on the reservation, they never accepted the program. After months of hard work, half-rations, and killing diseases, and crowded by their enemies, the Navajo, the Mescaleros simply left. They went one night in small groups and scattered over hundreds of miles of southern New Mexico. Pursuit was attempted but was fruitless.

Carleton, unable to believe he could be mistaken, had insisted on this location although its disadvantages had been strongly pointed out to him. Many who thought the Pecos land unsuitable argued for locating the Navajos in a reservation on their familiar canyonlands where they could support themselves. The critics proved fatally correct. Alternate drought and flood, too little arable land for too many Indians, and plagues of crop-destroying insects combined to bury Carleton's fantasy of the project's being self-supporting. Inadequate rations and disease decimated the bands of unfortunate internees.

An important element in the problem was the animosity between the military and the Indian Department. Throughout the Bosque Redondo experiment, the military, that is Carleton, and the Indian Department, represented principally by Michael Steck, the superintendent of Indian affairs, were fundamentally and angrily opposed to each other.

Native Americans and Steck were not the only ones who objected to Carleton's tactics. He angered white citizens by maintaining a tyrannical rule and martial law long after any Confederates had left the territory. After four despotic years he had lost the initial popularity gained from his victories over Native Americans. Scattered but increasingly numerous raids were attributed to deserters from Bosque Redondo, so the blame for the depredations fell on its creator. In the end, the management of the Navajo was returned to the Indian Department, and the surviving Navajo walked back to their own country.

In 1866 the legislature asked for Carleton's removal. Ruthless or not, the general's campaigns against the Apache and Navajo succeeded in shifting the initiative in the 250-year-old war between Native Americans and whites.

The Role of the Catholic Church

The Roman Catholic Church, like the military leaders, was a powerful group that resisted conceding any power to the territorial civil government. The Catholic Church had dictated the spiritual and moral values of Hispanic life in

North America for two hundred years. It recorded births, deaths, and marriages, controlled what education there was, and enjoyed unquestioned authority. After centuries of isolation from the discipline of Rome, however, some of the clergy had become lax and corrupt, and there were Catholics who yearned for reform. Many hoped the Anglo invasion would spur the church to renew its mission.

New Mexico's long run on the territorial stage produced a large and varied cast of characters, working both for and against statehood, and both sympathetic and antipathetic to the Americans. For generations, power in the region had been concentrated in a few Hispanic families, some of whom had close ties to the clergy. Because the interests of the Catholic Church and the interests of the Americans were at odds, these clergymen constituted an influential voice against Anglo ideas.

Padre Antonio José Martinez

One of these clergymen was Antonio José Martinez, a member of a prominent northern New Mexico family. Unusually well-educated for the time, he studied for the priesthood in Durango, Mexico. In 1830 he became curate of Taos, and in that and the following year served in the legislative assembly. A shrewd businessman with many connections, he became influential in New Mexico. Among his causes was his unsuccessful campaign against private land grants that deprived villagers of grazing lands. Wealthy Hispanic families had collected large ranch holdings, but the arrival of Anglo newcomers aggravated the situation. Martinez's objections to the invaders were so well known that he was suspected of complicity in the 1847 revolt. Martinez championed the poor and used his power to promote their rights, but his unorthodox and unclerical life style attracted the disapprobation of Bishop Lamy. The priest was estranged from the church in 1858, but he continued to live in Taos and to administer to his loyal followers.[12]

Donaciano Vigil

Donaciano Vigil was a native-born New Mexican with quite different and liberal views. Vigil figured in New Mexican politics for more than twenty years, including periods in which he was acting governor. From the beginning he was pro-American because he felt democratic government would further his sincere desires to reform the clergy and establish public education. At first working as a territorialist, he turned to the statehood party when they gained strength.

Vigil's long career resulted from an amiable and intelligent ability to cooperate with difficult leaders holding various viewpoints. He was military secretary to the last Mexican governor Armijo, advising against resistance to the American occupying force, and shortly thereafter was appointed secretary of the territory by Kearny. An indication of his flexibility is his retaining his position as secretary under the several military commandants before 1850. No doubt a factor in his tenure was his network of political and family ties throughout New Mexico.

Bishop Jean Baptiste Lamy

One ambition of Donaciano Vigil and other reform-minded New Mexicans was realized with the arrival of Bishop Jean Baptiste Lamy in 1852. With skill and diplomacy Lamy brought the outdated church in the territory up to standards more acceptable to Rome. He replaced unsuitable members of the clergy, some of whom, like Padre Martinez, were from prominent families, thereby causing still another rift in local allegiances. Among his accomplishments were the founding of a boy's academy in Santa Fe and the introduction of the Sisters of Loretto to establish a girls' academy. He also allowed priests to be the schoolmasters of "public" schools, so all education was under the influence of the Roman Catholic church.

Close federal rule was at odds with the church and Lamy on several matters, including the registry of marriages, baptisms, and burials and, importantly, jurisdiction over education. Because the elected territorial assembly was composed in great part of tradition-minded Hispanics, Lamy's influence on their actions was considerable. Repeatedly, governors pled with the assembly to enact an effective public school bill, and repeatedly the denunciations by the church and their own inclinations persuaded legislators to defeat the intention with a hollow piece of legislation. This attitude toward public education, known and condemned in Congress and the rest of the United States, was a serious blot on the territorial escutcheon.

GOVERNMENT BY CLIQUE

Party politics certainly influenced the political scene during New Mexico's territorial days, but not in an ordinary way. A two-party system played no part in the Spanish-Mexican tradition. There certainly were at least two sides to every question in the territory, but the terms "Republican" and "Democrat" figured principally to impress members of Congress.

Loyalty remained where it traditionally lay, with the long-time leading families: Martinez of Rio Arriba, Perea and Chavez of Rio Abajo, Pino, Sena, Archuleta, Ortiz, and Delgado of Santa Fe. These families composed the solid core of the statehood group who longed for the Americans to go back to Washington and let New Mexicans run their own state with their own leaders. Territorialists, meanwhile, feared Spanish-American domination from Santa Fe if locally elected officials were in charge. The territorial party also claimed the support of such old traders (and experienced Native American negotiators) as Ceran St. Vrain and Carlos Beaubien, who were convinced that the area required a permanent military presence. Complicating all affairs and confusing any observer were the divided loyalties and changing positions of all participants.

Delegates to Congress

The only official representation the territory had in Washington was the territorial delegate, a non-voting legislator elected every two years. Hotly contested, the coveted position usually went to a spokesman for the group in power in New Mexico, not necessarily the party in power in the nation's capital. Alleged chicanery in the close-run contests in New Mexico did not help the delegate's position in Washington; once the candidate's term was almost over before he was finally seated.

The first delegates were Anglo politicians, but an especially able man, Democrat Miguel A. Otero, was elected in 1855, 1857, and 1859. Otero, whose son of the same name became an even more prominent political power, represented the southern part of the territory and no doubt influenced the routing of the federally supported Butterfield stage route through that area. His sympathies, in contrast to the dominant loyalties in Santa Fe, pushed New Mexico toward the southern states in the critical period before the Civil War. The Confederate movement did not succeed. Otero the elder also supported the transcontinental railroad and was successful in furthering that project.

The election of Republican President Abraham Lincoln in 1860 ended Otero's effectiveness in Washington, and in 1861 a strong unionist and Republican won the delegacy. Succeeding delegate elections during the Civil War and Reconstruction illustrated the chameleon-like characteristic of New Mexican politics. Little pattern could be found other than the local leaders' willingness to thwart any orders from Washington that they disliked.

The Santa Fe Ring

In the early 1870s, Thomas Benton Catron and his partner and fellow Missourian, Stephen Benton Elkins, formed the group who controlled the power in New Mexico for the next twenty-five years, a coalition called the Santa Fe Ring. The motivation for the group was the money to be gained through manipulation of mining, railroad, and land grant schemes. The ring wielded economic and political power to control the law and judiciary on both territorial and local levels.

Their idea of law, unfortunately, seemed to encourage rather than mitigate the violence that plagued New Mexico during the post–Civil War period, the so-called Lincoln and Colfax County "wars" being a case in point. In Lincoln County, countywide violence erupted when feuding parties inflated a quarrel over money. Ring-controlled lawmen took sides rather than settling the conflict. Colfax County suffered bloodshed between large and small land-owners; because members of the ring were large owners, they naturally were prejudiced.

The statehood group elected Elkins delegate to Congress in 1871 for the purpose of influencing Washington not only toward statehood but also to promote the group's other interests—open-range cattle ranching, railroads, mining, and especially land grants. The land-grant operation, in its simplest terms, involved the speculator's buying a Spanish or Mexican land grant from the New Mexican owner. The buyer then arranged for suborned surveyors and judges to declare the grant to be two, three, or ten times its original size. The most egregious of these manipulations ballooned the Maxwell Grant from 97,000 to 2 million acres. For these enterprises the land grabbers called on the backing and expertise of lawyers, judges, surveyors, and bankers, all members of the ring.

Because the overriding interest was in money and power, the Santa Fe Ring favored the statehood party even though they often could control federal appointees under territorial rule. Catron's position was simply explained. In discussing a piece of land, he said the "selling price for the same is three dollars per acre and with the passage of the statehood bill for New Mexico it will be advanced to not less than $5 per acre."[13] Because he laid claim to millions of acres, the stakes were high. Catron was reported to be a partner in seventy-five grants, to be a part-owner or attorney for 4 million acres, and to own 2 million acres.[14]

From 1860 to 1885, ambitious businessmen such as Elkins and Catron enjoyed the advantage of a robber-baron attitude in Republican Washington that was favorable to rapacious operators. It was also favorable for New Mexico's admission, smoothly advanced by delegate Elkins. Smoothly advanced, that is, until a fateful handshake in 1876. During the congressional session of that year, Elkins happened to enter the House chamber just as Michigan representative Julius Caesar Burrows finished an impassioned speech. Elkins rushed up to Burrows and shook his hand in congratulation, unaware that the speech had supported civil rights for blacks. Appalled southern congressmen saw the handshake as support for prohibition of slavery and promptly changed their votes on admitting New Mexico from "yes" to "no." Elkins was again chosen delegate in 1877, but the momentum was lost, and there was no concerted effort for statehood for more than a decade. When Miguel Antonio Otero the younger won the governor's post in 1897 over Catron's candidacy, the latter's long-time control faded, but Catron held on to enough political prestige to become one of the state's first senators in 1912.

Some Democrats

Grover Cleveland became the U.S. president in 1884, the first Democrat in twenty-four years, and New Mexico elected a Democratic delegate, Antonio

Joseph. Joseph's victory was apparently the cause or the result of a split within the New Mexico Republican Party and in the Santa Fe Ring. This split did not mean that the power behind Joseph was not connected to the ring, because both Joseph and C. H. Gildersleeve, chairman of the Democratic central committee, were closely associated with the ring. Catron estimated two-thirds of Republicans in New Mexico were Spanish-American and one-third was Anglo-American. The demographics for Democrats were the reverse, with three-fourths being Anglo-Americans.[15] The ring always contained both Republicans and Democrats. With the Democrats in power in Washington, the ring showed its Democratic colors. Joseph remained in Congress for four terms between 1885 and 1895. Considered unenthusiastic about statehood at the beginning, he worked hard toward the goal during his last two terms, but with no final success.

Governor Edmund G. Ross

The appointed governors, of course, reflected the party in power nationally. Therefore most of them were Republican, and most of them were either actively or passively in league with the Santa Fe Ring, abetting its activities. There were exceptions, however.

Indianan Lew Wallace, appointed governor in 1878 to replace the unprincipled Samuel B. Axtell, fought to curb the lawlessness and violence but resigned in 1881, disillusioned with New Mexico. Both Wallace and Governor Edmund D. Ross, named by Democratic President Grover Cleveland in 1885, frustrated in their attempts to clean up the ring-controlled territory, came to believe that statehood was the only way to bring New Mexico to modern standards. The catch was that the territory had to make some progress toward modern standards to achieve admission.

Democrat Ross was appalled at the control exercised by the ring and denounced its venal objectives.

> From the land Grant ring grew others, as the opportunities for speculation and plunder were developed. Cattle rings. Public Land Stealing Rings, Mining Rings, Treasury Rings, and rings of almost every description, grew up, till the affairs of the Territory came to be run almost exclusively in the interest and for the benefit of combinations organized and headed by a few longheaded, ambitious and unscrupulous Americans.[16]

Ross was opposed to statehood as long as the power remained with the rings.

L. Bradford Prince

Succeeding Ross was L. Bradford Prince, another Republican and an ambitious politician but a man who worked to achieve modernity for the territory. In his address to the legislative assembly in 1890, Prince was explicit concerning

New Mexico's problems. The land title efforts were a "miserable failure," the school law was an "utter failure." About the judiciary he said there was "no country in the world, Christian or Pagan, in which the court practice was so antiquated, cumbersome and complicated."[17] That legislature finally passed an effective school bill.

Miguel Antonio Otero

President William McKinley was expected to make a standard Republican choice for governor in 1897, but instead he angered old-line Republicans like Tom Catron and made a watershed governor's appointment, Miguel Antonio Otero, the son of the 1850s delegate, the elder Miguel Antonio Otero.

This Otero was the first Spanish-American New Mexican to fill the governor's post, and he was particularly fitted to take the responsibility. With his background and connections, he could bridge the Anglo-Spanish gap and put together a government suited to his constituency. He was supported by a political machine, but it was a grass roots native New Mexican machine. It worked so well that Otero held the governor's position for nine years, until 1905. He supported and worked for statehood enthusiastically. In 1901 he called a statehood convention that passed resolutions toward that end, but without further progress. The next ten years saw a bitter, and sometimes ugly, resistance to New Mexico's admission to the Union.

THE FOUR CONSTITUTIONS OF NEW MEXICO

Four constitutions for New Mexico were written in the years 1850, 1872, 1889, and 1910. Each of the four New Mexican constitutions strikingly reflected hot current issues even though the constitutions were supposedly written for future generations. At a casual glance, the writing of a state constitution would seem to require a straightforward exposition of the organization and basic tenets of the state government. The reality was not that simple. The constitution not only had to set forth a plan for the structure of government but also had to satisfy the voting residents and the political factions and survive the scrutiny of the U.S. president and Congress.

In New Mexico, a basic problem that delayed admission and made the composition of the various constitutions so tricky was the considerable disparity between what the residents wanted—home rule, with their traditions unchanged—and what Washington wanted—complete "Americanization." In addition, the power factions, the church and the rings, were divided, each anxious to hold on to and augment their positions.

The 1850 Constitution

The constitution of 1850 was constructed in an atmosphere of urgency because Texas's claims to all the land east of the Rio Grande alarmed all New

Mexicans, both territorialists and statehood men. By emphasizing a strong anti-slavery statement in a constitution, New Mexicans hoped to assert their independence as a state and to separate themselves from the pro-slavery Texas and southern senators. In the document they also made counterclaims to land in the disputed Texas–New Mexico frontier, proposing a boundary that would have included in New Mexico all of the Texas panhandle and other land west of the one-hundredth meridian.[18] Both questions were settled by the Compromise of 1850.

Of prime concern also was subordinating the detested military regime to a civil government, another point on which all parties could agree. More controversial were the stipulations concerning the Catholic Church. Education would be supported by public taxes. Priests would not be required to serve in the army, on roads, or on juries. Divorce would require an act of the legislature. In a progressive move, "civilized" Native Americans were given the vote.

The structure of the government, with three branches, was classic: a bicameral legislature, an elected governor and lieutenant governor to serve four-year terms, and a court system with three judicial circuits. This constitution, endorsed by both the leading factions, was approved by voters but was overridden by the Compromise of 1850. An attempt to hold a constitutional convention in 1866 came to naught when it became apparent that President Andrew Johnson would do nothing about admitting new states during the turmoil of Reconstruction.

The 1872 Constitution

Michigan Republican Marsh Giddings became governor of New Mexico in September of 1871 after his nomination by President Ulysses S. Grant. In rare and temporary harmony, both parties welcomed him to the territory and applauded his first message to the territorial legislature the following December. On December 30, 1871, however, a note of discord sounded when both houses of the legislature voted to transfer Chief Justice Joseph G. Palen from the first, and most important, district in Santa Fe (the usual bench of the chief justice) to the third, remote district of Mesilla.

Governor Giddings believed, with sufficient reason, that Judge Palen was being removed to the southern district because it was known he could not be bought and gave equal justice to rich and poor. Several wealthy and prominent New Mexicans were under indictment or heavy bonds at the time, and they would prefer to appear in the court of the alcoholic and malleable incumbent from Mesilla. Giddings considered the proposed move "a blatant disregard for justice" and vetoed the measure.

This veto split New Mexican Republicans and Democrats into their usual adversarial positions as the Democrats tried to prevent the veto's being sustained. Some Republicans who had voted to move Palen now changed positions to support their Republican governor, and the house voted to sustain the veto. The Democrats were so angry that, with the collusion of some Republicans, they refused to seat four Republican representatives, thereby gaining control of the house.

From that point on, the legislative session began to resemble a comic opera. The governor, hoping to bring reason to bear, was seated beside the speaker when he was informed that the legislators were carrying arms. The next day, the session was so unruly that the speaker ordered the room cleared of spectators, but the crowd refused to leave. Finally, the speaker adjourned the session. As soon as the Republicans filed out of the room, the Democrats began to organize their own legislature and elected their own speaker.

The hostilities permeated the city, worrying Governor Giddings, who reported, "For many days a fight seemed inevitable. Riot and bloodshed were imminent and one day I was called on not less than three times by members of the House to go into the House to prevent a hand to hand fight, as it was declared to me every member was armed and at any moment a fight might occur."[19]

The Republican speaker, escorted by federal troops, declared the house Republican again by seating the four men whose places had been usurped. The governor recognized this Republican house, but the upper house, the council, recognized the Democratic group. The Democrats took over the actual chamber by stealing the doorkeeper's keys, but two nights later the Republican speaker sneaked into the building and replaced the lock. For the rest of the month New Mexico had two legislative houses, each passing laws and acting on official business. When there was an inquiry as to which should be paid, the U.S. attorney general answered that neither of the two groups was recognized as the lawful house of representatives. Two days before the end of the legislative session, the leaders negotiated a compromise. Surprisingly, the reunited house accomplished an astonishing amount in a short period, including the drafting of a new state constitution modeled after the constitution of Illinois. This constitution was approved by both Republicans and Democrats.[20] Aware of the imminent arrival of railroads in the territory, the framers included strict regulations on the railways, with provisions empowering the legislature to prevent abuses and enforce fair freight and passenger rates. Of course there were objections from those who wanted all corporations regulated equally, from those who thought it better to wait until the railroads arrived before passing such laws, and from those who thought too much restriction would hamper progress.

This constitution also called for free public schools. It forcefully separated church and state, eliminating any public support for church activities and specifying the tax exemptions that would be allowed the church. These provisions obviously had their opponents.

For the constitution to be submitted to Congress as part of the bid for statehood, it first had to be approved by the voters of New Mexico. By not approving a constitution, the voters nullified the bid for statehood. There were legitimate objections to the 1872 document, but in the end, in spite of chicanery and fraud by all parties, it seemed to be the indifference of the citizens that led to defeat at the polls.

The 1889 Constitution

At every constitutional convention the first arguments erupted over apportionment of delegates.[21] The 1889 convention was no exception, and as usual there were charges and countercharges, probably well founded, of every description of dishonest and unfair practices. The convention was dominated by the Republicans, with the Santa Fe Ring prominent.

Having control was not entirely to the Republicans' advantage. The major problem was the same as it had been for forty years, the necessity of providing a public school system in the face of the implacable opposition of the Catholic Church. Their control of the convention meant the Republicans would bear the onus of being enemies of the Catholic Church, an unfortunate position in New Mexico. Even before the convention was held, both a "secret" paper purportedly from church officials and a letter from the Archbishop of Santa Fe, the Most Reverend J. B. Salpointe, pointing out the dangers of secular education, circulated throughout the state. In spite of these warnings, the delegates included state support for public schools in the constitution. They had no choice. Congress would accept no less.

The 1889 constitution contained minimal regulations for corporations, not as effective as those in the 1872 version. The power of landholding delegates emerged with a ruling that taxes on land could never be higher than 1 percent, although mining and other property was liable for higher rates. None of these provisions went unnoticed or uncriticized, and the voters rejected the constitution. A proposal for the joint admission of New Mexico and Arizona, introduced in 1906, was rejected by Arizona voters and thereby was defeated before yet another new constitution was drafted.

The 1910 Constitution

In 1910 an Enabling Act for New Mexico was finally passed, allowing it to call a constitutional convention and containing the unusual condition that the constitution must be approved by both the president and Congress. The majority of delegates to the 1910 convention were Republicans and businessmen bent on gaining statehood, but they were also determined to retain their right to do things the way they always had done.[22] Republicans chaired and constituted the majority of every committee.

As always, national trends affected the process. Direct legislation was the Progressive thrust of the day. Progressive measures included the initiative (the right of the electorate to initiate legislation), the referendum (the right of the voters to accept or reject a measure), and the recall (the right of the voters to depose an elected official). Including these measures as part of the constitution occasioned a heated debate, but to a group of legislators who had previously balked at including even an amendment provision, the new ideas were unwelcome.

Democrat and former delegate to Congress Harvey Fergusson led a fight for direct legislation, vowing that the Hispanic citizens needed those protective measures and protesting that no right-minded Democrat could support a constitution that did not include these safeguards. On the other hand, traditionalists, including Catron, saw chaos in the majority being able to question laws and overturn decisions. Furthermore, they had been advised to write a "safe and sane constitution."[23]

The final result was a document considerably more conservative than the constitution of 1872. Women's issues received minimal support, with suffrage extended only to school elections, and prohibition was not supported. Not surprisingly, these businessmen delegates kept the regulation of business to a minimum. The provision for amending the constitution was so convoluted as to be unworkable, and the referendum clause was weak. Many Democrats voted against adopting this draft, but after it passed, most did sign it. In the following weeks, Harvey Fergusson led an unsuccessful public fight to defeat what he considered an inadequate instrument of government and a serious step backward for the territory. The framers, however, had done what they set out to do; they had written a constitution that would pass a traditionally conservative constituency and stand up to the examination in Washington. The only change made to the original draft was replacing the amendment procedure with a reasonable alternative.

Arizona, writing its constitution at the same time, developed an entirely different document, proving (if any further proof were necessary) that the two areas were far apart in philosophy. Arizona's constitution included direct legislation, even calling for the recall of judges. They were forced to remove this item before President William Taft would give his approval, but it was reinstituted by the first state legislature.

A FIGHT TO THE FINISH FOR STATEHOOD

Senator Albert J. Beveridge

For the last dozen years of her fight for statehood, New Mexico's nemesis was Indiana Senator Albert J. Beveridge, named chairman of the pivotal Committee on Territories in 1901. An impressive and able senator, he was a close and respected friend of President Theodore Roosevelt, with whom he shared an expansionist, imperialistic view of the United States' destiny. Unfortunately for the Southwest, Beveridge also held strong prejudices against non-Protestant, non-English-speaking peoples, even if they were native born. In addition, he represented the Progressive viewpoint and deeply distrusted certain connections between politicians in New Mexico and Arizona and money-men in northern states, convinced the mining and railroad interests planned to control the territory.

His prejudices negated the value of his so-called "fact-finding expedition" to the Southwest in 1902. Every effort by delegates, prominent New Mexicans, or supporters from the rest of the nation, failed to modify his hostility. He delayed reporting bills, filibustered, struck out the names of Arizona and New Mexico from omnibus bills, and in 1903 he even hid for a week so that a territorial bill could not be considered.[24]

'Statehood" Rodey and 'Bull" Andrews

Struggling to counteract Beveridge's opposition were two colorful and energetic delegates who carried New Mexico's message to Congress in the beginning of the twentieth century. Bernard S. Rodey, an Irishman, came to New Mexico in 1881 to work for the Atlantic and Pacific Railroad and became a part of Frank A. Hubbell's Republican machine in Albuquerque. By 1900 he was so active in politics and so popular that he was elected delegate, and he was reelected in 1902. His enthusiasm for the statehood cause earned him the nickname "Statehood" Rodey.

In 1904 even his immense popularity was undermined by political intrigue. Frank Hubbell and Governor Otero were feuding. Rodey was loyal to Hubbell, so Otero arranged for the Republicans to nominate William H. "Bull" Andrews, an accomplished politician newly arrived from Pennsylvania. Andrews had the backing of Catron as well as Otero (although those two were also feuding) and won the delegate's position. Unfortunately for New Mexico's image, Beveridge was particularly mistrustful of Andrews because of his intimate connections with big money interests.

Jointure Proposal

Both the Republican Party and President Roosevelt had made promises for statehood, but they did not want more, possibly radical, representatives of the West in Congress. In 1904, some eastern members of Congress, prominently Beveridge, along with President Roosevelt, decided that a happy solution would be to admit New Mexico and Arizona as one state, called Arizona. Obviously Beveridge, despising both territories, saw jointure only as a way of reducing the western representation in Congress and was able to ignore any flaw in his argument. Marcus Smith, a powerful figure in Arizona politics, pointed out that Beveridge was proceeding as if "one rotten egg is bad, but two rotten ones would make a fine omelet." Much maneuvering led to referendums on jointure in both states. New Mexico, anxious for statehood, passed the unpopular measure, but Arizona defied even the president, rejecting it when it came to a vote in 1906. Because it required passage by both territories, the Arizona vote was sufficient to kill jointure.

During the same period, Oklahoma applied for admission in consolidation with the Indian Territory adjoining it on the west. Voters approved its constitution, and Oklahoma became a state in 1907.

The Enabling Act

Undeterred by the failure of the jointure effort, and for the most part glad that it had failed, New Mexicans tried to gain statehood once again. By 1908 some factors had changed to their advantage. The Republican Party included separate statehood admissions as a plank in their platform, and President Roosevelt spoke in favor of separate states in his message to Congress. An omnibus bill advocating separate admissions for New Mexico and Arizona passed the House in 1909 but failed to make it through the Senate, principally because of obstruction by Beveridge.

In January 1910, a member of the House Committee on Territories, Edward L. Hamilton, presented an Enabling Act, a measure that would allow New Mexico and Arizona to call constitutional conventions in preparation for admittance. As passed by the House, the bill was generous in the land allotted to the states and other measures, but the Senate version differed significantly. Among other restrictions, Beveridge reduced the land allowance, fearing that the larger amount would lead to graft. He tried to insert a stipulation that any office holder would be required to speak and write English without an interpreter, but delegate Andrews and former Governor Curry were able to eliminate that clause, knowing it would endanger passage of the constitution. The Senate version was accepted, and President Taft signed the Enabling Act in June 1910.

Stumbling blocks remained, even at this late stage. Objections to Arizona's liberal constitution and Democratic objections to New Mexico's conservative document both required hearings and resolutions, an extra congressional session, public debate in the newspapers and, once more, Beveridge dragging his heels in the Senate. Finally, on January 6, 1912, a year and a half after the Enabling Act had been passed, Taft signed the proclamation admitting New Mexico to the Union.

Why Did Statehood Take So Long?

If the U.S. Congress had admitted New Mexico to the Union when it first petitioned in 1850, it would have become the thirty-second state and would have rivaled in size its giant neighbor Texas. As it happened, sixty-two tumultuous years passed before a much-reduced Territory of New Mexico joined the United States in 1912 as the forty-seventh state.

New Mexico's road to statehood reaches far back in the history of the continent, its Native Americans tracing their ancestry for thousands of years. Even the settlers of European origin were among the earliest to arrive, along with those of northern Florida, in the late sixteenth century. A local saying in Santa Fe surprises many visitors from the East: "When the Pilgrims landed on Plymouth Rock, the roof of our governor's palace was already leaking."

After this early settlement, there ensued more than 200 years during which the southwestern region was known as part of New Spain, its boundaries fluctuating with the vagaries of the Spanish Crown and the hostilities of those already occupying the ground. Considering its history, perhaps it is not surprising that integrating New Mexico into the United States took a very long time.

External Problems

The nation was not ready to accept New Mexico in 1850. First and foremost was the slavery question. As was proven within fifteen years when the Civil War erupted, the United States was fatally divided regarding slavery. The southern states' entire economy and way of life was based on the use of slave labor. On the other hand, many citizens of the northern states saw the practice as barbaric and immoral.

At the midpoint of the nineteenth century, an uneasy balance existed in Congress between pro- and anti-slavery states. Each faction felt it could not risk tilting the weight to the opposing side by admitting new states, with their representatives to Washington, unless they felt certain the particular state was on their side of the question. No such certainty could be felt in regard to New Mexico.

After the Civil War and Reconstruction had laid the slavery question to rest, uncertainty about New Mexico's position on other matters remained. Although New Mexico was basically conservative, it took a more radical view on some questions, such as Free Silver. Along with other western states, New Mexico had silver deposits that could help a struggling economy in a depressed period if coinage were allowed. Westerners could not convince the rest of the nation of the value of this approach, and the movement failed. To Republicans in Washington, New Mexico's support of Free Silver meant the state was unreliably insurgent.

Some Easterners, including some members of Congress, held prejudices against admitting any area to the Union that was not English-speaking and Protestant. Connected to these doubts were the serious questions of separation of church and state and of universal public, secular education. In addition, some powerful advocates of imperialism were attracted to the idea of "foreign colonies" rather than states.

The Progressive movement stood in the way of acceptance of both New Mexico and Arizona, because both areas were believed to be too closely connected with land and money manipulators based in the East. It was true that too many eastern politicians came west planning to exploit the region for personal advantage.

Internal Problems

Supporters of statehood also had problems closer to home. Beginning about 1700, citizens of New Mexico enjoyed a family-oriented, tradition-based life-style, its spiritual guidance provided principally by the Catholic Church. For the most part, people were not seeking change. An upheaval such as the takeover by the Americans was hardly welcome, and the more drastic the changes suggested, the less welcome they were.

Except for the oppressive regime during the U.S. military occupation, the most deeply resented change was the replacement of church authority with civil authority, a prerequisite for statehood. Although some Catholics saw the need for change and wished for reform in the church, most citizens were content with its role. They also were used to and satisfied with their systematic and legalistic judicial system and were unimpressed by the complicated judicial system of the United States.

New Mexicans and their children had been educated by the church, learning its precepts along with other skills. The fact that these skills might not include literacy was commonplace and disregarded by most citizens. The Catholic Church, of course, fought hard to maintain control, not only over education but also over sacramental records of baptisms, burials, and marriage. With the legislative assembly largely Catholic, the church's position was powerful, and it was able to protect its prerogatives, like public education, for decades. The lack of a public school system and widespread illiteracy presented a serious obstacle for promoters of statehood.

The usual doubts arose when people were faced with proposed changes in their leadership. They feared taxes would be higher, levied to support a public school system about which they were less than enthusiastic. Already the privatization of community land grants and village commons had disrupted their agricultural practices. For years, statehood seemed to be the pet project of a few Anglos, with the native-born New Mexicans content to stand by while the interlopers scuffled. As a writer remarked concerning more recent invasions, New Mexicans resist newcomers not by action but by "vast and collective inaction."

Very gradually, these attitudes changed. Statehood came to be viewed as a matter of status as well as a practical advantage, and New Mexicans wished for the recognition. Political battles continued to be hard fought, but a better-educated and literate citizenry tolerated less mischief. Life in New Mexico will never be a life in the forefront of innovation, but three-hundred-year-old traditions give it a variety not present in younger societies.

NOTES

1. U.S. Congress, Congressional Record, 51st Cong. 1st Sess., 1890, Part 3, pp. 2991–2995.

2. Richard N. Ellis, ed., "Proclamation of Stephen W. Kearny upon Occupying Santa Fe, 1846," in *New Mexico Historic Documents* (Albuquerque: University of New Mexico Press, 1975), p. 4.

3. Phillip St. George Cooke, *The Conquest of New Mexico and California, an Historical and Personal Narrative* (New York: G.P. Putnam's Sons, 1878), pp. 39–40.

4. "Northwest Ordinance of 1787," House Document No. 398 in *Documents Illustrative of the Formation of the Union of the American States* (Washington, DC: Government Printing Office, 1927).

5. Details of the 1847 rebellion are from Cooke, *The Conquest of New Mexico and California*, pp. 111–121.

6. Ellis, "Treaty of Guadalupe Hidalgo," in *New Mexico Historic Documents*, p. 10.

7. James E. Officer, *Hispanic Arizona, 1536–1856* (Tucson: University of Arizona Press, 1987), p. 3.

8. Edwin Charles Rozwenc, *Compromise of 1850* (Boston: Heath, 1957).

9. Ellis, "Organic Act Establishing the Territory of New Mexico," in *New Mexico Historic Documents*, p. 32.

10. *Congressional Globe*, 32nd Cong., 2d sess. (January 10, 1853), Appendix, p. 104.

11. Details of the Bosque Redondo are from Gerald Thompson, *The Army and the Navajo* (Tucson: University of Arizona Press, 1976).

12. Howard R. Lamar, *Encyclopedia of the American West* (New Haven: Yale University Press, 1998), pp. 679–680.

13. Catron to Don Matias Contreras, July 30, 1896, Catron Papers. University of New Mexico Library, Albuquerque.

14. *Santa Fe New Mexican*, October 31, 1894.

15. Howard R. Lamar, *The Far Southwest: 1846–1912; A Territorial History*, rev. ed. (Albuquerque: University of New Mexico Press, 2000), p. 165.

16. Ross to O'Grady, March 27, 1887 Ross Papers (Santa Fe, NM: New Mexico State Records Center and Archives).

17. Message of Governor Prince to Legislative Assembly, 1890 (Santa Fe, NM: New Mexico State Records Center and Archives).

18. *Constitution of the State of New Mexico, 1850* (reprint, Santa Fe: Stagecoach Press, 1965).

19. Robert W. Larson, *New Mexico's Quest for Statehood: 1846–1912* (Albuquerque: University of New Mexico Press, 1968), p. 97.

20. *Constitution of the State of New Mexico, 1872* (Santa Fe, NM: New Mexico State Records Center and Archives).

21. *Constitution of the State of New Mexico, 1889* (Santa Fe, NM: s.n., 1889).

22. *Constitution of the State of New Mexico, 1910* (Santa Fe, NM: Secretary of State, 1914).

23. Robert W. Larson, *New Mexico's Quest for Statehood*, p. 274.

24. Details of Beveridge's career are from Charles Edgar Maddox, "The Statehood Policy of Albert J. Beveridge, 1901–1911" (M.A. thesis, University of New Mexico, 1938).

BIBLIOGRAPHY

Cooke, Phillip St. George. *The Conquest of New Mexico and California, an Historical and Personal Narrative*. New York: G.P. Putnam's Sons, 1878.

Ellis, Richard N., ed. *New Mexico Historic Documents*. Albuquerque: University of New Mexico Press, 1975.

Lamar, Howard R. *Encyclopedia of the American West*. New Haven, CT: Yale University Press, 1998.

———. *The Far Southwest: 1846–1912; A Territorial History* . Rev. ed. Albuquerque: University of New Mexico Press, 2000.

Larson, Robert W. *New Mexico's Quest for Statehood: 1846–1912*. Albuquerque: University of New Mexico Press, 1968.

Officer, James E. *Hispanic Arizona, 1536–1856*. Tucson: University of Arizona Press, 1987.

New York

Territorial Development:

- Great Britain seizes New Netherland from the Dutch in 1624, renaming it New York in 1664
- Continental Congress approves Declaration of Independence from Great Britain, July 4, 1776
- Great Britain formally recognizes American independence through the Treaty of Paris, September 3, 1783
- New York becomes the eleventh state to ratify the U.S. Constitution, July 26, 1788

Territorial Capitals:

- Kingston, established in 1777 as the first official capital of New York, was sacked and burned by the British in the same year. After this, and throughout the Revolutionary War, the legislature met in Poughkeepsie as well as various other non-official locations. In 1783, after the Revolution, the legislature met in New York City, Poughkeepsie, Fishkill, and Albany, and finally settled on Albany as the permanent state capital in 1797.

State Capitals:

- Albany, 1797–present (for capitals prior to 1797 refer to paragraph above)

Origin of State Name: New York was named in honor of the Duke of York and Albany, the brother to England's Charles II.

First Governor: George Clinton
Governmental Organization: Bicameral
Population at Statehood: 340,241
Geographical Size: 47,214 square miles

THE STATE OF NEW YORK

Ratified the Constitution of the United States: July 26, 1788

Arthur Holst

INTRODUCTION

New York, the eleventh state to ratify the U.S. Constitution, has always been an integral component of the American experience through the colonial, revolutionary, confederation, and constitutional periods all the way up to modern times. One group of New York's original inhabitants, the Iroquois, was one of the New World's most powerful tribes, often effectively using the power wielded by their League of Nations. New York's first colonizers, the Dutch, settled and established a much more tolerant and easy-going lifestyle in North America than that of the rigid Puritan societies of New England and the strict Roman Catholic colony of New France. After some time, the village of New Amsterdam developed into the city of New York, which was beginning to outpace Philadelphia, Boston, and Baltimore in maritime importance. During the Revolution, New York suffered more than any other state. About one-third of all land and water battles were fought in New York, which was home to great victories like Saratoga and saddening losses like Brooklyn Heights. Under the Articles of Confederation, New York was the capital and the center of the young nation's loosely knit government. New York's journey to statehood is one full of heroism and importance and is an essential component of the founding and the growth of the United States.

THE IROQUOIS CONFEDERACY

Upon the arrival of Europeans to the New York area, the natives' population, economy, and government were particularly advanced. The most influential

Native American group at the time of the arrival of Europeans was the Iroquois Confederacy, known as the Five Nations. Iroquois settlements were numerous, often containing more than one thousand people in a village, and were positioned throughout the valleys and shores of northwestern New York.[1] Large populations were supported by agriculture, particularly the cultivation of maize, and by hunting and gathering.

The most important event in Iroquois history before colonization is believed to have occurred in 1570. On that date, members from the five major Native American tribes of central and western New York, the Onondaga, the Mohawk, the Seneca, the Cayuga, and the Oneida, held a meeting at which the union of the League of Five Nations was formed. Much later, between 1712 and 1714, the Tuscarora tribe, fleeing from enemies near present-day North Carolina, joined the Iroquois League.

Governmental power within the league was held by fifty chiefs, known as sachems, drawn from the tribes who made up the grand council. Originally, the Mohawk and the Oneida each had nine chiefs, the Onondaga had fourteen, the Cayuga had ten, and the Seneca had eight. Chiefs most often were the head of a village within their tribe and were selected by a council made up of the noble women from each village. Membership on the grand council was a great honor, because chiefs had the authority to maintain the peace and to coordinate the league's activities. Chiefs could be removed from the grand council, but removal required the approval of the noble women from the chief's home village.

The league established and distributed powers and responsibilities among its members. Most decisions required unanimous consent, so obtaining consensus was a complicated and politicized process. The league did, however, prevent the Iroquois tribes from battling among themselves, and it made the Iroquois Confederacy the most formidable counterweight to European colonists. Unfortunately, the league also gave the Iroquois a sense of superiority, resulting in continuous wars with other tribes and the refusal to admit tribes that did not speak an Iroquoian-based language into the league with full rights. Instead, they created a "covenant chain" system, as it was named by the Dutch, through which tribes relinquished all authority to the Iroquois without having representation on the grand council. The Iroquois, known for their ferocious warriors and their firm control of the fur trade, retained their influence in colonial affairs through politics and diplomacy. As a result, the Iroquois were able to resist European domination for many years, influencing the colony of New York's journey toward statehood.

DISCOVERY AND SETTLEMENT

Giovanni de Verrazano, sailing in the name of France in 1524, was the first European to explore New York harbor at the mouth of the Hudson River.

The region was not explored in detail, however, until Henry Hudson sailed his ship, *Half Moon*, up the Hudson River to an area near present-day Albany. Hudson, an English-born navigator hired by the Dutch to search for a northwest passage, described the newly discovered areas as being "as pleasant a land as one can tread upon."[2]

Although Hudson failed to discover a shorter route to the Spice Islands, his thorough descriptions of the New York area and its abundance of furs and fisheries spurred the interest of Dutch investors. At first, economic interests drew private merchants to the area. They were followed by the establishment of the New Netherland Company and its successor, the Dutch West India Company, established in 1621. In the following years, Dutch colonization spread slowly along the banks of the Hudson River.

DUTCH COLONIZATION, GOVERNMENT, AND CULTURE

Government for the Dutch territories in the New World was determined by the charter for the Dutch West India Company, which was approved by the States General, the legislative governing body of the United Provinces of the Netherlands in 1621. The first article of the charter granted the company a monopoly for twenty-four years over all "Dutch" territories in the New World, even though many of the lands were already occupied by other European powers, primarily the Spanish and Portuguese. The charter also stipulated an annual government commitment of 1 million guilders, but the company was underfinanced and unable to pursue large-scale operations from 1621 to 1623. Finances remained a major difficulty for the company, but the lack of government subsidization was not the only problem. For about the first twenty-five years of its life, the West India Company attempted to establish colonies in present-day Brazil, hoping to defeat the Amazon jungle and set up profitable sugar-producing plantations. Dutch plans for South America fell apart, resulting in millions of guilders in lost investments and thousands of lost lives.

Because of the company's preoccupation with South American and then with Caribbean colonies, the Hudson River Valley was primarily settled by private merchants abiding by the company's rules. The first two ships harboring a substantial number of European colonists, the *Mackereel* and the *Nieu Nederlandt*, both arrived near Manhattan Island by the spring of 1624. These first settlers were mostly Walloons, French Protestants who had fled to the United Provinces to escape religious intolerance in France. On March 29, 1624, the Walloons were read their Provisional Orders, a contract of responsibilities and regulations set down by company commissioners by which they agreed to live if they were to settle in New Netherlands. Incentives for settlement included free land, free passage, and the promise of available livestock. In the New World, the colonists were obligated "to obey and to carry out without any contradiction the orders of the company."[3] Other clauses gave the commander in charge of the colony the authority to distribute the free land and the power to decide what crops the colonists should grow. The Orders also offered rewards for the discovery of "mines of gold, silver, copper, or any other metals, as well as of precious stones, such as diamonds, rubies and the like."[4]

In the New Netherlands, the company commander held most of the authority in the colony, and he was responsible primarily to the commissioners in Amsterdam. The company commissioners appointed the commander, and he shared some of his authority with a council of other, more minor company employees and free colonists. During the first years of settlement, the council removed the company commander, Willem Verhulst, from his duties on a few occasions, an action that might be viewed as mutiny. Many believe the temporary removals were the result of disagreements and illegal profits from the fur trade.

Verhulst was removed permanently soon after by the proprietors of the West India Company in Europe, and he was replaced by Peter Minuit, who is famous for negotiating the purchase of Manhattan Island. Under Minuit's authority, the fur trade was steady, but the colony's agricultural support system faltered. Farmers were drawn to the easier profits realized in the fur trade and were burdened by heavy import taxes on farming tools and equipment. This failure in agriculture led to the rise of Kiliaen Van Rensselaer, a powerful diamond merchant from Amsterdam, who strongly advocated the use of a patroon system.

Rensselaer, who had invested heavily in New Amsterdam, was a principal shareholder in the West India Company. Under the proprietary government in Amsterdam, only shareholders could vote for or be directors of the company. Rensselaer had significant influence as an important member of the Amsterdam chamber of the Dutch West India Company that maintained authority over New Netherland. The system of patroonships that he advocated would establish fiefdoms owned entirely by an investor or group of investors, who would obtain the land free as long as they settled a certain number of tenants on their land. On their fiefdoms, the investors could maintain courts, collect rent, and claim portions of the tenants' grain.

Rensselaer's lobbying in favor of the patroonships was successful, and the final plan for implementation was agreed upon on June 7, 1629, by the West India Company directors and the Estates General. The plan was named the *Freedoms and Exemptions for the Patroons, Masters, and Private Individuals, who will Settle any Colonies and Cattle in New Netherland*, more simply known as the *Freedoms and Exemptions*. Under this plan patroons had almost total power over their tenants. Only in the event of a crime involving fifty florins or more could a case be appealed to the proprietors in Amsterdam. Patroons received a range of subsidies and concessions from the West India Company, including permission to engage in the fur trade, low, subsidized transport rates, and special credit rates. Under the *Freedoms and Exemptions*, private citizens were entitled to occupy "as much land as they shall be able to improve" with full hunting, fishing, and farming rights.[5]

Following the new charter's publication, there was a burst of activity in the shipyards of Amsterdam and throughout the United Provinces. Rensselaer and some of his wealthy associates had already chosen the sites of their respective fiefdoms, which were massive in size. Rensselaer's lands, established in 1629 and known as Rensselaerswyck, were situated 150 miles north of New Amsterdam on Manhattan Island, near Fort Orange. By 1632, he had a huge tract of land with stables, farms, cattle, a mill, a tannery, and numerous tenants. Whereas most of the other patroons failed for various reasons, Rensselaerswyck actually outlasted New Netherland and was the largest private estate in seventeenth-century North America.

Dutch colonization struggled, and the colony was plagued by inefficient leadership following the removal of Peter Minuit in 1631. Free colonists started to object to their lack of voice and rights in the colony. During the administration of William Kieft, now referred to as governor, there were numerous problems, including the provocation of a four-year war with the natives. In 1641, the fort at New Amsterdam was in a terrible state. Kieft decided to tax the natives for its repair, an action that resulted in a revolt.

Kieft finally acknowledged the desires of some of his colonists and called an unofficial council of twelve local men to decide how to deal with the revolt and the need to repair Fort Amsterdam. These men, however, had different plans. In return for their assistance in resolving the ongoing problems, they demanded some control over taxation and policy in the colony. Kieft rebuked them, and the council was disbanded; the Dutch colonists failed in their first attempt to gain some power in their colonial government.

Following Kieft's poor administration, the arrival of Governor Peter Stuyvesant signaled the most prosperous period for New Netherland. Overall, the Dutch West India Company began to concentrate less on its failed dream of New Holland in northeastern Brazil. After years of failed expeditions, military failures, and deadly diseases, the Dutch West India Company reevaluated its position in North America. Positioned between New England and Virginia, the increasingly valuable colony of New Netherland was placed between two strong colonies controlled by the United Provinces' biggest economic and military enemy.

Stuyvesant's first concerns were problems left over from Kieft's administration. Alcoholism was rampant in the colony, leading to widespread aggression and violence. Stuyvesant passed two ordinances, mandating closing times at every drinking place and attacking the colonial practice of home brewing. Next, Stuyvesant brought stability to local government by reestablishing the council that had been disbanded by Kieft and setting up a Board of Nine Men from leading citizens to supplement his complement of officials from the company.

Solving the critical problems, Stuyvesant and his council began a marketing campaign across Europe by creating and distributing pamphlets. A period of immigration and growth ensued, and the European population of New Netherland was around nine thousand, half of whom were not Dutch, by the time of the English conquest in 1664. Consequently, New Netherland had a much more complicated ethnic mix than the societies of New England and New France. During the 1650s, Dutch Jews, who had settled in Pernambuco, Brazil, when the Dutch West India Company controlled it, immigrated to New Netherland to avoid being forced to convert to Catholicism by the Portuguese. Governor Stuyvesant, who was anti-Semitic, requested permission from the Amsterdam chamber to ban Jews from the colony, breaking from the company's policy of religious tolerance and of ignoring religious issues.

The verdict was handed down in April 1655 to the disdain of Stuyvesant. The company judges ruled that it was "unreasonable and unfair" to force the Jews to leave after all their hardships, although the real reason they were permitted to stay was probably fiscal.[6] The judges' explanation acknowledged the "large amount of capital that [Jews] have invested in this company." A level of tolerance was once again unofficially established, but the Jews were barred from public positions, from owning stores, and from building a synagogue.[7]

The Quakers, however, were in a much worse situation, often receiving harsh treatment and banishment. Their treatment by Dutch officials evoked sympathy from English villagers who had begun settling Dutch lands after leaving New England. Stuyvesant was determined to rid the colony of Quakers; he issued a proclamation threatening seizure against ships that transported Quakers into the colony and fines against colonists who allowed Quakers into their homes. Throughout New Netherland, the proclamation was accepted, but not wholeheartedly. In the village of Flushing colonists composed a document known as the Flushing Remonstrance, which attacked the government's tactics against religious minorities and enunciated the principle of religious toleration. On December 27, 1657, thirty-one residents signed the document.

Stuyvesant's response was swift and predictable: he arrested everyone who signed the petition. Word of Stuyvesant's continued intolerance soon spread to the directors in the Amsterdam chamber, and he received a disciplinary letter. In it, the directors required that Stuyvesant "allow everyone to have his own belief, as long as he behaves quietly and legally, gives no offense to his neighbors, and does not oppose the government."[8] Eventually, Stuyvesant began to follow company policy of ignoring religious differences, as long as religion was practiced quietly and peacefully, giving New Netherland a level of religious tolerance far greater than in New England and New France at the time.

For Stuyvesant and New Netherland the real problems lay with the constant pressure on its boundaries by New England and its colonists. Before Stuyvesant could deal with that problem, however, further difficulties arose from within the colony. Stuyvesant's council, known as the Board of Nine Men, was in a state of crisis. In December 1648, Adriaen Van der Donck, proprietor of an estate near present-day Yonkers, was elected to the Board of Nine Men and became a thorn in Stuyvesant's side. Led by Van der Donck, the board set about planning a mission to Amsterdam to demand political reforms, because colonists were agitated by Stuyvesant's authoritarian rule.

Upon learning of the plan, Stuyvesant confiscated Van der Donck's papers and promptly expelled him from the council. Resolutely, Van der Donck prepared a petition that the other council members signed on July 26, 1649. Addressed to the Estates General, the petition attacked Stuyvesant and the Dutch West India Company, demanding a "suitable municipal government," which dealt better with border disputes and taxes.[9] Taken to the Estates General by three representatives of the Board of Nine Men, the demands in the petition were thwarted by Stuyvesant's secretary, Cornelis Van Tienhoven, who skillfully defended Stuyvesant and his administration.

With the Board of Nine Men rebuked and the potential takeover of the colony by the Estates General averted, Stuyvesant's attention once again turned to New England. In late September 1650, Stuyvesant concluded the Articles of Agreement, also known as the Hartford Treaty, which set enforceable boundaries for New Netherland, but at its severe expense. In the agreement, New Netherland lost its claim to the eastern portion of Long Island and the entire Connecticut Valley.

The treaty was tested soon after when the First Anglo-Dutch War erupted. Delegations were exchanged between the colonies to prevent war. The British colonies of Connecticut and New Haven advocated an invasion of New Netherland and tried to incite British citizens living in Dutch areas of Long Island to rebel. In contrast, the colonies of Massachusetts and New Plymouth advocated caution and peace. Stuyvesant attempted to defend the colony from attack from the south by sending delegates to Virginia, but a non-aggression pact could not be reached. Then, citizens from Providence, Rhode Island, fearing attacks by Dutch-supported Native American tribes, attacked a Dutch border fort. Unable to mount a significant military response to the act, Stuyvesant busied himself repairing Fort Amsterdam, which was in a poor state. A British invasion of New Amsterdam was in the final stages of planning, but word of a truce reached the colonies just in time to prevent the assault.

Finally responding to calls for improved government, the Estates General issued a new charter for the city of New Amsterdam, which came into effect in February of 1653. The charter worked to provide the more "suitable municipal government" called for by Van der Donck by giving the colony an array of municipal officials, each assuming some of Stuyvesant's authority.

A period of prosperity and expansion spread throughout New Netherland, particularly among the merchant class of New Amsterdam, but, ongoing problems signaled the beginning of the end for the Dutch presence in North America. English colonial settlements such as Hempstead, Flushing, Newton, and Gravesend, dotted throughout Dutch territory, began to push for more representation and authority. Finally in 1663, Stuyvesant granted them the right to elect their own magistrates.

By the first months of 1664, however, King Charles II of Great Britain had issued a charter to his brother, the Duke of York and Albany, entitling him to the area of New Netherland. Dutch denunciation of the British Navigation Act of 1660, which mandated tariffs on foreign shipping and required all British colonial goods to pass through Great Britain, precipitated another war. Rebellions were incited throughout the British-settled areas of New Netherlands. Stuyvesant once again tried but failed to resolve the disputes diplomatically. Dutch informants brought news of a fleet assembling at Portsmouth, England, but incorrectly reported that it was headed to New England to punish Puritans who did not agree with the restoration of the British monarchy. As a result, Stuyvesant and the defenses of New Amsterdam were completely unprepared when a British fleet dropped anchor off New Netherland's shores on August 18, 1664.

Stuyvesant was angered by the terms offered by the British and wished to fight, but his defenses were poor, and the majority of the population opposed fighting the British forces. Ninety-three of the wealthiest men in the colony signed a petition pleading with Stuyvesant to surrender. The rather generous terms that were finally agreed to on August 27, 1664, allowed the Dutch Reformed Church to continue undisturbed, respected all contracts and properties, and even allowed the Dutch West India Company to continue using its properties throughout the colony. On August 29, 1664, Stuyvesant and his troops boarded the *Gideon* and sailed to Amsterdam. New York's history as a British colony had begun.

New York retained its Dutch legacy for many years. The Dutch Reformed Church survived and helped the Dutch community to maintain its spoken language, although merchants, especially, quickly found that knowledge of English was a valuable business asset. Although the Dutch were viewed by some as "better subjects than [those] found in other colonies," they also contributed greatly to early colonial demands for religious tolerance and to early colonial insubordination.[10] Smuggling remained extremely profitable because of the constraints of the English Navigation Acts, and Dutch merchants stationed at Fort Orange, renamed to Albany upon the English takeover, continued to trade guns for furs, illegally arming the Iroquois.[11]

BRITISH RULE AND NEW YORK'S DEVELOPMENT

Under control of the Duke of York, Richard Nicolls, a successful royalist general, was dispatched to be the governor of the colony, holding the post at New York City. Upon his arrival, Nicolls was able to defuse potentially dangerous situations skillfully. The former magistrates of New Amsterdam proved to be one of Nicolls's first major problems. The magistrates refused to take an oath of allegiance to the British king but finally did so after Nicolls assured them that the oath would not void the terms of surrender or force them to fight against their country.

By 1665, Nicolls had established a government in New York that was centralized but also promoted regionalism. In addition to appointing Nicholls, the Duke of York appointed a council, but he did not plan to create a colonial assembly, because Dutch citizens far outnumbered English citizens, except in certain areas. Undaunted, in February 1665 Nicolls called for a colonial assembly composed of delegates from villages with an English majority, specifically towns on the Bronx Peninsula and on Long Island. After a short time, the assembly ratified a governmental plan known as the Duke's Laws of 1665.

Originally, the laws applied only to Yorkshire County, which was created within the laws and comprised Staten Island, Long Island, and West Chester. The Duke's Laws were not applied to New York City and Albany until 1674 nor to the entire colony until 1676. Hoping to not upset the Dutch colonists, the Duke's Laws were broad regulations that left many issues to be decided by local governments. For example, Nicolls allowed Rensselaerswyck to retain its own courts and local government officials. In other areas, the Dutch governmental structure remained intact, except that representatives would have to meet with the English commander for approval of their actions.

The Duke's Laws did provide courts, tax collection, and local government structures to Yorkshire County but did not establish a colonial assembly. The constables, the lowest officials of government who handled everyday affairs and disputes, could be chosen by taxpayers, but no other voice was given to the populace. The Duke of York still had the power to make all the laws, the only stipulation being that his laws agree with those of England. This lack of voice would prove problematic for New York's government in the future.

The Duke of York's primary concern with his colony was profit, but New York proved to be a disappointing investment because of the colonists' overall resistance to paying fees and respecting trading regulations. Nicolls guided the colony well, but he did not attempt to enforce trade regulations too fervently because he did not wish to stir up revolt in the English towns on Long Island, which had enjoyed a reasonable amount of autonomy under the Dutch. By the end of his tenure, Nicolls had succeeded in governing the colony "with humanity and gentleness" and he had solved most of the difficulties arising from the transition of power, but lingering issues remained.

Colonel Francis Lovelace was appointed governor after Nicolls. He held the position from 1668 to 1673, but his tenure was shortened by a Dutch invasion and takeover for fifteen months as a result of the Third Anglo-Dutch War. The colony was given back to England in 1674, and Major Edmund Andros was appointed governor. Andros's enforcement of all trading regulations met with resistance and uproar.

In response, the Duke of York sent out a new governor, Colonel Thomas Dongan, in 1683, with orders to establish a colonial assembly. According to the Duke's wishes, the assembly would have the power to raise money, but it would not have any control over expenditures.

When Dongan arrived, he called for delegates from across New York to sit with his council and discuss the formation of an assembly. In October 1683, a plan for a colonial assembly, known as the Charter of Liberties and Privileges, was agreed upon. The charter provided an assembly that shared legislative power with the governor and the proprietor and established the principles of trial by jury and freedom of worship. The charter was approved by the Duke of York, but it was revoked when the Duke ascended to the throne in 1685, becoming King James II of Great Britain. Advised by the Lords of Trade to take better control of merchants in the North American colonies, James added New York to the Dominion of New England, taking away some of the colony's powers.

Dongan granted more concessions in the charters for New York City and Albany, but these actions did not prevent colonists from pushing for revolt as early as 1688, stirred up by James's revocation of Charter of Liberties and Privileges and by economic difficulties. Rumors were also spreading that Dongan and King James II, both devout Catholics, were plotting to impose Catholicism on the entire colony.

The Glorious Revolution of 1688 in England, dethroning James II in favor of Protestant monarchs William and Mary, offered New Yorkers the opportunity to rebel. Prominent colonists formed a committee of safety to restore law in the colony, defend the colony, and prevent the alleged Catholic conspiracy. The committee selected Jacob Leisler, a wealthy merchant and religious zealot, to become commander.

At first, Leisler's rule was questioned further up the Hudson River, but after the French and Native American raid on Schenectady in February 1690, Albany and its outlying settlements overlooked their objections in return for the protection of Leisler's troops. Leisler moved to empower himself further by imprisoning and exiling critics. Although Leisler's rule did restore order to New York's colonial government, there was dissension between Leisler's supporters and his enemies, tempering New York politics for years after his demise. In 1691 King William's appointment of Henry Sloughter to take back control of New York ended Leisler's tenure as governor. Upon Sloughter's arrival in New York soon after, however, Leisler refused to surrender the city's fort, resulting in casualties on both sides. On May 16, 1691, Leisler and his second-in-command, Jacob Milburne, were hanged for treason.

Although some historians point to Leisler's rebellion as an early revolutionary movement, most analysts agree that the movement was religiously and economically motivated. Still, Leisler's Rebellion, along with similar rebellious activities in Maryland and New England during this period, reflected the increasingly unstable relationships between the colonies and the Crown as economic, governmental, and religious ties were being defined.

THE RISE OF THE COLONIAL ASSEMBLY

Upon his ascension to the throne, King William III disbanded his predecessor's plans for the Dominion of New England, setting the stage for the reestablishment of the colonial assembly that New York colonists fervently desired. Benjamin Fletcher, a new governor with military experience, arrived in New York to create the assembly. It was established before the end of 1691, putting New York on an even standing with other English colonies in North America, which had enjoyed the benefits of an assembly for quite some time. Notably, the governor's council became the upper house of the legislative assembly and also took over some judicial duties. Still, at the time, New York was not protected well from New France, it remained politically unstable, and its English population was far from being a majority.

Governor Fletcher did not follow his orders from King William III to the letter. Instead of remaining neutral on the emotionally charged issue of Leisler and his legacy, Fletcher allied himself openly with anti-Leislerians in the colonial assembly. Consequently, the assembly was able to pass vindictive laws against Leisler's supporters, further harming the stability of the colony. While the squabbling continued, Fletcher was unable to put together an army substantial enough to attack New France or even to support England's Iroquois allies, who were bearing the brunt of the French and Native American raids. By 1695, Leislerians were able to gain a majority in the assembly, revoking the penalties established against Leisler's former supporters. Soon after, complaints about Fletcher's close relationship with the aristocracy, his distribution of massive land grants to wealthy supporters, and his indifference to piracy reached England, leading to his dismissal in 1697.

In contrast, the next governor, Richard Coote, the Earl of Bellomont, allied himself with the Leislerians, who continued to stay in power in the assembly. Coote's actions were a cause for concern for New York's wealthy aristocracy, but Coote died soon after his appointment in 1701. Lord Edward Cornbury was appointed governor after Coote's death, and he ended the Leislerian domination in the assembly. Cornbury was notoriously greedy, enough to force even wealthy aristocrats to question his management of colony money. In the assembly, proponents of free trade, mostly wealthy merchants, lobbied for the removal of tariffs and for protections for local industries. In 1704, in reaction to Cornbury's mismanagement, the assembly called for the creation of a treasurer to handle money. The plan calling for a treasurer also disallowed the right of the governor's council to amend financial legislation. Although the Crown opposed removing the governor's ability to change monetary legislation, it did allow the colonists to create the position of treasurer and to deal with "extraordinary" monetary situations unchecked. Thereafter, the assembly deemed all spending "extraordinary," except for the essential provisioning for officials' salaries.

Throughout Cornbury's inefficient administration, assembly representatives worked slowly to transfer power away from the governor to the assembly. Representatives had realized that there was more to fear from the royal governors than from the opposite political party, as exemplified by the Leislerian Rebellion and the administrations of Fletcher, Bellomont, and Cornbury.

Disagreement between groups in the assembly continued, but there was common ground on the issues of taxes, salaries for British officials, and property rights.

When Governor Robert Hunter arrived in New York in 1710, he quickly found that the assembly was bent on continuing to accumulate power. Praised as one of the best royal governors, Hunter cemented his popularity in 1714 with a landmark compromise with the assembly. Hunter agreed to pass a naturalization law, which set conditions for conferring citizenship upon foreign-born colonists of New York, in exchange for a five-year revenue plan. Although the assembly desired the establishment of an annual revenue plan, representatives were unable to pass up a naturalization agreement, which would have prevented new citizens of the British Empire from being banned from trading in the colonies by the Navigation Acts. Economically, the naturalization measure spurred shipbuilding and trade at the port of New York City, which was rapidly expanding and prospering.

Years of steady growth and prosperity followed. From 1720 to 1728, Governor William Burnet worked to improve the English fur trade by banning trade with the French at Montreal and by establishing stronger ties with Native American tribes to the west. His plans were relatively successful but were popularly opposed, and Burnet and his allies lost their majority in the assembly. Confrontation over revenue between the governor and the assembly prompted Burnet to dissolve the body temporarily. The dissolution of the assembly further alarmed electors for the assembly, and it entrenched Burnet's opponents. Burnet's successor, Colonel John Montgomerie, tried to end the confrontation between the governor and his council and the assembly, but he died in 1731 after serving only three years as governor.

Controversy returned quickly when new governor William Cosby reached New York in 1732. During the interim, Rip Van Dam, head of Montgomerie's council, had assumed the powers of governor. Cosby informed Van Dam, whom he believed was embezzling money, that he had to return a sizeable portion of his salary. Van Dam refused. Cosby, who feared losing his case in front of a colonial jury, considered asserting his authority to set up courts. The Crown was in favor of the creation, because it would have offered a way for the British government to collect unpaid money, an issue that the colonial court did not pursue.

Instead of creating a new court, which would have caused a major uproar, Cosby decided to empower the supreme court to handle the case. He believed that Chief Justice Lewis Morris, a political appointee, would rule in his favor to maintain his position. To Cosby's surprise, Morris attacked the constitutionality of the supreme court's new powers and failed to return the verdict Cosby desired. In response, Cosby dismissed Morris from his position.

Soon afterward, in 1733, Morris and his son were elected to the assembly. New York's *Weekly Journal*, published by Peter Zenger, printed articles encouraging Morris's supporters. Cosby ordered the arrest of Zenger and had the paper burned. For Zenger's trial, Cosby disbarred all the lawyers who could possibly take his case. A group of powerful landowners rallied behind Zenger and hired Andrew Hamilton, a young and distinguished lawyer from Philadelphia, to fight Zenger's charges.

Hamilton argued that the jury, not the chief justice, should decide what was a seditious or libelous statement. He also proved that Zenger had never printed false stories, securing Zenger's acquittal and winning one of the landmark cases of colonial times. The precedent set by the case greatly strengthened the freedom of the press in America.

Morris's faction became more powerful in the assembly, forcing Cosby's successor, George Clarke, into an agreement with only one year of colonial revenue support. In return for even one year of support, Clarke agreed to a triennial act, which mandated new elections every three years, and he gave the assembly control over appropriations and expenditures.

The assembly had succeeded in gaining significant power, and it was successful in maintaining its power despite the efforts of the Crown and the British governors to reassert complete control. The Crown's ongoing need for colonial support in the wars with New France often gave the assembly the upper hand in debates.

Governor George Clinton, who presided over New York from 1743 to 1753, had one of the most turbulent and confrontational tenures of any royal governor. At first, he enlisted the support of James de Lancey, a wealthy and powerful colonial judge. De Lancey gave his support to, fought for, and won a one-year support bill for Clinton and received sizeable patronage in turn. Clinton hoped to build forts along New York's northern frontier and to mount an expedition against the French, but he was dismayed at the funding allocated, which he considered insufficient. Consequently, Clinton railed against Albany merchants and citizens, who continued to trade with the French and failed to supply ample food for troops stationed there. His attacks were so concerted that even de Lancey broke his ties with Clinton.

The confrontation that ensued dealt primarily with the issue of sovereignty. The political battle lasted from 1746 to 1750. The argument was relatively simple: the de Lanceys, who controlled the assembly, believed that the assembly had sole control over financial legislation, whereas Clinton and his supporters believed that the governor shared his powers with the assembly. By 1750, both sides were exhausted, particularly the de Lanceys, who had embezzled public money and did not want word of their actions to circulate. An agreement was signed, providing one year of support, allowing the leaders of Albany to determine their own fur trade policies, and providing payment for officials' salaries. In addition, the assembly also agreed to give up its more extreme claims, like the claim for complete control of finance and its refusal to allow the governor to introduce financial legislation.

Following Clinton and the suicide of his successor, Sir Danvers Osborne, James de Lancey became governor. He served for two years and was able to increase the governor's powers without sparking controversy with the assembly. Later, de Lancey returned to his position as chief justice, and a new governor, Sir Charles Hardy, was appointed. Hardy's main concern was the protection of New York against French and Native American raids. After Hardy, a controversy arose between the governor and the assembly on the issue of judges' tenure. The assembly's success in this disagreement was assured, because it controlled and paid the judges' salaries.

THE ROAD TO REVOLUTION

Following Great Britain's success in the French and Indian War, citizens throughout New York were proud of their accomplishments in the war and were also proud of their citizenship and empire. New York City's growth continued, spurred by an aggressive merchant class that enjoyed the benefits of the vast British Empire and its wide array of profitable goods. Land speculators and expansionists were optimistic about the opportunities offered by the surrender of New France and the collapse of French support for its Native American allies.

Soon, however, the merchants and the expansionists were disappointed. The Crown, fearing the need for further military action and recognizing the inconsistent Native American policies in the various colonies, issued the Proclamation of 1763. It provided strict controls for the fur trade and closed the lands west of the Appalachian Mountains to settlement. Although no serious rebellious activities resulted from the Proclamation of 1763, it affected a wealthy group of citizens—merchants and land speculators who were powerful and politically connected within the colony.

In 1764 the *Forsey v. Cunningham* case aroused hatred. Waddel Cunningham was found guilty of assaulting Thomas Forsey on a street in New York City. Forsey was awarded £1,500, but Cunningham appealed the verdict to Governor Cadwallader Colden and his council. Outrage arose when Colden considered the appeal, sparking harsh criticism by local lawyers and judges. Chief Justice Daniel Horsmanden was particularly opposed and expressed his belief that a verdict by a jury under English common law was unquestionable. In the end, the governor's council rebuked the governor's efforts to review the case, but Colden's actions had aroused opposition even though his efforts had failed.

Also in 1764, Parliament passed the Sugar Act, replacing the Molasses Act of 1733, further angering powerful and well-connected merchants. The Sugar Act reduced the duty on foreign molasses, forbade the importation of any rum that was not distilled within the British Empire, and set tax rates on other goods from the islands in the West Indies under foreign control. Although the Sugar Act was more liberal than its predecessor, merchants were angered because the new act was actually enforced. To worsen the situation, merchants at the time were fondly recalling the prosperity during the French and Indian War. The current economic times were difficult, even without the new regulations.

Reaction to the Sugar Act was quick and heated. Even before news of the Sugar Act reached the colony on April 6, 1764, colonial merchants were already protesting to the Board of Trade. Afterward, in October of the same year, the assembly sent letters to the Crown and Parliament denouncing the right of Parliament to tax citizens from New York without their consent. New Yorkers discussed the possibility of banning British imports and even made some plans to establish industries in the colony that would reduce dependence on British manufacturing.

When Lord Grenville estimated that it cost Great Britain £360,000 to maintain troops in the colonies and stated that the American colonies should pay one-third of the burden, relations were strained further, especially since the controversial Sugar Act raised only £45,000 of the estimated £120,000. Although the colonial assemblies were called upon to formulate a plan to pay the remaining £75,000, they refused to take action.

Parliament responded by passing the Stamp Act, which added a variety of fees that businessmen were forced to pay on certain documents and papers, effective November 1, 1765. News of the passage sparked an even larger controversy. Colonists, who maintained that Parliament had authority only to regulate trade, were angered by the act's obvious revenue intent. The act proved to be difficult and upsetting during the strenuous economic times. By 1765, some colonists were expressing their desire for independence for the first time, if the problem could not be ameliorated.

When the colonists learned of the Stamp Act, they had six months to organize resistance before it went into effect. New York's organization against the Stamp Act was so effective that it was never enforced within the colony. James McEvers, a New York merchant, was appointed to be the collector of the Stamp Act duties in New York City. By July 1, the public learned of his new position, and by August 30, about two months before the Stamp Act took effect, McEvers resigned, citing a fear of bodily harm. From October 7 to October 25, the Stamp Act Congress, convened by the General Court of Massachusetts, met in New York City, attended by delegates from nine of the colonies. At the conclusion of the meeting, after sessions of planning countermeasures, the group of delegates angrily denounced the Stamp Act.

In October 1765, a radical organization, known as the Sons of Liberty, that championed the use of force against the Crown and Parliament began to gain strength in New York, primarily among laborers and artisans. By October 23, 1765, probably in response to lobbying by the Sons of Liberty, the leading merchants of New York agreed that they would not purchase European goods until the Stamp Act was repealed.

When the effective date for Stamp Act enforcement finally arrived, New Yorkers responded with closed shops, flags at half-mast, tolling church bells, fiery pamphlets, and angry mobs. On November 5, Governor Cadwallader Colden promised not to enforce the Stamp Act and delivered the cargo of stamps to the mayor of New York City. By March 20, 1766, American boycotts of British goods had severely affected business in Great Britain, and the Stamp Act was revoked.

Embarrassed by the failure of the Stamp Act, Parliament passed legislation to reassert its authority over the colonies. The New York Restraining Act prevented the colonial assembly from conducting business until proper barracks and supplies were constructed and provisioned for the British troops stationed in the colony. There were large numbers of troops in the colony, because General Thomas Gage's headquarters were located in New York. New York eventually complied with the demands of the Quartering Act of 1765, which required the colonies to provide suitable housing for British troops, but only after the assembly was suspended temporarily. The New York Restraining Act was only one of the companion measures of the Townshend Acts, which also placed taxes on paper, tea, lead, paint, and glass.

Reaction to the Townshend Acts was minimal in New York, when compared with the uproar caused by the Stamp Act. It seemed that New Yorkers were waiting to see the reactions of Philadelphia and Boston before taking a position on the new acts. The new taxes were collected with only minor incidents for more than twelve months. The major problem at the time was economic. Farmers and merchants were struggling, and the Sons of Liberty took advantage of the situation, blaming the problems on the British. By August 27, 1768, the New York merchants finally answered calls for another boycott and again agreed not to purchase British goods until the Townshend Acts were repealed.

Meanwhile, elections for the assembly were held and marked a significant change in power for New York politics. The Livingstonite faction, led by popular merchant Philip Livingston, slowly began to lose its grip on power in the assembly, replaced by the rising DeLanceyite faction, led by James de Lancey, Jr. To challenge the Livingstonites, the DeLanceyites questioned its opposition's moderate position on the Stamp Act, presented them as wealthy manor lords, and spoke of better economic opportunities. Following the dissolution of the assembly as a result of the New York Restraining Act, James de Lancey solidified his reputation when he refused appointment by the governor to the Provincial Council, preferring instead to be an elected official of the people.

The Sons of Liberty, who were largely responsible for the DeLanceyites' control of the assembly, were increasingly gaining strength. In January 1770, tensions rose when British soldiers chopped down New York City's Liberty Tree, an action that enraged the Sons of Liberty. The Sons of Liberty quickly engineered an angry protest of about three thousand people. A few days later, on January 19, 1770, a group of New Yorkers engaged some British soldiers in a skirmish known as the Battle of Golden Hill, resulting in some minor injuries and bloodied clothing.

The sparks of anger and violence were quieted for the moment when news of the repeal of the Townshend Acts arrived in April 1770. The relative calm of 1771 and 1772 ended when news of the passage of the Tea Act reached New York. The Tea Act, which granted a monopoly on the tea trade to the East India Company and actually resulted in cheaper tea for the citizenry of New

York, angered merchants who lost tea customers and sparked outcries against "taxation without representation."

A boycott of tea from the East India Company resulted. News of the Boston Tea Party, during which colonists dressed as natives stormed a merchant ship and threw tons of tea into the harbor, strengthened New Yorkers' resolve to refuse to allow tea from the East India Company to be unloaded. In April of 1774, New Yorkers held their own version of the Boston Tea Party, when colonists boarded the cargo ship *London* and threw eighteen crates of tea into the harbor.

The British Parliament responded to the colonists' actions with the Intolerable Acts, five acts that punished Boston's insubordination by restructuring its government, closing its harbor, updating the hated Quartering Act, and allowing British officials accused of committing a crime in the colonies to be tried in Great Britain. The closing of Boston's harbor and the restructuring of Massachusetts' government particularly alarmed and angered New Yorkers, who had enjoyed the benefits of a strong legislative assembly for many years.

Meanwhile, a new committee of correspondence, independent of the colonial assembly, had been established in January of 1774 better to coordinate resistance to Parliament's actions among the colonies. On May 15, 1774, New York's committee of correspondence recommended that New York City host a congress made up of delegates from all the colonies to plan a common course of action. Virginia's House of Burgesses' call for a September meeting in Philadelphia, however, received support and won out.

The New York delegates to the First Continental Congress seem to have been chosen by the more radical elements of colonial society, without significant opposition from conservative groups. The delegates were Simon Boerum, John Haring, James Duane, John Jay, Philip Livingston, William Floyd, Henry Wisner, John Alsop, and Isaac Low. Low was chairman of the Committee of Fifty-One, an organization created by citizens to prevent the closure of New York City's harbor by the British. At the congress, however, New York's delegation, which simply sought a review of grievances with Great Britain, was more conservative than other delegations. At the conclusion of the sessions, the colonists had agreed to form the Continental Association, which banned trade with Great Britain. In accordance with the association, each town or city was called upon to form its own committee to observe the ban.

Soon after in New York City, a committee known as the Committee of Sixty replaced the Committee of Fifty-One. As the date for the Second Continental Congress in Philadelphia approached, the New York colonial assembly refused to appoint delegates to the meeting. In response, the Committee of Sixty called upon the local committees throughout New York to send delegates to a state convention. First meeting on April 20, 1775, the state convention, known as the First Provincial Congress, selected delegates to the Continental Congress and then adjourned within two days. Isaac Low and John Haring were not returned as delegates, but the others were, along with Philip Schuyler,

George Clinton, Lewis Morris, Francis Lewis, and Robert R. Livingston. News of the Battle of Lexington and Concord reached New York on the day after the adjournment of the First Provincial Congress.

On April 28, 1775, the Committee of Sixty expressed its desire to establish a permanent state government, but the committee was replaced soon after by the even more radical Committee of One Hundred, which controlled New York until the Second Provincial Congress began on May 25, 1775. In early May, before the meeting of the Second Provincial Congress, Ethan Allen and his group of Green Mountain Boys captured Fort Ticonderoga, and Seth Warner and a group of New Englanders seized Fort Crown Point only two days later.

Before the Second Provincial Congress met, military action had already taken place in New York. The formation of defense, most importantly a militia, was the principal issue that the Provincial Congress had to debate. During the meetings of the Provincial Congress, on June 6, 1775, British troops stationed at New York City were moved to secure Boston. By October, Acting Governor William Tryon fled, choosing to run what was left of his administration from a British warship.

Meanwhile, in late August, General Richard Montgomery and General Benedict Arnold began their ill-fated invasion of Quebec, capturing Montreal but failing to capture Quebec City. Another confrontation in New York occurred on August 23, 1775, when the cannons from the warship *Asia* fired on New York militia attempting to remove artillery from Fort George on Manhattan Island. The militia fired back, killing a British soldier and wounding others. Although the fighting intensified around the colony, New York's Provincial Congress, now in its third session, was reluctant to commit to independence, and statements by the congress reaffirmed its desire for rapprochement with the British until January 12, 1776, when the desire was confirmed in a letter to merchants in Quebec.

The position of rapprochement taken by the Third Provincial Congress proved problematic for New York's delegates at the Second Continental Congress. The delegates asked the Provincial Congress whether they had authority to debate the issue of independence. On June 11, 1776, the Provincial Congress informed the delegates that they were not empowered to speak in favor of independence. New York's stance was alarming to other prominent patriots, including John Adams of Massachusetts who asked, "Have they no sense, no feeling? No sentiment? No passions? While every other Colony is rapidly advancing, their motions seem to be rather retrograde."[12]

When the Declaration of Independence was adopted by the Continental Congress, New York's delegates refrained from voting. About the same time, following elections, the Fourth Provincial Congress met at White Plains on July 9, 1776, and quickly approved the Declaration of Independence. The next day, the congress changed its name to the Convention of the Representatives of the State of New York, completing the formation of an independent state. Only a few days before, on July 2, 1776, Sir William Howe began to land his troops on Staten Island. The forces were part of the largest fleet ever seen in North America.

INDEPENDENCE AND THE REVOLUTIONARY WAR

From the beginning of the Revolutionary War, New Yorkers understood the strategic value of their state's geographical position, specifically the north-south Hudson, Lake Champlain, and Richelieu waterway, which ensured that New England was not cut off from the rest of the colonies. New York City, with its magnificent harbor and central location, offered the British military an important base from which it could oversee actions and dispatch troops.

Soon after the landing of British troops at Staten Island, Sir William Howe's assembled force consisted of over 31,000 troops. Last-minute peace negotiations between Washington and Howe failed, and the British offensive began during the evening of August 26, 1776. Known as the Battle of Long Island, General George Washington's troops were badly defeated, a disaster that was lessened only by a well-planned retreat on the evening of August 29, 1776. After further attempts at peace failed, British forces occupied New York City on September 15, 1776.

New York City remained in British hands until November 25, 1783, even after the conclusion of the Revolutionary War, providing a strategic base for the British, a constant thorn in Washington's side, and a haven for Loyalists. Unfazed, the Fourth Provincial Congress formed a constitutional committee on August 1, 1776, charged with the task of formulating the state's government.

The constitution of 1777, which was the document produced by the committee, is believed to be primarily the work of John Jay, with the help of Robert R. Livingston, Gouverneur Morris, and James Duane. The group disliked, or was afraid of, the plan of government established by Pennsylvania, choosing rather to have a strong, popularly elected governor to counter the legislature, rather than a weak president. At the same time, the group believed that Maryland's new governmental plan was too reactionary, with extreme voting requirements and an odd election schedule.

The constitution of 1777 was clearly modeled after the governmental system of colonial New York. The legislature had two chambers, the senate and the assembly. Senators were elected from one of the four senatorial districts for terms of four years, and representatives in the assembly were selected from each county, based on population, for one-year terms. The court system remained relatively unchanged, except final appellate decisions were to be made by a Court of Errors and Impeachment. The position of governor remained, but certain powers and authorities were taken away. The governor was the commander of the military forces and had the power to call special meetings of the legislature, to postpone legislative sessions for up to sixty days, and to grant pardons. His veto power was lessened significantly; to veto legislation the governor needed the approval of the Council of Revision, which also included the chancellor, supreme court judges, and four senators nominated by the assembly. Even the veto by the Council of Revision could be overturned by a two-thirds majority in each chamber of the legislature.

In the end, the constitution of 1777 was noticeably undemocratic. To vote for the assembly, individuals had to own property valued at least £20.[13] To vote for the governor or senators, citizens had to own property valued at least £100.[14] Some individual rights, including the separation of church and state, freedom of religion, and trial by jury, were protected.

Elections were soon held, and George Clinton, a lawyer, general, former member of the colonial assembly, and a delegate at the Second Continental Congress, was chosen as governor, enjoying support from soldiers, laborers, and farmers. Clinton served as governor for the next eighteen years. A few months later, in September 1777, the legislature met in Kingston. It was soon forced to flee from Sir Henry Clinton and his army as they tried to march up the Hudson to meet with General Burgoyne.

Luckily for the Continental Army, the meeting between Clinton and Burgoyne never occurred. Instead, Burgoyne's troops were steadily worn down and were seriously defeated at Saratoga, resulting in his capitulation on October 17, 1777. Burgoyne's defeat and the resulting British failure to control the Hudson, Champlain, and Richelieu waterway raised American morale and led to France's entry into the war against Great Britain.

Battles continued to rage along New York's frontier, carried out by Iroquois and Loyalist raiding parties, but most of New York remained under patriot control, except for the state's only valuable seaport and largest city, New York. In February 1778 the state legislature responded to the Loyalist crisis by establishing the Commissioners for Detecting and Defeating Conspiracies. The announced policy was to convert Loyalists to the patriot cause, but harassment and imprisonment continued unabated.

Economic problems worsened the situation facing Loyalists. State funding for the war came from two sources, taxes and confiscation of Loyalists' property. In the fall of 1779, the legislature passed a cumbersome tax plan based upon "circumstances and abilities," which called for elected tax collectors to assess and to collect the amount that individuals could afford.[15] Loyalist property was targeted. In 1779 the official Loyalist policy changed from controlling Loyalists' activities to punishing them, resulting in the passage of a confiscation bill that Governor Clinton supported. Even with confiscation, the state had limited opportunities for revenue. As the war went on, price controls and embargoes were the options most often utilized.

On the national level, the Articles of Confederation formally defined the ties between each state government. New York was the second state to ratify the Articles. New York's delegates James Duane, William Duer, Francis Lewis, and Gouverneur Morris signed the Articles of Confederation on February 6, 1778, and the Continental Congress accepted them on November 15, 1777, but the Articles did not go into effect until Maryland ratified the plan on

March 1, 1781, after New York, Connecticut, and Virginia ceded their claims to northwest territories.

The Articles called for a single-chamber legislature composed of delegates from every state, gave each state one vote in the legislature, and called for an executive to oversee the legislature. The national legislature could conduct only limited foreign diplomacy and depended on tax donations from states; it was unable to regulate interstate trade or maintain an army. To New Yorkers, "the firm friendship" established between the states in the Articles granted more than enough power to the national government. At the time, while fighting the distant and centralized government in Great Britain, most New Yorkers believed their rights would be preserved better by the state than by a centralized government.

Militarily, the last major threat to New York's security ended with the discovery of Benedict Arnold's plan to surrender West Point in 1780. Soon after, General Cornwallis's surrender at Yorktown, Virginia, signaled the end of major fighting. After two years of impasse, on September 3, 1783, British and American diplomats signed a peace treaty ending the Revolutionary War and recognizing the United States as a separate nation.

THE ROAD TO STATEHOOD

When Governor George Clinton was sworn in for his third term of office in 1783, many pressing concerns needed his attention: dealing with Loyalists in New York City and other areas, settling claims to lands in current-day Vermont, and land and monetary policies.

A few people considered Governor Clinton himself to be one of the problems as partisanship quickly emerged following the defeat of the British. With the unifying threat gone, New Yorkers began to join public alliances in support of certain candidates, even though only a portion of the population was able to vote. Politically active citizens like Philip Schuyler, John Jay, and James Duane, were upset by Clinton's success and popular support. Clinton popularity was so great that he was able to run unopposed in 1780 and 1786, although he faced opposition in 1783, 1789, and 1792. Schuyler never pushed for a different office, Jay went to Congress and soon after became a diplomat, whereas Duane worked his way to the office of mayor of New York City following the British evacuation. Consequently, organization of a solid opposition to Clinton and his cohorts was led by Alexander Hamilton, a West Indies immigrant and a famous lawyer.

Hamilton attacked Clinton for his dealings with Loyalists and wealthy citizens and for the way he dealt with taxes, which continued to be collected on the basis of assessment. His views attracted wealthy landowners, particularly those who owned large estates in and around Albany. Hamilton's campaign proved reasonably successful, and all ten assemblymen elected from Albany County in 1785 were replaced by assemblymen more sympathetic to Hamilton's causes.

The same year, 1785, slavery became one of the major issues in New York. About 19,000 slaves lived in the state, and their owners were not eager to give them up. Political figures like Hamilton, Jay, and Clinton spoke out against slavery, but the issue was still highly contested. After numerous debates and numerous votes, the legislature passed a bill that would end slavery gradually but would not grant former slaves all the rights enjoyed by free men, including the right to vote and the right to hold public office. The Council of Revision vetoed the bill because it did not enfranchise freed slaves, and gradual emancipation was not approved in New York until 1799.

With the failure to abolish slavery and the failure to replace Clinton, Hamilton became disenchanted with state politics, instead setting his sights on national politics. Hamilton soon began to find other disaffected citizens with national political ambitions, including John Jay and James Madison. Collectively, they were alarmed by the quality of the assemblymen across the country, by the states that were deep in debt, and by the treatment of Loyalists. New York, in particular, blocked Congress's attempts to procure revenue from the states on two occasions. In Massachusetts, impoverished farmers, led by Daniel Shays, clashed with state troops, while calling for issuance of paper money, government assistance, and abolition of debtors' prisons. The uprising known as "Shays's Rebellion" worsened, forcing Clinton to mobilize a part of New York's militia, but it was quelled on January 25, 1787. Around the same time, New York placed tariffs and fees on ships arriving from New Jersey or Connecticut and on any international goods that reached New York by way of another state.

In addition to the campaigns of Alexander Hamilton and other disaffected politicians, interstate trade began to cause concern and led to a concerted effort to strengthen the central government. In response to these concerns, the legislature of Virginia called for a convention on interstate trade to be held at Annapolis, Maryland, in September of 1786. New York, along with four other states, sent representatives to the convention. Hamilton attended and had the opportunity to compose a report from the convention pointing out the serious defects of the current national government. Back in New York, Governor Clinton disapproved of the convention's report, in part because of party loyalties and also because New York continued to benefit from its collection of tariffs. Others questioned a strong central government's ability to protect a citizen's rights.

In response to the call for delegates to attend a convention in Philadelphia in May 1787, the New York legislature decided to send three delegates, Alexander Hamilton, Robert Yates, and John Lansing, with orders simply to revise the Articles of Confederation. Hamilton was the only member of the New York delegation who wanted to work toward a stronger central government. By early July, Yates and Lansing withdrew from the convention, stating that it had exceeded its authority by drawing up an entirely new constitution. As a result, New York did not have much input at the convention. Only Hamilton remained, playing a minor role in the framing and debate.

Soon after the convention ended, the Constitution was read before the Congress. Once again, a New York representative, Melancton Smith, attempted to stop the proposed Constitution, claiming that the lack of a Bill of Rights made the new document impossible to consider. Smith's protests failed, and Congress passed the Constitution on September 28, 1787, submitting it to each of the individual states for approval. Because of the scheduling of New York's legislature, the ratification debate in the legislature did not begin until January 1788, but the public fight for support began long before that time.

THE FIGHT FOR RATIFICATION

New York was considered one of the most important battlegrounds for ratification of the Constitution. On February 1, 1788, the New York legislature called for the election of delegates for a convention to meet in Poughkeepsie to debate the ratification of the new Constitution. The calling of elections for the convention was seen as a successful delaying tactic by Clinton, who opposed the new Constitution. Clinton believed that five states were likely to reject the new Constitution; if they did, the delay caused by elections would avoid the need for the convention, because the fate of the Constitution would have been decided before the convention could meet. To guarantee the opposition's success, Clinton and his followers in the New York legislature expanded suffrage in the election for the convention to all free, white males over the age of twenty-one.

The battle for public opinion and division into parties had begun long before the convention convened. The Federalists in New York were at a serious disadvantage from the beginning, because Governor Clinton had an immense following in New York. Alexander Hamilton, realizing the need to win supporters to the Federalist cause, asked for help from James Madison and John Jay. Together, the three composed the *Federalist Papers*, scholarly letters written under a pseudonym, but often the arguments in the expertly composed documents were too deep to have a serious effect on the common citizen.

Responding to the resolution, the counties elected their delegates, who assembled on June 17, 1788. The delegates unanimously selected George Clinton as president of the convention. The ratification debate had become so contested nationwide that Clinton was identified as a prominent Anti-Federalist, a developing political party that opposed ratification of the Constitution. The Federalists, who were in favor of ratification, were led at the convention by Alexander Hamilton. The election had been a success for Clinton and the Anti-Federalists: forty-six Anti-Federalists were chosen, compared with only nineteen Federalists.

Following Clinton's selection as president of the convention, a committee of regulations was chosen, and it soon made its recommendations for the rules of the convention. Oddly, the Anti-Federalists agreed to discuss the Constitution at great length instead of calling for an early vote. Once debate commenced, Alexander Hamilton fought passionately for the Federalist cause, supported by John Jay, James Duane, and Robert R. Livingston. The Anti-Federalists were not led in debate by Clinton, who was quiet publicly and preferred to work behind the scenes. Instead, Anti-Federalist debate was led by Melancton Smith, who had failed to delay the Constitution's adoption at the national Constitutional Convention, and by John Lansing.

Hamilton argued in favor of a stronger federal government, which offered better military protection for all states, common rules for interstate trade, and a national treasury to carry out the needs of the nation. On one occasion he asked, "we are brought to this dilemma—either a federal standing army is to enforce the requisitions, or the federal treasury is left without supplies, and the government without support. What, sir, is the cure for this great evil?"[16] Addressing the Anti-Federalists' concerns for a loss of personal liberties and their proposal to grant increased powers to the current Congress under the Articles, Hamilton stated,

> To take the old Confederation, and fashion upon it these principles, would be establishing a power that would destroy the liberties of the people. These considerations show clearly that a government totally different must be instituted. They had weight in the Convention who formed the new system. It was seen that the necessary powers were too great to be trusted to a single body; they therefore formed two branches, and divided the powers, that each might be a check upon the other.[17]

As debate commenced, it became more obvious that the delaying tactic pursued by the Anti-Federalists had failed. Eight of the nine state ratifications necessary to ensure the implementation of the Constitution had already occurred, whereas only North Carolina and Rhode Island had rejected ratification. Consequently, ratification hinged on the remaining states of Virginia, New York, and New Hampshire. New Hampshire ratified the Constitution on June 21, 1788, achieving the requisite number. When the news that Virginia had ratified the Constitution reached Poughkeepsie during the early morning of July 2, 1788, New York's conventional delegates were faced with a new question: whether or not the state would belong to the new government. Notably, there was a riot in Albany between Federalist and Anti-Federalist supporters on July 4, 1788, resulting in one dead and eighteen wounded.

Melancton Smith, an adamant Anti-Federalist, began to change his views on the Constitution as the situation changed. Instead of fighting not be part of the new Union under the Constitution, he started to search for ways to adjust the new Constitution to make it more acceptable. Smith believed that an increase in representation and a significant limitation of the legislative branch's powers were necessary, proposing both to guarantee the maintenance of personal rights and liberties.[18] Hamilton replied that these amendments were "speculative and useless," because no one could foresee how much population would grow and how the new legislature would operate concerning representation.[19] The flow of the debate at the convention indicates that opinion changed in favor of the Constitution's passage, but many deemed significant amendments to be necessary.

The Federalists at the convention were more than willing to concede to the Anti-Federalists' demands for amendments as long as they did not call for any serious changes to the Constitution or call for the framing convention at Philadelphia to reconvene. Meanwhile, gossip began to circulate that the southern district of the state, an area that was ardently Federalist, might separate from the rest of the state if the Constitution was not approved.

Samuel Jones, a delegate from Queen's County, came up with the biggest compromise at the convention. He proposed that Anti-Federalists vote in favor of the Constitution "in full confidence" that the new government would take New York's concerns into consideration, particularly in reference to the passage of a Bill of Rights to guarantee personal rights and liberties.[20] By the day of the final vote on ratification, a lengthy list of issues had been composed, describing New York's desire for better civilian control over the military and better guarantees of personal freedoms, among others. The list of grievances with the Constitution suggested a framework for the eventual Bill of Rights.

On July 26, 1788, the delegates voted in favor of the new Constitution, but it barely passed, thirty in favor and twenty against, after months of fierce debate. The necessary number of Anti-Federalists switched sides, and a significant number abstained. Nevertheless, New York's participation in the stronger Union was secured. Fittingly, George Washington was inaugurated as the first president of the United States on April 30, 1789, at New York City's Federal Hall.

CONCLUSION

New York was unique among the original thirteen colonies in not sharing their origin as a British colony. The Dutch patroon system that was set up in New Netherland, which created fiefdoms in which investor-owners controlled the law on their land, built an expectation for local governmental control. The Dutch also gave the colony a tradition of religious tolerance. British control of New York did not occur until 1664, when King Charles II of Britain gave his brother, the Duke of York and future King James II, the land occupied by the Dutch. In one of the more remarkable events in history, the Dutch handed over their successful colony to the British without a fight. By 1691, New York was on the same footing as the other British colonies in North America. New York City was the jewel of the colony, a major seaport with a thriving mercantile culture. During and after the Revolutionary War, until November 1783, the British occupied New York City, whereas the state was the scene of numerous battles. When the Revolutionary War was over, New

York, favoring a weak central government so that shipping revenues would remain in the state, became the second state to ratify the Articles of Confederation. New York's continuing reluctance to give up interstate and international commerce revenues to a strong central government continued as the U.S. Constitution was debated. New Yorkers were also unwilling to concede power to a centralized government without a statement of the rights of citizens. This tension caused Federalist supporters John Jay, Alexander Hamilton, and James Madison to compose the *Federalist Papers*, which endure as fundamental documents in American constitutional history. New York did not ratify the U.S. Constitution until July 1788, its decision merely affirming an already accomplished fact.

NOTES

1. The following sources have been consulted extensively and are separately cited only when directly quoted: David M. Ellis, *New York: State and City* (Ithaca, NY: Cornell University Press, 1979); David M. Ellis, James A. Frost, and William B. Fink, *New York: The Empire State*, 5th ed. (Englewood Cliffs, NJ: Prentice-Hall Inc., 1980); David M. Ellis et al., *A Short History of New York State* (Ithaca, NY: Cornell University Press, 1957); Milton M. Klein, ed., *The Empire State: A History of New York* (Ithaca, NY: Cornell University Press, 2001).

2. *Henry Hudson: Explorer of the Hudson River*, http://www.hudsonriver.com/ halfmoonpress/stories/hudson.html (accessed August 5, 2003).

3. Klein, *The Empire State*, p. 25.

4. Ibid.

5. Ibid., p. 34.

6. Ibid., pp. 83–84.

7. Ibid.

8. Ibid., p. 86.

9. Ellis, *Short History of New York State*, p. 24.

10. Klein, *The Empire State*, p. 114.

11. Francis Parkman, *Montcalm and Wolfe: The French and Indian War* (reprint, New York: Da Capo Press, 1984), p. 38.

12. Klein, *The Empire State*, p. 234.

13. "In Convention, Kingston, NY: 1777," in *The Constitution of New York: April 20, 1777*, The Avalon Project, Yale University School of Law, www.yale.edu/lawweb/ avalon/states/ny01.html (accessed August 20, 2003).

14. Ibid.

15. Klein, *The Empire State*, pp. 243–245.

16. "In Convention, Poughkeepsie, NY: 1788," in The *Debates in the Convention of the State of New York on the Adoption of the Federal Constitution*, www.constitution.org/ rc/rat_ny.html (accessed August 20, 2003).

17. Ibid.

18. Ibid.

19. Ibid.

20. Steve Mount, *New York's Ratification*, www.usconstitution.net/rat_ny.html (accessed August 20, 2003).

BIBLIOGRAPHY

Ellis, David M. *New York: State and City*. Ithaca, NY: Cornell University Press, 1979.

———, et al. *A Short History of New York State*. Ithaca, NY: Cornell University Press, 1957.

———, James A. Frost, and William B. Fink. *New York: The Empire State*. 5th ed. Englewood Cliffs, NJ: Prentice-Hall Inc., 1980.

Henry Hudson: Explorer of the Hudson River. May 1996. http://www.hudsonriver.com/halfmoonpress/stories/hudson.html (accessed August 5, 2003).

"In Convention, Kingston, NY: 1777." In *The Constitution of New York: April 20, 1777*. The Avalon Project, Yale University School of Law, www.yale.edu/lawweb/avalon/states/ny01.htm (accessed August 20, 2003).

"In Convention, Poughkeepsie, NY: 1788." In *The Debates in the Convention of the State of New York on the Adoption of the Federal Constitution*, www.constitution.org/rc/rat_ny.htm (accessed August 20, 2003).

Klein, Milton M., ed. *The Empire State: A History of New York*. Ithaca, NY: Cornell University Press, 2001.

Mount, Steve. *New York's Ratification*. www.usconstitution.net/rat_ny.html (accessed August 20, 2003).

Parkman, Francis. *Montcalm and Wolfe: The French and Indian War*. Reprint. New York: Da Capo Press, 1984.

North Carolina

Territorial Development:

- The Carolina Colony is separated from the Commonwealth of Virginia and King Charles II grants the land to eight English gentlemen who had helped him to the throne, 1663
- Carolina is divided into the two separate colonies of North Carolina and South Carolina, 1711
- North Carolina is made a Royal Province, 1729
- Continental Congress approves Declaration of Independence from Great Britain, July 4, 1776
- Great Britain formally recognizes American independence through the Treaty of Paris, September 3, 1783
- North Carolina becomes the twelfth state to ratify the United States Constitution, November 21, 1789

Territorial Capitals:

- New Bern, 1771–1776
- No fixed capital, 1776–1792

State Capitals:

- Raleigh, 1792–present

Origin of State Name: North Carolina was first named in honor of Charles IX of France, and subsequently so called in honor of Charles I and Charles II of England, both of whom made grants to the area.

First Governor: Samuel Johnston
Governmental Organization: Bicameral
Population at Statehood: 395,005
Geographical Size: 48,711 square miles

THE STATE OF NORTH CAROLINA

Ratified the Constitution of the United States: November 21, 1789

Chad Morgan

INTRODUCTION

The southern Appalachians have been called the "South's South" because all of the stereotypes and many of the realities that distinguished the South from the rest of the country were even more prevalent there than elsewhere in the region. It might similarly be said that North Carolina, at least in the Revolutionary and early national periods, could profitably be viewed as America's America. The state possessed more fully than any other the independent attitude and aversion to central authority that drove America's revolution. North Carolina was at the front of the movement to declare independence from Britain. Together with Rhode Island, it was last to ratify the in some ways counterrevolutionary document that was the Constitution. In the new era, North Carolina became a stronghold for Jeffersonian Republicanism and a bulwark against the centralizing impulse of federalism. This intense drive for independence alternately propelled and beset North Carolina on its long and tortuous road to statehood.[1]

Originally granted to eight "Lords Proprietors" as part of the Carolina Charter of 1663, the territory that became North Carolina was for most of the colonial period defined by what it was not—namely Virginia and South Carolina. In contrast to those two colonies, North Carolina evolved no large ersatz aristocracy and no comparable plantation economy. It was, in the famous phrase of the day, "a vale of humility between two mountains of conceit." Nor did the new state's reputation change with the Revolution. In the early national period, North Carolina earned the sobriquet the "Rip Van Winkle State." Like Washington Irving's most famous character, the state seemed to slumber for decades at a time while the world around marched forward.

Such stereotypes had their basis in truth. Numerous obstacles littered the path of North Carolina's early development. For one, the barrier islands known as the Outer Banks seriously restricted the state's connection to the world market, and early settlers' goods passed through Virginia ports. Not until the settlement of the Lower Cape Fear Valley in the 1720s did the state have a serviceable deep-water harbor. Dense woods and poor internal transportation made movement within the state difficult and increased settlers' isolation from both the wider world and one another. North Carolina also suffered from a relative lack of top-grade soils. Compared with Virginia and South Carolina, few large-scale plantations took root to buoy the colony's export economy. In the early Republic, another natural barrier to development surfaced. Located more than 150 miles inland, the remoteness of North Carolina's fall line (and thus the source of early mills' motor power) from coastal markets prevented the development of early manufactures. This distance was less of a problem in other southern states that shared North Carolina's liability but which also possessed vital plantation economies. Because of the slow pace of economic growth and development, North Carolina became proverbial for its social and economic backwardness. In this period, natives of the Old North State acquired an irksome and enduring reputation for malnutrition and illiteracy.[2]

The stereotypes, however, failed to convey what North Carolina had become, which was a diverse, populous, even prosperous colony. The English founders had originally populated the northeastern corner of the colony. They were followed by Highland Scots and Scotch-Irish who came in large numbers to southeastern North Carolina during the eighteenth century. Germans pushed into the interior, establishing important settlements at Salem and Charlotte. Finally, North Carolina's African American population grew geometrically as labor-hungry landlords imported slaves to work increasingly numerous plantations. Numbering fewer than 500 in 1700, the ranks of black North Carolinians had swelled to 33,554 in 1760 and to more than 100,000 by 1790. The state as a whole grew from 15,120 inhabitants in 1710 to 110,442 in 1760, attaining a higher population than Georgia, New Jersey, and rival South Carolina and becoming the fourth largest state when independence was declared. The burgeoning slave population also indicated the colony's rapidly expanding plantation economy. Still, compared with other southern colonies, a greater proportion of North Carolina farmers remained yeomen, growing enough for their own needs and rarely buying or selling goods in the market. A vigorous naval stores industry simultaneously blossomed, adding texture to the colonial economy.[3]

On the precipice of the revolution, North Carolina was a paradox: isolated, backward, and, through it all, prospering, but not to the extent of many of her sister colonies. The remoteness of the colonists, their general self-sufficiency, and the example of slavery in their midst made North Carolina whites averse to any form of dependence. A half-century after independence, one North Carolina matron admonished her half-brother, then just entering manhood, to accept no charity except as a matter of life and death: "Resolutely determine to submit to the narrowness of your means, rather than forfeit your independence by incurring obligations." (The writer of the letter also included instructions to her relation on the propriety of generosity to others, but realistically concluded that "Considering your prospects, Joe, I have been unnecessarily prolix on the subject of alms-giving.") The emphasis on personal independence was even more pronounced fifty years earlier.[4]

Jealous of their freedom from personal and economic obligations, North Carolinians proved equally unenthusiastic about the encroachment of distant governments, including that of their own state. One of the earliest prominent examples of this propensity came when Parliament passed the infamous Stamp Act. After a century of benign neglect toward its North American colonies, Britain decided in the early- to mid-1760s to change its policy. Having just fought the expensive and exhausting Seven Years' War, known on this side of the Atlantic as the French and Indian War, England determined it was time the colonies started contributing to their defense and paying their keep. The war, after all, had been largely fought for their security. The first measure taken to rein in the colonists was the Royal Proclamation of 1763, which prohibited them from settling beyond the Appalachian Mountains and thereby further antagonizing Native Americans. The following year, the Sugar Act, taxing coffee, indigo, molasses, sugar, and other luxuries, was passed. Neither of those actions provoked the colonists as much as the Stamp Act. Passed in 1765, that law placed a duty on paper to be used for contracts, deeds, playing cards, newspapers, and legal documents of virtually all descriptions. It was called the Stamp Act because all such paper required an official stamp. London was surprised that the new impost raised hackles in the New World, because a similar tax had been in place in Britain for years.[5]

Other colonies, notably Massachusetts, are better remembered for protests against the Stamp Act, but North Carolina's reaction was immediate and unmistakable. In Wilmington there were spontaneous demonstrations against that measure. A contemporary newspaper reported that "near Five Hundred People assembled together in this Town, and exhibited the Effigy of a certain HONOURABLE GENTLEMAN; and after letting it hang by the Neck for some Time, near the Court-House, they made a large Bonfire with a Number of Tar-Barrels &c. and committed it to the flames." The "honorable gentleman" in question, according to the report, was a local worthy who had "expressed himself much in Favour of the STAMP-DUTY." In October of the same year, "a great Number of People again assembled, and produced an Effigy of Liberty, which they put into a Coffin, and marched in solemn Procession with it to the Church-Yard." Finally, "three or four hundred people" greeted the first stamp distributors "with Drums beating and Colours flying, and repaired to the House the said STAMP-OFFICER put up at, and insisted upon knowing, 'Whether he intended to execute his said Office, or not?'" The officer replied that he would "be very sorry to execute any Office disagreeable to the People of the Province."

Still unsatisfied, the mob continued on to the houses of others associated with the act and harassed them. In February, Wilmington citizens joined together in a formal association to "mutually and solemnly plight our faith and honour, that we will risque whatever and whenever called upon, unite, and truly and faithfully assist each other to the best of our Power, in preventing entirely the operation of the Stamp Act." Faced with the tax, citizens of the port city avowed their preference of "death to slavery," and swore they would fight rather than be so oppressed.[6]

Wilmington was not the only quarter in which Stamp Act dissent flared. Indeed, the city's threat of armed resistance paled next to the mob activities in the temporary capital at Brunswick. Until the completion of Tryon Palace at New Bern in 1770, the colonial capital was located wherever the governor made his home. Governor William Tryon "observed" in Brunswick "a body of men in arms from four to five hundred move towards the house." Their complaint with the governor was that one Mr. Pennington, a royal official sent to exact the odious stamp tax, had taken refuge in the magistrate's home. Led by Wilmington assemblyman Cornelius Harnett, the mob requested Pennington come out. Before letting him go, Tryon accepted—demanded, really—the bureaucrat's resignation, hoping it would earn him softer treatment at the hands of the crowd. Apparently, the gambit helped: Pennington was made only to swear an oath "that he would never issue any stamped paper in this province," and then was released. Still, the presence of so substantial an "insurrection" testified to the colonists' keenness to challenge any authority they deemed illegitimate.[7]

The most notable revolt against governmental authority during colonial times, however, was the controversy over "Regulation" that gripped the North Carolina backcountry in the late 1760s and early 1770s. To assess the Regulation issue, a solid understanding of the colonial context and especially colonial government is necessary. Since its first European settlement, North Carolina had been quite loosely governed. Under the Lords Proprietors, the government consisted of a governor and his council, an elected assembly, and courts, but civil authority often seemed to disappear completely, as when an adventurer and thug named John Culpepper fomented a rebellion that nearly brought down the colonial administration in 1677. This laxity started to tighten when the English Crown assumed control of the colony in 1729. From that point forward, the mother country steadily tried to exert more control over a territory that had theretofore been an English colony in name only. To this end, it tried to diminish the power of the assembly by making the governor, judiciary, and all other colonial officials more independent of that body.[8]

The augmented power of the governor and judiciary weakened the popular voice within government. The movement toward a more centralized, less democratic government was the more galling in the western part of the state, because most officials tended to come from the ranks of the eastern elite. With time, the eastern-dominated colonial government became increasingly obnoxious to its citizens, especially in the rapidly developing Piedmont. There, a group calling themselves the Regulators—they wanted, they said, to "regulate" their own affairs—coalesced around the issue of excessive and unjust taxation. They objected most notably to the use of western taxes to defray the cost of building Tryon Palace in New Bern. Was the Regulation controversy a harbinger of the Revolution? Was it a class struggle? A sectional struggle? The best and most recent study of the movement emphasizes the class component of the struggle, especially different concepts of independence held by members of the elite and by commoners. For present purposes, it is enough to note that, faced with taxes they considered arbitrary, thousands of North Carolinians declined to pay them and inaugurated a sustained protest that became muted only when Regulator forces were defeated militarily at Alamance Creek in 1771.[9]

It is not surprising, therefore, that North Carolina was in the vanguard of states pushing for independence three years later. Nor was the movement for independence limited to groups who had previously protested taxation by the colony. In fact, much, if not most, of the protest against increased parliamentary taxation came from the Regulators' old enemies, the eastern elite. Their opposition was perhaps to have been expected, because, to the degree that Parliament encroached on the colony's power of self-government, it was impinging on a prerogative that had traditionally been reserved for wealthy, long-established easterners. As Edenton planter James Iredell wrote in his 1774 *Address to the Inhabitants of Great Britain*, the principal difficulty arose from "two independent legislatures...clash[ing] by different regulations about the same objects." That is, Iredell and other North Carolina nabobs balked at having to share or cede authority they felt rightfully theirs. Consternation over taxation was not confined to eastern men. At the so-called Edenton Tea Party in October 1774, fifty-one North Carolina women resolved to drink no more British tea and wear no more British cloth.[10]

Probably the more flamboyant protestations of independence emanated from the backcountry. The strongest remonstrance came from Mecklenburg County, where a citizens' committee declared in May 1775 that all "commissions civil and military heretofore granted by the Crown in these colonies are null and void" and that "all former laws are now suspended in this Province." It should be noted that the Mecklenburg Resolves, as this remarkable document came to be called, has not survived, and there are doubts as to its authenticity. Assuming the Resolves are legitimate, the Mecklenburg County body that drafted them obviously overreached its authority in declaring the independence, apparently, of all of Britain's American colonies. That task would have to fall to the Second Continental Congress.[11]

If a single North Carolina county could not by itself remove the colonies from the British Empire, more concerted action could, and the state actively promoted a united colonial front against the depredations of the Crown and Parliament. Following the Boston Tea Party, North Carolina moved swiftly to send representatives to the First Continental Congress. In defiance of Governor Josiah Martin, thirty counties and several cities elected delegates to the first provincial congress, to be held in New Bern in August, 1774. The location of the congress at the colonial capital, whence it had been moved from an initially designated inland location, was meant as a direct challenge to Martin's authority. Once in New Bern, the delegates took three days to elect Richard Caswell, Joseph Hewes, and William Hooper to represent North Carolina at the Continental Congress and to empower them to endorse whatever measure that body sponsored. Delegates also authorized moderator John Harvey to convoke a new provincial congress when necessary.[12]

It soon became so. After the Continental Congress adopted a Declaration of Rights in October 1774, events moved rapidly. The second provincial congress convened in the month the War for Independence erupted, April 1775, only to be peremptorily shut down by Martin. After the governor fled North Carolina in the summer, a third provincial congress gathered in the symbolically important town of Hillsborough, seedbed of the Regulation controversy. In August, that body, representing every county and town within the colony, made provision for the raising of troops and the reestablishment of government after the flight of Martin. It was decided, furthermore, that the provincial congress would serve temporarily as the lawmaking body and that executive responsibility would devolve on a provincial council. Judicial authority was dispersed among numerous district and local committees.[13]

These were dramatic measures for what was technically still a British colony. That status, of course, soon changed. At the Battle of Moore's Creek Bridge on February 27, 1776, North Carolina patriots became the first outside of Massachusetts to challenge British authority militarily. They distinguished themselves again by being the first to call for independence. In April, a fourth provincial congress met in Halifax. The delegates there drafted and passed the pivotal Halifax Resolves, which declared "the King and Parliament of Great Britain" to have "usurped a power over the persons and properties of the [American] people uncontrouled." And whereas it had been the former will of the "United Colonies…to be reconciled to the Mother Country on constitutional principles," that reconciliation had become impossible. Instead, North Carolina empowered the delegates it was sending to the Second Continental Congress "to concur with the delegates of the other Colonies in declaring independency." In Philadelphia, the Halifax Resolves met with enthusiastic approval. The swelling chorus for independence led to the declaration of July 4.[14]

Not all North Carolinians were patriots. The new state also had a substantial Tory population that remained loyal to Great Britain. Unsurprisingly, much of the Loyalists' support came from North Carolinians of English descent who were loath to separate from the mother country. More unexpected was the almost universal defense of the Crown offered up by Highland Scots in the Cape Fear Valley, an ethnic group that had come to the New World to escape English hegemony in their homeland. Their allegiance was more mysterious because many Sandhills Scots had tasted blood and witnessed British atrocities at the Battle of Culloden in 1746. Nevertheless, because so many former Highlanders benefited from British patronage of their naval stores industries, they shelved their former animosity. After his Pyrrhic victory at Guilford Court House in March 1781, Lord Cornwallis opted to retreat through the predominantly Scottish southeastern part of the state rather than risk traversing less friendly country. The price of remaining loyal to Britain was often great. Loyalists found guilty of lending succor to the enemy could be sentenced to death. Tory property was subject to frequent confiscation. After the war, many Loyalists, fearing for their life and property, moved to England or to another British colony.[15]

FROM COLONIAL TO INDEPENDENT GOVERNMENT

Despite the large population that stayed loyal to Britain, after 1776, North Carolina, with the rest of the colonies, was officially no longer a part of the British Empire. A more permanent government was needed to replace the colonial apparatus. Establishing a government was to be the Achilles' heel for the Tarheel State. However adept North Carolinians may have been at dissolving governmental authority—moving decisively, even rashly, to "regulate" their own interests and, later, to exit the empire—they showed themselves decidedly less proficient at reconstituting that authority in a different form. This tendency had social roots. The distinguished Revolutionary historian Gordon Wood has written that "[p]erhaps no ruling group in the eighteenth-century colonies was weaker and more vulnerable to challenge than that of North Carolina." The result had been a society and people profoundly suspicious of and resistant to constituted authority. This radically anti-authoritarian propensity played havoc with every effort made by North Carolina to replace the colonial administration.[16]

North Carolina's first attempt at building a viable government took place in November and December 1776. At that time, delegates from around the state met at the fifth provincial congress in Halifax and formulated the state's first independent plan of government. Approved on December 18, the new state constitution was, on the surface, similar to the old colonial plan. It divided the duties of government among the executive (governor), legislative (two-house assembly), and judicial (courts) branches. The key difference between the two governments lay in the relative power awarded to the executive and assembly. Whereas the colonial governor been largely independent of the legislature and had exercised considerable power, the state governor was to be elected by the legislature to a one-year term. Under the new system, moreover, the governor had no veto power. Consequently, the governorship under North Carolina's first state constitution was little more than a sinecure. Another notable aspect of the 1776 constitutional settlement was that it forbade non-Protestants from holding office, a provision that would ultimately require the drafting of a new state constitution in 1835.

Partly because of governmental weakness and partly because of general scarcity, raising adequate revenue was a difficult challenge for North Carolina. The state met this challenge by printing money. Like other governments who used the same tactic, North Carolina reaped a harvest of rampant inflation. The state's debts were paid, but the economy was devastated.[17]

Weakness on the state level was mirrored in the national government. During the war, the business of governing the colonies fell to the Second Continental Congress, but all understood this arrangement was only provisional. By 1777, Congress had set forth the contours of a more permanent national government, which, as it happened, did not go into effect until four years later. The Articles of Confederation were essentially the North Carolina government writ large: inefficient, impotent, and debilitating to the country. It is therefore fitting that North Carolina's delegation to Congress at the time—Thomas Burke, Cornelius Harnett, and John Penn—played a crucial role in rendering it so. These men argued consistently and heatedly for the limitation of the national government's power over individual states. Given the problems that would afflict the nation because of the Articles' weakness, the North Carolinians were more successful than they ought to have been. "Each state retains its sovereignty, freedom and independence, and every Power, Jurisdiction and right, which is not by this confederation expressly delegated to the United States, in Congress assembled" read the second article, for which Burke, North Carolina's most strident states' rights activist, was "almost solely" responsible. Under the Articles of Confederation, the national government could not directly tax the states or regulate commerce. It could only request funds. This arrangement predictably resulted in a chronically impecunious national government. Like North Carolina, but unlike most other states, the Confederation government resorted to printed money, with like results.

As the new nation fumbled into the latter half of the 1780s, it was a financial shambles, unable to pay its considerable debts or defend itself against the foreign powers that expected the infant republic to meet an early demise. Even with so dull an instrument as the Articles of Confederation, North Carolina's more moderate voices feared their recalcitrant compatriots would try to delay its ratification. Indeed, the inclusion of the second article and consequent ceding of almost every meaningful power to the states failed to appease Burke, who led the effort to defeat the Articles in the 1777 assembly. Fortunately, less fevered minds prevailed, and North Carolina ratified the Articles in April 1778.[18]

A weak national government exacerbated difficulties incurred by a long and draining war and an ineffectual state government. According to the foremost authorities on the colonial economy, a "truly disastrous" scenario unfolded during the Revolution. Whereas in 1774 the colonies' estimated per capita gross national product (adjusted to 1980 dollars) was $804, the 1790 figure came to only $437. The records for the Revolutionary era are sketchy at best, but if these numbers reflect anything approaching reality, the United States lost almost half of its productive capacity between the meeting of the First Continental Congress and the adoption of the Bill of Rights. In North Carolina, the economic downturn begot a general institutional breakdown. The few schools there languished, and no newspaper was published from 1778 to 1783. Still, it is easy to overstate the economic distress of the 1770s and 1780s, especially in the context of North Carolina's relatively anemic colonial development. Because North Carolina was less integrated into the Atlantic economy than other states, it suffered relatively fewer losses. In the same way that, 150 years later, Appalachian mountaineers who had lived largely outside the market economy suffered less from the onset of the Great Depression, so Revolutionary-era Tarheels endured fewer hardships from the decline of an economy in which, for the most part, they did not participate.[19]

REASONS FOR DISCONTENT

Little blame for the economic decline during the Revolutionary War can be attributed to the government under the Articles of Confederation, which were not adopted until 1781, the final year of actual fighting. The adoption of the Articles was delayed by conflicts over western land claims. Theoretically, the western borders of some states extended to the Mississippi or even the Pacific. At a time when white pioneers were already trickling over the North Carolina Appalachians into what would one day be Tennessee, states with no claim on western lands—especially Maryland, hemmed completely in on its western border by Virginia—balked at joining a Union in which there was no foreseeable limit to the expansion of other states. North Carolina, on the other hand, was understandably reluctant to cede its unusually promising western lands. Although the state agreed in principle to give the land to the Confederation after that government went into effect, in fact the issue was not settled for several more years. In 1784 conservatives defeated an act to cede the Tennessee country to the national government on the grounds that the decision had not been well thought through, although cession had been one of the most widely discussed issues within the state for half a decade. After this failure, representatives from four western counties met in Jonesboro to secede from North Carolina and establish the "Free State of Franklin" with John Sevier as governor.[20]

This action was received badly in North Carolina. Governor Alexander Martin addressed a "manifesto" to the seditious counties. In it, he declared his intention of "reclaim[ing] such Citizens, who by specious pretenses, and the

Acts of designing Men, have been seduced from their allegiance." Martin suggested that the Franklinites had acted rashly, had "seiz[ed] that by violence, which in time no doubt, would have been obtained by consent" when the issue of separation had been settled to the mutual satisfaction of the Mother and the new state." This rhetorical trick deferred meaningful action indefinitely, because the time never seemed quite right for action. Tennesseans of the eighteenth century had to wait on the national government for their rescue. Tennessee counties continued to be represented in the North Carolina legislature until North Carolina belatedly ratified the Constitution in 1789 and was thereby compelled to relinquish its western claims.[21]

The endless bickering over of North Carolina's western lands left out the group that had occupied them for centuries: North Carolina's Native American population. Historically, white settlers had ignored or minimized the claims of their Native American neighbors. Ever since the sixteenth century, when the first Europeans arrived in what was to become North Carolina, the story for the colony's Native Americans had mostly been one of epidemic, bad treaties, cultural devastation, and military defeat. Steadily, the small tribes who had populated the coastal and Piedmont regions receded to the west as English colonists advanced. The propensity of North Carolina's largest and most powerful tribe, the Cherokees, to pick the wrong side in important wars expedited the Native Americans' fate. Alarmed by the encroachment of English settlers, the Cherokees allied themselves with the French in the French and Indian War. From 1759 to 1761, the so-called "Cherokee War" saw British regulars and colonial troops drive Cherokees from their non-mountainous settlements. Although white settlers, led by Daniel Boone, started to slip across the Appalachians as early as 1769, the Cherokees presented a formidable obstacle to colonists' transmontane migration. Cherokee power was permanently broken during the American Revolution, opening the way for the white occupation of the southern interior.[22]

THE BATTLE OVER THE CONSTITUTION

As the nation's economic condition deteriorated, a movement emerged to strengthen the national government, culminating in the Constitutional Convention of 1787. From the start, North Carolina betrayed a marked caginess about any change in the Confederation government. The state was not even represented at the Annapolis trade convention that called for the 1787 Constitutional Convention in Philadelphia, and it only reluctantly agreed to send representatives to the convention. Finally, the assembly chose Governor Richard Caswell, William Davie, Willie Jones, Alexander Martin, and Richard Dobbs Spaight to represent the state in Philadelphia. In the end, Caswell was too ill to attend, and Jones was too averse to establishing a new government. Caswell appointed William Blount and Hugh Williamson in their places. The resulting delegation at least favored a stronger central government, but only Spaight and Williamson attended the convention from opening to closing gavel. Because the debates in Philadelphia were kept secret, one cannot know precisely what role North Carolinians played, but it can be assumed it was a minor one. The lack of a more meaningful Tarheel presence at this historic gathering and the state's relative indifference to its proceedings presaged an even greater ambivalence toward the document that the convention ultimately produced.[23]

The prompt eruption of controversy over the Constitution further reflected this ambivalence. The Constitution of 1787 was drafted to provide much-needed stability for the new nation, but that purpose was not at all apparent to many North Carolinians when the document was first introduced. Had not Americans just won independence from a similarly centralized and unresponsive government? Had not North Carolinians led this charge? And would it not be a betrayal of that gigantic effort to now endorse this new government? So, at any rate, went the reasoning of the opponents of the Constitution. At first, they spoke in just such nebulous phrases; opposition to the Constitution coalesced even before the new plan was made public, so these early critics could not have known what the document entailed. In North Carolina, the criers of doom included the prominent political personages Lemuel Burkitt, Thomas Person, and one of the originally named delegates to the Philadelphia convention, Willie Jones.[24]

Following the promulgation of the Constitution, arguments for and against its adoption grew more concrete. Supporters of the new government, calling themselves Federalists, famously won the ensuing debate. James Madison and Alexander Hamilton, with the occasional assistance of John Jay, carried the day in the crucial state of New York with the publication of the *Federalist Papers*, which was immediately recognized as an eloquent statement of political theory. In North Carolina, the discourse was not so sophisticated, but the Constitution had its defenders. Most prominent among these was James Iredell. "We admire in the new constitution a proper jealousy of liberty mixed with a due regard to the necessity of a strong authoritative government," the Edenton grandee proclaimed in his November 1787 defense of the document.

> Such a one is as requisite for a confederated, as for a single government, since it would not be more ridiculous or futile for our own Assembly to depend for a sanction to its laws on a unanimous concurrence of all the counties in the State, than for Congress to depend for any necessary exertion of power on the unanimous concurrence of all the States in the Union.

Partly for his efforts on behalf of the Constitution, Iredell was appointed to the Supreme Court during George Washington's presidency.[25]

Iredell's arguments in favor of a strong national government were, it must be said, fairly pedestrian, and they failed to mobilize much support in the Old North State. Initially, opponents of the Constitution outmatched its supporters.

The prosaic arguments of North Carolina Federalists are not totally to blame. The brilliant *Federalist Papers* were widely circulated in the state, but the arguments that swayed commercial New York were not suited to the social and political milieu of North Carolina, where undercurrents of section and class influenced the debate over the new government. Whereas Federalists usually came from wealthier, market-oriented, eastern families, most Anti-Federalists were stubborn backcountry agrarians. Section and class served as reliable but not absolute predictors of who lined up for and against the Constitution. Some eminent planters feared a strong central government, whereas some western subsistence farmers desired a powerful federal instrument to ameliorate conditions on the frontier. Generally, however, large planters urged creation of a powerful government, and yeomen pushed for decentralization. In a state where the propertied class had been historically weak, this situation did not augur well for the Federalist forces.[26]

When the state assembly met in November 1787, it ordered the election of delegates for a ratification convention to meet in Hillsborough the following July. There followed a heated campaign by both sides to secure the upper hand. In Kinston, a "riot" attended the voting when one Colonel Shepperd, an ardent Federalist, apparently upset that the tally was not going his way, "went upon the bench where the sheriffs, inspectors, and clerks were attending their business, and swore he would beat one of the inspectors...and having a number of clubs ready prepared," proceeded to carry out this threat. Thereupon, "The Antifederalist candidates...thought it advisable to retire privately in the dark." All but one escaped harm. Another "riot" accompanied polling in Dobbs County. Led statewide by Willie Jones, meanwhile, the Anti-Federalists won a smashing victory. When representatives met in Hillsborough the following summer, the eighty-four Federalists found themselves outnumbered by one hundred Anti-Federalists. The outcome of the convention's proceedings was never in doubt.[27]

The convention appointed Governor Samuel Johnston as president, less because of Johnston's politics—he was a Federalist, if a lukewarm one—than out of simple deference to the state's chief executive. It is also likely that, because the Federalists had no chance of victory, Johnston's chairmanship was an easy concession for their opponents to make. Once the delegates convened, Willie Jones moved an immediate vote on the question, arguing that "the Constitution had so long been the subject of the deliberation of every man in this country, and that the members of the Convention had had such ample opportunity to consider it." Jones added that he "believed every one of them was prepared to give his vote then upon the question: That the situation of the public funds would not admit of lavishing the public money, but required the utmost economy and frugality." Jones probably made this point for inclusion in the public record. The assembled gentlemen, many of whom had traveled days, had no intention of simply registering their votes and going back home. Rather, in the fashion of conventioneers since time immemorial, they relished the chance to spend a few days carousing with their peers (even Anti-Federalist delegates tended to come from the ranks of the elite) for a few days in the rowdy provincial town. (A year later, the hamlet of Chapel Hill was chosen over Hillsborough as the location as the location of the University of North Carolina for fear that the latter city would furnish students too much in the way of temptation.) The "desultory conversation" at Hillsborough was to last for more than a week longer.[28]

Although the result of the July 1788 meeting was a largely foregone conclusion, it is nevertheless instructive to recount some of the convention's more telling episodes. The record of the Hillsborough debate provides the fullest and best window on North Carolina's public discourse regarding the ratification of the Constitution. One of the most revealing incidents about North Carolina in particular and early American political culture in general occurred when James Iredell rose to contest Jones's motion for an immediate vote. It showed that there was a more substantive reason than carousing, at least in principle, for the delegates to spend a week in Hillsborough: "I trust we shall not go home and tell our constituents, that we met at Hillsborough; were afraid to enter into a discussion of the subject; but precipitated a decision without a moment's consideration," Iredell declaimed. To this, Jones responded that he had "believed that others were equally prepared as" he to vote, but that "[i]f gentlemen differ from me in the propriety of this motion, I will submit." Others did. Specifically, Iredell pointed out that if an immediate vote without discussion had been the purpose of the convention, "the Assembly might as well have required that the electors should vote or ballot for or against the Constitution in their respective counties."

Implicit in Iredell's riposte was the notion that pure democracy, no less than a monarchy or aristocracy, was a form of tyranny. Early Americans elected their social "betters" to decide matters for them, creating a buffer between the people and actual power. Hence, even the Anti-Federalist representatives were men of property, and state legislatures, not the people, elected representatives to Congress. Most colonists were only twelve years removed from pledging loyalty to a hereditary monarchy and nobility; for many, that interval had been far shorter. That authority had been replaced by an "aristocracy of talent" that dealt with important issues. It was the people's right only to choose among them. Even in relatively egalitarian North Carolina, a more truly democratic ethos had not prevailed by 1788. An authentically modern political system replete with vigorous popular participation, mass-based parties, and Jacksonian bluster remained, for better or worse, in the offing for the infant Republic.[29]

The democratic sentiment that activated the torchlight parades and campaign shenanigans of that later era, however, had already partially emerged in 1788. One delegate contested the legitimacy of the new Constitution by pointing out that, although it purported to speak for "*We, the People*—the people at large, I conceive the expression is improper. Were not they who framed this Constitution, the Representatives of the Legislatures of the different states? In my opinion they had no power from the people at large to use their name, or to act for them. They were not delegated for that purpose." If the Articles of Confederation were not quite an experiment with radical democracy, its authority was at least so diffuse that no excessively centralized, unresponsive government could form. Although it was generally unthinkable that the common yeoman or wheelwright should seek office, politics under the Articles remained decidedly local. The Constitution appeared to threaten this circumstance.[30]

In other states, Federalists successfully combated the argument that the Constitution threatened the people's sovereignty. Most notably in Federalist Paper No. 10, Madison argued that a large republic, far from being the enemy of the people, militated against any one faction's being able to impose its will on a helpless minority. Strangely, North Carolina Federalists made little use of this seminal and devastating argument. Nor did they utilize effectively the separation-of-powers argument presented best in Federalist Paper No. 51. Instead, they stuck to platitudes about "proper jealousy of liberty" and "due regard" for a strong central authority. The North Carolina Federalists' failure to use these arguments is somewhat puzzling. Madison and Hamilton's major points had been made by the time North Carolina's ratifying convention met, and leading Federalists, indeed the public at large, were well aware of them. No doubt one part of the explanation is that Iredell, Johnston, and the other Federalists in North Carolina were no Madisons or Hamiltons and could not express their position as forcefully or convincingly. Another factor, already mentioned, was that "Publius's" arguments scored more effectively in a relatively urban setting like New York than in North Carolina. Then, also, North Carolina had already paid off its debt by adopting an inflationary currency policy and did not require financial assistance from a national government. The failure of the Federalists did not result solely from unpropitious circumstances, however, and North Carolina's Anti-Federalists proved skilled at steering the debate toward their strongest arguments.

In the convention debate, the opponents of the Constitution kept its supporters continually on the defensive. As the unofficial spokesman of the state's Federalists, Iredell found himself having to fight for even the most basic considerations. First, he had to defend the notion that a debate should be held. Then, the planter fought for due consideration of all of the document's provisions. Another lengthy defense was required for the use of the phrase "We, the People." Thereafter, Anti-Federalists minutely criticized each section of each article, ensuring that Iredell and his allies remained perpetually on their heels. And rather than discussing the viability of the plan as a whole, the structure of the debate compelled Federalists to defend one small piece of the Constitution after another. Although the Anti-Federalists deserve credit for their management of the discussion, in the end the Constitution's supporters were hoisted by their own petard. Ironically, it was Iredell's early insistence that the Constitution be debated section by section that kept the Federalists bogged down in particulars and prevented them from essaying the arguments based in political theory that had proved so persuasive in the hands of Madison and Hamilton.[31]

When the convention adjourned on August 4, the Anti-Federalists carried the day by a count of 184 to 84. The debate had changed the mind of exactly no one. North Carolina nonetheless left the door open to eventual ratification. Before adjourning, the convention passed a declaration of rights and set of amendments that, if added to the Constitution, would make the state more likely to approve the document. The declaration enumerated rights that the government should preserve to each citizen. These rights included, naturally, "the enjoyment of life and liberty, with the means of acquiring, possessing and protecting property, and pursuing and obtaining happiness and safety." Notably, the convention delegates also added "security" to the rights of men and sought a guarantee of the right of revolution. The list of amendments, on the other hand, comprised tangible measures that would protect these rights against a newly expanded national government. The first proposed amendment tendered all powers not explicitly granted to the national government to the states. Subsequent provisos stipulated the precise popular distribution of representatives, required the regular publication of governmental revenues and expenditures, and prohibited the maintenance of a standing army. If the new government was inevitably to take effect, North Carolina wanted to place strict limits on its growth.[32]

Meanwhile, eleven states had ratified the Constitution as of July 1788. Thus began a year-long period during which North Carolina remained outside the Union. Men from other states now openly maligned North Carolina's patriotism. Having represented North Carolina in the Confederation congress, Hugh Williamson remained in New York after the new government formed to serve as the state's unofficial emissary and apologist. In that capacity, Williamson issued a statement to the *New York Daily Advertiser* defending his home state against charges that "during the war her exertions were trifling—that she had never contributed to the national expense—and that she now refuses to confederate, from a desire to promote the fraudulent tender of paper money." Williamson replied that "whenever the neighboring states were invaded, North Carolina was sure to lend them assistance." Fully 3,000 to 4,000 Tarheel militiamen had fallen in the defense of Georgia and South Carolina. Furthermore, "North Carolina has uniformly paid and supported her own militia, though they were in the continental service, and she has furnished provisions to a considerable part of the continental troops in the southern armies." As for North Carolina's love of paper money to the exclusion of her sister states, it was "true that paper money has been issued in that state, and it was made legal tender, but it [was] also true, that the general sense of the people is not in favour of fraudulent payments." On the all-important issue of the state's failure to ratify the Constitution, Williamson contended that because ten states had already ratified by the time of the Hillsborough convention, nine being the threshold for approval, North Carolina felt free to register some reservations about the document. North Carolina's refusal to ratify would not hold up the adoption of the Constitution in the states where it had been ratified, but it might gain some concessions, namely a bill of rights, for those who remained wary of excessively centralized national power.[33]

In a letter written August 1788, Anti-Federalist leader Thomas Person presented another view. Person assured his correspondent that had "total rejection been proposed, even in terms of Reprobation, the motion would have succeeded, but we conceived it more decent & moderate to refer it" in the way that they did, with a list of suggested amendments which left open the door to ultimate ratification. Person was not sanguine about this approach, however.

> There is so little Security left now for obtaining Amendments…that it may probably be wise…to oppose all representation until Amendments are obtained or to send into the new Congress only such men of unequivocal characters as to oppose every operation of the system until it is rendered consistent with the preservation of our Liberties too precious to be sacrificed to authority, name, ambition, or design.

The difference between Williamson's and Person's stances was less one of substance than of tone. Both explained non-ratification as a means of obtaining a bill of rights, but whereas Williamson stressed North Carolina's fundamental agreement with her sister states, Person emphasized North Carolina's refusal to ratify as a means of resisting the overweening and presumptuous authority that he believed the Constitution created. To the extent that such a course of massive resistance ever received serious consideration, events ensured that support for it steadily eroded over the next year.[34]

Member states of the federal Union elected George Washington president. For their obstinacy, North Carolina and Rhode Island were barred from voting in this election. Humiliated by this exclusion and not wishing to appear unpatriotic, North Carolina governor Samuel Johnston and his council directed a congratulatory address be sent to the new chief-of-state. Governor Johnson and his co-signers, Iredell and Clerk of the Council William Johnston Dawson, used the occasion to express their solidarity with the states that had already ratified. "Though this state be not yet a member of the union under the new form of government, we look forward with the pleasing hope of its shortly becoming such; and in the mean time consider ourselves bound in a common interest and affection with the other states." The North Carolinians were certain, moreover, that ratification "will be accelerated by your Excellency's appointment to the first office of the union." They meant, first, that Washington's eminence would dispel many misgivings among their fellows, but they also implied that the general's selection was auspicious because his "greatness of mind…will induce [him] to advise every measure calculated to compose party divisions, and to abate any animosity that may be excited by a mere difference of opinion." The subtext was unmistakable: Washington's election was a good start, but to carry North Carolina, a bill of rights might still be necessary.[35]

The president's reply was magnanimous but firm: "It is scarcely possible for an address to have given me greater pleasure than that which I have just received from you." The statement gratified Washington "because I consider it not only demonstrative of your approbation of my conduct in accepting the first office in the union, but also indicative of the good dispositions of the citizens of your state towards their sister states, and"—this was key—"of the probability of their speedily acceding to the new general government." To help appease North Carolina, he implied that a slate of amendments was in the works. Washington closed by returning to the adjuration that the state ratify the Constitution at once.[36]

With the new federal government in place, the movement in North Carolina for ratification was rekindled. Two crucial events added further fuel to the fire. First, Congress began to discuss amendments to the Constitution that would result ultimately in the proposal of a Bill of Rights in September 1789. This action allayed North Carolinians' fears of an overly powerful central government, and subsequent ratification vindicated Williamson's assertion that the state had refused to pass the document in the first instance only to gain a bill of rights. The second incident was the publication of the debate of the June 1788 ratification convention. Federalist stalwarts James Iredell and William Davie had hired a recorder for those proceedings. The resulting document stimulated interest in a new convention and showed the Constitution's advocates in the best possible light. Late in summer, the state held elections for a November convention in Fayetteville. In that contest, the Federalists won 195 seats to the Anti-Federalists' 77.[37]

After some preliminary debate, the state ratified the Constitution on November 21, 1789. As in the Hillsborough convention, the results in Fayetteville were settled before the opening gavel. Seeing the handwriting on the wall, some prominent Anti-Federalists such as Willie Jones refused to attend, and the Federalist path to victory was thus made smoother still.[38]

BRAVE NEW WORLD

Joining the Union was not wholly painless. North Carolina at last had to relinquish its claims to western lands. Supporters of the new order hoped that, through this and other concessions, especially acceding to a tariff, the state would get a break when it came to settling accounts with the national government. These hopes were disappointed. Debts paid with fiat currency were counted against the balance, according to historian J. Edwin Hendricks, "largely because of poor recordkeeping in the state and unfavorable interpretations of many of North Carolina's claims, when the accounts were tallied it was ruled that North Carolina owed the United States slightly more than $500,000." This debt was a tough pill to swallow for Tarheels who felt they had already sacrificed enough in joining the federal Union.[39]

Once it entered the Union, North Carolina showed itself distinctly uncomfortable with the bargain it had struck. Washington's first term is typically portrayed as remarkable for its lack of partisan division. During that same period, however, the seeds were sown for the most rancorous and important dispute of the early national period. The principals in the conflict were Washington's Secretary of the Treasury Alexander Hamilton and Secretary of State Thomas Jefferson. Hamilton advocated a loose construction of the Constitution, meaning he wished to arrogate, in the view of his adversaries, powers to the national government not explicitly granted in the document itself. By granting the federal government these extended powers, he hoped that America would become a strong, centralized nation-state, along the lines of the great European powers. Such a state was contingent on good public credit, tariff protection for America's fledgling manufacturers, and a standing army and navy. Jefferson, who had been in France during the drafting and ratification of the Constitution, envisaged for America a future as an egalitarian republic of independent smallholders who were not beholden to anyone for their living and thus were eligible for participation in popular government. A powerful national government and the urban, commercial polity it would promote threatened Jefferson's scheme. He wanted, therefore, to limit the powers of the federal government to those specifically enumerated in the Constitution.

No strict correlation can be made, but those who had supported ratification tended to coalesce around Hamilton in the infant Federalist Party, whereas the former Anti-Federalists gravitated toward Jefferson's Republicans. (It should be noted that during the 1790s these "parties" were inchoate. Nothing resembling a modern national political party appeared until at least the 1820s and, more probably, the 1830s.) Such was not the case in North Carolina, where even most of the former backers of the federal Union repudiated Hamilton's expansive vision and espoused Jefferson's. "This was evident in 1790," an eminent North Carolina scholar has written, "when the North Carolina House of Commons refused to take an oath to support the federal constitution." It was likewise evident when North Carolina assemblymen instructed national senators to vote almost always against taxes and held the senators strictly accountable to them. Even James Iredell, ensconced on the bench of the Supreme Court, shied away from the nationalism of his erstwhile allies. In the landmark case *Chisholm v. Georgia*, the justice wrote a passionate dissent, arguing that no citizen could sue a person from another state in federal court.[40]

In the years that followed, whatever Federalist sentiment existed in the state was snuffed out almost entirely. Because a powerful national government was at the core of Federalist doctrine, it is hard to see how matters could have turned out differently. Always resistant to what they perceived as the excessive concentration of authority, North Carolinians by and large parted company with Federalists on first, or nearly first, principles. Declining Federalist fortunes were little aided when the prominent national journalist Joseph Gales moved to the state's newly established capital in 1799 and established the *Raleigh Register*. The newspaper served as a reliable and powerful Republican voice for years to come, helping ensure that the ghost of federalism would rouse itself no more in North Carolina.[41]

Some historians have argued that North Carolina took several wildly inconsistent stances vis-à-vis the federal Union; that is, that the state was either for a robust national government or for strong states' rights depending on the circumstances. Superficially, it would seem self-evident that when required—as, for example, during the War for Independence or the ratification controversy— North Carolinians proved capable of putting aside narrow provincial concerns, albeit reluctantly, for the good of the larger entity. This perspective is false. In truth, North Carolina expressed a nationalist impulse only when it was in the state's self-interest to do so. Had Tarheels not banded together with other former colonists in the fight against the British army, it was unlikely that they could have retained their independence. Similarly, the ratification of the other states forced North Carolina's hand on the Constitution, but only after the state saw substantive action being taken on the Bill of Rights. All in all, it seems probable that, had the Old North State been able to go it alone, that is the course it would have chosen. As it was, North Carolina acceded to as much national government as was consistent with preserving the greatest possible autonomy for the state.[42]

This, then, was North Carolina during its long and winding passage from British colony to independent state: fiercely localistic, more so perhaps than any other state, yet pragmatic enough to know when to cast its lot with the larger whole. It was the state's localism that made it so quintessentially American in those early years. One of the more useful ways of viewing the American Revolution, that seismic eruption that began with the first tremors of discontent in 1765 and lasted until the consolidation of the United States with the adoption of the Constitution, is as an experiment that tested the limits of local power. In light of North Carolina's Revolutionary history, the state must be recognized for the central, if not indispensable, role it played in initiating and sustaining that grand experiment.

NOTES

1. See John Shelton Reed, *Southern Folk, Plain and Fancy: Native White Social Types* (Athens, GA: University of Georgia Press, 1986), p. 42.

2. William S. Price, Jr., "North Carolina in the First British Empire: Economy and Society in an Eighteenth-century Colony," in *The North Carolina Experience: An Interpretive and Documentary History*, ed. Lindley S. Butler and Alan D. Watson (Chapel

Hill: University of North Carolina Press, 1984), pp. 83–85; for the problems caused by the remoteness of Southern fall lines from the coast, see Stephen J. Goldfarb, "A Note on Limits to the Growth of the Cotton Textile Industry in the Old South," *Journal of Southern History* 48 (November 1982): 545–558.

3. Price, "North Carolina in the First British Empire," p. 84; population figures culled from Jack P. Greene, *Pursuits of Happiness: The Social Development of Early Modern British Colonies and the Formation of American Culture* (Chapel Hill: University of North Carolina Press, 1988), pp. 178–179.

4. Mary Ramsey to Joseph Ramsey, December 1828, Southern Historical Collection, University of North Carolina, Chapel Hill, NC.

5. William S. Powell, *North Carolina through Four Centuries* (Chapel Hill: University of North Carolina Press, 1991), pp. 161–163.

6. *North Carolina Gazette,* November 20, 1765, February 16, 1766, reprinted in Hugh Talmage Lefler, ed., *North Carolina History Told by Contemporaries* (Chapel Hill: University of North Carolina Press, 1934), pp. 85–86.

7. Tryon's Letter Book, February 21, 1866, reprinted in Lefler, *North Carolina History Told by Contemporaries,* pp. 86–87; Donna J. Spindel, "Law and Disorder: The North Carolina Stamp Act Crisis," *North Carolina Historical Review* 57 (1980): 203–221; see also Lawrence Lee, "Days of Defiance: Resistance to the Stamp Act in the Lower Cape Fear," *North Carolina Historical Review* 43 (April 1966): 186–202.

8. Powell, *North Carolina through Four Centuries,* pp. 87–103.

9. Alan D. Watson, "The Regulation: Society in Upheaval," in *The North Carolina Experience,* ed. Butler and Watson, pp. 101–124; see also Marjoleane Kars, *Breaking Loose Together: The Regulator Rebellion in Pre-Revolutionary North Carolina* (Chapel Hill: University of North Carolina Press, 2002).

10. Don Higginbotham, ed., *The Papers of James Iredell,* 2 vols. (Raleigh, NC: North Carolina Department of Cultural Resources, 1976), 1:266–267.

11. William L. Saunders, ed., *The Colonial Records of North Carolina,* 10 vols. (Raleigh, NC: P.M. Hale, State Printer, 1886–90) 9:1282–1285; for a sober look at the controversy over the Mecklenburg Resolves, see Richard N. Current, "That Other Declaration: May 20, 1775–May 20, 1975," *North Carolina Historical Review* 54 (April 1977): 169–191.

12. Powell, *North Carolina through Four Centuries,* p. 171.

13. Ibid., pp. 177–180.

14. Saunders, *Colonial Records,* 10:512; for a fuller explication of the evolution of the North Carolina delegation's position, see David T. Morgan and William J. Schmidt, "From Economic Sanctions to Political Separation: The North Carolina Delegation to the Continental Congress, 1774–1776," *North Carolina Historical Review* 52 (1975): 215–234.

15. Powell, *North Carolina through Four Centuries,* pp. 106–108.

16. Gordon S. Wood, *The Radicalism of the American Revolution* (New York: Alfred A. Knopf, 1991), p. 117.

17. Powell, *North Carolina through Four Centuries,* pp. 185–189.

18. J. Edwin Hendricks, "Joining the Federal Union," in *The North Carolina Experience,* ed. Butler and Watson, pp. 147–149.

19. John J. McCusker and Russell R. Menard, *The Economy of British America, 1607–1789* (Chapel Hill: University of North Carolina Press, 1985).

20. Hendricks, "Joining the Federal Union," pp. 150–151.

21. *State Records of North Carolina*, 28 vols. (Raleigh: P.M. Hale, 1886–1907), 22: 642–647.

22. Herbert R. Paschal, "The Tragedy of the North Carolina Indians," in *The North Carolina Experience*, ed. Butler and Watson, pp. 10–11; for another, marginally less tragic perspective, see Joffre L. Coe, "The Indian in North Carolina," *North Carolina Historical Review* 43 (April 1979): 158–161.

23. Powell, *North Carolina through Four Centuries*, pp. 221–225.

24. Hendricks, "Joining the Federal Union," pp. 153–154.

25. Griffith J. McRee, ed., *Life and Correspondence of James Iredell: One of the Associate Justices of the Supreme Court of the United States* (New York: P. Smith. 1949), 2:181–182.

26. Hendricks, "Joining the Federal Union," pp. 153–154.

27. The Kinston Election "Riot" is recounted in the *Norfolk and Portsmouth Journal*, April 30, 1788, reprinted in Lefler, *North Carolina History Told by Contemporaries*, pp.136–137; on the Dobbs County controversy, see *Proceedings and Debate of the Convention of North-Carolina, Convened at Hillsborough, on Monday the 21st Day of July, 1788, for the Purpose of Deliberating and Determining on the Constitution Recommended by the General Convention at Philadelphia, the 17th Day of September, 1787* (Edenton, NC, 1789), pp. 22–23; Powell, *North Carolina through Four Centuries*, p. 225.

28. *Proceedings and Debate of the Convention of North Carolina*, pp. 23, 27.

29. Ibid., pp. 26–27.

30. Ibid., p. 36.

31. Ibid., passim.

32. Ibid., pp. 271–277.

33. *New York Daily Advertiser*, September 17, 1788, reprinted in Butler and Watson, ed., *The North Carolina Experience*, pp. 165–166.

34. Thomas Person to John Lamb, August 6, 1788, reprinted in Butler and Watson, ed., *The North Carolina Experience*, pp. 164–165.

35. Governor's address reprinted in Butler and Watson, eds., *The North Carolina Experience*, pp. 165–167.

36. Reprinted in Butler and Watson, eds., *The North Carolina Experience*, p. 169.

37. Powell, *North Carolina through Four Centuries*, p. 228.

38. Hendricks, "Joining the Federal Union," in Butler and Watson, eds., *The North Carolina Experience*, pp. 156–157.

39. Ibid., p. 157.

40. Powell, *North Carolina through Four Centuries*, p. 231.

41. Ibid., p. 234.

42. For an example of the North-Carolina-as-inconsistent thesis, see especially, Hugh Talmage Lefler and Albert Ray Newsome, *North Carolina: The History of a Southern State*, 3rd ed. (Chapel Hill: University of North Carolina Press, 1973).

BIBLIOGRAPHY

Butler, Lindley S., and Alan D. Watson, eds. *The North Carolina Experience: An Interpretive and Documentary History*. Chapel Hill: University of North Carolina Press, 1984.

Coe, Joffre L. "The Indian in North Carolina." *North Carolina Historical Review* 43 (April 1979): 158–161.

Current, Richard N. "That Other Declaration: May 20, 1775–May 20, 1975." *North Carolina Historical Review* 54 (April 1977): 169–191.

Higginbotham, Don, ed. *The Papers of James Iredell.* 2 vols. Raleigh: North Carolina Department of Cultural Resources, 1978.

Kars, Marjoleine. *Breaking Loose Together: The Regulator Rebellion in Pre-Revolutionary North Carolina.* Chapel Hill: University of North Carolina Press, 2002.

Lee, Lawrence. "Days of Defiance: Resistance to the Stamp Act in the Lower Cape Fear." *North Carolina Historical Review* 43 (April 1966): 186–202.

Lefler, Hugh Talmage, and Albert Ray Newsome. *North Carolina: The History of a Southern State.* 3rd ed. Chapel Hill: University of North Carolina Press, 1973.

McLoughlin, William G. *Cherokee Renascence in the New Republic.* Princeton, NJ: Princeton University Press, 1986.

McRee, Griffith J., ed. *Life and Correspondence of James Iredell: One of the Associate Justices of the Supreme Court of the United States.* New York: P. Smith, 1949.

Morgan, David T., and William J. Schmidt. "From Economic Sanctions to Political Separation: The North Carolina Delegation to the Continental Congress, 1774–1776." *North Carolina Historical Review* 52 (1975): 215–234.

Morrill, James R. *The Practice and Politics of Fiat Finance: North Carolina in the Confederation, 1783–1789.* Chapel Hill: University of North Carolina Press, 1969.

Pool, William C. "An Economic Interpretation of the Ratification of the Federal Constitution in North Carolina." *North Carolina Historical Review* 27 (1950): 119–141, 289–313, 437–461.

Powell, William S. *North Carolina through Four Centuries.* Chapel Hill: University of North Carolina Press, 1989.

Saunders, Jennings B. "Thomas Burke in the Continental Congress." *North Carolina Historical Review* 9 (January 1932): 22–37.

Saunders, William L., ed. *The Colonial Records of North Carolina.* 10 vols. Raleigh, NC: P.M. Hale, State Printer, 1886–1890.

Sellers, Charles G. "Making of a Revolution: The North Carolina Whigs, 1765–1775." In *Studies in Southern History*, ed. J. Carlyle Sitterson, 29:23–46. Chapel Hill: University of North Carolina Press, 1957.

Spindel, Donna J. "Law and Disorder: The North Carolina Stamp Act Crisis." *North Carolina Historical Review* 57 (1980): 203–221.

THE STATE OF NORTH DAKOTA

Admitted to the Union as a State: November 2, 1889

David B. Danbom

INTRODUCTION

North Dakota was the thirty-ninth state admitted to the Union. Its admission came thirteen years and three months after the admission of the thirty-eighth state, Colorado, and it was accompanied in statehood by the other three "omnibus states," South Dakota, Montana, and Washington, all of which were admitted within nine days of one another in November of 1889.

North Dakota's road to statehood was a long and difficult one. It was lengthened by national political divisions, by differences between the northern and southern sections of Dakota Territory, and by the difficulties of attracting settlers to the northern plains. Statehood signified that the first two of these challenges had been surmounted and that the third had been managed. Statehood, however, failed to solve the problems of a physically remote and economically marginal region, whose early years in the Union were marked by economic hardship and intense political conflict.

AMERICAN ACQUISITION OF NORTH DAKOTA

North Dakota's location in the center of the North American continent, far distant from both the Atlantic and the Pacific oceans, dictated that European contact came relatively late in the colonial era. The first European known to have visited the future state was the Sieur de la Vérendrye, who was granted a monopoly over the fur trade west of Lake Superior by Louis XV of France in 1731. Vérendrye visited the region in 1738, establishing a trading relationship with the Mandan, who lived in agricultural villages on the Missouri River

North Dakota

Territorial Development:

- The United States obtains future North Dakotan territory west of the Missouri River from France through the Louisiana Purchase, April 30, 1803
- The United States obtains more land containing future North Dakotan territory east of the Missouri River from Great Britain through the Joint-Occupancy Treaty, 1818
- Future territory of North Dakota organized as part of the Louisiana Territory (or the District of Louisiana for a time in 1804), 1804–1812
- Reorganized as part of the Missouri Territory, 1812–1834
- East of the Missouri River, the future territory of North Dakota is reorganized as a part of the Michigan Territory, 1834–1836
- East of the Missouri River, the future territory of North Dakota is reorganized as a part of the Wisconsin Territory, 1836–1838
- Reorganized as a part of the Iowa Territory, 1838–1846; becomes unorganized territory, 1846–1849
- Reorganized as a part of the Minnesota Territory, 1849–1858
- West of the Missouri River, the future territory of North Dakota is reorganized as a part of the Nebraska Territory, 1854–1861
- Reorganized as the Dakota Territory, March 2, 1861
- Dakota Territory divided into North Dakota and South Dakota; North Dakota admitted into the Union as the thirty-ninth state, November 2, 1889

Territorial Capitals:

- Bismarck, 1883–1889

State Capitals:

- Bismarck, 1889–present

Origin of State Name: North Dakota received its name from the Sioux tribe, whose name means "allies," or "friends."

First Governor: John Miller
Governmental Organization: Bicameral
Population at Statehood: 182,719
Geographical Size: 68,976 square miles

northwest of present-day Bismarck. The Mandan served as middlemen in a fur trade that also involved the Hidatsa, Crow, Cheyenne, Assiniboine, Ojibwa, and Yanktonai and Teton Dakota.

The French claim over the future state was extinguished as a result of the Seven Years' War (also known as the French and Indian War, 1756–1763) and the subsequent Treaty of Paris of 1763. The treaty transferred French Canada, including the Red River Valley of the future state of North Dakota, to Great Britain, and Louisiana, defined as the territory drained by the Missouri River and its tributaries, to Spain.

Although Spain held legal title to most of the future state of North Dakota and attempted to assert its claim with a series of expeditions up the Missouri from St. Louis in the 1790s, the British enjoyed significant advantages of location. In the 1760s and 1770s the British Hudson's Bay Company erected a series of posts on the Assiniboine and Red rivers in present-day Manitoba from which they traded throughout the Red River Valley and as far west as the Mandan villages. Their rivals, the North West Company, also established fur trading posts, including one at Pembina, in the northeastern corner of present-day North Dakota, in 1801.

In 1803 the United States acquired most of North Dakota as a result of the purchase of Louisiana from France, which had secretly acquired the area from Spain in the 1800 Treaty of San Ildefonso. In 1804 and 1805, Meriwether Lewis and William Clark visited the future state as part of their celebrated expedition to the Pacific Coast, wintering at the Mandan villages. Lewis and Clark were followed quickly by Manuel Lisa, whose Missouri Company founded several trading posts in present-day North Dakota and Montana between 1808 and 1810. This activity hardly cancelled the substantial advantages the British continued to enjoy, as was illustrated early in the War of 1812 when the Hudson's Bay Company easily drove the American traders back to St. Louis.

In 1815 the Treaty of Ghent, which ended the War of 1812, resulted in the return of northern Louisiana to the United States. Three years later, in the Convention of 1818, Secretary of State John Quincy Adams and British negotiators agreed to simplify the border between the United States and Canada by drawing it at the 49th parallel between the Lake of the Woods and the crest of the Rocky Mountains. As a result of this agreement, the United States acquired the southern Red River Valley, whereas a portion of the Missouri River drainage went to Canada. The United States now possessed the future state of North Dakota.

CREATION OF DAKOTA TERRITORY

The region south of the 49th parallel did not appear particularly promising for several decades after the Convention of 1818. The most valuable resource in the region remained furs, but as a source of peltry it was second-rate, at best. Government treaties with Native American groups, especially the powerful Dakota, allowed a resumption of trading activity in the Upper Missouri country in the 1820s and the establishment of several posts by the American Fur Company, the most significant of which was Fort Union, at the junction of the Yellowstone and Missouri rivers. These posts traded mainly in buffalo hides, gathered by the Dakota men and prepared by their wives and other female dependents. Fur trading stimulated some minor European settlement on the Upper Missouri, mainly by "wood hawks," who supplied fuel to passing steamboats, but it did not form the basis for a thriving society.

To the east, in the Red River Valley, the fur trade was carried on mainly by Métis, a distinctive people of mixed Ojibwa and European—mostly French—ancestry, who numbered perhaps 5,000 by 1850. The Métis were classic go-betweens, mixing European and Native American cultures, serving as intermediaries between disparate groups, and passing easily between Canada and the United States. Over time, economic development on the American side of the border tended to orient them toward the United States. The establishment of Fort Snelling at the junction of the Minnesota and Mississippi rivers gave Métis traders an alternative to the Canadian trading outlets. Norman Kittson's trading post, which opened at Pembina in 1844, systematically gathered buffalo hides for shipment to St. Paul. In addition, by 1850 there was a well-established hide trade over ox-cart trails from the Red River Valley to St. Paul.

Eastern North Dakota was included in Minnesota Territory when it was organized in 1849. In recognition of increasing business activity there, the federal government began collecting customs at Pembina in 1851 and established mail service there and at St. Joseph's, a few miles to the west, in 1853. In the late 1850s stagecoach service connected St. Paul with Breckinridge, Minnesota, just across the Red River from what is now Wahpeton, North Dakota, and steamboat service began between Winnipeg and Georgetown, near present-day Fargo. By 1860 scattered farms had appeared along the Red River.

Although there was some settlement in the northern part of the region, more significant activity was taking place farther south. Rapid settlement in Iowa and Minnesota prompted land speculators and prospective pioneers to look to the West. In 1858 the government induced the Yanktonais Dakota to relinquish title to 14 million acres of land in what is now southeastern South Dakota. This land cession resulted in the founding of Yankton, Vermillion, and Sioux Falls and in a mini-boom in agricultural settlement. The movers and shakers of southeastern Dakota immediately sought creation of a territory by Congress, a move that would lead to a land survey and secure land titles. They were frustrated, however, by the crosscurrents of congressional politics in the chaotic sessions before the disintegration of the Union and by the desire of the largely Métis population in the Pembina vicinity to have the prospective territory divided into northern and southern halves. Finally, in March

1861, a bill organizing Dakota Territory passed Congress, and the territorial period was launched.

DAKOTA TERRITORY

The settlement of Dakota Territory was retarded by the disruptions and preoccupations of the Civil War as well as by Native American conflicts in the region beginning in 1862 and continuing through 1876. The rising of the Santee Dakota in the Minnesota River Valley in 1862 complicated Native American–white relationships throughout the region and led to a punitive expedition into Northern Dakota the next year under the leadership of generals Henry Sibley and Alfred Sully. In 1864, Sully built Fort Rice on the Missouri River, and over the course of the next eight years nine more forts were constructed in the northern part of the territory. These small posts, built for 100 to 500 men, were designed to facilitate control of the Dakota, but in fact they provoked and enraged the Native Americans, making life outside garrison walls dangerous. The Native American threat to white settlement was finally overcome by the winter campaigns that followed the battle of the Little Big Horn in 1876. By 1880 virtually all of the Native Americans in the region had been pacified and confined to reservations.

The end of the Civil War saw a resumption of interest in Dakota Territory. For the northern portion of the territory, physically remote and far distant from major settlements, the railroad was the key to substantial population growth. In 1871, the St. Paul and Pacific Railroad, which became the basis for the Great Northern, connected Breckinridge, Minnesota, with St. Paul, leading to the founding of Wahpeton across the river. More significantly, the Northern Pacific, building west from Duluth, crossed the Red River that year, bringing Fargo quickly to life. The Northern Pacific had a charter and received a significant land grant to build a railroad from Lake Superior to the mouth of the Columbia River. As it built west in 1872 and 1873, Valley City, Jamestown, Bismarck, and other settlements were founded. Settlement in northern Dakota received yet another boost in 1871 when a federal land office was opened in Pembina and surveying commenced there and at Fargo and Wahpeton.

This promising beginning came to a dramatic halt in 1873 when the Northern Pacific collapsed, going into receivership and plunging the country's economy into a depression. At this point James B. Power, the railroad's land agent, conceived a scheme to relieve the railroad of its debt and to demonstrate the agricultural possibilities of northern Dakota. Power proposed that bondholders exchange their depreciated bonds at par value for railroad lands, on which they would undertake large-scale wheat farming. In 1875 Power convinced two large bondholders and railroad board members, George Cass and Benjamin Cheney, to exchange bonds for 13,440 acres west of Fargo and to hire Oliver

Dalrymple, a St. Paul attorney and large-scale farmer, to manage it for them. This first "bonanza farm," which eventually was expanded to nearly 100,000 acres, was a spectacular success, drawing the attention of eastern and European journalists and agriculturists. It even brought about a visit from President Rutherford B. Hayes, who came in 1879 to watch Dalrymple harvest 600,000 bushels from 30,000 acres. As economic enterprises, the dozens of bonanza farms that were developed in the Northern Pacific land grant were of dubious value, but they did succeed in drawing widespread attention to northern Dakota and contributed mightily to the Great Dakota Boom by demonstrating the feasibility of grain farming in the region.

The Great Dakota Boom began about 1878, with the end of the economic downturn of the seventies, and ended about 1885. The railroads were central to the boom, as they were to most economic and political developments in northern Dakota's territorial days. Frederick Billings reorganized the Northern Pacific in 1875 and resumed construction of the main line and of branch lines, crossing the Missouri River in 1879 and reaching the Pacific in 1883. Of even greater significance, a consortium headed by St. Paul entrepreneur and Canadian immigrant James J. Hill gained control of the St. Paul and Pacific in 1878 and initiated an ambitious building program in the far northern portion of the region. In 1880 Hill's Great Northern crossed the Red River at Grand Forks and built to the west, reaching Minot in 1886.

Settlement and the railroads went hand in hand. Although settlements sometimes preceded the railroads, the railroads encouraged immigration from Europe and the East, provided attractive terms for land purchasers, sponsored agricultural experimentation, and built towns every twenty miles or so to gather the produce of the countryside effectively. The railroads and the settlers both benefited from a wet cycle in a normally dry country and from relatively high grain prices. The result was a boom that increased the population of northern Dakota from about 16,000 in 1878 to an estimated 152,000 in 1885. By 1890, 191,000 people were living in North Dakota. Most of these people were grain farmers living in the Red River Valley or in the Drift Prairie region just to its west. The 1890 census counted 27,600 farms in the state, encompassing 17 percent of available acreage.

Although settlement was concentrated in the eastern third of northern Dakota, there was also activity west of the Missouri as open-range cattle ranchers pushed into the region. Taking advantage of high beef prices and an open range on which buffalo no longer offered competition, large Texas outfits such as Berry, Boyce, and Continental, Europeans such as the romantic Frenchman, the Marquis deMores, and eastern adventurers such as Theodore Roosevelt tried their hands at ranching in the Little Missouri country west of Bismarck. There they introduced open-range methods from the southern plains and turned Dickinson into a rough-and-ready cow town.

The Great Dakota Boom had a marked impact on southern Dakota as well. There, the population rose from about 70,000 in 1878 to 262,000 in 1885 and to 349,000 in 1890. Most of the new southern Dakotans were farmers, like their northern counterparts, but there were some significant economic and demographic differences between the two halves of the territory. In the early territorial years, the significant population centers had been in the southeastern and northeastern corners of the territory. The people in the southeast were largely Yankees oriented to agriculture, whereas those in the northeast were Francophone Métis holding on to the remnants of the dying fur trade.

The Great Dakota Boom changed the demographics of the territory dramatically. Although Yankees continued to dominate the south politically and economically, many of the new settlers were immigrants from Germany or Scandinavia, sometimes by way of midwestern states such as Wisconsin or Illinois. In the north, new population groups that accompanied the railroads into the region rapidly eclipsed the folks at Pembina. As in southern Dakota, Yankees played a disproportionately significant role in the development and dominance of the area, but Canadian Scots, especially from Ontario, were also major figures in the north. In numbers, Norwegians and Germans, both "Reich" Germans from Germany proper and ethnic Germans from Russia, predominated, especially in agriculture. These immigrants were induced to come to northern Dakota by the railroads, which touted the economic possibilities of the region and the availability of land for free or at low prices. The engines of this propaganda were immigration offices opened by the railroads in Old World centers and pamphlets, broadsides, and advertisements celebrating the promise of northern Dakota.

Railroad appeals found receptive audiences in Europe. Norwegian farmers, mostly tenants without hope of acquiring farms of their own, were attracted by the promise of independence and prosperity. Germans from Russia, deprived of their privileges and subjected to conscription during the Czar's slavicization campaigns in the 1880s, were attracted by the prospect of re-creating strong and tightly knit communities in a region similar to the Russian steppes. The railroads encouraged their immigration by facilitating group settlement, providing liberal terms for land, and acquainting farmers with crops and methods appropriate for the peculiarities of the northern plains.

Germans and Norwegians were both able to fulfill their dreams in the northern half of Dakota Territory. The latter, who settled mainly in the Red River Valley and along the Great Northern line in the north, took readily to commercial production of wheat. They adapted relatively quickly and painlessly to American cultural values and participated eagerly in the political life of their new homes. Germans, who concentrated in the south central and central regions of northern Dakota, were able to recreate the diversified cattle and grain agriculture with which they were familiar and the tightly knit, insular communities that sustained them. Suspicious of outsiders and distrustful of government for good historic reasons, they were slow to embrace American culture or to participate in politics.

All of Dakota was predominantly agricultural, of course, and its development was part of a worldwide agricultural expansion that included the spread of settlement into the Canadian prairie provinces, the Australian outback, the Argentine pampas, and other areas as well. There were subtle but significant economic differences between the two Dakotas, however. Northern Dakota was wedded to a wheat monoculture. The hard red spring wheat grown there was sent mostly to Minneapolis, where the millers at St. Anthony Falls turned it into the finest bread flour in the world. Economically, the twin forces of wheat and the railroads fixed northern Dakota firmly within the orbit of the Twin Cities. Southern Dakota was mainly a wheat-producing region as well, but a more forgiving climate allowed greater diversification there, including the corn-hog production characteristic of the older Midwest. Southern Dakota also enjoyed mineral wealth, and the discovery of substantial gold deposits in the Black Hills in 1874 resulted in development of a major industry and substantial population there. Moreover, southern Dakota's railroads were based in Chicago, orienting the region's economy to that major urban center.

The demographic and economic differences that emerged within Dakota Territory during the Great Dakota Boom played a role in the long debate over whether Dakota Territory should become a state—or two states—or remain a territory. As early as 1877 political leaders in the southeastern part of the territory, known as the "Yankton Oligarchy" because of their concentration in the capital, had begun agitating for statehood. Statehood offered a number of advantages. Statehood would symbolize a degree of social and political maturity and would allow Dakota—or the Dakotas—to assume an equal place among the nation's other commonwealths. Statehood would allow the region to direct its own affairs under an elected rather than an appointed governor and to participate in Congress with voting representatives and senators rather than a non-voting delegate. Statehood would also allow greater leeway for locally generated economic efforts and would probably be accompanied by a substantial federal land grant earmarked for support of education or other public purposes.

There were also potential problems that would accompany statehood. With statehood, the people of the region would have to pay for their own government. In addition, ethnic or cultural minorities such as the Métis might be more comfortable as wards of the federal government than if left to the tender mercies of local neighbors, and economic interests such as the railroads might find a friendlier reception in Congress than they would in a local legislature.

From the beginning, the Yankton Oligarchy considered Dakota Territory to be too large, too diverse, and too unwieldy to be admitted as a single state. For a time they favored creating a state in southern Dakota and a new territory in northern Dakota. Through the mid-eighties, statehood efforts were thus based on the idea of separation and partial statehood.

The statehood movement was strengthened by territorial misgovernment. Territorial governors generally were a mixed lot. At best, they were well meaning and altruistic, but, because they served at the pleasure of the president rather than the voters, they were not always responsive to local wishes. The worst territorial governors were incompetent political hacks or venal self-servers looking to feather their own nests at the expense of the territory. A really bad territorial governor could advance a statehood movement substantially, and Nehemiah Ordway was, by all accounts, a really bad governor.

Nehemiah Ordway was a New Hampshire politician who was appointed governor in 1880 at the behest of Granite State land speculators who had holdings in Dakota. In addition to serving these masters, Ordway hoped for personal benefit through land speculation and graft. He contrived to get his son appointed to the crucial position of territorial auditor and used territorial printing contracts to build a supportive coterie of newspaper editors.

Ordway quickly understood that the Northern Pacific was the great corporate power in Dakota. He tied his wagon to the railroad's star. Northern Pacific President Henry Villard was interested in anything that might enhance the railroad's visibility and profitability. To further this goal, he advocated moving the territorial capital from Yankton to Bismarck, on the main line of the Northern Pacific. Villard entrusted the political task of moving the capital to Ordway.

In order to carry this project forward, Ordway enlisted the aid of the Northern Pacific's political agent in northern Dakota, Alexander McKenzie. McKenzie was a Canadian Scot who worked his way up from spikeman to construction foreman on the Northern Pacific as it moved west from Fargo. In 1873 McKenzie settled in Bismarck, where he became sheriff the next year. Although barely literate, McKenzie demonstrated a gift for political organization, coalition building, and buying elections when such unpleasant work was required. The political talents of the young sheriff caught the attention of the executives of the Northern Pacific, who established a relationship with him lasting for nearly thirty years.

In the 1883 session of the territorial legislature, Ordway supported a bill creating a commission of nine members to investigate the feasibility of removing the capital from Yankton and to suggest a replacement. Opposition to the commission was strong, but Ordway was able to secure passage of the bill by threatening to veto bills favoring particular localities unless their legislators agreed to creation of the commission.

The removal commission included three members from the north, all, including McKenzie, connected to the Northern Pacific. By law, the commission's organizational meeting had to take place in Yankton, where hostile citizens had induced a judge to issue a court order preventing the commission's meeting. Getting wind of this plan, McKenzie convened the meeting on a rail car passing through Yankton at five o'clock on an April morning, thus meeting the requirements of the law and dodging the court order. The Yankton Oligarchy had more than met its match in the canny Scot.

The removal commission proceeded to visit ten prospective capitals, including one with but a single building, enjoying lavish and mostly legal entertainment at every stop. Eventually the solidarity of the three Northern Pacific members and the judicious use of bribery had the anticipated result, and Bismarck was designated the new territorial capital in June of 1883. When Henry Villard laid the cornerstone of the capitol in September, one of the speakers predicted that Bismarck would become "the metropolitan hearth of the world's civilization." Bismarck is a nice town, but the "metropolitan hearth of the world's civilization" it is not![1]

The rampant corruption of the Ordway administration, as exemplified in the capital removal affair, disgusted political leaders in the south, especially because it failed to benefit their section. In 1882 the Yankton Oligarchy created the Dakota Citizens League to secure Ordway's removal and achieve statehood. In September 1883 the Dakota Citizens League spurred a convention that met at Sioux Falls to write a constitution for southern Dakota, an action implying that North Dakota would be separated and would continue its territorial status. A constitution was written and submitted to the voters, who approved it in October by nearly a two-to-one margin. Unfortunately, less than 40 percent of voters bothered to participate, indicating broad apathy among the southern public, and Congress demonstrated no more enthusiasm than the folk on the northern plains.

In 1885 the Citizens League tried again, holding another convention in Sioux Falls and writing a constitution virtually identical to that of 1883. In November the voters of southern Dakota again overwhelmingly approved a state constitution, but the vote was embarrassingly light. This time the U.S. Senate approved statehood, but the House of Representatives did not.

Much of the difficulty confronted by statehood forces was rooted in the national political standoff. Between 1875 and 1889 one party never simultaneously controlled the presidency and both houses of Congress. The likelihood that southern Dakota would become a Republican state with Republican electors, senators, and representatives dampened Democratic enthusiasm for the spread of self-government on the northern plains, particularly when another future Republican state would be created in the form of North Dakota Territory. Perhaps for strategic reasons, Democrats were willing to consider admission of a single state of Dakota, but that was anathema to the folk in the south. Unfortunately, Dakotans themselves were not united on the idea of dividing the territory into two states. Although there were substantial ethnic and economic differences between the two halves of the territory, northern Dakotans voted against division in 1887 by a margin of 18,000 to 8,000. At the same time nearly two-thirds of southern Dakotans favored division, but 15,000 of them opposed it.

The railroads, too were opposed to statehood for the Dakotas. With the rising tide of agrarian radicalism on the northern plains, the railroads became even less enthusiastic about the possibility of new state legislatures dominated by people who blamed the railroads for the farmers' troubles and who sought to regulate them, tax them, and generally rein them in. The railroads' point of view was ably represented in Washington by Nehemiah Ordway, who had been dismissed as governor of Dakota Territory by Chester Alan Arthur, only to appear in the federal district as a lobbyist for his old patron, the Northern Pacific railroad. Between the crosscurrents of partisan politics and the opposition of the railroads, statehood did not appear to stand a chance.

STATEHOOD ACHIEVED

The prospects for statehood for both halves of Dakota improved dramatically as a result of the election of 1888. After nearly two decades of divided government, the Republicans managed to elect their presidential candidate, Benjamin Harrison, and to secure majorities in both houses of Congress. Now there was a political incentive to admit as many potentially Republican states into the Union as possible and to do so quickly, before another election threatened to divide the government again.

The lame-duck session of Congress that sat in the winter of 1888 and 1889 quickly addressed the statehood issue. Democrats, seeing the handwriting on the wall and reluctant to alienate Dakotans who would soon be in the Union in any event, dropped their opposition to Senator—now President-elect—Harrison's plan to authorize the creation of two states out of Dakota Territory. On February 22, 1889, an Omnibus Bill was passed authorizing North Dakota, South Dakota, Montana, and Washington to write state constitutions for submission to Congress. President Grover Cleveland, now in the waning days of his term, signed the bill.

THE CONSTITUTIONAL CONVENTION
AND THE CONSTITUTION

North Dakotans went to the polls on May 14 to select seventy-five delegates to a constitutional convention to be held in Bismarck, beginning on July 4. The composition of the convention reflected the socioeconomic power structure of North Dakota better than it reflected its occupational or demographic make-up. The convention delegates were disproportionately Yankees, with fifty-two having been born in the United States. Thirteen of the delegates were natives of Wisconsin, and ten had been born in New York State. Of the twenty-three delegates who were immigrants, all but five were from the British Isles or Canada. Norwegians, Germans, and Germans from Russia were under-represented, and none of the seventy-five had been born in Dakota Territory. Over two-thirds of the delegates identified themselves as Republicans. Twenty-nine were farmers, which seems impressive until one realizes that three-fourths of North Dakotans farmed. Nearly as many lawyers as farmers served as delegates. Generally the delegates were young men, mostly in their thirties and forties. Most had moved to the region during the Great Dakota Boom and had tied their fortunes to it. They were typical of the boomers and boosters who played such a prominent role in so many of the territories.

Given the power of the railroads in northern Dakota, it should come as no surprise that the Northern Pacific, especially, was well represented. Such Northern Pacific water-bearers as Roger Allin and Burleigh Spalding played active and highly visible roles in the constitution-making process. It was noteworthy that Henry Villard, chairman of the Northern Pacific board, asked James Bradley Thayer, a professor at the Harvard Law School, to prepare a draft constitution for the future state. The draft constitution was presented to the delegates by Erastus Williams of Bismarck, who did not attempt to pass it off as his own work but refused to divulge its source.

Villard's motives in soliciting a constitution for North Dakota might have been altruistic, but some other factors may also have been in play. Villard probably recognized that time was of the essence in this process, and he may have doubted the abilities of the delegates. Clearly, his actions were presumptuous and demonstrated the Northern Pacific's proprietary attitude toward the area. As it turned out, however, his instincts were fairly sound, and the Thayer constitution formed the basis of the North Dakota constitution.

The railroads had great influence at the convention, but theirs was not the only agenda on the table. Moral reformers and good government advocates favored prohibition, woman suffrage, and a strict divorce law. More numerous and more threatening to the railroads' hopes and dreams were agrarian reformers, most of whom were active in the Farmers Alliance.

The Farmers Alliance was one organized response to the problems of money, markets, and middlemen that bedeviled farmers in the wheat and cotton belts in the late nineteenth century. The money problem involved the relative shortage of credit and the consequent high interest rates with which farmers struggled. Before the creation of the Federal Reserve system, money did not move easily around the country, and the further one was from a financial center, the more expensive the loan tended to be. Most territorial Dakotans borrowed through mortgage brokers, who arranged loans from eastern banks, insurance companies, and investors on a commission basis. Real interest rates frequently stood at 10 percent or even more. Exacerbating the difficult credit situation was the general deflation in prices, including farm prices, and the fact that loans were seldom made for periods longer than five or six years, entailing frequent visits by farmers to credit markets. The farmers' marketing problem was essentially that they sold their products on world markets over which they exercised no control and on which prices fluctuated wildly. Regional market controls worsened this difficult situation. The Minneapolis Chamber of Commerce, a closed cartel of grain buyers, set daily prices and maintained grading standards for grain that farmers believed harmed their interests. Because

Minneapolis was the flour-milling center of the country, farmers had few alternatives to marketing there. Finally, farmers complained of the depredations of middlemen, who frequently enjoyed a monopoly. Railroads, for example, were accused of excessive rates and inequitable rate structures, and line elevators were damned for downgrading wheat, short weighting, and excessive dockage (discounting wheat prices on the basis of dirt, broken kernels, and weed seed in the grain).

The Farmers Alliance organized in Dakota Territory in 1885 and gained adherents quickly, claiming 744 local chapters and 28,000 members by 1888. Its president was Henry Loucks, an energetic and charismatic Canadian immigrant. In the northern half of the territory the major figure in the alliance was Walter Muir, a Scottish immigrant of wide experience and substantial ability who farmed in Cass County, the largest county in the north.

The Farmers Alliance had an ambitious local program in addition to its national program of railroad regulation, currency inflation, and government warehousing of farm products and lending to farmers. In Dakota the alliance stressed economic cooperation. A cooperative buying enterprise, the Dakota Alliance Company, purchased binder twine, coal, plows, and buggies in bulk and offered them to members at reduced prices. The Hail Insurance Association offered relatively cheap coverage to protect grain farmers against a frequent calamity in the region. The alliance also bought or built a few dozen line elevators in Dakota. The ultimate goal of the Dakota alliance was to create an impressive cooperative marketing structure, including numerous warehouses and line elevators and a terminal elevator complex in Minneapolis. This goal was not realistic, requiring much more capital than the alliance had available and admission into the Minneapolis Chamber of Commerce, which was simply not going to happen. In addition to stressing cooperation, the alliance in Dakota pressed for regulation of railroad rates and practices and for territorial grading of grain and oversight of local elevators.

The program of the Dakota Farmers Alliance attracted members, but the organization offered other advantages as well. It was also a social organization that sponsored picnics, potlucks, and public speeches that helped relieve the isolation and tedium of life on the northern plains. It was a family organization, recognizing that in farming the home and the business are the same entity and shrewdly understanding that loyalty was likely to be stronger to an organization engaging the entire family than to one organized solely along economic lines. Finally, it tied members together with four locally published newspapers, including one printed in Norwegian.

Alliancemen and non-alliance delegates sensitive to their concerns were present at the constitutional convention and played a vital role in shaping the document. Indeed, convention president, Fred Fancher, was a vice president of the Dakota Farmers Alliance. The Alliance was antipathetic to monopolies and wary of corporate influence over government, favoring primacy for the genuine producers of wealth whom it claimed to represent.

Alliance distrust of government was reflected in a constitution that mandated independent boards and commissions to oversee state institutions, regulate railroads, and manage school lands, of which North Dakota was to receive nearly 3.2 million acres from Congress at the time of admission. Creation of these boards and commissions reflected the desire of the delegates for a weak governor, as did their decision to make virtually all executive offices—from secretary of state and attorney general to agriculture commissioner and superintendent of public instruction—elective rather than appointive. In a backhanded tribute to the memory of Nehemiah Ordway, the convention included a curious provision in the constitution making it illegal for the governor to threaten to veto legislation.

Distrust of the governor did not translate into trust for the legislature. That body was limited to one sixty-day session every two years. The legislature's ability to raise property taxes or to borrow money was severely limited, as was its ability to pass laws dealing with specific localities. The constitution outlawed bribery of legislators and legislators' acceptance of bribes, and even tried to make legislative log-rolling an offense warranting expulsion from the legislature. This measure was one of several pious but unenforceable hopes embodied in the document. In regard to the judicial branch, the framers of the constitution created a supreme court of three (now five) elected judges, who were given direct appellate and supervisory jurisdiction over district courts.

As the convention proceeded, the fairly simple and straightforward Thayer draft grew into an ungainly document, ultimately six times as long as the U.S. Constitution. Part of the problem lay in the determination of the delegates—distrustful of a legislature that did not even yet exist—to legislate in the constitution. Among other things, the constitution outlawed a series of abusive railroad practices, required the railroads to keep open records, and empowered the Board of Railroad Commissioners to regulate rates. The constitution also specified protected civil liberties, gave married women control of their own property, prohibited most non-farm child labor, and prohibited corporations from exchanging blacklists. The delegates considered and rejected numerous other measures, such as woman suffrage, prohibition of railroad passes for public officials, and compulsory arbitration of labor disputes.

Two articles in the constitution were especially controversial. One prohibited the manufacture and sale of alcoholic beverages in the new state. This prohibition was a favorite of Yankee moral reformers, such as the energetic Elizabeth Preston Anderson of the Women's Christian Temperance Union, but it was also supported by many Norwegian immigrants, especially those from the evangelical Lutheran churches. On the other side of the issue were German and German-Russian voters, especially, who viewed prohibition as a cultural assault and as an unwarranted governmental intrusion in their lives. The delegates approved the prohibition article, but they were so concerned that opposition to it would defeat the entire constitution that they required that it be voted on separately from the rest of the constitution.

The other controversial article was Article 19, which sought to locate thirteen state institutions—including colleges, normal schools, reformatories, veterans' homes, schools for the blind and deaf, and others—in designated cities and towns. This provision was probably bad government, because it gave the state many more institutions than it needed, and it limited legislative flexibility by embedding these institutions in the constitution. The opposition to Article 19, however, came mainly from those who were dissatisfied with the allocations as granted. Fargo, for example, complained that it received only an agricultural college, whereas Jamestown and Bismarck received the state mental hospital and the penitentiary respectively. Fargoans doubted that many agricultural students would enroll, but they were certain the state would produce plenty of lunatics and criminals. Article 19 mainly benefited towns along the Northern Pacific line, so the protest was most intense from the northeastern counties served by the Great Northern, who felt under-rewarded by the delegates dispensing the allocations.

Opposition to Article 19, although bitter, was not sufficient to scuttle the constitution, which was approved by the voters on October 1 by a vote of 27,441 to 8,107. The prohibition article, considered separately, was also approved, but by a much narrower margin, 18,552 to 17,393. The North Dakota constitution flew through the Republican Congress, and Benjamin Harrison signed the bill admitting North Dakota to the Union on November 2, a few moments before he signed the South Dakota statehood bill.

BRINGING THE STATE TO LIFE

North Dakota's early years as a state witnessed a continuation of the political struggles that had marked the constitutional convention. The Republican Party was dominant from the earliest days of the state, winning two-thirds of the votes cast for representative and the constitutional offices in November 1889, and would remain so until the 1950s. As is often the case in one-party states, however, the dominant party was divided into at least three identifiable and antagonistic factions.

The most stable and usually the largest faction of the new state's Republican party was the conservative one led by Northern Pacific operative Alexander McKenzie. Although it is tempting to identify the conservatives as railroad time-serves and toadies, they embraced the reasonable and defensible position that the state's economic development depended on maintaining a favorable environment for capital investment. Agrarian radicals, represented in 1889 by the Farmers Alliance, were the chief opponents of the McKenzie wing of the party. They, too, believed that economic development was essential for the state, but they argued that growth and prosperity would come only when North Dakota escaped such oppressive economic forces as the railroads and the Minneapolis grain traders. A third faction, much smaller than either of the others but strategically significant, was composed of good-government reformers such as Elizabeth Preston Anderson, Judge Charles Pollock of Fargo, and Grand Forks newspaper editor George Winship. The good-government faction was less interested in economic development per se than in preventing government corruption and maintaining a high moral tone through prohibition, extirpation of prostitution, and female suffrage.

The close balance between the two major factions was apparent in the first state elections and the inaugural legislative session. The Republicans nominated alliance leader John Miller for governor. Miller was a large farmer and land speculator in Richland County in the state's southeast corner, providing proof that the alliance was attractive to others than down-at-the-heels farmers. Miller was balanced by Henry Hansbrough, a newspaper editor aligned with the McKenzie faction, who was nominated for North Dakota's seat in the U.S. House of Representatives. The factional balancing act was also in evidence when the legislature chose the state's first U.S. senators. One seat went to Gilbert Pierce, a former territorial governor and close ally of the Northern Pacific. Alexander McKenzie hoped to deliver the other seat to his old friend and patron Nehemiah Ordway, but the alliance was strong enough to name one of its members, Lyman Casey, a rancher from Carrington.

Much of the work of the first legislative assembly involved bringing the new constitution to life. The legislature created a public school system and the institutions authorized in Article 19. Unfortunately, the legislature provided funding for only one of those institutions, the school for the deaf, setting a pattern that would obtain for many years. The legislature also delineated the structure for municipal and county governments and detailed the duties of state officials.

The alliance faction in the legislature sought to curb the abuses they saw in the railroads and the grain elevators. They were able to secure the passage of laws that empowered the Board of Railroad Commissioners to reduce rates, end long haul–short haul discrimination, curtail rate preferences, and prevent discrimination against farmer-owned elevators. The railroad commissioners were also empowered to create state grain grades, prevent collusion and price-fixing among elevators, and set storage rates. Elevators were also required to be licensed and bonded. Angered by these requirements, the major elevator firms threatened to shut down their North Dakota facilities. To prevent that from happening, the railroad commissioners and the attorney general traveled to the Twin Cities, where they promised the elevator companies that they would not enforce several of the new rules. Those who wondered where the real power of the new state lay had to look no further. The alliance-inspired laws respecting the railroads were no more effective than those dealing with grain elevators. Most of them were poorly framed—this legislature, filled with political amateurs, had written 210 laws in its special 120-day session—overly complex, and contradictory, allowing the railroads to evade them easily. The McKenzie faction, which offered little opposition to most of the restrictions on the railroads, probably knew all along that the laws would be dead letters.

Although the first legislature was largely characterized by the division between the alliance and McKenzie factions, good-government Republicans
also played a legislative role. They helped put prohibition into effect, defining
alcoholic beverages, determining who could be allowed to possess them, and
setting penalties for violations. Good-government advocates also played a role
in preventing the Louisiana Lottery from locating in the state.

The Louisiana Lottery, which sold tickets throughout the United States and
distributed $15 million in prize money annually, was due to lose its charter
in 1893 and was searching for a new home. Alexander McKenzie met with
lottery officials before the convening of the first legislative assembly, and
together they planned to move the lottery from the Gulf Coast to the northern
plains. In return for a charter in North Dakota, lottery officials promised a
one-time payment of $100,000 and an annual fee of $75,000 earmarked for
support of public education. These were substantial amounts of money in a
poor state that could not even afford to fund the institutions it had created.
In addition to lightening the burden on the state's taxpayers, the lottery also
promised economic development: the lottery had hundreds of employees
who would move to the state, and the money it promised to deposit in North
Dakota banks would alleviate the chronic capital shortage and would lower
interest rates.

All these factors endeared the lottery to the McKenzie faction, but good-
government Republicans were opposed. The lottery was believed to be corrupt,
and at best it promoted gambling, which lowered the moral tone of the community. Governor Miller became suspicious of the lottery, not least because he was
offered $100,000 to sign the lottery bill making its way through the legislature.
Enjoying strong support from George Winship and other advocates of good-
government, Miller hired the Pinkerton Detective Agency to investigate reports that legislators had been bribed. The agent posed as a journalist and
quickly gained access to several legislators, from whom he learned that money
had been applied liberally to lubricate the legislative process. Shortly after the
state senate passed the lottery charter bill by a veto-proof two-thirds majority,
Miller threatened McKenzie that he would expose the widespread bribery and
name names. In response to this threat, McKenzie ordered his lieutenants in
the House to table the bill, ending the possibility that North Dakota would
host the Louisiana Lottery.

The bitter failure of the alliance's legislative program in 1889 led some
members of that organization to contemplate creation of a third party similar
to those being created in Kansas, South Dakota, and other states where radical
agrarian impulses were strong. In September 1890, alliancemen led by Walter
Muir created the Independent Party, North Dakota's name for the Populists,
and nominated a slate of candidates for the legislature and statewide offices.

Many alliancemen, along with good-government Republicans, remained
loyal to the Grand Old Party, with the result that gubernatorial candidate
Muir got only 13 percent of the vote and only a handful of Independent

legislative candidates were successful. The second legislative assembly proved to be nearly as unsatisfactory as the first; however, convincing many heretofore-reluctant alliancemen that a third party was necessary.

By 1892 the Independent Party, now fully aligned with the new and rapidly growing Populist Party, was poised to make a significant impact in North Dakota. The Independents fused with the Democrats, working out an arrangement whereby each would endorse most of the other's candidates on the statewide ballot. The gubernatorial candidate was Eli Shortridge, former president of the North Dakota Farmers Alliance and an erstwhile Democrat. Promising to have the state build terminal elevator facilities on Lake Superior, Shortridge swept to victory along with most of the Independent-Democratic slate. The only Republican winner was the Norwegian-born candidate for secretary of state, who ran well among Norwegian-Americans otherwise drawn to agrarian radicalism. The Populist presidential candidate, James B. Weaver, defeated Republican Benjamin Harrison in the state by fewer than 150 votes out of more than 35,000 cast. One elector was assigned to Harrison, with the other two going to Weaver, although one of them, a fusion Democrat, cast his vote for Grover Cleveland. North Dakota thereby contrived to transform its minimal Electoral College influence into virtually none at all.

Shortridge took office freighted with the high expectations of the agrarian radicals, and it seemed for a time that he would satisfy them. Independents and sympathetic Republicans appropriated $100,000 to build terminal elevator facilities at Duluth or Superior and worked away at the biennial task of passing effective regulations for railroads and elevators. The previously unfunded state institutions, including the colleges and normal schools, finally received the appropriations implicitly promised in the constitution.

Overhanging the legislature, however, was a festering dispute between Democrats and formerly Republican Independents. The latter accused the former, who included the governor and the attorney general in their ranks, of gaining too many offices from the fusion arrangement. That suspicion was heightened when, after a struggle that consumed forty-eight days of the sixty-day legislative session, Democrat William Roach was sent to the U.S. Senate. With memories of the Civil War still fresh in many minds, honest cooperation between Democrats and Republicans was extremely difficult and was fraught with potential hazards, even when the principals styled themselves Independents or Populists.

The struggle over the Senate seat consumed so much of the legislature's limited time that scores of bills were passed in the assembly's waning hours. Indeed, 111 bills were sent to the governor on the final day of the session. Fire-alarm legislating was not good legislating, and the pell-mell conclusion of the session offered numerous opportunities for mischief. For example, several of the bills aimed at regulating the railroads and the grain elevators were lost or stolen between the legislature and the governor's desk, preventing him from signing them into law. An acrimonious dispute between the governor and the trustees of the agricultural college contributed further to the governor's image of incompetence and failure.

The legislature's adjournment coincided with a national stock market panic that quickly turned into a major depression. North Dakota's commodity-based economy was extremely sensitive to national and international economic trends, so the young state felt the full effect of the depression. A depleted treasury meant that funding promises to state institutions could not be fulfilled. It also meant that money was not available to build a terminal elevator in Duluth or Superior. (The terminal was only a wish anyway, because neither Minnesota nor Wisconsin was prepared to give North Dakota control over an elevator on their territory or allow it to apply its grain-grading standards there.)

The political and economic stresses of the Shortridge administration fractured the agrarian radical movement along partisan lines. The Independents refused fusion with the Democrats for the 1894 elections. Billing themselves as the party of prosperity and facing a divided opposition, the Republicans swept to victory with a predominantly conservative slate. Gubernatorial candidate Roger Allin won 57 percent of the vote; only 23 percent of the voters supported the Independent candidate. The Independent Party quickly declined, and a period of conservative Republican dominance ensued.

The collapse of agrarian radicalism seemed to conclude a struggle that had played out in the late territorial days, during the constitutional convention, and through the early years of statehood. The demise of agrarian radicalism proved to be temporary, however, and the early years of the twentieth century saw the American Society of Equity and then the Nonpartisan League repeating some of the themes the Farmers Alliance had developed. Indeed, in some ways agrarian radicalism remained a potent force in North Dakota politics into the 1950s.

CONCLUSION

The continuing potency of agrarian radicalism showed that problems confronting North Dakota in the territorial days were not quickly or easily solved. As historian Elwyn Robinson noted nearly half a century ago, such problems as physical remoteness, economic dependence, and disadvantage were glaringly apparent at the time of statehood, and they remained—and still remain—significant long afterward.[2]

Agrarian radicals provided one solution, and conservatives provided another for the economic problems that bedeviled the area. The radicals held out the prospect that North Dakotans could become masters of their own fates, escaping the clutches of outside bankers and corporations. Their proposals were popular because the problems confronting the territory and the young state were real and because they were addressing rural people who readily embraced cooperative solutions to their problems and who were not particularly frightened by governmental activism.

The agrarian radicals also spoke to people who were suspicious of politicians, as amply illustrated by the constitution, but who were quite willing to participate in politics themselves. In common with others in the upper Midwest, North Dakotans embraced the commonwealth political tradition, with its emphasis on a vital civic culture, widespread political participation, and direct democracy. It was quite in character that North Dakotans instituted and frequently used the initiative and the referendum shortly after the turn of the century, adopted the recall, and were the first people in the Union to remove a sitting governor from office through that device.

The territorial and early statehood period was of crucial significance to the state of North Dakota, highlighting a series of challenges with which the state would long struggle, and imparting a political culture that would long endure.

NOTES

1. Quoted in Richard A. Bartlett, *The New Country: A Social History of American Frontier* (New York: Oxford University Press, 1974), p. 431.
2. Elwyn B. Robinson, "The Themes of North Dakota's History," *North Dakota History* 26 (Winter 1959): 5–24.

BIBLIOGRAPHY

Bartlett, Richard A. *The New Country: A Social History of the American Frontier, 1776–1890* . New York: Oxford University Press, 1976.

Danbom, David B. "North Dakota: The Most Midwestern State." In *Heartland: Comparative Histories of the Midwestern States*, 107–126. Bloomington: Indiana University Press, 1999.

Lamar, Howard Roberts. *Dakota Territory, 1861–1889: A Study of Frontier Politics* . New Haven: Yale University Press, 1956.

Reid, Bill G. "Elizabeth Preston Anderson and the Politics of Social Reform." In *The North Dakota Political Tradition*, 183–202. Ames: Iowa State University Press, 1981.

Robinson, Elwyn B. *History of North Dakota*. Lincoln: University of Nebraska Press, 1966.

———. "The Themes of North Dakota's History." *North Dakota History* 26 (Winter 1959): 5–24.

Sherman, William C., and Thorson, Playford U., eds. *Plains Folk: North Dakota's Ethnic History*. Fargo: North Dakota Institute for Regional Studies, 1986.

Stradley, Scot Arthur. *The Broken Circle: An Economic History of North Dakota*. Grand Forks, North Dakota: Flat Earth Press, 1994.

Wilkins, Robert P., "Alexander McKenzie and the Politics of Bossism." In *The North Dakota Political Tradition*, 3–39. Ames: Iowa State University Press, 1981.

———, and H. Wynona. *North Dakota: A History*. New York: W.W. Norton, 1977.

THE STATE OF OHIO

Admitted to the Union as a State: March 1, 1803

Michael Mangus and Susan Mangus

INTRODUCTION

On February 19, 1803, Ohio became the seventeenth state to join the United States of America. Since the adoption of the U.S. Constitution in 1788, white Americans had focused their expansion on the southwest, especially Kentucky and Tennessee, which were admitted to statehood in 1792 and 1796, respectively. Following Tennessee's admittance, the nation's expansion shifted to the Northwest Territory, in particular to Ohio. As with the other early states, Ohio's admittance to the Union was fraught with difficulty. Tensions with Native Americans, differences of opinion between the two main political parties, the Democratic-Republicans and the Federalists, and arguments between landowners and squatters made Ohio statehood questionable during the late 1790s and the early 1800s. Slavery further complicated the situation, because some immigrants, especially from southern states, favored slavery, whereas settlers from the Northeast, were indifferent or, in some cases, vehemently opposed the institution of slavery. In 1802 and 1803, white Ohioans put aside their differences to create the seventeenth state, but these tensions continued to influence Ohio's development for the next several decades.[1]

SECURING THE OHIO COUNTRY
FOR WHITE AMERICANS

The Treaty of Paris of 1783, which formally concluded the American Revolution, recognized the American states' independence from Great Britain. The treaty also gave the new country possession of the Ohio Country,

Ohio

Territorial Development:

- Great Britain cedes future territory of Ohio to the United States through the Treaty of Paris, September 3, 1783
- The United States passes the Northwest Ordinance: territorial claims inherited from colonial charters ceded to the public domain; future territory of Ohio organized as a part of the Northwest Territory, July 13, 1787
- The Northwest Territory divided into the Indiana Territory and a new, smaller, Northwest Territory, Ohio, May 7, 1800
- Ohio admitted into the Union as the seventeenth state, March 1, 1803

Territorial Capitals:

- Marietta, 1788–1790
- Cincinnati, 1790–1800
- Chillicothe, 1800–1803

State Capitals:

- Chillicothe, 1803–1810
- Zanesville, 1810–1812
- Chillicothe, 1812–1817
- Columbus, 1817–present

Origin of State Name: The Iroquois referred to the river from which the state received its name as "Ohio," meaning "large" or "beautiful river."

First Governor: Edward Tiffin
Governmental Organization: Bicameral
Population at Statehood: 230,760 (figure taken from the 1810 census)
Geographical Size: 40,948 square miles

in addition to all other territory south of Canada, north of Florida, east of the Mississippi River, and west of the Atlantic Ocean. Encompassing modern-day Ohio and parts of Indiana, Pennsylvania, and West Virginia, the Ohio Country had been the center of conflict between various European and native powers since at least the 1740s. Both French and British citizens had moved into the region, hoping to engage in the fur trade with local natives, especially the Delaware, the Wyandot, and the Shawnee. The struggle for dominance of the Ohio Country peaked in the French and Indian War (1756–1763). The British emerged from this conflict victorious against the French and their native allies. The war left Great Britain in a severe financial crisis, however, and the British government sought to reduce its expenditures by reducing its military commitment to its North American colonies. Therefore, hoping to secure a lasting peace with the Ohio Country natives, Great Britain issued the Proclamation of 1763 that prohibited English colonists from moving west of the Appalachian Mountains. With the colonies' victory in the American Revolution, whites again gained access to the Ohio Country.

Although white Americans no longer faced government prohibitions on settlement west of the Appalachian Mountains, Native Americans contested the arrival of white migrants. During the American Revolution, numerous battles, relatively minor in comparison to those in the East, occurred between the Native Americans, their British allies, and the white Americans. The most significant of these battles was the Gnadenhutten Massacre. On March 8 and 9, 1782, Pennsylvania militiamen attacked a group of Christian Native Americans at Gnadenhutten. The Americans sought to revenge the deaths of several Pennsylvanians, although the Delaware at Gnadenhutten had not participated in the attacks. The Pennsylvanians murdered twenty-eight men, twenty-nine women, and thirty-nine children by crushing the skulls of the captive natives. Battles such as Gnadenhutten set the stage for widespread bloodshed as white settlers flooded the Ohio Country after 1783.[2]

With the American victory, settlers moved westward onto the natives' land with the blessing of the new federal government. The Articles of Confederation, the document that created the nation's first federal government, did not allow the national government to tax its citizens, and the government was in desperate need of money. To raise funds, the Confederation Congress intended to sell land in Ohio to white settlers.

The federal government also hoped to use land bounties in lieu of money to pay soldiers who had served in the Continental Army during the Revolution. By 1783, many of these men had not received payment for their services in several years. Rufus Putnam, a general in the Continental Army, drafted the Newburgh Petition to force the Confederation Congress to pay the soldiers with land grants in the Ohio Country. Putnam argued that these men would also help protect the young country from Native American attacks from the West. A total of 288 officers signed the petition, but the Confederation Congress refused to act. The officers threatened to overthrow the Confederation

Congress, but General George Washington easily prevented the uprising. With Native Americans in physical control of the land, government officials had to convince the natives to relinquish their land claims before any sales could take place and before the government could distribute any land bounties.[3]

The first step in convincing the natives to forsake their land was the Treaty of Fort Stanwix in 1784. In this treaty, the Tuscarora, the Mohawk, the Onondaga, the Oneida, the Seneca, and the Cayuga relinquished all their claims to the area. None of these tribes, however, actually resided in the Ohio Country. The natives who actually resided in the Ohio Country, including the Shawnee, the Mingo, the Delaware, and several other tribes, rejected the treaty. Bloodshed continued to stain the Ohio Country.[4]

The first treaty negotiated directly with Ohio Country natives was the Treaty of Fort McIntosh. Most of the Native American negotiators did not have permission from their respective tribes to discuss and sign a treaty, but the American commissioners demanded an agreement among the various parties. In 1785, after several weeks of negotiation, representatives of the Confederation Congress and the Delaware, Wyandot, Ottawa, and Chippewa Indians signed the treaty. The natives agreed to abide by the American government's dictates and not to form alliances with any other powers. The Native Americans relinquished their claims to lands in what is now southern and eastern Ohio, and the Confederation Congress agreed to prohibit white encroachment onto the natives' land in the northwestern portion of the present-day state.

Because the Native American negotiators did not have authority to sign the Treaty of Fort McIntosh, several tribes in the Ohio Country, most notably the Shawnee, refused to abide by the agreement. In 1785, Congress re-opened negotiations with the Shawnee at Fort Finney. During the negotiations, the Shawnees presented the Americans a belt of black wampum, a sign of war, and in response the whites threatened to attack the Shawnee. Under this threat, the Shawnee chieftains agreed to the Treaty of Fort Finney, also known as the Treaty at the Mouth of the Great Miami, on January 31, 1786. In it, the Shawnee and the white Americans agreed to abide by the Treaty of Fort McIntosh. In 1787, the Northwest Territory was created, encompassing present-day Ohio, Indiana, Illinois, Michigan, Wisconsin, and part of Minnesota.

The treaties of Fort McIntosh and Fort Finney resulted in a relatively brief period of peace in the Ohio Country. This peace quickly evaporated as thousands of whites flooded across the Appalachian Mountains during the late 1780s. Native Americans became alarmed as whites began to encroach on their land, in some cases settling on land guaranteed to the natives under earlier treaties. Violence erupted again, prompting Henry Knox, secretary of war under President George Washington, to order Arthur St. Clair, then serving as the governor of the Northwest Territory, to negotiate a new treaty with the Native Americans. The negotiations between St. Clair and representatives from the Wyandot, Delaware, Ottawa, Chippewa, Potawotami, and Sauk Indians took place at Fort Harmar, near present-day Marietta, Ohio. The

Native Americans hoped that the whites would agree to a new boundary between the whites and the natives that would give them all land north of the Ohio River and west of the Muskingum River, confining white settlement to the northeastern corner of modern-day Ohio. St. Clair instead demanded that the natives agree to the boundary established by the treaties of Fort McIntosh and Fort Finney. He also offered the Indians $3,000 in gifts. The tribal negotiators agreed to the treaty, the Treaty of Fort Harmar, on January 9, 1789, but it did not bring peace to the Northwest Territory. The Shawnee had not participated in the treaty negotiations and refused to abide by it.

Because of the Shawnees' refusal to adhere to the stipulations of the Treaty of Fort Harmar, Henry Knox ordered Josiah Harmar, the commander of the U.S. Army in the Northwest Territory, to remove the threat of a Native American attack in western Ohio. Although Native Americans living in Ohio claimed all of the territory as their own, most of them lived along the modern-day Ohio-Indiana border. In 1790 Harmar began his campaign from Fort Washington, present-day Cincinnati, with 320 regular soldiers and approximately 1,100 militiamen. The militiamen had limited training, with many not knowing how to fire a gun, and others did not even have firearms. Despite his poorly trained force, Harmar intended to destroy the villages of the Miami, the Shawnee, and the Delaware near modern-day Ft. Wayne, Indiana.[5]

The natives fled as Harmar's army approached. The Americans, facing no real resistance, burned several villages, but the Native Americans under the leadership of Little Turtle regrouped. On October 20, 1790, the natives ambushed a small portion of Harmar's army consisting of several hundred militiamen and a few regular soldiers. Most of the militiamen fled the battlefield without firing a shot, and some did not stop retreating until they had crossed the Ohio River into Kentucky, several hundred miles away. The regular soldiers fought valiantly, but most were killed. Harmar launched a counterattack against Little Turtle's warriors two days later. Again, the Native Americans easily defeated the whites. Harmar and the remainder of his command immediately retreated to Fort Washington. This disastrous campaign against the natives became known as Harmar's defeat.

As a result of Harmar's defeat, Governor St. Clair decided to lead his own military expedition against the Native Americans near present-day Ft. Wayne, Indiana. St. Clair's force also consisted primarily of unskilled militiamen. The army left Fort Washington in September 1791. Along the route St. Clair ordered the construction of forts Hamilton and Jefferson. He hoped the presence of these fortifications would intimidate the natives into retreating and also would provide security for white settlers who would, in theory, shortly move into the region. St. Clair's men faced harsh conditions in their northward march, enduring unseasonably low temperatures and heavy rain and snow. Many of the white soldiers deserted. The remainder of St. Clair's army reached the Miami's territory on October 24. By November 3, the American army had reached the Miami villages on the Wabash River. Little Turtle attacked

St. Clair's force the next morning. Again, the militiamen fled immediately. Some hid under wagons, and others immediately fled to Fort Jefferson. St. Clair rallied his remaining men, primarily regular soldiers, and launched an unsuccessful bayonet charge. In the fighting, St. Clair had two horses shot out from under him, and several bullets passed through his clothing, one taking off a lock of his hair. The Indians surrounded the Americans who were still resisting. After three hours of hand-to-hand combat, the remaining Americans pushed their way through the natives and joined the militiamen in retreat. With food and supplies short at Fort Jefferson, St. Clair led his men back to Fort Washington. St. Clair's defeat was one of the worst defeats ever experienced by the U.S. Army at the hands of Native Americans.

In 1792, President George Washington replaced St. Clair as the commander of the U.S. Army of the Northwest with Anthony Wayne. In May 1793, Wayne arrived at Fort Washington with additional regular soldiers to supplement the Army of the Northwest. Wayne intended to march against the natives immediately, but smallpox and influenza weakened his men. Five months later, Wayne's command left Fort Washington for Fort Jefferson. Upon his arrival at Fort Jefferson, Wayne and his force proceeded six miles farther north and constructed Fort Greene Ville. The army spent the winter of 1793–1794 inside this fort. During the winter, Wayne's men also constructed Fort Recovery at the site of St. Clair's defeat.

The Army of the Northwest was seen as a serious threat to Native Americans residing in the area of modern-day western Ohio and eastern Indiana. On June 30, more than one thousand Shawnee, Miami, Delaware, Ottawa, and Ojibwa led by Little Turtle attacked a supply train leaving Fort Recovery for Fort Greene Ville, where most of Wayne's men were stationed. The natives killed nearly fifty whites and seized numerous horses and cattle.

Until the successful assault on the supply train, the Native Americans had believed that Fort Recovery, with its four blockhouses, fifteen-foot-high stockade wall, and at least three cannon, was too strong for a direct assault, although only a small group of men garrisoned the fort. A small group of natives now believed that Fort Recovery would fall easily. They attacked, but the soldiers repelled the natives' assault, killing approximately seventeen braves. The siege of Fort Recovery led to dissention among the various tribes. Little Turtle became convinced that the Native Americans had no hope of victory and encouraged peace negotiations. Many of his supporters returned to their homes, unwilling to continue the struggle. Other natives continued the struggle under the leadership of Blue Jacket, a Shawnee who did not enjoy wide support among the other tribes.

In early August, Wayne's army moved against the Native Americans, destroying several villages and some crops. The white Americans pushed toward the Maumee River, and the Native Americans hoped to attack Wayne's force at the Fallen Timbers, so named because a tornado had uprooted many of the trees. The natives believed that the white Americans would arrive on August 19,

but the white soldiers failed to appear. The Native Americans fasted in anticipation of the battle, because they believed that a stomach wound was more likely to
become infected if a person had eaten recently. When Wayne and his force
arrived at Fallen Timbers on August 20, the natives were weak from hunger.
The white Americans easily forced them from their cover in the fallen trees.
Thirty-three whites were killed and approximately one hundred were wounded;
the Native Americans suffered nearly twice as many casualties. Blue Jacket's
force retreated to Fort Miamis, a British outpost in northwestern Ohio, believing
that the British garrison would protect them from Wayne's army. Fearful of
provoking Wayne, the British refused. But the British commander also refused
Wayne's demand that the British evacuate both the fort and the entire Northwest Territory. Rather than attack the British outpost, Wayne withdrew to
Fort Greene Ville.

As a result of Wayne's victory at the Battle of Fallen Timbers and the British
soldiers' refusal to assist the natives, most Indians residing in the northwestern
section of modern-day Ohio realized their precarious situation and sued for
peace with the U.S. government. In January 1795, chiefs from the Wyandot,
Delaware, Ottawa, Miami, Shawnee, Kaskaskia, Piankashaw, Eel River,
Chippewa, Kickapoo, Potawotami, and Wea tribes met with General Wayne
at Fort Greene Ville. Treaty negotiations continued for the next eight months.
On August 3, 1795, the chiefs and Wayne signed the Treaty of Greenville.
The various tribes in attendance agreed to forsake all claims to land east and
south of a boundary that began at the mouth of the Cuyahoga River on Lake
Erie, ran southward to Fort Laurens, then westward to Fort Loramie and Fort
Recovery. The boundary then turned in a southerly direction to the Ohio River.
The natives did retain hunting rights in this territory. In return, the Americans
agreed to forbid white settlement west of the boundary line. The natives were
promised $20,000 worth of goods for signing the treaty and an additional
$9,500 worth of goods every year to be distributed by the various tribes as
they saw fit. Although the Treaty of Greenville theoretically established peace
between the natives residing in what is now Ohio and the white settlers who
flooded the region, tensions continued to exist. Not all Native Americans and
not all whites abided by the treaty. Nevertheless, thanks to Anthony Wayne
and his victory at the Battle of Fallen Timbers, Americans now viewed the land
that encompasses modern-day Ohio as safe for settlement. Thousands of whites
crossed the Appalachian Mountains hoping to make Ohio their home.

PREPARING THE LAND FOR SETTLEMENT

During the 1780s, the Confederation Congress, replaced in 1789 by the U.S.
Congress, implemented legislation that determined exactly how the federal
government would develop the Ohio Country into territories and then into
states. The first piece of legislation pertaining to the Ohio Country was the

Ordinance of 1784. Numerous states, especially Connecticut and Virginia, claimed land west of the Appalachian Mountains that included large portions of the Ohio Country. While they were colonies of England, the king had granted some of these states control of all land between the East Coast colonies and the Pacific Ocean. For much of the colonial period, the colonists mistakenly believed that the Pacific Ocean was just a short distance west of the Appalachian Mountains. The Confederation Congress also endured financial difficulties, because the Articles of Confederation prohibited the federal government from taxing its citizens. Because of its inability to tax, the Confederation Congress desired to sell land in the Ohio Country to raise funds. The large number of squatters, settlers living illegally on land that they had not purchased, also concerned the federal government. Fearing that the Appalachian Mountains left these settlers so isolated from the remainder of the nation that these whites might choose to rebel against America and form their own nation, Congress determined that it had to act. The federal government immediately began negotiations with the states that claimed land in the Ohio Country. The Confederation Congress hoped to become the sole governmental entity in control of this land.[6]

While the negotiations with the states were taking place, the Confederation Congress passed the Ordinance of 1784. Thomas Jefferson authored the document, authorizing the federal government to divide all land under American control west of the Appalachian Mountains, east of the Mississippi River, south of Canada, and north of the Ohio River into ten separate states. The Ordinance of 1784 stipulated that these states would begin as territories. Once a territory attained the same population as the nation's least populous state, it would become a state with equal standing to all earlier states, including the original thirteen. The Ordinance of 1784 also granted the right to self-government to the residents of each territory. Although the Confederation Congress formally approved the Ordinance of 1784, the federal government failed to enact the legislation's provisions. The pertinent land area remained undivided, and the Congress created no new states based upon the legislation's stipulations.

The Ordinance of 1784 had established how people residing in American-controlled territory west of the Appalachian Mountains and north of the Ohio River could apply for statehood. It did not stipulate, however, how the federal government would distribute the land to potential settlers. Hoping to deal with this issue, the Confederation Congress supplemented the Ordinance of 1784 with the Land Ordinance of 1785. Under this legislation, government surveyors plotted the territory into townships. Each township was a square enclosing thirty-six square miles of territory. The surveyors then divided each township into one-square-mile sections, each of which encompassed 640 acres. Once the surveyors had subdivided the land to this point, they then assigned each section a number between one and thirty-six. Section sixteen was always set aside for public schools. Hoping finally to compensate veterans of the American

Revolution, the federal government also retained sections eight, eleven, twenty-six, and twenty-nine, intending to give land bounties in these sections to the former soldiers. To raise revenue for the government, the Confederation Congress planned to sell the remaining sections at public auction. The government would sell only entire one-square-mile sections of land with the minimum bid starting at $640 per section, or $1 per acre.[7]

The first portion of Ohio surveyed under the Land Ordinance of 1785 became known as the Seven Ranges. Thomas Hutchins, the geographer of the United States, conducted the survey, beginning where the eastern boundary of the Ohio Country crossed the Ohio River. Known as the "Point of Beginning," today this location is the site of modern-day East Liverpool, Ohio. The northern boundary stretched east and west from this point. Pennsylvania's western border served as the first north-to-south line. The surveyors proceeded to map a total of eight lines, each exactly six miles apart. Upon completion of this survey, seven north-to-south rows existed, thus the name "the Seven Ranges." Each range consisted of a vertical row of townships. Hutchins died before finishing the survey, but the federal government continued his work.[8]

On July 13, 1787, the Confederation Congress implemented the Northwest Ordinance. This legislation formally created the Northwest Territory, established a governmental system for the people residing in the area, and stipulated the procedure by which the region would eventually become states within the United States of America. The Northwest Ordinance, in essence, replaced the Ordinance of 1784, although the Land Ordinance of 1785 remained in place.[9]

Manasseh Cutler, Thomas Jefferson, Rufus King, and Nathan Dane provided the theoretical basis for the act. Cutler, serving on the board of the Ohio Company and Associates, spoke for the western migrants and land speculators. Jefferson's Ordinance of 1784 heavily influenced King and Dane, two members of the Confederation Congress selected to draft the Northwest Ordinance. The act specified that the land encompassed within the Northwest Territory would proceed through three different stages of government before becoming a state. Initially, the Confederation Congress, replaced with the U.S. Congress in 1789, would appoint the territory's leaders. Government officials were to include the governor, a secretary, and three judges. The governor and judges were responsible for establishing a legal code. The Confederation Congress would not permit the territorial government to create any new laws; instead, all laws must be taken from previously established state codes. In addition, the Confederation Congress had final approval of all laws. Any laws that the Confederation Congress found unsuitable would be declared unenforceable within the territory. Within the territorial government, the governor enjoyed the most power, having the authority to select law enforcement officials and judges for the lower courts as well as the ability to call out the militia and negotiate treaties with the Native Americans. The governor, secretary, and judges all had to be residents of the territory and possess sizable landholdings.

This form of government was to remain in operation until at least five thousand free persons had moved within the territory's borders. Once population surpassed that number, territorial government advanced to the second stage in which the federal government would authorize the formation of a territorial legislature. The territorial legislature would consist of two houses, including a house of representatives and a legislative council. The federal Congress would select five men to serve on the legislative council, chosen from a list of ten names provided by the territorial house of representatives. The members of the house of representatives were to be men twenty-one years of age or older who resided within the territory and who owned at least two hundred acres of land. Members of the legislative council had to meet the same requirements but had to own at least five hundred acres of land. Eligible voters, adult men who owned at least fifty acres of land, elected the members of the house of representatives.

The final stage of government was statehood. The Northwest Ordinance required the creation of at least three and no more than five states out of the Northwest Territory. Once the population of a territory reached sixty thousand people, the territory could apply for statehood. Eligible voters would select delegates to a constitutional convention, where they would draft a state constitution. The state constitution had to ensure the right to bail except in cases involving capital crimes, trial by jury, and religious freedom. The state constitution also should encourage education to create a literate population, but the Northwest Ordinance did not require states to provide free public education. In addition, the Northwest Ordinance prohibited slavery in all parts of the Northwest Territory. If the state constitution failed to outlaw slavery or did not guarantee the other rights as stipulated in the Northwest Ordinance, the U.S. Congress would not accept the state constitution. For a territory to become a state, the U.S. Congress had to approve the submitted constitution, and the president had to sign the bill passed by Congress. In 1803, Ohio became the seventeenth state within the United States of America. It was the first state to achieve statehood under the Northwest Ordinance. With some modifications, the Northwest Ordinance has provided the blueprint for how territories have become states ever since.

SETTLING THE LAND

With the Native Americans declining as a serious threat and the enactment of the Ordinance of 1784, the Land Ordinance of 1785, and the Northwest Ordinance, the Confederation Congress, and later the U.S. government, had established the process for Ohio's settlement and development. Thousands of white people flooded into what would eventually become Ohio beginning in the mid-1780s. Many of these earliest settlers hoped to make a fortune from the sale of Ohio's lands. These real estate speculators intended to buy the land for the relatively cheap price that the federal government had established under the Land Ordinance of 1785 and resell it at a significant profit to residents who arrived after the government-controlled land became privately owned.[10]

Most of the land that comprised the Northwest Territory was originally known as Congress Lands. The Confederation Congress and then the U.S. government controlled this land, and this was the land that the federal government offered for sale during the 1780s, 1790s, and later. The federal government hoped to use the proceeds from the land sales to pay the remaining debts from the American Revolution and to provide the capital for the government to operate effectively. In 1796, the U.S. government also created the U.S. Military District out of part of the Northwest Territory. Located in what is now central Ohio, the government gave this land to American Revolutionary War veterans as compensation for their military service. Most of these veterans accepted the offered land and then sold their land bounties to settlers who were more willing to endure life in the West. In 1798, the U.S. Congress also established the Refugee Tract, consisting of sixty thousand acres of land in present-day central Ohio. The federal government offered this land as compensation to British citizens who sided with the Americans in the Revolutionary War. Sixty-seven Canadian refugees eventually claimed the land. They had to prove that they had left Canada for the duration of the American Revolution and that they had actively assisted the Americans in securing independence.

Additional land in the Northwest Territory remained under the control of individual states, including Connecticut and Virginia. Although Connecticut, Virginia, and several other states ceded most of their claims to land in the Northwest Territory during the mid-1780s, Connecticut retained control of the Connecticut Western Reserve, located in modern-day northeastern Ohio, and Virginia remained in control of the Virginia Military District, located in central Ohio. The Connecticut government hoped to sell its land claims primarily to help finance public education within its state. It also gave some land as compensation to Connecticut residents who had lost everything they owned during the American Revolution. Virginia intended to use its area exclusively to pay its Revolutionary War veterans. The higher a soldier's rank in either the Continental Army or the Virginia militia, the more land to which he was entitled. Connecticut sold its land claims by 1800, but Virginia retained control of some of its territory for significantly longer. Eventually Virginia ceded its claims to the U.S. government, which then gave the remaining land to Ohio. In 1872, the Ohio legislature used this land to create an endowment for the Ohio State University.

In theory, settlers did not need to go through real estate speculators to purchase land in the Northwest Territory. Although the federal government currently sold the land for $1 per acre, with a minimum purchase of 640 acres, most white Americans could not afford to make such a large purchase. Real estate speculators were usually wealthy or middle-class men who pooled their resources. As a group, they could afford to make such a large purchase. They would then subdivide their property and sell smaller parcels to settlers at much higher prices per acre. Although some settlers could not pay one dollar per acre for 640 acres of land, they might be able to afford $5 or $10 per acre for twenty acres of land. Real estate speculators, although they took advantage of the situation for their own profit, actually helped make land more readily accessible to ordinary citizens.

Real estate speculation in Ohio began much earlier than the 1780s. The first European people to speculate in this area were the founders of the Ohio Company. In 1748, the King of England granted the Ohio Company 200,000 acres of land in the Ohio Country. Among the Ohio Company's investors were George Washington and Robert Dinwiddie, the lieutenant governor of Virginia. These men realized that land between the Atlantic Ocean and the Appalachian Mountains was becoming scarce, especially as the European population in England's North American colonies approached 2 million people. The Ohio Company investors hoped to sell the land in the Ohio Country at a tremendous profit to people who desired to move west of the Appalachian Mountains. Unfortunately for the investors, the French and Indian War and the resulting Proclamation of 1763, which forbade English colonists from settling west of the Appalachian Mountains, caused the Ohio Company to close its doors. This first attempt at real estate speculation ended in a dismal failure.

With the colonies' victory in the Revolution, the opportunity for whites to settle the Ohio Country returned, and real estate speculation began anew. Among the earliest companies formed to exploit the land was the Ohio Company and Associates, established in 1786. Among the company's organizers were Rufus Putnam, Benjamin Tupper, and Winthrop Sargent. All three of these men helped pave the way for Ohio's settlement and development. Tupper and Putnam had each assisted Thomas Hutchins as he surveyed the Seven Ranges. Their firsthand experience in the Ohio Country convinced the two men that highly desirable land existed for the taking. Sargent served in various governmental positions in the Northwest Territory, including secretary of the territory.

Company investors initially selected Samuel Holden Parsons to negotiate a land purchase with the Confederation government. Parsons proved unable to secure the desired agreement, and the company replaced him with Manasseh Cutler. Working with the president of the Confederation Congress, Arthur St. Clair, Cutler arranged for the Ohio Company and Associates to purchase 1.5 million acres of land for $1 million. The company had to pay $500,000 immediately and the remainder of the money once the surveying of the land was completed. The Confederation Congress permitted the Ohio Company and Associates to trade in military land grants that it had collected from American Revolutionary War veterans in lieu of paying cash for the land. As a result, the final cost to the company for the land amounted to 8.5 cents per acre. The Confederation Congress also permitted the company to use a slightly different survey pattern than the one used to map the Seven Ranges, although it still required each township to set aside parcels of land to promote education, religion, and government. Two townships were required to be set aside for the creation of a public university. In 1808, the company established Ohio University on the land, fulfilling the Confederation Congress's requirement. At first, because of the lack of qualified professors, Ohio University offered only a high school education. The university also experienced low enrollment during its first decade or so of existence, as Ohio residents struggled to establish homes, farms, and businesses on the frontier.

In addition to the land purchase, the Confederation Congress simply gave the Ohio Company and Associates an additional 100,000 acres of land. This land grant was located along the northern edge of the Ohio Company and Associates' land purchase. Known as the Donation Tract, the Congress required the company to give any adult white male who agreed to settle in this territory one hundred acres of land for free. The Congress hoped that white men would flood into the Donation Tract, providing a sizable population of white men to serve as a buffer between white settlements in the Ohio Company and Associates' tract and the Native American settlements further north and west. Being so close to the natives' villages caused the residents of the Donation Tract to live in constant fear. The Native American population clearly did not appreciate the flood of settlers coming across the Appalachian Mountains. On January 2, 1792, a combined force of Delaware and Wyandot attacked the community of Big Bottom, located in the Donation Tract along the Muskingum River. Most of the white settlers lived in a blockhouse, but they had failed to fill the large gaps between the logs with mud. The natives were able to sneak up on the settlers while they were inside the blockhouse preparing dinner. The Delawares and Wyandots surrounded the blockhouse and fired their weapons between the logs, killing eight whites and capturing five others. This event became known as the Big Bottom Massacre. The settlers living in the Donation Tract faced a formidable enemy in the native populace, but the whites fulfilled the Confederation Congress's goal of providing a buffer between the natives and the more populous centers of white settlement farther south and east.

In 1788, Rufus Putnam, one of the founders of the Ohio Company and Associates, established the Company's first settlement in the Northwest Territory. Originally known as Adelphia, the community quickly became known as Marietta, in honor of Marie Antoinette and France's contributions to the American Revolution. Although the Confederation Congress had taken steps to subdue the Native American population, the settlers still feared life on the western frontier and quickly built Campus Martius, a fort consisting of log walls and four blockhouses. Campus Martius originally served as the center of religion, education, and government for the settlement. One of the four blockhouses served as a school, and another served as the community's first church. On July 19, 1788, Arthur St. Clair, the first and longest-serving governor of the

Northwest Territory, arrived in Marietta and formally established the North-west Territory. During its first few years of existence, the community endured difficult times, as its residents struggled to build homes and establish productive farms. Nevertheless, Marietta quickly emerged as one of the most important governmental and economic centers in the Northwest Territory and then in Ohio. Fertile farmlands surrounded the community. Marietta is located on the Ohio River, and riverboat construction became one of the most important industries in the community, as many migrants used the Ohio River to transport themselves and their belongings westward.

Hoping to take advantage of opportunities in the Northwest Territory, numerous additional real estate speculators formed their own companies during the 1780s and the 1790s. One of these organizations was the Scioto Company, founded in 1789. Many of the men involved in the Ohio Company and Associates, among them Winthrop Sargent and Manasseh Cutler, also partici-pated in this and several other companies. The company had secured an agreement to purchase 4.5 million acres of land in the Northwest Territory from the federal government. Before the company had actually paid for the land and secured legal title to it, company representatives began selling the land, much of it to French purchasers who hoped to immigrate to the United States. The company's agents in France, William Playfair and Joel Barlow, embezzled the money they had taken in. As a result, the Scioto Company did not have the funds necessary to fulfill its agreement with the U.S. government.

The French settlers had no idea that the land that they had purchased was not legally theirs. When they arrived in the Northwest Territory, they quickly realized that Playfair and Barlow had swindled them. In reality, the land that the French had purchased was not even owned by the federal government. The Scioto Company's representatives had illegally sold the French migrants land belonging to the Ohio Company and Associates. Many of the settlers returned to the East Coast of the United States to earn a living there, others returned to France, and others tried to raise additional cash to purchase the land a second time, this time from the Ohio Company and Associates, the legitimate owners of the land in question. In 1795, the U.S. government authorized the creation of the French Grant, a gift of land near modern-day Gallipolis, Ohio, for the people whom the Scioto Company had swindled. By this point, most of the French settlers had either returned to the East, moved back to France, or had purchased land from the Ohio Company and Associates. As a result, most of the French settlers sold the land given to them under the French Grant to other white settlers.

In 1795, thirty-five investors organized the Connecticut Land Company. These men arranged to purchase the eastern portion of the Connecticut Western Reserve for $1.2 million. In 1796, the investors dispatched Moses Cleaveland and a group of surveyors to the area to establish townships. Rather than following the model set by the Land Ordinance of 1785, Cleaveland chose to limit townships to twenty-five square miles. In honor of Cleaveland, the first settlement in the Connecticut Western Reserve became known as Cleveland. Unlike the Ohio Company and Associates' land in southeastern Ohio, which quickly grew in population, the Connecticut Land Company's property experienced very slow growth. In 1800, Cleveland's population consisted of only three white men, and fewer than one thousand white people lived in the entire Connecticut Western Reserve. The primary reasons for this lethargic growth were the higher concentration of Native Americans living in north-central and northwestern Ohio and the lack of easy water access to the East and to the South to speed development. Marietta, located on the Ohio River in the Ohio Company and Associates' land, grew quickly. The Connecticut Western Reserve did not experience a burgeoning population until after the War of 1812. This conflict between the British and their Native American allies versus the white Americans destroyed the native resistance to white settlement in Ohio and also established amicable relations between the British and the Americans. No longer having to fear these two groups, white settlers eventually flooded into northern Ohio.

John Cleves Symmes was the final individual to purchase a sizable quantity of land for the purpose of real estate speculation in what would eventually become Ohio. Symmes was a U.S. congressman from New Jersey. In 1788, he and a small group of friends pooled their resources to purchase land in the Northwest Territory. Symmes hoped to purchase 1 million acres of land, but the final acreage amounted to one-third of the desired amount. The sale between Symmes and the U.S. government was formally concluded in 1794. The final purchase price amounted to approximately sixty-seven cents per acre, and Symmes and his partners had to agree to set aside land in each township for a school, a church, and the government's use. Symmes also had to establish a university within the land that he had acquired.

The Symmes purchase included land in western Ohio, some of which was along the Ohio River. At first, despite its strategic location along the river and the fertile farmland that comprised the area, the region grew slowly, primarily because the Native Americans actively contested the whites' claims to this land. In 1789, settlers built a small community on the Ohio River called Losantiville, which later became known as Cincinnati. Cincinnati quickly emerged as the most important community in the Symmes purchase and served as an important economic and governmental center. The population grew rapidly following Anthony Wayne's victory at the Battle of Fallen Timbers in 1794 and the subsequent signing of the Treaty of Greenville in 1795. Although problems with the natives had now diminished, new difficulties emerged. Symmes failed to follow the surveying criteria that the federal government had established in the Land Ordinance of 1785. Instead, he employed a more haphazard system. The end result was that Symmes and his agents commonly sold the same parcel of land more than once, creating a nightmare for the purchasers of the property. For example, Symmes sold the land that is now Dayton, Ohio, to Israel Ludlow. Unbeknownst to both Symmes and

Ludlow, this land was not part of the Symmes purchase. Most early settlers of Dayton ended up having to pay for their land twice, first when they purchased the property from Symmes and again when they bought the land from its rightful owners. During the late eighteenth century and the early nineteenth century, the court system first in the Northwest Territory and then in Ohio was inundated with land disputes.

Native Americans, the high prices of land, and questionable land sales all made settlement of the area that is present-day Ohio difficult. Complicating the situation even further were squatters who moved onto land in the Northwest Territory and did not purchase it from the legal owner. They simply claimed the land as their own. Squatters typically came from the working class and did not have the capital necessary to purchase the land legally. They believed that if they had settled and developed the land, they were entitled to retain it. It did not matter to the squatters that someone else, such as a real estate speculator like John Cleves Symmes, had legally purchased the land. If the legal owner had not actually settled upon the land, they believed anyone was entitled to it.

Squatters became a major difficulty for the federal government following the American Revolution. State governments, the federal government, and private citizens all claimed land in the Ohio Country. Where one entity's claims ended and the others' began remained unclear. With this uncertainty and desiring to improve their financial plight, many poverty-stricken people moved west of the Appalachian Mountains. Hoping to stem the tide, the Confederation Congress prohibited settlement in the Ohio Country without the approval of the individual states that claimed the land. Squatters ignored the government's dictate. In 1785, the Confederation Congress dispatched Josiah Harmar and a detachment of soldiers to push the illegal settlers from the region. Harmar's soldiers burned the homes and crops of several squatters, but other settlers convinced Harmar that they would relinquish the land after they had harvested their crops. Harmar agreed. The squatters harvested their fields but refused to leave once they had cleared their fields. To prevent the illegal settlers from remaining in the Ohio Country and to deter future migrants, Harmar ordered the construction of Fort Steuben and Fort Harmar near present-day Marietta. Rather than viewing the forts and the soldiers who manned them as deterrent to settlement, squatters considered them as protection against Native American attacks. Tensions between the squatters and the rightful landowner, whether it was a government entity, a private citizen, or a land corporation, further complicated the Northwest Territory's settlement.

GOVERNMENT IN THE NORTHWEST TERRITORY

The Northwest Ordinance of 1787 formally created the Northwest Territory. That same year, the Confederation Congress appointed Arthur St. Clair as the first territorial governor. He remained in this position until 1802, when President Thomas Jefferson removed him from office. Tensions with the Native Americans, squabbles between different political groups, and disagreements about when and if Ohio should become a state dominated St. Clair's fifteen years in office. As governor, St. Clair left an indelible mark on the social, political, and economic development of the Northwest Territory and the future state of Ohio.[11]

Born in Scotland in 1736, St. Clair arrived in North America as an ensign in the British Army during the French and Indian War. In 1762 he retired from the army and purchased four hundred acres of land in western Pennsylvania. His purchase made him the largest landholder in Pennsylvania residing west of the Appalachian Mountains. Because of his wealth and prestige, St. Clair played an active role in governmental affairs, including serving as a judge on the circuit court. During the American Revolution, St. Clair joined the Continental Army; upon the war's conclusion, he served in the Confederation Congress, including a term as president in 1787. Coming from a landed background and having served in several powerful positions, St. Clair was used to having his own way. As governor of the Northwest Territory, he ruled with an iron fist and commonly refused to work with the territorial legislature.

One of the first and perhaps greatest difficulties St. Clair and the other members of the territorial government faced was dealing with the Native Americans. St. Clair proved to be adept in negotiating treaties with the natives, as exemplified by the Treaty of Fort Harmar in 1789. Like most of the peace negotiators, however, St. Clair failed to convince all of the Native Americans to acquiesce to his demands. Intending to convince the natives who rejected the treaties to abide by them, St. Clair turned to violence. Although he was a veteran of both the French and Indian War and the American Revolution, St. Clair failed miserably in his military campaign against the Native Americans in 1791. President George Washington then demanded that St. Clair resign his military commission and replaced St. Clair with the more adept Anthony Wayne. With Wayne's victory at the Battle of Fallen Timbers in 1794, white Americans believed that peace had come to the Northwest Territory. Although they were mistaken in their belief, white settlers flooded into the region.[12]

Although St. Clair lost his military commission, President Washington permitted him to remain as governor of the Northwest Territory. The responsibility for establishing laws thus fell to St. Clair and the three federal judges overseeing legal disputes in the region. During the summer of 1795, St. Clair and two of the Northwest Territory's three judges, John Cleves Symmes and George Turner, met in Cincinnati to create a body of laws. Under the requirements set forth in the Northwest Ordinance, all laws chosen by these three men were to come from laws enforced in one of the original thirteen states. Any laws adopted by these men that were not enforced in one of these states were not to be enforceable under the Northwest Ordinance. This impromptu group adopted a total of thirty-seven laws that became known as Maxwell's Code, the first criminal and civil code for the Northwest Territory. Maxwell's Code established English common law as the basis for all legal decisions and laws within the Northwest Territory. It also guaranteed the territorial residents protection from excessive taxes, a fear that many Americans shared, having rebelled against Great Britain at least partly over taxation issues just twenty years before. In 1798, Governor St. Clair along with Winthrop Sargent, secretary of the Northwest Territory, and Joseph Gilman and Return Jonathan Meigs, Jr., judges on the Court of Common Pleas, adopted eleven additional laws. Although the creators of Maxwell Code originally determined that its laws had come from one of the original thirteen states, four of the laws adopted in 1798 came from Kentucky. The men realized that, as frontier regions, Kentucky and the Northwest Territory had many similarities. Conditions on the frontier of the United States of America differed dramatically from those in the more settled areas on the East Coast. These eleven new laws dealt primarily with criminal activities, landownership, and horse breeding.[13]

Maxwell's Code and the eleven additional laws helped establish law and order within the Northwest Territory. The legal code also represented one of the last times men of differing political beliefs worked together for the betterment of the Northwest Territory. During the late 1790s, white settlers within the Northwest Territory divided into two political parties, the Democratic-Republican Party and the Federalist Party. Both groups had been in existence at the national level for less than a decade, and they held very different visions for the future of the United States. These two competing views dominated the political arena in the Northwest Territory and eventually in Ohio until the late 1810s.[14]

During George Washington's administration, Alexander Hamilton, the first secretary of the treasury, established the Federalist Party. The Federalists believed that the Constitution was a "loose" document that permitted the federal government to adopt any powers necessary for it to govern the United States adequately. Although the Constitution might not expressly grant a power to the federal government, Hamilton and his supporters believed that government officials could assume any power that the Constitution did not specifically deny it. In essence, according to the Federalist Party, the Constitution established a strong, centralized government that was superior to the individual state governments. The Federalist Party also was elitist. Hamilton believed that only the most virtuous men should participate in government. To be virtuous, a man had to be able to put aside his own personal gain for his country's benefit. Federalists were concerned that, if working-class or even middle-class people received power, greed might corrupt them. Men from these social classes might view their political positions as a means to advance their own wealth, whereas men of property had already attained satisfactory wealth and would, supposedly, be less susceptible to bribes. Thus, only the wealthier and better-educated white men should serve in office or even vote.

Economically, the Federalists wanted the United States to model itself after England. The English had an industrialized economy and by the late 1700s had emerged as one of, if not the most, powerful nations on the face of the earth. The Federalists believed that the United States had to model itself after England if it ever hoped to rival its power. Most Federalists contended that farming was an antiquated and backward occupation. Although agricultural production was necessary to feed the American populace, Hamilton's supporters believed that for the United States to advance in power and prestige, a shift from farming to industrialization was necessary.

In opposition to the Federalist Party, Thomas Jefferson, Washington's secretary of state, founded the Democratic-Republican Party. The Democratic-Republicans, also known as the Jeffersonian Republicans, feared a strong national government. They believed that a strong federal government could usurp the rights of its people, as the British monarchy had done before the American Revolution. They proclaimed that the Constitution was a "strict" document that clearly delineated the federal government's powers. The Democratic-Republicans contended that the national government could not assume any powers that the Constitution did not expressly grant it. In essence, this political party believed that a federal government was necessary but that the citizens had circumscribed its powers. The states, the Democratic-Republicans concluded, could address the people's needs more adequately than could a strong, centralized federal government.

Democratic-Republicans also favored basing the U.S. economy on agriculture. Jefferson and his supporters believed that farmers could easily provide the American people with the basic necessities of life, including shelter and ample food, and would also grow an abundant surplus of crops that would provide the United States with marketable products overseas. The United States would serve as the breadbasket for the industrial economies of Great Britain and France; in return for American crops the British and French would provide the United States with manufactured goods.

The Democratic-Republicans' economic vision translated into a more egalitarian political and social system than the one the Federalists proposed. Jefferson believed that every adult white man should have the right to vote as long as he owned a minimal amount of property. If Americans were farmers, in theory, every adult white man would own his own family farm and qualify for suffrage. Unlike the Federalists, Democratic-Republicans believed that most white American men, as long as they could provide shelter and food for their families, were virtuous. The government could trust these men to put aside their own personal gain for the good of their nation. Nationally, the Democratic-Republicans emerged victorious over their Federalist counterparts, providing the United States with three of the first five presidents, Thomas Jefferson, James Madison, and James Monroe.

With the creation of the Northwest Territory in 1787, the Federalist Party emerged as the dominant political force in the region. By 1803, when Ohio attained statehood, the Democratic-Republican Party had triumphed over the Federalist Party. The chief point of contention between the two groups was not so much their competing economic visions nor their differing political visions. Rather it was when or if Ohio would become a state. Governor St. Clair belonged to the Federalist Party, as did the secretary of the Northwest Territory, Winthrop Sargent. During the late 1780s and the 1790s, Sargent routinely served as de facto governor when St. Clair was absent, usually because the governor was negotiating with or campaigning against the Native Americans or meeting with the U.S. Congress or the president. The judges in the Northwest Territory tended to favor the Democratic-Republican Party. The Democratic-Republican judges and the Federalist governor working together amicably to create Maxwell's Code remains surprising, especially considering the animosity that emerged between these two parties as Ohio moved toward statehood.

Much of the hatred that emerged between these two groups in what would become Ohio resulted from St. Clair's dictatorial nature. Democratic-Republicans John Cleves Symmes, Samuel Parsons, and James Varnum, three territorial judges, all contended that the governor exceeded his power by creating his own legal code in 1788, well before the formal acceptance of Maxwell's Code in 1795. Even some Federalists openly opposed St. Clair's policies. Among these men was Jacob Burnet, who argued that the territorial government should allow every adult male taxpayer to vote. He also endorsed town meetings as the preferred method of local government and opposed St. Clair's provision for secret ballots. St. Clair, for the most part, refused to budge from his position, setting the stage for a contentious move toward statehood.[15]

STATEHOOD

By the early 1800s, residents of what would become Ohio pushed for statehood. Fearing that the Federalist Party would not succeed in maintaining control of the state government as it had under the territorial government, Governor St. Clair proposed delaying statehood as long as possible. As the United States entered the nineteenth century, however, Ohio's population approached sixty thousand people, the number necessary for a territory to seek statehood. Despite all of St. Clair's efforts, the Democratic-Republicans and the supporters of statehood triumphed in 1803.

As pressure for statehood increased, the governor concocted a scheme to have the U.S. Congress agree that the future state of Ohio should actually become two separate states. The western boundary of the area to become states would remain the present-day, eastern border of Indiana, and the eastern boundary would be the western border of modern-day Pennsylvania. Lake Erie was to serve as the northern boundary, and the Ohio River would become the southern border. Under St. Clair's plan, the Scioto River, which roughly divides the modern-day state in two in a north-to-south direction, would serve as the dividing line between the two new states. If the Congress agreed, St. Clair believed that the Federalists would have more time to solidify their control in both potential states. Although approximately sixty thousand people resided within the border of the proposed state, if the same area became two states, the population of each would fall well below the required level. This action could potentially delay statehood for several years.[16]

Although St. Clair had managed to dominate the Northwest Territory's political life since the late 1780s, he faced increasing and more powerful opposition by the start of the nineteenth century. St. Clair, a New Englander, found strong enemies in recent immigrants from the southeastern portion of the United States, especially from Virginia. The most prominent of these influential men were Edward Tiffin and Thomas Worthington. Born in Virginia in 1773, Worthington became familiar with the Northwest Territory in 1796, when he helped survey the Virginia Military District. The Virginia legislature paid Worthington with a land grant near present-day Chillicothe, Ohio. Accompanied by Tiffin, his brother-in-law, who was a Methodist lay minister and a doctor, Worthington moved his family to the Northwest Territory in 1798. Before leaving Virginia, these two property owners freed their slaves, probably because of their religious beliefs. Several of their former bondsmen accompanied Worthington and Tiffin to the West, where they continued to work for the two men—now for a wage.[17]

These two men quickly emerged as strong political leaders in the Northwest Territory. Worthington served in the territorial legislature from 1799 to 1803, while Tiffin first became the chief clerk of the Northwest Territory's court of common pleas and, in 1799, became a member of the Northwest Territory's legislature. His fellow representatives admired him tremendously for his logical mind and elected him the first speaker of the house. Both men were committed members of the Democratic-Republican Party. They shared fellow Virginian Thomas Jefferson's vision for the new United States and actively lobbied against Governor St. Clair.

By 1801, St. Clair's attempts to prevent statehood had exhausted Democratic-Republicans residing in Ohio, including Tiffin and Worthington. Violence between the Democratic-Republicans and the Federalists seemed inevitable. On December 24, 1801, Michael Baldwin, a Democratic-Republican, led a group of like-minded followers known as the Bloodhounds to Governor St. Clair's residence. The Bloodhounds intended to threaten the governor by burning him in effigy. Fortunately for St. Clair, Worthington intervened and convinced the group to disperse. The Bloodhounds decided to continue their terrorist tactics the next evening, Christmas night, by attacking William R. Putnam, one of the governor's most avid supporters. Once again, bloodshed was avoided as more rational Democratic-Republicans and some Federalists intervened.[18]

Not all Democratic-Republicans were as hotheaded as Baldwin and his Bloodhounds. In 1801, several Democratic-Republicans, including Tiffin and Worthington, petitioned the U.S. government for assistance. In January 1802, the U.S. Congress responded by rejecting St. Clair's plan to divide Ohio into two separate states. The Congress passed the Enabling Act, which demanded that residents of what was to become Ohio apply for statehood as soon as possible and even set the date for Ohio's constitutional convention—November 1, 1802. The Enabling Act set the Pennsylvania state line as the eastern boundary of Ohio and the Ohio River as the southern border; the western border would begin at the mouth of the Great Miami River and extend due north to Lake Michigan. The northern boundary would be the border with Canada. Ohioans were to follow the Northwest Ordinance's stipulations to the letter in forming the new state constitution and government. The Northwest Ordinance required that a territory have a population of sixty thousand people before its citizens could apply for statehood. The census of 1800 set Ohio's population at 45,365 people, well below the number needed. The U.S. Congress decided that in the intervening two years since the census's completion, Ohio's population had undoubtedly surged well beyond sixty thousand. On April 30, 1802, Jefferson signed the Enabling Act, clearing the way for Ohio statehood.[19]

On November 1, 1802, thirty-five delegates met at Ohio's constitutional convention in Chillicothe to draft a state constitution. According to the Northwest Ordinance, representatives of the territory had to submit a constitution to the U.S. Congress for approval before Ohio could become a state. With twenty-six delegates, the Democratic-Republicans held a clear advantage at the convention. Among these men were Edward Tiffin, selected by the participants as the president of the convention, Thomas Worthington, and John Cleves Symmes. Federalists claimed seven seats, and two delegates remained uncommitted. Because of the Democratic-Republicans' dominance, their vision of a small government, dominated by a legislature with limited powers, triumphed over the Federalist vision of a strong, centralized government.[20]

Soon after the delegates selected Tiffin as the convention president, Governor St. Clair addressed the members, hoping to sway the representatives to his political viewpoint. He railed against the Enabling Act, claiming that the U.S. Congress and President Jefferson had illegally amended the Northwest Ordinance with this piece of legislation. St. Clair hoped that his speech would convince the Democratic-Republicans that the federal government had exceeded its authority and stood in clear violation of the Democratic-Republican Party's principles. St. Clair was gravely mistaken in his denunciation of the U.S. government. His opponents sent a copy of the speech to President Jefferson, who immediately removed St. Clair from office and replaced him with Virginian and Democratic-Republican Charles Byrd. The delegates also ignored St. Clair's call to delay statehood. Thirty-two delegates voted in favor of proceeding with the drafting of a state constitution. Two abstained, and only Federalist Ephraim Cutler opposed the resolution. Even St. Clair's fellow Federalists turned their backs on their former leader. They realized that Democratic-Republican principles had triumphed over their Federalist beliefs and that they were fighting a losing battle.[21]

The delegates drafted a state constitution that allowed all adult white men the right to vote, assuming that they paid their taxes or that they helped build and maintain the state's roads. Eligible voters would elect the state governor and legislature. The governor had few powers and was more a figurehead than a strong administrator. The governor could not veto acts of the legislature and had a term of only two years. The legislature, known as the General Assembly, contained two houses, the house of representatives and the senate. The constitution gave Ohio's eligible voters the opportunity to replace inadequate leaders, because representatives served only a single year before facing reelection; senators served two years. The General Assembly approved all the governor's appointments and also selected the judges.[22]

Rights for African Americans proved to be a much stickier point for the delegates than the type of government that they established. Honoring one of the Northwest Ordinance's stipulations and at the insistence of Federalist Ephraim Cutler, the proposed constitution outlawed slavery. Delegates agreed to this portion of the constitution with relative ease, because the Northwest Ordinance clearly stated that they had no choice. The question of whether or not Ohio's African American population would enjoy the right to suffrage was much more contentious. The delegates who originally immigrated to the Northwest Territory from the Northeast generally favored enfranchising African Americans, whereas those from the southeastern United States strongly opposed this action. The convention delegates divided evenly on this point— seventeen to seventeen—and Edward Tiffin cast the deciding vote that disenfranchised African American men. Tiffin was typical of many Northern whites during this time period. Although he had freed his slaves before moving to the Northwest Territory from Virginia, he still did not necessarily believe that black Ohioans deserved equal rights with whites. Even the most forward-thinking and egalitarian white men of this era held racist beliefs.[23]

The convention approved the constitution on November 29, 1802, and adjourned immediately. The delegates selected Thomas Worthington to transport the proposed constitution to the U.S. Congress at Washington, D.C. Illustrating the difficulty in traveling during this time period, Worthington did not arrive at the nation's capital until December 19. On December 22, he presented the document to the U.S. Congress. The Senate and the House of Representatives each approved the constitution in early 1803, and President Jefferson endorsed their decision on February 19, 1803, making Ohio officially the seventeenth state of the United States of America.[24]

SUMMARY

Ohio was the first part of the Northwest Territory to become a state within the United States of America. Ohio's path to statehood served as the model for every subsequent state within the Northwest Territory and beyond.

Ohio's constitution was relatively democratic and egalitarian, at least for white men. Several scholars have declared Ohio's constitution to be the most democratic of the first seventeen states. The statehood process was not an easy one. It involved the numerous divisions that existed within the United States during the late eighteenth and early nineteenth centuries. Even after the American Revolution, British subjects and white American citizens continued to struggle over the western frontier. Native Americans did not simply vacate the land in the late 1700s. They struggled against white settlement throughout this period and undoubtedly delayed Ohio's statehood by several years. Tensions between Federalists and Democratic-Republicans, the first two political parties in the United States, also divided the white population, and differences over slavery and African American rights widened the breach.[25]

These tensions did not prevent Ohio from gaining statehood. Differences over slavery, over rights for African American Ohioans, and with the Native Americans continued to cause difficulties well into the nineteenth century. Politically, the Democratic-Republicans dominated the government when Ohio attained statehood. Edward Tiffin became Ohio's first governor. Charles Byrd, former governor of the Northwest Territory, served as the first sitting justice on the U.S. District Court of Ohio, and Thomas Worthington became one of the state's first two U.S. senators. Even Michael Baldwin, leader of the Bloodhounds, attained a prominent position as speaker of the Ohio House of Representatives. The ideals of the Democratic-Republican Party dominated the political scene until after the War of 1812, but many of these men eventually became strong advocates of certain aspects of the Federalist Party's platform, including industrialization and the development of a transportation infrastructure. Ohio's white populace stood relatively united upon achieving statehood. They hoped to turn their frontier surroundings into more settled ones with prosperous businesses and relatively luxurious homes. On February 19, 1803, with Ohio about to be the seventeenth state of the United States of America, these people stood poised to fulfill their dreams.

NOTES

1. For a general overview of Ohio history, especially see Andrew R.L. Cayton, *Ohio: The History of a People* (Columbus: The Ohio State University Press, 2002); George W. Knepper, *Ohio and Its People* (Kent, OH: The Kent State University Press, 1997); Beverley W. Bond, Jr., *The Foundations of Ohio* (Columbus: Ohio Historical Society, 1941); William T. Utter, *The Frontier State, 1803–1825* (Columbus: Ohio Historical Society, 1942); Francis P. Weisenburger, *The Passing of the Frontier, 1825–1850* (Columbus: Ohio Historical Society, 1941); Eugene H. Roseboom, *The Civil War Era, 1850–1873* (Columbus: Ohio Historical Society, 1944); Philip D. Jordan, *Ohio Comes of Age, 1873–1900* (Columbus: Ohio Historical Society, 1943); Harlow Lindley, ed., *Ohio in the Twentieth Century* (Columbus: Ohio Historical Society, 1942); Emilius O.

Randall and Daniel J. Ryan, *History of Ohio: The Rise and Progress of an American State* (New York: The Century History Company, 1912).

2. For a discussion of the events that occurred at Gnadenhutten, see Knepper, *Ohio and Its People*, pp. 43–44; Earl P. Olmstead et al., *David Zeisberger: A Life Among the Indians* (Kent, OH: The Kent State University Press, 1997); Earl P. Olmstead, *Blackcoats Among the Delaware: David Zeisberger on the Ohio Frontier* (Kent, OH: The Kent State University Press, 1991).

3. On the Ohio Country under the Articles of Confederation, as well as the difficulties the Confederation Congress faced in paying soldiers who served in the Continental Army, especially see Randall and Ryan, *History of Ohio*, 2:379–600.

4. For a detailed accounting of the various treaties, including the actual text, that white Americans negotiated with the Ohio Country and Northwest Territory Native Americans, especially see www.ohiohistorycentral.org/ohc/history/h_indian/index.shtml.

5. For several contemporary accounts of the tensions between early white Ohioans and the Native Americans, see Thomas H. Smith, *An Ohio Reader: 1750 to the Civil War* (Grand Rapids, MI: William B. Eerdmans Publishing Company, 1975), pp. 67–95. This source contains some of the most pertinent documents for Ohio's early history. For additional primary accounts of life in Ohio during the late eighteenth and early nineteenth centuries, see R. Douglas Hurt, *The Ohio Frontier: Crucible of the Old Northwest, 1720–1830* (Bloomington: Indiana University Press, 1996). For a general overview of Harmar's defeat, St. Clair's defeat, and the Battle of Fallen Timbers, see Bond, *Foundations of Ohio*, pp. 312–348; Randall and Ryan, *History of Ohio*, 2:505–572.

6. For the text of the Ordinance of 1784, see Smith, *An Ohio Reader*, pp. 36–37.

7. For the text of the Land Ordinance of 1785; ibid., pp. 37–39.

8. On the surveying of the Seven Ranges, see Randall and Ryan, *History of Ohio*, 2:420–421.

9. For the text of the Northwest Ordinance, see Smith, *An Ohio Reader*, pp. 39–45.

10. On the various land divisions within the Northwest Territory and on the different companies that speculated on this land, see Bond, *Foundations of Ohio*, pp. 349–395; Randall and Ryan, *History of Ohio*, 2:439–470, 573–595.

11. For a general overview of Arthur St. Clair's life, see Simeon D. Fess, ed., *Ohio: A Four-Volume Reference Library on the History of a Great State*, vol. 4, *Ohio's Three Hundred* (Chicago, The Lewis Publishing Company, 1937), pp. 12–14.

12. On Native American conflict, see notes four and five.

13. For a discussion of Maxwell's Code and the difficulties St. Clair and the justices faced in establishing a legal code, see Bond, *The Foundations of Ohio*, pp. 396–436. To read the *Executive Journal* of the Northwest Territory, available at http://www.ohiohistory.org/ onlinedoc/northwest/exjournal. This source contains the official acts and correspondence of Arthur St. Clair and Winthrop Sargent.

14. On the Federalists and the Democratic-Republicans in the Northwest Territory and Ohio, see Cayton, *Ohio*, pp. 3–8; Bond, *The Foundations of Ohio*, pp. 396–476; Utter, *The Frontier State*, pp. 3–119.

15. For a discussion of the political battles between the Federalists and the Democratic-Republicans residing in the Northwest Territory, see note 14.

16. For Arthur St. Clair's reasoning behind dividing the area that was to become Ohio into two different territories, see Smith, *An Ohio Reader*, pp. 59–60.

17. For general overviews of the lives of Edward Tiffin and Thomas Worthington, see Fess, *Ohio*, 4:33–34, 45–49.

18. On the Bloodhounds and Michael Baldwin, see Knepper, *Ohio and Its People*, pp. 92–93.

19. On the Enabling Act, see Knepper, *Ohio and Its People*, pp. 92–93.

20. On Ohio's constitutional convention, see Utter, *The Frontier State*, pp. 3–31.

21. For Arthur St. Clair's speech, see Smith, *An Ohio Reader*, pp. 61–65.

22. On the Ohio constitution of 1803, see Utter, *The Frontier State*, pp. 13–18. For the text of the Ohio constitution of 1803, see www.ohiohistory.org/onlinedoc/ohgovernment/ constitution/cnst1802.html.

23. On the debate over African American rights within Ohio's constitutional convention, see Utter, *The Frontier State*, pp. 18–20. On treatment of African Americans in Ohio during the first half of the nineteenth century, see Smith, *An Ohio Reader*, pp. 249–287.

24. On Thomas Worthington's trip to Washington, D.C., and the actions of the U.S. Congress and President Jefferson, see Knepper, *Ohio and Its People*, pp. 95–97.

25. For two differing opinions on the democratic nature of Ohio's constitution, see Knepper, *Ohio and Its People*, pp. 95–97; Utter, *The Frontier State*, pp. 16–17.

BIBLIOGRAPHY

Bond, Beverley W., Jr. *The Foundations of Ohio*. Columbus: Ohio Historical Society, 1941.

Cayton, Andrew R. L. *Ohio: The History of a People*. Columbus: The Ohio State University Press, 2002.

Fess, Simeon D., ed. *Ohio: A Four-Volume Reference Library on the History of a Great State*. 4 vols. Chicago: The Lewis Publishing Company, 1937.

Hurt, R. Douglas. *The Ohio Frontier: Crucible of the Old Northwest, 1720–1830*. Bloomington: Indiana University Press, 1996.

Jordan, Philip D. *Ohio Comes of Age, 1873–1900*. Columbus: Ohio Historical Society, 1943.

Knepper, George W. *Ohio and Its People*. Kent, Ohio: The Kent State University Press, 1997.

Lindley, Harlow, ed. *Ohio in the Twentieth Century*. Columbus: Ohio Historical Society, 1942.

Randall, Emilius O., and Daniel J. Ryan. *History of Ohio: The Rise and Progress of an American State*. New York: The Century History Company, 1912.

Roseboom, Eugene H. *The Civil War Era, 1850–1873*. Columbus: Ohio Historical Society, 1944.

Smith, Thomas H. *An Ohio Reader: 1750 to the Civil War*. Grand Rapids, MI: William B. Eerdmans Publishing Company, 1975.

Utter, William T. *The Frontier State, 1803–1825*. Columbus: Ohio Historical Society, 1942.

Weisenburger, Francis P. *The Passing of the Frontier, 1825–1850*. Columbus: Ohio Historical Society, 1941.